THE PERSIAN WARS

MODERN LIBRARY COLLEGE EDITIONS

THE
PERSIAN
WARS

by

Herodotus

Translated by
GEORGE RAWLINSON

With an Introduction by
FRANCIS R. B. GODOLPHIN
Musgrave Professor of Latin, Princeton University

THE MODERN LIBRARY · *New York*

THE MODERN LIBRARY

is published by RANDOM HOUSE, INC.

Manufactured in the United States of America

Contents

Introduction

by Francis R. B. Godolphin

THE HORIZONS of our modern world have been enormously
extended in every way during the last hundred years. New scientific knowledge, new industrial techniques, new historical
knowledge, anthropological knowledge of races and civilisations
previously unsuspected, all combine to open up new intellectual
vistas. But, strangely enough, all these new avenues lead back
to the Greeks, the temporal and spiritual initiators of the great
movements of Western European culture. The eager curiosity
of the Greek mind speculating on every subject under the sun
made man something he had never been before and made him
something he has not ceased to be, whatever his particular race
and period, if only the influence of Greece has touched him,
however remotely. Interesting and important as the oriental
races are, there is an intellectual and spiritual difference which
conditions all our relationships with them. This is not true of
our relationship to Greece, and it is this underlying kinship
which makes it possible for us to return to the Greeks in one
generation and another, finding new insights and new inspiration from each renewal of contact. This does not mean that "the
Greeks thought of everything" or that "there is nothing new
under the sun." Rather it means that in the short span of their
history the greatest of the Greeks lived so intensely their physical, political, intellectual and aesthetic lives that they have left
intelligible remains to reassure man of the value of the struggle
to act and think as a man, and they have left suggestions of
ways in which man may actualise his desires and aspirations.

In all the varied interpretations man has put upon his experience in the world and in society, Greek history has never
ceased to possess a special fascination. What happened on that
small portion of the earth's surface within a comparatively short

period of time brought out certain continuing characteristics of human behavior in a fashion intelligible and interesting to a variety of people living under quite different circumstances. Our understanding of ourselves is increased by understanding these Greeks and we feel that this is important to us, just as men felt in other periods that they could predict their own future by following the course of Greek history, or receive a sound vocational training in military science by studying the campaigns in Greek history, or obtain sound moral training by learning the rewards of virtue or the consequences of vice as portrayed by the Greek historians. For others the pleasure and delight in a good story well told is freely offered to satisfy the aesthetic taste, as well as that *curiositas* about one's fellow man which is the source of so much human activity.

Much of this interest in Greek history is closely connected with the fact that the men who wrote that history were men like ourselves who were interested in many of the subjects which interest us, often subjects which we would say were not properly "history" if we were trying to be narrow and technical in our use of the term. However one cannot help wondering whether interest and curiosity alone would have preserved the works of Herodotus, Thucydides, Xenophon and Arrian, had they been unable to present their accounts of the life of the Greeks in a literary form which had an appeal beyond that of a bare list of facts, whatever the intrinsic interest of those facts. Such lists of facts did exist in the ancient world; we have some fragments of them, important to our knowledge of ancient history, but seldom consulted except by scholars. The appeal of the Greek historians, then, must mean that they have had something to say and a way of saying it which have found them audiences for nearly 2,400 years. Both of these aspects of history must be considered in any effort to appraise the existing evidence on the life process known to us as Greek history.

The belief that "the proper study of mankind is man" may be subject to justifiable attack by philosophy and theology, but it does succeed in expressing one aspect of human activity admirably. Man's interest in his fellows and in his predecessors is a persistent element in the human scene and the term history, used to describe both the process of life and the product of studying that life, is in constant danger of so great extension in use that it may confuse the unwary. As we tend to think of history, in the broader sense, everything, as well as everyone, has a history. Furthermore, as far as man himself is concerned, everyone is an historian, if only to collect and present to his own mind a history of himself. This wide range of possible subject-matter for history, however, is not really the cause of the greatest difficulty and confusion for the historian. The real problem is how the historian should deal with his subject-matter once he has determined upon it and worked out a technique to investigate it. What are the limits of his responsibilities as an historian in the presentation and interpretation of the evidence obtained by his research?

The Greek word ἱστορία, from which our word history is derived, originally seems to have meant research or investigation. This fact will account for the sense in which it may properly be applied to the sciences. A natural extension of the term results in its use to describe the product of the investigation. At this point the long-standing debate on the nature of history as an art or a science arises, since presentation of the results of investigation which cannot be formulated in strictly scientific terms necessarily involves the problem of form and interpretation. In passing we may note that much of the debate may have been caused by a sort of hypnotism induced through repetition of certain key terms and that much of the discussion is really beside the point.

Few scientists today would claim that science has keys to the ultimate problems of the universe, though such claims were characteristic of the optimism of nineteenth-century science and linger in the lay mind today. Scientists have realised that the methods of science are not adapted to formulation of answers to the questions, "Why?" and, "What is the value?" The scientists have, however, not only devised improved methods to obtain quantitative accuracy, but have also thrown new light on the problem of the nature of evidence. At this point the historian must be vitally concerned with the findings of the scientists. Realisation that the fact must be respected is axiomatic both in science and history, but not less so is the realisation that the fact must be respectable. It is always difficult to respect the fact which blocks the development of a pet hypothesis, but thanks to modern science the historian has been forced to a more rigorous standard of respect for evidence. He can no longer ignore or avoid the inconvenient fact. For example, Herodotus has a long and very interesting account of the relations between Croesus and Solon. Even in antiquity it was known that a meeting of the two was chronologically impossible. Herodotus ought to have known this if he had had a modern historian's conception of the necessity for investigation of evidence. On this count, then, he fails to measure up to modern standards in determining the validity of evidence. Quite possibly, however, he did know it, but this meeting was so well adapted to the reflections he wished to introduce on the subject of the mutability of human life and divine retribution that he felt under no obligation to respect the fact that the meeting was impossible. As a result he has written a very interesting passage which cannot qualify as history in the sense that Herodotus intended it to be history, despite its importance for other reasons.

In science the respectable fact is the fact which on further investigation proves to have certain inherent qualities by virtue of which it cannot be disregarded in any effort to interpret a given event, a fact, in short, which is a "crucial instance" or, if it can be tested statistically, a fact which is corroborated by repeated experiment, not a fact which is singular or exceptional in its occurrence.

The problem of respectability may be most difficult for the historian, since two facts may be relevant to a situation and not mutually exclusive. Under these circumstances it is easy to overvalue the fact which coincides with the historian's theory and undervalue the fact which is in conflict, regardless of the inherent respectability of the two facts. This problem is an essential part of Herodotus' account of the relation between the battles at Thermopylae and Artemisium. Herodotus believed that the Athenian navy withdrew because the Persians had turned the pass at Thermopylae and his evidence is presented in terms of that belief. A more respectable fact of the Persian invasion, however, is that there was no point in trying to hold the pass if the way to central Greece was open by sea because the Athenian navy had withdrawn. Herodotus here may have failed to determine which of the facts at his disposal was the more respectable, and by that failure completely obscured the actual nature of the campaign. The late treatise *On the Malignity of Herodotus*, included among the works of Plutarch, would attribute this not to human frailty on the part of Herodotus but to deliberate malice. Although the historian's personal bias is inevitably a factor in the weight he gives to particular facts, it is likely that here Herodotus merely evinces the factor of human error in calculation, against which modern science tries desperately to set up controls. In a laboratory repetitions of an experiment may serve to indicate the probable limits of such error; in the work of the historian it is often impossible to present the evidence in such a way as to make this calculation possible. In the particular instance of the battles of Thermopylae and Artemisium, however, Herodotus has preserved the material which makes it possible to show that the final battle at Artemisium had probably taken place before the final day at Thermopylae. This would serve to show that Herodotus' error was one of human frailty and not one of bias or malice. If his account had been inspired by malice, one would expect him to omit or conceal the evidence which serves to refute his interpretation.

What might be called systematic error is the source of enormous difficulty for the historian since it involves the presuppositions of his own thinking. It is likely to take the form of a general principle by means of which he interprets events, to the exclusion of contributing or material causes which should be assigned their proper place if the interpretation is not to be distorted. Fear of falling into some systematic error leads historians to stress the uniqueness of any given event and to deny any unity to history, along with the denial of any moral or didactic value. This particular form of the old problem of the one and the many is the chief obstacle which must be overcome by any valid philosophy of history. To obtain objectivity by stressing uniqueness is to lose significance; to obtain value and significance by stressing the unity of history, and history as instructive, is to risk falling into some systematic error. In any case the historian is working according to some hypothesis; his task is to evolve an hypothesis which will neither lead him into the systematic error of interpretation according to a general principle unsupported by evidence or insufficiently comprehensive, nor leave him with *disiecta membra* which cannot be brought into any intelligible relation with the actualities of human life.

The story of Croesus and Solon exhibits a systematic error in a form which today we can easily isolate and make allowance for. What leads Herodotus to give the account he does is his view of the world, his conception of the nature of divinity and the status of mankind in the phenomenal world. His account is determined by his belief in the power of Nemesis or divine retribution; just as the astronomers' accounts of the motions of the planets were determined by their acceptance of the Ptolemaic system when they had to resort to cycles and epicycles to make those motions intelligible. The modern scientist is likely to claim only that he has found certain hypotheses which account more accurately for observable phenomena or account for hitherto unexplainable phenomena. Since there is no pretence of finality in his accepted hypotheses of the present, his attitude is of great importance to the historian in devising an approach to his subject, not only in discerning sources of error in earlier historians, but also in his effort to define the nature and scope of history.

If the historian has tested his evidence and demonstrated that he is dealing with facts, if he has tested those facts to determine which are "respectable" facts and as such basic to his presentation of the subject he is treating, there is no absolute assurance that the product will convince his readers of the soundness of his interpretation. Or, to put it another way, propaganda, which has no factual basis in terms of the scientific approach, may be convincing where history is ignored. The presentation of the evidence must be considered an integral part of the job since it involves the use of a medium, words, which cannot be brought into combination without creating an emotional response because of the connotations of the words which must be used in the interpretation placed upon a fact, or because an aesthetic reaction of satisfaction or displeasure is inevitable whenever words are brought into grammatical relation. Occasionally historians have tried to avoid the contamination of art by sheer dullness in their effort to avoid being "popular" or literary. This was a part of the confusion between the technique of the historian as scientific, and the communication of his results to others, where inevitably the historian is in the position of T. S. Eliot's Sweeney, "I gotta use words when I talk to you." Unless the historian is prepared to work only for his own satisfaction with no effort to communicate, he must recognise the importance of his manner of expression and realise that his work is only half done if no one else is able to understand him. A chemical formula is intelligible to anyone who knows the language; an isolated historical fact may correspond to a chemical symbol, but an historian's formula requires a great deal more than the juxtaposition of several such symbols to be intelligible. Some of the later ancient historians may have become so absorbed in their manner of presentation that they forgot the importance of the matter, but at least they never lost sight of their audience, and never forgot that an important part of their effectiveness lay in the emotional and artistic responses they were able to evoke. Certainly we should not allow any pleasure in literary form, desirable as that is, to blind us to historical faults. Yet so strong is interest in form among the ancients that the inferior historians are likely to turn history into a series of rhetorical display pieces, building up an impressive mass of antitheses and arguments from probability to the exclusion of the facts, just as the orators argued cases from probability instead of citing the facts, even when the facts were in the orator's favour.

Our understanding of the importance of the ancient historians is complicated by added subjects, such as archaeology, which loom large in the interests of the man of today, and the added techniques which provide information unknown to the Greeks. It is necessary therefore to suggest some of the information available now, and the techniques of study developed in mod-ern times as a part of the background against which to read and understand just what the Greeks contributed. If the fifth-century Athenian knew the sites of earlier cities in Greece he certainly did not think it worthwhile to excavate them and study the remains. When a statue was broken it was no longer able to stand in its former place, so, after the Persian invasion, the Athenians used the broken statues to fill in a part of the Acropolis instead of building a museum to house the fragments, as we have done since modern excavation brought them to light. The whole study of archaeology with the great light it can throw on certain phases of Greek life was practically unknown to them. Much of the material for the knowledge of pre-history in Greece and Asia Minor was more accessible then than now, yet the Greeks were content to rely on folk-tales and poetic accounts of their own earlier history. For the majority of the Greeks, indeed, the myth was history. They never bothered to find evidence of living conditions, religious customs, and artis-tic development which the spade can uncover. The relative un-importance to them of such detailed knowledge of the past is also brought out by the evidence we can gather from epigraphy and numismatics. The inscriptions and coins which we can use to reconstruct treaties and tribute-lists, which provide evidence of trade and wealth, were necessarily available then, but it is surprising to see how seldom the ancient historian, with the ex-ception of Thucydides, used these sources directly. This fact should perhaps warn us against some of our own tendencies; many subjects of interest to us were simply irrelevant both to the historians and their readers, and we may wonder whether some classical archaeologists' passion for the exact measurement of every potsherd may not be a pseudo-scientific delusion. The character and distribution of potsherds is important for dating and showing trade relations, entirely apart from the artistic value of Greek vase painting, but it may be that much which can be measured, and hence appears to be a scientific occupation today, is really less important than the written records which can convey human insights and aspirations together with an expression of the values and limitations of human life.

Certain it is, and archaeology is responsible for the certainty, that the length of time and variety of races which make up the pre-Greek background of the eastern Mediterranean is a subject of infinitely greater complexity than the Greeks realised. Homer, despite the fact that he was writing poetry, and not history, provides many indications of the artistic development, interrelations, and prosperity of a variety of races and peoples in a period antedating his own. To a considerable extent the achievements of the classical archaeologists are based on a careful observance of Homer's hints as to the cities which were great, and the beautiful works of art found in these cities are those Homer said they possessed. What archaeology has not found is anything to equal Homer's portrayal of the confusion and difficulty attendant upon early man's effort to reach a coherent and worthy conception of the nature of the gods, or the human importance of the conflict of pride, loyalty, and honour. These subjects are still important to mankind, but it is not very important to know that Homer does not have any real conception of the chronological structure and relationships of what we call Minoan and Mycenaean civilisations. It is an excellent thing and very much worthwhile to the historian that we can now tell pretty accurately many of the stages of civilisation from about 2500 B. C. to 1200 B. C. In addition to many other Mediterranean races which were outside the sphere of interest of the early Greeks, we know a good deal about the Hittites, for instance, who indirectly took part in the whole movement which resulted in the decline and disappearance of the flourishing city of Troy in Asia Minor. We can also trace some stages

of the movement which led to the decline of Tiryns and Mycenae on the mainland of Greece. For this knowledge the historian is indebted to the archaeologist and to techniques of study
which simply did not exist for the Greeks.

No source has been found which will add much to our knowledge of the centuries of "Dark Ages" which follow the decline
of Mycenaean civilisation and precede the re-emergence of an
organised society in the eighth century. Within this period the
one startling phenomenon is of course the poetry of Homer.
Although few scholars today would hold the extreme patch-
work theory of the separatists of the last century, no one, I
think, would suppose that the *Iliad* and the *Odyssey* sprang
from the brain of Homer without the previous development
of a strong poetic tradition. Numerous poems on heroic themes
must have provided Homer with material which he incorporated
into his whole structure. In these so-called "Dark Ages" life
must have gone on in some reasonably ordered fashion which
enabled folk-lays and folk traditions to survive, for otherwise
how could the actual poetry picture a society so like that confirmed by the work of the archaeologists? The art of this period shows little evidence of vitality and very little can be
learned of the development of political institutions. Within this
period the earlier races and newcomers from northwest Greece
were fused into a new racial complex, whatever interpretation
is to be placed on the so-called Dorian Invasion. The art of
writing was acquired or re-acquired, and the stage set for the
historical period of Greek civilisation.

While these developments were taking place on the mainland
of Greece, the new oriental empires of Asia Minor were advancing to power and the Greek cities of the Asia Minor coast were
increasing in importance. It is significant that Greek culture
first shows signs of life on the Eastern coast of the Aegean, and
that Herodotus presents us with more facts, if facts they are,
about these cities than about the cities of Greece proper so far
as the early period is concerned. From scattered evidence in
later authors and from inference we gather that in many cities
the oligarchic rule which followed the period of the kings was

replaced by an era of tyrants in the seventh century. Hesiod's picture of the constant tasks and frustrations of agricultural life on the mainland is in sharp contrast to the fragments of the lyric poets from the Greek cities of Asia Minor, filled with their reactions to the political upheavals in the separate cities. In the lyric poets we also find evidence of continued incursions of barbarian races into the prosperous cities of Asia Minor. The only lyric poet from the mainland in this period, Tyrtaeus in Sparta, demonstrates the existence of the Spartan Kings and the elite group of warrior citizens who maintained the closest approach to a stable and strong society which Greece ever knew.

With the beginning of the sixth century we know a little more about the life in the chief cities. Certain distinct characteristics can be made out, and what we know of Solon's legislation for Athens in 594 B. C. enables us to infer with some confidence the steps which preceded it. The necessity of relieving debtors proves that the maladjustment of the economic order had reached considerable proportions. In the previous period extensive colonisation, proved by various types of evidence, had evidently provided an outlet for surplus population. The accumulation of land in the hands of the few powerful families points toward the development of an oligarchy of wealth in conflict with a large group of impoverished farmers who were forced to cultivate the less fertile land. The wide distribution of Euboeic coins shows that at this period the Athenians had not yet shifted their economy to one based on trade, but that the cities of Euboea, along with Corinth, as shown by the distribution of Corinthian pottery, were the centres of trade and commerce. In this period likewise we can trace the growth of the powerful Greek cities of Magna Graecia and Sicily by means of the archaeological remains. In fact we can set the stage for the problems of the fifth century without having to depend very much on Herodotus and Thucydides, who will be the chief interpreters of that period from the historical point of view. The Persian empire was expanding and adding to its subject races; many Greek city-states by the end of the sixth century had, with the aid of the tyrants, developed trade and commerce to supplement their agricultural economy. With the exception of Sparta, whose political and social structure was almost static, the period of the tyrants had passed without permanently settling the political and economic struggle between the haves and have-nots.

In Athens at least, the Pisistratids had exercised the tyranny in such a fashion that political reforms could be managed after their expulsion without the violence which seems, in the ancient accounts, characteristic of the period of transition. Consequently Cleisthenes was able to establish liberal policies essential to the development of Athenian democracy. It was the rapid development of the new constitution which enabled Athens to play such a large part in the struggle to repulse the Persian and maintain free institutions.

Athenian control of the Delian Confederacy after the Persian Wars brought Greece face to face with another great problem of the fifth century, the conflict between an imperialistic democracy based on maritime power and a conservative aristocracy based on military superiority. The exhaustion produced by the Peloponnesian War, the inadequacy of any Greek state as leader, combined with the failure of Pan-hellenism and the chronic inability of the Greeks to create a genuine federation leads to the political solution of the fourth century. A strong centralised control under Alexander maintained peace in Greece, and foreign conquest, using the professional soldiers developed in the long period of particularistic wars between the city-states, provided activity for surplus manpower. After Alexander's death, the long depression of the fourth century, partly caused by the loss of foreign markets, combined with the impossibility of genuine political activity, made the Greek cities subservient to one or another of Alexander's successors.

Alexander may have had a great conception of the possibility of a world-state embracing Greeks and "Barbarians," but the result of the process is a Greece under the power of a ruler whose control is symbolised by his adoption of the style and attributes of the Persian King. It is an ironic circumstance that originally the Persian alone had been able to arouse sufficient enmity in the Greek cities to lead them at least momentarily to submerge their passion for individual freedom and unite to defend that freedom.

Much of interest and importance is still being learned from Greek history between the death of Alexander and the final conquest by Rome. Most of the fundamental historical issues, however, are raised in the fifth and fourth centuries and, with the exception of the light Polybius throws on the later period in his treatment of Rome's destiny, the best extant work of the Greek historians is concentrated within this area. Consequently the period from the Persian Wars to the death of Alexander continues to be a most fascinating and profitable subject of study. This is above all true when one realises how much of the world's great literature and philosophy was created by this same race within this same period. Any epoch within which Aeschylus, Sophocles, Euripides and Aristophanes produced their drama, and Plato and Aristotle their philosophy, demands the historian's consideration.

Since any modern interpretation of the sixth and early fifth centuries must frequently depend on analysis of evidence presented and interpreted by Herodotus, it is necessary to learn what we can of his background and training to understand his conception of the aims and methods of history. Although we possess only scattered fragments of Herodotus' predecessors, it is possible to learn something of them and of one, Hecataeus, in particular. Herodotus frequently follows or corrects the account of Hecataeus so that we can be sure that geography and ethnology played a large part in the latter's work. We can be reasonably sure that the primary purpose of these earlier prose writers was narrative, and that they sought to entertain their audience and satisfy its curiosity. The present opening chapters of Herodotus show definitely that he has a new and different purpose, even though many passages in his history indicate that he had commenced his work simply to record his observations from extensive travel for the entertainment of his audience. He states flatly that he does not believe everything he has reported (Bk. VII. 152) but that it is his duty to recount everything that is said. It is also clear that from Hecataeus and the Ionian philosophers Herodotus had started with an idea of systematising geography and chronology, and of rationalising the myths. The typical Greek willingness to accept poetic accounts of the earlier period of the race is an indication of the difficulty they never quite outgrew in distinguishing myth from fact. This circumstance made it very hard for Herodotus to conceive himself as in any way bound by any laws of evidence in his account of the conflict between the Greeks and Persians.

To understand the influence of Hecataeus of Miletus and the Ionian philosophers we must go back to what can be learned of Herodotus' life. He was born in the Dorian city of Halicarnassus about 484 B. C. only four years before the battle of Thermopylae. He spent a good deal of time in the island of Samos, as the information in Book III indicates. He travelled in parts of the Persian empire, Scythia, and Egypt. He spent some time in Athens, travelling to Thurii in Magna Graecia as an Athenian colonist in 443 B. C., according to the ancient tradition. In Book VII. 133 he mentions an episode which took place in 430/429 B. C. These facts, though scattered, provide a considerable basis for understanding Herodotus' growth and development. His interest in the Persian empire and its ramifications is to be attributed to his birth and early residence on the Asia Minor coast.

The main structure of the early books, apart from the introduction to the first book, is in the tradition of his predecessors, and his later realisation of the significance of the Persian Wars may be attributed to his wider acquaintance with the Greek world and the part played by conceptions of liberty and freedom in that world. One can scarcely exaggerate the passion for autonomy which activated the Greeks on the mainland. For them the *polis* or city was the only unit which could supply the intellectual and spiritual environment essential for the good life- The Greek cities of Asia Minor had fallen away from their earlier political ideals into a period of petty quarrels and weak compliance with the will of a tyrant or overlord. Even the Ionian revolt shows few traces of devotion to a genuine ideal of political freedom. Only in Greece proper could Herodotus learn the full value attached to membership in the *polis*.

Since several different approaches to his subject are still evident, we may suppose that Herodotus revised his basic structure after considerable portions of his work had been written, and that some elements, such as the geographical sections, are imperfectly assimilated to the new structure. It would be unfair to describe the digressions as blemishes, however, for they are very skillfully worked in, and clearly a part of the tradition in which Herodotus was writing. His changed attitude toward the political significance of the war did not involve a change in his literary technique. In the same way he maintained a consistent religious attitude throughout the whole. The tragic sequence of prosperity, wanton insolence, blind folly, and disaster is illustrated for Herodotus on a far grander scale in the fate of the Persian monarch, but the moral is the same as in his stories of Solon and Croesus, Atys and Adrastus, and Polycrates and Cypselus. It is this dominating pattern, previously characterised as "systematic error" in Herodotus, which makes his work propaganda for the belief that the gods visit huge penalties on human arrogance.

As a result of the existing tradition and his own interests Herodotus possesses a merit as an historian which has often been overlooked in the past, especially in the nineteenth century, when his failure to measure up to scientific standards loomed so large. Herodotus was conscious of the influence of climate and social custom in racial development to such an extent that he often atones for weaknesses in his military and political accounts by supplying anthropological and sociological material of great importance. Even the inclusion of myth and the oriental tales may be accounted for in terms of Herodotus' interest in the whole culture and civilisation of each race and not merely in the details of military and political history. If the story has literary and artistic merit so much the better.

Apart from all deficiencies of historical technique and all merits of intrinsic interest, charm of literary style, and more or less accidental preservation of important historical facts, one solid and important achievement stands out in the work of Herodotus. He has succeeded once and for all in expressing the conflict between the ideal of the free man defending his autonomy and basing his state on the rule of law, and the despot who bases his rule on force and whose subjects have the status of slaves. As he says of the Athenians (V. 78), under the tyrants they were no better than their neighbours, but when they obtained freedom they became the first of all. That the conflict was between Greeks and Persians is an historical fact; that it was a conflict between East and West, as Herodotus saw it, is an unwarranted assumption which comes from Herodotus' hypostatising the concepts East and West. But in any case, it is Herodotus' great merit to have realised and presented in inescapable terms the conflict of two conceptions of man's relation to the state between which man must still choose.

In the translation of Herodotus a number of passages omitted by Rawlinson have been restored to the text, and the artificiality in diction in the speeches has been removed in favor of the direct and simple use of the second person.

HERODOTUS

THE PERSIAN WARS

The First Book, Entitled

CLIO

THESE are the researches of Herodotus of Halicarnassus,[1] which he publishes, in the hope of thereby preserving from decay the remembrance of what men have done, and of preventing the great and wonderful actions of the Greeks and the Barbarians from losing their due meed of glory; and withal to put on record what were their grounds of feud.

1. According to the Persians best informed in history, the Phoenicians began the quarrel. This people, who had formerly dwelt on the shores of the Red Sea,[2] having migrated to the Mediterranean and settled in the parts which they now inhabit, began at once, they say, to adventure on long voyages, freighting their vessels with the wares of Egypt and Assyria. They landed at many places on the coast, and among the rest at Argos, which was then pre-eminent above all the states included now under the common name of Hellas. Here they exposed

[1] This is the reading of all our MSS. Yet Aristotle, where he quotes the passage (Rhet. iii. 9), has Thurium in the place of Halicarnassus; that is, he cites the final residence instead of the birth-place of the writer. (See the sketch of Herodotus's Life prefixed to this volume.) The mention of the author's name and country in the first sentence of his history seems to have been usual in the age in which Herodotus wrote. The "Genealogies" of Hecataeus commenced with the words, Ἑκαταῖος Μιλήσιος ὧδε μυθεῖται. (Müller's Fragm. Hist. Gr. vol. i. Fr. 332.) And the practice is followed by Thucydides.

[2] By the Red Sea Herodotus intends, not our Red Sea, which he calls the Arabian Gulf, but the Indian Ocean, or rather both the Indian Ocean and the Persian Gulf, which latter he does not consider distinct from the Ocean, being ignorant of its shape.

3

their merchandise, and traded with the natives for five or six days; at the end of which time, when almost everything was sold, there came down to the beach a number of women, and among them the daughter of the king, who was, they say, agreeing in this with the Greeks, Io, the child of Inachus. The women were standing by the stern of the ship intent upon their purchases, when the Phoenicians, with a general shout, rushed upon them. The greater part made their escape, but some were seized and carried off. Io herself was among the captives. The Phoenicians put the women on board their vessel, and set sail for Egypt. Thus did Io pass into Egypt, according to the Persian story, which differs widely from the Phoenician: and thus commenced, according to their authors, the series of outrages.

2. At a later period, certain Greeks, with whose name they are unacquainted, but who would probably be Cretans, made a landing at Tyre, on the Phoenician coast, and bore off the king's daughter, Europe. In this they only retaliated; but afterwards the Greeks, they say, were guilty of a second violence. They manned a ship of war,[3] and sailed to Aea, a city of Colchis, on the river Phasis; from whence, after despatching the rest of the business on which they had come, they carried off Medea, the daughter of the king of the land. The monarch sent a herald into Greece to demand reparation of the wrong, and the restitution of his child; but the Greeks made answer, that having received no reparation of the wrong done them in the seizure of Io the Argive, they should give none in this instance.

3. In the next generation afterwards, according to the same authorities, Alexander the son of Priam, bearing these events in mind, resolved to procure himself a wife out of Greece by violence, fully persuaded, that as the Greeks had not given satisfaction for their outrages, so neither would he be forced to make any for his. Accordingly he made prize of Helen; upon which the Greeks decided that, before resorting to other measures, they would send envoys to reclaim the princess and require reparation of the wrong. Their demands were met by a reference to the violence which had been offered to Medea, and they were

---

[3] This is the expedition of Jason and the Argonauts.

asked with what face they could now require satisfaction, when they had formerly rejected all demands for either reparation or restitution addressed to them.[4]

4. Hitherto the injuries on either side had been mere acts of common violence; but in what followed the Persians consider that the Greeks were greatly to blame, since before any attack had been made on Europe, they led an army into Asia. Now as for the carrying off of women, it is the deed, they say, of a rogue; but to make a stir about such as are carried off, argues a man a fool. Men of sense care nothing for such women, since it is plain that without their own consent they would never be forced away. The Asiatics, when the Greeks ran off with their women, never troubled themselves about the matter; but the Greeks, for the sake of a single Lacedaemonian girl, collected a vast armament, invaded Asia, and destroyed the kingdom of Priam. Henceforth they ever looked upon the Greeks as their open enemies. For Asia, with all the various tribes of barbarians that inhabit it, is regarded by the Persians as their own; but Europe and the Greek race they look on as distinct and separate.[5]

5. Such is the account which the Persians give of these matters. They trace to the attack upon Troy their ancient enmity towards the Greeks. The Phoenicians, however, as regards Io, vary from the Persian statements. They deny that they used any violence to remove her into Egypt; she herself, they say, having formed an intimacy with the captain, while his vessel lay at Argos, and suspecting herself to be with child, of her own

---

[4] Aristophanes in the Acharnians (524-529) wittily parodies the opening of Herodotus' history. Professing to give the causes of the Peloponnesian war, he says, "But now some young drunkards go to Megara and carry off the harlot Simaetha; the Megarians, hurt to the quick, run off in turn with two harlots of the house of Aspasia: and so for three whores Greece is set ablaze." This is the earliest indication (425 B.C.) of a knowledge of the work of Herodotus on the part of any other Greek writer. Herodotus uses Homer's Alexander for the more familiar Paris, son of Priam.

[5] The claim made by the Persians to the natural lordship of Asia was convenient as furnishing them with pretexts for such wars as it suited their policy to engage in with non-Asiatic nations.

free will accompanied the Phoenicians on their leaving the shore, to escape the shame of detection and the reproaches of her parents. Which of these two accounts is true I shall not trouble to decide. I shall proceed at once to point out the person who first within my own knowledge commenced aggressions on the Greeks, after which I shall go forward with my history, describing equally the greater and the lesser cities. For the cities which were formerly great, have most of them become insignificant; and such as are at present powerful, were weak in the olden time.[6] I shall therefore discourse equally of both, convinced that human happiness never continues long in one stay.

6. Croesus, son of Alyattes, by birth a Lydian, was lord of all the nations to the west of the river Halys.[7] This stream, which separates Syria from Paphlagonia, runs with a course from south to north, and finally falls into the Euxine. So far as our knowledge goes, he was the first of the barbarians who held relations with the Greeks, forcing some of them to become his tributaries, and entering into alliance with others. He conquered the Aeolians, Ionians, and Dorians of Asia, and made a treaty with the Lacedaemonians. Up to that time all Greeks had been free. For the Cimmerian attack upon Ionia, which was earlier than Croesus, was not a conquest of the cities, but only an inroad for plundering.

7. The sovereignty of Lydia, which had belonged to the Heraclidae, passed into the family of Croesus, who were called the Mermnadae, in the manner which I will now relate. There was a certain king of Sardis, Candaules by name, whom the Greeks call Myrsilus. He was a descendant of Alcaeus, son of Heracles. The first king of this dynasty was Agron, son of Ninus, grandson of Belus, and great-grandson of Alcaeus; Candaules, son of Myrsus, was the last. The kings who reigned before Agron sprang from Lydus, son of Atys, from whom the people of the

[6] Thucydides (i. 10) remarks on the small size to which Mycenae had dwindled compared with its former power.

[7] By Syria Herodotus here means Cappadocia, the inhabitants of which he calls Syrians or Cappadocian Syrians. Herodotus regards the words Syria and Assyria, Syrians and Assyrians, as in reality the same.

land, called previously Maeonians, received the name of Lydians. The Heraclidae, descended from Heracles and the slavegirl of Jardanus, having been entrusted by these princes with the management of affairs, obtained the kingdom by an oracle. Their rule endured for twenty-two generations of men, a space of 505 years,⁸ during the whole of which period, from Agron to Candaules, the crown descended in the direct line from father to son.

8. Now it happened that this Candaules was in love with his own wife; and not only so, but thought her the fairest woman in the whole world. This fancy had strange consequences. There was in his bodyguard a man whom he specially favoured, Gyges, the son of Dascylus. All affairs of greatest moment were entrusted by Candaules to this person, and to him he was wont to extol the surpassing beauty of his wife. So matters went on for a while. At length, one day, Candaules, for he was fated to end ill, thus addressed his follower, "I see you do not credit what I tell you of my lady's loveliness; but come now, since men's ears are less credulous than their eyes, contrive some means whereby you may behold her naked." At this the other loudly exclaimed, saying, "What most unwise speech is this, master, which you have uttered? Would you have me behold my mistress when she is naked? Remember that a woman, with her clothes, puts off her bashfulness. Our fathers, in time past, distinguished right and wrong plainly enough, and it is our wisdom to submit to be taught by them. There is an old saying, 'Let each look on his own.' I hold your wife for the fairest of all womankind. Only, I beseech you, ask me not to do wickedly."

9. Gyges thus endeavoured to decline the king's proposal, trembling lest some dreadful evil should befall him through it. But the king replied to him, "Courage, friend; suspect me not of the design to prove you by this discourse; nor dread your mistress, lest mischief befall you at her hands. Be sure I will so

---

⁸ Herodotus professes to count three generations to the century (ii 142), thus making the generation thirty-three and one-third years. In this case the average of the generations is but twenty-three years. Herodotus does not here calculate, but intends to state facts though the figures have no historic value.

manage that she shall not even know that you have looked upon her. I will place you behind the open door of the chamber in which we sleep. When I enter to go to rest she will follow me. There stands a chair close to the entrance, on which she will lay her clothes one by one as she takes them off. You will be able thus at your leisure to peruse her person. Then, when she is moving from the chair towards the bed, and her back is turned on you, be it your care that she see you not as you pass through the door-way."

10. Gyges, unable to escape, could but declare his readiness. Then Candaules, when night came, led Gyges into his sleeping-chamber, and a moment after the queen followed. She came in, and laid her garments on the chair, and Gyges gazed on her. After a while she moved towards the bed, and her back being then turned, he glided stealthily from the apartment. As he was passing out, however, she saw him, and instantly divining what had happened, she neither screamed as her shame impelled her, nor even appeared to have noticed anything, purposing to take vengeance upon the husband who had so affronted her. For among the Lydians, and indeed among the barbarians generally, it is reckoned a deep disgrace, even to a man, to be seen naked.[9]

11. No sound or sign of intelligence escaped her at the time. But in the morning, as soon as day broke, she hastened to choose from among her retinue, such as she knew to be most faithful to her, and preparing them for what was to ensue, summoned Gyges into her presence. Now it had often happened before that the queen had desired to confer with him, and he was accustomed to come to her at her call. He therefore obeyed the summons, not suspecting that she knew what had occurred. Then she addressed these words to him, "Take your choice, Gyges, of two courses which are open to you. Slay Candaules, and thereby become my lord, and obtain the Lydian throne, or die this moment in his room. So you will not again, obeying all behests of your master, behold what is not lawful for you. It

[9] The contrast between the feelings of the Greeks and the barbarians on this point is noted by Thucydides (i. 6), where we learn that the exhibition of the naked person was recent, even with the Greeks.

must needs be, that either he perish by whose counsel this thing was done, or you, who saw me naked, and so did break our usages." At these words Gyges stood awhile in mute astonishment; recovering after a time, he earnestly besought the queen that she would not compel him to so hard a choice. But finding he implored in vain, and that necessity was indeed laid on him to kill or to be killed, he made choice of life for himself, and replied by this inquiry, "If it must be so, and you compel me against my will to put my lord to death, come, let me hear how you will have me set on him." "Let him be attacked," she answered, "on that spot where I was by him shown naked to you, and let the assault be made when he is asleep."

12. All was then prepared for the attack, and when night fell, Gyges, seeing that he had no retreat or escape, but must absolutely either slay Candaules, or himself be slain, followed his mistress into the sleeping-room. She placed a dagger in his hand, and hid him carefully behind the self-same door. Then Gyges, when the king was fallen asleep, entered privily into the chamber and struck him dead. Thus did the wife and kingdom of Candaules pass into the possession of his follower Gyges, of whom Archilochus the Parian, who lived about the same time, made mention in a poem written in Iambic trimeter verse.

13. Gyges was afterwards confirmed in the possession of the throne by an answer of the Delphic oracle. Enraged at the murder of their king, the people flew to arms, but after a while the partisans of Gyges came to terms with them, and it was agreed that if the Delphic oracle declared him king of the Lydians, he should reign; if otherwise, he should yield the throne to the Heraclidae. As the oracle was given in his favour he became king. The Pythian priestess, however, added that, in the fifth generation from Gyges, vengeance should come for the Heraclidae; a prophecy of which neither the Lydians nor their princes took any account till it was fulfilled. Such was the way in which the Mermnadae deposed the Heraclidae, and themselves obtained the sovereignty.

14. When Gyges was established on the throne, he sent no small presents to Delphi, as his many silver offerings at the

Delphic shrine testify. Besides this silver he gave a vast number
of vessels of gold, among which the most worthy of mention are
the goblets, six in number, and weighing altogether thirty talents, which stand in the Corinthian treasury, dedicated by him.
I call it the Corinthian treasury, though in strictness of speech
it is the treasury not of the whole Corinthian people, but of
Cypselus, son of Eetion. Excepting Midas, son of Gordias, king
of Phrygia, Gyges was the first of the barbarians whom we
know to have sent offerings to Delphi. Midas dedicated the
royal throne whereon he was accustomed to sit and administer
justice, an object well worth looking at. It lies in the same
place as the goblets presented by Gyges. The Delphians call the
whole of the silver and the gold which Gyges dedicated, after
the name of the donor, Gygian.

As soon as Gyges was king he made an inroad on Miletus and
Smyrna, and took the city of Colophon. Afterwards, however,
though he reigned thirty-eight years, he did not perform a single
notable exploit. I shall therefore make no further mention of
him, but pass on to his son and successor in the kingdom, Ardys.

15. Ardys took Priene and made war upon Miletus. In his
reign the Cimmerians, driven from their homes by the nomads
of Scythia, entered Asia and captured Sardis, all but the citadel.
He reigned forty-nine years, and was succeeded by his son,
Sadyattes, who reigned twelve years. At his death, his son
Alyattes mounted the throne.

16. This prince waged war with the Medes under Cyaxares,
the grandson of Deioces, drove the Cimmerians out of Asia, conquered Smyrna, the Colophonian colony, and invaded Clazomenae. From this last contest he did not come off as he could
have wished, but met with a severe defeat: still, however, in the
course of his reign, he performed other actions very worthy of
note, of which I will now proceed to give an account.

17. Inheriting from his father a war with the Milesians, he
pressed the siege against the city by attacking it in the following
manner. When the harvest was ripe on the ground he marched
his army into Milesia to the sound of pipes and harps, and flutes
masculine and feminine. The buildings that were scattered over

the country he neither pulled down nor burnt, nor did he even
tear away the doors, but left them standing as they were. He
cut down, however, and utterly destroyed all the trees and all
the corn throughout the land, and then returned to his own
dominions. It was idle for his army to sit down before the place,
as the Milesians were masters of the sea. The reason that he did
not demolish their buildings was, that the inhabitants might be
tempted to use them as homesteads from which to go forth to
sow and till their lands; and so each time that he invaded the
country he might find something to plunder.

18. In this way he carried on the war with the Milesians for
eleven years, in the course of which he inflicted on them two terrible blows; one in their own country in the district of Lim-
eneium, the other in the plain of the Maeander. During six of
these eleven years, Sadyattes, the son of Ardys, who first lighted
the flames of this war, was king of Lydia, and made the incursions. The five following years only belong to the reign of
Alyattes, son of Sadyattes, who (as I said before) inheriting the
war from his father, applied himself to it unremittingly. The
Milesians throughout the contest received no help at all from
any of the Ionians, excepting those of Chios, who lent them
troops in requital of a like service rendered them in former
times, the Milesians having fought on the side of the Chians
during the whole of the war between them and the people of
Erythrae.

19. It was in the twelfth year of the war that the following mischance occurred from the firing of the harvest-fields.
Scarcely had the corn been set a-light when a violent wind carried the flames against the temple of Athena Assesia, which
caught fire, and was burnt to the ground. At the time no one
made any account of the circumstance; but afterwards, on the
return of the army to Sardis, Alyattes fell sick. His illness continuing, either advised by some friend, or himself conceiving the
idea, he sent messengers to Delphi to inquire of the god concerning his malady. On their arrival the priestess declared that
no answer should be given them until they had rebuilt the
temple of Athena, burnt by the Lydians at Assesus in Milesia.

20. Thus much I know from information given me by the Delphians; the remainder of the story the Milesians add. The answer made by the oracle came to the ears of Periander, son of Cypselus, who was a very close friend to Thrasybulus, tyrant of Miletus at that period. He instantly despatched a messenger to report the oracle to him, that Thrasybulus forewarned of its tenor, might the better adapt his measures to the state of affairs.

21. Alyattes, the moment that the words of the oracle were reported to him, sent a herald to Miletus in hopes of concluding a truce with Thrasybulus and the Milesians for such a time as was needed to rebuild the temple. The herald went upon his way; but meantime Thrasybulus had been apprised of everything; and conjecturing what Alyattes would do, he contrived this artifice. He had all the corn that was in the city, whether belonging to himself or to private persons, brought into the market-place, and issued an order that the Milesians should hold themselves in readiness, and, when he gave the signal, should, one and all, fall to drinking and revelry.

22. The purpose for which he gave these orders was the following. He hoped that the Sardian herald, seeing so great store of corn upon the ground, and all the city given up to festivity, would inform Alyattes of it, which fell out as he anticipated. The herald observed the whole, and when he had delivered his message, went back to Sardis. This circumstance alone, as I gather, brought about the peace which ensued. Alyattes, who had hoped that there was now a great scarcity of corn in Miletus, and that the people were worn down to the last pitch of suffering, when he heard from the herald on his return from Miletus, tidings so contrary to those he had expected, made a treaty with the enemy by which the two nations became close friends and allies. He then built at Assesus two temples to Athena instead of one, and shortly after recovered from his malady. Such were the chief circumstances of the war which Alyattes waged with Thrasybulus and the Milesians.

23. This Periander, who apprised Thrasybulus of the oracle, was son of Cypselus, and tyrant of Corinth. In his time a very wonderful thing is said to have happened. The Corinthians and

the Lesbians agree in their account of the matter. They relate
that Arion of Methymna, who as a player on the harp was second to no man living at that time, and who was, so far as we
know, the first to invent the dithyrambic measure,[10] to give it
its name, and to recite in it at Corinth, was carried to Taenarum
on the back of a dolphin.

24. He had lived for many years at the court of Periander,
when a longing came upon him to sail across to Italy and Sicily.
Having made rich profits in those parts, he wanted to recross
the seas to Corinth. He therefore hired a vessel, the crew of
which were Corinthians, thinking that there was no people in
whom he could more safely confide; and, going on board, he set
sail from Tarentum. The sailors, however, when they reached
the open sea, formed a plot to throw him overboard and seize
upon his riches. Discovering their design, he fell on his knees,
beseeching them to spare his life, and making them welcome to
his money. But they refused; and required him either to kill
himself outright, if he wished for a grave on the dry land, or
without loss of time, to leap overboard into the sea. In this
strait Arion begged them, since such was their pleasure, to allow
him to mount upon the quarter-deck, dressed in his full costume, and there to play and sing, promising that, as soon as his
song was ended, he would destroy himself. Delighted at the
prospect of hearing the very best harper in the world, they consented, and withdrew from the stern to the middle of the vessel:
while Arion dressed himself in the full costume of his calling,
took his harp, and standing on the quarter-deck, chanted the

[10] The invention of the Dithyramb, or Cyclic chorus, was ascribed to
Arion, not only by Herodotus, but also by Aristotle, by Hellanicus, by
Dicaearchus, and, implicitly, by Pindar who said it was invented at
Corinth. Perhaps it is best to conclude that Arion did not invent, but
only improved the Dithyramb.

The dithyramb was originally a hymn in honour of Dionysus, with the
circumstances of whose birth the word is somewhat fancifully connected.
It was sung by a band of revellers, directed by a leader. It is thought
that Arion's improvement was to adapt it to the system of Doric choruses,
thereby making it anti-strophic, and substituting the accompaniment of
the harp for that of the flute. It was danced by a chorus of fifty men or
boys round an altar.

Orthian.[11] His strain ended, he flung himself, fully attired as he was, headlong into the sea. The Corinthians then sailed on to Corinth. As for Arion, a dolphin, they say, took him upon his back and carried him to Taenarum, where he went ashore, and thence walked to Corinth in his musician's dress, and told all that had happened to him. Periander, however, disbelieved the story, and put Arion in ward, to prevent his leaving Corinth, while he watched anxiously for the return of the mariners. On their arrival he summoned them before him and asked them if they could give him any tidings of Arion. They returned for answer that he was alive and in good health in Italy, and that they had left him at Tarentum, where he was doing well. Thereupon Arion appeared before them, just as he was when he jumped from the vessel: the men, astonished and detected in falsehood, could no longer deny their guilt. Such is the account which the Corinthians and Lesbians give; and there is to this day at Taenarum, an offering of Arion's at the shrine, which is a small figure in bronze, representing a man seated upon a dolphin.[12]

25. Having brought the war with the Milesians to a close, and reigned over the land of Lydia for fifty-seven years, Alyattes died. He was the second prince of his house who made offerings at Delphi. His gifts, which he sent on recovering from his sickness, were a great bowl of pure silver, with a salver in iron curiously inlaid, a work among all the offerings at Delphi the best worth looking at. Glaucus, the Chian, made it, the man who first invented the art of welding iron.

26. On the death of Alyattes, Croesus, his son, who was in his thirty-fifth year, succeeded to the throne. Of the Greek cities, Ephesus was the first that he attacked. The Ephesians, when he laid siege to the place, made an offering of their city to Artemis, by stretching a rope from the town wall to the temple of the Goddess, which was distant from the ancient city, then besieged

[11] The Orthian is mentioned as a particular sort of melody pitched in a high key, as the name would imply, and was a lively spirited air.

[12] The story of the dolphin is probably connected with a familiar coin type, a hero riding a dolphin.

by Croesus, a space of about a mile. They were, as I said, the first Greeks whom he attacked. Afterwards, on some pretext or other, he made war in turn upon every Ionian and Aeolian state, bringing forward, where he could, a substantial ground of complaint; where such failed him, advancing some poor excuse.

27. In this way he made himself master of all the Greek cities in Asia, and forced them to become his tributaries; after which he began to think of building ships, and attacking the islanders. Everything had been got ready for this purpose, when Bias of Priene (or, as some say, Pittacus the Mytilenean) put a stop to the project. The king had made inquiry of this person, who was lately arrived at Sardis, if there were any news from Greece; to which he answered, "Yes, sire, the islanders are gathering 10,000 horse, designing an expedition against you and against your capital." Croesus, thinking he spoke seriously, broke out, "Ah, might the gods put such a thought into their minds as to attack the sons of the Lydians with cavalry!" "It seems, O king," rejoined the other, "that you desire earnestly to catch the islanders on horseback upon the mainland, you know well what would come of it. But what think you the islanders desire better, now that they hear you are about to build ships and sail against them, than to catch the Lydians at sea, and there revenge on them the wrongs of their brothers upon the mainland, whom you hold in slavery?" Croesus was charmed with the turn of the speech; and thinking there was reason in what was said, gave up his shipbuilding and concluded a league of amity with the Ionians of the isles.

28. Croesus afterwards, in the course of many years, brought under his sway almost all the nations to the west of the Halys. The Lycians and Cilicians alone continued free; all the other tribes he reduced and held in subjection. They were the following: the Lydians, Phrygians, Mysians, Mariandynians, Chalybians, Paphlagonians, Thynian and Bithynian Thracians, Carians, Ionians, Dorians, Aeolians and Pamphylians.

29. When all these conquests had been added to the Lydian empire, and the prosperity of Sardis was now at its height, there

came thither, one after another, all the sages of Greece living at
the time, and among them Solon, the Athenian.[13] He was on his
travels, having left Athens to be absent ten years, under the
pretence of wishing to see the world, but really to avoid being
forced to repeal any of the laws which, at the request of the
Athenians, he had made for them. Without his sanction the
Athenians could not repeal them, as they had bound themselves
under a heavy curse to be governed for ten years by the laws
which should be imposed on them by Solon.

30. On this account, as well as to see the world, Solon set out
upon his travels, in the course of which he went to Egypt to the
court of Amasis,[14] and also came on a visit to Croesus at Sardis.
Croesus received him as his guest, and lodged him in the royal
palace. On the third or fourth day after, he bade his servants
conduct Solon over his treasuries, and show him all their greatness and magnificence. When he had seen them all, and, so far
as time allowed, inspected them, Croesus addressed this question to him, "Stranger of Athens, we have heard much of your
wisdom and of your travels through many lands, from love of
knowledge and a wish to see the world. I am curious therefore to
inquire of you, whom, of all the men that you have seen, you
consider the most happy?" This he asked because he thought
himself the happiest of mortals: but Solon answered him without flattery, according to his true sentiments, "Tellus of Athens,
sire." Full of astonishment at what he heard, Croesus demanded
sharply, "And wherefore do you deem Tellus happiest?" To
which the other replied, "First, because his country was flourishing in his days, and he himself had sons both beautiful and
good, and he lived to see children born to each of them, and

---

[13] Solon's visit to Croesus was rejected as fabulous before the time of
Plutarch (Solon. c. 27), on account of chronological difficulties. It is probably best to view the story as popular philosophy, based on ethical, and
not historical grounds. Herodotus' failure to mention Solon's constitutional
reforms is probably to be attributed to his lack of interest in such matters, not ignorance.

[14] Amasis began to reign 569 B. C. Solon might sail from Athens to
Egypt, thence to Cyprus, and from Cyprus to Lydia.

these children all grew up; and further because, after a life spent in what our people look upon as comfort, his end was surpassingly glorious. In a battle between the Athenians and their neighbours near Eleusis, he came to the assistance of his countrymen, routed the foe, and died upon the field most gallantly. The Athenians gave him a public funeral on the spot where he fell, and paid him the highest honours."

31. Thus did Solon admonish Croesus by the example of Tellus, enumerating the manifold particulars of his happiness. When he had ended, Croesus inquired a second time, who after Tellus seemed to him the happiest, expecting that, at any rate, he would be given the second place. "Cleobis and Bito," Solon answered, "they were of Argive race: their fortune was enough for their wants, and they were besides endowed with so much bodily strength that they had both gained prizes at the Games. Also this tale is told of them: There was a great festival in honour of the goddess Hera at Argos, to which their mother must needs be taken in a car. Now the oxen did not come home from the field in time: so the youths, fearful of being too late, put the yoke on their own necks, and themselves drew the car in which their mother rode. Five miles they drew her, and stopped before the temple. This deed of theirs was witnessed by the whole assembly of worshippers, and then their life closed in the best possible way. Herein, too, God showed forth most evidently, how much better a thing for man death is than life. For the Argive men stood thick around the car and extolled the vast strength of the youths; and the Argive women extolled the mother who was blessed with such a pair of sons; and the mother herself, overjoyed at the deed and at the praises it had won, standing straight before the image, besought the goddess to bestow on Cleobis and Bito, the sons who had so mightily honoured her, the highest blessing to which mortals can attain. Her prayer ended, they offered sacrifice, and partook of the holy banquet, after which the two youths fell asleep in the temple. They never woke more, but so passed from the earth. The Argives, looking on them as among the best of men, caused statues of them to be made, which they gave to the shrine at Delphi."

32. When Solon had thus assigned these youths the second place, Croesus broke in angrily, "What, stranger of Athens, is my happiness, then, valued so little by you, that you do not even put me on a level with private men?"

"Croesus," replied the other, "you asked a question concerning the condition of man, of one who knows that the power above us is full of jealousy,[15] and fond of troubling our lot. A long life gives one to witness much, and experience much oneself, that one would not choose. Seventy years I regard as the limit of the life of man. In these seventy years are contained, without reckoning intercalary months, 25,200 days. Add an intercalary month to every other year, that the seasons may come round at the right time, and there will be, besides the seventy years, thirty-five such months, making an addition of 1,050 days. The whole number of the days contained in the seventy years will thus be 26,250,[16] whereof not one but will produce events unlike the rest. Hence man is wholly accident. For yourself, Croesus, I see that you are wonderfully rich, and the lord of many nations; but with respect to your question, I have no answer to give, until I hear that you have closed your life happily. For assuredly he who possesses great store of riches is no nearer happiness than he who has what suffices for his daily

[15] The jealousy of God is a leading feature in Herodotus' conception of the Deity, and no doubt is one of the chief moral conclusions which he drew from his own survey of human events, and intended to impress on us by his history. The idea of an avenging God is included in the Herodotean conception, but it is far from being the whole of it. Prosperity, not pride, eminence, not arrogance, provokes him. He does not like any one to be great or happy but himself.

What is most remarkable is, that with such a conception of the Divine Nature, Herodotus could maintain such a placid, cheerful, childlike temper. Possibly he was serene because he felt secure in his mediocrity.

[16] Herodotus has made the solar year average 375 days. Two inaccuracies produce the error. In the first place he makes Solon count his months at thirty days each, whereas the Greek months, after the system of intercalation was introduced, were alternately of twenty-nine and thirty days. By this error his first number is raised from 24,780 to 25,200; and also his second number from 1,033 to 1,050. Secondly, he omits to mention that from time to time the intercalary month was omitted altogether.

needs, unless luck attend upon him, and so he continue in the
enjoyment of all his good things to the end of life. For many of
the wealthiest men have been unfavoured of fortune, and many
whose means were moderate, have had excellent luck. Men of
the former class excel those of the latter but in two respects;
these last excel the former in many. The wealthy man is better
able to content his desires, and to bear up against a sudden buf-
fet of calamity. The other has less ability to withstand these
evils (from which, however, his good luck keeps him clear), but
he enjoys all these following blessings: he is whole of limb, a
stranger to disease, free from misfortune, happy in his children,
and comely to look upon. If, in addition to all this, he end his
life well, he is of a truth the man of whom you are in search, the
man who may rightly be termed happy. Call him, however, until
he die, not happy but fortunate. Scarcely, indeed, can any man
unite all these advantages: as there is no country which contains within it all that it needs, but each, while it possesses some
things, lacks others, and the best country is that which contains
the most; so no single human being is complete in every respect
—something is always lacking. He who unites the greatest number of advantages, and retaining them to the day of his death,
then dies peaceably, that man alone, sire, is, in my judgment,
entitled to bear the name of 'happy.' But in every matter we
must mark well the end; for oftentimes God gives men a gleam
of happiness, and then plunges them into ruin."

33. Such was the speech which Solon addressed to Croesus, a
speech which brought him neither largess nor honour. The king
saw him depart with much indifference, since he thought that
a man must be an arrant fool who made no account of present
good, but bade men always wait and mark the end.

34. After Solon had gone away a dreadful vengeance, sent of
God, came upon Croesus, to punish him, it is likely, for considering himself the happiest of men. First he had a dream in the
night, which foreshowed him truly the evils that were about to
befall him in the person of his son. For Croesus had two sons,
one blasted by a natural defect, being deaf and dumb; the other,
distinguished far above all his mates in every pursuit. The name

of the last was Atys. It was this son concerning whom he
dreamed a dream, that he would die by the blow of an iron
weapon. When he woke, he considered earnestly with himself,
and, greatly alarmed at the dream, instantly made his son take
a wife, and whereas in former years the youth had been wont to
command the Lydian forces in the field, he now would not suffer
him to accompany them. All the spears and javelins, and weapons used in the wars, he removed out of the male apartments,
and laid them in heaps in the chambers of the women, fearing
lest perhaps one of the weapons that hung against the wall
might fall and strike him.

35. Now it chanced that while he was making arrangements
for the wedding, there came to Sardis a man under a misfortune,
who had upon him the stain of blood. He was by race a Phrygian, and belonged to the family of the king. Presenting himself
at the palace of Croesus, he prayed to be admitted to purifica-
tion according to the customs of the country. Now the Lydian
method of purifying is very nearly the same as the Greek. Croesus granted the request, and went through all the customary
rites, after which he asked the suppliant of his birth and country, addressing him as follows, "Who are you, stranger, and
from what part of Phrygia did you flee to take refuge at my
hearth? And whom, moreover, what man or what woman, have
you slain?" "O king," replied the Phrygian, "I am the son of
Gordias, son of Midas. I am named Adrastus.[17] The man I un-
intentionally slew was my own brother. For this my father
drove me from the land, and I lost all. Then fled I here to you."
"You are the offspring," Croesus rejoined, "of a house friendly
to mine, and you have come to friends. You shall want for nothing so long as you stay in my dominions. Bear your misfortune
as easily as you may, so will it go best with you." Thenceforth
Adrastus lived in the palace of the king.

36. It chanced that at this very same time there was in the
Mysian Olympus a huge monster of a boar, which went forth
often from this mountain-country, and wasted the corn-fields of

---

[17] Adrastus is "the doomed," "the man unable to escape." Atys is "the
youth under the influence of Até," "the man judicially blind."

the Mysians. Many a time had the Mysians collected to hunt the beast, but instead of doing him any hurt, they came off always with some loss to themselves. At length they sent ambassadors to Croesus, who delivered their message to him in these words, "O king, a mighty monster of a boar has appeared in our parts, and destroys the labour of our hands. We do our best to take him, but in vain. Now therefore we beseech you to let your son accompany us back, with some chosen youths and hounds, that we may rid our country of the animal." Such was the tenor of their prayer.

But Croesus thought of his dream, and answered, "Say no more of my son going with you; that may not be in any wise. He is but just joined in wedlock, and is busy enough with that. I will grant you a picked band of Lydians, and all my hunting array, and I will charge those whom I send to use all zeal in aiding you to rid your country of the brute."

37. With this reply the Mysians were content; but the king's son, hearing what the prayer of the Mysians was, came suddenly in, and on the refusal of Croesus to let him go with them, thus addressed his father, "Formerly, my father, it was considered the noblest and most suitable thing for me to frequent the wars and hunting-parties, and win myself glory in them; but now you keep me away from both, although you have never beheld in me either cowardice or lack of spirit. What face meanwhile must I wear as I walk to the agora or return from it? What must the citizens, what must my young bride think of me? What sort of man will she suppose her husband to be? Either, therefore, let me go to the chase of this boar, or give me a reason why it is best for me to do according to your wishes."

38. Then Croesus answered, "My son, it is not because I have seen in you either cowardice or anything else which has displeased me that I keep you back; but because a vision, which came before me in a dream as I slept, warned me that you were doomed to die young, pierced by an iron weapon. It was this which first led me to hasten on your wedding, and now it hinders me from sending you upon this enterprise. I would like to keep watch over you, if by any means I may cheat fate of you

during my own lifetime. For you are the one and only son that I possess; the other, whose hearing is destroyed, I regard as if he were not."

39. "Ah father," returned the youth, "I blame you not for keeping watch over me after a dream so terrible; but if you are mistaken, if you do not apprehend the dream rightly, it is no blame for me to show you your error. Now the dream, you said, foretold that I should die stricken by an iron weapon. But what hands has a boar to strike with? What iron weapon does he wield? Yet this is what you fear for me. Had the dream said that I should die pierced by a tusk, then you would have done well to keep me away; but it said a weapon. Now here we do not combat men, but a wild animal. I pray you, therefore, let me go with them."

40. "There you have me, my son," said Croesus, "your interpretation is better than mine. I yield to it, and change my mind, and consent to let you go."

41. Then the king sent for Adrastus the Phrygian, and said to him, "Adrastus, when you were smitten with the rod of affliction—no reproach, my friend—I purified you, and have taken you to live with me in my palace, and have been at every charge. Now, therefore, you should requite the good offices you have received at my hands by consenting to go with my son on this hunting-party, and to watch over him, in case you should be attacked upon the road by some band of daring robbers. Even apart from this, it were right for you to go where you may make yourself famous by noble deeds. They are the heritage of your family, and you too are stalwart and strong."

42. Adrastus answered, "Except for your request, O king, I would rather have kept away from this hunt, for it ill beseems a man under a misfortune such as mine to consort with his happier compeers, and besides, I have no heart to it. On many grounds I had stayed behind, but, as you urge it, and I am bound to pleasure you (for truly it does behove me to requite your good offices), I am content to do as you wish. For your son, whom you give into my charge, be sure you shall receive

him back safe and sound, so far as depends upon a guardian's carefulness."

43. Thus assured, Croesus let them depart, accompanied by a band of picked youths, and well provided with dogs of chase. When they reached Olympus, they scattered in quest of the animal; he was soon found, and the hunters, drawing round him in a circle, hurled their weapons at him. Then the stranger, the man who had been purified of blood, whose name was Adrastus, he also hurled his spear at the boar, but missed his aim, and struck Atys. Thus was the son of Croesus slain by the point of an iron weapon, and the warning of the vision was fulfilled. Then one ran to Sardis to bear the tidings to the king, and he came and informed him of the combat, and of the fate that had befallen his son.

44. If it was a heavy blow to the father to learn that his child was dead, it yet more strongly affected him to think that the very man whom he himself once purified had done the deed. In the violence of his grief he called aloud on Zeus the Purifier, to be a witness of what he had suffered at the stranger's hands. Afterwards he invoked the same god as Zeus the Protector of hearths and friendships, using the one term because he had unwittingly harboured in his house the man who had now slain his son; and the other, because the stranger, who had been sent as his child's guardian, had turned out his most cruel enemy.

45. Presently the Lydians arrived, bearing the body of the youth, and behind them followed the homicide. He took his stand in front of the corpse, and, stretching forth his hands to Croesus, delivered himself into his power with earnest entreaties that he would sacrifice him upon the body of his son, "his former misfortune was burden enough; now that he had added to it a second, and had brought ruin on the man who purified him, he could not bear to live." Then Croesus, when he heard these words, was moved with pity towards Adrastus, notwithstanding the bitterness of his own calamity; and so he answered, "Enough, my friend; I have all the revenge that I require, since you give sentence of death against yourself. But

indeed it is not you who have injured me, except so far as you accidentally dealt the blow. Some god is the author of my misfortune, and I was forewarned of it a long time ago." Croesus after this buried the body of his son, with such honours as fitted the occasion. Adrastus, son of Gordias, son of Midas, the destroyer of his brother in time past, the destroyer now of his purifier, regarding himself as the most unfortunate wretch whom he had ever known, as soon as all was quiet about the place, slew himself upon the tomb. Croesus, bereft of his son, gave himself up to mourning for two full years.

46. At the end of this time the grief of Croesus was interrupted by intelligence from abroad. He learned that Cyrus, the son of Cambyses, had destroyed the empire of Astyages, the son of Cyaxares; and that the Persians were becoming daily more powerful. This led him to consider with himself whether it were possible to check the growing power of that people before it came to a head. With this design he resolved to make instant trial of the several oracles in Greece, and of the one in Libya. So he sent his messengers in different directions, some to Delphi, some to Abae in Phocis, and some to Dodona; others to the oracle of Amphiaraus; others to that of Trophonius; others, again, to Branchidae in Milesia. These were the Greek oracles which he consulted. To Libya he sent another embassy, to consult the oracle of Ammon. These messengers were sent to test the knowledge of the oracles, that, if they were found really to return true answers, he might send a second time, and inquire if he ought to attack the Persians.

47. The messengers who were despatched to make trial of the oracles were given the following instructions: they were to keep count of the days from the time of their leaving Sardis, and, reckoning from that date, on the hundredth day they were to consult the oracles, and to inquire of them what Croesus the son of Alyattes, king of Lydia, was doing at that moment. The answers given them were to be taken down in writing, and brought back to him. None of the replies remain on record except that of the oracle at Delphi. There, the moment that the Lydians en-

tered the sanctuary, and before they put their questions, the priestess thus answered them in hexameter verse:

I can count the sands, and I can measure the ocean;
I have ears for the silent, and know what the dumb man mean-
    eth;
Lo! on my sense there striketh the smell of a shell-covered tor-
    toise,
Boiling now on a fire, with the flesh of a lamb, in a cauldron,
Brass is the vessel below, and brass the cover above it.

48. These words the Lydians wrote down at the mouth of the priestess as she prophesied, and then set off on their return to Sardis. When all the messengers had come back with the answers which they had received, Croesus undid the rolls, and read what was written in each. Only one approved itself to him, that of the Delphic oracle. This he had no sooner heard than he instantly made an act of adoration, and accepted it as true, declaring that the Delphic was the only really oracular shrine, the only one that had discovered in what way he was in fact employed. For on the departure of his messengers he had set himself to think what was most impossible for any one to conceive of his doing, and then, waiting till the day agreed on came, he acted as he had determined. He took a tortoise and a lamb, and cutting them in pieces with his own hands, boiled them both together in a brazen cauldron, covered over with a lid which was also of brass.

49. Such then was the answer returned to Croesus from Delphi. What the answer was which the Lydians who went to the shrine of Amphiaraus and performed the customary rites, obtained of the oracle there, I have it not in my power to mention, for there is no record of it. All that is known is, that Croesus believed himself to have found there also an oracle which spoke the truth.

50. After this Croesus, having resolved to propitiate the Delphic god with a magnificent sacrifice, offered up 3,000 of every kind of sacrificial beast, and besides made a huge pile, and

placed upon it couches coated with silver and with gold, and golden goblets, and robes and vests of purple; all which he burnt in the hope of thereby making himself more secure of the favour of the god. Further he issued his orders to all the people of the land to offer a sacrifice according to their means. When the sacrifice was ended, the king melted down a vast quantity of gold, and ran it into ingots, making them six palms long, three palms broad, and one palm in thickness. The number of ingots was 117, four being of refined gold, in weight two talents and a half; the others of pale gold, and in weight two talents. He also caused a statue of a lion to be made in refined gold, the weight of which was ten talents. At the time when the temple of Delphi was burnt to the ground, this lion fell from its place upon the ingots; it now stands in the Corinthian treasury, and weighs only six talents and a half, having lost three talents and a half by the fire.

51. On the completion of these works Croesus sent them away to Delphi, and with them two bowls of an enormous size, one of gold, the other of silver, which used to stand, the latter upon the right, the former upon the left, as one entered the temple. They too were moved after the fire; and now the golden one is in the Clazomenian treasury, and weighs eight talents and forty-two minae; the silver one stands in the corner of the ante-chapel, and holds 600 amphorae.[18] This is known, because the Delphians fill it at the time of the Theophania. It is said by the Delphians to be a work of Theodore the Samian,[19] and I think that they say true, for assuredly it is the work of no common artist. Croesus sent also four silver casks, which are in the Corinthian treasury, and two lustral vases, a golden and a silver one. On the former is inscribed the name of the Lacedaemonians, and they claim it as a gift of theirs, but wrongly, since it was really given by Croesus. The inscription upon it was cut by a Delphian, who wished to please the Lacedaemonians. His name

[18] Above 5,000 gallons (cf. iv. 81).
[19] Pausanias ascribed to Theodore of Samos the invention of casting in bronze, and spoke of him also as an architect.

is known to me, but I forbear to mention it. The boy, through
whose hand the water runs, is (I confess) a Lacedaemonian gift,
but they did not give either of the lustral vases. Besides these
various offerings, Croesus sent to Delphi many others of less account, among the rest a number of round silver basins. Also he
dedicated a female figure in gold, four and one-half feet high,
which is said by the Delphians to be the statue of his baking-
woman; and further, he presented the necklace and the girdles
of his wife.

52. These were the offerings sent by Croesus to Delphi. To
the shrine of Amphiaraus, with whose valour and misfortune he
was acquainted, he sent a shield entirely of gold, and a spear,
also of solid gold, both head and shaft. They were still existing
in my day at Thebes, laid up in the temple of Ismenian Apollo.

53. The messengers who had the charge of conveying these
treasures to the shrines, received instructions to ask the oracles
whether Croesus should go to war with the Persians, and if so,
whether he should strengthen himself by the forces of an ally.
Accordingly, when they had reached their destinations and presented the gifts, they proceeded to consult the oracles in the following terms, "Croesus, king of Lydia and other countries, believing that these are the only real oracles in all the world, has
sent you such presents as your discoveries deserved, and now
inquires of you whether he shall go to war with the Persians,
and if so, whether he shall strengthen himself by the forces of a
confederate." Both the oracles agreed in the tenor of their reply,
which was in each case a prophecy that if Croesus attacked the
Persians, he would destroy a mighty empire, and a recommendation to him to look and see who were the most powerful of the
Greeks, and to make alliance with them.

54. At the receipt of these oracular replies Croesus was overjoyed, and feeling sure now that he would destroy the empire of
the Persians, he sent once more to Pytho, and presented to the
Delphians, the number of whom he had ascertained, two gold
staters apiece. In return for this the Delphians granted to Croesus and the Lydians the privilege of precedency in consulting

the oracle, exemption from all charges, the most honourable seat
at the festivals, and the perpetual right of becoming at pleasure
citizens of their town.

55. After sending these presents to the Delphians, Croesus a
third time consulted the oracle, for having once proved its truthfulness, he wished to make constant use of it. The question
whereto he now desired an answer was, "Whether his kingdom
would be of long duration?" The following was the reply of the
priestess:

Wait till the time shall come when a mule is monarch of Media;
Then, thou delicate Lydian, away to the pebbles of Hermus;
Haste, oh! haste thee away, nor blush to behave like a coward.

56. Of all the answers that had reached him, this pleased him
far the best, for it seemed incredible that a mule should ever
come to be king of the Medes, and so he concluded that the sovereignty would never depart from himself or his seed after him.
Afterwards he turned his thoughts to the alliance which he had
been recommended to contract, and sought to ascertain by inquiry which was the most powerful of the Grecian states. His inquiries pointed out to him two states as pre-eminent above the
rest. These were the Lacedaemonians and the Athenians, the
former of Doric, the latter of Ionic blood. And indeed these two
nations had held from very early times the most distinguished
place in Greece, the one being a Pelasgic the other a Hellenic
people, and the one having never quitted its original seats, while
the other had been excessively migratory; for during the reign
of Deucalion, Phthiotis was the country in which the Hellenes
dwelt, but under Dorus, the son of Hellen, they moved to the
tract at the base of Ossa and Olympus, which is called Histiaeotis; forced to retire from that region by the Cadmeians,[20]
they settled, under the name of Macedni, in the chain of Pindus.
Hence they once more removed and came to Dryopis; and from

[20] The Cadmeians were the Graeco-Phoenician race (their name merely
signifying "the Easterns"), who in the ante-Trojan times, occupied the
country which was afterwards called Boeotia.

Dryopis having entered the Peloponnese in this way, they became known as Dorians.

57. What the language of the Pelasgi was I cannot say with any certainty. If, however, we may form a conjecture from the tongue spoken by the Pelasgi of the present day, those, for instance, who live at Creston above the Tyrrhenians, who formerly dwelt in the district named Thessaliotis, and were neighbours of the people now called the Dorians, or those again who founded Placia and Scylace upon the Hellespont, who had previously dwelt for some time with the Athenians, or those, in short, of any of the cities which have dropped the name but are in fact Pelasgian; if, I say, we are to form a conjecture from any of these, we must pronounce that the Pelasgi spoke a barbarous language. If this were really so, and the entire Pelasgic race spoke the same tongue, the Athenians, who were certainly Pelasgi, must have changed their language at the same time that they passed into the Hellenic body; for it is a certain fact that the people of Creston speak a language unlike any of their neighbours, and the same is true of the Placianians, while the language spoken by these two people is the same; which shows that they both retain the idiom which they brought with them into the countries where they are now settled.

58. The Hellenic race has never, since its first origin, changed its speech. This at least seems evident to me. It was a branch of the Pelasgic, which separated from the main body, and at first was scanty in numbers and of little power; but it gradually spread and increased to a multitude of nations, chiefly by the voluntary entrance into its ranks of numerous tribes of barbarians. The Pelasgi, on the other hand, were, as I think, a barbarian race which never greatly multiplied.

59. On inquiring into the condition of these two nations, Croesus found that one, the Athenian, was in a state of grievous oppression and distraction under Pisistratus, the son of Hippocrates, who was at that time tyrant of Athens. Hippocrates, when he was a private citizen, is said to have gone once upon a time to Olympia to see the games, when a wonderful prodigy

happened to him. As he was employed in sacrificing, the cauldrons which stood near, full of water and of the flesh of the victims, began to boil without the help of fire, and continued till
the water overflowed the pot. Chilon the Lacedaemonian, who
happened to be there and to witness the prodigy, advised Hippocrates, if he were unmarried, never to take into his house a
wife who could bear him a child; if he already had one, to send
her back to her friends; if he had a son, to disown him. Chilon's
advice did not at all please Hippocrates, who disregarded it,
and some time after became the father of Pisistratus. This Pisistratus, at a time when there was civil contention in Attica be
tween the party of the Seacoast headed by Megacles the son of
Alcmaeon, and that of the Plain headed by Lycurgus, one of the
Aristolaids, formed the project of making himself tyrant, and
with this view created a third faction. Gathering together a
band of partisans, and giving himself out for the protector of
the Highlanders, he contrived the following stratagem. He
wounded himself and his mules, and then drove his chariot into
the market-place, professing to have just escaped an attack of
his enemies, who had attempted his life as he was on his way
into the country. He besought the people to assign him a guard
to protect his person, reminding them of the glory which he had
gained when he led the attack upon the Megarians, and took the
town of Nisaea, at the same time performing many other exploits. The Athenians, deceived by his story, appointed him a
band of citizens to serve as a guard, who were to carry clubs instead of spears, and to accompany him wherever he went. Thus
strengthened, Pisistratus broke into revolt and seized the citadel. In this way he acquired the sovereignty of Athens, which he
continued to hold without disturbing the previously existing offices or altering any of the laws. He administered the state according to the established usages, and his arrangements were
wise and salutary.

60. However, after a little time, the partisans of Megacles
and those of Lycurgus agreed to forget their differences, and
united to drive him out. So Pisistratus, having by the means
described first made himself master of Athens, lost his power

again before it had time to take root. No sooner, however, was he departed than the factions which had driven him out quarrelled anew, and at last Megacles, wearied with the struggle, sent a herald to Pisistratus, with an offer to re-establish him on the throne if he would marry his daughter. Pisistratus consented, and on these terms an agreement was concluded between the two, after which they proceeded to devise the mode of his restoration. And here the device on which they hit was the silliest to be found in all history, more especially considering that the Greeks have been from very ancient times distinguished from the barbarians by superior sagacity and freedom from foolish simpleness, and remembering that the persons on whom this trick was played were not only Greeks but Athenians, who have the credit of surpassing all other Greeks in cleverness. There was in the Paeanian district a woman named Phya, whose height was almost six feet, and who was altogether comely to look upon. This woman they clothed in complete armour, and, instructing her as to the carriage which she was to maintain in order to beseem her part, they placed her in a chariot and drove to the city. Heralds had been sent forward to precede her, and to make proclamation to this effect, "Citizens of Athens, receive again Pisistratus with friendly minds. Athena, who of all men honours him the most, herself conducts him back to her own citadel." This they proclaimed in all directions, and immediately the rumour spread throughout the country districts that Athena was bringing back her favourite. They of the city also, fully persuaded that the woman was the veritable goddess, worshipped her, and received Pisistratus back.

61. Pisistratus, having thus recovered the sovereignty, married, according to agreement, the daughter of Megacles. As, however, he had already a family of grown-up sons, and the Alcmaeonidae were supposed to be under a curse,[21] he deter-

[21] The curse rested on them upon account of their treatment of the partisans of Cylon. The archon of the time, Megacles, not only broke faith with them after he had, by a pledge to spare their lives, induced them to leave the sacred precinct of Athena in the Acropolis, but also slew a number at the altar of the Eumenides.

mined that there should be no issue of the marriage, and he
consequently had intercourse with her in an abnormal fashion.
His wife at first kept this matter to herself, but after a time,
either her mother questioned her, or it may be that she told it
of her own accord. At any rate, she informed her mother, and so
it reached her father's ears. Megacles, indignant at receiving an
affront from such a quarter, in his anger instantly made up his
differences with the opposite faction, on which Pisistratus,
aware of what was planning against him, took himself out of
the country. Arrived at Eretria, he held a council with his children to decide what was to be done. The opinion of Hippias prevailed, and it was agreed to aim at regaining the sovereignty.
The first step was to obtain advances of money from such states
as were under obligations to them. By these means they collected large sums from several countries, especially from the
Thebans, who gave them far more than any of the rest. To be
brief, time passed, and all was at length got ready for their return. A band of Argive mercenaries arrived from the Peloponnese, and a certain Naxian named Lygdamis, who volunteered
his services, was particularly zealous in the cause, supplying
both men and money.

62. In the eleventh year of their exile the family of Pisistratus set sail from Eretria on their return home. They made the
coast of Attica, near Marathon, where they encamped, and were
joined by their partisans from the capital and by numbers from
the country districts, who loved tyranny better than freedom.
At Athens, while Pisistratus was obtaining funds, and even after
he landed at Marathon, no one paid any attention to his proceedings. When, however, it became known that he had left
Marathon, and was marching upon the city, preparations were
made for resistance, the whole force of the state was levied, and
led against the returning exiles. Meantime the army of Pisistratus, which had broken up from Marathon, meeting their adversaries near the temple of the Pallenian Athena, pitched their
camp opposite them. Here a certain soothsayer, Amphilytus by
name, an Acarnanian, moved by a divine impulse, came into the

presence of Pisistratus, and approaching him uttered this prophecy in the hexameter measure:

Now has the cast been made, the net is out-spread in the water,
Through the moonshiny night the tunnies will enter the meshes.

63. Such was the prophecy uttered under a divine inspiration. Pisistratus, apprehending its meaning, declared that he accepted the oracle, and instantly led on his army. The Athenians from the city had just finished their midday meal, after which they had betaken themselves, some to dice, others to sleep, when Pisistratus with his troops fell upon them and put them to the rout. As soon as the flight began, Pisistratus bethought himself of a most wise contrivance, whereby the Athenians might be induced to disperse and not unite in a body any more. He mounted his sons on horseback and sent them on in front to overtake the fugitives, and exhort them to be of good cheer, and return each man to his home. The Athenians took the advice, and Pisistratus became for the third time master of Athens.[22]

64. Upon this he set himslf to root his power more firmly, by the aid of a numerous body of mercenaries, and by keeping up a full exchequer, partly supplied from native sources, partly from the countries about the river Strymon. He also demanded hostages from many of the Athenians who had remained at home, and not left Athens at his approach; and these he sent to Naxos, which he had conquered by force of arms, and given over into the charge of Lygdamis. He also purified the island of Delos, according to the injunctions of an oracle, after the following fashion. All the dead bodies which had been interred within sight of the temple he dug up, and removed to another part of the isle. Thus was the tyranny of Pisistratus established at Athens, many of the Athenians having fallen in the battle, and many others having fled the country together with the sons of Alcmaeon.

[22] The probable dates of Pisistratid rule are as follows: First tyranny, 561–560; first exile, 559; second tyranny, 559; second exile, 556; third tyranny, 546; death, 527; expulsion of Hippias, 510.

65. Such was the condition of the Athenians when Croesus made inquiry concerning them. Proceeding to seek information concerning the Lacedaemonians, he learnt that, after passing through a period of great depression, they had lately been victorious in a war with the people of Tegea; for, during the joint reign of Leo and Hegesicles, kings of Sparta, the Lacedaemonians, successful in all their other wars, suffered continual defeats at the hands of the Tegeans. At a still earlier period they had been the very worst governed people in Greece, as well in matters of internal management as in their relations towards foreigners, from whom they kept entirely aloof. The circumstances which led to their being well governed were the following: Lycurgus, a man of distinction among the Spartans, had gone to Delphi, to visit the oracle. Scarcely had he entered into the inner fane, when the priestess exclaimed aloud:

O thou great Lycurgus, that com'st to my beautiful dwelling,
Dear to Zeus, and to all who sit in the halls of Olympus,
Whether to hail thee a god I know not, or only a mortal,
But my hope is strong that a god thou wilt prove, Lycurgus.

Some report besides, that the priestess delivered to him the entire system of laws which are still observed by the Spartans. The Lacedaemonians, however, themselves assert that Lycurgus,[26] when he was guardian of his nephew, Labotas, king of Sparta, and regent in his room, introduced them from Crete; for as soon as he became regent, he altered the whole of the existing customs, substituting new ones, which he took care should be observed by all. After this he arranged whatever appertained to war, establishing the companies of thirty, messmates, and sworn brotherhoods, besides which he instituted the senate, and the ephoralty. Such was the way in which the Lacedaemonians became a well-governed people.

66. On the death of Lycurgus they built him a temple, and

[26] Even if Lycurgus was a real person we know nothing about him and Herodotus' account is not historical. It is only valuable as the fifth century official Lacedaemonian account.

ever since they have worshipped him with the utmost reverence. Their soil being good and the population numerous, they sprang up rapidly to power, and became a flourishing people. In consequence they soon ceased to be satisfied to stay quiet; and, regarding the Arcadians as very much their inferiors, they sent to consult the oracle about conquering the whole of Arcadia. The priestess thus answered them:

Cravest thou Arcady? Bold is thy craving. I shall not content it.
Many the men that in Arcady dwell, whose food is the acorn—
They will never allow thee. It is not I that am niggard.
I will give thee to dance in Tegea, with noisy foot-fall,
And with the measuring line mete out the glorious champaign.

When the Lacedaemonians received this reply, leaving the rest of Arcadia untouched, they marched against the Tegeans, carrying with them fetters, so confident had this oracle (which was, in truth, but of base metal) made them that they would enslave the Tegeans. The battle, however, went against them, and many fell into the enemy's hands. Then these persons, wearing the fetters which they had themselves brought, and fastened together in a string. measured the Tegean plain as they executed their labours. The fetters in which they worked, were still, in my day, preserved at Tegea where they hung round the walls of the temple of Athena Alea.

67. Throughout the whole of this early contest with the Tegeans, the Lacedaemonians met with nothing but defeats; but in the time of Croesus, under the kings Anaxandrides and Ariston, fortune had turned in their favour, in the manner which I will now relate. Having been worsted in every engagement by their enemy, they sent to Delphi, and inquired of the oracle what god they must propitiate to prevail in the war against the Tegeans. The answer of the priestess was, that before they could prevail, they must remove to Sparta the bones of Orestes, the son of Agamemnon. Unable to discover his burial-place, they sent a second time, and asked the god where the body of the hero had been laid. The following was the answer they received:

Level and smooth is the plain where Arcadian Tegea standeth;
There two winds are ever, by strong necessity, blowing,
Counter-stroke answers stroke, and evil lies upon evil.
There all-teeming Earth doth harbour the son of Atrides;
Bring thou him to thy city, and then be Tegea's master.

After this reply, the Lacedaemonians were no nearer discovering
the burial-place than before, though they continued to search
for it diligently; until at last a man named Lichas, one of the
Spartans called Agathoergi, found it. The Agathoergi are citizens who have just served their time among the knights. The
five eldest of the knights go out every year, and are bound during the year after their discharge, to go wherever the State sends
them, and actively employ themselves in its service.

68. Lichas was one of this body when, partly by good luck,
partly by his own wisdom, he discovered the burial-place. Intercourse between the two States existing just at this time, he went
to Tegea, and, happening to enter into the workshop of a smith,
he saw him forging some iron. As he stood marvelling at what he
beheld, he was observed by the smith who, leaving off his work,
went up to him and said, "Certainly, then, you Spartan stranger,
you would have been wonderfully surprised if you had seen
what I have, since you make a marvel even of the working in
iron. I wanted to make myself a well in this room, and began to
dig it, when what think you? I came upon a coffin ten feet long.
I had never believed that men were taller in the olden times
than they are now, so I opened the coffin. The body inside was
of the same length; I measured it, and filled up the hole again."

Such was the man's account of what he had seen. The other,
on turning the matter over in his mind, conjectured that this
was the body of Orestes, of which the oracle had spoken. He
guessed so, because he observed that the smithy had two bellows, which he understood to be the two winds, and the hammer
and anvil would do for the stroke and the counter-stroke, and
the iron that was being wrought for the evil lying upon evil.
This he imagined might be so because iron had been discovered
to the hurt of man. Full of these conjectures, he sped back to

Sparta and laid the whole matter before his countrymen. Soon after, by a concerted plan, they brought a charge against him, and began a prosecution. Lichas betook himself to Tegea, and on his arrival acquainted the smith with his misfortune, and proposed to rent his room of him. The smith refused for some time; but at last Lichas persuaded him, and took up his abode in it. Then he opened the grave, and collecting the bones, returned with them to Sparta. From henceforth, whenever the Spartans and the Tegeans made trial of each other's skill in arms, the Spartans always had greatly the advantage; and by the time to which we are come now they were masters of most of the Peloponnese

69. Croesus, informed of all these circumstances, sent messengers to Sparta, with gifts in their hands, who were to ask the Spartans to enter into alliance with him. They received strict injunctions as to what they should say, and on their arrival at Sparta spoke as follows, "Croesus, king of the Lydians and of other nations, has sent us to speak thus to you, 'Lacedaemonians, the god has bidden me to make the Greek my friend; I therefore apply to you, in conformity with the oracle, knowing that you hold the first rank in Greece, and desire to become your friend and ally in all true faith and honesty.'"

Such was the message which Croesus sent by his heralds. The Lacedaemonians, who were aware beforehand of the reply given him by the oracle, were full of joy at the coming of the messengers, and at once took the oaths of friendship and alliance: this they did the more readily as they had previously contracted certain obligations towards him. They had sent to Sardis on one occasion to purchase some gold, intending to use it on a statue of Apollo—the statue, namely, which remains to this day at Thornax in Laconia, when Croesus, hearing of the matter, gave them as a gift the gold which they wanted.

70. This was one reason why the Lacedaemonians were so willing to make the alliance: another was, because Croesus had chosen them for his friends in preference to all the other Greeks. They therefore held themselves in readiness to come at his summons, and not content with so doing, they further had a huge

vase made in bronze, covered with figures of animals all round the outside of the rim, and large enough to contain 2,700 gallons, which they sent to Croesus as a return for his presents to them. The vase, however, never reached Sardis. Its miscarriage is accounted for in two quite different ways. The Lacedaemonian story is, that when it reached Samos, on its way towards Sardis, the Samians having knowledge of it, put to sea in their ships of war and made it their prize. But the Samians declare, that the Lacedaemonians who had the vase in charge, happening to arrive too late, and learning that Sardis had fallen and that Croesus was a prisoner, sold it in their island, and the purchasers (who were, they say, private persons) made an offering of it at the shrine of Hera: the sellers were very likely on their return to Sparta to have said that they had been robbed of it by the Samians. Such, then, was the fate of the vase.

71. Meanwhile Croesus, taking the oracle in a wrong sense, led his forces into Cappadocia, fully expecting to defeat Cyrus and destroy the empire of the Persians. While he was still engaged in making preparations for his attack, a Lydian named Sandanis, who had always been looked upon as a wise man, but who after this obtained a very great name indeed among his countrymen, came forward and counselled the king in these words, "You are about, king, to make war against men who wear leathern trousers, and have all their other garments of leather; who feed not on what they like, but on what they can get from a soil that is sterile and unkindly; who do not indulge in wine, but drink water; who possess no figs nor anything else that is good to eat. If, then, you conquer them, what can you get from them, seeing that they have nothing at all? But if they conquer you, consider how much that is precious you will lose: if they once get a taste of our pleasant things, they will keep such hold of them that we shall never be able to make them loose their grasp. For my part, I am thankful to the gods, that they have not put it into the hearts of the Persians to invade Lydia."

Croesus was not persuaded by this speech, though it was true

enough; for before the conquest of Lydia, the Persians possessed
none of the luxuries or delights of life.

72. The Cappadocians are known to the Greeks by the name
of Syrians. Before the rise of the Persian power, they had been
subject to the Medes; but at the present time they were within
the empire of Cyrus, for the boundary between the Median and
the Lydian empires was the river Halys. This stream, which
rises in the mountain country of Armenia, runs first through
Cilicia; afterwards it flows for a while with the Matieni on the
right, and the Phrygians on the left: then, when they are passed,
it proceeds with a northern course, separating the Cappadocian
Syrians from the Paphlagonians, who occupy the left bank, thus
forming the boundary of almost the whole of Lower Asia, from
the sea opposite Cyprus to the Euxine. Just there is the neck
of the peninsula, a journey of five days across for an active
walker.[24]

73. There were two motives which led Croesus to attack Cappadocia: firstly, he coveted the land, which he wished to add to
his own dominions; but the chief reason was, that he wanted to
revenge on Cyrus the wrongs of Astyages, and was made confident by the oracle of being able so to do: for the Astyages, son
of Cyaxares and king of the Medes, who had been dethroned by
Cyrus, son of Cambyses, was Croesus' brother by marriage.
This marriage had taken place under circumstances which I will
now relate. A band of Scythian nomads, who had left their own
land on occasion of some disturbance, had taken refuge in Media. Cyaxares, son of Phraortes, and grandson of Deioces, was
at that time king of the country. Recognising them as suppliants, he began by treating them with kindness, and coming
presently to esteem them highly, he intrusted to their care a
number of boys, whom they were to teach their language and to
instruct in the use of the bow. Time passed, and the Scythians

[24] Herodotus tells us in one place (iv. 101), that he reckons the day's
journey at about twenty-three of our miles. If we regard this as the
measure intended here, we must consider that Herodotus imagined the
isthmus to be but 115 miles across, 165 miles short of the truth.

employed themselves, day after day, in hunting, and always
brought home some game; but at last it chanced that one day
they took nothing. On their return to Cyaxares with empty
hands, that monarch, who was hot-tempered, as he showed upon
the occasion, received them very rudely and insultingly. In consequence of this treatment, which they did not conceive themselves to have deserved, the Scythians determined to take one of
the boys whom they had in charge, cut him in pieces, and then
dressing the flesh as they were wont to dress that of the wild
animals, serve it up to Cyaxares as game: after which they resolved to convey themselves with all speed to Sardis, to the
court of Alyattes, the son of Sadyattes. The plan was carried
out: Cyaxares and his guests ate of the flesh prepared by the
Scythians, and they themselves, having accomplished their purpose, fled to Alyattes in the guise of suppliants.

74. Afterwards, on the refusal of Alyattes to give up his suppliants when Cyaxares sent to demand them of him, war broke
out between the Lydians and the Medes, and continued for five
years, with various success. In the course of it the Medes gained
many victories over the Lydians, and the Lydians also gained
many victories over the Medes. Among their other battles there
was one night engagement. As, however, the balance had not inclined in favour of either nation, another combat took place in
the sixth year, in the course of which, just as the battle was
growing warm, day was on a sudden changed into night. This
event had been foretold by Thales, the Milesian, who forewarned the Ionians of it, fixing for it the very year in which it
actually took place.[25] The Medes and Lydians, when they observed the change, ceased fighting, and were alike anxious to
have terms of peace agreed on. Syennesis[26] of Cilicia, and Labynetus[27] of Babylon, were the persons who mediated between the
parties, who hastened the taking of the oaths, and brought

[25] This date is fixed by the astronomers as 28 May 585 B.C.
[26] The name Syennesis is common to all the kings of Cilicia mentioned in
history. It is not really a name, but, like Pharaoh, a title.
[27] The Babylonian monarch at this time was Nebuchadnezzar whose
reign began 604 B.C.

about the exchange of espousals. It was they who advised that
Alyattes should give his daughter Aryenis in marriage to Astyages the son of Cyaxares, knowing, as they did, that without
some sure bond of strong necessity, there is wont to be but little
security in men's covenants. Oaths are taken by these people in
the same way as by the Greeks, except that they make a slight
flesh wound in their arms, from which each sucks a portion of
the other's blood.

75. Cyrus had captured this Astyages, who was his mother's
father, and kept him prisoner, for a reason which I shall bring
forward in another part of my history. This capture formed the
ground of quarrel between Cyrus and Croesus, in consequence
of which Croesus sent his servants to ask the oracle if he should
attack the Persians; and when an evasive answer came, fancying it to be in his favour, carried his arms into the Persian territory. When he reached the river Halys, he transported his
army across it, as I maintain, by the bridges which exist there
at the present day; but, according to the general belief of the
Greeks, by the aid of Thales the Milesian. The tale is, that
Croesus was in doubt how he should get his army across, as the
bridges were not made at that time, and that Thales, who happened to be in the camp, divided the stream and caused it to
flow on both sides of the army instead of on the left only. This
he effected thus: Beginning some distance above the camp, he
dug a deep channel, which he brought round in a semicircle, so
that it might pass to rearward of the camp; and that thus the
river, diverted from its natural course into the new channel at
the point where this left the stream, might flow by the station
of the army, and afterwards fall again into the ancient bed. In
this way the river was split into two streams, which were both
easily fordable. It is said by some that the water was entirely
drained off from the natural bed of the river. But I am of a different opinion; for I do not see how, in that case, they could
have crossed it on their return.

76. Having passed the Halys with the forces under his command, Croesus entered the district of Cappadocia which is called

Pteria.[28] It lies in the neighbourhood of the city of Sinope upon the Euxine, and is the strongest position in the whole country thereabouts. Here Croesus pitched his camp, and began to ravage the fields of the Syrians. He besieged and took the chief city of the Pterians, and reduced the inhabitants to slavery: he likewise made himself master of the surrounding villages. Thus he brought ruin on the Syrians, who were guilty of no offence towards him. Meanwhile, Cyrus had levied an army and marched against Croesus, increasing his numbers at every step by the forces of the nations that lay in his way. Before beginning his march he had sent heralds to the Ionians, with an invitation to them to revolt from the Lydian king: they, however, had refused compliance. Cyrus, notwithstanding, marched against the enemy, and encamped opposite them in the district of Pteria, where the trial of strength took place between the contending powers. The combat was hot and bloody, and upon both sides the number of the slain was great; nor had victory declared in favour of either party, when night came down upon the battlefield. Thus both armies fought valiantly.

77. Croesus laid the blame of his ill success on the number of his troops, which fell very short of the enemy; and as on the next day Cyrus did not repeat the attack, he set off on his return to Sardis, intending to collect his allies and renew the contest in the spring. He meant to call on the Egyptians to send him aid, according to the terms of the alliance which he had concluded with Amasis, previous to his league with the Lacedaemonians. He intended also to summon to his assistance the Babylonians, under their king Labynetus,[29] for they too were bound to him by treaty: and further, he meant to send word to Sparta, and appoint a day for the coming of their succours. Having got together these forces in addition to his own, he would, as soon as the winter was past and springtime come, march once more

[28] Pteria is probably Boghaz Keui where modern excavations have uncovered a mass of inscriptions vital to the reconstruction of the history of the Hittite empire.

[29] Undoubtedly Nabonidus (556 B.C.), the last of the Babylonian monarchs.

against the Persians. With these intentions Croesus, immediately on his return, despatched heralds to his various allies, with a request that they would join him at Sardis in the course of the fifth month from the time of the departure of his messengers. He then disbanded the army—consisting of mercenary troops— which had been engaged with the Persians and had since accompanied him to his capital, and let them depart to their homes, never imagining that Cyrus, after a battle in which victory had been so evenly balanced, would venture to march upon Sardis.

78. While Croesus was still in this mind, all the suburbs of Sardis were found to swarm with snakes, on the appearance of which the horses left feeding in the pasture-grounds, and flocked to the suburbs to eat them. The king, who witnessed the unusual sight, regarded it very rightly as a prodigy. He therefore instantly sent messengers to the soothsayers of Telmessus, to consult them upon the matter. His messengers reached the city, and obtained from the Telmessians an explanation of what the prodigy portended, but fate did not allow them to inform their lord; for before they entered Sardis on their return, Croesus was a prisoner. What the Telmessians had declared was, that Croesus must look for the entry of an army of foreign invaders into his country, and that when they came they would subdue the native inhabitants; since the snake, said they, is a child of earth, and the horse a warrior and a foreigner. Croesus was already a prisoner when the Telmessians thus answered his inquiry, but they had no knowledge of what was taking place at Sardis, or of the fate of the monarch.

79. Cyrus, however, when Croesus broke up so suddenly from his quarters after the battle at Pteria, conceiving that he had marched away with the intention of disbanding his army, considered a little, and soon saw that it was advisable for him to advance upon Sardis with all haste, before the Lydians could get their forces together a second time. Having thus determined, he lost no time in carrying out his plan. He marched forward with such speed that he was himself the first to announce his coming to the Lydian king. That monarch, placed in the utmost diffi-

culty by the turn of events which had gone so entirely against all his calculations, nevertheless led out the Lydians to battle. In all Asia there was not at that time a braver or more warlike people. Their manner of fighting was on horseback; they carried long lances, and were clever in the management of their steeds.

80. The two armies met in the plain before Sardis. It is a vast flat, bare of trees, watered by the Hyllus and a number of other streams, which all flow into one larger than the rest, called the Hermus. This river rises in the sacred mountain of the Dindymenian Mother,[30] and falls into the sea near the town of Phocaea.[31]

When Cyrus beheld the Lydians arranging themselves in order of battle on this plan, fearful of the strength of their cavalry, he adopted a device which Harpagus, one of the Medes, suggested to him. He collected together all the camels that had come in the train of his army to carry the provisions and the baggage, and taking off their loads, he mounted riders upon them accoutred as horsemen. These he commanded to advance in front of his other troops against the Lydian horse; behind them were to follow the foot soldiers, and last of all the cavalry. When his arrangements were complete, he gave his troops orders to slay all the other Lydians who came in their way without mercy, but to spare Croesus and not kill him, even if he should be seized and offer resistance. The reason why Cyrus opposed his camels to the enemy's horse was, because the horse has a natural dread of the camel, and cannot abide either the sight or the smell of that animal. By this stratagem he hoped to make Croesus's horse useless to him, the horse being what he chiefly depended on for victory. The two armies then joined battle, and immediately the Lydian war-horses, seeing and smelling the camels, turned round and galloped off; and so it came to pass that all Croesus's hopes withered away. The Lydians, however, behaved manfully. As soon as they understood what was hap-

---

[30] The Dindymenian mother was Cybele, the special deity of Phrygia.

[31] The Hermus now falls into the sea very much nearer to Smyrna than to Phocaea. Its course is perpetually changing.

pening, they leaped off their horses, and engaged with the Persians on foot. The combat was long; but at last, after a great slaughter on both sides, the Lydians turned and fled. They were driven within their walls, and the Persians laid siege to Sardis.

81. Thus the siege began. Meanwhile Croesus, thinking that the place would hold out no inconsiderable time, sent off fresh heralds to his allies from the beleaguered town. His former messengers had been charged to bid them assemble at Sardis in the course of the fifth month; they whom he now sent were to say that he was already besieged, and to beseech them to come to his aid with all possible speed. Among his other allies Croesus did not omit to send to Lacedaemon.

82. It chanced, however, that the Spartans were themselves just at this time engaged in a quarrel with the Argives about a place called Thyrea, which was within the limits of Argolis, but had been seized on by the Lacedaemonians. Indeed, the whole country westward, as far as Cape Malea, belonged once to the Argives, and not only that entire tract upon the mainland, but also Cythera, and the other islands. The Argives collected troops to resist the seizure of Thyrea, but before any battle was fought, the two parties came to terms, and it was agreed that 300 Spartans and 300 Argives should meet and fight for the place, which should belong to the nation with whom the victory rested. It was stipulated also that the other troops on each side should return home to their respective countries, and not remain to witness the combat, as there was danger, if the armies stayed, that either the one or the other, on seeing their countrymen undergoing defeat, might hasten to their assistance. These terms being agreed on, the two armies marched off, leaving 300 picked men on each side to fight for the territory. The battle began, and so equal were the combatants, that at the close of the day, when night put a stop to the fight, of the whole 600 only three men remained alive, two Argives, Alcanor and Chromius, and a single Spartan, Othryadas. The two Argives, regarding themselves as the victors, hurried to Argos. Othryadas, the Spartan, remained upon the field, and, stripping the bodies of the Argives who had fallen, carried their armour to the Spartan camp. Next

day the two armies returned to learn the result. At first they disputed, both parties claiming the victory, the one, because they
had the greater number of survivors; the other, because their
man remained on the field, and stripped the bodies of the slain,
whereas the two men of the other side ran away; but at last they
fell from words to blows, and a battle was fought, in which both
parties suffered great loss, but at the end the Lacedaemonians
gained the victory. Upon this the Argives, who up to that time
had worn their hair long, cut it off close, and made a law, to
which they attached a curse, binding themselves never more to
let their hair grow, and never to allow their women to wear gold,
until they should recover Thyrea. At the same time the Lacedaemonians made a law the very reverse of this, namely, to wear
their hair long, though they had always before cut it close.
Othryadas himself, it is said, the sole survivor of the 300, prevented by a sense of shame from returning to Sparta after all
his comrades had fallen, laid violent hands upon himself in
Thyrea.

83. Although the Spartans were engaged with these matters
when the herald arrived from Sardis to entreat them to come to
the assistance of the besieged king, yet, notwithstanding, they
instantly set to work to afford him help. They had completed
their preparations, and the ships were just ready to start, when
a second message informed them that the place had already
fallen, and that Croesus was a prisoner. Deeply grieved at his
misfortune, the Spartans ceased their efforts.

84. The following is the way in which Sardis was taken. On
the fourteenth day of the siege Cyrus bade some horsemen ride
about his lines, and make proclamation to the whole army that
he would give a reward to the man who should first mount the
wall. After this he made an assault, but without success. His
troops retired, but a certain Mardian, Hyroeades by name, resolved to approach the citadel and attempt it at a place where
no guards were ever set. On this side the rock was so precipitous,
and the citadel (as it seemed) so impregnable, that no fear was
entertained of its being carried in this place. Here was the only
portion of the circuit round which their old king Meles did not

carry the lion[32] which his concubine bore to him. For when the
Telmessians had declared that if the lion were taken round the
defences, Sardis would be impregnable, and Meles, in consequence, carried it round the rest of the fortress where the citadel
seemed open to attack, he scorned to take it round this side,
which he looked on as a sheer precipice, and therefore absolutely
secure. It is on that side of the city which faces Mount Tmolus.
Hyroeades, however, having the day before observed a Lydian
soldier descend the rock after a helmet that had rolled down
from the top, and having seen him pick it up and carry it back,
thought over what he had witnessed, and formed his plan. He
climbed the rock himself, and other Persians followed in his
track, until a large number had mounted to the top. Thus was
Sardis taken,[33] and given up entirely to pillage.

85. With respect to Croesus himself, this is what befell him
at the taking of the town. He had a son, of whom I made mention above, a worthy youth, whose only defect was that he was
deaf and dumb. In the days of his prosperity Croesus had done
the utmost that he could for him, and among other plans which
he had devised, had sent to Delphi to consult the oracle on his
behalf. The answer which he had received from the priestess ran
thus:

Lydian, wide-ruling monarch, thou wondrous simple Croesus,
Wish not ever to hear in thy palace the voice thou hast prayed
for,
Utt'ring intelligent sounds. Far better thy son should be silent!
Ah! woe worth the day when thine ear shall first list to his ac-
cents.

When the town was taken, one of the Persians was just going
to kill Croesus, not knowing who he was. Croesus saw the man
coming, but under the pressure of his affliction, did not care to

---

[32] The germ of the story may be a native myth since the lion was the
sacred beast of the Lydian sun-god.

[33] Sardis was taken a second time in almost exactly the same way by
Antiochus the Great in 215 B.C.

avoid the blow, not minding whether he died beneath the stroke. Then this son of his, who was voiceless, beholding the Persian as he rushed towards Croesus, in the agony of his fear and grief burst into speech, and said, "Man, do not kill Croesus." This was the first time that he had ever spoken a word, but afterwards he retained the power of speech for the remainder of his life.

86. Thus was Sardis taken by the Persians, and Croesus himself fell into their hands, after having reigned fourteen years, and been besieged in his capital fourteen days; thus too did Croesus fulfil the oracle, which said that he should destroy a mighty empire, by destroying his own. Then the Persians who had made Croesus prisoner brought him before Cyrus. Now a vast pile had been raised by his orders, and Croesus, laden with fetters, was placed upon it, and with him twice seven of the sons of the Lydians. I know not whether Cyrus was minded to make an offering of the first-fruits to some god or other, or whether he had vowed a vow and was performing it, or whether, as may well be, he had heard that Croesus was a holy man, and so wished to see if any of the heavenly powers would appear to save him from being burnt alive. However it might be, Cyrus was thus engaged, and Croesus was already on the pile, when it entered his mind in the depth of his woe that there was a divine warning in the words which had come to him from the lips of Solon, "No one while he lives is happy." When this thought smote him he fetched a long breath, and breaking his deep silence, groaned out aloud, thrice uttering the name of Solon. Cyrus caught the sounds, and bade the interpreters inquire of Croesus who it was he called on. They drew near and asked him, but he held his peace, and for a long time made no answer to their questionings, until at length, forced to say something, he exclaimed, "One I would give much to see converse with every monarch." Not knowing what he meant by this reply, the interpreters begged him to explain himself; and as they pressed for an answer, and grew to be troublesome, he told them how, a long time before, Solon, an Athenian, had come and seen all his splendour, and made light of it; and how whatever he had said

to him had fallen out exactly as he foreshowed, although it was nothing that especially concerned him, but applied to all mankind alike, and most to those who seemed to themselves happy. Meanwhile, as he thus spoke, the pile was lighted, and the outer portion began to blaze. Then Cyrus, hearing from the interpreters what Croesus had said, relented, bethinking himself that he too was a man, and that it was a fellowman, and one who had once been as blessed by fortune as himself, that he was burning alive; afraid, moreover, of retribution, and full of the thought that whatever is human is insecure. So he bade them quench the blazing fire as quickly as they could, and take down Croesus and the other Lydians, which they tried to do, but the flames were not to be mastered.

87. Then, the Lydians say that Croesus, perceiving by the efforts made to quench the fire that Cyrus had relented, and seeing also that all was in vain, and that the men could not get the fire under, called with a loud voice upon the god Apollo, and prayed him, if he had ever received at his hands any acceptable gift, to come to his aid, and deliver him from his present danger. As thus with tears he besought the god, suddenly, though up to that time the sky had been clear and the day without a breath of wind, dark clouds gathered, and the storm burst over their heads with rain of such violence, that the flames were speedily extinguished. Cyrus, convinced by this that Croesus was a good man and a favourite of heaven, asked him after he was taken off the pile, "Who it was that had persuaded him to lead an army into his country, and so become his foe rather than continue his friend?" To which Croesus made answer as follows, "What I did, O King, was to thy advantage and to my own loss. If there be blame, it rests with the god of the Greeks, who encouraged me to begin the war. No one is so foolish as to prefer to peace war, in which, instead of sons burying their fathers, fathers bury their sons. But the gods willed it so."

88. Thus did Croesus speak. Cyrus then ordered his fetters to be taken off, and made him sit down near himself, and paid him much respect, looking upon him, as did also the courtiers, with a sort of wonder. Croesus, wrapped in thought, uttered no word.

After a while, happening to turn and perceive the Persian soldiers engaged in plundering the town, he said to Cyrus, "May I now tell you, O King, what I have in my mind, or is silence best?" Cyrus bade him speak his mind boldly. Then he put this question, "What is it, Cyrus, which those men yonder are doing so busily?" "Plundering your city," Cyrus answered, "and carrying off your riches." "Not my city," rejoined the other, "nor my riches. They are not mine any more. It is your wealth which they are pillaging."

89. Cyrus, struck by what Croesus had said, bade all the court to withdraw, and then asked Croesus what he thought it best for him to do as regarded the plundering. Croesus answered, "Now that the gods have made me your slave, Cyrus, it seems to me that it is my part, if I see anything to your advantage, to show it to you. Your subjects, the Persians, are a poor people with a proud spirit. If then you let them pillage and possess themselves of great wealth, I will tell you what you may expect at their hands. The man who gets the most, look to having him rebel against you. Now then, if my words please you, do thus: Let some of thy body-guards be placed as sentinels at each of the city gates, and let them take their booty from the soldiers as they leave the town, and tell them that they do so because the tenths are due to Zeus. So you will escape the hatred they would feel if the plunder were taken away from them by force; and they, seeing that what is proposed is just, will do it willingly."

90. Cyrus was beyond measure pleased with this advice, so excellent did it seem to him. He praised Croesus highly, and gave orders to his body-guard to do as he had suggested. Then, turning to Croesus, he said, "Croesus, I see that you are resolved both in speech and act to show yourself a virtuous prince: ask me, therefore, whatever you wish as a gift at this moment." Croesus replied, "My lord, if you will suffer me to send these fetters to the god of the Greeks, whom I once honoured above all other gods, and ask him if it is his wont to deceive his benefactors; that will be the highest favour you can confer on me." Cyrus upon this inquired what charge he had to

make against the god. Then Croesus gave him a full account of all his projects, and of the answers of the oracle, and of the offerings which he had sent, on which he dwelt especially, and told him how it was the encouragement given him by the oracle which had led him to make war upon Persia. All this he related, and at the end again besought permission to reproach the god with his behaviour. Cyrus answered with a laugh, "This I readily grant you, and whatever else you shall at any time ask at my hands." Croesus, finding his request allowed, sent certain Lydians to Delphi, enjoining them to lay his fetters upon the threshold of the temple, and ask the god, "If he were not ashamed of having encouraged him, as the destined destroyer of the empire of Cyrus, to begin a war with Persia, of which such were the first-fruits?" As they said this they were to point to the fetters; and further they were to inquire, "If it was the wont of the Greek gods to be ungrateful?"

91. The Lydians went to Delphi and delivered their message, on which the priestess is said to have replied, "It is not possible even for a god to escape the decree of destiny. Croesus has been punished for the sin of his fifth ancestor, who, when he was one of the body-guard of the Heraclidae, joined in a woman's fraud, and, slaying his master, wrongfully seized the throne. Apollo was anxious that the fall of Sardis should not happen in the lifetime of Croesus, but be delayed to his son's days; he could not, however, persuade the Fates. All that they were willing to allow he took and gave to Croesus. Let Croesus know that Apollo delayed the taking of Sardis three full years, and that he is thus a prisoner three years later than was his destiny. Moreover it was Apollo who saved him from the burning pile. Nor has Croesus any right to complain with respect to the oracular answer which he received. For when the god told him that, if he attacked the Persians, he would destroy a mighty empire, he ought, if he had been wise, to have sent again and inquired which empire was meant, that of Cyrus or his own; but if he neither understood what was said, nor took the trouble to seek for enlightenment, he has only himself to blame for the result. Besides, he had misunderstood the last answer which had been

given him about the mule. Cyrus was that mule. For the parents of Cyrus were of different races, and of different conditions, his mother a Median princess, daughter of King Astyages, and his father a Persian and a subject, who, though so far beneath her in all respects, had married his royal mistress."

Such was the answer of the priestess. The Lydians returned to Sardis and communicated it to Croesus, who confessed, on hearing it, that the fault was his, not the god's. Such was the way in which Ionia was first conquered, and so was the empire of Croesus brought to a close.

92. Besides the offerings which have been already mentioned, there are many others in various parts of Greece presented by Croesus; as at Thebes in Boeotia, where there is a golden tripod, dedicated by him to Ismenian Apollo; at Ephesus, where the golden heifers, and most of the columns are his gift; and at Delphi, in the temple of Pronaia, where there is a huge shield in gold, which he gave. All these offerings were still in existence in my day; many others have perished: among them those which he dedicated at Branchidae in Milesia, equal in weight, as I am informed, and in all respects like to those at Delphi. The Delphian presents, and those sent to Amphiaraus, came from his own private property, being the first-fruits of the fortune which he inherited from his father; his other offerings came from the riches of an enemy, who, before he mounted the throne, headed a party against him, with the view of obtaining the crown of Lydia for Pantaleon. This Pantaleon was a son of Alyattes, but by a different mother from Croesus; for the mother of Croesus was a Carian woman, but the mother of Pantaleon an Ionian. When, by the appointment of his father, Croesus obtained the kingly dignity, he seized the man who had plotted against him, and broke him upon the wheel. His property, which he had previously devoted to the service of the gods, Croesus applied in the way mentioned above. This is all I shall say about his offerings.

93. Lydia, unlike most other countries, scarcely offers any wonders for the historian to describe, except the gold-dust which is washed down from the range of Tmolus. It has, however, one

structure of enormous size, only inferior to the monuments of Egypt and Babylon. This is the tomb of Alyattes,[34] the father of Croesus, the base of which is formed of immense blocks of stone, the rest being a vast mound of earth. It was raised by the joint labour of the tradesmen, handicraftsmen, and courtesans of Sardis, and had at the top five stone pillars, which remained to my day, with inscriptions cut on them, showing how much of the work was done by each class of workpeople. It appeared on measurement that the portion of the courtesans was the largest. The daughters of the common people in Lydia, one and all, pursue this traffic, wishing to collect money for their portions. They continue the practice till they marry; and are wont to contract themselves in marriage. The tomb is 1,280 yards in circumference; its breadth is 440 yards. Close to the tomb is a large lake, which the Lydians say is never dry. They call it the Lake Gygaea.

94. The Lydians have very nearly the same customs as the Greeks, with the exception that these last do not bring up their girls in the same way. So far as we have any knowledge, they were the first nation to introduce the use of gold and silver coin,[35] and the first who sold goods by retail. They claim also the invention of all the games which are common to them with the Greeks. These they declare that they invented about the time when they colonised Tyrrhenia, an event of which they give the following account. In the days of Atys the son of Manes, there was great scarcity through the whole land of Lydia. For some time the Lydians bore the affliction patiently, but finding that it did not pass away, they set to work to devise remedies for the evil. Various expedients were discovered by various persons; dice, and knuckle-bones, and ball,[36] and all

---

[34] This monument still exists on the north bank of the Hermus, near the ruins of the ancient Sardis.

[35] It is probable that the Greeks derived their first knowledge of coined money from the Asiatics with whom they came into contact in Asia Minor, either Lydians or Phrygians.

[36] The ball was a very old game; it is mentioned by Homer and it was known in Egypt long before his time, as were the counters, used in a game resembling draughts.

such games were invented, except draughts, the invention of which they do not claim as theirs. The plan adopted against the famine was to engage in games one day so entirely as not to feel any craving for food, and the next day to eat and abstain from games. In this way they passed eighteen years. Still the affliction continued and even became more grievous. So the king determined to divide the nation in half, and to make the two portions draw lots, the one to stay, the other to leave the land. He would continue to reign over those whose lot it should be to remain behind; the emigrants should have his son Tyrrhenus for their leader. The lot was cast, and they who had to emigrate went down to Smyrna, and built themselves ships, in which, after they had put on board all needful stores, they sailed away in search of new homes and better sustenance. After sailing past many countries they came to Umbria,[37] where they built cities for themselves, and fixed their residence. Their former name of Lydians they laid aside, and called themselves after the name of the king's son, who led the colony, Tyrrhenians.[38]

95. Thus far I have been engaged in showing how the Lydians were brought under the Persian yoke. The course of my history now compels me to inquire who this Cyrus was by whom the Lydian empire was destroyed, and by what means the Persians had become the lords of Asia. And herein I shall follow those Persian authorities whose object it appears to be not to magnify the exploits of Cyrus, but to relate the simple truth. I know besides three ways in which the story of Cyrus is told, all differing from my own narrative.

The Assyrians had held the empire of Upper Asia for the space of 520 years,[39] when the Medes set the example of revolt

[37] The Umbria of Herodotus appears to include almost the whole of Northern Italy.

[38] That the Etruscans were Orientals and came by sea is one of the many points in which archaeology tends to confirm Herodotus against the scepticism of nineteenth-century scholars. Although the Etruscan alphabet presents no difficulties, the language cannot be read. The earliest settlements are dated about 1000 B.C. but the period of greatest influence in Italy begins about 700 B.C.

[39] The 520 years of Herodotus in this place represent the period 1229-709 B.C.

from their authority. They took arms for the recovery of their freedom, and fought a battle with the Assyrians, in which they behaved with such gallantry as to shake off the yoke of servitude, and to become a free people. Upon their success the other nations also revolted and regained their independence.

96. Thus the nations over that whole extent of country obtained the blessing of self-government, but they fell again under the sway of kings, in the manner which I will now relate. There was a certain Mede named Deioces, son of Phraortes, a man of much wisdom, who had conceived the desire of obtaining to himself the sovereign power. In furtherance of his ambition, therefore, he formed and carried into execution the following scheme. As the Medes at that time dwelt in scattered villages without any central authority, and lawlessness in consequence prevailed throughout the land, Deioces, who was already a man of mark in his own village, applied himself with greater zeal and earnestness than ever before to the practice of justice among his fellows. It was his conviction that justice and injustice are engaged in perpetual war with one another. He therefore began this course of conduct, and presently the men of his village, observing his integrity, chose him to be the arbiter of all their disputes. Bent on obtaining the sovereign power, he showed himself an honest and an upright judge, and by these means gained such credit with his fellow-citizens as to attract the attention of those who lived in the surrounding villages. They had long been suffering from unjust and oppressive judgments; so that, when they heard of the singular uprightness of Deioces, and of the equity of his decisions, they joyfully had recourse to him in the various quarrels and suits that arose, until at last they came to put confidence in no one else.

97. The number of complaints brought before him continually increasing, as people learnt more and more the fairness of his judgments, Deioces, feeling himself now all important, announced that he did not intend any longer to hear causes, and appeared no more in the seat in which he had been accustomed to sit and administer justice. "It did not square with his interests," he said, "to spend the whole day in regulating other men's

affairs to the neglect of his own." Hereupon robbery and law-lessness broke out afresh, and prevailed through the country even more than heretofore; wherefore the Medes assembled from all quarters, and held a consultation on the state of affairs. The speakers, as I think, were chiefly friends of Deioces. "We cannot possibly," they said, "go on living in this country if things continue as they now are; let us therefore set a king over us, that so the land may be well governed, and we ourselves may be able to attend to our own affairs, and not be forced to quit our country on account of anarchy." The assembly was per-suaded by these arguments, and resolved to appoint a king.

98. It followed to determine who should be chosen to the of-fice. When this debate began the claims of Deioces and his praises were at once in every mouth; so that presently all agreed that he should be king. Upon this he required a palace to be built for him suitable to his rank, and a guard to be given him for his person. The Medes complied, and built him a strong and large palace, on a spot which he himself pointed out, and like-wise gave him liberty to choose himself a body-guard from the whole nation.[40] Thus settled upon the throne, he further re-quired them to build a single great city, and, disregarding the petty towns in which they had formerly dwelt, make the new capital the object of their chief attention. The Medes were again obedient, and built the city now called Agbatana,[41] the walls of which are of great size and strength, rising in circles one within the other. The plan of the place is, that each of the walls should out-top the one beyond it by the battlements. The nature of the ground, which is a gentle hill, favours this arrangement in some

[40] The narrative of Herodotus presents to us Grecian society and ideas, not Oriental. The story of Deioces describes what may be called the despot's progress, first as candidate, and afterwards as fully established; he is athirst for despotism from the beginning, and is forward in mani-festing his rectitude and justice; he passes into a despot by the public vote, and receives what to the Greeks was the great symbol and instru-ment of such transition, a personal body-guard.

[41] The form Agbatana, given by Herodotus, in place of the more usual Ecbatana of other authors, is nearer to the Persian original, which is Hagmatan.

degree, but it was mainly effected by art. The number of the circles is seven, the royal palace and the treasuries standing within the last. The circuit of the outer wall is very nearly the same with that of Athens. Of this wall the battlements are white, of the next black, of the third scarlet, of the fourth blue, of the fifth orange; all these are coloured with paint. The two last have their battlements coated respectively with silver and gold.[42]

99. All these fortifications Deioces caused to be raised for himself and his own palace. The people were required to build their dwellings outside the circuit of the walls. When the town was finished, he proceeded to arrange the ceremonial. He allowed no one to have direct access to the person of the king, but made all communication pass through the hands of messengers, and forbade the king to be seen by his subjects. He also made it an offence for any one whatsoever to laugh or spit in the royal presence. This ceremonial, of which he was the first inventor, Deioces established for his own security, fearing that his compeers, who were brought up together with him, and were of as good family as he, and no whit inferior to him in manly qualities, if they saw him frequently would be pained at the sight, and would therefore be likely to conspire against him; whereas if they did not see him, they would think him quite a different sort of being from themselves.

100. After completing these arrangements, and firmly settling himself upon the throne, Deioces continued to administer justice with the same strictness as before. Causes were stated in writing, and sent in to the king, who passed his judgment upon the contents, and transmitted his decisions to the parties concerned: besides which he had spies and eavesdroppers in all parts of his dominions, and if he heard of any act of oppression, he sent for the guilty party, and awarded him the punishment meet for his offence.

---

[42] There is reason to believe that this account, though it may be greatly exaggerated, is not devoid of a foundation. The temple at Borsippa appears to have had its fourth and seventh stages actually coated with gold and silver respectively.

101. Thus Deioces collected the Medes into a nation, and ruled over them alone. Now these are the tribes of which they consist: the Busae, the Paretaceni, the Struchates, the Arizanti, the Budii, and the Magi.

102. Having reigned fifty-three years, Deioces was at his death succeeded by his son Phraortes. This prince, not satisfied with a dominion which did not extend beyond the single nation of the Medes, began by attacking the Persians; and marching an army into their country, brought them under the Median yoke before any other people. After this success, being now at the head of two nations, both of them powerful, he proceeded to conquer Asia, overrunning province after province. At last he engaged in war with the Assyrians—those Assyrians, I mean, to whom Nineveh belonged, who were formerly the lords of Asia. At present they stood alone by the revolt and desertion of their allies, yet still their internal condition was as flourishing as ever. Phraortes attacked them, but perished in the expedition with the greater part of his army, after having reigned over the Medes twenty-two years.

103. On the death of Phraortes his son Cyaxares ascended the throne. Of him it is reported that he was still more warlike than any of his ancestors, and that he was the first who gave organisation to an Asiatic army, dividing the troops into companies, and forming distinct bodies of the spearmen, the archers, and the cavalry, who before his time had been mingled in one mass, and confused together. He it was who fought against the Lydians on the occasion when the day was changed suddenly into night, and who brought under his dominion the whole of Asia beyond the Halys. This prince, collecting together all the nations which owned his sway, marched against Nineveh, resolved to avenge his father, and cherishing a hope that he might succeed in taking the town. A battle was fought, in which the Assyrians suffered a defeat, and Cyaxares had already begun the siege of the place, when a numerous horde of Scyths, under their king Madyes, son of Protothyes, burst into Asia in pursuit of the Cimmerians whom they had driven out of Europe, and entered the Median territory.

104. The distance from Lake Maeotis to the river Phasis and the Colchians is thirty days' journey for a lightly equipped traveller.[43] From Colchis to cross into Media does not take long—there is only a single intervening nation, the Saspirians, passing whom you find yourself in Media. This however was not the road followed by the Scythians, who turned out of the straight course, and took the upper route, which is much longer, keeping the Caucasus upon their right.[44] The Scythians, having thus invaded Media, were opposed by the Medes, who gave them battle, but, being defeated, lost their empire. The Scythians became masters of Asia.

105. After this they marched forward with the design of invading Egypt. When they had reached Palestine, however, Psammetichus the Egyptian king met them with gifts and prayers, and prevailed on them to advance no further. On their return, passing through Ascalon, a city of Syria, the greater part of them went their way without doing any damage; but some few who lagged behind pillaged the temple of Celestial Aphrodite.[45] I have inquired and find that the temple at Ascalon is the most ancient of all the temples to this goddess; for the one in Cyprus, as the Cyprians themselves admit, was built in imitation of it; and that in Cythera was erected by the Phoenicians, who belong to this part of Syria. The Scythians who plundered the temple were punished by the goddess with the female sickness,[46] which still attaches to their posterity. They

[43] From the mouth of Lake Maeotis, or Sea of Azov, to the river Rion is a distance of about 270 geographical miles, or but little more than the distance (240 miles) from the gulf of Issus to the Euxine, which was called (i. 72) "a journey of five days for a lightly equipped traveller." We may learn from this that Herodotus did not intend the day's journey for a measure of length.

[44] Herodotus, clearly, conceives the Cimmerians to have coasted the Black Sea, and appears to have thought that the Scythians entered Asia along the shores of the Caspian. He does not seem to have been aware of the existence of the Caucasian Gates.

[45] Herodotus probably intends the Syrian goddess Atergatis or Derceto, who was worshipped at Ascalon and elsewhere in Syria, under the form of a mermaid, or figure half woman half fish.

[46] This impotency Hippocrates ascribes to castration or excessive riding,

themselves confess that they are afflicted with the disease for this reason, and travellers who visit Scythia can see what sort of a disease it is. Those who suffer from it are called Enarees.

106. The dominion of the Scythians over Asia lasted twenty-eight years, during which time their insolence and oppression spread ruin on every side. For besides the regular tribute, they exacted from the several nations additional imposts, which they fixed at pleasure; and further, they scoured the country and plundered every one of whatever they could. At length Cyaxares and the Medes invited the greater part of them to a banquet, and made them drunk with wine, after which they were all massacred. The Medes then recovered their empire, and had the same extent of dominion as before. They took Nineveh—I will relate how in another history—and conquered all Assyria except the district of Babylonia. After this Cyaxares died, having reigned over the Medes, if we include the time of the Scythian rule, forty years.

107. Astyages, the son of Cyaxares, succeeded to the throne. He had a daughter who was named Mandane, concerning whom he had a wonderful dream. He dreamt that from her such a stream of water flowed forth as not only to fill his capital, but to flood the whole of Asia. This vision he laid before such of the Magi as had the gift of interpreting dreams, who expounded its meaning to him in full, whereat he was greatly terrified. On this account, when his daughter was now of ripe age, he would not give her in marriage to any of the Medes who were of suitable rank, lest the dream should be accomplished, but he married her to a Persian of good family indeed,[47] but of a quiet temper,

but he mentions that the natives believed it to be a judgment from the gods. It is said that traces of the disease are still found among the inhabitants of Southern Russia.

[47] Cambyses, the father of Cyrus, appears to have been not only a man of good family, but of royal race—the hereditary monarch of his nation, which, when it became subject to the Medes, still retained its line of native kings, the descendants of Achæmenes. In the Behistun Inscription (col. 1, par. 4) Darius carries up his genealogy to Achaemenes, and asserts that "eight of his race had been kings before himself—he was the ninth." Cambyses, the father of Cyrus, Cyrus himself, and Cambyses the son of Cyrus, are probably included in the eight.

whom he looked on as much inferior to a Mede of even middle condition.

108. Thus Cambyses (for so was the Persian called) wedded Mandane, and took her to his home, after which, in the very first year, Astyages saw another vision. He fancied that a vine grew from the womb of his daughter, and overshadowed the whole of Asia. After this dream, which he submitted also to the interpreters, he sent to Persia and fetched away Mandane, who was now with child and was not far from her time. On her arrival he set a watch over her, intending to destroy the child to which she should give birth; for the Magian interpreters had expounded the vision to foreshow that the offspring of his daughter would reign over Asia in his stead. To guard against this, Astyages, as soon as Cyrus was born, sent for Harpagus, a man of his own house and the most faithful of the Medes, to whom he was wont to entrust all his affairs, and addressed him thus, "Harpagus, I beseech you neglect not the business with which I am about to charge you; neither betray you the interests of your lord for others' sake, lest you bring destruction on your own head at some future time. Take the child born of Mandane my daughter; carry him with you to your home and slay him there. Then bury him as you please." "O king," replied the other, "never in time past did Harpagus disoblige you in anything, and be sure that through all future time he will be careful in nothing to offend. If therefore it be your will that this thing be done, it is for me to serve you with all diligence."

109. When Harpagus had thus answered, the child was given into his hands, clothed in the garb of death, and he hastened weeping to his home. There on his arrival he found his wife, to whom he told all that Astyages had said. "What then," said she, "do you intend to do?" "Not what Astyages requires," he an-

An inscription has been recently found upon a brick in lower Chaldaea, in which Cyrus the Great calls himself "the son of Cambyses, the powerful king." This then is decisive as to the royalty of the line of Cyrus the Great, and is confirmatory of the impression, derived from other evidence, that when Darius speaks of eight Achaemenian kings having preceded him, he alludes to the ancestry of Cyrus the Great, and not to his own immediate paternal line.

swered; "no, he may be madder and more frantic still than he is now, but I will not be the man to work his will, or lend a helping hand to such a murder as this. Many things forbid my slaying him. In the first place the boy is my own kith and kin; and next Astyages is old, and has no son. If then when he dies the crown should go to his daughter—that daughter whose child he now wishes to slay by my hand—what remains for me but danger of the fearfullest kind? For my own safety, indeed, the child must die; but some one belonging to Astyages must take his life, not I or mine."

110. So saying he sent off a messenger to fetch a certain Mitradates, one of the herdsmen of Astyages, whose pasturages he knew to be the best for his purpose, lying as they did among mountains infested with wild beasts. This man was married to one of the king's female slaves, whose Median name was Spaco, which is in Greek Cyno, since in the Median tongue the word Spaca means a bitch. The mountains, on the skirts of which his cattle grazed, lie to the north of Agbatana, towards the Euxine. That part of Media which borders on the Saspirians is an elevated tract, very mountainous, and covered with forests, while the rest of the Median territory is entirely level ground. On the arrival of the herdsman, who came at the hasty summons, Harpagus said to him, "Astyages requires you to take this child and lay him in the wildest part of the hills, where he will be sure to die speedily. And he bade me tell you that if you do not kill the boy, but anyhow allow him to escape, he will put you to the most painful of deaths. I myself am appointed to see the child exposed."

111. The herdsman on hearing this took the child in his arms, and went back the way he had come, till he reached the folds. There, providentially, his wife, who had been expecting daily to be put to bed, had just, during the absence of her husband, been delivered of a child. Both the herdsman and his wife were uneasy on each other's account, the former fearful because his wife was so near her time, the woman alarmed because it was a new thing for her husband to be sent for by Harpagus. When therefore he came into the house upon his return, his wife, seeing him

arrive so unexpectedly, was the first to speak, and begged to
know why Harpagus had sent for him in such a hurry. "Wife,"
said he, "when I got to the town I saw and heard such things as
I would to heaven I had never seen—such things as I would to
heaven had never happened to our masters. Every one was
weeping in Harpagus's house. It quite frightened me, but I went
in. The moment I stepped inside, what should I see but a baby
lying on the floor, panting and whimpering, and all covered with
gold, and wrapped in clothes of such beautiful colours? Harpagus observed me, and directly ordered me to take the child in
my arms and carry him off, and what was I to do with him,
think you? Why, to lay him in the mountains, where the wild
beasts are most plentiful. And he told me it was the king himself
that ordered it to be done, and he threatened me with dreadful
things if I failed. So I took the child up in my arms, and carried him along. I thought it might be the son of one of the household slaves. I did wonder certainly to see the gold and the beautiful baby-clothes, and I could not think why there was such a
weeping in Harpagus's house. Well, very soon, as I came along,
I got at the truth. They sent a servant with me to show me the
way out of the town, and to leave the baby in my hands; and he
told me that the child's mother is the king's daughter Mandane,
and his father Cambyses, the son of Cyrus; and that the king
orders him to be killed; and look, here the child is."

112. With this the herdsman uncovered the infant, and
showed him to his wife, who, when she saw him, and observed
how fine a child and how beautiful he was, burst into tears, and
clinging to the knees of her husband, besought him on no account to expose the babe; to which he answered, that it was not
possible for him to do otherwise, as Harpagus would be sure to
send persons to see and report to him, and he was to suffer a
most cruel death if he disobeyed. Failing thus in her first attempt to persuade her husband, the woman spoke a second time,
saying, "If then there is no persuading you, and a child must
needs be seen exposed upon the mountains, at least do thus. The
child of which I have just been delivered is still-born; take it
and lay it on the hills, and let us bring up as our own the child

of the daughter of Astyages. So you shall not be charged with
unfaithfulness to your lord, nor shall we have managed badly
for ourselves. Our dead babe will have a royal funeral, and this
living child will not be deprived of life."

113. It seemed to the herdsman that this advice was the best
under the circumstances. He therefore followed it without loss
of time. The child which he had intended to put to death he gave
over to his wife, and his own dead child he put in the cradle
wherein he had carried the other, clothing it first in all the
other's costly attire, and taking it in his arms he laid it in the
wildest place of all the mountain-range. When the child had
been three days exposed, leaving one of his helpers to watch the
body, he started off for the city, and going straight to Harpagus's house, declared himself ready to show the corpse of the
boy. Harpagus sent certain of his body-guard, on whom he had
the firmest reliance, to view the body for him, and, satisfied with
their seeing it, gave orders for the funeral. Thus was the herdsman's child buried, and the other child, who was afterwards
known by the name of Cyrus, was taken by the herdsman's wife,
and brought up under a different name.

114. When the boy was in his tenth year, an accident which
I will now relate, caused it to be discovered who he was. He
was at play one day in the village where the folds of the cattle
were, along with the boys of his own age, in the street. The
other boys who were playing with him chose the cowherd's son,
as he was called, to be their king. He then proceeded to order
them about—some he set to build him houses, others he made
his guards, one of them was to be the king's eye, another had
the office of carrying his messages, all had some task or other.
Among the boys there was one, the son of Artembares, a Mede
of distinction, who refused to do what Cyrus had set him. Cyrus
told the other boys to take him into custody, and when his
orders were obeyed, he chastised him most severely with the
whip. The son of Artembares, as soon as he was let go, full of
rage at treatment so little befitting his rank, hastened to the city
and complained bitterly to his father of what had been done to
him by Cyrus. He did not, of course, say "Cyrus," by which

name the boy was not yet known, but called him the son of the
king's cowherd. Artembares, in the heat of his passion, went to
Astyages, accompanied by his son, and made complaint of the
gross injury which had been done him. Pointing to the boy's
shoulders, he exclaimed, "Thus, O King, has your slave, the son
of a cowherd, heaped insult upon us."

115. At this sight and these words Astyages, wishing to
avenge the son of Artembares for his father's sake, sent for the
cowherd and his boy. When they came together into his presence, fixing his eyes on Cyrus, Astyages said, "Have you then,
the son of so mean a fellow as that, dared to behave thus rudely
to the son of yonder noble, one of the first in my court?" "My
lord," replied the boy, "I only treated him as he deserved. I was
chosen king in play by the boys of our village, because they
thought me the best for it. He himself was one of the boys who
chose me. All the others did according to my orders; but he refused, and made light of them, until at last he got his due reward. If for this I deserve to suffer punishment, here I am ready
to submit to it."

116. While the boy was yet speaking Astyages was struck
with a suspicion who he was. He thought he saw something in
the character of his face like his own, and there was a nobleness
about the answer he had made; besides which his age seemed to
tally with the time when his grandchild was exposed. Astonished
at all this, Astyages could not speak for a while. At last, recovering himself with difficulty, and wishing to be quit of Artembares, that he might examine the herdsman alone, he said to the
former, "I promise thee, Artembares, so to settle this business
that neither you nor your son shall have any cause to complain."
Artembares retired from his presence, and the attendants, at
the bidding of the king, led Cyrus into an inner apartment.
Astyages then being left alone with the herdsman, inquired of
him where he had got the boy, and who had given him to him;
to which he made answer that the lad was his own child, begot-
ten by himself, and that the mother who bore him was still alive,
and lived with him in his house. Astyages remarked that he was
very ill-advised to bring himself into such great trouble, and at

the same time signed to his body-guard to lay hold of him. Then
the herdsman, as they were dragging him to the rack, began at
the beginning and told the whole story exactly as it happened,
without concealing anything, ending with entreaties and prayers
to the king to grant him forgiveness.

117. Astyages, having got the truth of the matter from the
herdsman, was very little further concerned about him, but with
Harpagus he was exceedingly enraged. The guards were bidden
to summon him into the presence, and on his appearance Astyages asked him, "By what death was it, Harpagus, that you slew
the child of my daughter whom I gave into your hands?"
Harpagus, seeing the cowherd in the room, did not betake himself to lies, lest he should be confuted and proved false, but replied as follows, "Sire, when you gave the child into my hands
I instantly considered with myself how I could contrive to execute your wishes, and yet, while guiltless of any unfaithfulness
towards you, avoid imbruing my hands in blood which was in
truth your daughter's and your own. And this was how I contrived it. I sent for this cowherd, and gave the child over to
him, telling him that by the king's orders it was to be put to
death. And in this I told no lie, for you had so commanded.
Moreover, when I gave him the child, I enjoined him to lay it
somewhere in the wilds of the mountains, and to stay near and
watch till it was dead; and I threatened him with all manner of
punishment if he failed. Afterwards, when he had done according to all that I commanded him, and the child had died, I sent
some of the most trustworthy of my eunuchs, who viewed the
body for me, and then I had the child buried. This, sire, is the
simple truth, and this is the death by which the child died."

118. Thus Harpagus related the whole story in a plain,
straightforward way; upon which Astyages, letting no sign escape him of the anger that he felt, began by repeating to him
all that he had just heard from the cowherd, and then concluded
with saying, "So the boy is alive, and it is best as it is. For the
child's fate was a great sorrow to me, and the reproaches of my
daughter went to my heart. Truly fortune has played us a good
turn in this. Go home then, and send your son to be with the

new comer, and tonight, as I mean to sacrifice thank-offerings
for the child's safety to the gods to whom such honour is due,
I look to have you a guest at the banquet."

119. Harpagus, on hearing this, made obeisance, and went
home rejoicing to find that his disobedience had turned out so
fortunately, and that, instead of being punished, he was invited
to a banquet given in honour of the happy occasion. The moment he reached home he called for his son, a youth of about
thirteen, the only child of his parents, and bade him go to the
palace, and do whatever Astyages should direct. Then, in the
gladness of his heart, he went to his wife and told her all that
had happened. Astyages, meanwhile, took the son of Harpagus,
and slew him, after which he cut him in pieces, and roasted
some portions before the fire, and boiled others; and when all
were duly prepared, he kept them ready for use. The hour for
the banquet came, and Harpagus appeared, and with him the
other guests, and all sat down to the feast. Astyages and the
rest of the guests had joints of meat served up to them; but on
the table of Harpagus, nothing was placed except the flesh of his
own son. This was all put before him, except the hands and feet
and head, which were laid by themselves in a covered basket.
When Harpagus seemed to have eaten his fill, Astyages called
out to him to know how he had enjoyed the repast. On his reply
that he had enjoyed it excessively, they whose business it was
brought him the basket, in which were the hands and feet and
head of his son, and bade him open it, and take out what he
pleased. Harpagus accordingly uncovered the basket, and saw
within it the remains of his son. The sight, however, did not
scare him, or rob him of his self-possession. Being asked by
Astyages if he knew what beast's flesh it was that he had been
eating, he answered that he knew very well, and that whatever
the king did was agreeable. After this reply, he took with him
such morsels of the flesh as were uneaten, and went home, intending, as I conceive, to collect the remains and bury them.

120. Such was the mode in which Astyages punished Harpagus: afterwards, proceeding to consider what he should do with
Cyrus, his grandchild, he sent for the Magi, who formerly in-

terpreted his dream in the way which alarmed him so much, and asked them how they had expounded it. They answered, without varying from what they had said before, that the boy would be a king if he grew up, and did not die too soon. Then Astyages addressed them thus, "The boy has escaped, and lives; he has been brought up in the country, and the lads of the village where he lives have made him their king. All that kings commonly do he has done. He has had his guards, and his doorkeepers, and his messengers, and all the other usual officers. Tell me, then, to what, think you, does all this tend?" The Magi answered, "If the boy survives, and has ruled as a king without any craft or contrivance, in that case we bid you cheer up, and feel no more alarm on his account. He will not reign a second time. For we have found even oracles sometimes fulfilled in an unimportant way; and dreams, still oftener, have wondrously mean accomplishments." "It is what I myself most incline to think," Astyages rejoined, "the boy having been already king, the dream is out, and I have nothing more to fear from him. Nevertheless, take good heed and counsel me the best you can for the safety of my house and your own interests." "Truly," said the Magi in reply, "it very much concerns our interests that your kingdom be firmly established; for if it went to this boy it would pass into foreign hands, since he is a Persian: and then we Medes should lose our freedom, and be quite despised by the Persians, as being foreigners. But so long as you, our fellow-countryman, are on the throne, all manner of honours are ours, and we are even not without some share in the government. Much reason therefore have we to forecast well for you and for your sovereignty. If then we saw any cause for present fear, be sure we would not keep it back from you. But truly we are persuaded that the dream has had its accomplishment in this harmless way; and so our own fears being at rest, we recommend you to banish yours. As for the boy, our advice is, that you send him away to Persia, to his father and mother."

121. Astyages heard their answer with pleasure, and calling Cyrus into his presence, said to him, "My child, I was led to do you a wrong by a dream which has come to nothing; from that

wrong you were saved by your own good fortune. Go now with
a light heart to Persia; I will provide your escort. Go, and when
you get to your journey's end, you will behold your father and
your mother, quite other people from Mitradates the cowherd
and his wife."

122. With these words Astyages dismissed his grandchild. On
his arrival at the house of Cambyses, he was received by his
parents, who, when they learned who he was, embraced him
heartily, having always been convinced that he died almost as
soon as he was born. So they asked him by what means he had
chanced to escape; and he told them how that till lately he had
known nothing at all about the matter, but had been greatly
mistaken and how he had learned his history by the way, as he
came from Media. He had been quite sure that he was the son
of the king's cowherd, but on the road the king's escort had told
him all the truth; and then he spoke of the cowherd's wife who
had brought him up, and filled his whole talk with her praises;
in all that he had to tell them about himself, it was always Cyno
—Cyno was everything. So it happened that his parents, catching the name at his mouth, and wishing to persuade the Persians
that there was a special providence in his preservation, spread
the report that Cyrus, when he was exposed, was suckled by a
bitch. This was the sole origin of the rumour.[48]

123. Afterwards, when Cyrus grew to manhood, and became
known as the bravest and most popular of all his compeers,
Harpagus, who was bent on revenging himself upon Astyages,
began to pay him court by gifts and messages. His own rank
was too humble for him to hope to obtain vengeance without
some foreign help. When therefore he saw Cyrus, whose wrongs
were so similar to his own, growing up expressly (as it were)
to be the avenger whom he needed, he set to work to procure his
support and aid in the matter. He had already paved the way
for his designs, by persuading, severally, the great Median nobles, whom the harsh rule of their monarch had offended, that

---

[48] The exposure of a future king and his suckling by an animal are common features of popular fiction. Herodotus' version represents a subsequent rationalising tendency of the Greeks.

the best plan would be to put Cyrus at their head, and dethrone
Astyages. These preparations made, Harpagus being now ready
for revolt, was anxious to make known his wishes to Cyrus, who
still lived in Persia; but as the roads between Media and Persia
were guarded, he had to contrive a means of sending word secretly, which he did in the following way. He took a hare, and
cutting open its belly without hurting the fur, he slipped in a
letter containing what he wanted to say, and then carefully
sewing up the paunch, he gave the hare to one of his most faithful slaves, disguising him as a hunter with nets, and sent him
off to Persia to take the game as a present to Cyrus, bidding
him tell Cyrus, by word of mouth, to cut open the animal himself, and let no one be present at the time.

124. All was done as he wished, and Cyrus, on cutting the
hare open, found the letter inside, and read as follows, "Son of
Cambyses, the gods assuredly watch over you, or never would
you have passed through your many wonderful adventures—
now is the time when you may avenge yourself upon Astyages,
your murderer. He willed your death, remember; to the gods
and to me you owe it that you are still alive. I think you are
not ignorant of what he did to you, nor of what I suffered at his
hands because I committed you to the cowherd, and did not put
you to death. Listen now to me, and obey my words, and all the
empire of Astyages shall be yours. Raise the standard of revolt
in Persia, and then march straight on Media. Whether Astyages
appoint me to command his forces against you, or whether he
appoint any other of the princes of the Medes, all will go as
you could wish. They will be the first to fall away from him, and
joining your side, exert themselves to overturn his power. Be
sure that on our part all is ready; wherefore do your part, and
that speedily."

125. Cyrus, on receiving the tidings contained in this letter,
set himself to consider how he might best persuade the Persians
to revolt. After much thought, he hit on the following as the
most expedient course: he wrote what he thought proper upon
a roll, and then calling an assembly of the Persians, he unfolded
the roll, and read out of it that Astyages appointed him their

general. "And now," said he, "since it is so, I command you to go and bring each man his reaping-hook." With these words he dismissed the assembly.

Now the Persian nation is made up of many tribes. Those which Cyrus assembled and persuaded to revolt from the Medes, were the principal ones on which all the others are dependent. These are the Pasargadae, the Maraphians, and the Maspians, of whom the Pasargadae are the noblest. The Achaemenidae,[49] from which spring all the Perseid kings, is one of their clans. The rest of the Persian tribes are the following: the Panthialaeans, the Derusiaeans, the Germanians, who are engaged in husbandry; the Daans, the Mardians, the Dropicans, and the Sagartians, who are Nomads.

126. When, in obedience to the orders which they had received, the Persians came with their reaping-hooks, Cyrus led them to a tract of ground, about three miles square, covered with thorns, and ordered them to clear it before the day was out. They accomplished their task, upon which he issued a second order to them, to take the bath the day following, and again come to him. Meanwhile he collected together all his father's flocks, both sheep and goats, and all his oxen, and slaughtered them, and made ready to give an entertainment to the entire Persian army. Wine, too, and bread of the choicest kinds were prepared for the occasion. When the morrow came, and the Persians appeared, he bade them recline upon the grass, and enjoy themselves. After the feast was over, he requested them to tell him which they liked best, today's work, or yesterday's. They answered that the contrast was indeed strong: yesterday brought them nothing but what was bad, today everything that was good. Cyrus instantly seized on their reply, and laid bare his purpose in these words, "Men of Persia, thus do matters stand with you. If you choose to hearken to my words, you may enjoy these and ten thousand similar delights, and never condescend to any slavish toil; but if you will not hearken, prepare

---

[49] The Achaemenidae were the royal family of Persia, the descendants of Achaemenes, who was probably the leader under whom the Persians first settled in the country which has ever since borne their name

yourselves for unnumbered toils as hard as yesterday's. Now therefore follow my bidding, and be free. For myself I feel that I am destined by Providence to undertake your liberation; and you, I am sure, are no whit inferior to the Medes in anything, least of all in bravery. Revolt, therefore, from Astyages, without a moment's delay."

127. The Persians, who had long been impatient of the Median dominion, now that they had found a leader, were delighted to shake off the yoke. Meanwhile Astyages, informed of the doings of Cyrus, sent a messenger to summon him to his presence. Cyrus replied, "Tell Astyages that I shall appear in his presence sooner than he will like." Astyages, when he received this message, instantly armed all his subjects, and, as if God had deprived him of his senses, appointed Harpagus to be their general, forgetting how greatly he had injured him. So when the two armies met and engaged, only a few of the Medes, who were not in the secret, fought; others deserted openly to the Persians; while the greater number counterfeited fear, and fled.

128. Astyages, on learning the shameful flight and dispersion of his army, broke out into threats against Cyrus, saying, "Cyrus shall nevertheless have no reason to rejoice;" and directly he seized the Magian interpreters, who had persuaded him to allow Cyrus to escape, and impaled them; after which, he armed all the Medes who had remained in the city, both young and old; and leading them against the Persians, fought a battle, in which he was utterly defeated, his army being destroyed, and he himself falling into the enemy's hands.

129. Harpagus then, seeing him a prisoner, came near, and exulted over him with many gibes and jeers. Among other cutting speeches which he made, he alluded to the supper where the flesh of his son was given him to eat, and asked Astyages to answer him now, how he enjoyed being a slave instead of a king? Astyages looked in his face, and asked him in return, why he claimed as his own the achievements of Cyrus? "Because," said Harpagus, "it was my letter which made him revolt, and so I am entitled to all the credit of the enterprise." Then Asty-

ages declared, that "in that case he was at once the silliest and the most unjust of men: the silliest, if when it was in his power to put the crown on his own head, as it must assuredly have been, if the revolt was entirely his doing, he had placed it on the head of another; the most unjust, if on account of that supper he had brought slavery on the Medes. For, supposing that he was obliged to invest another with the kingly power, and not retain it himself, yet justice required that a Mede, rather than a Persian, should receive the dignity. Now, however, the Medes, who had been no parties to the wrong of which he complained, were made slaves instead of lords, and slaves moreover of those who till recently had been their subjects."

130. Thus after a reign of thirty-five years, Astyages lost his crown, and the Medes, in consequence of his cruelty, were brought under the rule of the Persians. Their empire over the parts of Asia beyond the Halys had lasted 128 years, except during the time when the Scythians had the dominion. Afterwards the Medes repented of their submission, and revolted from Darius, but were defeated in battle, and again reduced to subjection.[50] Now, however, in the time of Astyages, it was the Persians who under Cyrus revolted from the Medes, and became thenceforth the rulers of Asia. Cyrus kept Astyages at his court during the remainder of his life, without doing him any further injury. Such then were the circumstances of the birth and bringing up of Cyrus, and such were the steps by which he mounted the throne. It was at a later date that he was attacked by Croesus, and overthrew him, as I have related in an earlier portion of this history. The overthrow of Croesus made him master of the whole of Asia.

131. The customs which I know the Persians to observe are the following. They have no images of the gods, no temples nor altars, and consider the use of them a sign of folly. This comes, I think, from their not believing the gods to have the same nature with men, as the Greeks imagine. Their wont, however, is to ascend the summits of the loftiest mountains, and there to offer sacrifice to Zeus, which is the name they give to the

---

[50] This revolt took place in 528 B.C.

whole circuit of the firmament. They likewise offer to the sun and moon, to the earth, to fire, to water, and to the winds. These are the only gods whose worship has come down to them from ancient times. At a later period they began the worship of Aphrodite, which they borrowed [51] from the Arabians and Assyrians. Mylitta is the name by which the Assyrians know this goddess, whom the Arabians call Alitta, and the Persians Mitra.[52]

132. To these gods the Persians offer sacrifice in the following manner: they raise no altar, light no fire, pour no libations, there is no sound of the flute, no putting on of chaplets, no consecrated barley-cake; but the man who wishes to sacrifice brings his victim to a spot of ground which is pure from pollution, and there calls upon the name of the god to whom he intends to offer. It is usual to have the turban encircled with a wreath, most commonly of myrtle. The sacrificer is not allowed to pray for blessings on himself alone, but he prays for the welfare of the king, and of the whole Persian people, among whom he is of necessity included. He cuts the victim in pieces, and having boiled the flesh, he lays it out upon the softest grass that he can find, trefoil especially. When all is ready, one of the Magi comes forward and chants a hymn, which they say recounts the origin of the gods. It is not lawful to offer sacrifice unless there is a Magus present. After waiting a short time the sacrificer carries the flesh of the victim away with him, and makes whatever use of it he pleases.

133. Of all the days in the year, the one which they celebrate most is their birthday. It is customary to have the board furnished on that day with an ampler supply than common. The richer Persians cause an ox, a horse, a camel, and an ass to be baked whole and so served up to them: the poorer classes use instead the smaller kinds of cattle. They eat little solid food

[51] The readiness of the Persians to adopt foreign customs, even in religion, is very remarkable.

[52] This identification is altogether a mistake. The Persians, like their Vedic brethren, worshipped the sun under the name of Mithra. His worship became most important in the later developments of the Persian religion.

but abundance of dessert, which is set on table a few dishes at a time; this it is which makes them say that "the Greeks, when they eat, leave off hungry, having nothing worth mention served up to them after the meats; whereas, if they had more put before them, they would not stop eating." They are very fond of wine, and drink it in large quantities. To vomit or obey natural calls in the presence of another, is forbidden among them. Such are their customs in these matters.

It is also their general practice to deliberate upon affairs of weight when they are drunk; and then on the morrow, when they are sober, the decision to which they came the night before is put before them by the master of the house in which it was made; and if it is then approved of, they act on it; if not, they set it aside. Sometimes, however, they are sober at their first deliberation, but in this case they always reconsider the matter under the influence of wine.

134. When they meet each other in the streets, you may know if the persons meeting are of equal rank by the following token; if they are, instead of speaking, they kiss each other on the lips. In the case where one is a little inferior to the other, the kiss is given on the cheek; where the difference of rank is great, the inferior prostrates himself upon the ground. Of nations, they honour most their nearest neighbours whom they esteem next to themselves; those who live beyond these they honour in the second degree; and so with the remainder, the further they are removed, the less the esteem in which they hold them. The reason is, that they look upon themselves as very greatly superior in all respects to the rest of mankind, regarding others as approaching to excellence in proportion as they dwell nearer to them; whence it comes to pass that those who are the farthest off must be the most degraded of mankind. Under the dominion of the Medes, the several nations of the empire exercised authority over each other in this order. The Medes were lords over all, and governed the nations upon their borders, who in their turn governed the States beyond, who likewise bore rule over the nations which adjoined on them.[53] And this is the order

[53] It is quite inconceivable that there should have been any such exact

which the Persians also follow in their distribution of honour; for that people, like the Medes, has a progressive scale of administration and government.

135. There is no nation which so readily adopts foreign customs as the Persians. Thus, they have taken the dress of the Medes, considering it superior to their own; and in war they wear the Egyptian breastplate. As soon as they hear of any luxury, they instantly make it their own: and hence, among other novelties, they have learned pederasty from the Greeks. Each of them has several wives, and a still larger number of concubines.

136. Next to prowess in arms, it is regarded as the greatest proof of manly excellence, to be the father of many sons. Every year the king sends rich gifts to the man who can show the largest number: for they hold that number is strength. Their sons are carefully instructed from their fifth to their twentieth year, in three things alone,—to ride, to draw the bow, and to speak the truth. Until their fifth year they are not allowed to come into the sight of their father, but pass their lives with the women. This is done that, if the child die young, the father may not be afflicted by its loss.

137. To my mind it is a wise rule, as also is the following—that the king shall not put any one to death for a single fault, and that none of the Persians shall visit a single fault in a slave with any extreme penalty; but in every case the services of the offender shall be set against his misdoings; and, if the latter be found to outweigh the former, the aggrieved party shall then proceed to punishment.

138. The Persians maintain that never yet did any one kill his own father or mother; but in all such cases they are quite sure that, if matters were sifted to the bottom, it would be found that the child was either a changeling or else the fruit of adultery; for it is not likely they say that the real father should perish by the hands of his child.

139. They hold it unlawful to talk of any thing which it is

system of government, either in Media or Persia, as Herodotus here indicates.

unlawful to do. The most disgraceful thing in the world, they think, is to tell a lie; the next worse, to owe a debt: because, among other reasons, the debtor is obliged to tell lies. If a Persian has the leprosy he is not allowed to enter into a city, or to have any dealings with the other Persians; he must, they say, have sinned against the sun. Foreigners attacked by this disorder, are forced to leave the country: even white pigeons are often driven away, as guilty of the same offence. They never defile a river with the secretions of their bodies, nor even wash their hands in one; nor will they allow others to do so, as they have a great reverence for rivers. There is another peculiarity, which the Persians themselves have never noticed, but which has not escaped my observation. Their names, which are expressive of some bodily or mental excellence, all end with the same letter—the letter which is called San by the Dorians, and Sigma by the Ionians. Any one who examines will find that the Persian names, one and all without exception, end with this letter.[54]

140. Thus much I can declare of the Persians with entire certainty, from my own actual knowledge. There is another custom which is spoken of with reserve, and not openly, concerning their dead. It is said that the body of a male Persian is never buried, until it has been torn either by a dog or a bird of prey.[55] That the Magi have this custom is beyond a doubt, for they practise it without any concealment. The dead bodies are covered with wax, and then buried in the ground.

The Magi are a very peculiar race, differing entirely from the Egyptian priests, and indeed from all other men whatsoever. The Egyptian priests make it a point of religion not to kill any live animals except those which they offer in sacrifice. The Magi, on the contrary, kill animals of all kinds with their own

---

[54] Here Herodotus was again mistaken. The Persian names of men which terminate with a consonant end indeed invariably with the letter *s*, but a large number of Persian names of men were pronounced with a vowel termination, not expressed in writing, and in these the last consonant might be almost any letter.

[55] This strange custom, still prevails among the Parsees wherever they are found, whether in Persia or in India.

hands, excepting dogs[56] and men. They even seem to take a delight in the employment, and kill, as readily as they do other animals, ants and snakes, and such like flying or creeping things. However, since this has always been their custom, let them keep to it. I return to my former narrative.

141. Immediately after the conquest of Lydia by the Persians, the Ionian and Aeolian Greeks sent ambassadors to Cyrus at Sardis, and prayed to become his lieges on the footing which they had occupied under Croesus. Cyrus listened attentively to their proposals, and answered them by a fable. "There was a certain piper," he said, "who was walking one day by the seaside, when he espied some fish; so he began to pipe to them, imagining they would come out to him upon the land. But as he found at last that his hope was vain, he took a net, and enclosing a great draught of fishes, drew them ashore. The fish then began to leap and dance; but the piper said, 'Cease your dancing now, as you did not choose to come and dance when I piped to you.'" Cyrus gave this answer to the Ionians and Aeolians, because, when he urged them by his messengers to revolt from Croesus, they refused; but now, when his work was done, they came to offer their allegiance. It was in anger, therefore, that he made them this reply. The Ionians, on hearing it, set to work to fortify their towns, and held meetings at the Panionium, which were attended by all excepting the Milesians, with whom Cyrus had concluded a separate treaty, by which he allowed them the terms they had formerly obtained from Croesus. The other Ionians resolved, with one accord, to send ambassadors to Sparta to implore assistance.

142. Now the Ionians of Asia, who meet at the Panionium, have built their cities in a region where the air and climate are the most beautiful in the whole world; for no other region is equally blessed with Ionia, neither above it nor below it, nor east nor west of it. For in other countries either the climate is over cold and damp, or else the heat and drought are sorely op-

[56] The dog is represented in the Zendavesta as the special animal of Ormazd, and is still regarded with peculiar reverence by the Parsees.

pressive. The Ionians do not all speak the same language, but use in different places four different dialects. Towards the south their first city is Miletus, next to which lie Myus and Priene; all these three are in Caria and have the same dialect. Their cities in Lydia are the following: Ephesus, Colophon, Lebedus, Teos, Clazomenae, and Phocaea.[57] The inhabitants of these towns have none of the peculiarities of speech which belong to the three first-named cities, but use a dialect of their own. There remain three other Ionian towns, two located on islands, namely, Samos and Chios; one upon the mainland, which is Erythrae. Of these Chios and Erythrae have the same dialect, while Samos possesses a language peculiar to itself. Such are the four varieties of which I spoke.

143. Of the Ionians at this period, one people, the Milesians, were in no danger of attack, as Cyrus had received them into alliance. The islanders also had as yet nothing to fear, since Phoenicia was still independent of Persia, and the Persians themselves were not a seafaring people. The Milesians had separated from the common cause solely on account of the extreme weakness of the Ionians: for, feeble as the power of the entire Hellenic race was at that time, of all its tribes the Ionic was by far the feeblest and least esteemed, not possessing a single city of any mark except Athens. The Athenians and most of the other Ionic states over the world, went so far in their dislike of the name as actually to lay it aside; and even at the present day the greater number of them seem to me to be ashamed of it. But the twelve cities in Asia have always gloried in the appellation; they gave the temple which they built for themselves the name of the Panionium, and decreed that it should not be open to any of the other Ionic states; no state, however, except Smyrna, has craved admission to it.

144. In the same way the Dorians of the region which is now called the Five Cities, but which was formerly known as the

[57] These cities are enumerated in the order in which they stood, from south to north. Erythrae lay on the coast opposite Chios, between Teos and Clazomenae.

Doric Six Cities, exclude all their Dorian neighbours from their temple, the Triopium:[58] nay, they have even gone so far as to shut out from it certain of their own body who were guilty of an offence against the customs of the place. In the games which were anciently celebrated in honour of the Triopian Apollo, the prizes given to the victors were tripods of brass; and the rule was that these tripods should not be carried away from the temple, but should then and there be dedicated to the god. Now a man of Halicarnassus, whose name was Agasicles, being declared victor in the games, in open contempt of the law, took the tripod home to his own house and there hung it against the wall. As a punishment for this fault, the five other cities, Lindus, Ialysus, Cameirus, Cos, and Cnidus, deprived the sixth city, Halicarnassus, of the right of entering the temple.[59]

145. The Ionians founded twelve cities in Asia, and refused to enlarge the number, on account (as I imagine) of their having been divided into twelve States when they lived in the Peloponnese; just as the Achaeans, who drove them out, are at the present day. The first city of the Achaeans after Sicyon, is Pellene, next to which are Aegeira, Aegae upon the Crathis, a stream which is never dry, and from which the Italian Crathis received its name, Bura, Helice where the Ionians took refuge on their defeat by the Achaean invaders, Aegium, Rhypes, Patreis, Phareis, Olenus on the Peirus, which is a large river, Dyme and Tritaeeis, all sea-port towns except the last two, which lie up the country.

146. These are the twelve divisions of what is now Achaea, and was formerly Ionia; and it was owing to their coming from a country so divided that the Ionians, on reaching Asia, founded their twelve States: for it is the height of folly to maintain that these Ionians are more Ionian than the rest, or in any respect

[58] The Triopium was built on a promontory of the same name within the territory of the Cnidians.

[59] Lindus, Ialysus, and Cameirus were in Rhodes, Cos was on the island of the same name, at the mouth of the Ceramic Gulf. Cnidus and Halicarnassus were on the mainland, the former near to the Triopium, the latter on the north shore of the Ceramic Gulf.

better born, since the truth is that no small portion of them
were Abantians from Euboea, who are not even Ionians in
name; and, besides, there were mixed up with the emigration,
Minyae from Orchomenus, Cadmeians, Dryopians, Phocians
from the several cities of Phocis, Molossians, Arcadian Pelasgi,
Dorians from Epidaurus, and many other distinct tribes. Even
those who came from the prytaneum of Athens,[60] and reckon
themselves the purest Ionians of all, brought no wives with
them to the new country, but married Carian girls, whose fathers they had slain. Hence these women made a law, which
they bound themselves by an oath to observe, and which they
handed down to their daughters after them, that none should
ever sit at meat with her husband, or call him by his name, because the invaders slew their fathers, their husbands, and their
sons, and then forced them to become their wives. It was at
Miletus that these events took place.

147. The kings, too, whom they set over them, were either
Lycians, of the blood of Glaucus, son of Hippolochus, or Pylian
Caucons of the blood of Codrus, son of Melanthus; or else from
both those families. But since these Ionians set more store by
the name than any of the others, let them pass for the pure bred
Ionians; though truly all are Ionians who have their origin from
Athens, and keep the Apaturia.[61] This is a festival which all
the Ionians celebrate, except the Ephesians and the Colophoni-
ans, whom a certain act of bloodshed excludes from it.

148. The Panionium is a place in Mycale, facing the north,
which was chosen by the common voice of the Ionians and made
sacred to Heliconian Poseidon. Mycale itself is a promontory

[60] This expression alludes to the solemnities which accompanied the
sending out of a colony in Herodotus' own time. In the prytaneum of
each state was preserved the sacred fire, which was never allowed to go
out, whereon the life of the State was supposed to depend. When a colony
took its departure, the leaders went in solemn procession to the prytaneum
of the mother city, and took fresh fire from the sacred hearth, which was
conveyed to the prytaneum of the new settlement.

[61] The Apaturia was the solemn annual meeting of the phratries, for the
purpose of registering the children of the preceding year whose birth entitled them to citizenship.

of the mainland, stretching out westward towards Samos, in which the Ionians assemble from all their States to keep the feast of the Panionia.[62] The names of festivals, not only among the Ionians but among all the Greeks, end, like the Persian proper names, in one and the same letter.

149. The above-mentioned, then, are the twelve towns of the Ionians. The Aeolic cities are the following: Cyme, called also Phriconis, Larissa, Neonteichus, Temnus, Cilla, Notium, Aegiroessa, Pitane, Aegaeae, Myrina, and Gryneia. These are the eleven ancient cities of the Aeolians. Originally, indeed, they had twelve cities upon the mainland, like the Ionians, but the Ionians deprived them of Smyrna, one of the number. The soil of Aeolis is better than that of Ionia, but the climate is less agreeable.

150. The following is the way in which the loss of Smyrna happened. Certain men of Colophon had been engaged in a sedition there, and being the weaker party, were driven by the others into banishment. The Smyrnaeans received the fugitives, who, after a time, watching their opportunity, while the inhabitants were celebrating a feast to Dionysus outside the walls, shut to the gates, and so got possession of the town. The Aeolians of the other States came to their aid, and terms were agreed on between the parties, the Ionians consenting to give up all the movables, and the Aeolians making a surrender of the place. The expelled Smyrnaeans were distributed among the other states of the Aeolians, and were everywhere admitted to citizenship.

151. These, then, were all the Aeolic cities upon the mainland, with the exception of those about Mount Ida, which made no part of this confederacy. As for the islands, Lesbos contains five cities. Arisba, the sixth, was taken by the Methymnaeans, their kinsmen, and the inhabitants reduced to slavery. Tenedos contains one city, and there is another which is built on what

---

[62] It is remarkable that Thucydides, writing so shortly after Herodotus, should speak of the Pan-Ionic festival at Mycale as no longer of any importance, and regard it as practically superseded by the festival held near Ephesus.

are called the Hundred Isles. The Aeolians of Lesbos and Tenedos, like the Ionian islanders, had at this time nothing to fear. The other Aeolians decided in their common assembly to follow the Ionians, whatever course they should pursue.

152. When the deputies of the Ionians and Aeolians, who had journeyed with all speed to Sparta, reached the city, they chose one of their number, Pythermus, a Phocaean, to be their spokesman. In order to draw together as large an audience as possible, he clothed himself in a purple garment, and so attired stood forth to speak. In a long discourse he besought the Spartans to come to the assistance of his countrymen, but they were not to be persuaded, and voted against sending any succour. The deputies accordingly went their way, while the Lacedaemonians, notwithstanding the refusal which they had given to the prayer of the deputation, despatched a fifty-oared ship to the Asiatic coast with certain Spartans on board, for the purpose, as I think, of watching Cyrus and Ionia. These men, on their arrival at Phocaea, sent to Sardis Lacrines, the most distinguished of their number, to prohibit Cyrus, in the name of the Lacedaemonians, from offering molestation to any city of Greece, since they would not allow it.

153. Cyrus is said, on hearing the speech of the herald, to have asked some Greeks who were standing by, "Who these Lacedaemonians were, and what was their number, that they dared to send him such a notice?" When he had received their reply, he turned to the Spartan herald and said, "I have never yet been afraid of any men, who have a set place in the middle of their city, where they come together to cheat each other and forswear themselves. If I live, the Spartans shall have troubles enough of their own to talk of, without concerning themselves about the Ionians." Cyrus intended these words as a reproach against all the Greeks, because of their having market-places where they buy and sell, which is a custom unknown to the Persians, who never make purchases in open marts, and indeed have not in their whole country a single market-place.[63]

---

[63] Markets in the strict sense of the word are still unknown in the East, where the bazaars, which are collections of shops, take their place.

After this interview Cyrus quitted Sardis, leaving the city under the charge of Tabalus, a Persian, but appointing Pactyas, a native, to collect the treasure belonging to Croesus and the other Lydians, and bring it after him. Cyrus himself proceeded towards Agbatana, carrying Croesus along with him, not regarding the Ionians as important enough to be his immediate object. Larger designs were in his mind. He wished to war in person against Babylon, the Bactrians, the Sacae, and Egypt; he therefore determined to assign to one of his generals the task of conquering the Ionians.

154. No sooner, however, was Cyrus gone from Sardis than Pactyas induced his countrymen to rise in open revolt against him and his deputy Tabalus. With the vast treasures at his disposal he then went down to the sea, and employed them in hiring mercenary troops, while at the same time he engaged the people of the coast to enrol themselves in his army. He then marched upon Sardis, where he besieged Tabalus, who shut himself up in the citadel.

155. When Cyrus, on his way to Agbatana, received these tidings, he turned to Croesus and said, "Where will all this end, Croesus? It seems that these Lydians will not cease to cause trouble both to themselves and others, I wonder if it were not best to sell them all for slaves. Perhaps what I have now done is as if a man were to 'kill the father and then spare the child.' You, who were something more than a father to your people, I have seized and carried off, and to that people I have entrusted their city. Can I then feel surprise at their rebellion?" Thus did Cyrus open to Croesus his thoughts; the latter, full of alarm lest Cyrus should lay Sardis in ruins, replied as follows, "O king, your words are reasonable; but do not, I beseech you, give full vent to your anger, nor doom to destruction an ancient city, guiltless alike of the past and of the present trouble. I caused the one, and in my own person now pay the forfeit. Pactyas has caused the other, he to whom you gave Sardis in charge; let him bear the punishment. Grant, then, forgiveness to the Lydians, and to make sure of their never rebelling against you, or alarming you more, send and forbid them to keep any

weapons of war, command them to wear tunics under their cloaks, and to put buskins upon their legs, and make them bring up their sons to lyre-playing, harping, and shop-keeping. So you will soon see them become women instead of men, and there will be no more fear of their revolting from you."

156. Croesus thought the Lydians would even so be better off than if they were sold for slaves, and therefore gave the above advice to Cyrus, knowing that, unless he brought forward some notable suggestion, he would not be able to persuade him to alter his mind. He was likewise afraid lest, after escaping the danger which now pressed, the Lydians at some future time might revolt from the Persians and so bring themselves to ruin. The advice pleased Cyrus, who consented to forego his anger and do as Croesus had said. Thereupon he summoned to his presence a certain Mede, Mazares by name, and charged him to issue orders to the Lydians in accordance with the terms of Croesus' discourse. Further, he commanded him to sell for slaves all who had joined the Lydians in their attack upon Sardis, and above all else to be sure that he brought Pactyas with him alive on his return. Having given these orders Cyrus continued his journey towards the Persian territory.

157. Pactyas, when news came of the near approach of the army sent against him, fled in terror to Cyme. Mazares, therefore, the Median general, who had marched on Sardis with a detachment of the army of Cyrus, finding on his arrival that Pactyas and his troops were gone, immediately entered the town. And first of all he forced the Lydians to obey the orders of his master, and change (as they did from that time) their entire manner of living.[64] Next, he despatched messengers to Cyme, and required to have Pactyas delivered up to him. On this the Cymaeans resolved to send to Branchidae and ask the advice of the god. Branchidae[65] is situated in the territory of

---

[64] The conversation here reported is evidently an hypothesis to explain the contrast between the Lydians whom the Greeks saw before them, and the old irresistible horsemen of whom they had heard in fame.

[65] The temple of Apollo at Branchidae and the port Panormus still remain. The former is a magnificent ruin of Ionic architecture.

Miletus, above the port of Panormus. There was an oracle there,
established in very ancient times, which both the Ionians and
Aeolians were wont often to consult.

158. Hither therefore the Cymaeans sent their deputies to
make inquiry at the shrine, "What the gods would like them to
do with the Lydian, Pactyas?" The oracle told them, in reply,
to give him up to the Persians. With this answer the messengers
returned, and the people of Cyme were ready to surrender him
accordingly; but as they were preparing to do so, Aristodicus,
son of Heraclides, a citizen of distinction, hindered them. He
declared that he distrusted the response, and believed that the
messengers had reported it falsely; until at last another embassy, of which Aristodicus himself made part, was despatched,
to repeat the former inquiry concerning Pactyas.

159. On their arrival at the shrine of the god, Aristodicus,
speaking on behalf of the whole body, thus addressed the oracle,
"O king, Pactyas the Lydian, threatened by the Persians with
a violent death, has come to us for sanctuary, and lo, they ask
him at our hands, calling upon our nation to deliver him up.
Now, though we greatly dread the Persian power, yet have we
not been bold to give up our suppliant, till we have certain
knowledge of your mind, what you would have us do." The
oracle thus questioned gave the same answer as before, bidding
them surrender Pactyas to the Persians; whereupon Aristodicus,
who had come prepared for such an answer, proceeded to make
the circuit of the temple, and to take all the nests of young
sparrows and other birds that he could find about the building.
As he was thus employed, a voice, it is said, came forth from
the inner sanctuary, addressing Aristodicus in these words,
"Most impious of men, what is this you dare to do? Do you tear
my suppliants from my temple?" Aristodicus, at no loss for a
reply, rejoined, "O king, are you so ready to protect your suppliants, and do you command the Cymaeans to give up a suppliant?" "Yes," returned the god, "I do command it, that so for
the impiety you may the sooner perish, and not come here again
to consult my oracle about the surrender of suppliants."

160. On the receipt of this answer the Cymaeans, unwilling
to bring the threatened destruction on themselves by giving up
the man, and afraid of having to endure a siege if they continued to harbour him, sent Pactyas away to Mytilene. On this
Mazares despatched envoys to the Mytilenaeans to demand the
fugitive of them, and they were preparing to give him up for a
reward (I cannot say with certainty how large, as the bargain
was not completed), when the Cymaeans, hearing what the
Mytilenaeans were about, sent a vessel to Lesbos, and conveyed
away Pactyas to Chios. From hence it was that he was surrendered. The Chians dragged him from the temple of Athena,
Guardian of the citadel and gave him up to the Persians, on
condition of receiving the district of Atarneus, a tract of Mysia
opposite to Lesbos, as the price of the surrender. Thus did
Pactyas fall into the hands of his pursuers, who kept a strict
watch upon him, that they might be able to produce him before
Cyrus. For a long time afterwards none of the Chians would
use the barley of Atarneus to place on the heads of victims, or
make sacrificial cakes of the corn grown there, but the whole
produce of the land was excluded from all their temples.

161. Meanwhile Mazares, after he had recovered Pactyas
from the Chians, made war upon those who had taken part in
the attack on Tabalus, and in the first place took Priene and
sold the inhabitants for slaves, after which he overran the whole
plain of the Maeander and the district of Magnesia,[66] both of
which he gave up for pillage to the soldiery. He then suddenly
sickened and died.

162. Upon his death Harpagus was sent down to the coast
to succeed to his command. He also was of the race of the
Medes, being the man whom the Median king, Astyages, feasted
at the unholy banquet, and who lent his aid to place Cyrus
upon the throne. Appointed by Cyrus to conduct the war in
these parts, he entered Ionia, and took the cities by means of
mounds. Forcing the enemy to shut themselves up within their
defences, he heaped mounds of earth against their walls, and

[66] Not Magnesia under Sipylus, but Magnesia on the Maeander, one of
the few ancient Greek settlements situated far inland.

thus carried the towns. Phocaea was the city against which he
directed his first attack.

163. Now the Phocaeans were the first of the Greeks who
performed long voyages, and it was they who made the Greeks
acquainted with the Adriatic and with Tyrrhenia, with Iberia,
and the city of Tartessus.[67] The vessel which they used in their
voyages was not the round-built merchant-ship, but the long
fifty-oared galley. On their arrival at Tartessus, the king of the
country, whose name was Arganthonius, took a liking to them.
This monarch reigned over the Tartessians for eighty years, and
lived to be 120 years old. He regarded the Phocaeans with so
much favour as, at first, to beg them to quit Ionia and settle in
whatever part of his country they liked. Afterwards, finding
that he could not prevail upon them to agree to this, and hearing that the Mede was growing great in their neighbourhood,
he gave them money to build a wall about their town, and certainly he must have given it with a bountiful hand, for the
town is many furlongs in circuit, and the wall is built entirely
of great blocks of stone skilfully fitted together. The wall, then,
was built by his aid.

164. Harpagus, having advanced against the Phocaeans with
his army, laid siege to their city, first, however, offering them
terms. "It would content him," he said, "if the Phocaeans would
agree to throw down one of their battlements, and dedicate one
dwelling-house to the king." The Phocaeans, sorely vexed at the
thought of becoming slaves, asked a single day to deliberate on
the answer they should return, and besought Harpagus during
that day to draw off his forces from the walls. Harpagus replied
that he understood well enough what they were about to do, but
nevertheless he would grant their request. Accordingly the
troops were withdrawn, and the Phocaeans forthwith took advantage of their absence to launch their fifty-oared ships, and
put on board their wives and children, their household goods,
and even the images of their gods, with all the votive offerings

---

[67] The Iberia of Herodotus is the Spanish Peninsula. Tartessus was a
colony founded there very early by the Phoenicians. It was situated beyond the Straits, near the site of the modern Cadiz.

from the temples, except the paintings and the works in stone
or brass, which were left behind. With the rest they embarked,
and putting to sea, set sail for Chios. The Persians, on their
return, took possession of an empty town.

165. Arrived at Chios, the Phocaeans made offers for the purchase of the islands called the Oenussae, but the Chians refused
to part with them, fearing lest the Phocaeans should establish
a market there, and exclude their merchants from the commerce
of those seas. On their refusal, the Phocaeans, as Arganthonius
was now dead, made up their minds to sail to Cyrnus (Corsica),
where, twenty years before, following the direction of an oracle,[68] they had founded a city, which was called Alalia. Before
they set out, however, on this voyage they sailed once more to
Phocaea, and surprising the Persian troops appointed by Harpagus to garrison the town, put them all to the sword. After this
they laid the heaviest curses on the man who should draw back
and forsake the armament; and having dropped a heavy mass
of iron into the sea, swore never to return to Phocaea till that
mass reappeared upon the surface. Nevertheless, as they were
preparing to depart for Cyrnus, more than half of their number
were seized with such sadness and so great a longing to see once
more their city and their ancient homes, that they broke the
oath by which they had bound themselves and sailed back to
Phocaea.

166. The rest of the Phocaeans, who kept their oath, proceeded without stopping upon their voyage, and when they
came to Cyrnus established themselves along with the earlier
settlers at Alalia and built temples in the place. For five years
they annoyed their neighbours by plundering and pillaging on
all sides, until at length the Carthaginians and Tyrrhenians[69]

[68] A most important influence was exercised by the Greek oracles, especially that of Delphi, over the course of Hellenic colonisation. Herodotus lets fall a remark which shows that it was almost the invariable
practice to consult the oracle as to the place to be colonised.

[69] The naval power of the Etruscans was about this time at its height.
Populonia and Caere were the most important of their maritime towns.
Corsica probably was under their dominion before the Phocaeans made

leagued against them, and sent each a fleet of sixty ships to attack the town. The Phocaeans, on their part, manned all their vessels, sixty in number, and met their enemy on the Sardinian sea. In the engagement which followed the Phocaeans were victorious, but their success was only a sort of Cadmeian victory. They lost forty ships in the battle, and the twenty which remained came out of the engagement with beaks so bent and blunted as to be no longer serviceable. The Phocaeans therefore sailed back again to Alalia, and taking their wives and children on board, with such portion of their goods and chattels as the vessels could bear, bade adieu to Cyrnus and sailed to Rhegium.

167. The Carthaginians and Tyrrhenians, who had got into their hands many more than the Phocaeans from among the crews of the forty vessels that were destroyed, landed their captives upon the coast after the fight, and stoned them all to death. Afterwards, when sheep, or oxen, or even men of the district of Agylla passed by the spot where the murdered Phocaeans lay, their bodies became distorted, or they were seized with palsy, or they lost the use of some of their limbs. On this the people of Agylla sent to Delphi to ask the oracle how they might expiate their sin. The answer of the priestess required them to institute the custom, which they still observe, of honouring the dead Phocaeans with magnificent funeral rites, and solemn games, both gymnic and equestrian. Such, then, was the fate that befell the Phocaean prisoners. The other Phocaeans, who had fled to Rhegium, became after a while the founders of the city called Vela,[70] in the district of Oenotria. This city they colonised, upon the showing of a man of Posidonia,[71] who suggested that the oracle had not meant to bid

their settlement at Alalia. A fresh body of emigrants, with a powerful navy, would exasperate the Tyrrhenians. Hitherto they had shared the commerce of the Western half of the Mediterranean with the Carthaginians.

[70] This is the town more commonly called Velia or Elea, where soon afterwards the great Eleatic school of philosophy arose.

[71] This is the place now known as Paestum, so famous for its beautiful ruins.

them set up a town in Cyrnus the island, but set up the worship
of Cyrnus the hero.

168. Thus fared it with the men of the city of Phocaea in
Ionia. They of Teos did and suffered almost the same; for they
too, when Harpagus had raised his mound to the height of their
defences, took ship, one and all, and sailing across the sea to
Thrace, founded there the city of Abdera. The site was one
which Timesius of Clazomenae had previously tried to colonise,
but without any lasting success, for he was expelled by the
Thracians. Still the Teians of Abdera worship him to this day
as a hero.

169. Of all the Ionians these two states alone, rather than
submit to slavery, forsook their fatherland. The others (I except
Miletus) resisted Harpagus no less bravely than those who fled
their country, and performed many feats of arms, each fighting
in their own defence, but one after another they suffered defeat;
the cities were taken, and the inhabitants submitted, remaining
in their respective countries, and obeying the behests of their
new lords. Miletus, as I have already mentioned, had made
terms with Cyrus, and so continued at peace. Thus was continental Ionia once more reduced to servitude; and when the
Ionians of the islands saw their brethren upon the mainland
subjugated, they also, dreading the like, gave themselves up to
Cyrus.[72]

170. It was while the Ionians were in this distress, but still,
amid it all, held their meetings, as of old, at the Panionium,
that Bias of Priene, who was present at the festival, recommended (as I am informed) a project of the very highest wisdom, which would, had it been embraced, have enabled the
Ionians to become the happiest and most flourishing of the
Greeks. He exhorted them "to join in one body, set sail for
Sardinia, and there found a single Pan-Ionic city; so they would
escape from slavery and rise to great fortune, being masters of
the largest island in the world,[73] and exercising dominion even

---

[72] This statement appears to be too general. Samos certainly maintained
her independence till the reign of Darius.

[73] Herodotus appears to have been entirely convinced that there was no

beyond its bounds; whereas if they stayed in Ionia, he saw no prospect of their ever recovering their lost freedom." Such was the counsel which Bias gave the Ionians in their affliction. Before their misfortunes began, Thales, a man of Miletus, of Phoenician descent, had recommended a different plan. He counselled them to establish a single seat of government, and pointed out Teos as the fittest place for it, "for that," he said, "was the centre of Ionia. Their other cities might still continue to enjoy their own laws, just as if they were independent states." This also was good advice.

171. After conquering the Ionians, Harpagus proceeded to attack the Carians, the Caunians, and the Lycians. The Ionians and Aeolians were forced to serve in his army. Now, of the above nations the Carians are a race who came into the mainland from the islands. In ancient times they were subjects of king Midos, and went by the name of Leleges, dwelling among the isles, and, so far as I have been able to push my inquiries, never liable to give tribute to any man. They served on board the ships of king Minos whenever he required; and thus, as he was a great conqueror and prospered in his wars, the Carians were in his day the most famous by far of all the nations of the earth. They likewise were the inventors of three things, the use of which was borrowed from them by the Greeks; they were the first to fasten crests on helmets and to put devices on shields, and they also invented handles for shields. In the earlier times shields were without handles, and their wearers managed them by the aid of a leathern thong, by which they were slung round the neck and left shoulder. Long after the time of Minos, the Carians were driven from the islands by the Ionians and Dorians, and so settled upon the mainland. The above is the ac-

island in the world so large as Sardinia. He puts the assertion into the mouth of Histiaeus (v. 106), and again (vi. 2) repeats the statement, without expressing any doubt of the fact. We need not be surprised that he was not aware of the size of the British Islands (the Cassiterides, with which the Carthaginians traded, iii. 115), since the south coast was probably all that the Carthaginians themselves had visited; but it does seem extraordinary that he should have lived so long in Italy, and been ignorant that Sicily was a larger island than Sardinia.

count which the Cretans give of the Carians: the Carians themselves say very differently. They maintain that they are the
aboriginal inhabitants of the part of the mainland where they
now dwell,[74] and never had any other name than that which
they still bear: and in proof of this they show an ancient temple
of Carian Zeus in the country of the Mylasians, in which the
Mysians and Lydians have the right of worshipping, as brother
races to the Carians: for Lydus and Mysus, they say, were
brothers of Car. These nations, therefore, have the aforesaid
right; but such as are of a different race, even though they have
come to use the Carian tongue, are excluded from this temple.

172. The Caunians, in my judgment, are aboriginals; but by
their own account they came from Crete. In their language,
either they have approximated to the Carians, or the Carians to
them—on this point I cannot speak with certainty. In their customs, however, they differ greatly from the Carians, and not
only so, but from all other men. They think it a most honourable practice for friends or persons of the same age, whether
they be men, women, or children, to meet together in large companies, for the purpose of drinking wine. Again, on one occasion
they determined that they would no longer make use of the foreign temples which had been long established among them, but
would worship their own old ancestral gods alone. Then their
whole youth took arms, and striking the air with their spears,
marched to the Calyndic frontier, declaring that they were driving out the foreign gods.

173. The Lycians are in good truth anciently from Crete;
which island, in former days, was wholly peopled with barbarians. A quarrel arising there between the two sons of Europa,
Sarpedon and Minos, as to which of them should be king,
Minos, whose party prevailed, drove Sarpedon and his follow-

[74] It seems probable that the Carians, who were a kindred nation to
the Lydians and the Mysians belonged originally to the Asiatic continent, and thence spread to the islands. When the Greek colonisation of
the islands began, the native Carian population would naturally fall back
upon the main mass of the nation which had continued in Asia. Thus both
the Carian and the Greek accounts would have truth in them.

ers into banishment. The exiles sailed to Asia,[75] and landed on
the Milyan territory. Milyas was the ancient name of the country now inhabited by the Lycians: the Milyae of the present
day were, in those times, called Solymi. So long as Sarpedon
reigned, his followers kept the name which they brought with
them from Crete, and were called Termilae, as the Lycians still
are by those who live in their neighbourhood. But after Lycus,
the son of Pandion, banished from Athens by his brother
Aegeus, had found a refuge with Sarpedon in the country of
these Termilae, they came, in course of time, to be called from
him Lycians. Their customs are partly Cretan, partly Carian.
They have, however, one singular custom in which they differ
from every other nation in the world. They take the mother's
and not the father's name. Ask a Lycian who he is, and he answers by giving his own name, that of his mother, and so on in
the female line. Moreover, if a free woman marry a man who is
a slave, their children are full citizens; but if a free man marry
a foreign woman, or live with a concubine, even though he be
the first person in the State, the children forfeit all the rights of
citizenship.

174. Of these nations, the Carians submitted to Harpagus
without performing any brilliant exploits. Nor did the Greeks
who dwelt in Caria behave with any greater gallantry. Among
them were the Cnidians, colonists from Lacedaemon, who occupy a district facing the sea, which is called Triopium. This region adjoins upon the Bybassian Chersonese; and, except a very
small space, is surrounded by the sea, being bounded on the
north by the Ceramic Gulf, and on the south by the channel
towards the islands of Syme and Rhodes. While Harpagus was
engaged in the conquest of Ionia, the Cnidians, wishing to make
their country an island, attempted to cut through this narrow
neck of land, which was about half a mile across from sea to

[75] It is doubtful whether there is any truth at all in this tale, which
would connect the Greeks with Lycia. One thing is clear, namely, that the
Lycian people of history were an entirely distinct race from the Greeks.
The Lycian language cannot be read, though the inscriptions are written
in an alphabet borrowed from the Greek; it may be related to the
Etruscan.

sea. Their whole territory lay inside the isthmus; for where Cnidia ends towards the mainland, the isthmus begins which they were now seeking to cut through. The work had been commenced, and many hands were employed upon it, when it was observed that there seemed to be something unusual and unnatural in the number of wounds that the workmen received, especially about their eyes, from the splintering of the rock. The Cnidians, therefore, sent to Delphi, to inquire what it was that hindered their efforts; and received, according to their own account, the following answer from the oracle:

> Fence not the isthmus off, nor dig it through—
> Zeus would have made an island, had he wished.

So the Cnidians ceased digging, and when Harpagus advanced with his army, they gave themselves up to him without striking a blow.

175. Above Halicarnassus, and further from the coast, were the Pedasians. With this people, when any evil is about to befall either themselves or their neighbours, the priestess of Athena grows an ample beard. Three times has this marvel happened. They alone, of all the dwellers in Caria, resisted Harpagus for awhile, and gave him much trouble, maintaining themselves in a certain mountain called Lida, which they had fortified; but in course of time they also were forced to submit.

176. When Harpagus, after these successes, led his forces into the Xanthian plain, the Lycians of Xanthus went out to meet him in the field: though but a small band against a numerous host, they engaged in battle, and performed many glorious exploits. Overpowered at last, and forced within their walls, they collected into the citadel their wives and children, all their treasures, and their slaves; and having so done, fired the building, and burnt it to the ground. After this, they bound themselves together by dreadful oaths, and sallying forth against the enemy, died sword in hand, not one escaping. Those Lycians who now claim to be Xanthians, are foreign immigrants, except eighty families, who happened to be absent from the country,

and so survived the others. Thus was Xanthus taken by Harpagus, and Caunus fell in like manner into his hands; for the Caunians in the main followed the example of the Lycians.

177. While the lower parts of Asia were in this way brought under by Harpagus, Cyrus in person subjected the upper regions, conquering every nation, and not suffering one to escape. Of these conquests I shall pass by the greater portion, and give an account of those only which gave him the most trouble, and are the worthiest of mention. When he had brought all the rest of the continent under his sway, he made war on the Assyrians.[76]

178. Assyria possesses a vast number of great cities, whereof the most renowned and strongest at this time was Babylon, whither, after the fall of Nineveh, the seat of government had been removed. The following is a description of the place: The city stands on a broad plain, and is an exact square, fifteen miles in length each way, so that the entire circuit is sixty miles.[77] While such is its size, in magnificence there is no other city that approaches to it. It is surrounded, in the first place, by a broad and deep moat, full of water, behind which rises a wall fifty royal cubits in width, and 200 in height.[78] (The royal cubit is longer by three fingers' breadth than the common cubit.)

179. And here I may not omit to tell the use to which the mould dug out of the great moat was turned, nor the manner wherein the wall was wrought. As fast as they dug the moat the soil which they got from the cutting was made into bricks, and when a sufficient number were completed they baked the bricks in kilns. Then they set to building, and began with bricking the borders of the moat, after which they proceeded to construct the wall itself, using throughout for their cement hot bitumen, and interposing a layer of wattled reeds at every thirtieth course of the bricks. On the top, along the edges of the wall, they constructed buildings of a single chamber facing one another, leav-

[76] Herodotus includes Babylonia in Assyria.

[77] This figure must include outlying moats and fortifications.

[78] These figures, 335 feet by eighty-five feet, are probably exaggerations to be attributed to Herodotus' guide.

ing between them room for a four-horse chariot to turn. In the circuit of the wall are 100 gates, all of brass, with brazen lintels and side-posts. The bitumen used in the work was brought to Babylon from the Is, a small stream which flows into the Euphrates at the point where the city of the same name stands, eight days' journey from Babylon. Lumps of bitumen are found in great abundance in this river.

180. The city is divided into two portions by the river which runs through the midst of it. This river is the Euphrates, a broad, deep, swift stream, which rises in Armenia, and empties itself into the Red sea. The city wall is brought down on both sides to the edge of the stream: thence from the corners of the wall, there is carried along each bank of the river a fence of burnt bricks. The houses are mostly three and four stories high; the streets all run in straight lines, not only those parallel to the river, but also the cross streets which lead down to the waterside. At the river end of these cross streets are low gates in the fence that skirts the stream, which are, like the great gates in the outer wall, of brass, and open on the water.

181. The outer wall is the main defence of the city. There is, however, a second inner wall, of less thickness than the first, but very little inferior to it in strength. The centre of each division of the town was occupied by a fortress. In the one stood the palace of the kings, surrounded by a wall of great strength and size: in the other was the sacred precinct of Zeus Belus,[79] an enclosure a quarter of a mile square, with gates of solid brass; which was also remaining in my time. In the middle of the precinct there was a tower of solid masonry, a furlong in length and breadth, upon which was raised a second tower, and on that a third, and so on up to eight. The ascent to the top is on the outside, by a path which winds round all the towers. When one is about half way up, one finds a resting-place and seats, where persons are wont to sit some time on their way to the summit. On the topmost tower there is a spacious temple, and inside the

[79] The Babylonian worship of Bel is well known; there is little doubt that he was the recognised head of the Babylonian Pantheon, and therefore properly identified by the Greeks with their Zeus.

temple stands a couch of unusual size, richly adorned, with a golden table by its side. There is no statue of any kind set up in the place, nor is the chamber occupied of nights by any one but a single native woman, who, as the Chaldaeans, the priests of this god, affirm, is chosen for himself by the deity out of all the women of the land.

182. They also declare (but I do not believe it) that the god comes down in person into this chamber, and sleeps upon the couch. This is like the story told by the Egyptians of what takes place in their city of Thebes, where a woman always passes the night in the temple of the Theban Zeus. In each case the woman is said to be debarred all intercourse with men. It is also like the custom at Patara, in Lycia, where the priestess who delivers the oracles, during the time that she is so employed—for at Patara there is not always an oracle,[80] is shut up in the temple every night.

183. Below, in the same precinct, there is a second temple, in which is a sitting figure of Zeus, all of gold. Before the figure stands a large golden table, and the throne whereon it sits, and the base on which the throne is placed, are likewise of gold. The Chaldaeans told me that all the gold together was 800 talents' weight. Outside the temple are two altars, one of solid gold, on which it is only lawful to offer sucklings; the other a common altar, but of great size, on which the full-grown animals are sacrificed. It is also on the great altar that the Chaldaeans burn the frankincense, which is offered to the amount of 1,000 talents' weight, every year, at the festival of the god. In the time of Cyrus there was likewise in this temple the figure of a man, eighteen feet high, entirely of solid gold. I myself did not see this figure, but I relate what the Chaldaeans report concerning it. Darius, the son of Hystaspes, plotted to carry the statue off, but had not the hardihood to lay his hands upon it. Xerxes, however, the son of Darius, killed the priest who forbade him to move the statue, and took it away. Besides the ornaments which

---

[80] Apollo delivered oracles here during the six winter months, while during the six summer months he gave responses at Delos.

I have mentioned, there are a large number of private offerings in this holy precinct.

184. Many sovereigns have ruled over this city of Babylon, and lent their aid to the building of its walls and the adornment of its temples, of whom I shall make mention in my Assyrian history. Among them two were women. Of these, the earlier, called Semiramis,[81] held the throne five generations before the later princess. She raised certain embankments well worthy of inspection, in the plain near Babylon, to control the river, which, till then, used to overflow, and flood the whole country round about.

185. The later of the two queens, whose name was Nitocris,[82] a wiser princess than her predecessor, not only left behind her, as memorials of her occupancy of the throne, the works which I shall presently describe, but also, observing the great power and restless enterprise of the Medes, who had taken so large a number of cities, and among them Nineveh, and expecting to be attacked in her turn, made all possible exertions to increase the defences of her empire. And first, whereas the river Euphrates, which traverses the city, ran formerly with a straight course to Babylon, she, by certain excavations which she made at some distance up the stream, rendered it so winding that it comes three several times in sight of the same village, a village in Assyria, which is called Ardericca;[83] and to this day, they who would go from our sea to Babylon, on descending to the river touch three times, and on three different days, at this very place. She also made an embankment along each side of the Euphrates, wonderful both for breadth and height, and dug a basin for a lake a great way above Babylon, close alongside of the stream, which was sunk everywhere to the point where they came to water, and was of such breadth that the whole circuit measured

[81] Semiramis was the wife of Rammannirari III (812-783 B.C.), and seems to have introduced the worship of Nebo into Nineveh. Herodotus gives none of the wild tales attached to the mythical Semiramis.

[82] No such queen as Nitocris is found either in the Babylonian inscriptions or in Berosus.

[83] No such cuttings as those here described by Herodotus ever existed.

fifty-three miles. The soil dug out of this basin was made use of in the embankments along the waterside. When the excavation was finished, she had stones brought, and bordered with them the entire margin of the reservoir. These two things were done, the river made to wind, and the lake excavated, that the stream might be slacker by reason of the number of curves, and the voyage be rendered circuitous, and that at the end of the voyage it might be necessary to skirt the lake and so make a long round. All these works were on that side of Babylon where the passes lay, and the roads into Media were the straightest, and the aim of the queen in making them was to prevent the Medes from holding intercourse with the Babylonians, and so to keep them in ignorance of her affairs.

186. While the soil from the excavation was being thus used for the defence of the city, Nitocris engaged also in another undertaking, a mere by-work compared with those we have already mentioned. The city, as I said, was divided by the river into two distinct portions. Under the former kings, if a man wanted to pass from one of these divisions to the other, he had to cross in a boat; which must, it seems to me, have been very troublesome. Accordingly, while she was digging the lake, Nitocris bethought herself of turning it to a use which should at once remove this inconvenience, and enable her to leave another monument of her reign over Babylon. She gave orders for the hewing of immense blocks of stone, and when they were ready and the basin was excavated, she turned the entire stream of the Euphrates into the cutting, and thus for a time, while the basin was filling, the natural channel of the river was left dry. Forthwith she set to work, and in the first place lined the banks of the stream within the city with quays of burnt brick, and also bricked the landing-places opposite the river-gates, adopting throughout the same fashion of brickwork which had been used in the town wall; after which, with the materials which had been prepared, she built, as near the middle of the town as possible, a stone bridge, the blocks whereof were bound together with iron and lead. In the daytime square wooden platforms were laid

along from pier to pier, on which the inhabitants crossed the
stream; but at night they were withdrawn, to prevent people
passing from side to side in the dark to commit robberies. When
the river had filled the cutting, and the bridge was finished, the
Euphrates was turned back again into its ancient bed; and thus
the basin, transformed suddenly into a lake, was seen to answer
the purpose for which it was made, and the inhabitants, by help
of the basin, obtained the advantage of a bridge.

187. It was this same princess by whom a remarkable decep-
tion was planned. She had her tomb constructed in the upper
part of one of the principal gateways of the city, high above the
heads of the passers-by, with this inscription cut upon it, "If
there be one among my successors on the throne of Babylon
who is in want of treasure, let him open my tomb, and take as
much as he chooses, not, however, unless he be truly in want,
for it will not be for his good." This tomb continued untouched
until Darius came to the kingdom. To him it seemed a monstrous thing that he should be unable to use one of the gates of
the town, and that a sum of money should be lying idle, and
moreover inviting his grasp, and he not seize upon it. Now he
could not use the gate because, as he drove through, the dead
body would have been over his head. Accordingly he opened the
tomb; but instead of money, found only the dead body, and a
writing which said, "Had you not been insatiate of pelf, and
careless how you got it, you would not have broken open the
sepulchres of the dead."

188. The expedition of Cyrus was undertaken against the son
of this princess, who bore the same name as his father Labynetus,[84] and was king of the Assyrians. The Great King, when
he goes to the wars, is always supplied with provisions carefully
prepared at home, and with cattle of his own. Water too from
the river Choaspes, which flows by Susa, is taken with him for
his drink, as that is the only water which the kings of Persia
taste. Wherever he travels, he is attended by a number of four-

---

[84] Herodotus regards this Labynetus (Nabonidus, 556 B.C.) as the son of
the king mentioned in i. 74.

wheeled cars drawn by mules, in which the Choaspes water, ready boiled for use, and stored in flagons of silver, is moved with him from place to place.

189. Cyrus on his way to Babylon came to the banks of the Gyndes, a stream which, rising in the Matienian mountains, runs through the country of the Dardanians, and empties itself into the river Tigris. The Tigris, after receiving the Gyndes, flows on by the city of Opis, and discharges its waters into the Erythraean sea. When Cyrus reached this stream, which could only be passed in boats, one of the sacred white horses accompanying his march, full of spirit and high mettle, walked into the water, and tried to cross by himself; but the current seized him, swept him along with it, and drowned him in its depths. Cyrus, enraged at the insolence of the river, threatened so to break its strength that in future even women should cross it easily without wetting their knees. Accordingly he put off for a time his attack on Babylon, and, dividing his army into two parts, he marked out by ropes 180 trenches on each side of the Gyndes, leading off from it in all directions, and setting his army to dig, some on one side of the river, some on the other, he accomplished his threat by the aid of so great a number of hands, but not without losing thereby the whole summer season.

190. Having, however, thus wreaked his vengeance on the Gyndes by dispersing it through 360 channels, Cyrus, with the first approach of the ensuing spring, marched forward against Babylon. The Babylonians, encamped without their walls, awaited his coming. A battle was fought at a short distance from the city, in which the Babylonians were defeated by the Persian king, whereupon they withdrew within their defences. Here they shut themselves up, and made light of his siege, having laid in a store of provisions for many years in preparation against this attack; for when they saw Cyrus conquering nation after nation, they were convinced that he would never stop, and that their turn would come at last.

191. Cyrus was now reduced to great perplexity, as time went on and he made no progress against the place. In this distress either some one made the suggestion to him, or he bethought

himself of a plan, which he proceeded to put in execution. He
placed a portion of his army at the point where the river enters
the city, and another body at the back of the place where it
issues forth, with orders to march into the town by the bed of
the stream, as soon as the water became shallow enough: he
then himself drew off with the unwarlike portion of his host, and
made for the place where Nitocris dug the basin for the river,
where he did exactly what she had done formerly: he turned the
Euphrates by a canal into the basin, which was then a marsh, on
which the river sank to such an extent that the natural bed of
the stream became fordable. Hereupon the Persians who had
been left for the purpose at Babylon by the river-side, entered
the stream, which had now sunk so as to reach about midway
up a man's thigh, and thus got into the town. Had the Babylonians been apprised of what Cyrus was about, or had they
noticed their danger, they would not have allowed the entrance
of the Persians within the city, which was what ruined them utterly, but would have made fast all the street-gates which gave
upon the river, and mounting upon the walls along both sides of
the stream, would so have caught the enemy as it were in a trap.
But, as it was, the Persians came upon them by surprise and so
took the city. Owing to the vast size of the place, the inhabitants
of the central parts (as the residents at Babylon declare) long
after the outer portions of the town were taken, knew nothing of
what had chanced, but as they were engaged in a festival, continued dancing and revelling until they learnt the capture but
too certainly. Such, then, were the circumstances of the first
taking of Babylon.

192. Among many proofs which I shall bring forward of the
power and resources of the Babylonians, the following is of special account. The whole country under the dominion of the Persians, besides paying a fixed tribute, is parcelled out into divisions, which have to supply food to the Great King and his army
during different portions of the year. Now out of the twelve
months which go to a year, the district of Babylon furnishes
food during four, the other regions of Asia during eight; by
which it appears that Assyria, in respect of resources, is one-

third of the whole of Asia. Of all the Persian governments, or
satrapies as they are called by the natives, this is by far the
best. When Tritantaechmes, son of Artabazus, held it of the
king, it brought him in an artaba of silver every day. The artaba
is a Persian measure, and holds three choenixes more than the
medimnus of the Athenians. He also had, belonging to his own
private stud, besides war-horses, 800 stallions and 16,000 mares,
twenty to each stallion. Besides which he kept so great a number
of Indian hounds, that four large villages of the plain were ex-
empted from all other charges on condition of finding them in
food.

193. But little rain falls in Assyria, enough, however, to make
the corn begin to sprout, after which the plant is nourished and
the ears formed by means of irrigation from the river. For the
river does not, as in Egypt, overflow the corn-lands of its own
accord, but is spread over them by the hand, or by the help of
engines. The whole of Babylonia is, like Egypt, intersected with
canals. The largest of them all, which runs towards the winter
sun, and is impassable except in boats, is carried from the Euphrates into another stream, called the Tigris, the river upon
which the town of Nineveh formerly stood. Of all the countries
that we know there is none which is so fruitful in grain It
makes no pretension indeed of growing the fig, the olive, the
vine, or any other tree of the kind; but in grain it is so fruitful
as to yield commonly two-hundred-fold, and when the produc-
tion is the greatest, even three-hundred-fold. The blade of the
wheat-plant and barley-plant is often four fingers in breadth. As
for the millet and the sesame, I shall not say to what height they
grow, though within my own knowledge; for I am not ignorant
that what I have already written concerning the fruitfulness of
Babylonia must seem incredible to those who have never visited
the country. The only oil they use is made from the sesame-
plant. Palm-trees grow in great numbers over the whole of the
flat country, mostly of the kind which bears fruit, and this fruit
supplies them with bread, wine, and honey. They are cultivated
like the fig-tree in all respects, among others in this. The natives
tie the fruit of the male-palms, as they are called by the Greeks,

to the branches of the date-bearing palm, to let the gall-fly enter the dates and ripen them, and to prevent the fruit from falling off. The male-palms, like the wild fig-trees, have usually the gall-fly in their fruit.

194. But the greatest wonder of all that I saw in the land, after the city itself, I will now proceed to mention. The boats which come down the river to Babylon are circular, and made of skins. The frames, which are of willow, are cut in the country of the Armenians above Assyria, and on these, which serve for hulls, a covering of skins is stretched outside, and thus the boats are made, without either stem or stern, quite round like a shield. They are then entirely filled with straw, and their cargo is put on board, after which they are suffered to float down the stream. Their chief freight is wine, stored in casks made of the wood of the palm-tree. They are managed by two men who stand upright in them, each plying an oar, one pulling and the other pushing. The boats are of various sizes, some larger, some smaller; the biggest reach as high as 150 tons burthen. Each vessel has a live ass on board; those of larger size have more than one. When they reach Babylon, the cargo is landed and offered for sale; after which the men break up their boats, sell the straw and the frames, and loading their asses with the skins, set off on their way back to Armenia. The current is too strong to allow a boat to return up-stream, for which reason they make their boats of skins rather than wood. On their return to Armenia they build fresh boats for the next voyage.

195. The dress of the Babylonians is a linen tunic reaching to the feet, and above it another tunic made in wool, besides which they have a short white cloak thrown round them, and shoes of a peculiar fashion, not unlike those worn by the Boeotians. They have long hair, wear turbans on their heads, and anoint their whole body with perfumes. Every one carries a seal and a walking-stick, carved at the top into the form of an apple, a rose, a lily, an eagle, or something similar; for it is not their habit to use a stick without an ornament.

196. Of their customs, whereof I shall now proceed to give an account, the following (which I understand belongs to them

in common with the Illyrian tribe of the Eneti[85]) is the wisest in my judgment. Once a year in each village the maidens of age to marry were collected all together into one place; while the men stood round them in a circle. Then a herald called up the damsels one by one, and offered them for sale. He began with the most beautiful. When she was sold for no small sum of money, he offered for sale the one who came next to her in beauty. All of them were sold to be wives. The richest of the Babylonians who wished to wed bid against each other for the loveliest maidens, while the humbler wife-seekers, who were in different about beauty, took the more homely damsels with marriage-portions. For the custom was that when the herald had gone through the whole number of the beautiful damsels, he should then call up the ugliest—a cripple, if there chanced to be one—and offer her to the men, asking who would agree to take her with the smallest marriage-portion. And the man who offered to take the smallest sum had her assigned to him. The marriage-portions were furnished by the money paid for the beautiful damsels, and thus the fairer maidens portioned out the uglier. No one was allowed to give his daughter in marriage to the man of his choice, nor might any one carry away the damsel whom he had purchased without finding bail really and truly to make her his wife; if, however, it turned out that they did not agree, the money might be paid back. All who liked might come even from distant villages and bid for the women. This was the best of all their customs, but it has now fallen into disuse. They have lately hit upon a very different plan to save their maidens from violence, and prevent their being torn from them and carried to distant cities, which is to bring up their daughters to be prostitutes. This is now done by all the poorer of the common people, who since the conquest have been maltreated by their lords, and have had ruin brought upon their families.

197. The following custom seems to me the wisest of their institutions next to the one lately praised. They have no physicians, but when a man is ill, they lay him in the public square,

[85] The Eneti or Heneti are the same with the Venetians of later times. This information Herodotus probably obtained in Italy.

and the passers-by come up to him, and if they have ever had his disease themselves or have known any one who has suffered from it, they give him advice, recommending him to do whatever they found good in their own case, or in the case known to them. And no one is allowed to pass the sick man in silence without asking him what his ailment is.

198. They bury their dead in honey, and have funeral lamentations like the Egyptians. When a Babylonian has had intercourse with his wife, he sits down before a censer of burning incense, and the woman sits opposite to him. At dawn of day they wash; for till they are washed they will not touch any of their common vessels. This practice is observed also by the Arabians.

199. The Babylonians have one most shameful custom. Every woman born in the country must once in her life go and sit down in the precinct of Aphrodite, and there have intercourse with a stranger. Many of the wealthier sort, who are too proud to mix with the others, drive in covered carriages to the precinct, followed by a goodly train of attendants, and there take their station. But the larger number seat themselves within the holy enclosure with wreaths of string about their heads, and here there is always a great crowd, some coming and others going; lines of cord mark out paths in all directions among the women, and the strangers pass along them to make their choice. A woman who has once taken her seat is not allowed to return home till one of the strangers throws a silver coin into her lap, and takes her with him beyond the holy ground. When he throws the coin he says these words, "I summon you in the name of the goddess Mylitta." (Aphrodite is called Mylitta by the Assyrians.) The silver coin may be of any size; it cannot be refused, for that is forbidden by the law, since once thrown it is sacred. The woman goes with the first man who throws her money, and rejects no one. When she has had intercourse with him, and so satisfied the goddess, she returns home, and from that time on no gift however great will prevail with her. Such of the women as are tall and beautiful are soon released, but others who are ugly have to stay a long time before they can fulfil the

law. Some have waited three or four years in the precinct. A custom very much like this is found also in certain parts of the island of Cyprus.

200. Such are the customs of the Babylonians generally. There are likewise three tribes among them who eat nothing but fish. These are caught and dried in the sun, after which they are brayed in a mortar, and strained through a linen sieve. Some prefer to make cakes of this material, others bake it into a kind of bread.

201. When Cyrus had achieved the conquest of the Babylonians, he conceived the desire of bringing the Massagetae under his dominion. Now the Massagetae are said to be a great and warlike nation, dwelling eastward, towards the rising of the sun, beyond the river Araxes, and opposite the Issedonians. By many they are regarded as a Scythian race.

202. As for the Araxes, it is, according to some accounts, larger, according to others smaller than the Ister (Danube). It has islands in it, many of which are said to be equal in size to Lesbos. The men who inhabit them feed during the summer on roots of all kinds, which they dig out of the ground, while they store up the fruits, which they gather from the trees at the fitting season, to serve them as food in the wintertime. Besides the trees whose fruit they gather for this purpose, they have also a tree which bears the strangest produce. When they are met together in companies they throw some of it upon the fire round which they are sitting, and presently, by the mere smell of the fumes[86] which it gives out in burning, they grow drunk, as the Greeks do with wine. More of the fruit is then thrown on the fire, and, their drunkenness increasing, they often jump up and begin to dance and sing. Such is the account which I have heard of this people.

The river Araxes, like the Gyndes, which Cyrus dispersed into 360 channels, has its source in the country of the Matienians. It has forty mouths, whereof all, except one, end in bogs and swamps. These bogs and swamps are said to be inhabited by a race of men who feed on raw fish, and clothe themselves with

---

[86] This intoxicant was obviously hashish.

the skins of seals. The other mouth of the river flows with a clear course into the Caspian Sea.[87]

203. The Caspian is a sea by itself, having no connexion with any other.[88] The sea frequented by the Greeks, that beyond the pillars of Heracles, which is called the Atlantic, and also the Red Sea, are all one and the same sea. But the Caspian is a distinct sea, lying by itself, in length fifteen days' voyage with a row-boat, in breadth, at the broadest part, eight days' voyage.[89] Along its western shore runs the chain of the Caucasus, the most extensive and loftiest of all mountain-ranges. Many and various are the tribes by which it is inhabited, most of whom live entirely on the wild fruits of the forest. In these forests certain trees are said to grow, from the leaves of which, pounded and mixed with water, the inhabitants make a dye, wherewith they paint upon their clothes the figures of animals; and the figures so impressed never wash out, but last as though they had been inwoven in the cloth from the first, and wear as long as the garment. These people are said to copulate in public, like cattle.

204. On the west then, as I have said, the Caspian Sea is bounded by the range of Caucasus. On the east it is followed by a vast plain, stretching out interminably before the eye, the greater portion of which is possessed by those Massagetae, against whom Cyrus was now so anxious to make an expedition. Many strong motives weighed with him and urged him on—his birth especially, which seemed something more than human, and

[87] The geographical knowledge of Herodotus seems to be nowhere so much at fault as in his account of this river. He appears to have confused together the information which had reached him concerning four distant streams.

[88] Here the geographical knowledge of Herodotus was much in advance of his age. False information received at the time of Alexander's conquests seems to have made geographical knowledge retrograde. It was reserved for Ptolemy to restore the Caspian to its true position of an inland sea.

[89] It is impossible to make any exact comparison between the actual size of the Caspian and the estimate of Herodotus, since we do not know what distance he intends by the day's voyage of a row-boat.

his good fortune in all his former wars, wherein he had always found, that against what country soever he turned his arms, it was impossible for that people to escape.

205. At this time the Massagetae were ruled by a queen, named Tomyris, who at the death of her husband, the late king, had mounted the throne. To her Cyrus sent ambassadors, with instructions to court her on his part, pretending that he wished to take her to wife. Tomyris, however, aware that it was her kingdom, and not herself, that he courted, forbade the men to approach. Cyrus, therefore, finding that he did not advance his designs by this deceit, marched towards the Araxes, and openly displaying his hostile intentions, set to work to construct a bridge on which his army might cross the river, and began building towers upon the boats which were to be used in the passage.

206. While the Persian leader was occupied in these labours, Tomyris sent a herald to him, who said, "King of the Medes, cease to press this enterprise, for you cannot know if what you are doing will be of real advantage to you. Be content to rule in peace your kingdom, and bear to see us reign over the countries that are ours to govern. As, however, I know you will not choose to hearken to this counsel, since there is nothing you less desire than peace and quietness, come now, if you are so mightily desirous of meeting the Massagetae in arms, leave your useless toil of bridge-making; let us retire three days' march from the river bank, and you come across with your soldiers; or, if you like better to give us battle on your side the stream, retire an equal distance." Cyrus, on this offer, called together the chiefs of the Persians, and laid the matter before them, requesting them to advise him what he should do. All the votes were in favour of his letting Tomyris cross the stream, and giving battle on Persian ground.

207. But Croesus the Lydian, who was present at the meeting of the chiefs, disapproved of this advice; he therefore rose, and thus delivered his sentiments in opposition to it, "O king I promised you long since, that, as Zeus had given me into your hands, I would, to the best of my power, avert impending dan-

ger from your house. Alas, my own sufferings, by their very bitterness, have taught me to be keen-sighted of dangers. If you
deem yourself an immortal, and your army an army of immortals, my counsel will doubtless be thrown away upon you.
But if you feel yourself to be a man, and a ruler of men, lay this
first to heart, that there is a wheel on which the affairs of men
revolve, and that its movement forbids the same man to be
always fortunate. Now concerning the matter in hand, my judgment runs counter to the judgment of your other counsellors.
For if you agree to give the enemy entrance into your country,
consider what risk is run! Lose the battle, and your whole kingdom is lost. For assuredly, the Massagetae, if they win the fight,
will not return to their homes, but will push forward against the
states of your empire. Or if you win the battle, why, then you
gain far less than if you were across the stream, where you
might follow up your victory. For against your loss, if they defeat you on your own ground, must be set theirs in like case.
Rout their army on the other side of the river, and you may
push at once into the heart of their country. Moreover, were it
not disgrace intolerable for Cyrus the son of Cambyses to retire
before and yield ground to a woman? My counsel therefore is,
that we cross the stream, and pushing forward as far as they
shall fall back, then seek to get the better of them by stratagem.
I am told they are unacquainted with the good things on which
the Persians live, and have never tasted the great delights of
life. Let us then prepare a feast for them in our camp; let sheep
be slaughtered without stint, and the wine-cups be filled full of
noble liquor, and let all manner of dishes be prepared: then
leaving behind us our worst troops, let us fall back towards the
river. Unless I very much mistake, when they see the good fare
set out, they will forget all else and fall to. Then it will remain
for us to do our parts manfully."

208. Cyrus, when the two plans were thus placed in contrast
before him, changed his mind, and preferring the advice which
Croesus had given, returned for answer to Tomyris, that she
should retire, and that he would cross the stream. She therefore
retired, as she had engaged; and Cyrus, giving Croesus into the

care of his son Cambyses (whom he had appointed to succeed him on the throne), with strict charge to pay him all respect and treat him well, if the expedition failed of success; and sending them both back to Persia, crossed the river with his army.

209. The first night after the passage, as he slept in the enemy's country, a vision appeared to him. He seemed to see in his sleep the eldest of the sons of Hystaspes, with wings upon his shoulders, shadowing with the one wing Asia, and Europe with the other. Now Hystaspes, the son of Arsames, was of the race of the Achaemenidae, and his eldest son, Darius, was at that time scarce twenty years old; wherefore, not being of age to go to the wars, he had remained behind in Persia. When Cyrus woke from his sleep, and turned the vision over in his mind, it seemed to him no light matter. He therefore sent for Hystaspes, and taking him aside, said, "Hystaspes, your son is discovered to be plotting against me and my crown. I will tell you how I know it so certainly. The gods watch over my safety, and warn me beforehand of every danger. Now last night, as I lay in my bed, I saw in a vision the eldest of your sons with wings upon his shoulders, shadowing with the one wing Asia, and Europe with the other. From this it is certain, beyond all possible doubt, that he is engaged in some plot against me. Return then at once to Persia, and be sure, when I come back from conquering the Massagetae, to have your son ready to produce before me, that I may examine him."

210. Thus Cyrus spoke, in the belief that he was plotted against by Darius; but he missed the true meaning of the dream, which was sent by God to forewarn him, that he was to die then and there, and that his kingdom was to fall at last to Darius.

Hystaspes made answer to Cyrus in these words, "Heaven forbid, sire, that there should be a Persian living who would plot against you! If such an one there be, may a speedy death overtake him! You found the Persians a race of slaves, you made them free men: you found them subject to others, you made them lords of all. If a vision has announced that my son is practising against you, I resign him into your hands to deal with as

you will." Hystaspes, when he had thus answered, recrossed the
Araxes and hastened back to Persia, to keep a watch on his son
Darius.

211. Meanwhile Cyrus, having advanced a day's march from
the river, did as Croesus had advised him, and, leaving the
worthless portion of his army in the camp, drew off with his
good troops towards the river. Soon afterwards, a detachment
of the Massagetae, one-third of their entire army, led by Spargapises, son of the queen Tomyris, coming up, fell upon the
body which had been left behind by Cyrus, and on their resistance put them to the sword. Then, seeing the banquet prepared, they sat down and began to feast. When they had eaten
and drunk their fill, and were now sunk in sleep, the Persians
under Cyrus arrived, slaughtered a great multitude, and made
even a larger number prisoners. Among these last was Spargapises himself.

212. When Tomyris heard what had befallen her son and her
army, she sent a herald to Cyrus, who thus addressed the conqueror, "Bloodthirsty Cyrus, pride not yourself on this poor
success: it was the grapejuice—which, when you drink it, makes
you so mad, and as you swallow it down brings up to your lips
such bold and wicked words—it was this poison wherewith you
ensnared my child, and so overcame him, not in fair open fight.
Now hearken what I advise, and be sure I advise you for your
good. Restore my son to me and leave the land unharmed, tri-
umphant over a third part of the host of the Massagetae. Refuse, and I swear by the sun, the sovereign lord of the Massagetae, bloodthirsty as you are, I will give you your fill of blood."

213. To the words of this message Cyrus paid no manner of
regard. As for Spargapises, the son of the queen, when the wine
went off, and he saw the extent of his calamity, he made request
to Cyrus to release him from his bonds; then, when his prayer
was granted, and the fetters were taken from his limbs, as soon
as his hands were free, he destroyed himself.

214. Tomyris, when she found that Cyrus paid no heed to
her advice, collected all the forces of her kingdom, and gave him
battle. Of all the combats in which the barbarians have engaged

among themselves, I reckon this to have been the fiercest. The following, as I understand, was the manner of it: First, the two armies stood apart and shot their arrows at each other; then, when their quivers were empty, they closed and fought hand-to-hand with lances and daggers; and thus they continued fighting for a length of time, neither choosing to give ground. At length the Massagetae prevailed. The greater part of the army of the Persians was destroyed and Cyrus himself fell, after reigning twenty-nine years. Search was made among the slain by order of the queen for the body of Cyrus, and when it was found she took a skin, and, filling it full of human blood, she dipped the head of Cyrus in the gore, saying, as she thus insulted the corpse, "I live and have conquered you in fight, and yet by you am I ruined, for you took my son with guile; but thus I make good my threat, and give you your fill of blood." Of the many different accounts which are given of the death of Cyrus, this which I have followed appears to me most worthy of credit.[90]

215. In their dress and mode of living the Massagetae resemble the Scythians. They fight both on horseback and on foot, neither method is strange to them: they use bows and lances, but their favourite weapon is the battle-axe. Their arms are all either of gold or brass. For their spearpoints, and arrowheads, and for their battle-axes, they make use of brass; for head-gear, belts, and girdles, of gold. So too with the caparison of their horses, they give them breastplates of brass, but employ gold about the reins, the bit, and the cheek-plates. They use neither iron nor silver, having none in their country; but they have brass and gold in abundance.[91]

216. The following are some of their customs: Each man has but one wife, yet all the wives are held in common; for this is a custom of the Massagetae and not of the Scythians, as the Greeks wrongly say. When a man desires a woman he hangs his quiver in front of her waggon and has intercourse with her unhindered. Human life does not come to its natural close with

[90] It may be questioned whether the account, which out of many seemed to our author most worthy of credit, was really the most credible.
[91] Both the Ural and the Altai mountains abound in gold.

this people; but when a man grows very old, all his kinsfolk collect together and offer him up in sacrifice; offering at the same time some cattle also. After the sacrifice they boil the flesh and feast on it; and those who thus end their days are reckoned the happiest. If a man dies of disease they do not eat him, but bury him in the ground, bewailing his ill-fortune that he did not come to be sacrificed. They sow no grain, but live on their herds, and on fish, of which there is great plenty in the Araxes. Milk is what they chiefly drink. The only god they worship is the sun, and to him they offer the horse in sacrifice; under the notion of giving to the swiftest of the gods the swiftest of all mortal creatures.

The Second Book, Entitled

EUTERPE

1. On the death of Cyrus, Cambyses his son by Cassandane daughter of Pharnaspes took the kingdom. Cassandane had died in the lifetime of Cyrus, who had made a great mourning for her at her death, and had commanded all the subjects of his empire to observe the like. Cambyses, the son of this woman and of Cyrus, regarding the Ionian and Aeolian Greeks as vassals of his father, took them with him in his expedition against Egypt[1] among the other nations which owned his sway.

2. Now the Egyptians, before the reign of their king Psammetichus, believed themselves to be the most ancient of mankind.[2] Since Psammetichus, however, made an attempt to discover who were actually the primitive race, they have been of opinion that while they surpass all other nations, the Phrygians surpass them in antiquity. This king, finding it impossible to make out by dint of inquiry what men were the most ancient, contrived the following method of discovery: He took two children of the common sort, and gave them over to a herdsman to bring up at his folds, strictly charging him to let no one utter a word in their presence, but to keep them in a sequestered cottage, and from time to time introduce goats to their apartment,

[1] The date of the expedition of Cambyses against Egypt cannot be fixed with absolute certainty. 525 B.C. is, on the whole, the most probable date.
[2] This affectation of extreme antiquity is strongly put by Plato in his Timaeus, where the Greek nation is taxed by the Egyptians with being in its infancy as compared with them. The Egyptian claims to a high relative antiquity had, no doubt, a solid basis of truth.

see that they got their fill of milk, and in all other respects look
after them. His object herein was to know, after the indistinct
babblings of infancy were over, what word they would first
articulate. It happened as he had anticipated. The herdsman
obeyed his orders for two years, and at the end of that time, on
his one day opening the door of their room and going in, the
children both ran up to him with outstretched arms, and distinctly said Becos. When this first happened the herdsman took
no notice; but afterwards when he observed, on coming often to
see after them, that the word was constantly in their mouths, he
informed his lord, and by his command brought the children
into his presence. Psammetichus then himself heard them say
the word, upon which he proceeded to make inquiry what people
there was who called anything becos, and hereupon he learnt
that becos was the Phrygian name for bread. In consideration
of this circumstance the Egyptians yielded their claims, and admitted the greater antiquity of the Phrygians.

3. That these were the real facts I learnt at Memphis from
the priests of Hephaestus. The Greeks, among other foolish
tales, relate that Psammetichus had the children brought up by
women whose tongues he had previously cut out; but the priests
said their bringing up was such as I have stated above. I got
much other information also from conversation with these
priests while I was at Memphis, and I even went to Heliopolis
and to Thebes, expressly to try whether the priests of those
places would agree in their accounts with the priests at Memphis. The Heliopolitans have the reputation of being the best
skilled in history of all the Egyptians. What they told me concerning their religion it is not my intention to repeat, except the
names of their deities, since I believe all men know equally
little about the gods. If I relate anything else concerning these
matters, it will only be when compelled to do so by the course
of my narrative.

4. Now with regard to mere human matters, the accounts
which they gave, and in which all agreed, were the following.
The Egyptians, they said, were the first to discover the solar
year, and to portion out its course into twelve parts. They ob-

tained this knowledge from the stars. (To my mind they contrive their year much more cleverly than the Greeks, for these
last every other year intercalate a whole month, but the Egyptians, dividing the year into twelve months of thirty days each,
add every year a space of five days besides, whereby the circuit
of the seasons is made to return with uniformity.[3]) The Egyptians, they went on to affirm, first brought into use the names
of the twelve gods, which the Greeks adopted from them; and
first erected altars, images, and temples to the gods; and also
first engraved upon stone the figures of animals. In most of
these cases they proved to me that what they said was true. And
they told me that the first man who ruled over Egypt was Min,[4]
and that in his time all Egypt, except the Thebaic nome, was a
marsh, none of the land below lake Moeris then showing itself
above the surface of the water. This is a distance of seven days'
sail from the sea up the river.

5. What they said of their country seemed to me very reasonable. For any one who sees Egypt, without having heard a word
about it before, must perceive, if he has only common powers
of observation, that the Egypt to which the Greeks go in their
ships is an acquired country, the gift of the river. The same is
true of the land above the lake, to the distance of three days'
voyage, concerning which the Egyptians say nothing, but which
is exactly the same kind of country.

The following is the general character of the region. In the
first place, on approaching it by sea, when you are still a day's
sail from the land, if you let down a sounding-line you will bring
up mud, and find yourself in eleven fathoms'[5] water, which

---

[3] The difficulty of all calendars is to reconcile a lunar and a solar system of reckoning since a lunar year has 354 days, eight hours, forty-eight
minutes and thirty-six seconds as compared with the solar year of 365
days, five hours, forty-eight minutes and forty-eight seconds. The Greeks
made the months alternately of thirty and twenty-nine days, inserting an
intercalary month three times in eight years. The Egyptian "Sothic period" of 1,460 years compensated for the additional quarter of a day.

[4] Min, the Menes of most Greek authors, is usually taken for a legendary
figure compounded of two or three different kings.

[5] A day's sail, according to Herodotus is about 61 miles, where the
soundings would be at least the same number of fathoms.

shows that the soil washed down by the stream extends to that distance.

6. The length of the country along shore, according to the bounds that we assign to Egypt, namely from the Plinthinetic gulf to lake Serbonis, which extends along the base of Mount Casius, is sixty schoenes. The nations whose territories are scanty measure them by the fathom; those whose bounds are less confined, by the furlong; those who have an ample territory, by the parasang; but if men have a country which is very vast, they measure it by the schoene. Now the length of the parasang is thirty furlongs, but the schoene, which is an Egyptian measure, is sixty furlongs. Thus the coast-line of Egypt would extend a length of 420 miles.[6]

7. From the coast inland as far as Heliopolis the breadth of Egypt is considerable, the country is flat, without springs, and full of swamps. The length of the route from the sea up to Heliopolis is almost exactly the same as that of the road which runs from the altar of the twelve gods at Athens to the temple of Olympian Zeus at Pisa. If a person made a calculation he would find but a very little difference between the two routes, not more than about two miles;[7] for the road from Athens to Pisa falls short of 173 miles by exactly two, whereas the distance of Heliopolis from the sea is just the round number.

8. As one proceeds beyond Heliopolis up the country, Egypt becomes narrow, the Arabian range of hills, which has a direction from north to south, shutting it in upon the one side, and the Libyan range upon the other. The former ridge runs on without a break, and stretches away to the sea called the Red Sea; it contains the quarries whence the stone was cut for the pyramids of Memphis: and this is the point where it ceases its first direction, and bends away in the manner above indicated. In its greatest length from east to west, it is, as I have been informed, a distance of two months' journey; towards the extreme east its skirts produce frankincense. Such are the chief features

---

[6] The actual length is about 275 miles.

[7] This measurement is correct as compared with others in Herodotus, but the real distance of Heliopolis from the sea is about 110 miles.

of this range. On the Libyan side, the other ridge whereon the pyramids stand, is rocky and covered with sand; its direction is the same as that of the Arabian ridge in the first part of its course. Above Heliopolis, then, there is no great breadth of territory for such a country as Egypt, but during four days' sail Egypt is narrow; the valley between the two ranges is a level plain, and seemed to me to be, at the narrowest point, not more than two hundred furlongs across from the Arabian to the Libyan hills. Above this point Egypt again widens.

9. From Heliopolis to Thebes is nine days' sail up the river; the distance is eighty-one schoenes, or 552 miles. If we now put together the several measurements of the country we shall find that the distance along shore is, as I stated above, 420 miles, and the distance from the sea inland to Thebes 700 miles. Further, it is a distance of 206 miles from Thebes to the place called Elephantine.[8]

10. The greater portion of the country above described seemed to me to be, as the priests declared, a tract gained by the inhabitants. For the whole region above Memphis, lying between the two ranges of hills that have been spoken of, appeared evidently to have formed at one time a gulf of the sea. It resembles (to compare small things with great) the parts about Ilium and Teuthrania, Ephesus, and the plain of the Maeander. In all these regions the land has been formed by rivers, whereof the greatest is not to compare for size with any one of the five mouths of the Nile.[9] I could mention other rivers also, far inferior to the Nile in magnitude, that have effected very great changes. Among these not the least is the Achelous, which, after passing through Acarnania, empties itself into the sea opposite the islands called Echinades, and has already joined one half of them to the continent.

[8] In addition to other geographical inaccuracies, Herodotus has overestimated these distances; Heliopolis to Thebes, 421 miles; sea to Thebes, 566 miles; Thebes to Elephantine, 124 miles.

[9] This signifies the natural branches of the Nile; and when seven are reckoned, they include the two artificial ones, the Bolbitine and Bucolic or Phatmetic, which Herodotus says were the work of man.

11. In Arabia, not far from Egypt, there is a long and narrow gulf running inland from the sea called the Red Sea,[10] of which I will here set down the dimensions. Starting from its innermost recess, and using a row-boat, you take forty days to reach the open main, while you may cross the gulf at its widest part in the space of half a day. In this sea there is an ebb and flow of the tide every day. My opinion is, that Egypt was formerly very much such a gulf as this—one gulf penetrated from the sea that washes Egypt on the north, and extended itself towards Ethiopia; another entered from the southern ocean, and stretched towards Syria; the two gulfs ran into the land so as almost to meet each other, and left between them only a very narrow tract of country. Now if the Nile should choose to divert his waters from their present bed into this Arabian gulf, what is there to hinder it from being filled up by the stream within, at the utmost, 20,000 years? For my part, I think it would be filled in half the time. How then should not a gulf, even of much greater size, have been filled up in the ages that passed before I was born, by a river that is at once so large and so given to working changes?

12. Thus I give credit to those from whom I received this account of Egypt, and am myself, moreover, strongly of the same opinion, since I remarked that the country projects into the sea further than the neighbouring shores, and I observed that there were shells upon the hills,[11] and that salt exuded from the soil to such an extent as even to injure the pyramids; and I noticed also that there is but a single hill in all Egypt where sand is found, namely, the hill above Memphis; and further, I found the country to bear no resemblance either to its border-land Arabia, or to Libya—nay, nor even to Syria, which forms

[10] The Greeks generally did not give the name Red Sea to the Arabian Gulf, but to all that part of the Indian Ocean reaching from the Persian Gulf to India. It was also applied to the Persian Gulf and Herodotus sometimes gives it to the Arabian Gulf, and even the western branch between Mount Sinai and Egypt.

[11] Herodotus' geological remarks in this chapter are mainly right and show his excellence as an observer.

the seaboard of Arabia; but whereas the soil of Libya is, we know, sandy and of a reddish hue, and that of Arabia and Syria inclines to stone and clay, Egypt has a soil that is black and crumbly, as being alluvial and formed of the deposits brought down by the river from Ethiopia.

13. One fact which I learnt of the priests is to me a strong evidence of the origin of the country. They said that when Moeris was king, the Nile overflowed all Egypt below Memphis, as soon as it rose so little as twelve feet. Now Moeris had not been dead 900 years at the time when I heard this of the priests;[12] yet at the present day, unless the river rise twenty-four feet, or, at the very least, twenty-two feet, it does not over-flow the lands. It seems to me, therefore, that if the land goes on rising and growing at this rate, the Egyptians who dwell be-low lake Moeris, in the Delta (as it is called) and elsewhere, will one day, by the stoppage of the inundations, suffer per-manently the fate which they told me they expected would some time or other befall the Greeks. On hearing that the whole land of Greece is watered by rain from heaven, and not, like their own, inundated by rivers, they observed, "Some day the Greeks will be disappointed of their grand hope, and then they will be wretchedly hungry;" which was as much as to say, "If God shall some day see fit not to grant the Greeks rain, but shall afflict them with a long drought, the Greeks will be swept away by a famine, since they have nothing to rely on but rain from Zeus, and have no other resource for water."

14. And in thus speaking of the Greeks the Egyptians say nothing but what is true. But now let me tell the Egyptians how the case stands with themselves. If, as I said before, the country below Memphis, which is the land that is always rising, continues to increase in height at the rate at which it has risen in times gone by, how will it be possible for the inhabitants of that region to avoid hunger, when they will certainly have no rain, and the river will not be able to overflow their corn-lands? At present, it must be confessed, they obtain the fruits of the

[12] Herodotus' date is incorrect for he probably means Amenemhet III of the twelfth dynasty (1849-1801 B.C.).

field with less trouble than any other people in the world, the rest of the Egyptians included, since they have no need to break up the ground with the plough, nor to use the hoe, nor to do any of the work which the rest of mankind find necessary if they are to get a crop; but the husbandman waits till the river has of its own accord spread itself over the fields and withdrawn again to its bed, and then sows his plot of ground, and after sowing turns his swine into it (the swine tread in the corn) after which he has only to await the harvest. The swine serve him also to thrash the grain, which is then carried to the garner.

15. If then we choose to adopt the views of the Ionians concerning Egypt, we must come to the conclusion that the Egyptians had formerly no country at all. For the Ionians say that nothing is really Egypt but the Delta, which extends along shore from the Watch-tower of Perseus, as it is called, to the Pelusiac Salt-pans, a distance of 300 miles, and stretches inland as far as the city of Cercasorus, where the Nile divides into the two streams which reach the sea at Pelusium and Canobus respectively. The rest of what is accounted Egypt belongs, they say, either to Arabia or Libya. But the Delta, as the Egyptians affirm, and as I myself am persuaded, is formed of the deposits of the river, and has only recently, if I may use the expression, come to light. If then they had formerly no territory at all, how came they to be so extravagant as to fancy themselves the most ancient race in the world? Surely there was no need of their making the experiment with the children to see what language they would first speak. But in truth I do not believe that the Egyptians came into being at the same time with the Delta, as the Ionians call it; I think they have always existed ever since the human race began; as the land went on increasing, part of the population came down into the new country, part remained in their old settlements. In ancient times the Thebais bore the name of Egypt, a district of which the entire circumference is but 700 miles.

16. If then my judgment on these matters be right, the Ionians are mistaken in what they say of Egypt. If, on the contrary, it is they who are right, then I undertake to show that neither

the Ionians nor any of the other Greeks know how to count. For they all say that the earth is divided into three parts, Europe, Asia, and Libya, whereas they ought to add a fourth part, the Delta of Egypt, since they do not include it either in Asia or Libya. For is it not their theory that the Nile separates Asia from Libya? As the Nile therefore splits in two at the apex of the Delta, the Delta itself must be a separate country, not contained in either Asia or Libya.

17. Here I take my leave of the opinions of the Ionians, and proceed to deliver my own sentiments on these subjects. I consider Egypt to be the whole country inhabited by the Egyptians, just as Cilicia is the tract occupied by the Cilicians, and Assyria that possessed by the Assyrians. And I regard the only proper boundary-line between Libya and Asia to be that which is marked out by the Egyptian frontier. For if we take the boundary-line commonly received by the Greeks, we must regard Egypt as divided, along its whole length from Elephantine and the Cataracts to Cercasorus, into two parts, each belonging to a different portion of the world, one to Asia, the other to Libya; since the Nile divides Egypt in two from the Cataracts to the sea, running as far as the city of Cercasorus in a single stream, but at that point separating into three branches, whereof the one which bends eastward is called the Pelusiac mouth, and that which slants to the west, the Canobic. Meanwhile the straight course of the stream, which comes down from the upper country, and meets the apex of the Delta, continues on, dividing the Delta down the middle, and empties itself into the sea by a mouth, which is as celebrated, and carries as large a body of water, as most of the others, the mouth called the Sebennytic. Besides these there are two other mouths which run out of the Sebennytic called respectively the Saitic and the Mendesian. The Bolbitine mouth, and the Bucolic, are not natural branches, but channels made by excavation.

18. My judgment as to the extent of Egypt is confirmed by an oracle delivered at the shrine of Ammon, of which I had no knowledge at all until after I had formed my opinion. It happened that the people of the cities Marea and Apis, who live in

the part of Egypt that borders on Libya, took a dislike to the religious usages of the country concerning sacrificial animals, and wished no longer to be restricted from eating the flesh of cows. So, as they believed themselves to be Libyans and not Egyptians, they sent to the shrine to say that, having nothing in common with the Egyptians, neither inhabiting the Delta nor using the Egyptian tongue, they claimed to be allowed to eat whatever they pleased. Their request, however, was refused by the god, who declared in reply that Egypt was the entire tract of country which the Nile overspreads and irrigates, and the Egyptians were the people who lived below Elephantine, and drank the waters of that river.

19. So said the oracle. Now the Nile, when it overflows, floods not only the Delta, but also the tracts of country on both sides of the stream which are thought to belong to Libya and Arabia, in some places reaching to the extent of two days' journey from its banks, in some even exceeding that distance, but in others falling short of it.

Concerning the nature of the river, I was not able to gain any information either from the priests or from others. I was particularly anxious to learn from them why the Nile, at the commencement of the summer solstice, begins to rise,[13] and continues to increase for a hundred days—and why, as soon as that number is past, it forthwith retires and contracts its stream, continuing low during the whole of the winter until the summer solstice comes round again. On none of these points could I obtain any explanation from the inhabitants,[14] though I made every inquiry, wishing to know what was commonly reported— they could neither tell me what special virtue the Nile has which

[13] Herodotus was surprised that the Nile should rise in the summer solstice and become low in winter. In the latitude of Memphis it begins to rise at the end of June, about the 10th of August it attains to the height requisite for cutting the canals and admitting it into the interior of the plain; and it is generally at its highest about the end of September. This makes from 92 to 100 days, as Herodotus states.

[14] The cause of the inundation is the water that falls during the rainy season in Abyssinia; and the range of the tropical rains extends even as far N. as latitude 17° 43'.

makes it so opposite in its nature to all other streams, nor why, unlike every other river, it gives forth no breezes from its surface.

20. Some of the Greeks, however, wishing to get a reputation for cleverness, have offered explanations of the phenomena of the river, for which they have accounted in three different ways. Two of these I do not think it worth while to speak of, further than simply to mention what they are. One pretends that the Etesian winds cause the rise of the river by preventing the Nile-water from running off into the sea. But in the first place it has often happened, when the Etesian winds did not blow, that the Nile has risen according to its usual wont; and further, if the Etesian winds produced the effect, the other rivers which flow in a direction opposite to those winds ought to present the same phenomena as the Nile, and the more so as they are all smaller streams, and have a weaker current. But these rivers, of which there are many both in Syria and Libya, are entirely unlike the Nile in this respect.

21. The second opinion is even more unscientific than the one just mentioned, and also, if I may so say, more marvellous. It is that the Nile acts so strangely, because it flows from the ocean, and that the ocean flows all round the earth.

22. The third explanation, which is very much more plausible than either of the others, is positively the furthest from the truth; for there is really nothing in what it says, any more than in the other theories. It is, that the inundation of the Nile is caused by the melting of snows.[15] Now, as the Nile flows out of Libya, through Ethiopia, into Egypt, how is it possible that it can be formed of melted snow, running, as it does, from the hottest regions of the world into cooler countries? Many are the proofs whereby any one capable of reasoning on the subject may be convinced that it is most unlikely this should be the

---

[15] This was the opinion of Anaxagoras, as well as of his pupil Euripides and others. Herodotus is wrong in supposing snow could not be found on mountains in the hot climate of Africa. Throughout this chapter he is trying to apply critical tests to a fact which seems to him insufficiently supported by evidence.

case. The first and strongest argument is furnished by the winds, which always blow hot from these regions. The second is, that rain and frost are unknown there. Now, whenever snow falls, it must of necessity rain within five days; so that, if there were snow, there must be rain also in those parts. Thirdly, it is certain that the natives of the country are black with the heat, that the kites and the swallows remain there the whole year, and that the cranes, when they fly from the rigours of a Scythian winter, flock thither to pass the cold season. If then, in the country whence the Nile has its source, or in that through which it flows, there fell ever so little snow, it is absolutely impossible that any of these circumstances could take place.

23. As for the writer who attributes the phenomenon to the ocean, his account is involved in such obscurity, that it is impossible to disprove it by argument. For my part I know of no river called Ocean, and I think that Homer, or one of the earlier poets, invented the name, and introduced it into his poetry.

24. Perhaps, after censuring all the opinions that have been put forward on this obscure subject, one ought to propose some theory of one's own. I will therefore proceed to explain what I think to be the reason of the Nile's swelling in the summer time. During the winter, the sun is driven out of his usual course by the storms, and removes to the upper parts of Libya. This is the whole secret in the fewest possible words; for it stands to reason that the country to which the Sun-god approaches the nearest, and which he passes most directly over, will be scantest of water, and that there the streams which feed the rivers will shrink the most.

25. To explain, however, more at length, the case is this. The sun, in his passage across the upper parts of Libya, affects them in the following way. As the air in those regions is constantly clear, and the country warm through the absence of cold winds, the sun in his passage across them acts upon them exactly as he is wont to act elsewhere in summer, when his path is in the middle of heaven—that is, he attracts the water. After attracting it, he again repels it into the upper regions, where the winds lay hold of it, scatter it, and reduce it to a vapour, whence it natu-

rally enough comes to pass that the winds which blow from this quarter—the south and south-west—are of all winds the most rainy. And my own opinion is that the sun does not get rid of all the water which he draws year by year from the Nile, but retains some about him. When the winter begins to soften, the sun goes back again to his old place in the middle of the heaven, and proceeds to attract water equally from all countries. Till then the other rivers run big, from the quantity of rain-water which they bring down from countries where so much moisture falls that all the land is cut into gullies; but in summer, when the showers fail, and the sun attracts their water, they become low. The Nile, on the contrary, not deriving any of its bulk from rains, and being in winter subject to the attraction of the sun, naturally runs at that season, unlike all other streams, with a less burthen of water than in the summer time. For in summer it is exposed to attraction equally with all other rivers, but in winter it suffers alone. The sun, therefore, I regard as the sole cause of the phenomenon.

26. It is the sun also, in my opinion, which, by heating the space through which it passes, makes the air in Egypt so dry. There is thus perpetual summer in the upper parts of Libya. Were the position of the heavenly regions reversed, so that the place where now the north wind and the winter have their dwelling became the station of the south wind and of the noon-day, while, on the other hand, the station of the south wind became that of the north, the consequence would be that the sun, driven from the mid-heaven by the winter and the northern gales, would betake himself to the upper parts of Europe, as he now does to those of Libya, and then I believe his passage across Europe would affect the Ister exactly as the Nile is affected at the present day.

27. And with respect to the fact that no breeze blows from the Nile, I am of the opinion that no wind is likely to arise in very hot countries, for breezes love to blow from some cold quarter.

28. Let us leave these things, however, to their natural course, to continue as they are and have been from the begin-

ning. With regard to the sources of the Nile, I have found no
one among all those with whom I have conversed, whether
Egyptians, Libyans, or Greeks, who professed to have any
knowledge, except a single person. He was the scribe who kept
the register of the sacred treasures of Athena in the city of Sais,
and he seemed to me to be joking when he said that he knew
them perfectly well. His story was as follows, "Between Syene,
a city of the Thebais, and Elephantine,[16] there are two hills
with sharp conical tops; the name of the one is Crophi, of the
other, Mophi. Midway between them are the fountains of the
Nile, fountains which it is impossible to fathom. Half the water
runs northward into Egypt, half to the south towards Ethiopia."
The fountains were known to be unfathomable, he declared,
because Psammetichus, an Egyptian king, had made trial of
them. He had caused a rope to be made, many thousand fathoms in length, and had sounded the fountain with it, but could
find no bottom. By this the scribe gave me to understand, if
there was any truth at all in what he said, that in this fountain
there are certain strong eddies, and a regurgitation, owing to the
force wherewith the water dashes against the mountains, and
hence a sounding-line cannot be got to reach the bottom of the
spring.

29. No other information on this head could I obtain from
any quarter. All that I succeeded in learning further of the more
distant portions of the Nile, by ascending myself as high as
Elephantine, and making inquiries concerning the parts beyond,
was the following: As one advances beyond Elephantine, the
land rises. Hence it is necessary in this part of the river to at-
tach a rope to the boat on each side, as men harness an ox, and
so proceed on the journey. If the rope snaps, the vessel is borne
away down stream by the force of the current. The navigation
continues the same for four days, the river winding greatly, like
the Maeander, and the distance traversed amounting to eighty
miles. Here you come upon a smooth and level plain, where the
Nile flows in two branches, round an island called Tachompso.

---

[16] Herodotus apparently thought that the town of Syene opposite Elephantine was a part of it and believed that Syene was farther south.

The country above Elephantine is inhabited by the Ethiopians, who possess one half of this island, the Egyptians occupying the other. Above the island there is a great lake, the shores of which are inhabited by Ethiopian nomads; after passing it, you come again to the stream of the Nile, which runs into the lake. Here you land, and travel for forty days along the banks of the river, since it is impossible to proceed further in a boat on account of the sharp peaks which jut out from the water, and the sunken rocks which abound in that part of the stream. When you have passed this portion of the river in the space of forty days, you go on board another boat, and proceed by water for twelve days more, at the end of which time you reach a great city called Meroe, which is said to be the capital of the other Ethiopians. The only gods worshipped by the inhabitants are Zeus and Dionysus; to whom great honours are paid. There is an oracle of Zeus in the city, which directs the warlike expeditions of the Ethiopians; when it commands they go to war, and in whatever direction it bids them march, thither straightway they carry their arms.

30. On leaving this city, and again mounting the stream, in the same space of time which it took you to reach the capital from Elephantine, you come to the Deserters, who bear the name of Asmach. This word, translated into our language, means "the men who stand on the left hand of the king." These Deserters are Egyptians of the warrior cast, who, to the number of 240,000, went over to the Ethiopians in the reign of king Psammetichus. The cause of their desertion was the following: Three garrisons were maintained in Egypt at that time, one in the city of Elephantine against the Ethiopians, another in the Pelusiac Daphnae, against the Syrians and Arabians, and a third, against the Libyans, in Marea. (The very same posts are to this day occupied by the Persians, whose forces are in garrison both in Daphnae and in Elephantine.) Now it happened, that on one occasion the garrisons were not relieved during the space of three years; the soldiers, therefore, at the end of that time, consulted together, and having determined by common consent to revolt, marched away towards Ethiopia. Psammeti-

chus, informed of the movement, set out in pursuit, and coming up with them, besought them with many words not to desert the gods of their country, nor abandon their wives and children. "Nay, but," said one of the deserters pointing to his genitals, "wherever we go, we are sure enough of finding wives and children." Arrived in Ethiopia, they placed themselves at the disposal of the king. In return, he made them a present of a tract of land which belonged to certain Ethiopians with whom he was at feud, bidding them expel the inhabitants and take possession of their territory. From the time that this settlement was formed, their acquaintance with Egyptian manners has tended to civilise the Ethiopians.

31. Thus the course of the Nile is known, not only throughout Egypt, but to the extent of four months' journey either by land or water above the Egyptian boundary; for on calculation it will be found that it takes that length of time to travel from Elephantine to the country of the Deserters. There the direction of the river is from west to east. Beyond, no one has any certain knowledge of its course, since the country is uninhabited by reason of the excessive heat.

32. I did hear, indeed, what I will now relate, from certain natives of Cyrene. Once upon a time, they said, they were on a visit to the oracular shrine of Ammon,[17] when it chanced that in the course of conversation with Etearchus, the Ammonian king, the talk fell upon the Nile, how that its sources were unknown to all men. Etearchus upon this mentioned that some Nasamonians had once come to his court, and when asked if they could give any information concerning the uninhabited parts of Libya, had told the following tale. (The Nasamonians are a Libyan race who occupy the Syrtis, and a tract of no great size towards the east.) They said there had grown up among them some wild young men, the sons of certain chiefs, who, when they came to man's estate, indulged in all manner of extravagancies, and among other things drew lots for five of their number to go and explore the desert parts of Libya, and try if

---

[17] This was in the modern Oasis of Siwah, where remains of the temple are still seen. The oracle long continued in great repute.

they could not penetrate further than any had done previously. (The coast of Libya along the sea which washes it to the north, throughout its entire length from Egypt to Cape Soloeis, which is its furthest point, is inhabited by Libyans of many distinct tribes, who possess the whole tract except certain portions which belong to the Phoenicians and the Greeks. Above the coast-line and the country inhabited by the maritime tribes, Libya is full of wild beasts; while beyond the wild beast region there is a tract which is wholly sand, very scant of water, and utterly and entirely a desert.) The young men therefore, despatched on this errand by their comrades with a plentiful supply of water and provisions, travelled at first through the inhabited region, passing which they came to the wild beast tract, whence they finally entered upon the desert, which they proceeded to cross in a direction from east to west. After journeying for many days over a wide extent of sand, they came at last to a plain where they observed trees growing; approaching them, and seeing fruit on them, they proceeded to gather it. While they were thus engaged, there came upon them some dwarfish men,[18] under the middle height, who seized them and carried them off. The Nasamonians could not understand a word of their language, nor had they any acquaintance with the language of the Nasamonians. They were led across extensive marshes, and finally came to a town, where all the men were of the height of their conductors, and black-complexioned. A great river flowed by the town, running from west to east, and containing crocodiles.

33. Here let me dismiss Etearchus the Ammonian, and his story, only adding that (according to the Cyrenaeans) he declared that the Nasamonians got safe back to their country, and that the men whose city they had reached were a nation of sorcerers. With respect to the river which ran by their town, Etearchus conjectured it to be the Nile; and reason favours that view. For the Nile certainly flows out of Libya, dividing it down the middle, and as I conceive, judging the unknown from the

[18] Herodotus does not exaggerate the smallness of the pygmies as other writers do.

known, rises at the same distance from its mouth as the Ister.[19] This latter river has its source in the country of the Celts near the city Pyrene, and runs through the middle of Europe, dividing it into two portions. The Celts live beyond the pillars of Heracles, and border on the Cynesians, who dwell at the extreme west of Europe. Thus the Ister flows through the whole of Europe before it finally empties itself into the Euxine at Istria,[20] one of the colonies of the Milesians.

34. Now as this river flows through regions that are inhabited, its course is perfectly well known; but of the sources of the Nile no one can give any account, since Libya, the country through which it passes, is desert and without inhabitants. As far as it was possible to get information by inquiry, I have given a description of the stream. It enters Egypt from the parts beyond. Egypt lies almost exactly opposite the mountainous portion of Cilicia,[21] whence a lightly equipped traveller may reach Sinope on the Euxine in five days by the direct route. Sinope lies opposite the place where the Ister falls into the sea. My opinion therefore is that the Nile, as it traverses the whole of Libya, is of equal length with the Ister. And here I take my leave of this subject.

35. Concerning Egypt itself I shall extend my remarks to a great length, because there is no country that possesses so many wonders,[22] nor any that has such a number of works which defy

[19] The meaning of this passage has been much disputed, but Herodotus does not intend any exact correspondency between the Nile and the Danube. He is only speaking of the comparative length of the two streams, and conjectures that they are equal in this respect.

[20] If the Danube in the time of Herodotus entered the Euxine at Istria, it must have changed its course very greatly since he wrote.

[21] Herodotus gives all Africa, as far as the Lesser Syrtis, too easterly a position.

[22] By this statement Herodotus prepares his readers for what he is about to relate; but the desire to tell of the wonders in which it differed from all other countries led Herodotus to indulge in his love of antithesis, so that in some cases he confines to one sex what was done by both (a singular instance being noted down by him as an invariable custom), and in others he has indulged in the marvellous at a sacrifice of truth. In many cases where Herodotus tells improbable tales, they are on the authority

description. Not only is the climate different from that of the rest of the world, and the rivers unlike any other rivers, but the people also, in most of their manners and customs, exactly reverse the common practice of mankind. The women attend the markets and trade, while the men sit at home at the loom; and here, while the rest of the world works the woof up the warp, the Egyptians work it down; the women likewise carry burdens upon their shoulders, while the men carry them upon their heads. Women stand up to urinate, men sit down. They eat their food out of doors in the streets, but relieve themselves in their houses, giving as a reason that what is unseemly, but necessary, ought to be done in secret, but what has nothing unseemly about it, should be done openly. A woman cannot serve the priestly office, either for god or goddess, but men are priests to both; sons need not support their parents unless they choose, but daughters must, whether they choose or no.

36. In other countries the priests have long hair, in Egypt their heads are shaven; elsewhere it is customary, in mourning, for near relations to cut their hair close; the Egyptians, who wear no hair at any other time, when they lose a relative, let their beards and the hair of their heads grow long. All other men pass their lives separate from animals, the Egyptians have animals always living with them; others make barley and wheat their food, it is a disgrace to do so in Egypt, where the grain they live on is spelt, which some call zea. Dough they knead with their feet, but they mix mud, and even take up dung with their hands. They are the only people in the world—they at least, and such as have learnt the practice from them—who use circumcision. Their men wear two garments apiece, their women but one. They put on the rings and fasten the ropes to sails inside, others put them outside. When they write or calculate, instead of going, like the Greeks, from left to right, they move their hand from right to left; and they insist, notwithstanding, that it is they who go to the right, and the Greeks who go to the

of others, or mere heresay reports, for which he at once declares himself not responsible, and he justly pleads that his history was not only a relation of facts, but the result of an *"ἱστορία,"* or "inquiry," in which all he heard was inserted.

left. They have two quite different kinds of writing, one of which is called sacred, the other common.

37. They are religious to excess, far beyond any other race of men,[23] and use the following ceremonies: They drink out of brazen cups, which they scour every day: there is no exception to this practice. They wear linen garments, which they are specially careful to have always fresh washed. They practise circumcision for the sake of cleanliness, considering it better to be cleanly than comely. The priests shave their whole body every other day, that no lice or other impure thing may adhere to them when they are engaged in the service of the gods. Their dress is entirely of linen, and their shoes of the papyrus plant: it is not lawful for them to wear either dress or shoes of any other material. They bathe twice every day in cold water, and twice each night. Besides which they observe, so to speak, thousands of ceremonies. They enjoy, however, not a few advantages. They consume none of their own property, and are at no expense for anything; but every day bread is baked for them of the sacred corn, and a plentiful supply of beef and of goose's flesh is assigned to each, and also a portion of wine made from the grape. Fish they are not allowed to eat;[24] and beans, which none of the Egyptians ever sow, or eat, if they come up of their own accord, either raw or boiled, the priests will not even endure to look on, since they consider it an unclean kind of pulse. Instead of a single priest, each god has the attendance of a college, at the head of which is a chief priest; when one of these dies, his son is appointed in his room.

38. Male kine are reckoned to belong to Epaphus, and are therefore tested in the following manner: One of the priests appointed for the purpose searches to see if there is a single black hair on the whole body, since in that case the beast is unclean. He examines him all over, standing on his legs, and again laid

---

[23] The extreme religious views of the Egyptians became at length a gross superstition, and were naturally a subject for ridicule and contempt.

[24] Though fish were so generally eaten by the rest of the Egyptians, they were forbidden to the priests. The custom of forbidding beans to the priests was borrowed from Egypt by Pythagoras.

upon his back; after which he takes the tongue out of his mouth, to see if it be clean in respect of the prescribed marks (what they are I will mention elsewhere); he also inspects the hairs of the tail, to observe if they grow naturally. If the animal is pronounced clean in all these various points, the priest marks him by twisting a piece of papyrus round his horns, and attaching thereto some sealing-clay, which he then stamps with his own signet-ring. After this the beast is led away; and it is forbidden, under the penalty of death, to sacrifice an animal which has not been marked in this way.

39. The following is their manner of sacrifice: They lead the victim, marked with their signet, to the altar where they are about to offer it, and setting the wood alight, pour a libation of wine upon the altar in front of the victim, and at the same time invoke the god. Then they slay the animal, and cutting off his head, proceed to flay the body. Next they take the head, and heaping imprecations on it, if there is a market-place and a body of Greek traders in the city, they carry it there and sell it instantly; if, however, there are no Greeks among them, they throw the head into the river. The imprecation is to this effect: They pray that if any evil is impending either over those who sacrifice, or over universal Egypt, it may be made to fall upon that head. These practices, the imprecations upon the heads, and the libations of wine, prevail all over Egypt, and extend to victims of all sorts; and hence the Egyptians will never eat the head of any animal.

40. The disembowelling and burning are however different in different sacrifices. I will mention the mode in use with respect to the goddess whom they regard as the greatest, and honour with the chiefest festival. When they have flayed their steer they pray, and when their prayer is ended they take the paunch of the animal out entire, leaving the intestines and the fat inside the body; they then cut off the legs, the end of the loins, the shoulders, and the neck; and having so done, they fill the body of the steer with clean bread, honey, raisins, figs, frankincense, myrrh, and other aromatics. Thus filled, they burn the body, pouring over it great quantities of oil. Before offering the

sacrifice they fast, and while the bodies of the victims are being consumed they beat themselves. Afterwards, when they have concluded this part of the ceremony, they have the other parts of the victim served up to them for a repast.

41. The male kine, therefore, if clean, and the male calves, are used for sacrifice by the Egyptians universally; but the female they are not allowed to sacrifice, since they are sacred to Isis. The statue of this goddess has the form of a woman but with horns like a cow, resembling thus the Greek representations of Io; and the Egyptians, one and all, venerate cows much more highly than any other animal. This is the reason why no native of Egypt, whether man or woman, will give a Greek a kiss, or use the knife of a Greek, or his spit, or his cauldron, or taste the flesh of an ox, known to be pure, if it has been cut with a Greek knife. When kine die, the following is the manner of their sepulture: The females are thrown into the river; the males are buried in the suburbs of the towns, with one or both of their horns appearing above the surface of the ground to mark the place. When the bodies are decayed, a boat comes, at an appointed time, from the island called Prosopitis, which is a portion of the Delta, sixty miles in circumference,—and calls at the several cities in turn to collect the bones of the oxen. Prosopitis is a district containing several cities; the name of that from which the boats come is Atarbechis. Aphrodite has a temple there of much sanctity. Great numbers of men go forth from this city and proceed to the other towns, where they dig up the bones, which they take away with them and bury together in one place. The same practice prevails with respect to the interment of all other cattle—the law so determining; they do not slaughter any of them.

42. Such Egyptians as possess a temple of the Theban Zeus, or live in the Thebaic nome, offer no sheep in sacrifice, but only goats; for the Egyptians do not all worship the same gods, excepting Isis and Osiris, the latter of whom they say is the Grecian Dionysus. Those, on the contrary, who possess a temple dedicated to Mendes, or belong to the Mendesian nome, abstain from offering goats, and sacrifice sheep instead. The Thebans,

and such as imitate them in their practice, give the following account of the origin of the custom, "Heracles," they say, "wished of all things to see Zeus, but Zeus did not choose to be seen of him. At length, when Heracles persisted, Zeus hit on a device—to flay a ram, and, cutting off his head, hold the head before him, and cover himself with the fleece. In this guise he showed himself to Heracles." Therefore the Egyptians give their statues of Zeus the face of a ram; and from them the practice has passed to the Ammonians, who are a joint colony of Egyptians and Ethiopians, speaking a language between the two; hence also, in my opinion, the latter people took their name of Ammonians, since the Egyptian name for Zeus is Amun. Such then is the reason why the Thebans do not sacrifice rams, but consider them sacred animals. Upon one day in the year, however, at the festival of Zeus, they slay a single ram, and stripping off the fleece, cover with it the statue of that god, as he once covered himself, and then bring up to the statue of Zeus an image of Heracles. When this has been done, the whole assembly beat their breasts in mourning for the ram, and afterwards bury him in a holy sepulchre.

43. The account which I received of this Heracles makes him one of the twelve gods. Of the other Heracles, with whom the Greeks are familiar, I could hear nothing in any part of Egypt. That the Greeks, however (those I mean who gave the son of Amphitryon that name), took the name[25] from the Egyptians, and not the Egyptians from the Greeks, is I think clearly proved, among other arguments, by the fact that both the parents of Heracles, Amphitryon as well as Alcmena, were of Egyptian origin. Again, the Egyptians disclaim all knowledge of the names of Poseidon and the Dioscuri,[26] and do not include them in the number of their gods; but had they adopted the name of any god from the Greeks, these would have been the likeliest to

---

[25] Herodotus, who derived his knowledge of the Egyptian religion from the professional interpreters, seems to have regarded the word "Heracles" as Egyptian.

[26] Herodotus is quite right in saying that these gods were not in the Egyptian Pantheon.

obtain notice, since the Egyptians, as I am well convinced, practised navigation at that time, and the Greeks also were some of them mariners, so that they would have been more likely to know the names of these gods than that of Heracles. But the Egyptian Heracles is one of their ancient gods. 17,000 years before the reign of Amasis, the twelve gods were, they affirm, produced from the eight: and of these twelve, Heracles is one.

44. In the wish to get the best information that I could on these matters, I made a voyage to Tyre in Phoenicia, hearing there was a temple of Heracles at that place, very highly venerated. I visited the temple, and found it richly adorned with a number of offerings, among which were two pillars, one of pure gold, the other of emerald, shining with great brilliancy at night. In a conversation which I held with the priests, I inquired how long their temple had been built, and found by their answer that they too differed from the Greeks. They said that the temple was built at the same time that the city was founded, and that the foundation of the city took place 2,300 years ago. In Tyre I remarked another temple where the same god was worshipped as the Thasian Heracles. So I went on to Thasos, where I found a temple of Heracles which had been built by the Phoenicians who colonised that island when they sailed in search of Europa. Even this was five generations earlier than the time when Heracles, son of Amphitryon, was born in Greece. These researches show plainly that there is an ancient god Heracles; and my own opinion is, that those Greeks act most wisely who build and maintain two temples of Heracles, in the one of which the Heracles worshipped is known by the name of Olympian, and has sacrifice offered to him as an immortal, while in the other the honours paid are such as are due to a hero.

45. The Greeks tell many tales without due investigation, and among them the following silly fable respecting Heracles. "Heracles," they say, "went once to Egypt, and there the inhabitants took him, and putting a chaplet on his head, led him out in solemn procession, intending to offer him a sacrifice to Zeus. For a while he submitted quietly; but when they led him up to the altar, and began the ceremonies, he put forth his

strength and slew them all." Now to me it seems that such a
story proves the Greeks to be utterly ignorant of the character
and customs of the people. The Egyptians do not think it allow-
able even to sacrifice cattle, excepting sheep, and the male kine
and calves, provided they be pure, and also geese. How then can
it be believed that they would sacrifice men? And again, how
would it have been possible for Heracles alone, and, as they confess, a mere mortal, to destroy so many thousands? In saying
thus much concerning these matters, may I incur no displeasure
either of god or hero!

46. I mentioned above that some of the Egyptians abstain
from sacrificing goats, either male or female. The reason is the
following: These Egyptians, who are the Mendesians, consider
Pan to be one of the eight gods who existed before the twelve,
and Pan is represented in Egypt by the painters and the sculp-
tors, just as he is in Greece, with the face and legs of a goat.
They do not, however, believe this to be his shape, or consider
him in any respect unlike the other gods; but they represent
him thus for a reason which I prefer not to relate. The Mendesians hold all goats in veneration, but the male more than
the female, giving the goatherds of the males especial honour.
One is venerated more highly than all the rest, and when he dies
there is a great mourning throughout all the Mendesian nome.
In Egyptian, the goat and Pan are both called Mendes. In my
own lifetime a monstrous thing took place in this nome when a
woman had intercourse with a goat in public so that it became
a matter of common knowledge.

47. The pig is regarded among them as an unclean animal,
so much so that if a man in passing accidentally touch a pig, he
instantly hurries to the river, and plunges in with all his clothes
on. Hence too the swineherds, notwithstanding that they are of
pure Egyptian blood, are forbidden to enter into any of the
temples, which are open to all other Egyptians; and further, no
one will give his daughter in marriage to a swineherd, or take
a wife from among them, so that the swineherds are forced to
intermarry among themselves. They do not offer swine in sacrifice to any of their gods, excepting Dionysus and the Moon,

whom they honour in this way at the same time, sacrificing pigs
to both of them at the same full moon, and afterwards eating
of the flesh. There is a reason alleged by them for their detesta-
tion of swine at all other seasons, and their of them at this
festival, with which I am well acquainted, but which I do not
think it proper to mention. The following is the mode in which
they sacrifice the swine to the Moon: As soon as the victim is
slain, the tip of the tail, the spleen, and the caul are put together, and having been covered with all the fat that has been
found in the animal's belly, are straightway burnt. The remainder of the flesh is eaten on the same day that the sacrifice is
offered, which is the day of the full moon: at any other time
they would not so much as taste it. The poorer sort, who cannot
afford live pigs, form pigs of dough, which they bake and offer
in sacrifice.

48. To Dionysus, on the eve of his feast, every Egyptian
sacrifices a hog before the door of his house, which is then given
back to the swineherd by whom it was furnished, and by him
carried away. In other respects the festival is celebrated almost
exactly as Dionysiac festivals are in Greece, excepting that the
Egyptians have no choral dances. They also use instead of phalli
another invention, consisting of images eighteen inches high,
pulled by strings, which the women carry round to the villages.
These images have male members of about the same size also
operated by strings. A piper goes in front, and the women follow, singing hymns in honour of Dionysus. They give a religious
reason for the peculiarities of the image.

49. Melampus, the son of Amytheon, cannot (I think) have
been ignorant of this ceremony—nay, he must, I should conceive, have been well acquainted with it. He it was who introduced into Greece the name of Dionysus, the ceremonial of his
worship, and the procession of the phallus. He did not, however,
so completely apprehend the whole doctrine as to be able to
communicate it entirely, but various sages since his time have
carried out his teaching to greater perfection. Still it is certain
that Melampus introduced the phallus, and that the Greeks
learnt from him the ceremonies which they now practise. I

therefore maintain that Melampus, who was a wise man, and had acquired the art of divination, having become acquainted with the worship of Dionysus through knowledge derived from Egypt, introduced it into Greece, with a few slight changes, at the same time that he brought in various other practices. For I can by no means allow that it is by mere coincidence that the ceremonies of Dionysus in Greece are so nearly the same as the Egyptian—they would then have been more Greek in their character, and less recent in their origin. Much less can I admit that the Egyptians borrowed these customs, or any other, from the Greeks. My belief is that Melampus got his knowledge of them from Cadmus the Tyrian, and the followers whom he brought from Phoenicia into the country which is now called Boeotia.

50. Almost all the names of the gods came into Greece from Egypt.[27] My inquiries prove that they were all derived from a foreign source, and my opinion is that Egypt furnished the greater number. For with the exception of Poseidon and the Dioscuri, whom I mentioned above, and Hera, Hestia, Themis, the Graces, and the Nereids, the other gods have been known from time immemorial in Egypt. This I assert on the authority of the Egyptians themselves. The gods, with whose names they profess themselves unacquainted, the Greeks received, I believe, from the Pelasgi, except Poseidon. Of him they got their knowledge from the Libyans, by whom he has been always honoured, and who were anciently the only people that had a god of the name. The Egyptians differ from the Greeks also in paying no divine honours to heroes.

51. Besides these which have been here mentioned, there are many other practices whereof I shall speak hereafter, which the Greeks have borrowed from Egypt. The erection of the phallus, however, which they observe in their statues of Hermes they did not derive from the Egyptians, but from the Pelasgi; from

---

[27] There is no doubt that the Greeks borrowed sometimes the names, sometimes the attributes, of their deities from Egypt; but when Herodotus says the names of the Greek gods were always known in Egypt, it is evident that he does not mean they were the same as the Greek, since he gives in other places the Egyptian name to which those very gods agree, whom he mentions in Egypt.

them the Athenians first adopted it, and afterwards it passed from the Athenians to the other Greeks. For just at the time when the Athenians were entering into the Hellenic body, the Pelasgi came to live with them in their country, whence it was that the latter came first to be regarded as Greeks. Whoever has been initiated into the mysteries of the Cabeiri[28] will understand what I mean. The Samothracians received these mysteries from the Pelasgi, who, before they went to live in Attica, were dwellers in Samothrace, and imparted their religious ceremonies to the inhabitants. The Athenians, then, who were the first of all the Greeks to make their statues of Hermes with phallus erect, learnt the practice from the Pelasgians; and by this people a religious account of the matter is given, which is explained in the Samothracian mysteries.

52. In early times the Pelasgi, as I know by information which I got at Dodona, offered sacrifices of all kinds, and prayed to the gods, but had no distinct names or appellations for them, since they had never heard of any. They called them gods, because they had disposed and arranged all things in such a beautiful order. After a long lapse of time the names of the gods came to Greece from Egypt, and the Pelasgi learnt them, only as yet they knew nothing of Dionysus, of whom they first heard at a much later date. Not long after the arrival of the names they sent to consult the oracle at Dodona about them. This is the most ancient oracle in Greece, and at that time there was no other. To their question, "Whether they should adopt the names that had been imported from the foreigners?" the oracle replied by recommending their use. Thenceforth in their sacrifices the Pelasgi made use of the names of the gods, and from them the names passed afterwards to the Greeks.

53. Whence the gods severally sprang, whether or no they had all existed from eternity, what forms they bore—these are questions of which the Greeks knew nothing until the other day,

---

[28] Nothing is known for certain respecting the Cabeiri. Most authorities agree that they varied in number, and that their worship, which was very ancient in Samothrace and in Phrygia, was carried to Greece from the former by the Pelasgi.

so to speak. For Homer and Hesiod were the first to compose genealogies and give the gods their epithets, to allot them their several offices and occupations, and describe their forms; and they lived but 400 years before my time,[29] as I believe. As for the poets, who are thought by some to be earlier than these, they are, in my judgment, decidedly later writers. In these matters I have the authority of the priestesses of Dodona for the former portion of my statements; what I have said of Homer and Hesiod is my own opinion.

54. The following tale is commonly told in Egypt concerning the oracle of Dodona in Greece, and that of Ammon in Libya. My informants on the point were the priests of Zeus at Thebes. They said that two of the sacred women were once carried off from Thebes by the Phoenicians, and that the story went that one of them was sold into Libya and the other into Greece, and these women were the first founders of the oracles in the two countries. On my inquiring how they came to know so exactly what became of the women, they answered, that diligent search had been made after them at the time, but that it had not been found possible to discover where they were; afterwards, however, they received the information which they had given me.

55. This was what I heard from the priests at Thebes; at Dodona, however, the women who deliver the oracles relate the matter as follows, "Two black doves flew away from Egyptian Thebes, and while one directed its flight to Libya, the other came to them. She alighted on an oak, and sitting there began to speak with a human voice, and told them that on the spot where she was, there should thenceforth be an oracle of Zeus. They understood the announcement to be from heaven, so they set to work at once and erected the shrine. The dove which flew to Libya bade the Libyans to establish there the oracle of Ammon." This likewise is an oracle of Zeus. The persons from

[29] It is plain from the expressions which Herodotus here uses that in his time the general belief assigned to Homer an earlier date than that which he considered the true one. His date would place the poet about 850 B.C., which is very nearly the mean between the earliest and the latest epochs that are assigned to him. The time of Hesiod is probably to be placed at least 100 years after Homer.

whom I received these particulars were three priestesses of the Dodonaeans, the eldest Promeneia, the next Timarete, and the youngest Nicandra—what they said was confirmed by the other Dodonaeans who dwell around the temple.

56. My own opinion of these matters is as follows: I think that, if it be true that the Phoenicians carried off the holy women, and sold them for slaves, the one into Libya and the other into Greece, or Pelasgia (as it was then called), this last must have been sold to the Thesprotians. Afterwards, while undergoing servitude in those parts, she built under a real oak a temple to Zeus, her thoughts in her new abode reverting—as it was likely they would do, if she had been an attendant in a temple of Zeus at Thebes—to that particular god. Then, having acquired a knowledge of the Greek tongue, she set up an oracle. She also mentioned that her sister had been sold for a slave into Libya by the same persons as herself.

57. The Dodonaeans called the women doves because they were foreigners, and seemed to them to make a noise like birds. After a while the dove spoke with a human voice, because the woman, whose foreign talk had previously sounded to them like the chattering of a bird, acquired the power of speaking what they could understand. For how can it be conceived possible that a dove should really speak with the voice of a man? Lastly, by calling the dove black the Dodonaeans indicated that the woman was an Egyptian. And certainly the character of the oracles at Thebes and Dodona is very similar. Besides this form of divination, the Greeks learnt also divination by means of victims from the Egyptians.

58. The Egyptians were also the first to introduce solemn assemblies, processions, and litanies to the gods; of all which the Greeks were taught the use by them. It seems to me a sufficient proof of this, that in Egypt these practices have been established from remote antiquity, while in Greece they are only recently known.

59. The Egyptians do not hold a single solemn assembly, but several in the course of the year. Of these the chief, which is better attended than any other, is held at the city of Bubastis

in honour of Artemis. The next in importance is that which takes place at Busiris, a city situated in the very middle of the Delta; it is in honour of Isis, who is called in the Greek tongue Demeter. There is a third great festival in Sais to Athena, a fourth in Heliopolis to the Sun, a fifth in Buto to Leto, and a sixth in Papremis to Ares.

60. The following are the proceedings on occasion of the assembly at Bubastis: Men and women come sailing all together, vast numbers in each boat, many of the women with castanets, which they strike, while some of the men pipe during the whole time of the voyage; the remainder of the voyagers, male and female, sing the while, and make a clapping with their hands. When they arrive opposite any of the towns upon the banks of the stream, they approach the shore, and, while some of the women continue to play and sing, others call aloud to the females of the place and load them with abuse, while a certain number dance, and some standing up expose themselves. After proceeding in this way all along the river-course, they reach Bubastis, where they celebrate the feast with abundant sacrifices. More grapewine is consumed at this festival than in all the rest of the year besides. The number of those who attend, counting only the men and women and omitting the children, amounts, according to the native reports, to 700,000.

61. The ceremonies at the feast of Isis in the city of Busiris[30] have been already spoken of. It is there that the whole multitude, both of men and women, many thousands in number, beat themselves at the close of the sacrifice, in honour of a god, whose name a religious scruple forbids me to mention.[31] The Carian dwellers in Egypt proceed on this occasion to still greater lengths, even cutting their faces with their knives, whereby they let it be seen that they are not Egyptians but foreigners.

[30] There were several places called Busiris in Egypt. It signifies the burial-place of Osiris, and many places claim the honour of having the body of Osiris, the chief of which were Memphis, Busiris, Philae, Taposiris, and Abydus.

[31] This was Osiris, and men are often represented doing this in the paintings of the tombs.

62. At Sais, when the assembly takes place for the sacrifices, there is one night on which the inhabitants all burn a multitude of lights in the open air round their houses. They use lamps, which are flat saucers filled with a mixture of oil and salt, on the top of which the wick floats. These burn the whole night, and give to the festival the name of the Feast of Lamps. The Egyptians who are absent from the festival observe the night of the sacrifice, no less than the rest, by a general lighting of lamps; so that the illumination is not confined to the city of Sais but extends over the whole of Egypt. And there is a religious reason assigned for the special honour paid to this night, as well as for the illumination which accompanies it.

63. At Heliopolis and Buto the assemblies are merely for the purpose of sacrifice; but at Papremis, besides the sacrifices and other rites which are performed there as elsewhere, the following custom is observed. When the sun is getting low, a few only of the priests continue occupied about the image of the god, while the greater number, armed with wooden clubs, take their station at the portal of the temple. Opposite to them is drawn up a body of men, in number above a thousand, armed, like the others, with clubs, consisting of persons engaged in the performance of their vows. The image of the god, which is kept in a small wooden shrine covered with plates of gold, is conveyed from the temple into a second sacred building the day before the festival begins. The few priests still in attendance upon the image place it, together with the shrine containing it, on a four-wheeled car, and begin to drag it along; the others, stationed at the gateway of the temple, oppose its admission. Then the votaries come forward to espouse the quarrel of the god, and set upon the opponents, who are sure to offer resistance. A sharp fight with clubs ensues, in which heads are commonly broken on both sides. Many, I am convinced, die of the wounds that they receive, though the Egyptians insist that no one is ever killed.

64. The natives give the subjoined account of this festival. They say that the mother of the god Ares once dwelt in the temple. Brought up at a distance from his parent, when he grew

to man's estate he conceived a wish for intercourse with her. Accordingly he came, but the attendants, who had never seen him before, refused him entrance, and succeeded in keeping him out. So he went to another city and collected a body of men, with whose aid he handled the attendants very roughly, and forced his way in to his mother. Hence they say arose the custom of a fight with sticks in honour of Ares at this festival.

The Egyptians first made it a point of religion to have no intercourse with women in the sacred places, and not to enter them without washing, after such intercourse. Almost all other nations, except the Greeks and the Egyptians, act differently, regarding man as in this matter under no other law than the brutes. Many animals, they say, and various kinds of birds may be seen to couple in the temples and the sacred precincts, which would certainly not happen if the gods were displeased at it. Such are the arguments by which they defend their practice, but I nevertheless can by no means approve of it. In these points the Egyptians are specially careful, as they are indeed in every thing which concerns their sacred edifices.

65. Egypt, though it borders upon Libya, is not a region abounding in wild animals.[32] The animals that do exist in the country, whether domesticated or otherwise, are all regarded as sacred. If I were to explain why they are consecrated to the several gods, I should be led to speak of religious matters, which I particularly shrink from mentioning; the points whereon I have touched slightly hitherto have all been introduced from sheer necessity. Their custom with respect to animals is as follows. For every kind there are appointed certain guardians, some male, some female, whose business it is to look after them; and this honour is made to descend from father to son. The inhabitants of the various cities, when they have made a vow to any god, pay it to his animals in the way which I will now explain.

[32] This was thought to be extraordinary, because Africa abounded in wild animals; but it was on the west and south, and not on the confines of Egypt that they were numerous. Though Herodotus abstains from saying why the Egyptians held some animals sacred, he explains it in some degree by observing that Egypt did not abound in animals.

At the time of making the vow they shave the head of the child, cutting off all the hair, or else half, or sometimes a third part, which they then weigh in a balance against a sum of silver; and whatever sum the hair weighs is presented to the guardian of the animals, who thereupon cuts up some fish, and gives it to them for food—such being the stuff whereon they are fed. When a man has killed one of the sacred animals, if he did it with malice prepense, he is punished with death; if unwittingly, he has to pay such a fine as the priests choose to impose. When an ibis, however, or a hawk is killed, whether it was done by accident or on purpose, the man must die.

66. The number of domestic animals in Egypt is very great, and would be still greater were it not for what befalls the cats. As the females, when they have kittened, no longer seek the company of the males, these last, to obtain once more their companionship, practise a curious artifice. They seize the kittens, carry them off, and kill them, but do not eat them afterwards. Upon this the females, being deprived of their young, and longing to supply their place, seek the males once more, since they are particularly fond of their offspring. On every occasion of a fire in Egypt the strangest prodigy occurs with the cats. The inhabitants allow the fire to rage as it pleases, while they stand about at intervals and watch these animals, which, slipping by the men or else leaping over them, rush headlong into the flames. When this happens, the Egyptians are in deep affliction. If a cat dies in a private house by a natural death, all the inmates of the house shave their eyebrows; on the death of a dog they shave the head and the whole of the body.

67. The cats on their decease are taken to the city of Bubastis, where they are embalmed, after which they are buried in certain sacred repositories. The dogs are interred in the cities to which they belong, also in sacred burial-places. The same practice obtains with respect to the ichneumons; the hawks and shrew-mice, on the contrary, are conveyed to the city of Buto for burial, and the ibises to Hermopolis. The bears, which are scarce in Egypt, and the wolves, which are not much bigger than foxes, they bury wherever they happen to find them lying.

68. The following are the peculiarities of the crocodile: During the four winter months they eat nothing; they are four-footed, and live indifferently on land or in the water. The female lays and hatches her eggs ashore, passing the greater portion of the day on dry land, but at night retiring to the river, the water of which is warmer than the night-air and the dew. Of all known animals this is the one which from the smallest size grows to be the greatest: for the egg of the crocodile is but little bigger than that of the goose, and the young crocodile is in proportion to the egg; yet when it is full grown, the animal measures frequently twenty-five feet and even more. It has the eyes of a pig, teeth large and tusk-like, of a size proportioned to its frame; unlike any other animal, it is without a tongue; it cannot move its under-jaw, and in this respect too it is singular, being the only animal in the world which moves the upper-jaw but not the under. It has strong claws and a scaly skin, impenetrable upon the back. In the water it is blind, but on land it is very keen of sight. As it lives chiefly in the river, it has the inside of its mouth constantly covered with leeches; hence it happens that, while all the other birds and beasts avoid it, with the trochilus it lives at peace, since it owes much to that bird: for the crocodile, when he leaves the water and comes out upon the land, is in the habit of lying with his mouth wide open, facing the western breeze: at such times the trochilus goes into his mouth and devours the leeches. This benefits the crocodile, who is pleased, and takes care not to hurt the trochilus.

69. The crocodile is esteemed sacred by some of the Egyptians, by others he is treated as an enemy. Those who live near Thebes, and those who dwell around lake Moeris, regard them with especial veneration. In each of these places they keep one crocodile in particular, who is taught to be tame and tractable. They adorn his ears with ear-rings of molten stone[33] or gold, and put bracelets on his forepaws, giving him daily a set portion of bread, with a certain number of victims; and, after having thus treated him with the greatest possible attention while alive,

[33] By molten stone seems to be meant glass, which was well known to the Egyptians.

they embalm him when he dies and bury him in a sacred reposi-
tory. The people of Elephantine, on the other hand, are so far
from considering these animals as sacred that they even eat their
flesh. In the Egyptian language they are not called crocodiles,
but champsae. The name of crocodiles was given them by the
Ionians, who remarked their resemblance to the lizards, which
in Ionia live in the walls, and are called crocodiles.

70. The modes of catching the crocodile are many and various. I shall only describe the one which seems to me most
worthy of mention. They bait a hook with a chine of pork and
let the meat be carried out into the middle of the stream, while
the hunter upon the bank holds a living pig, which he belabours.
The crocodile hears its cries and, making for the sound, encounters the pork, which he instantly swallows down. The men
on the shore haul, and when they have got him to land, the first
thing the hunter does is to plaster his eyes with mud. This once
accomplished, the animal is despatched with ease, otherwise he
gives great trouble.

71. The hippopotamus,[34] in the nome of Papremis, is a sacred
animal, but not in any other part of Egypt. It may be thus described: It is a quadruped, cloven-footed, with hoofs like an ox,
and a flat nose. It has the mane and tail of a horse, huge tusks
which are very conspicuous, and a voice like a horse's neigh. In
size it equals the biggest oxen, and its skin is so tough that when
dried it is made into javelins.

72. Otters also are found in the Nile, and are considered
sacred. Only two sorts of fish are venerated, that called the lepi-
dotus and the eel. These are regarded as sacred to the Nile, as
likewise among birds is the fox-goose.

73. They have also another sacred bird called the phoenix,
which I myself have never seen, except in pictures. Indeed it is
a great rarity even in Egypt, only coming there (according to
the accounts of the people of Heliopolis) once in five hundred
years, when the old phoenix dies. Its size and appearance, if it is

---

[34] This animal was formerly common in Egypt, but is now rarely seen
as low as the second cataract. The description of the hippopotamus by
Herodotus is far from correct.

like the pictures, are as follows: The plumage is partly red, partly golden, while the general make and size are almost exactly that of the eagle. They tell a story of what this bird does, which does not seem to me to be credible: that he comes all the way from Arabia, and brings the parent bird, all plastered over with myrrh, to the temple of the Sun, and there buries the body. In order to bring him, they say, he first forms a ball of myrrh as big as he finds that he can carry; then he hollows out the ball, and puts his parent inside, after which he covers over the opening with fresh myrrh, and the ball is then of exactly the same weight as at first; so he brings it to Egypt, plastered over as I have said, and deposits it in the temple of the Sun. Such is the story they tell of the doings of this bird.

74. In the neighbourhood of Thebes there are some sacred serpents which are perfectly harmless. They are of small size, and have two horns[35] growing out of the top of the head. These snakes, when they die, are buried in the temple of Zeus, the god to whom they are sacred.

75. I went once to a certain place in Arabia, almost exactly opposite the city of Buto, to make inquiries concerning the winged serpents.[36] On my arrival I saw the back-bones and ribs of serpents in such numbers as it is impossible to describe: of the ribs there were a multitude of heaps, some great, some small, some middle-sized. The place where the bones lie is at the entrance of a narrow gorge between steep mountains, which there open upon a spacious plain communicating with the great plain of Egypt. The story goes that with the spring the winged snakes come flying from Arabia towards Egypt, but are met in this gorge by the birds called ibises, who forbid their entrance and destroy them all. The Arabians assert, and the Egyptians also admit, that it is on account of the service thus rendered that the Egyptians hold the ibis in so much reverence.

---

[35] The bite of the cerastes or horned snake is deadly; but of the many serpents in Egypt, three only are poisonous, the cerastes, the asp and the common viper.

[36] The winged serpents of Herodotus have puzzled many persons but Herodotus only saw the bones; the rest of the story he was told.

76. The ibis is a bird of deep-black colour, with legs like a crane; its beak is strongly hooked, and its size is about that of the landrail. This is a description of the black ibis which contends with the serpents. The commoner sort, for there are two quite distinct species, has the head and the whole throat bare of feathers; its general plumage is white, but the head and neck are jet black, as also are the tips of the wings and the extremity of the tail; in its beak and legs it resembles the other species. The winged serpent is shaped like the water-snake. Its wings are not feathered, but resemble very closely those of the bat. And thus I conclude the subject of the sacred animals.

77. With respect to the Egyptians themselves, it is to be remarked that those who live in the corn country,[37] devoting themselves, as they do, far more than any other people in the world, to the preservation of the memory of past actions, are the best skilled in history of any men that I have ever met. The following is the mode of life habitual to them: For three successive days in each month they purge the body by means of emetics and clysters, which is done out of a regard for their health, since they have a persuasion that every disease to which men are liable is occasioned by the substances whereon they feed. Apart from any such precautions, they are, I believe, next to the Libyans, the healthiest people in the world—an effect of their climate, in my opinion, which has no sudden changes. Diseases almost always attack men when they are exposed to a change, and never more than during changes of the weather. They live on bread made of spelt, which they form into loaves called in their own tongue cyllestis. Their drink is a wine which they obtain from barley, as they have no vines in their country. Many kinds of fish they eat raw, either salted or dried in the sun. Quails also, and ducks and small birds, they eat uncooked,

[37] This is in contradistinction to the marsh-lands; and signifies Upper Egypt as it includes the city of Chemmis; but when he says they have no vines in the country and only drink beer, his statement is opposed to fact, and to the ordinary habits of the Egyptians. In the neighbourhood of Memphis, at Thebes, and the places between those two cities, as well as at Eileithyias, all corn-growing districts, they ate wheaten bread and cultivated the vine.

merely first salting them. All other birds and fishes, excepting those which are set apart as sacred, are eaten either roasted or boiled.

78. In social meetings among the rich, when the banquet is ended, a servant carries round to the several guests a coffin, in which there is a wooden image of a corpse, carved and painted to resemble nature as nearly as possible, about a cubit or two cubits in length. As he shows it to each guest in turn, the servant says, "Gaze here, and drink and be merry; for when you die, such will you be."

79. The Egyptians adhere to their own national customs, and adopt no foreign usages. Many of these customs are worthy of note: among others their song, the Linus, which is sung under various names not only in Egypt but in Phoenicia, in Cyprus, and in other places; and which seems to be exactly the same as that in use among the Greeks, and by them called Linus. There were very many things in Egypt which filled me with astonishment, and this was one of them. Whence could the Egyptians have got the Linus? It appears to have been sung by them from the very earliest times. For the Linus in Egyptian is called Maneros; and they told me that Maneros was the only son of their first king, and that on his untimely death he was honoured by the Egyptians with these dirgelike strains, and in this way they got their first and only melody.

80. There is another custom in which the Egyptians resemble a particular Greek people, namely the Lacedaemonians. Their young men, when they meet their elders in the streets, give way to them and step aside; and if an elder come in where young men are present, these latter rise from their seats. In a third point they differ entirely from all the nations of Greece. Instead of speaking to each other when they meet in the streets, they make an obeisance, sinking the hand to the knee.

81. They wear a linen tunic fringed about the legs, and called calasiris; over this they have a white woollen garment thrown on afterwards. Nothing of woollen, however, is taken into their temples or buried with them, as their religion forbids it. Here their practice resembles the rites called Orphic and Bacchic, but

which are in reality Egyptian and Pythagorean; for no one initiated in these mysteries can be buried in a woollen shroud, a religious reason being assigned for the observance.

82. The Egyptians likewise discovered to which of the gods each month and day is sacred; and found out from the day of a man's birth, what he will meet with in the course of his life,[38] and how he will end his days, and what sort of man he will be—discoveries whereof the Greeks engaged in poetry have made a use. The Egyptians have also discovered more prognostics than all the rest of mankind besides. Whenever a prodigy takes place, they watch and record the result; then, if anything similar ever happens again, they expect the same consequences.

83. With respect to divination, they hold that it is a gift which no mortal possesses, but only certain of the gods; thus they have an oracle of Heracles, one of Apollo, of Athena, of Artemis, of Ares, and of Zeus. Besides these, there is the oracle of Leto at Buto, which is held in much higher repute than any of the rest. The mode of delivering the oracles is not uniform, but varies at the different shrines.

84. Medicine is practised among them on a plan of separation; each physician treats a single disorder, and no more:[39] thus the country swarms with medical practitioners, some undertaking to cure diseases of the eye, others of the head, others again of the teeth, others of the intestines, and some those which are not local.

85. The following is the way in which they conduct their mournings and their funerals: On the death in any house of a man of consequence, forthwith the women of the family beplaster their heads, and sometimes even their faces, with mud; and then, leaving the body indoors, sally forth and wander through the city, with their dress fastened by a band, and their

[38] Horoscopes were of very early use in Egypt, as well as the interpretation of dreams; and Cicero speaks of the Egyptians and Chaldees predicting future events, as well as a man's destiny at his birth, by their observations of the stars.

[39] The medical profession being so divided indicates a great advancement of civilisation, as well as of medicinal knowledge.

bosoms bare, beating themselves as they walk. All the female
relations join them and do the same. The men too, similarly be-
girt, beat their breasts separately. When these ceremonies are
over, the body is carried away to be embalmed.

86. There are a set of men in Egypt who practise the art of
embalming, and make it their proper business. These persons,
when a body is brought to them, show the bearers various
models of corpses, made in wood, and painted so as to resemble
nature. The most perfect is said to be after the manner of him
whom I do not think it religious to name in connexion with
such a matter; the second sort is inferior to the first, and less
costly; the third is the cheapest of all. All this the embalmers
explain, and then ask in which way it is wished that the corpse
should be prepared. The bearers tell them, and having concluded their bargain, take their departure, while the embalmers,
left to themselves, proceed to their task. The mode of embalming,[40] according to the most perfect process, is the following:
They take first a crooked piece of iron, and with it draw out the
brain through the nostrils, thus getting rid of a portion, while
the skull is cleared of the rest by rinsing with drugs; next they
make a cut along the flank with a sharp Ethiopian stone, and
take out the whole contents of the abdomen, which they then
cleanse, washing it thoroughly with palm-wine, and again frequently with an infusion of pounded aromatics. After this they
fill the cavity with the purest bruised myrrh, with cassia, and
every other sort of spicery except frankincense, and sew up the
opening. Then the body is placed in natrum for seventy days,[41]
and covered entirely over. After the expiration of that space of
time, which must not be exceeded, the body is washed, and
wrapped round, from head to foot, with bandages of fine linen
cloth, smeared over with gum, which is used generally by the
Egyptians in the place of glue, and in this state it is given back
to the relations, who enclose it in a wooden case which they
have had made for the purpose, shaped into the figure of a man.

[40] Herodotus' account of embalming is on the whole very accurate.
[41] This included the whole period of mourning. The embalming in natrum (saltpetre or soda) only occupied forty days.

Then fastening the case, they place it in a sepulchral chamber, upright against the wall. Such is the most costly way of embalming the dead.

87. If persons wish to avoid expense, and choose the second process, the following is the method pursued: Syringes are filled with oil made from the cedar-tree, which is then, without any incision or disembowelling, injected into the bowel. The passage is stopped, and the body laid in natrum the prescribed number of days. At the end of the time the cedar-oil is allowed to make its escape; and such is its power that it brings with it the whole stomach and intestines in a liquid state. The natrum meanwhile has dissolved the flesh, and so nothing is left of the dead body but the skin and the bones. It is returned in this condition to the relatives, without any further trouble being bestowed upon it.

88. The third method of embalming, which is practised in the case of the poorer classes, is to clear out the intestines with a purge, and let the body lie in natrum the seventy days, after which it is at once given to those who come to fetch it away.

89. The wives of men of rank are not given to be embalmed immediately after death, nor indeed are any of the more beautiful and valued women. It is not till they have been dead three or four days that they are carried to the embalmers. This is done to prevent the embalmers having intercourse with them. It is said that once a man was detected in the act with a woman newly dead and denounced by his fellow-workman.

90. Whensoever any one, Egyptian or foreigner, has lost his life by falling a prey to a crocodile, or by drowning in the river, the law compels the inhabitants of the city near which the body is cast up to have it embalmed, and to bury it in one of the sacred repositories with all possible magnificence. No one may touch the corpse, not even any of the friends or relatives, but only the priests of the Nile, who prepare it for burial with their own hands—regarding it as something more than the mere body of a man—and themselves lay it in the tomb.

91. The Egyptians are averse to adopt Greek customs, or, in a word, those of any other nation. This feeling is almost uni-

versal among them. At Chemmis,[42] however, which is a large
city in the Thebaic nome, near Neapolis, there is a square enclosure sacred to Perseus, son of Danae. Palm trees grow all
round the place, which has a gateway of stone of an unusual
size, surmounted by two colossal statues, also in stone. Inside
this precinct is a temple, and in the temple an image of Perseus.
The people of Chemmis say that Perseus often appears to them,
sometimes within the sacred enclosure, sometimes in the open
country: one of the sandals which he has worn is frequently
found—three feet in length, as they affirm—and then all Egypt
flourishes greatly. In the worship of Perseus Greek ceremonies
are used; gymnastic games are celebrated in his honour, com-
prising every kind of contest, with prizes of cattle, cloaks, and
skins. I made inquiries of the Chemmites why it was that Perseus appeared to them and not elsewhere in Egypt, and how
they came to celebrate gymnastic contests unlike the rest of the
Egyptians: to which they answered, "that Perseus belonged to
their city by descent. Danaus and Lynceus were Chemmites before they set sail for Greece, and from them Perseus was descended," they said, tracing the genealogy, "and he, when he
came to Egypt for the purpose" (which the Greeks also assign)
"of bringing away from Libya the Gorgon's head, paid them a
visit, and acknowledged them for his kinsmen—he had heard
the name of their city from his mother before he left Greece—he
bade them institute a gymnastic contest in his honour, and that
was the reason why they observed the practice."

92. The customs hitherto described are those of the Egyptians who live above the marsh-country. The inhabitants of the
marshes have the same customs as the rest, as well in those matters which have been mentioned above as in respect of marriage,
each Egyptian taking to himself, like the Greeks, a single wife;
but for greater cheapness of living the marsh-men practise certain peculiar customs, such as these following. They gather the
blossoms of a certain water-lily, which grows in great abundance
all over the flat country at the time when the Nile rises and

[42] Chem, the god of Chemmis, being supposed to answer to Pan, this
city was called Panopolis by the Greeks and Romans.

floods the regions along its banks—the Egyptians call it the lotus⁺³—they gather, I say, the blossoms of this plant and dry them in the sun, after which they extract from the centre of each blossom a substance like the head of a poppy, which they crush and make into bread. The root of the lotus is likewise eatable, and has a pleasant sweet taste: it is round, and about the size of an apple. There is also another species of the lily in Egypt, which grows, like the lotus, in the river, and resembles the rose. The fruit springs up side by side with the blossom, on a separate stalk, and has almost exactly the look of the comb made by wasps. It contains a number of seeds, about the size of an olive-stone, which are good to eat: and these are eaten both green and dried. The papyrus, which grows year after year in the marshes, they pull up, and, cutting the plant in two, reserve the upper portion for other purposes, but take the lower, which is about eighteen inches long, and either eat it or else sell it. Such as wish to enjoy the papyrus in full perfection bake it first in a closed vessel, heated to a glow. Some of these folk, however, live entirely on fish, which are gutted as soon as caught, and then hung up in the sun: when dry, they are used as food.

93. Gregarious fish are not found in any numbers in the rivers; they frequent the lagoons, whence, at the season of breeding, they proceed in shoals towards the sea. The males lead the way, and drop their milt as they go, while the females, following close behind, eagerly swallow it down. From this they conceive,⁴⁴ and when, after passing some time in the sea, they begin to be in spawn, the whole shoal sets off on its return to its ancient haunts. Now, however, it is no longer the males, but the females, who take the lead: they swim in front in a body, and do exactly as the male did before, dropping, little by little, their grains of spawn as they go, while the males in the rear devour

⁴⁰ This Nymphaèa Lotus grows in ponds and small channels in the Delta during the inundation, which are dry during the rest of the year; but it is not found in the Nile itself. It is nearly the same as our white water-lily.

⁴⁴ Aristotle (de Gen. Anim. iii. 5) shows the absurdity of this statement, quoting Herodotus by name. and giving his exact words.

the grains, each one of which is a fish.[45] A portion of the spawn escapes and is not swallowed by the males, and hence come the fishes which grow afterwards to maturity. When any of this sort of fish are taken on their passage to the sea, they are found to have the left side of the head scarred and bruised; while if taken cn their return, the marks appear on the right. The reason is, that as they swim down the Nile seaward, they keep close to the bank of the river upon their left, and returning again up stream they still cling to the same side hugging it and brushing in against it constantly, to be sure that they miss not their road through the great force of the current. When the Nile begins to rise, the hollows in the land and the marshy spots near the river are flooded before any other places by the percolation of the water through the river banks; and these, almost as soon as they become pools, are found to be full of numbers of little fishes. I think that I understand how it is this comes to pass. On the subsidence of the Nile the year before, though the fish retired with the retreating waters, they had first deposited their spawn in the mud upon the banks; and so, when at the usual season the water returns, small fry are rapidly engendered out of the spawn of the preceding year. So much concerning the fish.

94. The Egyptians who live in the marshes use for the anointing of their bodies an oil made from the castor berry, which is known among them by the name of "kiki." To obtain this they plant the castor (which grows wild in Greece) along the banks of the rivers and by the sides of the lakes, where it produces fruit in great abundance, but with a very disagreeable smell. This fruit is gathered, and then bruised and pressed, or else boiled down after roasting: the liquid which comes from it is collected and is found to be unctuous, and as well suited as olive-oil for lamps, only that it gives out an unpleasant odour.

95. The contrivances which they use against gnats, wherewith the country swarms, are the following. In the parts of

---

[45] The male fish deposits the milt after the female has deposited the spawn, and thus renders it prolific. The swallowing of the spawn is simply the act of any hungry fish, male or female, who happens to find it The bruised heads are a fable.

Egypt above the marshes the inhabitants pass the night upon
lofty towers, which are of great service, as the gnats are unable
to fly to any height on account of the winds. In the marsh-
country, where there are no towers, each man possesses a net
instead. By day it serves him to catch fish, while at night he
spreads it over the bed in which he is to rest, and creeping in,
goes to sleep underneath. The gnats, which, if he rolls himself
up in his dress or in a piece of muslin, are sure to bite through
the covering, do not so much as attempt to pass the net.

96. The vessels used in Egypt for the transport of merchandise are made of the acacia, a tree which in its growth is very
like the Cyrenaic lotus, and from which there exudes a gum.
They cut a quantity of planks about three feet in length from
this tree, and then proceed to their ship-building, arranging the
planks like bricks, and attaching them by ties to a number of
long stakes or poles till the hull is complete, when they lay the
cross-planks on the top from side to side. They give the boats
no ribs, but caulk the seams with papyrus on the inside. Each
has a single rudder, which is driven straight through the keel.
The mast is a piece of acacia-wood, and the sails are made of
papyrus. These boats cannot make way against the current unless there is a brisk breeze; they are, therefore, towed up-stream
from the shore: down-stream they are managed as follows.
There is a raft belonging to each, made of the wood of the
tamarisk, fastened together with a wattling of reeds; and also a
stone bored through the middle about 100 pounds in weight.
The raft is fastened to the vessel by a rope, and allowed to float
down the stream in front, while the stone is attached by another
rope astern. The result is, that the raft, hurried forward by the
current, goes rapidly down the river, and drags the baris (for so
they call this sort of boat) after it; while the stone, which is
pulled along in the wake of the vessel, and lies deep in the
water, keeps the boat straight. There are a vast number of these
vessels in Egypt, and some of them are of many tons' burden.

97. When the Nile overflows, the country is converted into a
sea, and nothing appears but the cities, which look like the
islands in the Aegean. At this season boats no longer keep the

course of the river, but sail right across the plain. On the voyage from Naucratis to Memphis at this season, you pass close to the pyramids, whereas the usual course is by the apex of the Delta, and the city of Cercasorus. You can sail also from the maritime town of Canobus across the flat to Naucratis, passing by the cities of Anthylla and Archandropolis.

98. The former of these cities, which is a place of note, is assigned expressly to the wife of the ruler of Egypt for the time being, to keep her in shoes. Such has been the custom ever since Egypt fell under the Persian yoke. The other city seems to me to have got its name of Archandropolis from Archander the Phthian, son of Achaeus, and son-in-law of Danaus. There might certainly have been another Archander; but, any rate, the name is not Egyptian.

99. Thus far I have spoken of Egypt from my own observation, relating what I myself saw, the ideas that I formed, and the results of my own researches. What follows rests on the accounts given me by the Egyptians, which I shall now repeat, adding thereto some particulars which fell under my own notice.

The priests said that Min was the first king of Egypt,[46] and that it was he who raised the dyke which protects Memphis from the inundations of the Nile. Before his time the river flowed entirely along the sandy range of hills which skirts Egypt on the side of Libya. He, however, by banking up the river at the bend which it forms about eleven miles south of Memphis, laid the ancient channel dry, while he dug a new course for the stream half-way between the two lines of hills. To this day, the elbow which the Nile forms at the point where it is forced aside into the new channel is guarded with the greatest care by the Persians, and strengthened every year; for if the river were to burst out at this place, and pour over the mound, there would be danger of Memphis being completely overwhelmed by the flood. Min, the first king, having thus, by turning the river, made the tract where it used to run, dry land, proceeded in the first place to build the city now called Memphis,[47] which lies in

---

[46] The gods were said to have reigned before Menes.

[47] The early foundation of Memphis is proved by the names of the kings of the oldest dynasties being found there.

the narrow part of Egypt; after which he further excavated a
lake outside the town, to the north and west, communicating
with the river, which was itself the eastern boundary. Besides
these works he also, the priests said, built the temple of Hephaestus which stands within the city, a vast edifice, very
worthy of mention.

100. Next, they read me from a papyrus, the names of 330
monarchs, who (they said) were his successors upon the throne.
In this number of generations there were eighteen Ethiopian
kings, and one queen who was a native: all the rest were kings
and Egyptians. The queen bore the same name as the Babylonian princess, namely, Nitocris.[48] They said that she succeeded her brother; he had been king of Egypt, and was put to
death by his subjects, who then placed her upon the throne.
Bent on avenging his death, she devised a cunning scheme by
which she destroyed a vast number of Egyptians. She constructed a spacious underground chamber, and, on pretence of
inaugurating it, contrived the following: Inviting to a banquet
those of the Egyptians whom she knew to have had the chief
share in the murder of her brother, she suddenly, as they were
feasting, let the river in upon them, by means of a secret duct
of large size. This, and this only, did they tell me of her, except
that, when she had done as I have said, she threw herself into
an apartment full of ashes, that she might escape the vengeance
whereto she would otherwise have been exposed.

101. The other kings, they said, were personages of no note
or distinction,[49] and left no monuments of any account, with the
exception of the last, who was named Moeris.[50] He left several

[48] Nitocris was an early Egyptian queen if the word Neitakri, occurring
in the Turin Papyrus and as the last sovereign of Manetho's 6th dynasty,
is feminine in gender.

[49] Their obscurity was owing to Egypt being part of the time under the
domination of the Shepherds, who finding Egypt divided into several
kingdoms, invaded the country, and succeeded at length in dispossessing
the Memphite kings of their territories.

[50] Herodotus passes over the Old Kingdom whose prominent rulers are
misplaced in chapter 124. Moeris (Amenemhet) belongs to the Twelfth
Dynasty.

memorials of his reign—the northern gateway of the temple of Hephaestus, the lake excavated by his orders, whose dimensions I shall give presently, and the pyramids built by him in the lake, the size of which will be stated when I describe the lake itself wherein they stand. Such were his works: the other kings left absolutely nothing.

102. Passing over these monarchs, therefore, I shall speak of the king who reigned next, whose name was Sesostris.[51] He, the priests said, first of all proceeded in a fleet of ships of war from the Arabian gulf along the shores of the Red sea, subduing the nations as he went, until he finally reached a sea which could not be navigated by reason of the shoals. Hence he returned to Egypt, where, they told me, he collected a vast armament, and made a progress by land across the continent, conquering every people which fell in his way. In the countries where the natives withstood his attack, and fought gallantly for their liberties, he erected pillars,[52] on which he inscribed his own name and country, and how that he had here reduced the inhabitants to subjection by the might of his arms: where, on the contrary, they submitted readily and without a struggle, he inscribed on the pillars, in addition to these particulars, female genitalia to mark that they were a nation of women, that is, unwarlike and effeminate.

103. In this way he traversed the whole continent of Asia, whence he passed on into Europe, and made himself master of Scythia and of Thrace, beyond which countries I do not think that his army extended its march. For thus far the pillars which he erected are still visible, but in the remoter regions they are no longer found. Returning to Egypt from Thrace, he came, on his way, to the banks of the river Phasis. Here I cannot say with any certainty what took place. Either he of his own accord detached a body of troops from his main army and left them to colonise the country, or else a certain number of his soldiers.

[51] It is probable that the exploits of Senusret I, Senusret III and Rameses II are amalgamated under the name of Sesostris.
[52] These memorials, which belong to Rameses II, are found in Syria, on the rocks above the mouth of the Lycus.

wearied with their long wanderings, deserted, and established themselves on the banks of this stream.

104. There can be no doubt that the Colchians are an Egyptian race. Before I heard any mention of the fact from others, I had remarked it myself. After the thought had struck me, I made inquiries on the subject both in Colchis and in Egypt, and I found that the Colchians had a more distinct recollection of the Egyptians, than the Egyptians had of them. Still the Egyptians said that they believed the Colchians to be descended from the army of Sesostris. My own conjectures were founded, first, on the fact that they are black skinned and have woolly hair; which certainly amounts to but little, since several other nations are so too; but further and more especially, on the circumstance that the Colchians, the Egyptians, and the Ethiopians, are the only nations who have practised circumcision from the earliest times. The Phoenicians and the Syrians of Palestine[53] themselves confess that they learnt the custom of the Egyptians; and the Syrians who dwell about the rivers Thermodon and Parthenius, as well as their neighbours the Macronians, say that they have recently adopted it from the Colchians. Now these are the only nations who use circumcision, and it is plain that they all imitate herein the Egyptians. With respect to the Ethiopians, indeed, I cannot decide whether they learnt the practice of the Egyptians, or the Egyptians of them—it is undoubtedly of very ancient date in Ethiopia—but that the others derived their knowledge of it from Egypt is clear to me, from the fact that the Phoenicians, when they come to have commerce with the Greeks, cease to follow the Egyptians in this custom, and allow their children to remain uncircumcised.

105. I will add a further proof of the identity of the Egyptians and the Colchians. These two nations weave their linen in exactly the same way, and this is a way entirely unknown to the rest of the world; they also in their whole mode of life and in their language resemble one another. The Colchian linen is

---

[53] Herodotus apparently alludes to the Jews. He may be excused for supposing that the Jews borrowed circumcision from the Egyptians, since they did not practise it as a regular and universal custom until after they left Egypt.

called by the Greeks Sardonian, while that which comes from
Egypt is known as Egyptian.

106. The pillars, which Sesostris erected in the conquered
countries, have for the most part disappeared, but in the part of
Syria called Palestine, I myself saw them still standing, with the
writing above mentioned, and the genitals distinctly visible. In
Ionia also, there are two representations of this prince engraved
upon rocks, one on the road from Ephesus to Phocaea, the other
between Sardis and Smyrna. In each case the figure is that of a
man, seven feet high, with a spear in his right hand and a bow
in his left, the rest of his costume being likewise half Egyptian,
half Ethiopian. There is an inscription across the breast from
shoulder to shoulder, in the sacred character of Egypt, which
says, "With my own shoulders I conquered this land." The conqueror does not tell who he is, or whence he comes, though elsewhere Sesostris records these facts. Hence it has been imagined
by some of those who have seen these forms, that they are
figures of Memnon;[54] but such as think so err very widely from
the truth.

107. This Sesostris, the priests went on to say, upon his return home accompanied by vast multitudes of the people whose
countries he had subdued, was received by his brother, whom he
had made viceroy of Egypt on his departure, at Daphnae near
Pelusium, and invited by him to a banquet, which he attended,
together with his sons. Then his brother piled a quantity of
wood all round the building, and having so done set it alight.
Sesostris, discovering what had happened, took counsel instantly
with his wife, who had accompanied him to the feast, and was
advised by her to lay two of their six sons upon the fire, and so
make a bridge across the flames, whereby the rest might effect
their escape. Sesostris did as she recommended, and thus while
two of his sons were burnt to death, he himself and his other
children were saved.

[54] Herodotus shows his discrimination in rejecting the notion of his being Memnon, which had already become prevalent among the Greeks,
who saw Memnon everywhere in Egypt merely because he was mentioned in Homer.

108. The king then returned to his own land and took vengeance upon his brother, after which he proceeded to make use of the multitudes whom he had brought with him from the conquered countries, partly to drag the huge masses of stone which were moved in the course of his reign to the temple of Hephaestus—partly to dig the numerous canals with which the whole of Egypt is intersected. By these forced labours the entire face of the country was changed; for whereas Egypt had formerly been a region suited both for horses and carriages, henceforth it became entirely unfit for either. Though a flat country throughout its whole extent, it is now unfit for either horse or carriage, being cut up by the canals, which are extremely numerous and run in all directions. The king's object was to supply Nile water to the inhabitants of the towns situated in the mid-country, and not lying upon the river; for previously they had been obliged, after the subsidence of the floods, to drink a brackish water which they obtained from the wells.

109. Sesostris also, they declared, made a division of the soil of Egypt among the inhabitants, assigning square plots of ground of equal size to all, and obtaining his chief revenue from the rent which the holders were required to pay him every year. If the river carried away any portion of a man's lot, he appeared before the king, and related what had happened; upon which the king sent persons to examine, and determine by measurement the exact extent of the loss; and thenceforth only such a rent was demanded of him as was proportionate to the reduced size of his land. From this practice, I think, geometry first came to be known in Egypt, whence it passed into Greece. The sundial, however, and the gnomon, with the division of the day into twelve parts, were received by the Greeks from the Babylonians.

110. Sesostris was king not only of Egypt, but also of Ethiopia. He was the only Egyptian monarch who ever ruled over the latter country.[55] He left, as memorials of his reign, the stone statues which stand in front of the temple of Hephaestus, two of which, representing himself and his wife, are forty-five feet

[55] The Egyptians evidently overran all Ethiopia, and part of the interior of Africa, in the time of the 18th and 19th dynasties.

in height, while the remaining four, which represent his sons, are thirty feet. These are the statues, in front of which the priest of Hephaestus, very many years afterwards, would not allow Darius the Persian[56] to place a statue of himself; "because," he said, "Darius had not equalled the achievements of Sesostris the Egyptian: for while Sesostris had subdued to the full as many nations as ever Darius had brought under, he had likewise conquered the Scythians, whom Darius had failed to master. It was not fair, therefore, that he should erect his statue in front of the offerings of a king, whose deeds he had been unable to surpass." Darius, they say, pardoned the freedom of this speech.

111. On the death of Sesostris, his son Pheros,[57] the priests said, mounted the throne. He undertook no warlike expeditions; being struck with blindness, owing to the following circumstance. The river had swollen to the unusual height of twenty-seven feet, and had overflowed all the fields, when, a sudden wind arising, the water rose in great waves. Then the king, in a spirit of impious violence, seized his spear, and hurled it into the strong eddies of the stream. Instantly he was smitten with disease of the eyes, from which after a little while he became blind, continuing without the power of vision for ten years. At last, in the eleventh year, an oracular announcement reached him from the city of Buto, to the effect, that "the time of his punishment had run out, and he should recover his sight by washing his eyes with urine. He must find a woman who had been faithful to her husband, and had never had intercourse with another man." The king, therefore, first of all made trial of his wife, but to no purpose—he continued as blind as before. So he made the experiment with other women, until at length he succeeded, and in this way recovered his sight. Hereupon he assembled all the women, except the last, and bringing them to the city which now

[56] The name of Darius occurs in the sculptures, and great part of the principal Temple of El Khargeh, in the Great Oasis, was built by him, his name being the oldest there.

[57] Pheros is probably not a name but a corruption of Pharaoh and the whole tale a satire on women developed from an actual Egyptian remedy for ophthalmia.

bears the name of Red-soil, he there burnt them all, together with the place itself. The woman to whom he owed his cure, he married, and after his recovery was complete, he presented offerings to all the temples of any note, among which the best worthy of mention are the two stone obelisks which he gave to the temple of the Sun.[58] These are magnificent works; each is made of a single stone, twelve feet broad, and 150 feet in height.

112. Pheros, they said, was succeeded by a man of Memphis, whose name, in the language of the Greeks, was Proteus. There is a sacred precinct of this king in Memphis, which is very beautiful, and richly adorned, situated south of the great temple of Hephaestus. Phoenicians from the city of Tyre dwell all round this precinct, and the whole place is known by the name of the camp of the Tyrians. Within the enclosure stands a temple, which is called that of Aphrodite the Stranger. I conjecture the building to have been erected to Helen, the daughter of Tyndarus; first, because she, as I have heard say, passed some time at the court of Proteus; and secondly, because the temple is dedicated to Aphrodite the Stranger; for among all the many temples of Aphrodite there is no other where the goddess bears this title.

113. The priests, in answer to my inquiries on the subject of Helen,[59] informed me of the following particulars. When Alexander had carried off Helen from Sparta, he took ship and sailed homewards. On his way across the Aegean a gale arose, which drove him from his course and took him down to the sea of Egypt; hence, as the wind did not abate, he was carried on to the coast, when he went ashore, landing at the Salt-Pans, in that mouth of the Nile which is now called the Canobic. At this place there stood upon the shore a temple, which still exists, dedicated to Heracles. If a slave runs away from his master, and taking

[58] They were therefore most probably at Heliopolis. The height far exceeds that of any found in Egypt, the highest being less than 100 feet.

[59] The eagerness of the Greeks to "inquire" after events mentioned by Homer, and the readiness of the Egyptians to take advantage of it, are shown in this story related to Herodotus. The fact of Homer having believed that Helen went to Egypt, only proves that the story was not invented in Herodotus' time, but was current long before.

sanctuary at this shrine gives himself up to the god, and receives
certain sacred marks upon his person, whosoever his master may
be, he cannot lay hand on him. This law still remained unchanged to my time. Hearing, therefore, of the custom of the
place, the attendants of Alexander deserted him, and fled to the
temple where they sat as suppliants. While there, wishing to
damage their master, they accused him to the Egyptians, nar-
rating all the circumstances of the rape of Helen and the wrong
done to Menelaus. These charges they brought, not only before
the priests, but also before the warden of that mouth of the
river, whose name was Thonis.

114. As soon as he received the intelligence, Thonis sent a
message to Proteus, who was at Memphis, to this effect, "A
stranger is arrived from Greece; he is by race a Teucrian, and
has done a wicked deed in the country from which he is come.
Having beguiled the wife of the man whose guest he was, he
carried her away with him, and much treasure also. Compelled
by stress of weather, he has now put in here. Are we to let him
depart as he came, or shall we seize what he has brought?" Proteus replied, "Seize the man, be he who he may, that has dealt
thus wickedly with his friend, and bring him before me, that I
may hear what he will say for himself."

115. Thonis, on receiving these orders, arrested Alexander,
and stopped the departure of his ships; then, taking with him
Alexander, Helen, the treasures, and also the fugitive slaves, he
went up to Memphis. When all were arrived, Proteus asked
Alexander, "Who he was, and whence he had come?" Alexander
replied by giving his descent, the name of his country, and a
true account of his late voyage. Then Proteus questioned him as
to how he got possession of Helen. In his reply Alexander became confused, and diverged from the truth, whereon the slaves
interposed, confuted his statements, and told the whole history
of the crime. Finally, Proteus delivered judgment as follows,
"Did I not regard it as a matter of the utmost consequence that
no stranger driven to my country by adverse winds should ever
be put to death, I would certainly have avenged the Greek by

slaying you, basest of men, after accepting hospitality, to do so wicked a deed! First, you did seduce the wife of your own host —then, not content therewith, you must violently excite her mind, and steal her away from her husband. Nay, even so you were not satisfied, but on leaving, you plundered the house in which you had been a guest. Now then, as I think it of the greatest importance to put no stranger to death, I suffer you to depart; but the woman and the treasures I shall not permit to be carried away. Here they must stay, till the Greek stranger comes in person and takes them back with him. For yourself and your companions, I command you to leave my land within the space of three days—and I warn you, that otherwise at the end of that time you will be treated as enemies."

116. Such was the tale told me by the priests concerning the arrival of Helen at the court of Proteus. It seems to me that Homer was acquainted with this story, and while discarding it, because he thought it less adapted for epic poetry than the version which he followed, showed that it was not unknown to him. This is evident from the travels which he assigns to Alexander in the *Iliad*—and let it be borne in mind that he has nowhere else contradicted himself—making him be carried out of his course on his return with Helen, and after divers wanderings come at last to Sidon in Phoenicia. The passage is in the Bravery of Diomede,[60] and the words are as follows:

There were the robes, many-coloured, the work of Sidonian
    women:
They from Sidon had come, what time god-shaped Alexander
Over the broad sea brought, that way, the high-born Helen.

In the *Odyssey*[61] also the same fact is alluded to, in these words:

[60] The objection that the passage quoted is from *Iliad* vi., and not *Iliad* v., which now bears the title of "Diomede's Bravery," is of no importance, for our present division of the books dates from Aristarchus, and in the time of Herodotus a portion of the sixth book may have been included under the heading confined afterwards to the fifth.

[61] iv. 227-230.

Such, so wisely prepared, were the drugs that her stores afforded,
Excellent; gift which once Polydamna, partner of Thonis,
Gave her in Egypt, where many the simples that grow in the
 meadows,
Potent to cure in part, in part as potent to injure.

Menelaus too, in the same poem,[62] thus addresses Telemachus:

Much did I long to return, but the gods still kept me in Egypt—
Angry because I had failed to pay them their hecatombs duly.

 In these places Homer shows himself acquainted with the
voyage of Alexander to Egypt, for Syria borders on Egypt,
and the Phoenicians, to whom Sidon belongs, dwell in Syria.
 117. From these various passages, and from that about Sidon
especially, it is clear that Homer did not write the *Cypria*.[63] For
there it is said that Alexander arrived at Ilium with Helen on
the third day after he left Sparta, the wind having been favourable, and the sea smooth; whereas in the *Iliad,* the poet makes
him wander before he brings her home. Enough, however, for
the present of Homer and the *Cypria.*
 118. I made inquiry of the priests, whether the story which
the Greeks tell about Ilium is a fable, or no. In reply they related the following particulars, of which they declared that
Menelaus had himself informed them. After the rape of Helen,
a vast army of Greeks, wishing to render help to Menelaus, set
sail for the Teucrian territory; on their arrival they disembarked, and formed their camp, after which they sent ambassadors to Ilium, of whom Menelaus was one. The embassy was
received within the walls, and demanded the restoration of
Helen with the treasures which Alexander had carried off, and
likewise required satisfaction for the wrong done. The Teucrians gave at once the answer in which they persisted ever
afterwards, backing their assertions sometimes even with oaths,

[62] iv. 351-352.
[63] The criticism here is better than the argument. The *Cypria* was probably written by Stasinus about 700 B.C.

to wit, that neither Helen, nor the treasures claimed, were in their possession, both the one and the other had remained, they said, in Egypt; and it was not just to come upon them for what Proteus, king of Egypt, was detaining. The Greeks, imagining that the Teucrians were merely laughing at them, laid siege to the town, and never rested until they finally took it. As, however, no Helen was found, and they were still told the same story, they at length believed in its truth, and despatched Menelaus to the court of Proteus.

119. So Menelaus travelled to Egypt, and on his arrival sailed up the river as far as Memphis, and related all that had happened. He met with the utmost hospitality, received Helen back unharmed, and recovered all his treasures. After this friendly treatment Menelaus, they said, behaved most unjustly towards the Egyptians; for as it happened that at the time when he wanted to take his departure, he was detained by the wind being contrary, and as he found this obstruction continue, he had recourse to a most wicked expedient. He seized, they said, two children of the people of the country, and offered them up in sacrifice. When this became known, the indignation of the people was stirred, and they went in pursuit of Menelaus, who, however, escaped with his ships to Libya, after which the Egyptians could not say whither he went. The rest they knew full well, partly by the inquiries which they had made, and partly from the circumstances having taken place in their own land, and therefore not admitting of doubt.

120. Such is the account given by the Egyptian priests, and I am myself inclined to regard as true all that they say of Helen from the following considerations: If Helen had been at Troy, the inhabitants would, I think, have given her up to the Greeks, whether Alexander consented to it or no. For surely neither Priam, nor his family, could have been so infatuated as to endanger their own persons, their children, and their city, merely that Alexander might possess Helen. At any rate, if they determined to refuse at first, yet afterwards when so many of the Trojans fell on every encounter with the Greeks, and Priam too in each battle lost a son, or sometimes two, or three, or even

more, if we may credit the epic poets,[64] I do not believe that
even if Priam himself had been married to her he would have
declined to deliver her up, with the view of bringing the series
of calamities to a close. Nor was it as if Alexander had been heir
to the crown, in which case he might have had the chief management of affairs, since Priam was already old. Hector, who was
his elder brother, and a far braver man, stood before him, and
was the heir to the kingdom on the death of their father Priam.
And it could not be Hector's interest to uphold his brother in
his wrong, when it brought such dire calamities upon himself
and the other Trojans. But the fact was that they had no Helen
to deliver, and so they told the Greeks, but the Greeks would
not believe what they said—Divine Providence, as I think, so
willing, that by their utter destruction it might be made evident
to all men that when great wrongs are done, the gods will surely
visit them with great punishments. Such, at least, is my view of
the matter.

121. When Proteus died, Rhampsinitus,[65] the priests informed me, succeeded to the throne. His monuments were, the
western gateway of the temple of Hephaestus, and the two statues which stand in front of this gateway, called by the Egyptians, the one Summer, the other Winter, each forty feet in
height. The statue of Summer, which is the northernmost of the
two, is worshipped by the natives, and has offerings made to it;
that of Winter, which stands towards the south, is treated in
exactly the contrary way. King Rhampsinitus was possessed,
they said, of great riches in silver, indeed to such an amount,
that none of the princes, his successors, surpassed or even
equalled his wealth. For the better custody of this money, he
proposed to build a vast chamber of hewn stone, one side of
which was to form a part of the outer wall of his palace. The
builder, therefore, having designs upon the treasures, contrived,
as he was making the building, to insert in this wall a stone,
which could easily be removed from its place by two men, or

---

[64] The whole chapter is an instance of Greek rationalising criticism.

[65] This is evidently the name of a Rameses of the twentieth dynasty
with whom Herodotus has connected a familiar piece of folklore.

even by one. So the chamber was finished, and the king's money stored away in it. Time passed, and the builder fell sick, when finding his end approaching, he called for his two sons, and related to them the contrivance he had made in the king's treasure-chamber, telling them it was for their sakes he had done it, that so they might always live in affluence. Then he gave them clear directions concerning the mode of removing the stone, and communicated the measurements, bidding them carefully keep the secret, whereby they would be Stewards of the royal treasury so long as they lived. Then the father died, and the sons were not slow in setting to work; they went by night to the palace, found the stone in the wall of the building, and having removed it with ease, plundered the treasury of a round sum.

When the king next paid a visit to the apartment, he was astonished to see that the money was sunk in some of the vessels wherein it was stored away. Whom to accuse, however, he knew not, as the seals were all perfect, and the fastenings of the room secure. Still each time that he repeated his visits, he found that more money was gone. The thieves in truth never stopped, but plundered the treasury ever more and more. At last the king determined to have some traps made, and set near the vessels which containd his wealth. This was done, and when the thieves came, as usual, to the treasure-chamber, and one of them entering through the aperture, made straight for the jars, suddenly he found himself caught in one of the traps. Perceiving that he was lost, he instantly called his brother, and telling him what had happened, entreated him to enter as quickly as possible and cut off his head, that when his body should be discovered it might not be recognised, which would have the effect of bringing ruin upon both. The other thief thought the advice good, and was persuaded to follow it; then, fitting the stone into its place, he went home, taking with him his brother's head.

When day dawned, the king came into the room, and marvelled greatly to see the body of the thief in the trap without a head, while the building was still whole, and neither entrance nor exit was to be seen anywhere. In this perplexity he commanded the body of the dead man to be hung up outside the

palace wall, and set a guard to watch it, with orders that if any
persons were seen weeping or lamenting near the place, they
should be seized and brought before him. When the mother
heard of this exposure of the corpse of her son, she took it sorely
to heart, and spoke to her surviving child, bidding him devise
some plan or other to get back the body, and threatening, that
if he did not exert himself, she would go herself to the king, and
denounce him as the robber.

The son said all he could to persuade her to let the matter
rest, but in vain: she still continued to trouble him, until at last
he yielded to her importunity, and contrived as follows: Filling
some skins with wine, he loaded them on donkeys, which he
drove before him till he came to the place where the guards were
watching the dead body, when pulling two or three of the skins
towards him, he untied some of the necks which dangled by the
asses' sides. The wine poured freely out, whereupon he began to
beat his head, and shout with all his might, seeming not to know
which of the donkeys he should turn to first. When the guards
saw the wine running, delighted to profit by the occasion, they
rushed one and all into the road, each with some vessel or other,
and caught the liquor as it was spilling. The driver pretended
anger, and loaded them with abuse; whereon they did their best
to pacify him, until at last he appeared to soften, and recover
his good humour, drove his asses aside out of the road, and set
to work to rearrange their burdens; meanwhile, as he talked and
chatted with the guards, one of them began to rally him, and
make him laugh, whereupon he gave them one of the skins as a
gift. They now made up their minds to sit down and have a
drinking-bout where they were, so they begged him to remain
and drink with them. Then the man let himself be persuaded,
and stayed. As the drinking went on, they grew very friendly
together, so presently he gave them another skin, upon which
they drank so copiously that they were all overcome with the
liquor, and growing drowsy lay down, and fell asleep on the
spot. The thief waited till it was the dead of the night, and then
took down the body of his brother; after which, in mockery, he
shaved off the right side of all the soldiers' beards, and so left

them. Laying his brother's body upon the asses, he carried it home to his mother, having thus accomplished the thing that she had required of him.

When it came to the king's ears that the thief's body was stolen away, he was sorely vexed. Wishing therefore, whatever it might cost, to catch the man who had contrived the trick, he had recourse (the priests said) to an expedient, which I can scarcely credit. He sent his own daughter to the common stews, with orders to admit all comers, but first to require every man to tell her what was the cleverest and wickedest thing he had done in the whole course of his life. If any one in reply told her the story of the thief, she was to lay hold of him, and not allow him to get away. The daughter did as her father willed, whereon the thief, who was well aware of the king's motive, felt a desire to outdo him in craft and cunning. Accordingly he contrived the following plan: He procured the corpse of a man lately dead, and cutting off one of the arms at the shoulder, put it under his dress, and so went to the king's daughter. When she put the question to him as she had done to all the rest, he replied, that the wickedest thing he had ever done was cutting off the head of his brother when he was caught in a trap in the king's treasury, and the cleverest was making the guards drunk and carrying off the body. As he spoke, the princess caught at him, but the thief took advantage of the darkness to hold out to her the hand of the corpse. Imagining it to be his own hand, she seized and held it fast; while the thief, leaving it in her grasp, made his escape by the door.

The king, when word was brought him of this fresh success, amazed at the sagacity and boldness of the man, sent messengers to all the towns in his dominions to proclaim a free pardon for the thief, and to promise him a rich reward, if he came and made himself known. The thief took the king at his word, and came boldly into his presence; whereupon Rhampsinitus, greatly admiring him, and looking on him as the most knowing of men, gave him his daughter in marriage. "The Egyptians," he said, "excelled all the rest of the world in wisdom, and this man excelled all other Egyptians."

122. The same king, I was also informed by the priests, afterwards descended alive into the region which the Greeks call Hades, and there played at dice with Demeter, sometimes winning and sometimes suffering defeat. After a while he returned to earth, and brought with him a golden napkin, a gift which he had received from the goddess. From this descent of Rhampsinitus into Hades, and return to earth again, the Egyptians, I was told, instituted a festival, which they certainly celebrated in my day. On what occasion it was that they instituted it, whether upon this or upon any other, I cannot determine. The following are the ceremonies: On a certain day in the year the priests weave a mantle, and binding the eyes of one of their number with a fillet, they put the mantle upon him, and take him with them into the roadway conducting to the temple of Demeter, when they depart and leave him to himself. Then the priest, thus blindfolded, is led (they say) by two wolves[66] to the temple of Demeter, distant three miles from the city, where he stays a while, after which he is brought back from the temple by the wolves, and left upon the spot where they first joined him.

123. Such as think the tales told by the Egyptians credible are free to accept them for history. For my own part, I propose to myself throughout my whole work faithfully to record the traditions of the several nations. The Egyptians maintain that Demeter and Dionysus[67] preside in the realms below. They were also the first to broach the opinion, that the soul of man is immortal, and that, when the body dies, it enters into the form of an animal [68] which is born at the moment, thence passing on from one animal into another, until it has circled through the forms of all the creatures which tenant the earth, the water, and the air, after which it enters again into a human frame, and is born anew. The whole period of the transmigration is (they say)

[66] The animal is not a wolf; it is a jackal, the emblem of Anubis.

[67] Answering to Isis and Osiris, who were the principal deities of Amenti, the Egyptian Hades.

[68] Herodotus has apparently confused the doctrine of immortality with metempsychosis.

3,000 years. There are Greek writers, some of an earlier, some of a later date, who have borrowed this doctrine from the Egyptians, and put it forward as their own. I could mention their names, but I abstain from doing so.

124. Till the death of Rhampsinitus, the priests said, Egypt was excellently governed, and flourished greatly; but after him Cheops succeeded to the throne,[69] and plunged into all manner of wickedness. He closed the temples, and forbade the Egyptians to offer sacrifice, compelling them instead to labour, one and all, in his service. Some were required to drag blocks of stone down to the Nile from the quarries in the Arabian range of hills; others received the blocks after they had been conveyed in boats across the river, and drew them to the range of hills called the Libyan. One hundred thousand men laboured constantly, and were relieved every three months by a fresh lot. It took ten years' oppression of the people to make the causeway for the conveyance of the stones, a work not much inferior, in my judgment, to the pyramid itself. This causeway is half a mile in length, sixty feet wide, and in height, at the highest part, forty-eight feet. It is built of polished stone, and is covered with carvings of animals. To make it took ten years, as I said—or rather to make the causeway, the works on the mound where the pyramid stands, and the underground chambers, which Cheops intended as vaults for his own use: these last were built on a sort of island, surrounded by water introduced from the Nile by a canal. The pyramid itself was twenty years in building. It is a square, 800 feet each way,[70] and the height the same, built entirely of polished stone, fitted together with the utmost care. The stones of which it is composed are none of them less than thirty feet in length.

125. The pyramid was built in steps, battlement-wise, as it is called, or, according to others, altar-wise. After laying the

[60] The pyramid builders are placed roughly 2,000 years too late.

[70] The dimensions of the great pyramid were—each face, 756 ft., now reduced to 732 ft.; original height when entire, 480 ft. 9 in., now 460 ft. 9 in.; angles at the base, 51° 50'; angle at the apex, 76° 20'; it covered an area of 571,536 square feet, now 535,824 square feet.

stones for the base, they raised the remaining stones to their places by means of machines formed of short wooden planks. The first machine raised them from the ground to the top of the first step. On this there was another machine, which received the stone upon its arrival, and conveyed it to the second step, whence a third machine advanced it still higher. Either they had as many machines as there were steps in the pyramid, or possibly they had but a single machine, which, being easily moved, was transferred from tier to tier as the stone rose—both accounts are given, and therefore I mention both. The upper portion of the pyramid was finished first, then the middle, and finally the part which was lowest and nearest the ground. There is an inscription in Egyptian characters[71] on the pyramid which records the quantity of radishes, onions, and garlic consumed by the labourers who constructed it; and I perfectly well remember that the interpreter who read the writing to me said that the money expended in this way was 1,600 talents of silver. If this then is a true record, what a vast sum must have been spent on the iron tools used in the work, and on the feeding and clothing of the labourers, considering the length of time the work lasted, which has already been stated, and the additional time—no small space, I imagine—which must have been occupied by the quarrying of the stones, their conveyance, and the formation of the underground apartments.

126. The wickedness of Cheops reached to such a pitch that, when he had spent all his treasures and wanted more, he sent his daughter to the stews, with orders to procure him a certain sum—how much I cannot say, for I was not told; she procured it, however, and at the same time, bent on leaving a monument which should perpetuate her own memory, she required each man who sought intercourse to make her a present of a stone towards the works which she contemplated. With these stones she built the pyramid which stands midmost of the three that

---

[71] This must have been in hieroglyphics, the monumental character. The outer stones being gone, it is impossible to verify, or disprove, the assertion of Herodotus, which, however, would have nothing improbable in it, provided it was not confined to the simple inscription he gives.

are in front of the great pyramid, measuring along each side 150 feet.

127. Cheops reigned, the Egyptians said, fifty years, and was succeeded at his demise by Chephren, his brother.

Chephren imitated the conduct of his predecessor, and, like him, built a pyramid, which did not, however, equal the dimensions of his brother's.[72] Of this I am certain, for I measured them both myself. It has no subterraneous apartments, nor any canal from the Nile to supply it with water as the other pyramid has. In that, the Nile water, introduced through an artificial duct, surrounds an island, where the body of Cheops is said to lie. Chephren built his pyramid close to the great pyramid of Cheops, and of the same dimensions, except that he lowered the height forty feet. For the basement he employed the many-coloured stone of Ethiopia. These two pyramids stand both on the same hill, an elevation not far s¹ ⋅ of 100 feet in height. The reign of Chephren lasted fifty-six years.

128. Thus the affliction of Egypt endured for the space of 106 years, during the whole of which time the temples were shut up and never opened. The Egyptians so detest the memory of these kings that they do not much like even to mention their names. Hence they commonly call the pyramids after Philitis, a shepherd who at that time fed his flocks about the place.

129. After Chephren, Mycerinus (they said) son of Cheops, ascended the throne. This prince disapproved the conduct of his father, re-opened the temples, and allowed the people, who were ground down to the lowest point of misery, to return to their occupations, and to resume the practice of sacrifice. His justice in the decision of causes was beyond that of all the former kings. The Egyptians praise him in this respect more highly than any of their other monarchs, declaring that he not only gave his judgments with fairness, but also, when any one was dissatisfied with his sentence, made compensation to him out of his own purse, and thus pacified his anger. Mycerinus had es-

---

[72] The measurements of the second pyramid are: present base, 690 ft.; former base, 707 ft. 9 in.; present perpendicular height (calculating the angle 52° 20′), 446 ft. 9 in.; former height, 454 ft. 3 in.

tablished his character for mildness, and was acting as I have described, when the stroke of calamity fell on him. First of all his daughter died, the only child that he possessed. Experiencing a bitter grief at this visitation, in his sorrow he conceived the wish to entomb his child in some unusual way. He therefore caused a cow to be made of wood, and after the interior had been hollowed out, he had the whole surface coated with gold; and in this novel tomb laid the dead body of his daughter.

130. The cow was not placed underground, but continued visible to my times: it was at Sais, in the royal palace, where it occupied a chamber richly adorned. Every day there are burnt before it aromatics of every kind; and all night long a lamp is kept burning in the apartment. In an adjoining chamber are statues which the priests at Sais declared to represent the various concubines of Mycerinus. They are colossal figures in wood, of the number of about twenty, and are represented naked. Whose images they really are, I cannot say—I can only repeat the account which was given to me.

131. Concerning these colossal figures and the sacred cow, there is also another tale narrated, which runs thus, "Mycerinus was enamoured of his daughter, and raped her—the damsel for grief hanged herself, and Mycerinus entombed her in the cow. Then her mother cut off the hands of all her tiring-maids, because they had sided with the father, and betrayed the child; and so the statues of the maids have no hands." All this is mere fable in my judgment, especially what is said about the hands of the colossal statues. I could plainly see that the figures had only lost their hands through the effect of time. They had dropped off, and were still lying on the ground about the feet of the statues.

132. As for the cow, the greater portion of it is hidden by a scarlet coverture; the head and neck, however, which are visible, are coated very thickly with gold, and between the horns there is a representation in gold of the orb of the sun. The figure is not erect, but lying down, with the limbs under the body; the dimensions being fully those of a large animal of the kind. Every year it is taken from the apartment where it is kept, and

exposed to the light of day—this is done at the season when the Egyptians beat themselves in honour of one of their gods, whose name I am unwilling to mention in connexion with such a matter. They say that the daughter of Mycerinus requested her father in her dying moments to allow her once a year to see the sun.

133. After the death of his daughter, Mycerinus was visited with a second calamity, of which I shall now proceed to give an account. An oracle reached him from the town of Buto, which said, "Six years only shall you live upon the earth, and in the seventh you shall end your days." Mycerinus, indignant, sent an angry message to the oracle, reproaching the god with his injustice, "My father and uncle," he said, "though they shut up the temples, took no thought of the gods, and destroyed multitudes of men, nevertheless enjoyed a long life; I, who am pious, am to die so soon!" There came in reply a second message from the oracle, "For this very reason is your life brought so quickly to a close. Egypt was fated to suffer affliction 150 years—the two kings who preceded you upon the throne understood this— you have not understood it." Mycerinus, when this answer reached him, perceiving that his doom was fixed, had lamps prepared, which he lighted every day at eventime, and feasted and enjoyed himself unceasingly both day and night, moving about in the marsh-country and the woods, and visiting all the places that he heard were agreeable sojourns. His wish was to prove the oracle false, by turning the nights into days, and so living twelve years in the space of six.

134. He too left a pyramid, but much inferior in size to his father's. It is a square, each side of which is 280 feet, and is built for half its height of the stone of Ethiopia. Some of the Greeks call it the work of Rhodopis the courtesan, but they report falsely. It seems to me that these persons cannot have any real knowledge who Rhodopis was; otherwise they would scarcely have ascribed to her a work on which uncounted treasures, so to speak, must have been expended. Rhodopis also lived during the reign of Amasis, not of Mycerinus, and was thus very many years later than the time of the kings who built the

pyramids. She was a Thracian by birth, and was the slave of
Iadmon, son of Hephaestopolis, a Samian. Aesop, the fable-
writer, was one of her fellow-slaves. That Aesop belonged to
Iadmon is proved by many facts—among others, by this. When
the Delphians, in obedience to the command of the oracle, made
proclamation that if any one claimed compensation for the murder of Aesop he should receive it, the person who at last came
forward was Iadmon, grandson of the former Iadmon, and he
received the compensation. Aesop therefore must certainly have
been the former Iadmon's slave.

135. Rhodopis really arrived in Egypt under the conduct of
Xantheus the Samian; she was brought there to exercise her
trade, but was redeemed for a vast sum by Charaxus, a Mytilenaean, the son of Scamandronymus, and brother of Sappho the
poetess.[73] After thus obtaining her freedom, she remained in
Egypt, and as she was very beautiful, amassed great wealth, for
a courtesan; not, however, enough to enable her to erect such a
work as this pyramid. Any one who likes may go and see to
what the tenth part of her wealth amounted, and he will thereby
learn that her riches must not be imagined to have been very
wonderfully great. Wishing to leave a memorial of herself in
Greece, she determined to have something made the like of
which was not to be found in any temple, and to offer it at the
shrine at Delphi. So she set apart a tenth of her possessions,
and purchased with the money a quantity of iron spits, such as
are fit for roasting oxen whole, whereof she made a present to
the oracle. They are still to be seen there, lying of a heap, behind the altar which the Chians dedicated, opposite the sanctuary. Naucratis seems somehow to be the place where such
women are most attractive. First there was this Rhodopis of
whom we have been speaking, so celebrated a person that
her name came to be familiar to all the Greeks; and, afterwards, there was another, called Archidice, notorious throughout Greece, though not so much talked of as her predecessor.

[73] Charaxus, the brother of Sappho, traded in wine from Lesbos, which
he was in the habit of taking to Naucratis. It is probable that both he
and Rhodopis were lampooned by Sappho.

Charaxus, after ransoming Rhodopis, returned to Mytilene, and was often lashed by Sappho in her poetry. But enough has been said on the subject of this courtesan.

136. After Mycerinus, the priests said, Asychis ascended the throne. He built the eastern gateway of the temple of Hephaestus, which in size and beauty far surpasses the other three. All the four gateways have figures graven on them, and a vast amount of architectural ornament, but the gateway of Asychis is by far the most richly adorned. In the reign of this king, money being scarce and commercial dealings straitened, a law was passed that the borrower might pledge his father's body to raise the sum whereof he had need. A proviso was appended to this law, giving the lender authority over the entire sepulchre of the borrower, so that a man who took up money under this pledge, if he died without paying the debt, could not obtain burial either in his own ancestral tomb, or in any other, nor could he during his lifetime bury in his own tomb any member of his family. The same king, desirous of eclipsing all his predecessors upon the throne, left as a monument of his reign a pyramid of brick. It bears an inscription, cut in stone, which runs thus, "Despise me not in comparison with the stone pyramids; for I surpass them all, as much as Zeus surpasses the other gods. A pole was plunged into a lake, and the mud which clave thereto was gathered; and bricks were made of the mud, and so I was formed." Such were the chief actions of this prince.

137. He was succeeded on the throne, they said, by a blind man, a native of Anysis, whose own name also was Anysis. Under him Egypt was invaded by a vast army of Ethiopians, led by Sabacos,[74] their king. The blind Anysis fled away to the marsh-country, and the Ethiopian was lord of the land for fifty years, during which his mode of rule was the following: When an Egyptian was guilty of an offence, his plan was not to punish him with death: instead of so doing, he sentenced him, according to the nature of his crime, to raise the ground to a greater or a less extent in the neighbourhood of the city to which he

[74] Herodotus mentions only one Sabacos who must represent the twenty-fifth dynasty (725-667 B.C.) of Manetho.

belonged. Thus the cities came to be elevated even more than they were before. As early as the time of Sesostris, they had been raised by those who dug the canals in his reign; this second elevation of the soil under the Ethiopian king gave them a very lofty position. Among the many cities which thus attained to a great elevation, none (I think) was raised so much as the town called Bubastis, where there is a temple of the goddess Bubastis, which well deserves to be described. Other temples may be grander, and may have cost more in the building, but there is none so pleasant to the eye as this of Bubastis. The Bubastis of the Egyptians is the same as the Artemis of the Greeks.

138. The following is a description of this edifice:[75] Excepting the entrance, the whole forms an island. Two artificial channels from the Nile, one on either side of the temple, encompass the building, leaving only a narrow passage by which it is approached. These channels are each 100 feet wide, and are thickly shaded with trees. The gateway is sixty feet in height, and is ornamented with figures cut upon the stone, nine feet high and well worthy of notice. The temple stands in the middle of the city, and is visible on all sides as one walks round it; for as the city has been raised up by embankment, while the temple has been left untouched in its original condition, you look down upon it wheresoever you are. A low wall runs round the enclosure, having figures engraved upon it, and inside there is a grove of beautiful tall trees growing round the shrine, which contains the image of the goddess. The enclosure is 200 yards in length, and the same in breadth. The entrance to it is by a road paved with stone for a distance of about three-eighths of a mile, which passes straight through the market-place with an easterly direction, and is 400 feet in width. Trees of an extraordinary height grow on each side of the road, which conducts from the temple of Bubastis to that of Hermes.

139. The Ethiopian finally quitted Egypt, the priests said, by a hasty flight under the following circumstances. He saw in

[75] This account of the position of the temple of Bubastis is very accurate.

his sleep a vision; a man stood by his side, and counselled him
to gather together all the priests of Egypt and cut every one of
them asunder. On this, according to the account which he himself gave, it came into his mind that the gods intended hereby
to lead him to commit an act of sacrilege, which would be sure
to draw down upon him some punishment either at the hands
of gods or men. So he resolved not to do the deed suggested
to him, but rather to retire from Egypt, as the time during
which it was fated that he should hold the country had now (he
thought) expired. For before he left Ethiopia he had been told
by the oracles which are venerated there, that he was to reign
fifty years over Egypt. The years were now fled, and the dream
had come to trouble him; he therefore of his own accord withdrew from the land.

140. As soon as Sabacos was gone, the blind king left the
marshes, and resumed the government. He had lived in the
marsh-region the whole time, having formed for himself an
island there by a mixture of earth and ashes. While he remained,
the natives had orders to bring him food unbeknown to the
Ethiopian, and latterly, at his request, each man had brought
him, with the food, a certain quantity of ashes. Before Amyrtaeus, no one was able to discover the site of this island, which
continued unknown to the kings of Egypt who preceded him on
the throne for the space of 700 years and more. The name
which it bears is Elbo. It is about a mile across in each direction.

141. The next king, I was told, was a priest of Hephaestus,
called Sethos.[76] This monarch despised and neglected the warrior class of the Egyptians, as though he did not need their
services. Among other indignities which he offered them, he took
from them the lands which they had possessed under all the
previous kings, consisting of twelve acres of choice land for each
warrior. Afterwards, therefore, when Sanacharib, king of the

---

[76] No mention is made by Herodotus of Bocchoris and the lists of Manetho omit the Asychis and Anysis of Herodotus. Sethos again, whom
Herodotus calls a contemporary of Sennacherib [Sanacharib] is unnoticed
in Manetho's lists. Herodotus probably has given to a priest of Pthah the
title of king.

Arabians and Assyrians, marched his vast army into Egypt, the
warriors one and all refused to come to his aid. On this the
monarch, greatly distressed, entered into the inner sanctuary,
and before the image of the god, bewailed the fate which impended over him. As he wept he fell asleep, and dreamt that the
god came and stood at his side, bidding him be of good cheer,
and go boldly forth and meet the Arabian host, which would
do him no hurt, as he himself would send those who should
help him. Sethos, then, relying on the dream, collected such of
the Egyptians as were willing to follow him, who were none of
them warriors, but traders, artisans, and market-people; and
with these marched to Pelusium, which commands the entrance
into Egypt, and there pitched his camp. As the two armies lay
here opposite one another, there came in the night a multitude
of field-mice, which devoured all the quivers and bow-strings
of the enemy, and ate the thongs by which they managed their
shields. Next morning they commenced their flight, and great
multitudes fell, as they had no arms with which to defend themselves. There stands to this day in the temple of Hephaestus, a
stone statue of Sethos, with a mouse in his hand, and an inscription to this effect, "Look on me, and learn to reverence the
gods."

142. Thus far I have spoken on the authority of the Egyptians and their priests. They declare that from their first king to
this last-mentioned monarch, the priest of Hephaestus, was a
period of 341 generations; such, at least, they say, was the
number both of their kings and of their high priests, during this
interval. Now 300 generations of men make 10,000 years, three
generations filling up the century; and the remaining forty-one
generations make 1,340 years. Thus the whole number of years
is 11,340; in which entire space, they said, no god had ever
appeared in a human form; nothing of this kind had happened
either under the former or under the later Egyptian kings. The
sun, however, had within this period of time, on four several
occasions, moved from his wonted course, twice rising where he
now sets, and twice setting where he now rises. Egypt was in no
degree affected by these changes; the productions of the land,

and of the river, remained the same; nor was there anything unusual either in the diseases or the deaths.

143. When Hecataeus the prose-writer[77] was at Thebes, and, discoursing of his genealogy, traced his descent to a god in the person of his sixteenth ancestor, the priests of Zeus did to him exactly as they afterwards did to me, though I made no boast of my family. They led me into the inner sanctuary, which is a spacious chamber, and showed me a multitude of colossal statues, in wood, which they counted up, and found to amount to the exact number they had said; the custom being for every high priest during his lifetime to set up his statue in the temple. As they showed me the figures and reckoned them up, they assured me that each was the son of the one preceding him; and this they repeated throughout the whole line, beginning with the representation of the priest last deceased, and continuing till they had completed the series. When Hecataeus, in giving his genealogy, mentioned a god as his sixteenth ancestor, the priests opposed their genealogy to his, going through this list, and refusing to allow that any man was ever born of a god. Their colossal figures were each, they said, a Piromis, born of a Piromis, and the number of them was 345; through the whole series Piromis followed Piromis, and the line did not run up either to a god or a hero. The word Piromis may be rendered "gentleman."

144. Of such a nature were, they said, the beings represented by these images—they were very far indeed from being gods. However, in the times anterior to them it was otherwise; then Egypt had gods for its rulers, who dwelt upon the earth with men, one being always supreme above the rest. The last of these was Horus, the son of Osiris, called by the Greeks Apollo. He

[77] This is the first distinct mention of Hecataeus, who had done far more than any other writer to pave the way for Herodotus. His works were of two kinds, geographical and historical. Under the former head he wrote a description of the known world, chiefly the result of his own travels, which must have been of considerable service to our author. Under the latter he wrote his genealogies, which were for the most part mythical, but contained occasionally important history.

deposed Typhon, and ruled over Egypt as its last god-king. Osiris is named Dionysus by the Greeks.

145. The Greeks regard Heracles, Dionysus, and Pan as the youngest of the gods. With the Egyptians, contrariwise, Pan is exceedingly ancient, and belongs to those whom they call "the eight gods," who existed before the rest. Heracles is one of the gods of the second order, who are known as "the twelve;" and Dionysus belongs to the gods of the third order, whom the twelve produced. I have already mentioned how many years intervened according to the Egyptians between the birth of Heracles and the reign of Amasis. From Pan to this period they count a still longer time; and even from Dionysus, who is the youngest of the three, they reckoned 15,000 years to the reign of that king. In these matters they say they cannot be mistaken, as they have always kept count of the years, and noted them in their registers. But from the present day to the time of Dionysus, the reputed son of Semele, daughter of Cadmus, is a period of not more than 1,600 years; to that of Heracles, son of Alcmena, is about 900; while to the time of Pan, son of Penelope (Pan, according to the Greeks, was her child by Hermes), is a shorter space than to the Trojan war, 800 years or thereabouts.

146. It is open to all to receive whichever he may prefer of these two traditions; my own opinion about them has been already declared. If indeed these gods had been publicly known, and had grown old in Greece, as was the case with Heracles, son of Amphitryon, Dionysus, son of Semele, and Pan, son of Penelope, it might have been said that the last-mentioned personages were men who bore the names of certain previously existing deities. But Dionysus, according to the Greek tradition, was no sooner born than he was sewn up in Zeus's thigh, and carried off to Nysa, above Egypt, in Ethiopia; and as to Pan, they do not even profess to know what happened to him after his birth. To me, therefore, it is quite manifest that the names of these gods became known to the Greeks after those of their other deities, and that they count their birth from the time when they first acquired a knowledge of them. Thus far my narrative rests on the accounts given by the Egyptians.

147. In what follows I have the authority, not of the Egyptians only, but of others also who agree with them. I shall speak likewise in part from my own observation. When the Egyptians regained their liberty after the reign of the priest of Hephaestus, unable to continue any while without a king, they divided Egypt into twelve districts, and set twelve kings over them. These twelve kings, united together by intermarriages, ruled Egypt in peace, having entered into engagements with one another not to depose any of their number, nor to aim at any aggrandisement of one above the rest, but to dwell together in perfect amity. Now the reason why they made these stipulations, and guarded with care against their infraction, was, because at the very first establishment of the twelve kingdoms, an oracle had declared, "That he among them who should pour in Hephaestus' temple a libation from a cup of bronze, would become monarch of the whole land of Egypt." Now the twelve held their meetings at all the temples.

148. To bind themselves yet more closely together, it seemed good to them to have a common monument. In pursuance of this resolution they made the Labyrinth which lies a little above lake Moeris, in the neighbourhood of the place called the city of Crocodiles. I visited this place, and found it to surpass description; for if all the walls and other great works of the Greeks could be put together in one, they would not equal, either for labour or expense, this Labyrinth; and yet the temple of Ephesus is a building worthy of note, and so is the temple of Samos. The pyramids likewise surpass description, and are severally equal to a number of the greatest works of the Greeks, but the Labyrinth surpasses the pyramids. It has twelve courts, all of them roofed, with gates exactly opposite to one another, six looking to the north, and six to the south. A single wall surrounds the entire building. There are two different sorts of chambers throughout—half under ground, half above ground, the latter built upon the former; the whole number of these chambers is 3,000, 1,500 of each kind. The upper chambers I myself passed through and saw, and what I say concerning them is from my own observation; of the underground chambers I

can only speak from report: for the keepers of the building could not be got to show them, since they contained (as they said) the sepulchres of the kings who built the Labyrinth, and also those of the sacred crocodiles. Thus it is from hearsay only that I can speak of the lower chambers. The upper chambers, however, I saw with my own eyes, and found them to excel all other human productions; for the passages through the houses, and the varied windings of the paths across the courts, excited in me infinite admiration, as I passed from the courts into chambers, and from the chambers into colonnades, and from the colonnades into fresh houses, and again from these into courts unseen before. The roof was throughout of stone, like the walls; and the walls were covered all over with figures; every court was surrounded with a colonnade, which was built of white stones exquisitely fitted together. At the corner of the Labyrinth stands a pyramid, 240 feet high, with large figures engraved on it; which is entered by a subterranean passage.

149. Wonderful as is the Labyrinth, the work called the lake Moeris,[78] which is close by the Labyrinth, is yet more astonishing. The measure of its circumference is sixty schoenes, or 400 miles, which is equal to the entire length of Egypt along the sea-coast. The lake stretches in its longest direction from north to south, and in its deepest parts is of the depth of 300 feet. It is manifestly an artificial excavation, for nearly in the centre there stand two pyramids, rising to the height of 300 feet above the surface of the water, and extending as far beneath, crowned each of them with a colossal statue sitting upon a throne. Thus these pyramids are 100 fathoms high, which is exactly a furlong of 600 feet: the fathom being six feet in length, or four cubits, which is the same thing, since a cubit measures six, and a foot four, palms. The water of the lake does not come out of the ground, which is here excessively dry, but is introduced by a canal from the Nile. The current sets for six months into the lake from the river, and for the next six months into the river from the lake. While it runs outward it returns a talent of silver

[78] Lake Moeris was used to regulate the flow of the Nile. Its size and the size of the statues are much exaggerated by Herodotus.

daily to the royal treasury from the fish that are taken, but
when the current is the other way the return sinks to one-third
of that sum.

150. The natives told me that there was a subterranean passage from this lake to the Libyan Syrtis, running westward into
the interior by the hills above Memphis. As I could not anywhere see the earth which had been taken out when the excavation was made, and I was curious to know what had become
of it, I asked the Egyptians who live closest to the lake where
the earth had been put. The answer that they gave me I readily
accepted as true, since I had heard of the same thing being
done in Nineveh of the Assyrians. There, once upon a time,
certain thieves having formed a plan to get into their possession
the vast treasures of Sardanapalus, the Ninevite king, which
were laid up in subterranean treasuries, proceeded to tunnel
a passage from the house where they lived into the royal palace,
calculating the distance and the direction. At nightfall they took
the earth from the excavation and carried it to the river Tigris,
which ran by Nineveh, continuing to get rid of it in this manner
until they had accomplished their purpose. It was exactly in the
same way that the Egyptians disposed of the mould from their
excavation, except that they did it by day and not by night;
for as fast as the earth was dug, they carried it to the Nile,
which they knew would disperse it far and wide. Such was the
account which I received of the formation of this lake.

151. The twelve kings for some time dealt honourably by
one another, but at length it happened that on a certain occasion, when they had met to worship in the temple of Hephaestus, the high-priest on the last day of the festival, in bringing
forth the golden goblets from which they were wont to pour the
libations, mistook the number, and brought eleven goblets only
for the twelve princes. Psammetichus was standing last, and
being left without a cup, he took his helmet, which was of
bronze, from off his head, stretched it out to receive the liquor,
and so made his libation. All the kings were accustomed to wear
helmets, and all indeed wore them at this very time. Nor was
there any crafty design in the action of Psammetichus. The

eleven, however, when they came to consider what had been done, and bethought them of the oracle which had declared that he who, of the twelve, should pour a libation from a cup of bronze, the same would be king of the whole land of Egypt, doubted at first if they should not put Psammetichus to death. Finding, however, upon examination, that he had acted in the matter without any guilty intent, they did not think it would be just to kill him; but determined, instead, to strip him of the chief part of his power and to banish him to the marshes, forbidding him to leave them, or to hold any communication with the rest of Egypt.

152. This was the second time that Psammetichus had been driven into banishment. On a former occasion he had fled from Sabacos the Ethiopian, who had put his father Necos to death; and had taken refuge in Syria, from whence, after the retirement of the Ethiop in consequence of his dream, he was brought back by the Egyptians of the Saitic nome. Now it was his ill-fortune to be banished a second time by the eleven kings, on account of the libation which he had poured from his helmet; on this occasion he fled to the marshes. Feeling that he was an injured man, and designing to avenge himself upon his persecutors, Psammetichus sent to the city of Buto, where there is an oracle of Leto, the most veracious of all the oracles of the Egyptians, and having inquired concerning means of vengeance, received for answer, "Vengeance would come from the sea, when brazen men should appear." Great was his incredulity when this answer arrived, for never, he thought, would brazen men arrive to be his helpers. However, not long afterwards certain Carians and Ionians, who had left their country on a voyage of plunder, were carried by stress of weather to Egypt, where they disembarked, all equipped in their brazen armour, and were seen by the natives, one of whom carried the tidings to Psammetichus, and, as he had never before seen men clad in brass, he reported that brazen men had come from the sea and were plundering the plain. Psammetichus, perceiving at once that the oracle was accomplished, made friendly advances to the strangers, and engaged them, by splendid promises, to enter into his service. He

then, with their aid and that of the Egyptians who espoused his cause, attacked the eleven and vanquished them.

153. When Psammetichus had thus become sole monarch of Egypt, he built the southern gateway of the temple of Hephaestus in Memphis, and also a court for Apis, in which Apis is kept whenever he makes his appearance in Egypt. This court is opposite the gateway of Psammetichus, and is surrounded with a colonnade and adorned with a multitude of figures. Instead of pillars, the colonnade rests upon colossal statues, eighteen feet in height. The Greek name for Apis is Epaphus.

154. To the Ionians and Carians who had lent them their assistance Psammetichus assigned as abodes two places opposite to each other, one on either side of the Nile, which received the name of the Camps. He also made good all the splendid promises by which he had gained their support; and further, he entrusted to their care certain Egyptian children, whom they were to teach the language of the Greeks. These children, thus instructed, became the parents of the entire class of interpreters in Egypt. The Ionians and Carians occupied for many years the places assigned them by Psammetichus, which lay near the sea, a little below the city of Bubastis, on the Pelusiac mouth of the Nile.[79] King Amasis, long afterwards, removed the Greeks hence, and settled them at Memphis to guard him against the native Egyptians. From the date of the original settlement of these persons in Egypt, we Greeks, through our intercourse with them, have acquired an accurate knowledge of the several events in Egyptian history, from the reign of Psammetichus downwards; but before his time no foreigners had ever taken up their residence in that land. The docks where their vessels were laid up, and the ruins of their habitations, were still to be seen in my day at the place where they dwelt originally, before they were removed by Amasis. Such was the mode by which Psammetichus became master of Egypt.

155. I have already made mention more than once of the Egyptian oracle, and as it well deserves notice, I shall now pro-

---

[79] The site chosen for the Greek camps shows that they were thought necessary as a defence against foreign invasion from the eastward.

ceed to give an account of it more at length. It is a temple of Leto, situated in the midst of a great city on the Sebennytic mouth of the Nile, at some distance up the river from the sea. The name of the city, as I have before observed, is Buto; and in it are two other temples also, one of Apollo and one of Artemis. Leto's temple, which contains the oracle, is a spacious building with a gateway sixty feet in height. The most wonderful thing that was actually to be seen about this temple was a chapel in the enclosure made of a single stone, the length and height of which were the same, each wall being sixty feet square, and the whole a single block! Another block of stone formed the roof, and projected at the eaves to the extent of six feet.

156. This, as I have said, was what astonished me the most, of all the things that were actually to be seen about the temple. The next greatest marvel was the island called Chemmis. This island lies in the middle of a broad and deep lake close by the temple, and the natives declare that it floats. For my own part I did not see it float, or even move; and I wondered greatly, when they told me concerning it, whether there be really such a thing as a floating island.[80] It has a grand temple of Apollo built upon it, in which are three distinct altars. Palm-trees grow on it in great abundance, and many other trees, some of which bear fruit, while others are barren. The Egyptians tell the following story in connexion with this island, to explain the way in which it first came to float, "In former times, when the isle was still fixed and motionless, Leto, one of the eight gods of the first order, who dwelt in the city of Buto, where now she has her oracle, received Apollo as a sacred charge from Isis, and saved him by hiding him in what is now called the floating island. Typhon meanwhile was searching everywhere in hopes of finding the child of Osiris." (According to the Egyptians, Apollo and Artemis are the children of Dionysus and Isis; while Leto is their nurse and their preserver. They call Apollo, in their language, Horus; Demeter they call Isis; Artemis, Bubastis.

[80] Hecataeus had related the marvels of this island, which he called Chembis, without any appearance of incredulity. There is a tacit allusion to him in this passage.

From this Egyptian tradition, and from no other, it must have been that Aeschylus, the son of Euphorion, took the idea, which is found in none of the earlier poets, of making Artemis the daughter of Demeter.) The island, therefore, in consequence of this event, was first made to float. Such at least is the account which the Egyptians give.

157. Psammetichus ruled Egypt for fifty-four years, during twenty-nine of which he pressed the siege of Azotus without intermission, till finally he took the place. Azotus is a great town in Syria. Of all the cities that we know, none ever stood so long a siege.

158. Psammetichus left a son called Necos, who succeeded him upon the throne. This prince was the first to attempt the construction of the canal to the Red Sea, a work completed afterwards by Darius the Persian, the length of which is four days' journey, and the width such as to admit of two triremes being rowed along it abreast. The water is derived from the Nile, which the canal leaves a little above the city of Bubastis, near Patumus, the Arabian town, being continued thence until it joins the Red Sea. At first it is carried along the Arabian side of the Egyptian plain, as far as the chain of hills opposite Memphis, whereby the plain is bounded, and in which lie the great stone quarries; here it skirts the base of the hills running in a direction from west to east; after which it turns, and enters a narrow pass, trending southwards from this point, until it enters the Arabian Gulf. From the northern sea to that which is called the southern or Red Sea, the shortest and quickest passage, which is from Mount Casius, the boundary between Egypt and Syria, to the Gulf of Arabia, is a distance of exactly 115 miles.[81] But the way by the canal is very much longer, on account of the crookedness of its course. One hundred and twenty thousand of the Egyptians, employed upon the work in the reign of Necos, lost their lives in making the excavation. He

---

[81] The length of the canal was about eighty miles, or, if measured from the Bubastite branch to the Red Sea, about ninety-six. The shortest distance from the Mediterranean to the Red Sea overland is about seventy-six miles.

at length desisted from his undertaking, in consequence of an oracle which warned him that he was labouring for the barbarian. The Egyptians call by the name of barbarians all such as speak a language different from their own.

159. Necos, when he gave up the construction of the canal, turned all his thoughts to war, and set to work to build a fleet of triremes, some intended for service in the northern sea, and some for the navigation of the Red Sea. These last were built in the Arabian Gulf, where the dry docks in which they lay are still visible. These fleets he employed wherever he had occasion; while he also made war by land upon the Syrians, and defeated them in a pitched battle at Magdolus, after which he made himself master of Cadytis, a large city of Syria. The dress which he wore on these occasions he sent to Branchidae in Milesia, as an offering to Apollo. After having reigned in all sixteen years, Necos died, and at his death bequeathed the throne to his son Psammis.

160. In the reign of Psammis, ambassadors from Elis arrived in Egypt, boasting that their arrangements for the conduct of the Olympic games were the best and fairest that could be devised, and fancying that not even the Egyptians, who surpassed all other nations in wisdom, could add anything to their perfection. When these persons reached Egypt, and explained the reason of their visit, the king summoned an assembly of all the wisest of the Egyptians. They met, and the Eleans having given them a full account of all their rules and regulations with respect to the contests, said that they had come to Egypt for the express purpose of learning whether the Egyptians could improve the fairness of their regulations in any particular. The Egyptians considered a while, and then made inquiry, "If they allowed their own citizens to enter the lists?" The Eleans answered, "That the lists were open to all Greeks, whether they belonged to Elis or to any other state." Hereupon the Egyptians observed, "That if this were so, they departed from justice very widely, since it was impossible but that they would favour their own countrymen, and deal unfairly by foreigners. If therefore

they really wished to manage the games with fairness, and if this was the object of their coming to Egypt, they advised them to confine the contests to strangers, and allow no native of Elis to be a candidate." Such was the advice which the Egyptians gave to the Eleans.

161. Psammis reigned only six years. He attacked Ethiopia, and died almost directly afterwards. Apries, his son, succeeded him upon the throne, who, excepting Psammetichus, his great-grandfather, was the most prosperous of all the kings that ever ruled over Egypt. The length of his reign was twenty-five years, and in the course of it he marched an army to attack Sidon, and fought a battle with the king of Tyre by sea. When at length the time came that was fated to bring him woe, an occasion arose which I shall describe more fully in my Libyan history, only touching it very briefly here. An army despatched by Apries to attack Cyrene having met with a terrible reverse, the Egyptians laid the blame on him, imagining that he had deliberately sent the troops into the jaws of destruction. They believed he had wished a vast number of them to be slain, in order that he himself might reign with more security over the rest of the Egyptians. Indignant therefore at this usage, the soldiers who returned and the friends of the slain broke instantly into revolt.

162. Apries, on learning these circumstances, sent Amasis to the rebels, to appease the tumult by persuasion. Upon his arrival, as he was seeking to restrain the malcontents by his exhortations, one of them, coming behind him, put a helmet on his head, saying, as he put it on, that he thereby crowned him king. Amasis was not altogether displeased at the action, as his conduct soon made manifest: for no sooner had the insurgents agreed to make him actually their king, than he prepared to march with them against Apries. That monarch, on tidings of these events reaching him, sent Patarbemis, one of his courtiers, a man of high rank, to Amasis, with orders to bring him alive into his presence. Patarbemis, on arriving at the place where Amasis was, called on him to come back with him to the king,

whereupon Amasis farted and said, "Take that back to your master." When the envoy, notwithstanding this reply, persisted in his request, exhorting Amasis to obey the summons of the king, he answered that this was exactly what he had long been intending to do; Apries would have no reason to complain of him on the score of delay; he would shortly come himself to the king, and bring others with him. Patarbemis, upon this, comprehending the intention of Amasis, partly from his replies, and partly from the preparations which he saw in progress, departed hastily, wishing to inform the king with all speed of what was going on. Apries, however, when he saw him approaching without Amasis, fell into a paroxysm of rage; and not giving himself time for reflection, commanded the nose and ears of Patarbemis to be cut off. Then the rest of the Egyptians, who had hitherto sided with Apries, when they saw a man of such note among them so shamefully outraged, without a moment's hesitation went over to the rebels, and put themselves at the disposal of Amasis.

163. Apries, informed of this new calamity, armed his mercenaries, and led them against the Egyptians: this was a body of Carians and Ionians, numbering 30,000 men, which was now with him at Sais, where his palace stood—a vast building, well worthy of notice. The army of Apries marched out to attack the host of the Egyptians, while that of Amasis went forth to fight the strangers; and now both armies drew near the city of Momemphis, and prepared for the coming fight.

164. The Egyptians are divided into seven distinct classes—these are, the priests, the warriors, the cowherds, the swineherds, the tradesmen, the interpreters, and the boatmen. Their titles indicate their occupations. The warriors consist of Hermotybians and Calasirians, who come from different nomes, the whole of Egypt being parcelled out into districts bearing this name.

165. The following nomes furnish the Hermotybians—the nomes of Busiris, Sais, Chemmis, Papremis, that of the island called Prosopitis, and half of Natho. They number, when most

numerous, 160,000. None of them ever practises a trade, but all are given wholly to war.

166. The nomes of the Calasirians are different—they include the following: the nomes of Thebes, Bubastis, Aphthis, Tanis, Mendes, Sebennytus, Athribis, Pharbaethus, Thmuis, Onuphis, Anysis, and Myecphoris—this last nome consists of an island which lies over against the town of Bubastis. The Calasirians, when at their greatest number, have amounted to 250,000. Like the Hermotybians they are forbidden to pursue any trade, and devote themselves entirely to warlike exercises, the son following the father's calling.

167. Whether the Greeks borrowed from the Egyptians their notions about trade, like so many others, I cannot say for certain. I have remarked that the Thracians, the Scyths, the Persians, the Lydians, and almost all other barbarians, hold the citizens who practise trades, and their children, in less repute than the rest, while they esteem as noble those who keep aloof from handicrafts, and especially honour such as are given wholly to war. These ideas prevail throughout the whole of Greece, particularly among the Lacedaemonians. Corinth is the place where mechanics are least despised.

168. The warrior class in Egypt had certain special privileges in which none of the rest of the Egyptians participated except the priests. In the first place each man had twelve arurae[82] of land assigned him free from tax. (The arura is a square of a hundred Egyptian cubits, the Egyptian cubit being of the same length as the Samian.) All the warriors enjoyed this privilege together; but there were other advantages which came to each in rotation, the same man never obtaining them twice. A thousand Calasirians, and the same number of Hermotybians, formed in alternate years the body-guard of the king; and during their year of service these persons, besides their arurae, received a daily portion of meat and drink, consisting of five pounds of baked bread, two pounds of beef, and four cups of wine.

[82] The arura was about two-thirds of an English acre and was only a land measure.

169. When Apries, at the head of his mercenaries, and Amasis, in command of the whole native force of the Egyptians, en-
countered one another near the city of Momemphis, an engagement presently took place. The foreign troops fought bravely,
but were overpowered by numbers, in which they fell very far
short of their adversaries. It is said that Apries believed that
there was not a god who could cast him down from his eminence,
so firmly did he think that he had established himself in his
kingdom. But at this time the battle went against him, and,
his army being worsted, he fell into the enemy's hands, and was
brought back a prisoner to Sais, where he was lodged in what
had been his own house, but was now the palace of Amasis.
Amasis treated him with kindness, and kept him in the palace
for a while; but, finding his conduct blamed by the Egyptians,
who charged him with acting unjustly in preserving a man who
had shown himself so bitter an enemy both to them and him,
he gave Apries over into the hands of his former subjects, to
deal with as they chose. Then the Egyptians took him and
strangled him, but having so done, they buried him in the
sepulchre of his fathers. This tomb is in the temple of Athena,
very near the sanctuary, on the left hand as one enters. The
Saites buried all the kings who belonged to their nome inside
this temple; and thus it even contains the tomb of Amasis as
well as that of Apries and his family. The latter is not so close
to the sanctuary as the former, but still it is within the temple.
It stands in the court, and is a spacious cloister, built of stone,
and adorned with pillars carved so as to resemble palm-trees,
and with other sumptuous ornaments. Within the cloister is a
chamber with folding doors, behind which lies the sepulchre
of the king.

170. Here too, in this same precinct of Athena at Sais, is the
burial-place of one whom I think it not right to mention in such
a connexion.[83] It stands behind the temple, against the back-
wall, which it entirely covers. There are also some large stone

---

[83] This was Osiris, in honor of whom many ceremonies were performed
at Sais, as in some other towns.

obelisks in the enclosure, and there is a lake near them, adorned with an edging of stone. In form it is circular, and in size, as it seemed to me, about equal to the lake in Delos called the Hoop.

171. On this lake it is that the Egyptians represent by night his sufferings[84] whose name I refrain from mentioning, and this representation they call their Mysteries. I know well the whole course of the proceedings in these ceremonies, but they shall not pass my lips. So too, with regard to the mysteries of Demeter, which the Greeks term the Thesmophoria, I know them, but I shall not mention them, except so far as may be done without impiety. The daughters of Danaus brought these rites from Egypt, and taught them to the Pelasgic women of the Peloponnese. Afterwards when the inhabitants of the peninsula were driven from their homes by the Dorians, the rites perished. Only in Arcadia, where the natives remained and were not compelled to migrate, their observance continued.

172. After Apries had been put to death in the way that I have described above, Amasis reigned over Egypt. He belonged to the nome of Sais, being a native of the town called Siouph. At first his subjects looked down on him and held him in small esteem, because he had been a mere private person, and of a house of no great distinction: but after a time Amasis succeeded in reconciling them to his rule, not by severity, but by cleverness. Among his other splendour he had a golden foot-pan, in which his guests and himself were wont upon occasion to wash their feet. This vessel he caused to be broken in pieces, and

[84] The Egyptians and the Syrians had each the myth of a dying god; but they selected a different phenomenon for its basis; the former the Nile, the Syrians, the aspect of nature, or the sun; which, during one part of the year manifesting its vivifying effects on the earth's surface, seemed to die on the approach of winter; and hence the notion of a god, who was both mortal and immortal. The sufferings and death of Osiris were the great mystery of the Egyptian religion; and some traces of it are perceptible among other people of antiquity. His being the divine goodness, and the abstract idea of 'good,' his manifestation upon earth, his death, and resurrection, and his office as judge of the dead in a future state, are not less remarkable than that notion of the Egyptians mentioned by Plutarch that a woman might conceive by the approach of some divine spirit.

made of the gold an image of one of the gods, which he set up in the most public place in the whole city; upon which the Egyptians flocked to the image, and worshipped it with the utmost reverence. Amasis, finding this was so, called an assembly, and opened the matter to them, explaining how the image had been made of the foot-pan, wherein they had been wont formerly to wash their feet, vomit and piss, yet now it was greatly reverenced. "And truly," he went on to say, "it had gone with him as with the foot-pan. If he was a private person formerly, yet now he had come to be their king. And so he bade them honour and reverence him." Such was the mode in which he won over the Egyptians, and brought them to be content to do him service.

173. The following was the general habit of his life: From early dawn to the time when the market place is wont to fill, he sedulously transacted all the business that was brought before him; during the remainder of the day he drank and joked with his guests, passing the time in witty and, sometimes, scarce seemly conversation. It grieved his friends that he should thus demean himself, and accordingly some of them chid him on the subject, saying to him, "O king, you demean your royal dignity while you allow yourself such levities. You should sit in state upon a stately throne, and busy yourself with affairs the whole day long. So would the Egyptians feel that a great man rules them, and you would be better spoken of. But now you conduct yourself in no kingly fashion." Amasis answered them thus, "Bowmen bend their bows when they wish to shoot; unbrace them when the shooting is over. Were they kept always strung they would break, and fail the archer in time of need. So it is with men. If they give themselves constantly to serious work, and never indulge a while in pastime or sport, they lose their senses, and become mad or moody. Knowing this, I divide my life between pastime and business." Thus he answered his friends.

174. It is said that Amasis, even while he was a private man, had the same tastes for drinking and jesting, and was averse to engaging in any serious employment. He lived in constant

feasts and revelries, and whenever his means failed him, he roamed about and robbed people. On such occasions the persons from whom he had stolen would bring him, if he denied the charge, before the nearest oracle; sometimes, the oracle would pronounce him guilty of the theft, at other times it would acquit him. When afterwards he came to be king, he neglected the temples of such gods as had declared that he was not a thief, and neither contributed to their adornment, nor frequented them for sacrifice; since he regarded them as utterly worthless, and their oracles as wholly false: but the gods who had detected his guilt he considered to be true gods whose oracles did not deceive; and these he honoured exceedingly.

175. First of all, therefore, he built the gateway of the temple of Athena at Sais, which is an astonishing work, far surpassing all other buildings of the same kind both in extent and height, and built with stones of rare size and excellency. In the next place, he presented to the temple a number of large colossal statues, and several prodigious man-headed sphinxes, besides certain stones for the repairs, of a most extraordinary size. Some of these he got from the quarries over against Memphis, but the largest were brought from Elephantine, which is twenty days' voyage from Sais. Of all these wonderful masses that which I most admire is a chamber made of a single stone, which was quarried at Elephantine. It took three years to convey this block from the quarry to Sais; and in the conveyance were employed no fewer than 2,000 labourers, who were all from the class of boatmen. The length of this chamber on the outside is thirty-one feet, its breadth twenty-one feet, and its height twelve feet. The measurements inside are the following: the length, twenty-eight feet; the breadth, eighteen feet; and the height, nine feet. It lies near the entrance of the temple, where it was left in consequence of the following circumstance: It happened that the architect, just as the stone had reached the spot where it now stands, heaved a sigh, considering the length of time that the removal had taken, and feeling wearied with the heavy toil. The sigh was heard by Amasis, who regarding it as an omen, would not allow the chamber to be moved forward

any further. Some, however, say, that one of the workmen engaged at the levers was crushed and killed by the mass, and that
this was the reason of its being left where it now stands.

176. To the other temples of much note Amasis also made
magnificent offerings—at Memphis, for instance, he gave the
recumbent colossus[85] in front of the temple of Hephaestus,
which is seventy-five feet long. Two other colossal statues stand
on the same base, each twenty feet high, carved in the stone of
Ethiopia, one on either side of the temple. There is also a stone
colossus of the same size at Sais, recumbent like that at Memphis. Amasis finally built the temple of Isis at Memphis, a vast
structure, well worth seeing.

177. It is said that the reign of Amasis was the most prosperous time that Egypt ever saw,[86] the river was more liberal to
the land, and the land brought forth more abundantly for the
service of man than had ever been known before; while the
number of inhabited cities was not less than 20,000. It was this
king Amasis who established the law that every Egyptian
should appear once a year before the governor of his nome,[87]
and show his means of living; or, failing to do so, and to prove
that he got an honest livelihood, should be put to death. Solon
the Athenian borrowed this law from the Egyptians, and im-

[85] It was an unusual position for an Egyptian statue; and this, as well
as the other at Memphis, and the monolith, may have been left on the
ground, in consequence of the troubles which came upon Egypt at the
time; and which the Egyptians concealed from Herodotus.

[86] This can only relate to the internal state of the country; and what
Herodotus afterwards says shows this was his meaning. The flourishing
internal condition of Egypt is certainly proved by the monuments, and
the wealth of private individuals was very remarkable; but Egypt had lost
all its power abroad, and had long been threatened, if not actually invaded, by the Babylonians. Indeed the civil war between Apries and
Amasis had probably given Nebuchadnezzar an opportunity for interfering
in Egypt.

[87] Each nome was governed by a monarch. Herodotus attributes this
law to Amasis; but it appears to have been much older; since we find in
the sculptures of the eighteenth dynasty bodies of men presenting themselves before the magistrates for registration.

posed it on his countrymen, who have observed it ever since. It is indeed an excellent custom.

178. Amasis was partial to the Greeks, and among other favours which he granted them, gave to such as liked to settle in Egypt the city of Naucratis for their residence. To those who only wished to trade upon the coast, and did not want to fix their abode in the country, he granted certain lands where they might set up altars and erect temples to the gods. Of these temples the grandest and most famous, which is also the most frequented, is that called the Hellenium. It was built conjointly by the Ionians, Dorians, and Aeolians, the following cities taking part in the work, the Ionian states of Chios, Teos, Phocaea, and Clazomenae; Rhodes, Cnidus, Halicarnassus, and Phaselis of the Dorians; and Mytilene of the Aeolians. These are the states to whom the temple belongs, and they have the right of appointing the governors of the port; the other cities which claim a share in the building, claim what in no sense belongs to them. Three nations, however, consecrated for themselves separate temples, the Aeginetans one to Zeus, the Samians to Hera, and the Milesians to Apollo.

179. In ancient times there was no trading port but Naucratis in the whole of Egypt; and if a person entered one of the other mouths of the Nile, he was obliged to swear, that he had not come there of his own free will. Having so done, he was bound to sail in his ship to the Canobic mouth, or, were that impossible owing to contrary winds, he must take his wares by boat all round the Delta, and so bring them to Naucratis, which had an exclusive privilege.

180. It happened in the reign of Amasis that the temple of Delphi had been accidentally burnt,[88] and the Amphictyons had contracted to have it rebuilt for 300 talents, of which sum one-fourth was to be furnished by the Delphians. Under these circumstances the Delphians went from city to city begging contri-

---

[88] The temple at Delphi was burnt in the year 548 B.C., consequently in the twenty-first year of Amasis. Herodotus is apparently refuting the story that it was purposely destroyed by the Pisistratidae.

butions, and among their other wanderings came to Egypt, and
asked for help. From few other places did they obtain so much
—Amasis gave them a thousand talents of alum, and the Greek
settlers, twenty minae.

181. A league was concluded by Amasis with the Cyrenaeans,
by which Cyrene and Egypt became close friends and allies. He
likewise took a wife from that city, either as a sign of his
friendly feeling, or because he had a fancy to marry a Greek
woman. However this may be, certain it is that he espoused a
lady of Cyrene, by name Ladice, daughter, some say, of Battus
or Arcesilaus, the king—others, of Critobulus, one of the chief
citizens. When Amasis went to bed with her he was unable to
have intercourse with her, though he had shown no lack of viril-
ity with other women. Astonished the king thus addressed his
bride, "Woman, you have certainly bewitched me—now therefore be sure you shall perish more miserably than ever woman
perished yet." Ladice protested her innocence, but in vain; Amasis was not softened. Hereupon she made a vow internally, that
if he had intercourse with her that night (for no longer time was
allowed her), she would present a statue to the temple of Aphrodite at Cyrene. Immediately she obtained her wish, and the
king's weakness disappeared. Amasis loved her greatly ever
after, and Ladice performed her vow. The statue which she
caused to be made, and sent to Cyrene, continued there to my
day, standing with its face looking outwards from the city.
Ladice herself, when Cambyses conquered Egypt, suffered no
wrong; for Cambyses, on learning of her who she was, sent her
back unharmed to her country.

182. Besides the marks of favour already mentioned, Amasis also enriched with offerings many of the Greek temples. He
sent to Cyrene a statue of Athena covered with plates of gold,
and a painted likeness of himself. To the Athena of Lindus he
gave two statues in stone, and a linen corslet well worth inspection. To the Samian Hera he presented two statues of himself,
made in wood, which stood in the great temple to my day, behind the doors. Samos was honoured with these gifts on account
of the bond of friendship subsisting between Amasis and Polyc-

rates, the son of Aeaces; Lindus, for no such reason, but because of the tradition that the daughters of Danaus touched there in their flight from the sons of Aegyptus, and built the temple of Athena. Such were the offerings of Amasis. He likewise took Cyprus, which no man had ever done before, and compelled it to pay him a tribute.

The Third Book, Entitled

THALIA

1. The above-mentioned Amasis was the Egyptian king against whom Cambyses, son of Cyrus, made his expedition; and with him went an army composed of the many nations under his rule, among them being included both Ionic and Aeolic Greeks. The reason of the invasion was the following.[1] Cambyses, by the advice of a certain Egyptian, who was angry with Amasis for having torn him from his wife and children, and given him over to the Persians, had sent a herald to Amasis to ask his daughter in marriage. His adviser was a physician, whom Amasis, when Cyrus had requested that he would send him the most skilful of all the Egyptian eye-doctors, singled out as the best from the whole number. Therefore the Egyptian bore Amasis a grudge, and his reason for urging Cambyses to ask the hand of the king's daughter was, that if he complied, it might cause him annoyance; if he refused, it might make Cambyses his enemy. When the message came, Amasis, who much dreaded the power of the Persians, was greatly perplexed whether to give his daughter or no; for that Cambyses did not intend to make her his wife, but would only receive her as his concubine, he knew for certain. He therefore cast the matter in his mind, and finally resolved what he would do. There was a daughter of

[1] Herodotus has already told us that the subjugation of Egypt was among the designs of Cyrus (i. 153). Indeed, two motives of a public character, each by itself enough to account for the attack, urged the Persian arms in this direction; revenge, and the lust of conquest.

the late king Apries, named Nitetis,[2] a tall and beautiful woman, the last survivor of that royal house. Amasis took this woman, and, decking her out with gold and costly garments, sent her to Persia as if she had been his own child. Some time afterwards, Cambyses, as he gave her an embrace, happened to call her by her father's name, whereupon she said to him, "I see, O king, you know not how you have been cheated by Amasis; who took me, and, tricking me out with gauds, sent me to you as his own daughter. But I am in truth the child of Apries, who was his lord and master, until he rebelled against him, together with the rest of the Egyptians, and put him to death." It was this speech, and the cause of quarrel it disclosed, which roused the anger of Cambyses, son of Cyrus, and brought his arms upon Egypt. Such is the Persian story.

2. The Egyptians, however, claim Cambyses as belonging to them, declaring that he was the son of this Nitetis. It was Cyrus, they say, and not Cambyses, who sent to Amasis for his daughter. But here they mis-state the truth. Acquainted as they are beyond all other men with the laws and customs of the Persians, they cannot but be well aware, first, that it is not the Persian custom to allow a bastard to reign when there is a legitimate heir; and next, that Cambyses was the son of Cassandane, the daughter of Pharnaspes, an Achaemenian, and not of this Egyptian. But the fact is, that they pervert history, in order to claim relationship with the house of Cyrus. Such is the truth of this matter.

3. I have also heard another account, which I do not at all believe, that a Persian lady came to visit the wives of Cyrus, and seeing how tall and beautiful were the children of Cassandane, then standing by, broke out into loud praise of them, and admired them exceedingly. But Cassandane, wife of Cyrus, answered, "Though such the children I have borne him, yet Cyrus

---

[2] This account, which Herodotus says was that of the Persians, is utterly inadmissible. That of the Egyptians, who pretended that Cambyses was the son of a daughter of Apries, is quite eastern, and resembles the Persian story of Alexander the Great having been born of a Persian princess.

slights me and gives all his regard to the newcomer from Egypt."
Thus did she express her vexation on account of Nitetis; whereupon Cambyses, the eldest of her boys, exclaimed, "Mother,
when I am a man, I will turn Egypt upside down for you." He
was but ten years old, as the tale runs, when he said this, and
astonished all the women, yet he never forgot it afterwards; and
on this account, they say, when he came to be a man, and
mounted the throne, he made his expedition against Egypt.

4. There was another matter, quite distinct, which helped to
bring about the expedition. One of the mercenaries of Amasis, a
Halicarnassian, Phanes by name, a man of good judgment, and
a brave warrior, dissatisfied for some reason or other with his
master, deserted the service, and, taking ship, fled to Cambyses,
wishing to get speech with him. As he was a person of no small
account among the mercenaries, and one who could give very
exact intelligence about Egypt, Amasis, anxious to recover him,
ordered that he should be pursued. He gave the matter in charge
to one of the most trusty of the eunuchs, who went in quest of
the Halicarnassian in a vessel of war. The eunuch caught him
in Lycia, but did not contrive to bring him back to Egypt, for
Phanes outwitted him by making his guards drunk, and then
escaping into Persia. Now it happened that Cambyses was meditating his attack on Egypt, and doubting how he might best
pass the desert, when Phanes arrived, and not only told him all
the secrets of Amasis, but advised him also how the desert
might be crossed. He counselled him to send an ambassador to
the king of the Arabs, and ask him for safe-conduct through the
region.

5. Now the only entrance into Egypt is by this desert: the
country from Phoenicia to the borders of the city Cadytis belongs to the people called the Palestine Syrians; from Cadytis,
which it appears to me is a city almost as large as Sardis, the
marts upon the coast till you reach Ienysus are the Arabian
king's; after Ienysus the Syrians again come in, and extend to
Lake Serbonis, near the place where Mount Casius juts out into
the sea. At Lake Serbonis, where the tale goes that Typhon hid

himself, Egypt begins. Now the whole tract between Ienysus on
the one side, and Lake Serbonis and Mount Casius on the other,
and this is no small space, being as much as three days' journey,
is a dry desert without a drop of water.

6. I shall now mention a thing of which few of those who sail
to Egypt are aware. Twice a year wine is brought into Egypt
from every part of Greece, as well as from Phoenicia, in earthen
jars; and yet in the whole country you will nowhere see, as I
may say, a single jar. What then, every one will ask, becomes of
the jars? This, too, I will clear up. The mayor of each town has
to collect the wine-jars within his district, and to carry them to
Memphis, where they are all filled with water by the Mem-
phians, who then convey them to this desert tract of Syria. And
so it comes to pass that all the jars which enter Egypt year by
year, and are there put up to sale, find their way into Syria,
whither all the old jars have gone before them.

7. This way of keeping the passage into Egypt fit for use by
storing water there, was begun by the Persians so soon as they
became masters of that country. As, however, at the time of
which we speak the tract had not yet been so supplied, Cambyses took the advice of his Halicarnassian guest, and sent messengers to the Arabian to beg a safe-conduct through the region.
The Arabian granted his prayer, and each pledged faith to the
other.

8. The Arabs keep such pledges more religiously than almost
any other people. They plight faith with the forms following.
When two men would swear a friendship, they stand on each
side of a third: he with a sharp stone makes a cut on the inside
of the hand of each near the middle finger, and, taking a piece
from their dress, dips it in the blood of each, and moistens therewith seven stones lying in the midst, calling the while on Dionysus and Heavenly Aphrodite. After this, the man who makes
the pledge commends the stranger (or the citizen, if citizen he
be) to all his friends, and they deem themselves bound to stand
to the engagement. They have but these two gods, to wit,
Dionysus and Heavenly Aphrodite; and they say that in their

mode of cutting the hair, they follow Dionysus. Now their practice is to cut it in a ring, away from the temples. Dionysus they call in their language Orotal, and Aphrodite, Alilat.

9. When, therefore, the Arabian had pledged his faith to the messengers of Cambyses, he straightway contrived as follows: he filled a number of camels' skins with water, and loading therewith all the live camels that he possessed, drove them into the desert, and awaited the coming of the army. This is the more likely of the two tales that are told. The other is an improbable story, but, as it is related, I think that I ought not to pass it by. There is a great river in Arabia, called the Corys, which empties itself into the Red Sea. The Arabian king, they say, made a pipe of the skins of oxen and other beasts, reaching from this river all the way to the desert, and so brought the water to certain cisterns which he had had dug in the desert to receive it. It is a twelve days' journey from the river to this desert tract. And the water, they say, was brought through three different pipes to three separate places.

10. Psammenitus, son of Amasis, lay encamped at the mouth of the Nile, called the Pelusiac, awaiting Cambyses. For Cambyses, when he went up against Egypt, found Amasis no longer in life: he had died after ruling Egypt forty-four years, during all which time no great misfortune had befallen him. When he died, his body was embalmed, and buried in the tomb which he had himself caused to be made in the temple. After his son Psammenitus had mounted the throne, a strange prodigy occurred in Egypt: Rain fell at Egyptian Thebes, a thing which never happened before, and which, to the present time, has never happened again, as the Thebans themselves testify. In Upper Egypt it does not usually rain at all; but on this occasion, rain fell at Thebes in small drops.

11. The Persians crossed the desert, and, pitching their camp close to the Egyptians, made ready for battle. Hereupon the mercenaries in the pay of Psammenitus, who were Greeks and Carians, full of anger against Phanes for having brought a foreign army upon Egypt, bethought themselves of a mode whereby they might be revenged on him. Phanes had left sons in Egypt.

The mercenaries took these, and leading them to the camp, displayed them before the eyes of their father; after which they brought out a bowl, and, placing it in the space between the two hosts, they led the sons of Phanes, one by one, to the vessel, and slew them over it. When the last was dead, water and wine were poured into the bowl, and all the soldiers tasted of the blood, and so they went to the battle. Stubborn was the fight which followed, and it was not till vast numbers had been slain upon both sides, that the Egyptians turned and fled.

12. On the field where this battle was fought I saw a very wonderful thing which the natives pointed out to me. The bones of the slain lie scattered upon the field in two lots, those of the Persians in one place by themselves, as the bodies lay at the first—those of the Egyptians in another place apart from them: if, then, you strike the Persian skulls, even with a pebble, they are so weak, that you break a hole in them; but the Egyptian skulls are so strong, that you may smite them with a stone and you will scarcely break them in. They gave me the following reason for this difference, which seemed to me likely enough: The Egyptians (they said) from early childhood have the head shaved, and so by the action of the sun the skull becomes thick and hard. The same cause prevents baldness in Egypt, where you see fewer bald men than in any other land. Such, then, is the reason why the skulls of the Egyptians are so strong. The Persians, on the other hand, have feeble skulls, because they keep themselves shaded from the first, wearing turbans upon their heads. What I have here mentioned I saw with my own eyes, and I observed also the like at Papremis, in the case of the Persians who were killed with Achaemenes, the son of Darius, by Inarus the Libyan.

13. The Egyptians who fought in the battle, no sooner turned their backs upon the enemy, than they fled away in complete disorder to Memphis, where they shut themselves up within the walls. Hereupon Cambyses sent a Mytilenaean vessel, with a Persian herald on board, who was to sail up the Nile to Memphis, and invite the Egyptians to a surrender. They, however, when they saw the vessel entering the town, poured forth in

crowds from the castle, destroyed the ship, and, tearing the
crew limb from limb, so bore them into the fortress. After this
Memphis was besieged, and in due time surrendered. Hereon
the Libyans who bordered upon Egypt, fearing the fate of that
country, gave themselves up to Cambyses without a battle,
made an agreement to pay tribute to him, and forthwith sent
him gifts. The Cyrenaeans too, and the Barcaeans, having the
same fear as the Libyans, immediately did the like. Cambyses
received the Libyan presents very graciously, but not so the
gifts of the Cyrenaeans. They had sent no more than five hundred minae of silver, which Cambyses, I imagine, thought too
little. He therefore snatched the money from them, and with his
own hands scattered it among his soldiers.

14. Ten days after the fort had fallen, Cambyses resolved to
try the spirit of Psammenitus, the Egyptian king, whose whole
reign had been but six months. He therefore had him set in one
of the suburbs, and many other Egyptians with him, and there
subjected him to insult. First of all he sent his daughter out
from the city, clothed in the garb of a slave, with a pitcher to
draw water. Many virgins, the daughters of the chief nobles, accompanied her, wearing the same dress. When the damsels came
opposite the place where their fathers sat, shedding tears and
uttering cries of woe, the fathers, all but Psammenitus, wept
and wailed in return, grieving to see their children in so sad a
plight; but he, when he had looked and seen, bent his head towards the ground. In this way passed by the water-carriers.
Next to them came Psammenitus' son, and 2,000 Egyptians of
the same age with him—all of them having ropes round their
necks and bridles in their mouths—and they too passed by on
their way to suffer death for the murder of the Mytilenaeans
who were destroyed, with their vessel, in Memphis. For so had
the royal judges given their sentence, for each Mytilenaean ten
of the noblest Egyptians must forfeit life. King Psammenitus
saw the train pass on, and knew his son was being led to death,
but, while the other Egyptians who sat around him wept and
were sorely troubled, he showed no further sign than when he
saw his daughter. And now, when they too were gone, it chanced

that one of his former boon-companions, a man advanced in years, who had been stripped of all that he had and was a beggar, came where Psammenitus, son of Amasis, and the rest of the Egyptians were, asking alms from the soldiers. At this sight the king burst into tears, and, weeping out aloud, called his friend by his name, and smote himself on the head. Now there were some who had been set to watch Psammenitus and see what he would do as each train went by; so these persons went and told Cambyses of his behaviour. Then he, astonished at what was done, sent a messenger to Psammenitus, and questioned him, saying, "Psammenitus, Cambyses asks you why, when you saw your daughter brought to shame, and your son on his way to death, you neither cried nor wept, while to a beggar, who is, he hears, a stranger to your race, you gave those marks of honour." To this question Psammenitus made answer, "O son of Cyrus, my own misfortunes were too great for tears; but the woe of my friend deserved them. When a man falls from splendour and plenty into beggary at the threshold of old age, one may well weep for him." When the messenger brought back this answer, Cambyses owned it was just; Croesus, likewise, the Egyptians say, burst into tears—for he too had come into Egypt with Cambyses—and the Persians who were present wept. Even Cambyses himself was touched with pity, and he forthwith gave an order, that the son of Psammenitus should be spared from the number of those appointed to die, and Psammenitus himself brought from the suburb into his presence.

15. The messengers were too late to save the life of Psammenitus' son, who had been cut in pieces the first of all; but they took Psammenitus himself and brought him before the king. Cambyses allowed him to live with him, and gave him no more harsh treatment; indeed, could he have kept from meddling with affairs, he might have recovered Egypt, and ruled it as governor. For the Persian custom is to treat the sons of kings with honour, and even to give their fathers' kingdoms to the children of such as revolt from them. There are many cases from which one may collect that this is the Persian rule, and especially those of Pausiris and Thannyras. Thannyras was son

of Inarus the Libyan, and was allowed to succeed his father, as was also Pausiris, son of Amyrtaeus; yet certainly no two persons ever did the Persians more damage than Amyrtaeus and Inarus.[3] In this case Psammenitus plotted evil, and received his reward accordingly. He was discovered to be stirring up revolt in Egypt, wherefore Cambyses, when his guilt clearly appeared, compelled him to drink bull's blood,[4] which presently caused his death. Such was the end of Psammenitus.

16. After this Cambyses left Memphis, and went to Sais, wishing to do that which he actually did on his arrival there. He entered the palace of Amasis, and straightway commanded that the body of the king should be brought forth from the sepulchre. When the attendants did according to his commandment, he further bade them scourge the body, and prick it with goads, and pluck the hair from it, and heap upon it all manner of insults. The body, however, having been embalmed, resisted, and refused to come apart, do what they would to it; so the attendants grew weary of their work; whereupon Cambyses bade them take the corpse and burn it. This was truly an impious command to give, for the Persians hold fire to be a god, and never by any chance burn their dead. Indeed this practice is unlawful, both with them and with the Egyptians—with them for the reason above-mentioned, since they deem it wrong to give the corpse of a man to a god; and with the Egyptians, because they believe fire to be a live animal which eats whatever it can seize, and then, glutted with the food, dies with the matter which it feeds upon. Now to give a man's body to be devoured by beasts is in no wise agreeable to their customs, and indeed this is the very reason why they embalm their dead; namely, to prevent them from being eaten in the grave by worms. Thus Cambyses commanded what both nations accounted unlawful. According to the Egyptians it was not Amasis

[3] It is not unlikely that Manetho's six years of Amyrtaeus the Saite are the six years (from 460 B.C. to 455 B.C.) in the reign of Artaxerxes during which Egypt is known to have been independent of Persia, through the exertions of Inarus and Amyrtaeus.

[4] Bull's blood was supposed to coagulate and choke the drinker.

who was thus treated, but another of their nation who was of about the same height. The Persians, believing this man's body to be the king's, abused it in the fashion described above. Amasis, they say, was warned by an oracle of what would happen to him after his death: in order, therefore, to prevent the impending fate, he buried the body, which afterwards received the blows, inside his own tomb near the entrance, commanding his son to bury him, when he died, in the farthest recess of the same sepulchre. For my own part I do not believe that these orders were ever given by Amasis; the Egyptians, as it seems to me, falsely assert it, to save their own dignity.

17. After this Cambyses took counsel with himself, and planned three expeditions. One was against the Carthaginians, another against the Ammonians, and a third against the long-lived Ethiopians, who dwelt in that part of Libya which borders upon the southern sea. He judged it best to despatch his fleet against Carthage and to send some portion of his land army to act against the Ammonians, while his spies went into Ethiopia, under the pretence of carrying presents to the king, but in reality to take note of all they saw, and especially to observe whether there was really what is called the table of the sun in Ethiopia.

18. Now the table of the sun, according to the accounts given of it, may be thus described: It is a meadow in the skirts of their city full of the boiled flesh of all manner of beasts, which the magistrates are careful to store with meat every night, and where whoever likes may come and eat during the day. The people of the land say that the earth itself brings forth the food. Such is the description which is given of this table.

19. When Cambyses had made up his mind that the spies should go, he forthwith sent to Elephantine for certain of the Fish-eaters who were acquainted with the Ethiopian tongue; and, while they were being fetched, issued orders to his fleet to sail against Carthage. But the Phoenicians said they would not go, since they were bound to the Carthaginians by solemn oaths, and since besides it would be wicked in them to make war on their own children. Now when the Phoenicians refused the rest

of the fleet was unequal to the undertaking; and thus it was that the Carthaginians escaped, and were not enslaved by the Persians. Cambyses thought it not right to force the war upon the Phoenicians, because they had yielded themselves to the Persians, and because upon the Phoenicians all his sea-service depended. The Cyprians had also joined the Persians of their own accord, and took part with them in the expedition against Egypt.

20. As soon as the Fish-eaters arrived from Elephantine, Cambyses, having told them what they were to say, forthwith despatched them into Ethiopia with these following gifts: a purple robe, a gold chain for the neck, armlets, an alabaster box of myrrh, and a cask of palm wine. The Ethiopians to whom this embassy was sent, are said to be the tallest and handsomest men in the whole world. In their customs they differ greatly from the rest of mankind, and particularly in the way they choose their kings; for they find out the man who is the tallest of all the citizens, and of strength equal to his height, and appoint him to rule over them.

21. The Fish-eaters, on reaching this people, delivered the gifts to the king of the country, and spoke as follows, "Cambyses, king of the Persians, anxious to become your ally and sworn friend, has sent us to address you, and to bear you the gifts you see, which are the things wherein he himself delights the most." Hereon the Ethiopian, who knew they came as spies, made answer, "The king of the Persians sent you not with these gifts, because he much desired to become my sworn friend—nor is the account which you give of yourselves true, for you have come to search out my kingdom. Also your king is not a just man—for were he so, he had not coveted a land which is not his own, nor brought slavery on a people who never did him any wrong. Bear him this bow, and say, 'The king of the Ethiops thus advises the king of the Persians—when the Persians can pull a bow of this strength easily, then let them come with an army of superior strength against the long-lived Ethiopians— till then, let them thank the gods that they have not put it into the heart of the sons of the Ethiops to covet countries which do not belong to them.' "

22. So speaking, he unstrung the bow, and gave it into the hands of the messengers. Then, taking the purple robe, he asked them what it was, and how it had been made. They answered truly, telling him concerning the purple, and the art of the dyer —whereat he observed that the men were deceitful, and their garments also. Next he took the necklace and the armlets, and asked about them. So the Fish-eaters explained their use as ornaments. Then the king laughed, and fancying they were fetters, said that the Ethiopians had much stronger ones. Thirdly, he inquired about the myrrh, and when they told him how it was made and rubbed upon the limbs, he said the same concerning it that he had said of the robe. Last of all he came to the wine, and having learnt their way of making it, he drank a draught, which greatly delighted him; whereupon he asked what the Persian king ate, and to what age the longest-lived of the Persians had been known to attain. They told him that the king ate bread, and described the nature of wheat—adding that eighty years was the longest term of man's life among the Persians. Hereat he remarked, "It did not surprise him if they fed on manure, that they died so soon; indeed he was sure they never would have lived so long as eighty years, except for the refreshment they got from that drink (meaning the wine), wherein he confessed that the Persians surpassed the Ethiopians."

23. The Fish-eaters then in their turn questioned the king concerning the term of life and diet of his people, and were told that most of them lived to be 120 years old, while some even went beyond that age—they ate boiled flesh, and had for their drink nothing but milk. When the Fish-eaters showed wonder at the number of the years, he led them to a fountain, wherein, when they had washed, they found their flesh all glossy and sleek, as if they had bathed in oil—and a scent came from the spring like that of violets. The water was so weak, they said, that nothing would float in it, neither wood, nor any lighter substance, but all went to the bottom. If their account of this fountain be true, it would be their constant use of the water from it which makes them so long-lived. When they quitted the fountain the king led them to a prison, where the prisoners were

all bound with fetters of gold.[5] Among these Ethiopians copper is of all metals the most scarce and valuable. After they had seen the prison, they were likewise shown what is called the table of the sun.

24. Also, last of all, they were allowed to behold the coffins of the Ethiopians, which are made (according to report) of crystal, after the following fashion: When the dead body has been dried, either in the Egyptian, or in some other manner, they cover the whole with gypsum, and adorn it with painting until it is as like the living man as possible. Then they place the body in a crystal pillar which has been hollowed out to receive it, crystal being dug up in great abundance in their country, and of a kind very easy to work. You may see the corpse through the pillar within which it lies; and it neither gives out any unpleasant odour, nor is it in any respect unseemly; yet there is no part that is not as plainly visible as if the body was bare. The next of kin keep the crystal pillar in their houses a full year from the time of the death, and give it the first fruits continually, and honour it with sacrifice. After the year is out they bear the pillar forth, and set it up near the town.

25. When the spies had now seen everything, they returned back to Egypt, and made report to Cambyses, who was stirred to anger by their words. Forthwith he set out on his march against the Ethiopians without having made any provision for the sustenance of his army, or reflected that he was about to wage war in the uttermost parts of the earth. Like a senseless madman as he was, no sooner did he receive the report of the Fish-eaters than he began his march, bidding the Greeks who were with his army remain where they were, and taking his land force with him. At Thebes, which he passed through on his way, he detached from his main body some 50,000 men, and sent them against the Ammonians with orders to carry the people into captivity, and burn the oracle of Zeus. Meanwhile he himself went on with the rest of his forces against the Ethiopians. Before, however, he had accomplished one-fifth part of the distance, all that the army had in the way of provisions failed;

[5] This is probably all a traveller's tale; but gold was found in Ethiopia.

whereupon the men began to eat the pack animals, which shortly
failed also. If then, at this time, Cambyses, seeing what was
happening, had confessed himself in the wrong, and led his army
back, he would have done the wisest thing that he could after
the mistake made at the outset; but as it was, he took no manner of heed, but continued to march forward. So long as the
earth gave them anything, the soldiers sustained life by eating
the grass and herbs; but when they came to the bare sand, a
portion of them were guilty of a horrid deed: by tens they cast
lots for a man, who was slain to be the food of the others. When
Cambyses heard of these doings, alarmed at such cannibalism,
he gave up his attack on Ethiopia, and retreating by the way he
had come, reached Thebes, after he had lost vast numbers of his
soldiers. From Thebes he marched down to Memphis, where he
dismissed the Greeks, allowing them to sail home. And so ended
the expedition against Ethiopia.

26. The men sent to attack the Ammonians, started from
Thebes, having guides with them, and may be clearly traced as
far as the city Oasis, which is inhabited by Samians, said to be
of the tribe Aeschrionia. The place is distant from Thebes seven
days' journey across the sand, and is called in our tongue the
Island of the Blessed. Thus far the army is known to have made
its way; but thenceforth nothing is to be heard of them, except
what the Ammonians, and those who get their knowledge from
them, report. It is certain they neither reached the Ammonians,
nor ever came back to Egypt. Further than this, the Ammonians
relate as follows: That the Persians set forth from Oasis across
the sand, and had reached about half way between that place
and themselves, when, as they were at their midday meal, a
wind arose from the south, strong and deadly, bringing with it
vast columns of whirling sand, which entirely covered up the
troops, and caused them wholly to disappear. Thus, according
to the Ammonians, did it fare with this army.

27. About the time when Cambyses arrived at Memphis,
Apis appeared to the Egyptians. Now Apis is the god whom the
Greeks call Epaphus. As soon as he appeared, straightway all
the Egyptians arrayed themselves in their gayest garments, and

fell to feasting and jollity: which when Cambyses saw, making sure that these rejoicings were on account of his own ill success, he called before him the officers, who had charge of Memphis, and demanded of them, "Why, when he was in Memphis before, the Egyptians had done nothing of this kind, but waited until now, when he had returned with the loss of so many of his troops?" The officers made answer, "One of their gods had appeared to them, a god who at long intervals of time had been accustomed to show himself in Egypt—and that always on his appearance, the whole of Egypt feasted and kept jubilee." When Cambyses heard this, he told them that they lied, and as liars he condemned them all to suffer death.

28. When they were dead, he called the priests to his presence, and questioning them received the same answer; whereupon he observed, that he would soon know whether a tame god had really come to dwell in Egypt and straightway, without another word, he bade them bring Apis to him. So they went out from his presence to fetch the god. Now this Apis, or Epaphus, is the calf of a cow which is never afterwards able to bear young. The Egyptians say that fire comes down from heaven upon the cow, which thereupon conceives Apis. The calf which is so called, has the following marks: He is black, with a square spot of white upon his forehead, and on his back the figure of an eagle; the hairs in his tail are double, and there is a beetle upon his tongue.

29. When the priests returned bringing Apis with them, Cambyses, like the harebrained person that he was, drew his dagger, and aimed at the belly of the animal, but missed his mark, and stabbed him in the thigh. Then he laughed, and said to the priests, "Blockheads, do you think that gods become like this, of flesh and blood, and sensible to steel? A fit god indeed for Egyptians, such an one! But it shall cost you dear that you have made me your laughing-stock." When he had so spoken, he ordered those whose business it was to scourge the priests, and if they found any of the Egyptians keeping festival to put them to death. Thus was the feast stopped throughout the land of Egypt, and the priests suffered punishment. Apis, wounded in

the thigh, lay some time pining in the temple; at last he died of his wound, and the priests buried him secretly without the knowledge of Cambyses.

30. And now Cambyses, who even before had not been quite in his right mind, was forthwith, as the Egyptians say, smitten with madness for this crime. The first of his outrages was the slaying of Smerdis,[6] his full brother, whom he had sent back to Persia from Egypt out of envy, because he drew the bow brought from the Ethiopians by the Fish-eaters (which none of the other Persians were able to bend) the distance of two fingers' breadth. When Smerdis was departed into Persia, Cambyses had a vision in his sleep—he thought a messenger from Persia came to him with tidings, that Smerdis sat upon the royal throne, and with his head touched the heavens. Fearing therefore for himself, and thinking it likely that his brother would kill him, and rule in his stead, Cambyses sent into Persia Prexaspes, whom he trusted beyond all the other Persians, bidding him put Smerdis to death. So this Prexaspes went up to Susa and slew Smerdis.[7] Some say he killed him as they hunted together, others, that he took him down to the Red Sea, and there drowned him.

31. This, it is said, was the first outrage which Cambyses committed. The second was the slaying of his sister, who had accompanied him into Egypt, and lived with him as his wife, though she was his full sister, the daughter both of his father and of his mother. The way wherein he had made her his wife was the following: It was not the custom of the Persians, before his time, to marry their sisters—but Cambyses, happening to fall in love with one of his, and wishing to take her to wife, as he knew that it was an uncommon thing, called together the royal judges, and asked them, whether there was any law which allowed a brother, if he wished, to marry his sister? Now the royal judges are certain picked men among the Persians, who hold their office

[6] The Persian name of this prince was Bardiya.

[7] The Behistun inscription expressly confirms the fact of the putting to death of Smerdis by his brother, and also states that the death was not generally known.

for life, or until they are found guilty of some misconduct. By
them justice is administered in Persia, and they are the interpreters of the old laws, all disputes being referred to their decision. When Cambyses, therefore, put his question to these
judges, they gave him an answer which was at once true and
safe, "They did not find any law," they said, "allowing a brother
to take his sister to wife, but they found a law, that the king of
the Persians might do whatever he pleased." And so they neither
warped the law through fear of Cambyses, nor ruined themselves by over stiffly maintaining the law; but they brought another quite distinct law to the king's help, which allowed him to
have his wish. Cambyses, therefore, married the object of his
love,[8] and no long time afterwards he took to wife another sister. It was the younger of these who went with him into Egypt,
and there suffered death at his hands.

32. Concerning the manner of her death, as concerning that
of Smerdis, two different accounts are given. The story which
the Greeks tell, is, that Cambyses had set a young dog to fight
the cub of a lioness—his wife looking on at the time. Now the
dog was getting the worse, when a pup of the same litter broke
his chain, and came to his brother's aid—then the two dogs together fought the lion, and conquered him. The thing greatly
pleased Cambyses, but his sister who was sitting by shed tears.
When Cambyses saw this, he asked her why she wept: whereon
she told him, that seeing the young dog come to his brother's
aid made her think of Smerdis, whom there was none to help.
For this speech, the Greeks say, Cambyses put her to death. But
the Egyptians tell the story thus: The two were sitting at table,
when the sister took a lettuce, and stripping the leaves off, asked
her brother when he thought the lettuce looked the prettiest—
when it had all its leaves on, or now that it was stripped? He
answered, "When the leaves were on." "But you," she rejoined,
"have done as I did to the lettuce, and made bare the house of
Cyrus." Then Cambyses was angry, and sprang fiercely upon

[8] This was Atossa, the mother of Xerxes, who was the wife successively
of Cambyses, the Pseudo-Smerdis, and Darius Hystaspes.

her, though she was with child at the time. And so it came to
pass that she miscarried and died.

33. Thus mad was Cambyses upon his own kindred, and this
either from his usage of Apis, or from some other among the
many causes from which calamities are wont to arise. They say
that from his birth he was afflicted with a dreadful disease, the
disorder which some call the sacred sickness.[9] It would be by no
means strange, therefore, if his mind were affected in some degree, seeing that his body laboured under so sore a malady.

34. He dealt madly with others besides his kindred; among
the rest, upon Prexaspes, the man whom he esteemed beyond all
the rest of the Persians, who carried his messages, and whose
son held the office—an honour of no small account in Persia—
of his cupbearer. Him Cambyses is said to have once addressed
as follows, "What sort of man, Prexaspes, do the Persians think
me? What do they say of me?" Prexaspes answered, "Sire, they
praise you greatly in all things but one—they say you are too
much given to love of wine." Such Prexaspes told him was the
judgment of the Persians; whereupon Cambyses, full of rage,
answered, "What? they say now that I drink too much wine,
and so have lost my senses, and am gone out of my mind! Then
their former speeches about me were untrue." For once, when
the Persians were sitting with him, and Croesus also, he had
asked them, "What sort of man they thought him compared to
his father Cyrus?" Hereon they had answered, "That he surpassed his father, for he was lord of all that his father ever
ruled, and further had made himself master of Egypt, and the
sea." Then Croesus, who was standing near, and disliked the
comparison, spoke thus to Cambyses, "In my judgment, son of
Cyrus, you are not equal to your father, for you have not yet
left behind you such a son as he." Cambyses was delighted when
he heard this reply, and praised the judgment of Croesus.

35. Recollecting these answers, Cambyses spoke fiercely to
Prexaspes, saying, "Judge now, Prexaspes, whether the Persians
tell the truth, or whether it is not they who are mad for speaking

[9] The disease known under this name was epilepsy.

as they do. Look there now at your son standing in the vestibule —if I shoot and hit him right in the middle of the heart, it will be plain the Persians have no grounds for what they say: if I miss him, then I allow that the Persians are right, and that I am out of my mind." So speaking he drew the bow to the full, and struck the boy, who straightway fell down dead. Then Cambyses ordered the body to be opened, and the wound examined; and when the arrow was found to have entered the heart, the king was quite overjoyed, and said to the father with a laugh, "Now you see plainly, Prexaspes, that it is not I who am mad, but the Persians who have lost their senses. I pray you tell me, did you ever see a man send an arrow with a better aim?" Prexaspes, seeing that the king was not in his right mind, and fearing for himself, replied, "My lord, I do not think that god himself could shoot so dexterously." Such was the outrage which Cambyses committed at this time: at another, he took twelve of the noblest Persians, and, without bringing any charge worthy of death against them, buried them all up to the neck.

36. Hereupon Croesus the Lydian thought it right to admonish Cambyses, which he did in these words following, "O king, do not give way entirely to youth, and the heat of your temper, but check and control yourself. It is well to look to consequences, and in forethought is true wisdom. You lay hold of men, who are your fellow-citizens, and without cause of complaint, slay them—you even put children to death—think now, if you often do things like these, will not the Persians rise in revolt against you? It is by your father's wish that I offer you advice; he charged me strictly to give you such counsel as I might see to be good." In thus advising Cambyses, Croesus meant nothing but what was friendly. But Cambyses answered him, "Do you presume to offer me advice? Right well you ruled your own country when you were a king, and right sage advice you gave my father Cyrus, bidding him cross the Araxes and fight the Massagetae in their own land, when they were willing to have passed over into ours. By your misdirection of your own affairs you brought ruin upon yourself, and by your bad counsel which he followed, you brought ruin upon Cyrus, my father.

But you shall not escape punishment now, for I have long been seeking to find some occasion against you." As he thus spoke, Cambyses took up his bow to shoot at Croesus; but Croesus ran hastily out, and escaped. So when Cambyses found that he could not kill him with his bow, he ordered his servants to seize him, and put him to death. The servants, however, who knew their master's humour, thought it best to hide Croesus; that so, if Cambyses relented, and asked for him, they might bring him out, and get a reward for having saved his life—if, on the other hand, he did not relent, or regret the loss, they might then despatch him. Not long afterwards, Cambyses did in fact regret the loss of Croesus, and the servants, perceiving it, let him know that he was still alive. "I am glad," said he, "that Croesus lives, but as for you who saved him, you shall not escape my vengeance, but shall all of you be put to death." And he did even as he had said.

37. Many other wild outrages of this sort did Cambyses commit, both upon the Persians and the allies, while he still stayed at Memphis; among the rest he opened the ancient sepulchres, and examined the bodies that were buried in them. He likewise went into the temple of Hephaestus, and made great sport of the image. For the image of Hephaestus is very like the Pataici of the Phoenicians, wherewith they ornament the prows of their ships of war. If persons have not seen these, I will explain in a different way—it is a figure resembling that of a pigmy. He went also into the temple of the Cabeiri, which it is unlawful for any one to enter except the priests, and not only made sport of the images, but even burnt them. They are made like the statue of Hephaestus, who is said to have been their father.

38. Thus it appears certain to me, by a great variety of proofs, that Cambyses was raving mad; he would not else have set himself to make a mock of holy rites and long-established usages. For if one were to offer men to choose out of all the customs in the world such as seemed to them the best, they would examine the whole number, and end by preferring their own; so convinced are they that their own usages far surpass those of all others. Unless, therefore, a man was mad, it is not likely that he

would make sport of such matters. That people have this feeling about their laws may be seen by very many proofs: among others, by the following. Darius, after he had got the kingdom, called into his presence certain Greeks who were at hand, and asked what he should pay them to eat the bodies of their fathers when they died. To which they answered, that there was no sum that would tempt them to do such a thing. He then sent for certain Indians, of the race called Callatians, men who eat their fathers, and asked them, while the Greeks stood by, and knew by the help of an interpreter all that was said, what he should give them to burn the bodies of their fathers at their decease. The Indians exclaimed aloud, and bade him forbear such language. Such is men's custom; and Pindar was right, in my judgment, when he said, "Law is king over all."

39. While Cambyses was carrying on this war in Egypt, the Lacedaemonians likewise sent a force to Samos against Polycrates, the son of Aeaces, who had by insurrection made himself master of that island.[10] At the outset he divided the state into three parts, and shared the kingdom with his brothers, Pantagnotus and Syloson; but later, having killed the former and banished the latter, who was the younger of the two, he held the whole island. Hereupon he made a contract of friendship with Amasis the Egyptian king, sending him gifts, and receiving from him others in return. In a little while his power so greatly increased, that the fame of it went abroad throughout Ionia and the rest of Greece. Wherever he turned his arms, success waited on him. He had a fleet of 100 fifty-oared ships, and bowmen to the number of 1,000. Herewith he plundered all, without distinction of friend or foe; for he argued that a friend was better pleased if you gave him back what you had taken from him, than if you spared him at the first. He captured many of the islands and several towns upon the mainland. Among his other doings he overcame the Lesbians in a sea-fight, when they came with all their forces to the help of Miletus, and made a

---

[10] The date of Polycrates' accession is about 532 B.C. Herodotus' story bears marks of personal observation but he has concealed the treachery of Samos by stressing the Nemesis attendant on good fortune.

number of them prisoners. These persons, laden with fetters, dug the moat which surrounds the castle at Samos.

40. The exceeding good fortune of Polycrates did not escape the notice of Amasis, who was much disturbed thereat. When therefore his successes continued increasing, Amasis wrote him the following letter, and sent it to Samos. "Amasis to Polycrates speaks thus: It is a pleasure to hear of a friend and ally prospering, but your exceeding prosperity does not cause me joy, for as much as I know that the gods are envious. My wish for myself, and for those whom I love, is, to be now successful, and now to meet with a check; thus passing through life amid alternate good and ill, rather than with perpetual good fortune. For never yet did I hear tell of any one succeeding in all his undertakings, who did not meet with calamity at last, and come to utter ruin. Now, therefore, give ear to my words, and meet your good luck in this way. Think which of all your treasures you value most and can least bear to part with; take it, whatsoever it be, and throw it away, so that it may be sure never to come any more into the sight of man. Then, if your good fortune be not thenceforth chequered with ill, save yourself from harm by again doing as I have counselled."

41. When Polycrates read this letter, and perceived that the advice of Amasis was good, he considered carefully with himself which of the treasures that he had it would grieve him most to lose. After much thought he made up his mind that it was a signet-ring which he wore, an emerald set in gold, the workmanship of Theodore, son of Telecles, a Samian. So he determined to throw this away; and, manning a fifty-oared ship, he went on board, and bade the sailors put out into the open sea. When he was now a long way from the island, he took the ring from his finger, and, in the sight of all those who were on board, flung it into the deep. This done, he returned home, and gave vent to his sorrow.

42. Now it happened five or six days afterwards that a fisherman caught a fish so large and beautiful, that he thought it well deserved to be made a present of to the king. So he took it with him to the gate of the palace, and said that he wanted to see

Polycrates. Then Polycrates allowed him to come in, and the fisherman gave him the fish with these words, "O king, when I took this prize, I thought I would not carry it to market, though I am a poor man who live by my trade. I said to myself, it is worthy of Polycrates and his greatness; and so I brought it here to give it to you." The speech pleased the king, who thus spoke in reply, "You did right well, friend, and I am doubly indebted, both for the gift and for the speech. Come now, and sup with me." So the fisherman went home, esteeming it a high honour that he had been asked to sup with the king. Meanwhile the servants, on cutting open the fish, found the signet of their master in its belly. No sooner did they see it than they seized upon it, and, hastening to Polycrates with great joy, restored it to him, and told him in what way it had been found. The king, who saw something providential in the matter, forthwith wrote a letter to Amasis, telling him all that had happened, what he had himself done, and what had been the upshot—and despatched the letter to Egypt.

43. When Amasis had read the letter of Polycrates, he perceived that it does not belong to man to save his fellow-man from the fate which is in store for him; likewise he felt certain that Polycrates would end ill, as he prospered in everything, even finding what he had thrown away. So he sent a herald to Samos, and dissolved the contract of friendship.[11] This he did, that when the great and heavy misfortune came, he might escape the grief which he would have felt if the sufferer had been his bond-friend.

44. It was with this Polycrates, so fortunate in every undertaking, that the Lacedaemonians now went to war. Certain Samians, the same who afterwards founded the city of Cydonia in Crete, had earnestly entreated their help. For Polycrates, at the time when Cambyses, son of Cyrus, was gathering together an armament against Egypt, had sent to beg him not to omit to ask aid from Samos; whereupon Cambyses with much readiness despatched a messenger to the island, and made request that

[11] It was probably Polycrates who broke off his friendship with Amasis finding it suitable to his policy to cultivate the alliance of Cambyses.

Polycrates would give some ships to the naval force which he was collecting against Egypt. Polycrates straightway picked out from among the citizens such as he thought most likely to stir revolt against him, and manned with them forty triremes,[12] which he sent to Cambyses, bidding him keep the men safe, and never allow them to return home.

45. Now some accounts say that these Samians did not reach Egypt; for that when they were off Carpathus, they took counsel together and resolved to sail no further. But others maintain that they did go to Egypt, and, finding themselves watched, deserted, and sailed back to Samos. There Polycrates went out against them with his fleet, and a battle was fought and gained by the exiles; after which they disembarked upon the island and engaged the land forces of Polycrates, but were defeated, and so sailed off to Lacedaemon. Some relate that the Samians from Egypt overcame Polycrates, but it seems to me untruly; for had the Samians been strong enough to conquer Polycrates by themselves, they would not have needed to call in the aid of the Lacedaemonians. And moreover, it is not likely that a king who had in his pay so large a body of foreign mercenaries, and maintained likewise such a force of native bowmen, would have been worsted by an army so small as that of the returned Samians. As for his own subjects, to hinder them from betraying him and joining the exiles, Polycrates shut up their wives and children in the sheds built to shelter his ships, and was ready to burn sheds and all in case of need.

46. When the banished Samians reached Sparta, they had audience of the magistrates, before whom they made a long speech, as was natural with persons greatly in want of aid. Accordingly at this first sitting the Spartans answered them, that they had forgotten the first half of their speech, and could make nothing of the remainder. Afterwards the Samians had another audience, whereat they simply said, showing a bag which they

---

[12] The naval force of Polycrates was said to have consisted of vessels propelled by fifty rowers but his ships are now called triremes, or vessels having three banks of oars. Polycrates probably had a fleet of 100 vessels, some few of which—certainly not forty—were triremes.

had brought with them, "The bag wants flour." The Spartans answered that they did not need to have said the bag; however, they resolved to give them aid.

47. Then the Lacedaemonians made ready and set forth to the attack of Samos, from a motive of gratitude, if we may believe the Samians, because the Samians had once sent ships to their aid against the Messenians, but as the Spartans themselves say, not so much from any wish to assist the Samians who begged their help, as from a desire to punish the people who had seized the bowl which they sent to Croesus, and the corslet which Amasis, king of Egypt, sent as a present to them. The Samians made prize of this corslet the year before they took the bowl—it was of linen, and had a vast number of figures of animals inwoven into its fabric, and was likewise embroidered with gold and cotton. What is most worthy of admiration in it is, that each of the twists, although of fine texture, contains within it 360 threads, all of them clearly visible. The corslet which Amasis gave to the temple of Athena in Lindus is just such another.

48. The Corinthians likewise right willingly lent a helping hand towards the expedition against Samos; for a generation earlier, about the time of the seizure of the wine-bowl, they too had suffered insult at the hands of the Samians. It happened that Periander, son of Cypselus, had taken 300 boys, children of the chief nobles among the Corcyraeans, and sent them to Alyattes for eunuchs; the men who had them in charge touched at Samos on their way to Sardis; whereupon the Samians, having found out what was to become of the boys when they reached that city, first prompted them to take sanctuary at the temple of Artemis; and after this, when the Corinthians, as they were forbidden to tear the suppliants from the holy place, sought to cut off from them all supplies of food, invented a festival in their behalf, which they celebrate to this day with the self-same rites. Each evening, as night closed in, during the whole time that the boys continued there, choirs of youths and virgins were placed about the temple, carrying in their hands cakes made of sesame and honey, in order that the Corcyraean boys might snatch the cakes, and so get enough to live upon.

49. And this went on for so long, that at last the Corinthians who had charge of the boys gave them up, and took their departure, upon which the Samians conveyed them back to Corcyra. If, now, after the death of Periander, the Corinthians and Corcyraeans had been good friends, it is not to be imagined that the former would ever have taken part in the expedition against Samos for such a reason as this; but as, in fact, the two people have always, ever since the first settlement of the island, been enemies to one another, this outrage was remembered, and the Corinthians bore the Samians a grudge for it. Periander had chosen the youths from among the first families in Corcyra, and sent them to Sardis for castration, to revenge a wrong which he had received. For it was the Corcyraeans who began the quarrel and injured Periander by an outrage of a horrid nature.

50. After Periander had put to death his wife Melissa, it chanced that on this first affliction a second followed of a different kind. His wife had borne him two sons, and one of them had now reached the age of seventeen, the other of eighteen years, when their mother's father, Procles, tyrant of Epidaurus, asked them to his court. They went, and Procles treated them with much kindness, as was natural, considering they were his own daughter's children. At length, when the time for parting came, Procles, as he was sending them on their way, said, "Know you now, my children, who it was that caused your mother's death?" The elder son took no account of this speech, but the younger, whose name was Lycophron, was sorely troubled at it—so much so, that when he got back to Corinth, looking upon his father as his mother's murderer, he would neither speak to him, nor answer when spoken to, nor utter a word in reply to all his questionings. So Periander at last growing furious at such behaviour, banished him from his house.

51. The younger son gone, he turned to the elder and asked him what it was that their grandfather had said to them. Then he related in how kind and friendly a fashion he had received them; but, not having taken any notice of the speech which Procles had uttered at parting, he quite forgot to mention it. Periander insisted that it was not possible this should be all—

their grandfather must have given them some hint or other—and he went on pressing him, till at last the lad remembered the parting speech and told it. Periander, after he had turned the whole matter over in his thoughts, and felt unwilling to give way at all, sent a messenger to the persons who had opened their houses to his outcast son, and forbade them to harbour him. Then the boy, when he was chased from one friend, sought refuge with another, but was driven from shelter to shelter by the threats of his father, who menaced all those that took him in, and commanded them to shut their doors against him. Still, as fast as he was forced to leave one house he went to another, and was received by the inmates; for his acquaintance, although in no small alarm, yet gave him shelter, as he was Periander's son.

52. At last Periander made proclamation that whoever harboured his son or even spoke to him, should forfeit a certain sum of money to Apollo. On hearing this no one any longer liked to take him in, or even to converse with him, and he himself did not think it right to seek to do what was forbidden; so, abiding by his resolve, he made his lodging in the public porticos. When four days had passed in this way, Periander, seeing how wretched his son was, that he neither washed nor took any food, felt moved with compassion towards him; wherefore, foregoing his anger, he approached him, and said, "Which is better, my son, to fare as now you fare, or to receive my crown and all the good things that I possess, on the one condition of submitting to your father? See, now, though my own child, and lord of this wealthy Corinth, you have brought yourself to a beggar's life, because you resist and treat with anger him whom you should least oppose. If there has been a calamity, and you bear me ill will on that account, think that I too feel it, and am the greatest sufferer, in as much as it was by me that the deed was done. For yourself, now that you know how much better a thing it is to be envied than pitied, and how dangerous it is to indulge anger against parents and superiors, come back with me to your home." With such words as these did Periander chide his son; but the son made no reply except to remind his father that he

owed the god the penalty for coming and talking with him. Then Periander knew that there was no cure for the youth's malady, nor means of overcoming it; so he prepared a ship and sent him away out of his sight to Corcyra, which island at that time belonged to him. As for Procles, Periander, regarding him as the true author of all his present troubles, went to war with him as soon as his son was gone, and not only made himself master of his kingdom Epidaurus, but also took Procles himself, and carried him into captivity.

53. As time went on, and Periander came to be old, he found himself no longer equal to the oversight and management of affairs. Seeing, therefore, in his eldest son no manner of ability, but knowing him to be dull and blockish, he sent to Corcyra and recalled Lycophron to take the kingdom. Lycophron, however, did not even ask the bearer of this message a question. But Periander's heart was set upon the youth, so he sent again to him, this time by his own daughter, the sister of Lycophron, who would, he thought, have more power to persuade him than any other person. Then she, when she reached Corcyra, spoke thus with her brother, "Do you wish the kingdom, brother, to pass into strange hands, and our father's wealth to be made a prey, rather than yourself return to enjoy it? Come back home with me, and cease to punish yourself. It is scant gain, this obstinacy. Why seek to cure evil by evil? Mercy, remember, is by many set above justice. Many, also, while pushing their mother's claims have forfeited their father's fortune. Power is a slippery thing—it has many suitors; and he is old and stricken in years—let not your inheritance go to another." Thus did the sister, who had been tutored by Periander what to say, urge all the arguments most likely to have weight with her brother. He however answered, that so long as he knew his father to be still alive, he would never go back to Corinth. When the sister brought Periander this reply, he sent to his son a third time by a herald, and said he would come himself to Corcyra, and let his son take his place at Corinth as heir to his kingdom. To these terms Lycophron agreed; and Periander was making ready to pass into Corcyra and his son to return to Corinth, when the

Corcyraeans, being informed of what was taking place, to keep Periander away, put the young man to death. For this reason it was that Periander took vengeance on the Corcyraeans.

54. The Lacedaemonians arrived before Samos with a mighty armament, and laid siege to the place. In one of the assaults upon the walls, they forced their way to the top of the tower which stands by the sea on the side where the suburb is, but Polycrates came in person to the rescue with a strong force, and beat them back. Meanwhile at the upper tower, which stood on the ridge of the hill, the besieged, both mercenaries and Samians, made a sally; but after they had withstood the Lacedaemonians a short time, they fled backwards, and the Lacedaemonians, pressing upon them, slew numbers.

55. If now all who were present had behaved that day like Archias and Lycopas, two of the Lacedaemonians, Samos might have been taken. For these two heroes, following hard upon the flying Samians, entered the city along with them, and, being all alone, and their retreat cut off, were slain within the walls of the place. I myself once fell in with the grandson of this Archias, a man named Archias like his grandsire, and the son of Samius, whom I met at Pitana, to which township he belonged. He respected the Samians beyond all other foreigners, and he told me that his father was called Samius, because his grandfather Archias died in Samos so gloriously, and that the reason why he respected the Samians so greatly was, that his grandsire was buried with public honours by the Samian people.

56. The Lacedaemonians besieged Samos during forty days, but not making any progress before the place, they raised the siege at the end of that time, and returned home to the Peloponnese. There is a silly tale told, that Polycrates struck a quantity of the coin of his country in lead, and, coating it with gold, gave it to the Lacedaemonians, who on receiving it took their departure.

This was the first expedition into Asia of the Lacedaemonian Dorians.[13]

---

[13] These words are emphatic. They mark the place which this expedition occupies in the mind of Herodotus. It is an aggression of the Greeks upon

57. The Samians who had fought against Polycrates, when
they knew that the Lacedaemonians were about to forsake
them, left Samos themselves, and sailed to Siphnos. They happened to be in want of money; and the Siphnians at that time
were at the height of their greatness, no islanders having so
much wealth as they. There were mines of gold and silver in
their country, and of so rich a yield, that from a tithe of the
ores the Siphnians furnished out a treasury at Delphi which was
on a par with the grandest there. What the mines yielded was
divided year by year among the citizens. At the time when they
formed the treasury, the Siphnians consulted the oracle, and
asked whether their good things would remain to them many
years. The priestess made answer as follows:

When the Prytanies' seat shines white in the island of Siphnos,
White-browed all the market—need then of a true seer's wis-
    dom—
Danger will threat from a wooden host, and a herald in scarlet.

Now about this time the market-place of the Siphnians and
their town-hall or prytaneum had been adorned with Parian
marble.

58. The Siphnians, however, were unable to understand the
oracle, either at the time when it was given, or afterwards on
the arrival of the Samians. For these last no sooner came to
anchor off the island than they sent one of their vessels, with
ambassadors on board, to the city. All ships in these early times
were painted with vermilion; and this was what the priestess
had meant when she told them to beware of danger from a
wooden host, and a herald in scarlet. So the ambassadors came
ashore and besought the Siphnians to lend them ten talents,
but the Siphnians refused, whereupon the Samians began to
plunder their lands. Tidings of this reached the Siphnians, who
straightway sallied forth to save their crops; then a battle was
fought, in which the Siphnians suffered defeat, and many of
their number were cut off from the city by the Samians, after

Asia, and therefore a passage in the history of the great quarrel between
Persia and Greece, for all Asia is the King's.

which these latter forced the Siphnians to give them 100 talents.

59. With this money they bought of the Hermionians the island of Hydrea, off the coast of the Peloponnese, and this they gave in trust to the Troezenians, to keep for them, while they themselves went on to Crete, and founded the city of Cydonia. They had not meant, when they set sail, to settle there, but only to drive out the Zacynthians from the island. However they rested at Cydonia, where they flourished greatly for five years. It was they who built the various temples that may still be seen at that place, and among them the temple of Dictyna.[14] But in the sixth year they were attacked by the Aeginetans, who beat them in a sea-fight, and, with the help of the Cretans, reduced them all to slavery. The beaks of their ships, which carried the figure of a wild boar, they sawed off and laid them up in the temple of Athena in Aegina. The Aeginetans took part against the Samians on account of an ancient grudge, since the Samians had first, when Amphicrates was king of Samos, made war on them and done great harm to their island, suffering, however, much damage also themselves. Such was the reason which moved the Aeginetans to make this attack.

60. I have dwelt the longer on the affairs of the Samians, because three of the greatest works in all Greece were made by them. One is a tunnel, under a hill 900 feet high, carried entirely through the base of the hill, with a mouth at either end.[15] The length of the cutting is almost a mile—the height and width are each eight feet. Along the whole course there is a second cutting, thirty feet deep and three feet broad, whereby water is brought, through pipes, from an abundant source into the city. The architect of this tunnel was Eupalinus, son of Naustrophus, a Megarian. Such is the first of their great works: the second is a mole in the sea, which goes all round the harbour, nearly 120 feet deep, and in length over 400 yards. The

[14] Dictyna, or Dictynna, was the same as Britomartis, an ancient goddess of the Cretans. The Greeks usually regarded her as identical with their Artemis.

[15] Discovery of the tunnel has confirmed 'the accuracy of Herodotus' account except in the matter of length which is only 1,100 feet.

third is a temple; the largest of all the temples known to us, whereof Rhoecus, son of Phileus, a Samian, was first architect. Because of these works I have dwelt the longer on the affairs of Samos.[16]

61. While Cambyses, son of Cyrus, after losing his senses, still lingered in Egypt, two Magi, brothers, revolted against him. One of them had been left in Persia by Cambyses as comptroller of his household; and it was he who began the revolt. Aware that Smerdis was dead, and that his death was hid, and known to few of the Persians, while most believed that he was still alive, he laid his plan, and made a bold stroke for the crown. He had a brother—the same of whom I spoke before as his partner in the revolt—who happened greatly to resemble Smerdis the son of Cyrus, whom Cambyses his brother had put to death. And not only was this brother of his like Smerdis in person, but he also bore the selfsame name, to wit Smerdis.[17] Patizeithes, the other Magus, having persuaded him that he would carry the whole business through, took him and made him sit upon the royal throne. Having so done, he sent heralds through all the land, to Egypt and elsewhere, to make proclamation to the troops that henceforth they were to obey Smerdis the son of Cyrus, and not Cambyses.

62. The other heralds therefore made proclamation as they were ordered, and likewise the herald whose place it was to proceed into Egypt. He, when he reached Agbatana in Syria, finding Cambyses and his army there, went straight into the middle of the host, and standing forth before them all, made the proclamation which Patizeithes the Magus had commanded. Cambyses no sooner heard him, than believing that what the herald said was true, and imagining that he had been betrayed by

[16] Aristotle looks upon these works as marks of the grinding tyranny under which the Samians groaned at this period, but it may be questioned whether they were really of an oppressive character. The policy of Polycrates seems to have been to conciliate the masses and his works were doubtless in great part to give employment to the poorer classes.

[17] Here Herodotus was most certainly mistaken. The pretender's name was Gaumata.

Prexaspes (who, he supposed, had not put Smerdis to death when sent into Persia for that purpose), he turned his eyes full upon Prexaspes, and said, "Is this the way, Prexaspes, that you did my errand?" "My liege," answered the other, "there is no truth in the tidings that Smerdis your brother has revolted against you, nor need you to fear in time to come any quarrel, great or small, with that man. With my own hands I did what you commanded, and with my own hands I buried him. If of a truth the dead can leave their graves, expect Astyages the Mede to rise and fight against you; but if the course of nature be the same as formerly, then be sure no ill will ever come upon you from this quarter. Now therefore my counsel is, that we send in pursuit of the herald, and strictly question him who it was that charged him to bid us obey king Smerdis."

63. When Prexaspes had so spoken, and Cambyses had approved his words, the herald was forthwith pursued, and brought back to the king. Then Prexaspes said to him, "You bear us a message, you say, from Smerdis, son of Cyrus. Now answer truly, and go your way in safety. Did Smerdis have you in his presence and give you your orders, or had you them from one of his officers?" The herald answered, "Truly I have not set eyes on Smerdis son of Cyrus, since the day when king Cambyses led the Persians into Egypt. The man who gave me my orders was the Magus that Cambyses left in charge of the household; but he said that Smerdis son of Cyrus sent you the message." In all this the herald spoke nothing but the strict truth. Then Cambyses said thus to Prexaspes, "You are free from all blame, Prexaspes, since, as a right good man, you have not failed to do the thing which I commanded. But tell me now, which of the Persians can have taken the name of Smerdis, and revolted from me?" "I think, my liege," he answered, "that I apprehend the whole business. The men who have risen in revolt against you are the two Magi, Patizeithes, who was left comptroller of your household, and his brother, who is named Smerdis."

64. Cambyses no sooner heard the name of Smerdis than he was struck with the truth of Prexaspes' words, and the fulfil-

ment of his own dream—the dream, I mean, which he had in
former days, when one appeared to him in his sleep and told
him that Smerdis sat upon the royal throne, and with his head
touched the heavens. So when he saw that he had needlessly
slain his brother Smerdis, he wept and bewailed his loss: after
which, smarting with vexation as he thought of all his ill luck,
he sprang hastily upon his steed, meaning to march his army
with all haste to Susa against the Magus. As he made his spring,
the button of his sword-sheath fell off, and the bared point
entered his thigh, wounding him exactly where he had himself
once wounded the Egyptian god Apis.[18] Then Cambyses, feeling
that he had got his death-wound, inquired the name of the
place where he was, and was answered, "Agbatana." Now before this it had been told him by the oracle at Buto that he
should end his days at Agbatana. He, however, had understood
the Median Agbatana, where all his treasures were, and had
thought that he should die there at a good old age, but the
oracle meant Agbatana in Syria. So when Cambyses heard the
name of the place, the double shock that he had received, from
the revolt of the Magus and from his wound, brought him back
to his senses. And he understood now the true meaning of the
oracle, and said, "Here then Cambyses, son of Cyrus, is doomed
to die."

65. At this time he said no more; but twenty days afterwards he called to his presence all the chief Persians who were
with the army, and addressed them as follows, "Persians, I
must tell you now what hitherto I have striven with the greatest
care to keep concealed. When I was in Egypt I saw in my sleep
a vision, which would that I had never beheld. I thought a messenger came to me from my home, and said that Smerdis sat
upon the royal throne, and with his head touched the heavens.
Then I feared to be cast from my throne by Smerdis my brother,
and I did what was more hasty than wise. Truly, do what they
may, it is impossible for men to turn aside the coming fate. I,

---

[18] The details here are suspicious, since they evidently come from the
Egyptian priests, who wish to represent the death of Cambyses as a
judgment upon him for his impiety.

in my folly, sent Prexaspes to Susa to put my brother to death.
So this great woe was accomplished, and I then lived without
fear, never imagining that, after Smerdis was dead, I need dread
revolt from any other. But herein I had quite mistaken what
was about to happen, and so I slew my brother without any
need, and nevertheless have lost my crown. For it was Smerdis
the Magus, and not Smerdis my brother, of whose rebellion God
forewarned me by the vision. The deed is done, however, and
Smerdis, son of Cyrus, be sure is lost to you. The Magi have the
royal power—Patizeithes, whom I left at Susa to oversee my
household, and Smerdis his brother. There was one who would
have been bound beyond all others to avenge the wrongs I have
suffered from these Magians, but he, alas! has perished by a
horrid fate, deprived of life by those nearest and dearest to him.
In his default, nothing now remains for me but to tell you, O
Persians, what I would wish to have done after I have breathed
my last. Therefore, in the name of the gods that watch over our
royal house, I charge you all, and especially such of you as are
Achaemenids, that you do not tamely allow the kingdom to go
back to the Medes. Recover it one way or another, by force or
fraud; by fraud, if it is by fraud that they have seized on it; by
force, if force has helped them in their enterprise. Do this, and
then may your land bring you forth fruit abundantly, and your
wives bear children, and your herds increase, and freedom be
your portion for ever: but do it not—make no brave struggle to
regain the kingdom—and then my curse be on you, and may the
opposite of all these things happen to you—and not only so, but
may you, one and all, perish at the last by such a fate as mine!"
Then Cambyses, when he left speaking, bewailed his whole misfortune from beginning to end.

66. Whereupon the Persians, seeing their king weep, rent the
garments that they had on, and uttered cries of lamentation;
after which, as the bone presently grew carious, and the limb
gangrened, Cambyses, son of Cyrus, died. He had reigned in all
seven years and five months, and left no issue behind him, male
or female. The Persians who had heard his words, put no faith
in anything that he said concerning the Magi having the royal

power; but believed that he spoke out of hatred towards Smerdis, and had invented the tale of his death to cause the whole
Persian race to rise up in arms against him. Thus they were convinced that it was Smerdis the son of Cyrus who had rebelled
and now sat on the throne. For Prexaspes stoutly denied that he
had slain Smerdis, since it was not safe for him, after Cambyses
was dead, to allow that a son of Cyrus had met death at his
hands.

67. Thus then Cambyses died, and the Magus now reigned
in security, and passed himself off for Smerdis the son of Cyrus.
And so went by the seven months which were wanting to complete the eighth year of Cambyses. The Magus' subjects, while
his reign lasted, received great benefits from him, insomuch
that, when he died, all the dwellers in Asia mourned his loss exceedingly, except only the Persians. For no sooner did he come
to the throne than forthwith he sent round to every nation under his rule, and granted them freedom from war-service and
from taxes for the space of three years.

68. In the eighth month, however, it was discovered who he
was in the mode following. There was a man called Otanes, the
son of Pharnaspes, who for rank and wealth was equal to the
greatest of the Persians. This Otanes was the first to suspect
that the Magus was not Smerdis the son of Cyrus, and to surmise moreover who he really was. He was led to guess the truth
by the king never quitting the citadel, and never calling before
him any of the Persian noblemen. As soon therefore as his sus-
picions were aroused, he adopted the following measures: One
of his daughters, who was called Phaedima, had been married to
Cambyses, and was taken to wife, together with the rest of Cambyses' wives, by the Magus. To this daughter Otanes sent a message, and inquired of her who it was whose bed she shared, was
it Smerdis the son of Cyrus, or was it some other man. Phaedima
in reply declared that she did not know—Smerdis the son of Cyrus she had never seen, and so she could not tell whose bed she
shared. Upon this Otanes sent a second time, and said, "If you
do not know Smerdis son of Cyrus yourself, ask queen Atossa
who it is with whom you both live—she cannot fail to know her

own brother." To this the daughter made answer, "I can neither get speech with Atossa, nor with any of the women who lodge in the palace. For no sooner did this man, be he who he may, obtain the kingdom, than he parted us from one another, and gave us all separate chambers."

69. This made the matter seem still more plain to Otanes. Nevertheless he sent a third message to his daughter in these words following, "Daughter, you are of noble blood—you will not shrink from a risk which your father bids you encounter. If this fellow be not Smerdis the son of Cyrus, but the man whom I think him to be, his boldness in taking you as his wife, and lording it over the Persians, must not be allowed to pass unpunished. Now therefore do as I command—when next he passes the night with you, wait till you are sure he is fast asleep, and then feel for his ears. If you find him to have ears, then believe him to be Smerdis the son of Cyrus, but if he has none, know him for Smerdis the Magian." Phaedima answered that, it would be a great risk. If he was without ears, and caught her feeling for them, she well knew he would make away with her— nevertheless she would venture. So Otanes got his daughter's promise that she would do as he desired. Now Smerdis the Magian had had his ears cut off in the lifetime of Cyrus son of Cambyses, as a punishment for a crime of no slight heinousness. Phaedima therefore, Otanes' daughter, bent on accomplishing what she had promised her father, when her turn came, and she was taken to the bed of the Magus (in Persia a man's wives sleep with him in their turns), waited till he was sound asleep, and then felt for his ears. She quickly perceived that he had no ears; and of this, as soon as day dawned, she sent word to her father.

70. Then Otanes took to him two of the chief Persians, Aspathines and Gobryas, men whom it was most advisable to trust in such a matter, and told them everything. Now they had already of themselves suspected how the matter stood. When Otanes therefore laid his reasons before them they at once came into his views; and it was agreed that each of the three should take as companion in the work the Persian in whom he placed

the greatest confidence. Then Otanes chose Intaphernes, Gobryas Megabyzus, and Aspathines Hydarnes. After the number had thus become six, Darius, the son of Hystaspes, arrived at Susa from Persia, whereof his father was governor.[19] On his coming it seemed good to the six to take him likewise into their counsels.

71. After this, the men, being now seven in all, met together to exchange oaths, and hold discourse with one another. And when it came to the turn of Darius to speak his mind, he said as follows, "I thought no one but I knew that Smerdis, the son of Cyrus, was not now alive, and that Smerdis the Magian ruled over us; on this account I came hither with speed, to compass the death of the Magian. But as it seems the matter is known to you all, and not to me only, my judgment is that we should act at once, and not any longer delay. For to do so were not well." Otanes spoke upon this, "Son of Hystaspes," said he, "you are the child of a brave father, and seem likely to show yourself as bold as he. Beware, however, of rash haste in this matter; do not hurry so, but proceed with soberness. We must add to our number before we venture to strike the blow." "Not so," Darius rejoined, "for let all present be well assured, that if the advice of Otanes guide our acts, we shall perish most miserably. Some one will betray our plot to the Magians for gain. You ought to have kept the matter to yourselves, and so made the venture; but as you have chosen to take others into your secret, and have opened the matter to me, take my advice and make the attempt today—or if not, if a single day be suffered to pass by, be sure that I will let no one betray me to the Magian. I myself will go to him, and plainly denounce you all."

72. Otanes, when he saw Darius so hot, replied, "But if you will force us to action, and not allow a day's delay, tell us, I pray you, how we shall get entrance into the palace, so as to set upon them. Guards are placed every where as you yourself well know —for if you have not seen, at least you have heard of them. How

---

[19] The curious fact, that Darius became king in his father's lifetime, is confirmed by the great inscription, where we find Hystaspes employed as one of his son's generals in subduing the rebellious Parthians.

are we to pass these guards, I ask you?" "Otanes," answered Darius, "there are many things easy enough in act, which by speech it is hard to explain. There are also things concerning which speech is easy, but no noble action follows when the speech is done. As for these guards, you know well that we shall not find it hard to make our way through them. Our rank alone would cause them to allow us to enter—shame and fear alike forbidding them to say us nay. But besides, I have the fairest plea that can be conceived for gaining admission. I can say that I have just come from Persia, and have a message to deliver to the king from my father. An untruth must be spoken, where need requires. For whether men lie, or say true, it is with one and the same object. Men lie, because they think to gain by deceiving others; and speak the truth, because they expect to get something by their true speaking, and to be trusted afterwards in more important matters. Thus, though their conduct is so opposite, the end of both is alike. If there were no gain to be got, your true-speaking man would tell untruths as much as your liar, and your liar would tell the truth as much as your true-speaking man. The doorkeeper, who lets us in readily, shall have his reward some day or other; but woe to the man who resists us, he must forthwith be declared an enemy. Forcing our way past him, we will press in and go straight to our work."

73. After Darius had thus said, Gobryas spoke as follows, "Dear friends, when will a fitter occasion offer for us to recover the kingdom, or, if we are not strong enough, at least die in the attempt? Consider that we Persians are governed by a Median Magus, and one, too, who has had his ears cut off. Some of you were present when Cambyses lay upon his deathbed—such, doubtless, remember what curses he called down upon the Persians if they made no effort to recover the kingdom. Then, indeed, we paid but little heed to what he said, because we thought he spoke out of hatred to set us against his brother. Now, however, my vote is, that we do as Darius has counselled —march straight in a body to the palace from the place where we now are, and forthwith set upon the Magian." So Gobryas spoke, and the others all approved.

74. While the seven were thus taking counsel together, it so chanced that the following events were happening: The Magi had been thinking what they had best do, and had resolved for many reasons to make a friend of Prexaspes. They knew how cruelly he had been outraged by Cambyses, who slew his son with an arrow; they were also aware that it was by his hand that Smerdis the son of Cyrus fell, and that he was the only person privy to that prince's death; and they further found him to be held in the highest esteem by all the Persians. So they called him to them, made him their friend, and bound him by a promise and by oaths to keep silence about the fraud which they were practising upon the Persians, and not discover it to any one; and they pledged themselves that in this case they would give him thousands of gifts of every sort and kind. So Prexaspes agreed; and the Magi, when they found that they had persuaded him so far, went on to another proposal, and said they would assemble the Persians at the foot of the palace wall, and he should mount one of the towers and harangue them from it, assuring them that Smerdis the son of Cyrus, and none but he, ruled the land. This they bade him do, because Prexaspes was a man of great weight with his countrymen, and had often declared in public that Smerdis the son of Cyrus was still alive, and denied being his murderer.

75. Prexaspes said he was quite ready to do their will in the matter; so the Magi assembled the people, and placed Prexaspes upon the top of the tower, and told him to make his speech. Then this man, forgetting of set purpose all that the Magi had entreated him to say, began with Achaemenes, and traced down the descent of Cyrus; after which, when he came to that king, he recounted all the services that had been rendered by him to the Persians, from whence he went on to declare the truth, which hitherto he had concealed, he said, because it would not have been safe for him to make it known, but now necessity was laid on him to disclose the whole. Then he told how, forced to it by Cambyses, he had himself taken the life of Smerdis, son of Cyrus, and how that Persia was now ruled by the Magi. Last of all, with many curses upon the Persians if they did not recover

the kingdom, and wreak vengeance on the Magi, he threw him-self headlong from the tower into the abyss below. Such was the end of Prexaspes, a man all his life of high repute among the Persians.

76. And now the seven Persians, having resolved that they would attack the Magi without more delay, first offered prayers to the gods and then set off for the palace, quite unacquainted with what had been done by Prexaspes. The news of his doings reached them upon their way, when they had accomplished about half the distance. Hereupon they turned aside out of the road, and consulted together. Otanes and his party said they must certainly put off the business, and not make the attack when affairs were in such a ferment. Darius, on the other hand, and his friends, were against any change of plan, and wished to go straight on, and not lose a moment. Now, as they strove to-gether, suddenly there came in sight two pairs of vultures, and seven pairs of hawks, pursuing them, and the hawks tore the vultures both with their claws and bills. At this sight the seven with one accord came in to the opinion of Darius, and encour-aged by the omen hastened on towards the palace.

77. At the gate they were received as Darius had foretold. The guards, who had no suspicion that they came for any ill purpose, and held the chief Persians in much reverence, let them pass without difficulty—it seemed as if they were under the spe-cial protection of the gods—none even asked them any question. When they were now in the great court they fell in with certain of the eunuchs, whose business it was to carry the king's mes-sages, who stopped them and asked what they wanted, while at the same time they threatened the doorkeepers for having let them in. The seven sought to press on, but the eunuchs would not suffer them. Then these men, with cheers encouraging one another, drew their daggers, and stabbing those who strove to withstand them, rushed forward to the men's apartment.

78. Now both the Magi were at this time within, holding counsel upon the matter of Prexaspes. So when they heard the stir among the eunuchs, and their loud cries, they ran out them-selves, to see what was happening. Instantly perceiving their

danger, they both flew to arms; one had just time to seize his bow, the other got hold of his lance; when straightway the fight began. The one whose weapon was the bow found it of no serv- ice at all, the foe was too near, and the combat too close to al- low of his using it. But the other made a stout defence with his lance, wounding two of the seven, Aspathines in the leg, and Intaphernes in the eye. This wound did not kill Intaphernes, but it cost him his sight. The other Magus, when he found his bow of no avail, fled into a chamber which opened out into the men's apartment, intending to shut to the doors. But two of the seven entered the room with him, Darius and Gobryas. Gobryas seized the Magus and grappled with him, while Darius stood over them, not knowing what to do, for it was dark, and he was afraid that if he struck a blow he might kill Gobryas. Then Go- bryas, when he perceived that Darius stood doing nothing, asked him why his hand was idle. "I fear to hurt you," he an- swered. "Fear not," said Gobryas, "strike, though it be through both." Darius did as he desired, drove his dagger home, and by good luck killed the Magus.

79. Thus were the Magi slain, and the seven, cutting off both the heads, and leaving their own wounded in the palace, partly because they were disabled, and partly to guard the citadel, went forth from the gates with the heads in their hands, shout- ing and making an uproar. They called out to all the Persians that they met, and told them what had happened, showing them the heads of the Magi, while at the same time they slew every Magus who fell in their way. Then the Persians, when they knew what the seven had done, and understood the fraud of the Magi, thought it but just to follow the example set them, and, drawing their daggers, they killed the Magi wherever they could find any. Such was their fury, that, unless night had closed in, not a single Magus would have been left alive. The Persians ob- serve this day with one accord, and keep it more strictly than any other in the whole year. It is then that they hold the great festi- val, which they call the Slaughter of the Magi. No Magus may show himself abroad during the whole time that the feast lasts; but all must remain at home the entire day.

80. And now when five days were gone, and the hubbub had settled down, the conspirators met together to consult about the situation of affairs. At this meeting speeches were made, to which many of the Greeks give no credence, but they were made nevertheless.[20] Otanes recommended that the management of public affairs should be entrusted to the whole nation. "To me," he said, "it seems advisable, that we should no longer have a single man to rule over us —the rule of one is neither good nor pleasant. You cannot have forgotten to what lengths Cambyses went in his haughty tyranny, and the haughtiness of the Magi you have experienced. How indeed is it possible that monarchy should be a well-adjusted thing, when it allows a man to do as he likes without being answerable? Such licence is enough to stir strange and unwonted thoughts in the heart of the worthiest of men. Give a person this power, and straightway his manifold good things puff him up with pride, while envy is so natural to human kind that it cannot but arise in him. But pride and envy together include all wickedness; both leading on to deeds of savage violence. True it is that kings, possessing as they do all that heart can desire, ought to be void of envy, but the contrary is seen in their conduct towards the citizens. They are jealous of the most virtuous among their subjects, and wish their death; while they take delight in the meanest and basest, being ever ready to listen to the tales of slanderers. A king, besides, is beyond all other men inconsistent with himself. Pay him court in moderation, and he is angry because you do not show him more profound respect—show him profound respect, and he is offended again, because (as he says) you fawn on him. But the worst of all is, that he sets aside the laws of the land, puts men to death without trial, and rapes women. The rule of the many, on the other hand, has, in the first place, the fairest of names, equality before the law; and further it is free from all those outrages which a king is wont to commit. There, places are given by lot, the magistrate is answerable for what he does, and measures rest with the commonalty. I vote, therefore, that we do away

[20] Moderns have generally seen the unhistorical character of the narrative but it is interesting as an example of Greek political philosophy.

with monarchy, and raise the people to power. For the people are all in all."

81. Such were the sentiments of Otanes. Megabyzus spoke next, and advised the setting up of an oligarchy. "In all that Otanes has said to persuade you to put down monarchy," he observed, "I fully concur; but his recommendation that we should call the people to power seems to me not the best advice. For there is nothing so void of understanding, nothing so full of wantonness as the unwieldy rabble. It were folly not to be borne for men, while seeking to escape the wantonness of a tyrant, to give themselves up to the wantonness of a rude unbridled mob. The tyrant, in all his doings, at least knows what he is about, but a mob is altogether devoid of knowledge; for how should there be any knowledge in a rabble, untaught, and with no natural sense of what is right and fit? It rushes wildly into state affairs with all the fury of a stream swollen in the winter, and confuses everything. Let the enemies of the Persians be ruled by democracies; but let us choose out from the citizens a certain number of the worthiest, and put the government into their hands. For thus both we ourselves shall be among the governors, and power being entrusted to the best men, it is likely that the best counsels will prevail in the state."

82. This was the advice which Megabyzus gave, and after him Darius came forward, and spoke as follows, "All that Megabyzus said against democracy was well said, I think; but about oligarchy he did not speak advisedly; for take these three forms of government, democracy, oligarchy, and monarchy, and let them each be at their best, I maintain that monarchy far surpasses the other two. What government can possibly be better than that of the very best man in the whole state? The counsels of such a man are like himself, and so he governs the mass of the people to their heart's content; while at the same time his measures against evil-doers are kept more secret than in other states. Contrariwise, in oligarchies, where men vie with each other in the service of the commonwealth, fierce enmities are apt to arise between man and man, each wishing to be leader, and to carry his own measures; whence violent quarrels come, which

lead to open strife, often ending in bloodshed. Then monarchy is sure to follow; and this too shows how far that rule surpasses all others. Again, in a democracy, it is impossible but that there will be malpractices: these malpractices, however, do not lead to enmities, but to close friendships, which are formed among those engaged in them, who must hold well together to carry on their villanies. And so things go on until a man stands forth as champion of the commonalty, and puts down the evil-doers. Straightway the author of so great a service is admired by all, and from being admired soon comes to be appointed king; so that here too it is plain that monarchy is the best government. Lastly, to sum up all in a word, whence, I ask, was it that we got the freedom which we enjoy?—did democracy give it us, or oligarchy, or a monarch? As a single man recovered our freedom for us, my sentence is that we keep to the rule of one. Even apart from this, we ought not to change the laws of our forefathers when they work fairly; for to do so, is not well."

83. Such were the three opinions brought forward at this meeting; the four other Persians voted in favour of the last. Otanes, who wished to give his countrymen a democracy, when he found the decision against him, arose a second time, and spoke thus before the assembly, "Brother conspirators, it is plain that the king who is to be chosen will be one of ourselves, whether we make the choice by casting lots for the prize, or by letting the people decide which of us they will have to rule over them, or in any other way. Now, as I have neither a mind to rule nor to be ruled, I shall not enter the lists with you in this matter. I withdraw, however, on one condition—none of you shall claim to exercise rule over me or my seed for ever." The six agreed to these terms, and Otanes withdrew and stood aloof from the contest. And still to this day the family of Otanes continues to be the only free family in Persia; those who belong to it submit to the rule of the king only so far as they themselves choose; they are bound, however, to observe the laws of the land like the other Persians.

84. After this the six took counsel together, as to the fairest way of setting up a king: and first, with respect to Otanes, they

resolved, that if any of their own number got the kingdom, Otanes and his seed after him should receive year by year, as a mark of special honour, a Median robe, and all such other gifts as are accounted the most honourable in Persia. And these they resolved to give him, because he was the man who first planned the outbreak, and who brought the seven together. These privileges, therefore, were assigned specially to Otanes. The following were made common to them all: It was to be free to each, whenever he pleased, to enter the palace unannounced, unless the king were sleeping with a woman; and the king was to be bound to marry into no family excepting those of the conspirators. Concerning the appointment of a king, the resolve to which they came was the following: They would ride out together next morning into the skirts of the city, and he whose steed first neighed after the sun was up should have the kingdom.

85. Now Darius had a sharp-witted groom called Oebares. After the meeting had broken up, Darius sent for him, and said, "Oebares, this is the way in which the king is to be chosen—we are to mount our horses, and the man whose horse first neighs after the sun is up is to have the kingdom. If then you have any cleverness, contrive a plan whereby the prize may fall to us, and not go to another." "Truly, master," Oebares answered, "if it depends on this whether you shall be king or no, set your heart at ease, and fear nothing: I have a charm which is sure not to fail." "If you really have anything of the kind," said Darius, "hasten to get it ready. The matter does not brook delay, for the trial is to be tomorrow." So Oebares when he heard that, did as follows: When night came, he took one of the mares, the chief favourite of the horse which Darius rode, and tethering it in the suburb, brought his master's horse to the place; then, after leading him round and round the mare several times, nearer and nearer at each circuit, he ended by letting him cover her.

86. And now, when the morning broke, the six Persians, according to agreement, met together on horseback, and rode out to the suburb. As they went along they neared the spot where the mare was tethered the night before, whereupon the horse of Darius sprang forward and neighed. Just at the same time,

though the sky was clear and bright, there was a flash of lightning, followed by a thunder-clap. It seemed as if the heavens conspired with Darius, and hereby inaugurated him king: so the five other nobles leaped with one accord from their steeds, and bowed down before him and owned him for their king.[21]

87. This is the account which some of the Persians gave of the contrivance of Oebares; but there are others who relate the matter differently. They say that in the morning he stroked the mare's genitals with his hand, which he then hid in his trousers until the sun rose and the horses were about to start, when he suddenly drew his hand forth and put it to the nostrils of his master's horse, which immediately snorted and neighed.

88. Thus was Darius, son of Hystaspes, appointed king; and, except the Arabians, all they of Asia were subject to him; for Cyrus, and after him Cambyses, had brought them all under. The Arabians were never subject as slaves to the Persians, but had a league of friendship with them from the time when they brought Cambyses on his way as he went into Egypt; for had they been unfriendly the Persians could never have made their invasion.

Darius married, first of all, the following women, who were all of them Persians, namely, two daughters of Cyrus, Atossa and Artystone; of these, Atossa had been twice married before, once to Cambyses, her brother, and once to the Magus; the other, Artystone, was a virgin. He married also Parmys, daughter of Smerdis, son of Cyrus; and he likewise took to wife the daughter of Otanes, who had made the discovery about the Magus. And now when his power was established firmly throughout all the kingdoms, the first thing that he did was to set up a carving in stone, which showed a man mounted upon a horse, with an inscription in these words following: "Darius, son

---

[21] It has been already observed that Darius probably succeeded to the throne by right of birth. Failing the line of Cyrus, which was now extinct, the line of Darius was next in succession. Of course, if this view be correct, Hystaspes was the rightful heir; but, as his years prevented him from undertaking the post of leader in the conspiracy, he ceded his rights to his son

of Hystaspes, by aid of his good horse" (here followed the horse's name), "and of his good groom Oebares, got himself the kingdom of the Persians."

89. This he set up in Persia, and afterwards he proceeded to establish twenty governments of the kind which the Persians call satrapies, assigning to each its governor, and fixing the tribute which was to be paid him by the several nations. And generally he joined together in one satrapy the nations that were neighbours, but sometimes he passed over the nearer tribes, and put in their stead those which were more remote. The following is an account of these governments, and of the yearly tribute which they paid to the king:[22] Such as brought their tribute in silver were ordered to pay according to the Babylonian talent; while the Euboic was the standard measure for such as brought gold. Now the Babylonian talent contains seventy Euboic minae. During all the reign of Cyrus, and afterwards when Cambyses ruled, there were no fixed tributes, but the nations severally brought gifts to the king. On account of this and other like doings, the Persians say that Darius was a huckster, Cambyses a master, and Cyrus a father; for Darius looked to making a gain in everything; Cambyses was harsh and reckless; while Cyrus was gentle, and procured them all manner of goods.

90. The Ionians, the Magnesians of Asia, the Aeolians, the Carians, the Lycians, the Milyans, and the Pamphylians, paid their tribute in a single sum, which was fixed at 400 talents of silver. These formed together the first satrapy.

The Mysians, Lydians, Lasonians, Cabalians, and Hygennians paid the sum of 500 talents. This was the second satrapy.

The Hellespontians, of the right coast as one enters the straits, the Phrygians, the Asiatic Thracians, the Paphlagonians, the Mariandynians, and the Syrians paid a tribute of 360 talents. This was the third satrapy.

The Cilicians gave 360 white horses, one for each day in the

---

[22] Chapters 89-96 give an official statistical account of the empire; chapters 97-117 describe remote dependencies and are mostly travellers' tales.

year, and 500 talents of silver. Of this sum 140 talents went to pay the cavalry which guarded the country, while the remaining 360 were received by Darius. This was the fourth satrapy.

91. The country reaching from the city of Posideium (built by Amphilocus, son of Amphiaraus, on the confines of Syria and Cilicia) to the borders of Egypt, excluding therefrom a district which belonged to Arabia, and was free from tax, paid a tribute of 350 talents. All Phoenicia, Palestine Syria, and Cyprus, were herein contained. This was the fifth satrapy.

From Egypt, and the neighbouring parts of Libya, together with the towns of Cyrene and Barca, which belonged to the Egyptian satrapy, the tribute which came in was 700 talents. These 700 talents did not include the profits of the fisheries of Lake Moeris, nor the corn furnished to the troops at Memphis. Corn was supplied to 120,000 Persians, who dwelt at Memphis in the quarter called the White Castle, and to a number of auxiliaries. This was the sixth satrapy.

The Sattagydians, the Gandarians, the Dadicae, and the Aparytae, who were all reckoned together, paid a tribute of 170 talents. This was the seventh satrapy.

Susa, and the other parts of Cissia, paid 300 talents. This was the eighth satrapy.

92. From Babylonia, and the rest of Assyria, were drawn 1,000 talents of silver, and 500 boy-eunuchs. This was the ninth satrapy.

Agbatana, and the other parts of Media, together with the Paricanians, and Orthocorybantes, paid in all 450 talents. This was the tenth satrapy.

The Caspians, Pausicae, Pantimathi, and Daritae, were joined in one government, and paid the sum of 200 talents. This was the eleventh satrapy.

From the Bactrian tribes as far as the Aegli, the tribute received was 360 talents. This was the twelfth satrapy.

93. From Pactyica, Armenia, and the countries reaching thence to the Euxine, the sum drawn was 400 talents. This was the thirteenth satrapy.

The Sagartians, Sarangians, Thamanaeans, Utians, and My-cians, together with the inhabitants of the islands in the Red Sea, where the king sends those whom he banishes, furnished al-together a tribute of 600 talents. This was the fourteenth sa-trapy.

The Sacans and Caspians gave 250 talents. This was the fif-teenth satrapy.

The Parthians, Chorasmians, Sogdians, and Arians, gave 300. This was the sixteenth satrapy.

94. The Paricanians and Ethiopians of Asia furnished a trib-ute of 400 talents. This was the seventeenth satrapy.

The Matienians, Saspeires, and Alarodians were rated to pay 200 talents. This was the eighteenth satrapy

The Moschi, Tibareni, Macrones, Mosynoeci, and Mares had to pay 300 talents. This was the nineteenth satrapy.

The Indians, who are more numerous than any other nation with which we are acquainted, paid a tribute exceeding that of every other people, 360 talents of gold-dust. This was the twentieth satrapy.

95. If the Babylonian money here spoken of be reduced to the Euboic scale, it will make 9,540 such talents; and if the gold be reckoned at thirteen times the worth of silver, the Indian gold-dust will come to 4,680 talents. Add these two amounts to-gether, and the whole revenue which came in to Darius year by year will be found to be in Euboic money 14,560 talents, not to mention parts of a talent.[23]

96. Such was the revenue which Darius derived from Asia

[23] It is impossible to reconcile Herodotus' numbers, and equally im-possible to say where the mistake lies. According to the items of his ac-count the sum total of the silver amounts to 7,740 Babylonian talents. This would equal 9,030 Euboic talents; instead of which he gives, in his present text, 9,540; being an excess over the items of 510 Euboic talents. Again, having stated the silver to amount to 9,540 Euboic talents, and the gold-dust to be equal to 4,680 Euboic talents (a correct estimate on his premises), he gives the whole amount as 14,560 instead of 14,220 talents; so that again he is in excess, this time, by 340 talents. Thus we seem to have a double error, which it is quite impossible to remedy.

and a small part of Libya. Later in his reign the sum was increased by the tribute of the islands, and of the nations of Europe as far as Thessaly. The great king stores away the tribute which he receives after this fashion—he melts it down, and while it is in a liquid state runs it into earthen vessels, which are afterwards removed, leaving the metal in a solid mass. When money is wanted, he coins as much of this bullion as the occasion requires.

97. Such then were the governments, and such the amounts of tribute at which they were assessed respectively. Persia alone has not been reckoned among the tributaries—and for this reason, because the country of the Persians is altogether exempt from tax. The following peoples paid no settled tribute, but brought gifts to the king: first, the Ethiopians bordering upon Egypt, who were reduced by Cambyses when he made war on the long-lived Ethiopians, and who dwell about the sacred city of Nysa, and have festivals in honour of Dionysus. The grain on which they and their next neighbours feed is the same as that used by the Calantian Indians. Their dwelling houses are underground. Every third year these two nations brought—and they still bring to my day—two quarts of virgin gold, 200 logs of ebony, five Ethiopian boys, and twenty elephant tusks. The Colchians, and the neighbouring tribes who dwell between them and the Caucasus—for so far the Persian rule reaches, while north of the Caucasus no one fears them any longer—undertook to furnish a gift, which in my day was still brought every fifth year, consisting of 100 boys, and the same number of maidens. The Arabs brought every year 1,000 talents of frankincense. Such were the gifts which the king received over and above the tribute-money.

98. The way in which the Indians get the plentiful supply of gold, which enables them to furnish year by year so vast an amount of gold-dust to the king is the following: Eastward of India lies a tract which is entirely sand. Indeed of all the inhabitants of Asia, concerning whom anything certain is known, the Indians dwell the nearest to the east, and the rising of the sun. Beyond them the whole country is desert on account of the

sand.[24] The tribes of Indians are numerous, and do not all speak the same language—some are nomads, others not. They who dwell in the marshes along the river,[25] live on raw fish, which they take in boats made of reeds, each formed out of a single joint. These Indians wear a dress of sedge, which they cut in the river and bruise; afterwards they weave it into mats, and wear it as we wear a breast-plate.

99. Eastward of these Indians are another tribe, called Padaeans, who are wanderers, and live on raw flesh. This tribe is said to have the following customs: If one of their number be ill, man or woman, they take the sick person, and if he be a man, the men of his acquaintance proceed to put him to death, because, they say, his flesh would be spoilt for them if he pined and wasted away with sickness. The man protests he is not ill in the least; but his friends will not accept his denial—in spite of all he can say, they kill him, and feast themselves on his body. So also if a woman be sick, the women, who are her friends, take her and do with her exactly the same as the men. If one of them reaches to old age, about which there is seldom any question, as commonly before that time they have had some disease or other, and so have been put to death—but if a man, notwithstanding, comes to be old, then they offer him in sacrifice to their gods, and afterwards eat his flesh.

100. There is another set of Indians whose customs are very different. They refuse to put any live animal to death,[26] they sow no corn, and have no dwelling-houses. Vegetables are their only food. There is a plant which grows wild in their country, bearing seed about the size of millet-seed in a calyx: their wont is to gather this seed and having boiled it, calyx and all, to use

[24] The India of Herodotus is the true ancient India, the region about the Upper Indus, best known to us at present under the name of the Punjab. Herodotus knows nothing of the great southern peninsula.

[25] By the river is meant the Indus. It does not appear that Herodotus was aware of the existence of the Ganges, which only became known to the Greeks by the expedition of Alexander.

[26] The repugnance of true Brahmins to take away life is well known. The Mahrattas are said to have the same prejudice.

it for food. If one of them is attacked with sickness, he goes forth into the wilderness, and lies down to die; no has the least concern either for the sick or for the dead.

101. All the tribes which I have mentioned copulate openly like the brute beasts: they have also all the same tint of skin, which approaches that of the Ethiopians. Their semen too is not white like other men's but black like that of the Ethiopians. Their country is a long way from Persia towards the south: nor had king Darius ever any authority over them.

102. Besides these, there are Indians of another tribe, who border on the city Caspatyrus, and the country of Pactyica; these people dwell northward of all the rest of the Indians, and follow nearly the same mode of life as the Bactrians. They are more warlike than any of the other tribes, and from them the men are sent forth who go to procure the gold. For it is in this part of India that the sandy desert lies. Here, in this desert, there lived amid the sand great ants,[27] in size somewhat less than dogs, but bigger than foxes. The Persian king has a number of them, which have been caught by the hunters in the land whereof we are speaking. These ants make their dwellings underground, and like the Greek ants, which they very much resemble in shape, throw up sand-heaps as they burrow. Now the sand which they throw up is full of gold. The Indians, when they go into the desert to collect this sand, take three camels and harness them together, a female in the middle and a male on either side, in a leading-rein. The rider sits on the female, and they are particular to choose for the purpose one that has but just dropped her young; for their female camels can run as fast as horses, while they bear burdens very much better.

103. As the Greeks are well acquainted with the shape of the camel, I shall not trouble to describe it; but I shall mention what seems to have escaped their notice. The camel has in its hind legs four thigh-bones and four knee-joints,[28] and the geni-

---

[27] It is curious to find the same narrative, told gravely by Prester John in the 12th century. He gives the ants seven legs and four wings.

[28] This is of course untrue, but Herodotus was deceived by the way the camel kneels to receive a load.

tals, which lie between its hind legs, are turned towards the tail.

104. When the Indians therefore have thus equipped themselves they set off in quest of the gold, calculating the time so
that they may be engaged in seizing it during the most sultry
part of the day, when the ants hide themselves to escape the
heat. The sun in those parts shines fiercest in the morning, not,
as elsewhere, at noonday; the greatest heat is from the time
when he has reached a certain height, until the hour at which
the market closes. During this space he burns much more furiously than at midday in Greece, so that the men there are said
at that time to drench themselves with water. At noon his heat
is much the same in India as in other countries, after which, as
the day declines, the warmth is only equal to that of the morning sun elsewhere. Towards evening the coolness increases, till
about sunset it becomes very cold.

105. When the Indians reach the place where the gold is,
they fill their bags with the sand, and ride away at their best
speed: the ants, however, scenting them, as the Persians say,
rush forth in pursuit. Now these animals are so swift, they declare, that there is nothing in the world like them: if it were not,
therefore, that the Indians get a start while the ants are muster-
ing, not a single gold-gatherer could escape. During the flight
the male camels, which are not so fleet as the females, grow
tired, and begin to drag, first one, and then the other; but the
females recollect the young which they have left behind, and
never give way or flag. Such, according to the Persians, is the
manner in which the Indians get the greater part of their gold,
some is dug out of the earth, but of this the supply is more
scanty.

106. It seems as if the extreme regions of the earth were
blessed by nature with the most excellent productions, just in
the same way that Greece enjoys a climate more excellently
tempered than any other country. In India, which, as I observed lately, is the furthest region of the inhabited world towards the east, all the four-footed beasts and the birds are very
much bigger than those found elsewhere, except only the horses,
which are surpassed by the Median breed called the Nisaean.

Gold too is produced there in vast abundance, some dug from the earth, some washed down by the rivers, some carried off in the mode which I have but now described. And further, there are trees which grow wild there, the fruit whereof is a wool exceeding in beauty and goodness that of sheep. The natives make their clothes of this tree-wool.[29]

107. Arabia is the last of inhabited lands towards the south, and it is the only country which produces frankincense, myrrh, cassia, cinnamon, and laudanum. The Arabians do not get any of these, except the myrrh, without trouble. The frankincense they procure by means of the gum storax, which the Greeks obtain from the Phoenicians; this they burn, and thereby obtain the spice. For the trees which bear the frankincense are guarded by winged serpents, small in size, and of varied colours, whereof vast numbers hang about every tree. They are of the same kind as the serpents that invade Egypt; and there is nothing but the smoke of the storax which will drive them from the trees.

108. The Arabians say that the whole world would swarm with these serpents, if they were not kept in check in the way in which I know that vipers are. Of a truth divine Providence does appear to be, as indeed one might expect beforehand, a wise contriver. For timid animals which are a prey to others are all made to produce young abundantly, that so the species may not be entirely eaten up and lost; while savage and noxious creatures are made very unfruitful. The hare, for instance, which is hunted alike by beasts, birds, and men, breeds so abundantly as even to conceive while pregnant, a thing which is true of no other animal. You find in a hare's belly, at one and the same time, some of the young all covered with fur, others quite naked, others again just fully formed in the womb, while the hare perhaps has lately conceived afresh. The lioness, on the other hand, which is one of the strongest and boldest of brutes, brings forth young but once in her lifetime,[30] and then a single cub; she

---

[29] Tree-wool is the Greek word for cotton.
[30] Aristotle observes that the lioness breeds once a year, and usually has three cubs.

cannot possibly conceive again, since she loses her womb at the same time that she drops her young. The reason of this is, that as soon as the cub begins to stir inside the dam, his claws, which are sharper than those of any other animal, scratch the womb; as time goes on, he grows bigger, he tears it ever more and more; so that at last, when the birth comes, there is not a morsel in the whole womb that is sound.

109. Now with respect to the vipers and the winged snakes of Arabia, if they increased as fast as their nature would allow, impossible were it for man to maintain himself upon the earth. Accordingly it is found that when the male and female couple together, at the very moment of impregnation, the female seizes the male by the neck, and having once fastened, cannot be brought to leave go till she has bit the neck entirely through. And so the male perishes; but after a while he is revenged upon the female by means of the young, which, while still unborn, gnaw a passage through the womb, and then through the belly of their mother, and so make their entrance into the world. Contrariwise, other snakes, which are harmless, lay eggs, and hatch a vast number of young. Vipers are found in all parts of the world, but the winged serpents are nowhere seen except in Arabia, where they are all congregated together. This makes them appear so numerous.

110. Such, then, is the way in which the Arabians obtain their frankincense; their manner of collecting the cassia is the following: They cover all their body and their face with the hides of oxen and other skins, leaving only holes for the eyes, and thus protected go in search of the cassia, which grows in a lake of no great depth. All round the shores and in the lake itself there dwell a number of winged animals, much resembling bats, which screech horribly, and are very valiant. These creatures they must keep from their eyes all the while that they gather the cassia.

111. Still more wonderful is the mode in which they collect the cinnamon. Where the wood grows, and what country produces it, they cannot tell—only some, following probability, relate that it comes from the country in which Dionysus was

brought up. Great birds, they say, bring the sticks which w\
Greeks, taking the word from the Phoenicians, call cinnamon,
and carry them up into the air to make their nests. These are
fastened with a sort of mud to a sheer face of rock, where no
foot of man is able to climb. So the Arabians, to get the cinnamon, use the following artifice. They cut all the oxen and asses
and beasts of burden that die in their land into large pieces,
which they carry with them into those regions, and place near
the nests: then they withdraw to a distance, and the old birds,
swooping down, seize the pieces of meat and fly with them up to
their nests; which, not being able to support the weight, break
off and fall to the ground.[31] Hereupon the Arabians return and
collect the cinnamon, which is afterwards carried from Arabia
into other countries.

112. Ledanum, which the Arabs call ladanon, is procured in
a yet stranger fashion. Found in a most inodorous place, it is
the sweetest-scented of all substances. It is gathered from the
beards of he-goats, where it is found sticking like gum, having
come from the bushes on which they browse. It is used in many
sorts of unguents, and is what the Arabs burn chiefly as incense.

113. Concerning the spices of Arabia let no more be said. The
whole country is scented with them, and exhales an odour mar-
vellously sweet. There are also in Arabia two kinds of sheep
worthy of admiration, the like of which is nowhere else to be
seen; the one kind has long tails, not less than four and one-half
feet in length, which, if they were allowed to trail on the ground,
would be bruised and fall into sores. As it is, all the shepherds
know enough of carpentering to make little trucks for their
sheep's tails. The trucks are placed under the tails, each sheep
having one to himself, and the tails are then tied down upon
them. The other kind has a broad tail, which is eighteen inches
across sometimes.

114. Where the south declines towards the setting sun lies
the country called Ethiopia, the last inhabited land in that direction. There gold is obtained in great plenty, huge elephants

---

[31] The story evidently belongs to a whole class of Eastern tales, wherein
an important part is played by great birds.

abound, with wild trees of all sorts, and ebony; and the men are taller, handsomer, and longer lived than anywhere else.

115. Now these are the furthest regions of the world in Asia and Libya. Of the extreme tracts of Europe towards the west I cannot speak with any certainty; for I do not allow that there is any river, to which the barbarians give the name of Eridanus, emptying itself into the northern sea, whence (as the tale goes) amber is procured; nor do I know of any islands called the Tin Islands,[32] whence the tin comes which we use. For in the first place the name Eridanus is manifestly not a barbarian word at all, but a Greek name, invented by some poet or other; and secondly, though I have taken vast pains, I have never been able to get an assurance from an eye-witness that there is any sea on the further side of Europe. Nevertheless, tin and amber[33] do certainly come to us from the ends of the earth.

116. The northern parts of Europe are very much richer in gold than any other region:[34] but how it is procured I have no certain knowledge. The story runs, that the one-eyed Arimaspi purloin it from the griffins; but here too I am incredulous, and cannot persuade myself that there is a race of men born with one eye, who in all else resemble the rest of mankind. Nevertheless it seems to be true that the extreme regions of the earth, which surround and shut up within themselves all other countries, produce the things which are the rarest, and which men reckon the most beautiful.

117. There is a plain in Asia which is shut in on all sides by a mountain-range, and in this mountain-range are five openings. The plain lies on the confines of the Chorasmians, Hyrcanians, Parthians, Sarangians, and Thaminaeans, and belonged formerly

[32] This name was applied to the Selinae, or Scilly Isles; and the imperfect information respecting the site of the mines of tin led to the belief that they were there, instead of on the mainland of Cornwall.

[33] Herodotus is quite correct in his information respecting amber being found at the extremity of Europe, though not at the West.

[34] It appears, by the mention of the Arimaspi, that the European gold region of which Herodotus here speaks, is the district east of the Ural Mountains, which modern geography would assign to Asia. Herodotus regards Europe as extending the whole length of both Africa and Asia.

to the first-mentioned of those peoples. Ever since the Persians, however, obtained the mastery of Asia, it has been the property of the Great King. A mighty river, called the Aces,[35] flows from the hills inclosing the plain; and this stream, formerly, splitting into five channels, ran through the five openings in the hills, and watered the lands of the five nations which dwell around. The Persian came, however, and conquered the region, and then it went ill with the people of these lands. The Great King blocked up all the passages between the hills with dykes and flood-gates, and so prevented the water from flowing out. Then the plain within the hills became a sea, for the river kept rising, and the water could find no outlet. From that time the five nations which were wont formerly to have the use of the stream, losing their accustomed supply of water, have been in great distress. In winter, indeed, they have rain from heaven like the rest of the world, but in summer, after sowing their millet and their sesame, they always stood in need of water from the river. When, therefore, they suffer from this want, hastening to Persia, men and women alike, they take their station at the gate of the king's palace, and wail aloud. Then the king orders the flood-gates to be opened towards the country whose need is greatest, and lets the soil drink until it has had enough; after which the gates on this side are shut, and others are unclosed for the nation which, of the remainder, needs it most. It has been told me that the king never gives the order to open the gates till the suppliants have paid him a large sum of money over and above the tribute.

118. Of the seven Persians who rose up against the Magus, one, Intaphernes, lost his life very shortly after the outbreak, for an act of insolence. He wished to enter the palace and transact a certain business with the king. Now the law was that all those who had taken part in the rising against the Magus might enter unannounced into the king's presence, unless he happened

* No river çan be found which at all answers the description; but the origin of the tale may be found in the distribution by the Persians of the waters. Under a strong government, the water supply would of course have been regulated, and so good an opportunity of raising a revenue was seized with alacrity.

to be having intercourse. So Intaphernes would not have any
one announce him, but, as he belonged to the seven, claimed it
as his right to go in. The doorkeeper, however, and chief usher
forbade his entrance, since the king, they said, was lying with a
woman. But Intaphernes thought they told lies; so drawing his
scimitar, he cut off their noses and their ears, and, hanging them
on the bridle of his horse, put the bridle round their necks, and
so let them go.

119. Then these two men went and showed themselves to the
king, and told him how it had come to pass that they were thus
treated. Darius trembled lest it was by the common consent of
the six that the deed had been done; he therefore sent for them
all in turn, and sounded them to know if they approved the conduct of Intaphernes. When he found by their answers that there
had been no concert between him and them, he laid hands on
Intaphernes, his children, and all his near kindred; strongly
suspecting that he and his friends were about to raise a revolt.
When all had been seized and put in chains, as malefactors condemned to death, the wife of Intaphernes came and stood continually at the palace-gates, weeping and wailing sore. So Darius
after a while, seeing that she never ceased to stand and weep,
was touched with pity for her, and bade a messenger go to her
and say, "Lady, king Darius gives you as a boon the life of one
of your kinsmen—choose which you will of the prisoners." Then
she pondered awhile before she answered, "If the king grants
me the life of one alone, I make choice of my brother." Darius
when he heard the reply, was astonished, and sent again, saying,
"Lady, the king bids you tell him why it is that you pass by
your husband and your children, and prefer to have the life of
your brother spared. He is not so near to you as your children,
nor so dear as your husband." She answered, "O king, if the
gods will, I may have another husband and other children when
these are gone. But as my father and my mother are no more, it
is impossible that I should have another brother.[36] This was my
thought when I asked to have my brother spared." Then it

---

[36] The resemblance of this to Antigone's speech (Sophocles, *Antigone*
909-912) is very striking.

seemed to Darius that the lady spoke well, and he gave her, besides the life that she had asked, the life also of her eldest son, because he was greatly pleased with her. But he slew all the rest. Thus one of the seven died, in the way I have described, very shortly after the insurrection.

120. About the time of Cambyses' last sickness, the following events happened. There was a certain Oroetes, a Persian, whom Cyrus had made governor of Sardis. This man conceived a most unholy wish. He had never suffered wrong or had an ill word from Polycrates the Samian—nay, he had not so much as seen him in all his life; yet, notwithstanding, he conceived the wish to seize him and put him to death. This wish, according to the account which the most part give, arose from what happened one day as he was sitting with another Persian in the gate of the king's palace. The man's name was Mitrobates, and he was ruler of the satrapy of Dascyleium. He and Oroetes had been talking together, and from talking they fell to quarrelling and comparing their merits; whereupon Mitrobates said to Oroetes reproachfully, "Are you worthy to be called a man, when, near as Samos lies to your government, and easy as it is to conquer, you have omitted to bring it under the dominion of the king? Easy to conquer, said I? Why, a mere common citizen, with the help of fifteen men-at-arms, mastered the island, and is still king of it." Oroetes, they say, took this reproach greatly to heart; but, instead of seeking to revenge himself on the man by whom it was uttered, he conceived the desire of destroying Polycrates, since it was on Polycrates' account that the reproach had fallen on him.

121. Another less common version of the story is that Oroetes sent a herald to Samos to make a request, the nature of which is not stated; Polycrates was at the time reclining in the men's apartment, and Anacreon the Teian was with him; when therefore the herald came forward to converse, Polycrates, either out of studied contempt for the power of Oroetes, or it may be merely by chance, was lying with his face turned away towards the wall; and so he lay all the time that the herald spoke, and when he ended, did not even vouchsafe him a word.

122. Such are the two reasons alleged for the death of Polycrates; it is open to all to believe which they please. What is certain is, that Oroetes, while residing at Magnesia on the Maeander, sent a Lydian, by name Myrsus, the son of Gyges, with a message to Polycrates at Samos, well knowing what that monarch designed. For Polycrates entertained a design which no other Greek, so far as we know, ever formed before him, unless it were Minos the Cnossian, and those (if there were any such) who had the mastery of the Aegean at an earlier time—Polycrates, I say, was the first of mere human birth who conceived the design of gaining the empire of the sea, and aspired to rule over Ionia and the islands. Knowing then that Polycrates was thus minded, Oroetes sent his message, which ran as follows:

"Oroetes to Polycrates speaks thus: I hear you raised your thoughts high, but your means are not equal to your ambition. Listen then to my words, and learn how you may at once serve yourself and preserve me. King Cambyses is bent on my destruction—of this I have warning from a sure hand. Come, therefore, and fetch me away, men and all my wealth—share my wealth with me, and then, so far as money can aid, you may make yourself master of the whole of Greece. But if you doubt my wealth, send the trustiest of your followers, and I will show my treasures to him."

123. Polycrates, when he heard this message, was full of joy, and straightway approved the terms; but, as money was what he chiefly desired, before stirring in the business he sent his secretary, Maeandrius, son of Maeandrius, a Samian, to look into the matter. This was the man who, not very long afterwards, made an offering at the temple of Hera of all the furniture which had adorned the male apartments in the palace of Polycrates, an offering well worth seeing. Oroetes learning that one was coming to view his treasures, contrived as follows: he filled eight great chests almost brimful of stones, and then covering over the stones with gold, corded the chests, and so held them in readiness. When Maeandrius arrived, he was shown this as Oroetes' treasure, and having seen it returned to Samos.

124. On hearing his account, Polycrates, notwithstanding

many warnings given him by the soothsayers, and much dissuasion of his friends, made ready to go in person Even the dream which visited his daughter failed to check him. She had dreamed that she saw her father hanging high in air, washed by Zeus, and anointed by the sun. Having therefore thus dreamed, she used every effort to prevent her father from going; even as he went on board his fifty-oared galley crying after him with words of evil omen. Then Polycrates threatened her that, if he returned in safety, he would keep her unmarried many years. She answered that he might perform his threat; far better for her to remain long unmarried than to be bereft of her father!

125. Polycrates, however, making light of all the counsel offered him, set sail and went to Oroetes. Many friends accompanied him; among the rest, Democedes, the son of Calliphon, a native of Croton, who was a physician, and the best skilled in his art of all men then living. Polycrates, on his arrival at Magnesia, perished miserably, in a way unworthy of his rank and of his lofty schemes. For, if we except the Syracusans, there has never been one of the Greek tyrants who was to be compared with Polycrates for magnificence. Oroetes, however, slew him and in a mode which is not fit to be described, and then hung his dead body upon a cross. His Samian followers Oroetes let go free, bidding them thank him that they were allowed their liberty; the rest, who were in part slaves, in part free foreigners, he alike treated as his slaves by conquest. Then was the dream of the daughter of Polycrates fulfilled; for Polycrates, as he hung upon the cross, and rain fell on him, was washed by Zeus; and he was anointed by the sun, when his own moisture overspread his body. And so the vast good fortune of Polycrates came at last to the end which Amasis the Egyptian king had prophesied in days gone by.

126. It was not long before retribution for the murder of Polycrates overtook Oroetes. After the death of Cambyses, and during all the time that the Magus sat upon the throne, Oroetes remained in Sardis, and brought no help to the Persians, whom the Medes had robbed of the sovereignty. On the contrary, amid the troubles of this season, he slew Mitrobates, the satrap of

Dascyleium, who had cast the reproach upon him in the matter of Polycrates; and he slew also Mitrobates' son, Cranaspes, both men of high repute among the Persians. He was likewise guilty of many other acts of insolence; among the rest, of the following: There was a courier sent to him by Darius whose message was not to his mind—Oroetes had him waylaid and murdered on his road back to the king; the man and his horse both disappeared, and no traces were left of either.

127. Darius therefore was no sooner settled upon the throne than he longed to take vengeance upon Oroetes for all his misdoings, and especially for the murder of Mitrobates and his son. To send an armed force openly against him, however, he did not think advisable, as the whole kingdom was still unsettled, and he too was but lately come to the throne, while Oroetes, as he understood, had a great power. In truth 1,000 Persians attended on him as a body-guard, and he held the satrapies of Phrygia, Lydia, and Ionia. Darius therefore proceeded by artifice. He called together a meeting of all the chief of the Persians, and thus addressed them, "Who among you, Persians, will undertake to accomplish me a matter by skill without force or tumult? Force is misplaced where the work wants skilful management. Who, then, will undertake to bring me Oroetes alive, or else to kill him? He never did the Persians any good in his life, and he has wrought us abundant injury. Two of our number, Mitrobates and his son, he has slain; and when messengers go to recall him, even though they have their mandate from me, with an insolence which is not to be endured, he puts them to death. We must kill this man, therefore, before he does the Persians any greater hurt."

128. Thus spoke Darius; and straightway thirty of those present came forward and offered themselves for the work. As they strove together, Darius interfered, and bade them have recourse to the lot. Accordingly lots were cast, and the task fell to Bagaeus, son of Artontes. Then Bagaeus caused many letters to be written on various matters, and sealed them all with the king's signet; after which he took the letters with him, and departed for Sardis. On his arrival he was shown into the presence

of Oroetes, when he uncovered the letters one by one, and giving them to the king's secretary—every satrap has with him a king's secretary—commanded him to read their contents. Herein his design was to try the fidelity of the body-guard, and to see if they would be likely to fall away from Oroetes. When therefore he saw that they showed the letters all due respect, and even more highly reverenced their contents, he gave the secretary a paper in which was written, "Persians, king Darius forbids you to guard Oroetes." The soldiers at these words laid aside their spears. So Bagaeus, finding that they obeyed this mandate, took courage, and gave into the secretary's hands the last letter, wherein it was written, "King Darius commands the Persians who are in Sardis to kill Oroetes." Then the guards drew their swords and slew him upon the spot. Thus did retribution for the murder of Polycrates the Samian overtake Oroetes the Persian.

129. Soon after the treasures of Oroetes had been conveyed to Sardis it happened that king Darius, as he leaped from his horse during the chase, sprained his foot. The sprain was one of no common severity, for the ankle-bone was forced quite out of the socket. Now Darius already had at his court certain Egyptians whom he reckoned the best-skilled physicians in all the world; to their aid, therefore, he had recourse; but they twisted the foot so clumsily, and used such violence, that they only made the mischief greater. For seven days and seven nights the king lay without sleep, so grievous was the pain he suffered. On the eighth day of his indisposition, one who had heard before leaving Sardis of the skill of Democedes the Crotoniat, told Darius, who commanded that he should be brought with all speed into his presence. When, therefore, they had found him among the slaves of Oroetes, quite uncared for by any one, they brought him just as he was, clanking his fetters, and all clothed in rags, before the king.

130. As soon as he was entered into the presence, Darius asked him if he knew medicine—to which he answered, "No," for he feared that if he made himself known he would lose all chance of ever again beholding Greece. Darius, however, perceiving that he dealt deceitfuly, and really understood the art,

bade those who had brought him to the presence, go fetch the scourges and the pricking-irons. Upon this Democedes confessed, but at the same time said, that he had no thorough knowledge of medicine—he had but lived some time with a physician, and in this way had gained a slight smattering of the art. However, Darius put himself under his care, and Democedes, by using the remedies customary among the Greeks, and exchanging the violent treatment of the Egyptians for milder means, first enabled him to get some sleep, and then in a very little time restored him altogether, after he had quite lost the hope of ever having the use of his foot. Hereupon the king presented Democedes with two sets of fetters wrought in gold; so Democedes asked if he meant to double his sufferings, because he had brought him back to health? Darius was pleased at the speech, and bade the eunuchs take Democedes to see his wives, which they did accordingly, telling them all that this was the man who had saved the king's life. Then each of the wives dipped with a saucer into the chest of gold, and gave so bountifully to Democedes, that a slave named Sciton, who followed him, and picked up the staters which fell from the saucers, gathered together a great heap of gold.

131. This Democedes left his country and became attached to Polycrates in the following way: His father, who dwelt at Croton, was a man of a savage temper, and treated him cruelly. When, therefore, he could no longer bear such constant illusage, Democedes left his home, and sailed away to Aegina. There he set up in business, and succeeded the first year in surpassing all the best-skilled physicians of the place, notwithstanding that he was without instruments, and had with him none of the appliances needful for the practice of his art. In the second year the state of Aegina hired his services at the price of a talent; in the third the Athenians engaged him at a hundred minae; and in the fourth Polycrates at two talents. So he went to Samos, and there took up his abode. It was in no small measure from his success that the Crotoniats came to be reckoned such good physicians; for about this period the physicians of Croton had the name of being the best, and those of Cyrene the

second best, in all Greece. The Argives, about the same time, were thought to be the first musicians in Greece.

132. After Democedes had cured Darius at Susa, he dwelt there in a large house, and feasted daily at the king's table, nor did he lack anything that his heart desired, excepting liberty to return to his country. By interceding for them with Darius, he saved the lives of the Egyptian physicians who had had the care of the king before he came, when they were about to be impaled, because they had been surpassed by a Greek: and further, he succeeded in rescuing an Elean soothsayer, who had followed the fortunes of Polycrates, and was lying in utter neglect among his slaves. In short there was no one who stood so high as Democedes in the favour of the king.

133. Moreover, within a little while it happened that Atossa, the daughter of Cyrus, who was married to Darius, had a boil form upon her breast, which, after it burst, began to spread and increase. Now so long as the sore was of no great size, she hid it through shame and made no mention of it to any one; but when it became worse, she sent at last for Democedes, and showed it to him. Democedes said that he would make her well, but she must first promise him with an oath that if he cured her she would grant him whatever request he might prefer; assuring her at the same time that it should be nothing which she could blush to hear.

134. On these terms Democedes applied his art, and soon cured the abscess; and Atossa, when she had heard his request, spoke thus one night to Darius, "It seems to me strange, my lord, that, with the mighty power which is yours, you sit idle, and neither make any conquest, nor advance the power of the Persians. I think that one who is so young, and so richly endowed with wealth, should perform some noble achievement to prove to the Persians that it is a man who governs them. Another reason, too, should urge you to attempt some enterprise. Not only does it befit you to show the Persians that a man rules them, but for your own peace you should waste their strength in wars lest idleness breed revolt against your authority. Now, too, while you are still young, you may well accomplish some ex-

ploit; for as the body grows in strength the mind too ripens, and as the body ages, the mind's powers decay, till at last it becomes dulled to everything."

So spake Atossa, as Democedes had instructed her. Darius answered, "Dear lady, you have uttered the very thoughts that occupy my brain. I am minded to construct a bridge which shall join our continent with the other, and so carry war into Scythia. In a brief space and all will be accomplished as you desire."

But Atossa rejoined, "Look now, this war with Scythia were best reserved awhile—for the Scythians may be conquered at any time. Lead your host first into Greece. I long to be served by some of those Lacedaemonian maids of whom I have heard so much. I want also Argive, and Athenian, and Corinthian women. There is now at the court a man who can tell you better than any one else in the whole world whatever you would know concerning Greece, and who might serve you right well as guide: I mean him who performed the cure on your foot."

"Dear lady," Darius answered, "since it is your wish that we try first the valour of the Greeks, it were best, I think, before marching against them, to send some Persians to spy out the land; they may go in company with the man you mention, and when they have seen and learned all, they can bring us back a full report. Then, having a more perfect knowledge of them, I will begin the war."

135. Darius, having so spoke, put no long distance between the word and the deed, but as soon as day broke he summoned to his presence fifteen Persians of note, and bade them take Democedes for their guide, and explore the sea-coasts of Greece. Above all, they were to be sure to bring Democedes back with them, and not suffer him to run away and escape. After he had given these orders, Darius sent for Democedes, and asked him to serve as guide to the Persians, and when he had shown them the whole of Greece to come back to Persia. He should take, he said, all the valuables he possessed as presents to his father and his brothers, and he should receive on his return a far more abundant store. Moreover, the king added, he would give him, as his contribution towards the presents, a merchant-ship laden

with all manner of precious things, which should accompany him on his voyage. Now I do not believe that Darius, when he made these promises, had any guile in his heart: Democedes, however, who suspected that the king spoke to try him, took care not to snatch at the offers with any haste; but said he would leave his own goods behind to enjoy upon his return—the merchant-ship which the king proposed to grant him to carry gifts to his brothers, that he would accept at the king's hands. So when Darius had laid his orders upon Democedes, he sent him and the Persians away to the coast.

136. The men went down to Phoenicia, to Sidon, the Phoenician town, where straightway they fitted out two triremes and a trading vessel, which they loaded with all manner of precious merchandise; and, everything being now ready, they set sail for Greece. When they had made the land, they kept along the shore and examined it, taking notes of all that they saw; and in this way they explored the greater portion of the country, and all the most famous regions, until at last they reached Tarentum in Italy. There Aristophilides, king of the Tarentines, out of kindness to Democedes, took the rudders off the Median ships, and detained their crews as spies. Meanwhile Democedes escaped to Croton, his native city, whereupon Aristophilides released the Persians from prison, and gave their rudders back to them.

137. The Persians now quitted Tarentum, and sailed to Croton in pursuit of Democedes; they found him in the market place, where they straightway laid violent hands on him. Some of the Crotoniats, who greatly feared the power of the Persians, were willing to give him up; but others resisted, held Democedes fast, and even struck the Persians with their walking-sticks. They, on their part, kept crying out, "Men of Croton, beware what you do. It is the king's runaway slave that you are rescuing. Think you Darius will tamely submit to such an insult? Think you, that if you carry off the man from us, it will hereafter go well with you? Will you not rather be the first persons on whom we shall make war? Will not your city be the first we shall seek to lead away captive?" Thus they spoke, but the

Crotoniats did not heed them: they rescued Democedes, and seized also the trading-ship which the Persians had brought with them from Phoenicia. Thus robbed, and bereft of their guide, the Persians gave up all hope of exploring the rest of Greece, and set sail for Asia. As they were departing, Democedes sent to them and begged they would inform Darius that the daughter of Milo was affianced to him as his bride. For the name of Milo the wrestler was in high repute with the king. My belief is, that Democedes hastened his marriage by the payment of a large sum of money for the purpose of showing Darius that he was a man of mark in his own country.

138. The Persians weighed anchor and left Croton, but being wrecked on the coast of Iapygia, were made slaves by the inhabitants. From this condition they were rescued by Gillus, a banished Tarentine, who ransomed them at his own cost, and took them back to Darius. Darius offered to repay this service by granting Gillus whatever boon he chose to ask; whereupon Gillus told the king of his misfortune, and begged to be restored to his country. Fearing, however, that he might bring trouble on Greece if a vast armament were sent to Italy on his account, he added that it would content him if the Cnidians undertook to obtain his recall. Now the Cnidians were close friends of the Tarentines, which made him think there was no likelier means of procuring his return. Darius promised, and performed his part; for he sent a messenger to Cnidus, and commanded the Cnidians to restore Gillus. The Cnidians did as he wished, but found themselves unable to persuade the Tarentines, and were too weak to attempt force. Such, then, was the course which this matter took. These were the first Persians who ever came from Asia to Greece;[37] and they were sent to spy out the land for the reason which I have before mentioned.

139. After this, king Darius besieged and took Samos, which

[37] In the mind of Herodotus this voyage is of the greatest importance. It is the first step towards the invasion of Greece, and so a chief link in the chain of his history. Whether Darius attached much importance to it is a different matter. We must bear in mind that the details have evidently come from the descendants of Democedes, with whom Herodotus would have been brought into contact in Magna Graecia.

was the first city, Greek or Barbarian, that he conquered. The cause of his making war upon Samos was the following: At the time when Cambyses, son of Cyrus, marched against Egypt, vast numbers of Greeks flocked thither, some, as might have been looked for, to push their trade; others, to serve in his army; others again, merely to see the land: among these last was Syloson, son of Aeaces, and brother of Polycrates, at that time an exile from Samos. This Syloson, during his stay in Egypt, met with a singular piece of good fortune. He happened one day to put on a scarlet cloak, and thus attired to go into the market-place at Memphis, when Darius, who was one of Cambyses' body-guard, and not at that time a man of any account, saw him, and taking a strong liking to the dress, went up and offered to purchase it. Syloson perceived how anxious he was, and by a lucky inspiration answered, "There is no price at which I would sell my cloak, but I will give it to you for nothing, if you wish it." Darius thanked him, and accepted the garment.

140. Poor Syloson felt at the time that he had fooled away his cloak in a very simple manner; but afterwards, when in the course of years Cambyses died, and the seven Persians rose in revolt against the Magus, and Darius was the man chosen out of the seven to have the kingdom, Syloson learnt that the person to whom the crown had come was the very man who had coveted his cloak in Egypt, and to whom he had freely given it. So he made his way to Susa, and seating himself at the portal of the royal palace, gave out that he was a benefactor of the king. Then the doorkeeper went and told Darius. Amazed at what he heard, the king said thus within himself, "What Greek can have been my benefactor, or to which of them do I owe anything, so lately as I have got the kingdom? Scarcely a man of them all has been here, not more than one or two certainly, since I came to the throne. Nor do I remember that I am in the debt of any Greek. However, bring him in, and let me hear what he means by his boast." So the doorkeeper ushered Syloson into the presence, and the interpreters asked him who he was, and what he had done that he should call himself a benefactor of the king.

Then Syloson told the whole story of the cloak, and said that it was he who had made Darius the present. Hereupon Darius exclaimed, "Most generous of men, are you indeed he who, when I had no power at all, gave me something, albeit little? Truly the favour is as great as a very grand present would be nowadays. I will therefore give you in return gold and silver without stint, that you may never repent of having rendered a service to Darius, son of Hystaspes." "Give me not, O king," replied Syloson, "either silver or gold, but recover me Samos, my native land, and let that be your gift to me. It belongs now to a slave of ours, who, when Oroetes put my brother Polycrates to death, became its master. Give me Samos, I beg; but give it unharmed, with no bloodshed—no leading into captivity."

141. When he heard this, Darius sent off an army, under Otanes, one of the seven, with orders to accomplish all that Syloson had desired. And Otanes went down to the coast and made ready to cross over.

142. The government of Samos was held at this time by Maeandrius, son of Maeandrius, whom Polycrates had appointed as his deputy. This person conceived the wish to act like the justest of men, but it was not allowed him to do so. On receiving tidings of the death of Polycrates, he forthwith raised an altar to Zeus the Protector of Freedom, and assigned it the piece of ground which may still be seen in the suburb. This done, he assembled all the citizens, and spoke to them as follows:

"You know, friends, that the sceptre of Polycrates, and all his power, has passed into my hands, and if I choose I may rule over you. But what I condemn in another I will, if I may, avoid myself. I never approved the ambition of Polycrates to lord it over men as good as himself, nor looked with favour on any of those who have done the like. Now therefore, since he has fulfilled his destiny, I lay down my office, and proclaim equal rights. All that I claim in return is six talents from the treasures of Polycrates, and the priesthood of Zeus the Protector of Freedom, for myself and my descendants for ever. Allow me this, as the man by whom his temple has been built, and by whom you yourselves are now restored to liberty." As soon as Maeandrius had ended, one of the Samians rose up and said, "As if you were fit to rule us, baseborn and rascal as you are! Think rather of accounting for the moneys which you have fingered."

143. The man who thus spoke was a certain Telesarchus, one of the leading citizens. Maeandrius, therefore, feeling sure that if he laid down the sovereign power some one else would become tyrant in his room, gave up the thought of relinquishing it. Withdrawing to the citadel, he sent for the chief men one by one, under pretence of showing them his accounts, and as fast as they came arrested them and put them in irons. So these men were bound; and Maeandrius within a short time fell sick: whereupon Lycaretus, one of his brothers, thinking that he was going to die, and wishing to make his own accession to the throne the easier, slew all the prisoners. It seemed that the Samians did not choose to be a free people.

144. When the Persians whose business it was to restore Syloson reached Samos, not a man was found to lift up his hand against them. Maeandrius and his partisans expressed themselves willing to quit the island upon certain terms, and these terms were agreed to by Otanes. After the treaty was made, the most distinguished of the Persians had their thrones brought, and seated themselves over against the citadel.

145. Now the king Maeandrius had a lightheaded brother—Charilaus by name—whom for some offence or other he had shut up in prison: this man heard what was going on, and peering through his bars, saw the Persians sitting peacefully upon their seats, whereupon he exclaimed aloud, and said he must speak with Maeandrius. When this was reported to him, Maeandrius gave orders that Charilaus should be released from prison and brought into his presence. No sooner did he arrive than he began reviling and abusing his brother, and strove to persuade him to attack the Persians. "Meanest-spirited of men," he said, "you can keep me, your brother, chained in a dungeon, notwithstanding that I have done nothing worthy of bonds; but when the Persians come and drive you forth a houseless wanderer from your native land, you look on, and lack the heart to seek revenge, though they might so easily be subdued. If you, how-

ever, are afraid, lend me your soldiers, and I will make them pay
dearly for their coming here. I engage too to send you first safe
out of the island."

146. So spoke Charilaus, and Maeandrius gave consent; not
(I believe) that he was so void of sense as to imagine that his
own forces could overcome those of the king, but because he was
jealous of Syloson, and did not wish him to get so quietly an
unharmed city. He desired therefore to rouse the anger of the
Persians against Samos, that so he might deliver it up to Syloson
with its power at the lowest possible ebb; for he knew well that
if the Persians met with a disaster they would be furious against
the Samians, while he himself felt secure of a retreat at any
time that he liked, since he had a secret passage underground
leading from the citadel to the sea. Maeandrius accordingly
took ship and sailed away from Samos; and Charilaus, having
armed all the mercenaries, threw open the gates, and fell upon
the Persians, who looked for nothing less, since they supposed
that the whole matter had been arranged by treaty. At the first
onslaught therefore all the Persians of most note, men who were
in the habit of using litters, were slain by the mercenaries; the
rest of the army, however, came to the rescue, defeated the mercenaries, and drove them back into the citadel.

147. Then Otanes, the general, when he saw the great calamity which had befallen the Persians, made up his mind to forget
the orders which Darius had given him not to kill or enslave a
single Samian, but to deliver up the island unharmed to Syloson,
and gave the word to his army that they should slay the Samians, both men and boys, wherever they could find them. Upon
this some of his troops laid siege to the citadel, while others began the massacre, killing all they met, some outside, some inside
the temples.

148. Maeandrius fled from Samos to Lacedaemon, and conveyed thither all the riches which he had brought away from the
island, after which he acted as follows. Having placed upon his
board all the gold and silver vessels that he had, and bade his
servants employ themselves in cleaning them, he himself went
and entered into conversation with Cleomenes, son of Anaxan-

drides, king of Sparta, and as they talked brought him along to his house. There Cleomenes, seeing the plate, was filled with wonder and astonishment; whereon the other begged that he would carry home with him any of the vessels that he liked. Maeandrius said this two or three times; but Cleomenes here displayed surpassing honesty. He refused the gift, and thinking that if Maeandrius made the same offers to others he would get the aid he sought, the Spartan king went straight to the ephors and told them it would be best for Sparta that the Samian stranger should be sent away from the Peloponnese; for otherwise he might perchance persuade himself or some other Spartan to be base. The ephors took his advice, and let Maeandrius know by a herald that he must leave the city.

149. Meanwhile the Persians netted Samos, and delivered it up to Syloson, stripped of all its men. After some time, however, this same general Otanes was induced to repeople it by a dream which he had, and a loathsome disease that seized on his genitals.

150. After the armament of Otanes had set sail for Samos, the Babylonians revolted, having made every preparation for defence. During all the time that the Magus was king, and while the seven were conspiring, they had profited by the troubles, and had made themselves ready against a siege. And it happened somehow or other that no one perceived what they were doing. At last when the time came for rebelling openly, they did as follows: having first set apart their mothers, each man chose besides out of his whole household one woman, whomsoever he pleased; these alone were allowed to live, while all the rest were brought to one place and strangled. The women chosen were kept to make bread for the men; the others were strangled that they might not consume the stores.

151. When tidings reached Darius of what had happened, he drew together all his power, and began the war by marching straight upon Babylon, and laying siege to the place. The Babylonians, however, cared not a whit for his siege. Mounting upon the battlements that crowned their walls, they insulted and

jeered at Darius and his mighty host. One even shouted to them and said, "Why do you sit there, Persians? Why not go back to your homes? Till mules foal you will not take our city." This was said by a Babylonian who thought that a mule would never foal.

152. Now when a year and seven months had passed, Darius and his army were quite wearied out, finding that they could not anyhow take the city. All stratagems and all arts had been used, and yet the king could not prevail—not even when he tried the means by which Cyrus made himself master of the place. The Babylonians were ever upon the watch, and he found no way of conquering them.

153. At last, in the twentieth month, a marvellous thing happened to Zopyrus, son of the Megabyzus who was among the seven men that overthrew the Magus. One of his sumpter-mules gave birth to a foal. Zopyrus, when they told him, not thinking that it could be true, went and saw the colt with his own eyes; after which he commanded his servants to tell no one what had come to pass, while he himself pondered the matter. Calling to mind then the words of the Babylonian at the beginning of the siege, "Till mules foal you shall not take our city"—he thought, as he reflected on this speech, that Babylon might now be taken. For it seemed to him that there was a divine providence in the man having used the phrase, and then his mule having foaled.

154. As soon therefore as he felt within himself that Babylon was fated to be taken, he went to Darius and asked him if he set a very high value on its conquest. When he found that Darius did indeed value it highly, he considered further with himself how he might make the deed his own, and be the man to take Babylon. Noble exploits in Persia are ever highly honoured and bring their authors to greatness. He therefore reviewed all ways of bringing the city under, but found none by which he could hope to prevail, unless he maimed himself and then went over to the enemy. To do this seeming to him a light matter, he mutilated himself in a way that was utterly without remedy.

For he cut off his own nose and ears, and then, clipping his hair close and flogging himself with a scourge, he came in this plight before Darius.

155. Wrath stirred within the king at the sight of a man of his lofty rank in such a condition; leaping down from his throne, he exclaimed aloud, and asked Zopyrus who it was that had disfigured him, and what he had done to be so treated. Zopyrus answered, "There is not a man in the world, but you, king, that could reduce me to such a plight—no stranger's hands have wrought this work on me but my own only. I maimed myself because I could not endure that the Assyrians should laugh at the Persians." "Wretched man," said Darius, "you cover the foulest deed with the fairest possible name, when you say your maiming is to help our siege forward. How will your disfigurement, simpleton, induce the enemy to yield one day the sooner? Surely you had gone out of your mind when you so misused yourself." "Had I told you," rejoined the other, "what I was bent on doing, you would not have suffered it; as it is, I kept my own counsel, and so accomplished my plans. Now, therefore, if there be no failure on your part, we shall take Babylon. I will desert to the enemy as I am, and when I get into their city I will tell them that it is by you I have been thus treated. I think they will believe my words, and entrust me with a command of troops. You, on your part, must wait till the tenth day after I am entered within the town, and then place near to the gates of Semiramis a detachment of your army, troops for whose loss you will care little, 1,000 men. Wait, after that, seven days, and post me another detachment, 2,000 strong, at the Nineveh gates; then let twenty days pass, and at the end of that time station near the Chaldaean gates a body of 4,000. Let neither these nor the former troops be armed with any weapons but their swords —those you may leave them. After the twenty days are over, bid your whole army attack the city on every side, and put me two bodies of Persians, one at the Belian, the other at the Cissian gates; for I expect, that, on account of my successes, the Babylonians will entrust everything, even the keys of their

gates, to me. Then it will be for me and my Persians to do the rest." [38]

156. Having left these instructions, Zopyrus fled towards the gates of the town, often looking back, to give himself the air of a deserter. The men upon the towers, whose business it was to keep a look-out, observing him, hastened down, and setting one of the gates slightly ajar, questioned him who he was, and on what errand he had come. He replied that he was Zopyrus, and had deserted to them from the Persians. Then the doorkeepers, when they heard this, carried him at once before the magistrates. Introduced into the assembly, he began to bewail his misfortunes, telling them that Darius had maltreated him in the way they could see, only because he had given advice that the siege should be raised, since there seemed no hope of taking the city. "And now," he went on to say, "my coming to you, Babylonians, will prove the greatest gain that you could possibly receive, while to Darius and the Persians it will be the severest loss. Verily he by whom I have been so mutilated, shall not escape unpunished. And truly all the paths of his counsels are known to me." Thus did Zopyrus speak.

157. The Babylonians, seeing a Persian of such exalted rank in so grievous a plight, his nose and ears cut off, his body red with marks of scourging and with blood, had no suspicion but that he spoke the truth, and was really come to be their friend and helper. They were ready, therefore, to grant him anything that he asked; and on his suing for a command, they entrusted to him a body of troops, with the help of which he proceeded to do as he had arranged with Darius. On the tenth day after his flight he led out his detachment, and surrounding the thousand men, whom Darius according to agreement had sent first, he fell upon them and slew them all. Then the Babylonians, seeing that his deeds were as brave as his words, were beyond measure pleased, and set no bounds to their trust. He waited, however, and when the next period agreed on had elapsed, again with a

---

[38] The stratagem of Zopyrus has small claim to be considered a historic fact.

band of picked men he sallied forth, and slaughtered the two thousand. After this second exploit, his praise was in all mouths. Once more, however, he waited till the interval appointed had gone by, and then leading the troops to the place where the four thousand were, he put them also to the sword. This last victory gave the finishing stroke to his power, and made him all in all with the Babylonians: accordingly they committed to him the command of their whole army, and put the keys of their city into his hands.

158. Darius now, still keeping to the plan agreed upon, attacked the walls on every side, whereupon Zopyrus played out the remainder of his stratagem. While the Babylonians, crowding to the walls, did their best to resist the Persian assault, he threw open the Cissian and the Belian gates, and admitted the enemy. Such of the Babylonians as witnessed the treachery, took refuge in the temple of Zeus Belus; the rest, who did not see it, kept at their posts, till at last they too learned that they were betrayed.

159. Thus was Babylon taken for the second time. Darius, having become master of the place, destroyed the wall, and tore down all the gates; for Cyrus had done neither the one nor the other when he took Babylon. He then chose out 3,000 of the leading citizens, and caused them to be crucified, while he allowed the remainder still to inhabit the city. Further, wishing to prevent the race of the Babylonians from becoming extinct, he provided wives for them in the room of those whom (as I explained before) they strangled, to save their stores. These he levied from the nations bordering on Babylonia, who were each required to send so large a number to Babylon, that in all there were collected no fewer than 50,000. It is from these women that the Babylonians of our times are sprung.

160. As for Zopyrus, he was considered by Darius to have surpassed, in the greatness of his achievements, all other Persians, whether of former or of later times, except only Cyrus—with whom no Persian ever yet thought himself worthy to compare. Darius, as the story goes, would often say that he had rather Zopyrus were unmaimed, than be master of twenty more

Babylons. And he honoured Zopyrus greatly; year by year he presented him with all the gifts which are held in most esteem among the Persians; he gave him likewise the government of Babylon for his life, free from tribute; and he also granted him many other favours. Megabyzus, who held the command in Egypt against the Athenians and their allies, was a son of this Zopyrus. And Zopyrus, who fled from Persia to Athens, was a son of this Megabyzus.

The Fourth Book, Entitled

MELPOMENE

1. After the taking of Babylon, an expedition was led by Darius into Scythia.[1] Asia abounding in men, and vast sums flowing into the treasury, the desire seized him to exact vengeance from the Scyths, who had once in days gone by invaded Media, defeated those who met them in the field, and so begun the quarrel. During the space of twenty-eight years, as I have before mentioned, the Scyths continued lords of the whole of Upper Asia. They entered Asia in pursuit of the Cimmerians, and overthrew the empire of the Medes, who till they came possessed the sovereignty. On their return to their homes after the long absence of twenty-eight years, a task awaited them little less troublesome than their struggle with the Medes. They found an army of no small size prepared to oppose their entrance. For the Scythian women, when they saw that time went on, and their husbands did not come back, had intermarried with their slaves.

2. Now the Scythians blind all their slaves, to use them in preparing their milk. The plan they follow is to thrust tubes made of bone, not unlike our musical pipes, up the vulva of the mare, and then to blow into the tubes with their mouths, some milking while the others blow. They say that they do this because when the veins of the animal are full of air, the udder is forced down. The milk thus obtained is poured into deep wooden casks, about which the blind slaves are placed, and then

---

[1] The date of Darius' campaign seems to be 512 B.C. Although chapters 1-144 have little to do with Herodotus' main subject, they are important as the earliest study we possess of an uncivilised people.

the milk is stirred round. That which rises to the top is drawn off, and considered the best part; the under portion is of less account. Such is the reason why the Scythians blind all those whom they take in war; it arises from their not being tillers of the ground, but a pastoral race.

3. When therefore the children sprung from these slaves and the Scythian women, grew to manhood, and understood the circumstances of their birth, they resolved to oppose the army which was returning from Media. And first of all, they cut off a tract of country from the rest of Scythia by digging a broad dyke from the Tauric mountains to the vast lake of the Maeotis. Afterwards, when the Scythians tried to force an entrance, they marched out and engaged them. Many battles were fought, and the Scythians gained no advantage, until at last one of them thus addressed the remainder, "What are we doing, Scythians? We are fighting our slaves, diminishing our own number when we fall, and the number of those that belong to us when they fall by our hands. Take my advice—lay spear and bow aside, and let each man fetch his horse-whip, and go boldly up to them. So long as they see us with arms in our hands, they imagine themselves our equals in birth and bravery; but let them behold us with no other weapon but the whip, and they will feel that they are our slaves, and flee before us."

4. The Scythians followed this counsel, and the slaves were so astounded, that they forgot to fight, and immediately ran away. Such was the mode in which the Scythians, after being for a time the lords of Asia, and being forced to quit it by the Medes, returned and settled in their own country. This inroad of theirs it was that Darius was anxious to avenge, and such was the purpose for which he was now collecting an army to invade them.

5. According to the account which the Scythians themselves give, they are the youngest of all nations. Their tradition is as follows. A certain Targitaus was the first man who ever lived in their country, which before his time was a desert without inhabitants. He was a child—I do not believe the tale, but it is told nevertheless—of Zeus and a daughter of the Borysthenes.

Targitaus, thus descended, begat three sons, Leipoxais, Arpoxais, and Colaxais, who was the youngest born of the three. While
they still ruled the land, there fell from the sky four implements,
all of gold,—a plough, a yoke, a battle-axe, and a drinking-cup.
The eldest of the brothers perceived them first, and approached
to pick them up; as he came near, the gold took fire, and blazed.
He therefore went his way, and the second coming forward
made the attempt, but the same thing happened again. The gold
rejected both the eldest and the second brother. Last of all the
youngest brother approached, and immediately the flames were
extinguished; so he picked up the gold, and carried it to his
home. Then the two elder agreed together, and made the whole
kingdom over to the youngest born.

6. From Leipoxais sprang the Scythians of the race called
Auchatae; from Arpoxais, the middle brother, those known as
the Catiari and Traspians; from Colaxais, the youngest, the
Royal Scythians, or Paralatae. All together they are named Sco-
loti, after one of their kings: the Greeks, however, call them
Scythians.

7. Such is the account which the Scythians give of their origin. They add that from the time of Targitaus, their first king,
to the invasion of their country by Darius, is a period of 1,000
years, neither less nor more. The Royal Scythians guard the
sacred gold with most especial care, and year by year offer great
sacrifices in its honour. At this feast, if the man who has the
custody of the gold should fall asleep in the open air, he is sure
(the Scythians say) not to outlive the year. His pay therefore is
as much land as he can ride round on horseback in a day. As the
extent of Scythia is very great, Colaxais gave each of his three
sons a separate kingdom, one of which was of ampler size than
the other two: in this the gold was preserved. Above, to the
northward of the farthest dwellers in Scythia, the country is said
to be concealed from sight and made impassable by reason of
the feathers which are shed abroad abundantly. The earth and
air are alike full of them, and this it is which prevents the eye
from obtaining any view of the region.[2]

---

[2] Herodotus explains (iv. 31) that the so-called feathers are snow-flakes.

8. Such is the account which the Scythians give of themselves, and of the country which lies above them. The Greeks
who dwell about the Pontus tell a different story. According to
them, Heracles, when he was carrying off the cows of Geryon,
arrived in the region which is now inhabited by the Scyths, but
which was then a desert. Geryon lived outside the Pontus, in an
island called by the Greeks Erytheia, near Gades,[3] which is beyond the Pillars of Heracles upon the Ocean. Now some say that
the Ocean begins in the east, and runs the whole way round the
world; but they give no proof that this is really so.[4] Heracles
came from thence into the region now called Scythia, and being
overtaken by storm and frost, drew his lion's skin about him,
and fell fast asleep. While he slept, his mares, which he had
loosed from his chariot to graze, by some wonderful chance disappeared.

9. On waking, he went in quest of them, and, after wandering
over the whole country, came at last to the district called the
Woodland, where he found in a cave a strange being, between a
maiden and a serpent, whose form from the buttocks upwards
was like that of a woman, while all below was like a snake. He
looked at her wonderingly; but nevertheless inquired, whether
she had chanced to see his strayed mares anywhere. She answered him, "Yes, and they were now in her keeping; but never
would she consent to give them back, before he had intercourse
with her." So Heracles, to get his mares back, agreed; but afterwards she put him off and delayed restoring the mares, since
she wished to keep him with her as long as possible. He, on the
other hand, was only anxious to secure them and to get away.
At last, when she gave them up, she said to him, "When your
mares strayed hither, it was I who saved them for you: now you
have paid a reward; for I bear in my womb three sons of yours.
Tell me therefore when your sons grow up, what must I do with
them? Would you wish that I should settle them here in this

[3] The modern Cadiz.

[4] Herodotus considered that the eastern and northern boundaries of the
earth were unknown, and that the general belief that the sea encompassed
the land was a pure conjecture resting on no certain data.

land, whereof I am mistress, or shall I send them to you?"
Thus questioned, they say, Heracles answered, "When the lads
have grown to manhood, do thus, and assuredly you will not
err. Watch them, and when you see one of them bend this bow
as I now bend it, and gird himself with this girdle thus, choose
him to remain in the land. Those who fail in the trial, send
away. Thus you will at once please yourself and obey me."

10. Hereupon he strung one of his bows—up to that time he
had carried two—and showed her how to fasten the belt. Then
he gave both bow and belt into her hands. Now the belt had a
golden goblet attached to its clasp. So after he had given them
to her, he went his way; and the woman, when her children grew
to manhood, first gave them severally their names. One she
called Agathyrsus, one Gelonus, and the other, who was the
youngest Scythes. Then she remembered the instructions she
had received from Heracles, and, in obedience to his orders, she
put her sons to the test. Two of them, Agathyrsus and Gelonus,
proving unequal to the task enjoined, their mother sent them
out of the land; Scythes, the youngest, succeeded, and so he was
allowed to remain. From Scythes, the son of Heracles, were descended the after kings of Scythia; and from the circumstance
of the goblet which hung from the belt, the Scythians to this day
wear goblets at their girdles. This was the only thing which the
mother of Sythes did for him. Such is the tale told by the
Greeks who dwell around the Pontus.

11. There is also another different story, now to be related,
in which I am more inclined to put faith than in any other. It is
that the wandering Scythians once dwelt in Asia, and there
warred with the Massagetae, but with ill success; they therefore
quitted their homes, crossed the Araxes,[5] and entered the land
of Cimmeria. For the land which is now inhabited by the Scyths
was formerly the country of the Cimmerians. On their coming,
the natives, who heard how numerous the invading army was,
held a council. At this meeting opinion was divided, and both
parties stiffly maintained their own view, but the counsel of the
Royal tribe was the braver. For the others urged that the best

[5] It seems that the Araxes here represents the Volga.

thing to be done was to leave the country and avoid a contest
with so vast a host; but the Royal tribe advised remaining and
fighting for the soil to the last. As neither party chose to give
way, the one determined to retire without a blow and yield their
lands to the invaders; but the other, remembering the good
things which they had enjoyed in their homes, and picturing to
themselves the evils which they had to expect if they gave them
up, resolved not to flee, but rather to die and at least be buried
in their fatherland. Having thus decided, they drew apart in two
bodies, the one as numerous as the other, and fought together.
All of the Royal tribe were slain, and the people buried them
near the river Tyras, where their grave is still to be seen. Then
the rest of the Cimmerians departed, and the Scythians, on their
coming, took possession of a deserted land.

12. Scythia still retains traces of the Cimmerians; there are
Cimmerian walls, and a Cimmerian ferry, also a tract called
Cimmeria,[6] and a Cimmerian Bosporus. It appears likewise that
the Cimmerians, when they fled into Asia to escape the Scyths,
made a settlement in the peninsula where the Greek city of Sinope was afterwards built. The Scyths, it is plain, pursued them,
and missing their road, poured into Media. For the Cimmerians
kept the line which led along the sea-shore, but the Scyths in
their pursuit held the Caucasus upon their right, thus proceeding inland, and falling upon Media. This account is one which
is common both to Greeks and barbarians.

13. Aristeas also, son of Caystrobius, a native of Proconnesus,[7] says in the course of his poem, that inspired by Phoebus,
he went as far as the Issedones. Above them dwelt the Arimaspi,
men with one eye; still further, the gold-guarding Griffins; and
beyond these, the Hyperboreans, who extended to the sea. Except the Hyperboreans, all these nations, beginning with the
Arimaspi, were continually encroaching upon their neighbours.
Hence it came to pass that the Arimaspi drove the Issedonians from their country, while the Issedonians dispossessed the

[6] The Cimmerians have given their name to the Crimea.
[7] Proconnesus is the island now called Marmora, which gives its modern
appellation to the Sea of Marmora.

Scyths; and the Scyths, pressing upon the Cimmerians, who dwelt on the shores of the Southern sea,[8] forced them to leave their land. Thus even Aristeas does not agree in his account of this region with the Scythians.

14. The birthplace of Aristeas, the poet who sung of these things, I have already mentioned. I will now relate a tale which I heard concerning him both at Proconnesus and at Cyzicus. Aristeas, they said, who belonged to one of the noblest families in the island, had entered one day into a fuller's shop, when he suddenly dropped down dead. Hereupon the fuller shut up his shop, and went to tell Aristeas' kindred what had happened. The report of the death had just spread through the town, when a certain Cyzicenian, lately arrived from Artaca, contradicted the rumour, affirming that he had met Aristeas on his road to Cyzicus, and had spoken with him. This man, therefore, strenuously denied the rumour; the relations, however, proceeded to the fuller's shop with all things necessary for the funeral, intending to carry the body away. But on the shop being opened, no Aristeas was found, either dead or alive. Seven years afterwards he reappeared, they told me, in Proconnesus, and wrote the poem called by the Greeks the *Arimaspeia*, after which he disappeared a second time. This is the tale current in the two cities above mentioned.

15. What follows I know to have happened to the Metapontines of Italy, 240 years after the second disappearance of Aristeas, as I collect by comparing the accounts given me at Proconnesus and Metapontum. Aristeas then, as the Metapontines affirm, appeared to them in their own country, and ordered them to set up an altar in honour of Apollo, and to place near it a statue to be called that of Aristeas the Proconnesian. "Apollo," he told them, "had come to their country once, though he had visited no other Italiots; and he had been with Apollo at the time, not however in his present form, but in the shape of a crow." Having said so much, he vanished. Then the Metapontines, as they relate, sent to Delphi, and inquired of the god, in

8 That is, the Euxine, in contradistinction from the Northern Sea, on the shores of which dwelt the Hyperboreans, according to Aristeas.

what light they were to regard the appearance of this ghost of a man. The priestess, in reply, bade them attend to what the spectre said, "for so it would go best with them." Thus advised, they did as they had been directed: and there is now a statue bearing the name of Aristeas, close by the image of Apollo in the market-place of Metapontum, with baytrees standing around it. But enough has been said concerning Aristeas.

16. With regard to the regions which lie above the country whereof this portion of my history treats, there is no one who possesses any exact knowledge. Not a single person can I find who professes to be acquainted with them by actual observation. Even Aristeas, the traveller of whom I lately spoke, does not claim—and he is writing poetry—to have reached any farther than the Issedonians. What he relates concerning the regions beyond is, he confesses, mere hearsay, being the account which the Issedonians gave him of those countries. However, I shall proceed to mention all that I have learnt of these parts by the most exact inquiries which I have been able to make concerning them.

17. Above the trading-port of the Borysthenites, which is situated in the very centre of the whole sea-coast of Scythia, the first people who inhabit the land are the Callippidae, a Graeco-Scythic race. Next to them, as you go inland, dwell the people called the Alazonians. These two nations in other respects resemble the Scythians in their usages, but sow and eat corn, also onions, garlic, lentils, and millet. Beyond the Alazonians reside Scythian cultivators, who grow corn, not for their own use, but for sale.[9] Still higher up are the Neuri. Northwards of the Neuri the continent, as far as it is known to us, is uninhabited. These are the nations along the course of the river Hypanis, west of the Borysthenes.

18. Across the Borysthenes, the first country after you leave the coast is the Woodland. Above this dwell the Scythian Husbandmen, whom the Greeks living near the Hypanis call Borys-

---

[9] The corn-trade of the Scythians appears to have been chiefly with the Greeks. Its extent is indicated in Herodotus by his assignment of the whole country west, and a portion of that east, of the Borysthenes to Scythian husbandmen, who raised corn only for sale.

thenites, while they call themselves Olbiopolites. These Husbandmen extend eastward a distance of three days' journey to a river bearing the name of Panticapes,[10] while northward the country is theirs for eleven days' sail up the course of the Borysthenes. Further inland there is a vast tract which is uninhabited. Above this desolate region dwell the Cannibals, who are a people apart, much unlike the Scythians. Above them the country becomes an utter desert; not a single tribe, so far as we know, inhabits it.

19. Crossing the Panticapes, and proceeding eastward of the Husbandmen, we come upon the wandering Scythians, who neither plough nor sow. Their country, and the whole of this region, except the Woodlands, is quite bare of trees. They extend towards the east a distance of fourteen days' journey, occupying a tract which reaches to the river Gerrhus.

20. On the opposite side of the Gerrhus is the Royal district, as it is called: here dwells the largest and bravest of the Scythian tribes, which looks upon all the other tribes in the light of slaves. Its country reaches on the south to Taurica, on the east to the trench dug by the sons of the blind slaves, the mart upon Lake Maeotis, called the Cliffs, and in part to the river Tanais.[11] North of the country of the Royal Scythians are the Blackcloaks, a people of a quite different race from the Scythians. Beyond them lie marshes and a region without inhabitants, so far as our knowledge reaches.

21. When one crosses the Tanais, one is no longer in Scythia; the first region on crossing is that of the Sauromatae, who, beginning at the upper end of Lake Maeotis, stretch northward a distance of fifteen days' journey, inhabiting a country which is entirely bare of trees, whether wild or cultivated. Above them, possessing the second region, dwell the Budini, whose territory is thickly wooded with trees of every kind.

22. Beyond the Budini, as one goes northward, first there is a desert, seven days' journey across; after which, if one inclines

[10] Here the description of Herodotus, which has been hitherto excellent, begins to fail.
[11] Now the Don.

somewhat to the east, the Thyssagetae are reached, a numerous nation quite distinct from any other, and living by the chase. Adjoining them, and within the limits of the same region, are the people who bear the name of Iyrcae; they also support themselves by hunting, which they practise in the following manner. The hunter climbs a tree, the whole country abounding in wood, and there sets himself in ambush; he has a dog at hand, and a horse, trained to lie down upon its belly, and thus make itself low; the hunter keeps watch, and when he sees his game, lets fly an arrow; then mounting his horse, he gives the beast chase, his dog following hard all the while. Beyond these people, a little to the east, dwells a distinct tribe of Scyths, who revolted once from the Royal Scythians, and migrated into these parts.

23. As far as their country, the tract of land whereof I have been speaking is all a smooth plain, and the soil deep; beyond you enter on a region which is rugged and stony. Passing over a great extent of this rough country, you come to a people dwelling at the foot of lofty mountains, who are said to be all—both men and women—bald from their birth, to have flat noses, and very long chins. These people speak a language of their own, but the dress which they wear is the same as the Scythian. They live on the fruit of a certain tree, the name of which is Ponticum; in size it is about equal to our fig-tree, and it bears a fruit like a bean, with a stone inside. When the fruit is ripe, they strain it through cloths; the juice which runs off is black and thick, and is called by the natives "aschy." They lap this up with their tongues, and also mix it with milk for a drink; while they make the lees, which are solid, into cakes, and eat them instead of meat; for they have but few sheep in their country, in which there is no good pasturage. Each of them dwells under a tree, and they cover the tree in winter with a cloth of thick white felt, but take off the covering in the summer-time. No one harms these people, for they are looked upon as sacred,—they do not even possess any warlike weapons. When their neighbours fall out, they make up the quarrel; and when one flies to them for refuge, he is safe from all hurt. They are called the Argippaeans.

24. Up to this point the territory of which we are speaking is

very completely explored, and all the nations between the coast and the bald-headed men are well known to us. For some of the Scythians are accustomed to penetrate as far, of whom inquiry may easily be made, and Greeks also go there from the trading-station on the Borysthenes, and from the other trading-stations along the Euxine. The Scythians who make this journey communicate with the inhabitants by means of seven interpreters and seven languages.

25. Thus far therefore the land is known; but beyond the bald-headed men lies a region of which no one can give any exact account. Lofty and precipitous mountains, which are never crossed, bar further progress. The bald men say, but it does not seem to me credible, that the people who live in these mountains have feet like goats; and that after passing them you find another race of men, who sleep during one half of the year. This latter statement appears to me quite unworthy of credit. The region east of the bald-headed men is well known to be inhabited by the Issedonians, but the tract that lies to the north of these two nations is entirely unknown, except by the accounts which they give of it.

26. The Issedonians are said to have the following customs. When a man's father dies, all the near relatives bring sheep to the house; which are sacrificed, and their flesh cut in pieces, while at the same time the dead body undergoes the like treatment. The two sorts of flesh are afterwards mixed together, and the whole is served up at a banquet. The head of the dead man is treated differently: it is stripped bare, cleansed, and set in gold. It then becomes an ornament on which they pride themselves, and is brought out year by year at the great festival which sons keep in honour of their fathers' death, just as the Greeks keep their feast of the dead. In other respects the Issedonians are reputed to be observers of justice: and it is to be remarked that their women have equal authority with the men. Thus our knowledge extends as far as this nation.

27. The regions beyond are known only from the accounts of the Issedonians, by whom the stories are told of the one-eyed race of men and the gold-guarding griffins. These stories are re-

ceived by the Scythians from the Issedonians, and by them
passed on to us Greeks: whence it arises that we give the one-
eyed race the Scythian name of Arimaspi, arima being the
Scythic word for one, and spu for the eye.

28. The whole district whereof we have here discoursed has
winters of exceeding rigour. During eight months the frost is so
intense, that water poured upon the ground does not form mud,
but if a fire be lighted on it mud is produced. The sea freezes,
and the Cimmerian Bosporus is frozen over. At that season the
Scythians who dwell inside the trench make warlike expeditions
upon the ice, and even drive their waggons across to the country
of the Sindians. Such is the intensity of the cold during eight
months out of the twelve, and even in the remaining four the
climate is still cool. The character of the winter likewise is unlike that of the same season in any other country; for at that
time, when the rains ought to fall, in Scythia there is scarcely
any rain worth mentioning, while in summer it never gives over
raining; and thunder, which elsewhere is frequent then, in
Scythia is unknown in that part of the year, coming only in
summer, when it is very heavy. Thunder in the wintertime is
there accounted a prodigy; as also are earthquakes, whether
they happen in winter or summer. Horses bear the winter well,
cold as it is, but mules and asses are quite unable to bear it;
whereas in other countries mules and asses are found to endure
the cold, while horses, if they stand still, are frost-bitten.

29. To me it seems that the cold may likewise be the cause
which prevents the oxen in Scythia from having horns. There is
a line of Homer's in the *Odyssey*[12] which gives a support to my
opinion:

Libya too, where horns bud quick on the foreheads of lambkins.

He means to say, what is quite true, that in warm countries the
horns come early. So too in countries where the cold is severe
animals either have no horns, or grow them with difficulty—the
cold being the cause in this instance.

[12] *Odyssey* iv. 85.

30. Here I must express my wonder—additions being what my work always from the very first affected—that in Elis, where the cold is not remarkable, and there is nothing else to account for it, mules are never produced. The Eleans say it is in consequence of a curse,[13] and their habit is, when the breeding-time comes, to take their mares into one of the adjoining countries, and there keep them till they are in foal, when they bring them back again into Elis.

31. With respect to the feathers which are said by the Scythians to fill the air, and to prevent persons from penetrating into the remoter parts of the continent, or even having any view of those regions, my opinion is, that in the countries above Scythia it always snows, less, of course, in the summer than in the wintertime. Now snow when it falls looks like feathers, as every one is aware who has seen it come down close to him. These northern regions, therefore, are uninhabitable by reason of the severity of the winter; and the Scythians, with their neighbours, call the snow-flakes feathers because, I think, of the likeness which they bear to them. I have now related what is said of the most distant parts of this continent whereof any account is given.

32. Of the Hyperboreans nothing is said either by the Scythians or by any of the other dwellers in these regions, unless it be the Issedonians. But in my opinion, even the Issedonians are silent concerning them; otherwise the Scythians would have repeated their statements, as they do those concerning the one-eyed men. Hesiod, however, mentions them, and Homer also in the *Epigoni,* if that be really a work of his.

33. But the persons who have by far the most to say on this subject are the Delians. They declare that certain offerings, packed in wheaten straw, were brought from the country of the Hyperboreans into Scythia, and that the Scythians received them and passed them on to their neighbours upon the west, who continued to pass them on, until at last they reached the Adriatic. From hence they were sent southward, and when they came to

[13] According to Plutarch, Oenomaus, king of Elis, out of his love for horses, laid heavy curses on the breeding of mules.

Greece, were received first of all by the Dodonaeans. Thence they descended to the Maliac Gulf, from which they were carried across into Euboea, where the people handed them on from city to city, till they came at length to Carystus. The Carystians took them over to Tenos, without stopping at Andros; and the Tenians brought them finally to Delos. Such, according to their own account, was the road by which the offerings reached the Delians. Two damsels, they say, named Hyperoche and Laodice, brought the first offerings from the Hyperboreans; and with them the Hyperboreans sent five men, to keep them from all harm by the way; these are the persons whom the Delians call Perpherees, and to whom great honours are paid at Delos. Afterwards the Hyperboreans, when they found that their messengers did not return, thinking it would be a grievous thing always to be liable to lose the envoys they should send, adopted the following plan: they wrapped their offerings in the wheaten straw, and bearing them to their borders, charged their neighbours to send them forward from one nation to another, which was done accordingly, and in this way the offerings reached Delos. I myself know of a practice like this, which obtains with the women of Thrace and Paeonia. They in their sacrifices to the Queenly Artemis bring wheaten straw always with their offerings. Of my own knowledge I can testify that this is so.

34. The damsels sent by the Hyperboreans died in Delos, and in their honour all the Delian girls and youths are wont to cut off their hair. The girls, before their marriage-day, cut off a curl, and twining it round a distaff, lay it upon the grave of the strangers. This grave is on the left as one enters the precinct of Artemis, and has an olive-tree growing on it. The youths wind some of their hair round a kind of grass, and, like the girls, place it upon the tomb. Such are the honours paid to these damsels by the Delians.

35. They add that, once before, there came to Delos by the same road as Hyperoche and Laodice, two other virgins from the Hyperboreans, whose names were Arge and Opis. Hyperoche and Laodice came to bring to Eilithyia the offering which they had laid upon themselves, in acknowledgment of their

quick labours; but Arge and Opis came at the same time as the
gods of Delos, and are honoured by the Delians in a different
way. For the Delian women make collections in these maidens'
names, and invoke them in the hymn which Olen, a Lycian,
composed for them; and the rest of the islanders, and even the
Ionians, have been taught by the Delians to do the like. This
Olen, who came from Lycia, made the other old hymns also
which are sung in Delos. The Delians add, that the ashes from
the thigh-bones burnt upon the altar are scattered over the tomb
of Opis and Arge. Their tomb lies behind the temple of Artemis,
facing the east, near the banqueting-hall of the Ceians. Thus
much then, and no more, concerning the Hyperboreans.

36. As for the tale of Abaris, who is said to have been a Hy-
perborean, and to have gone with his arrow all round the world
without once eating, I shall pass it by in silence. Thus much,
however, is clear: if there are men beyond the north wind, there
must also be men beyond the south wind.[14] For my part, I cannot but laugh when I see numbers of persons drawing maps of
the world without having any reason to guide them; making, as
they do, the ocean-stream to run all round the earth, and the
earth itself to be an exact circle, as if described by a pair of
compasses,[15] with Europe and Asia just of the same size. The
truth in this matter I will now proceed to explain in a very few
words, making it clear what the real size of each region is, and
what shape should be given them.

37. The Persians inhabit a country upon the southern or Red
Sea; above them, to the north, are the Medes; beyond the
Medes, the Saspirians; beyond them, the Colchians, reaching to
the northern sea, into which the Phasis empties itself. These
four nations fill the whole space from one sea to the other.

[14] Herodotus cannot, even while combating, escape from the prevalent
notion that in geography there was some absolute symmetry and paral-
lelism.
[15] That there is a special allusion to Hecataeus here seems very probable. The belief which Herodotus ridicules is not that of the world's spher-
ical form, which had not yet been suspected by the Greeks, but a false
notion of the configuration of the land on the earth's surface.

38. West of these nations there project into the sea two tracts which I will now describe; one beginning at the river Phasis on the north, stretches along the Euxine and the Hellespont to Sigeum in the Troas; while on the south it reaches from the Myriandrian gulf, which adjoins Phoenicia, to the Triopic promontory. This is one of the tracts, and is inhabited by thirty different nations.

39. The other starts from the country of the Persians, and stretches into the Red Sea, containing first Persia, then Assyria, and after Assyria, Arabia. It ends, that is to say it is considered to end, though it does not really come to a termination, at the Arabian gulf—the gulf whereinto Darius conducted the canal which he made from the Nile. Between Persia and Phoenicia lies a broad and ample tract of country, after which the region I am describing skirts our sea, stretching from Phoenicia along the coast of Palestine-Syria till it comes to Egypt, where it terminates. This entire tract contains but three nations.[16] The whole of Asia west of the country of the Persians is comprised in these two regions.

40. Beyond the tract occupied by the Persians, Medes, Saspirians, and Colchians, towards the east and the region of the sunrise, Asia is bounded on the south by the Red Sea, and on the north by the Caspian and the river Araxes, which flows towards the rising sun. Till you reach India the country is peopled, but further east it is void of inhabitants, and no one can say what sort of region it is. Such then is the shape, and such the size of Asia.

41. Libya belongs to one of the above-mentioned tracts, for it adjoins on Egypt. In Egypt the tract is at first a narrow neck, the distance from our sea to the Red Sea not exceeding 100,000 fathoms, or, in other words, 115 miles; but from the point where the neck ends, the tract which bears the name of Libya is of very great breadth.

42. For my part I am astonished that men should ever have divided Libya, Asia, and Europe as they have, for they are exceedingly unequal. Europe extends the entire length of the other

---

[16] The Assyrians, the Arabians, and the Phoenicians.

two, and for breadth will not even (as I think) bear to be compared to them. As for Libya, we know it to be washed on all sides by the sea, except where it is attached to Asia. This discovery was first made by Necos,[17] the Egyptian king, who on desisting from the canal which he had begun between the Nile and the Arabian gulf, sent to sea a number of ships manned by Phoenicians, with orders to make for the Pillars of Heracles, and return to Egypt through them, and by the Mediterranean. The Phoenicians took their departure from Egypt by way of the Red Sea, and so sailed into the southern ocean. When autumn came, they went ashore, wherever they might happen to be, and having sown a tract of land with corn, waited until the grain was fit to cut. Having reaped it, they again set sail; and thus it came to pass that two whole years went by, and it was not till the third year that they doubled the Pillars of Heracles, and made good their voyage home. On their return, they declared—I for my part do not believe them, but perhaps others may—that in sailing round Libya they had the sun upon their right hand. In this way was the extent of Libya first discovered.

43. Next to these Phoenicians the Carthaginians, according to their own accounts, made the voyage. For Sataspes, son of Teaspes the Achaemenian, did not circumnavigate Libya, though he was sent to do so; but, fearing the length and desolateness of the journey, he turned back and left unaccomplished the task which had been set him by his mother. This man had raped a virgin daughter of Zopyrus, son of Megabyzus, and King Xerxes was about to impale him for the offence, when his mother, who was a sister of Darius, begged him off, undertaking to punish his crime more heavily than the king himself had designed. She would force him, she said, to sail round Libya and return to Egypt by the Arabian gulf. Xerxes gave his consent,

[17] We may infer, from Necos' ordering the Phoenicians to come round by the Pillars of Heracles, that the form of Africa was already known, and that this was not the first expedition which had gone round it. The fact of their seeing the sun rise on their right as they returned northwards, which Herodotus doubted, is the very proof of their having gone round the Cape, and completed the circuit.

and Sataspes went down to Egypt, and there got a ship and crew, with which he set sail for the Pillars of Heracles. Having passed the Straits, he doubled the Libyan headland, known as Cape Soloeis, and proceeded southward. Following this course for many months over a vast stretch of sea, and finding that more water than he had crossed still lay ever before him, he put about, and came back to Egypt. Thence proceeding to the court, he made report to Xerxes, that at the farthest point to which he had reached, the coast was occupied by a dwarfish race, who wore a dress made from the palm-tree. These people, whenever he landed, left their towns and fled away to the mountains; his men, however, did them no wrong, only entering into their cities and taking some of their cattle. The reason why he had not sailed quite round Libya was, he said, because the ship stopped, and would not go any further. Xerxes, however, did not accept this account for true; and so Sataspes, as he had failed to accomplish the task set him, was impaled by the king's orders in accordance with the former sentence. One of his eunuchs, on hearing of his death, ran away with a great portion of his wealth, and reached Samos, where a certain Samian seized the whole. I know the man's name well, but I shall willingly forget it here.

44. Of the greater part of Asia Darius was the discoverer. Wishing to know where the Indus (which is the only river save one that produces crocodiles) emptied itself into the sea, he sent a number of men, on whose truthfulness he could rely, and among them Scylax of Caryanda, to sail down the river. They started from the city of Caspatyrus, in the region called Pactyica, and sailed down the stream in an easterly direction to the sea. Here they turned westward, and after a voyage of thirty months, reached the place from which the Egyptian king, of whom I spoke above, sent the Phoenicians to sail round Libya. After this voyage was completed, Darius conquered the Indians,[18] and made use of the sea in those parts. Thus all Asia,

---

[18] The conquest of the Indians, by which we are to understand the reduction of the Punjab, preceded (as may be proved by the Inscriptions) the Scythian expedition.

except the eastern portion, has been found to be similarly cir-
cumstanced with Libya.

45. But the boundaries of Europe are quite unknown, and
there is not a man who can say whether any sea girds it round
either on the north or on the east, while in length it undoubtedly
extends as far as both the other two. For my part I cannot conceive why three names, and women's names especially, should
ever have been given to a tract which is in reality one, or why
the Egyptian Nile and the Colchian Phasis (or according to
others the Maeotic Tanais and Cimmerian ferry) should have
been fixed upon for the boundary lines; nor can I even say who
gave the three tracts their names, or whence they took the epithets. According to the Greeks in general, Libya was so called
after a certain Libya, a native woman, and Asia after the wife
of Prometheus. The Lydians, however, put in a claim to the latter name, which, they declare, was not derived from Asia the
wife of Prometheus, but from Asies, the son of Cotys, and
grandson of Manes, who also gave name to the tribe Asias at
Sardis. As for Europe, no one can say whether it is surrounded
by the sea or not, neither is it known whence the name of Europe was derived, nor who gave it name, unless we say that Europe was so called after the Tyrian Europa, and before her time
was nameless, like the other divisions. But it is certain that Europa was an Asiatic, and never even set foot on the land which
the Greeks now call Europe, only sailing from Phoenicia to
Crete, and from Crete to Lycia. However let us quit these matters. We shall ourselves continue to use the names which custom
sanctions.

46. The Euxine sea, where Darius now went to war, has nations dwelling around it, with the one exception of the Scythians, more unpolished than those of any other region that we
know of. For, setting aside Anacharsis and the Scythian people,
there is not within this region a single nation which can be put
forward as having any claims to wisdom, or which has produced
a single person of any high repute. The Scythians indeed have
in one respect, and that the very most important of all those
that fall under man's control, shown themselves wiser than any

nation upon the face of the earth. Their customs otherwise are
not such as I admire. The one thing of which I speak, is the contrivance whereby they make it impossible for the enemy who in-
vades them to escape destruction, while they themselves are
entirely out of his reach, unless it please them to engage with
him. Having neither cities nor forts, and carrying their dwellings with them wherever they go; accustomed, moreover, one
and all of them, to shoot from horseback; and living not by husbandry but on their cattle, their waggons the only houses that
they possess, how can they fail of being unconquerable, and un-
assailable even?

47. The nature of their country, and the rivers by which it
is intersected, greatly favour this mode of resisting attacks. For
the land is level, well-watered, and abounding in pasture; while
the rivers which traverse it are almost equal in number to the
canals of Egypt. Of these I shall only mention the most famous
and such as are navigable to some distance from the sea. They
are, the Ister, which has five mouths; the Tyras, the Hypanis,
the Borysthenes, the Panticapes, the Hypacyris, the Gerrhus,
and the Tanais. The courses of these streams I shall now proceed to describe.

48. The Ister is of all the rivers with which we are acquainted
the mightiest. It never varies in height, but continues at the
same level summer and winter. Counting from the west it is the
first of the Scythian rivers, and the reason of its being the greatest is, that it receives the waters of several tributaries. Now the
tributaries which swell its flood are the following: first, on the
side of Scythia, these five—the stream called by the Scythians
Porata, and by the Greeks Pyretus, the Tiarantus, the Ararus,
the Naparis, and the Ordessus. The first-mentioned is a great
stream, and is the easternmost of the tributaries. The Tiarantus
is of less volume, and more to the west. The Ararus, Naparis,
and Ordessus fall into the Ister between these two. All the
above-mentioned are genuine Scythian rivers, and go to swell
the current of the Ister.

49. From the country of the Agathyrsi comes down another
river, the Maris, which empties itself into the same; and from

the heights of Haemus descend with a northern course three large streams, the Atlas, the Auras, and the Tibisis, and pour their waters into it. Thrace gives it three tributaries, the Athrys, the Noes, and the Artanes, which all pass through the country of the Crobyzian Thracians. Another tributary is furnished by Paeonia, namely the Scius; this river, rising near Mount Rhodope, forces its way through the chain of Haemus, and so reaches the Ister. From Illyria comes another stream, the Angrus, which has a course from south to north, and after watering the Triballian plain, falls into the Brongus, which falls into the Ister. So the Ister is augmented by these two streams, both considerable. Besides all these, the Ister receives also the waters of the Carpis and the Alpis, two rivers running in a northerly direction from the country above the Umbrians. For the Ister flows through the whole extent of Europe, rising in the country of the Celts[19] (the most westerly of all the nations of Europe, excepting the Cynetians), and thence running across the continent till it reaches Scythia, whereof it washes the flanks.

50. All these streams, then, and many others, add their waters to swell the flood of the Ister, which thus increased becomes the mightiest of rivers; for undoubtedly if we compare the stream of the Nile with the single stream of the Ister, we must give the preference to the Nile, of which no tributary river, nor even rivulet, augments the volume. The Ister remains at the same level both summer and winter—owing to the following reasons, as I believe. During the winter it runs at its natural height, or a very little higher, because in those countries there is scarcely any rain in winter, but constant snow. When summer comes, this snow, which is of great depth, begins to melt, and flows into the Ister, which is swelled at that season, not only by this cause but also by the rains, which are heavy and frequent

[19] As Herodotus plunges deeper into the European continent, his knowledge is less and less exact. He knows that the Danube receives two great tributaries from the south in the upper part of its course, but he conceives the rivers, of which he had heard the Umbrians tell as running northwards from the Alps above their country, to be identical with the great tributaries whereof the dwellers on the middle Danube spoke. The length of the Nile is 4,000 miles; of the Danube, 1,760 miles.

at that part of the year. Thus the various streams which go to form the Ister, are higher in summer than in winter, and just so much higher as the sun's power and attraction are greater; so that these two causes counteract each other, and the effect is to produce a balance, whereby the Ister remains always at the same level.

51. This, then, is one of the great Scythian rivers; the next to it is the Tyras, which rises from a great lake separating Scythia from the land of the Neuri, and runs with a southerly course to the sea. Greeks dwell at the mouth of the river, who are called Tyritae.

52. The third river is the Hypanis. This stream rises within the limits of Scythia, and has its source in another vast lake, around which wild white horses graze. The lake is called, properly enough, the Mother of the Hypanis. The Hypanis, rising here, during the distance of five days' navigation is a shallow stream, and the water sweet and pure; thence, however, to the sea, which is a distance of four days, it is exceedingly bitter. This change is caused by its receiving into it at that point a brook the waters of which are so bitter that, although it is but a tiny rivulet, it nevertheless taints the entire Hypanis, which is a large stream among those of the second order. The source of this bitter spring is on the borders of the Scythian Husbandmen, where they adjoin upon the Alazonians; and the place where it rises is called in the Scythic tongue Exampaeus, which means in our language, the Sacred Ways. The spring itself bears the same name. The Tyras and the Hypanis approach each other in the country of the Alazonians, but afterwards separate, and leave a wide space between their streams.

53. The fourth of the Scythian rivers is the Borysthenes. Next to the Ister, it is the greatest of them all; and, in my judgment, it is the most productive river, not merely in Scythia, but in the whole world, excepting only the Nile, with which no stream can possibly compare. It has upon its banks the loveliest and most excellent pasturages for cattle; it contains abundance of the most delicious fish; its water is most pleasant to the taste; its stream is limpid, while all the other rivers near it are

muddy; the richest harvests spring up along its course, and where the ground is not sown, the heaviest crops of grass; while salt forms in great plenty about its mouth without human aid,[20] and large fish are taken in it of the sort called sturgeon, without any prickly bones, and good for pickling. Nor are these the whole of its marvels. As far inland as the place named Gerrhus, which is distant forty days' voyage from the sea,[21] its course is known, and its direction is from north to south; but above this no one has traced it, so as to say through what countries it flows. It enters the territory of the Scythian Husbandmen after running for some time across a desert region, and continues for ten days' navigation to pass through the land which they inhabit. It is the only river besides the Nile the sources of which are unknown to me, as they are also (I believe) to all the other Greeks. Not long before it reaches the sea, the Borysthenes is joined by the Hypanis, which pours its waters into the same lake. The land that lies between them, a narrow point like the beak of a ship, is called Cape Hippolaus. Here is a temple dedicated to Demeter, and opposite the temple upon the Hypanis is the dwelling-place of the Borysthenites. But enough has been said of these streams.

54. Next in succession comes the fifth river, called the Panticapes, which has, like the Borysthenes, a course from north to south, and rises from a lake. The space between this river and the Borysthenes is occupied by the Scythians who are engaged in husbandry. After watering their country, the Panticapes flows through the Woodland, and empties itself into the Borysthenes.

55. The sixth stream is the Hypacyris, a river rising from a lake, and running directly through the middle of the Nomadic Scythians. It falls into the sea near the city of Carcinitis, leaving the Woodland and the Race-course of Achilles to the right.

56. The seventh river is the Gerrhus, which is a branch thrown out by the Borysthenes at the point where the course of that stream first begins to be known, the region called by the

---

[20] The salt of Kinburn is still of the greatest importance to Russia.

[21] The Dnieper is navigable for barges all the way from Smolensk to its mouth, a distance of not less than 1,500 miles.

same name as the stream itself, Gerrhus. This river on its passage towards the sea divides the country of the Nomadic from that of the Royal Scyths. It runs into the Hypacyris.

57. The eighth river is the Tanais,[22] a stream which has its source, far up the country, in a lake of vast size, and which empties itself into another still larger lake, the Palus Maeotis, whereby the country of the Royal Scythians is divided from that of the Sauromatae. The Tanais receives the waters of a tributary stream, called the Hyrgis.

58. Such then are the rivers of chief note in Scythia. The grass which the land produces is more apt to generate gall in the beasts that feed on it than any other grass which is known to us, as plainly appears on the opening of their carcases.

59. Thus abundantly are the Scythians provided with the most important necessaries. Their manners and customs come now to be described. They worship only the following gods, namely, Hestia, whom they reverence beyond all the rest, Zeus and Earth, whom they consider to be the wife of Zeus; and after these Apollo, Celestial Aphrodite, Heracles, and Ares. These gods are worshipped by the whole nation: the Royal Scythians offer sacrifice likewise to Poseidon. In the Scythic tongue Hestia is called *Tabiti*, Zeus (very properly, in my judgment) *Papaeus*, Earth *Apia*, Apollo *Oetosyrus*, Celestial Aphrodite *Artimpasa*, and Poseidon *Thamimasadas*. They use no images, altars, or temples, except in the worship of Ares; but in his worship they do use them.

60. The manner of their sacrifices is everywhere and in every case the same; the victim stands with its two fore-feet bound together by a cord, and the person who is about to offer, taking his station behind the victim, gives the rope a pull, and thereby throws the animal down; as it falls he invokes the god to whom he is offering; after which he puts a noose round the animal's neck, and, inserting a small stick, twists it round, and so strangles him. No fire is lighted, there is no consecration, and no pouring out of drink-offerings; but directly that the beast is

* The modern Don.

strangled the sacrificer flays him, and then sets to work to boil the flesh.

61. As Scythia, however, is utterly barren of firewood, a plan has had to be contrived for boiling the flesh, which is the following. After flaying the beasts, they take out all the bones, and (if they possess such gear) put the flesh into boilers made in the country, which are very like the cauldrons of the Lesbians, except that they are of a much larger size; then, placing the bones of the animals beneath the cauldron, they set them alight, and so boil the meat. If they do not happen to possess a cauldron, they make the animal's paunch hold the flesh, and pouring in at the same time a little water, lay the bones under and light them. The bones burn beautifully, and the paunch easily contains all the flesh when it is stripped from the bones, so that by this plan the ox is made to boil himself, and other victims also to do the like. When the meat is all cooked, the sacrificer offers a portion of the flesh and of the entrails, by casting it on the ground before him. They sacrifice all sorts of cattle, but most commonly horses.

62. Such are the victims offered to the other gods, and such is the mode in which they are sacrificed; but the rites paid to Ares are different. In every district, at the seat of government, there stands a temple of this god, whereof the following is a description. It is a pile of brushwood, made of a vast quantity of faggots, in length and breadth 600 yards; in height somewhat less, having a square platform upon the top, three sides of which are precipitous, while the fourth slopes so that men may walk up it. Each year 150 waggon-loads of brushwood are added to the pile, which sinks continually by reason of the rains. An antique iron sword is planted on the top of every such mound, and serves as the image of Ares; yearly sacrifices of cattle and of horses are made to it, and more victims are offered thus than to all the rest of their gods. When prisoners are taken in war, out of every hundred men they sacrifice one, not however with the same rites as the cattle, but with different. Libations of wine are first poured upon their heads, after which they are slaughtered over a vessel; the vessel is then carried up to the top of the pile,

and the blood poured upon the scimitar. While this takes place at the top of the mound, below, by the side of the temple, the right hands and arms of the slaughtered prisoners are cut off, and tossed on high into the air. Then the other victims are slain, and those who have offered the sacrifice depart, leaving the hands and arms where they may chance to have fallen, and the bodies also, separate.

63. Such are the observances of the Scythians with respect to sacrifice. They never use swine for the purpose, nor indeed is it their wont to breed them in any part of their country.

64. In what concerns war, their customs are the following. The Scythian soldier drinks the blood of the first man he over-throws in battle. Whatever number he slays, he cuts off all their heads, and carries them to the king; since he is thus entitled to a share of the booty, whereto he forfeits all claim if he does not produce a head. In order to strip the skull of its covering, he makes a cut round the head above the ears, and, laying hold of the scalp, shakes the skull out; then with the rib of an ox he scrapes the scalp clean of flesh, and softening it by rubbing be-tween the hands, uses it thenceforth as a napkin. The Scyth is proud of these scalps, and hangs them from his bridle-rein; the greater the number of such napkins that a man can show, the more highly is he esteemed among them. Many make themselves cloaks, like the sheepskins of our peasants, by sewing a quantity of these scalps together. Others flay the right arms of their dead enemies, and make of the skin, which is stripped off with the nails hanging to it, a covering for their quivers. Now the skin of a man is thick and glossy, and would in whiteness surpass al-most all other hides. Some even flay the entire body of their en-emy, and, stretching it upon a frame, carry it about with them wherever they ride. Such are the Scythian customs with respect to scalps and skins.

65. The skulls of their enemies, not indeed of all, but of those whom they most detest, they treat as follows. Having sawn off the portion below the eyebrows, and cleaned out the inside, they cover the outside with leather. When a man is poor, this is all that he does; but if he is rich, he also lines the inside with gold:

in either case the skull is used as a drinking cup. They do the same with the skulls of their own kith and kin if they have been at feud with them, and have vanquished them in the presence of the king. When strangers whom they deem of any account come to visit them, these skulls are handed round, and the host tells how that these were his relations who made war upon him, and how that he got the better of them; all this being looked upon as proof of bravery.

66. Once a year the governor of each district, at a set place in his own province, mingles a bowl of wine, of which all Scythians have a right to drink by whom foes have been slain; while they who have slain no enemy are not allowed to taste of the bowl, but sit aloof in disgrace. No greater shame than this can happen to them. Such as have slain a very large number of foes, have two cups instead of one, and drink from both.

67. Scythia has an abundance of soothsayers, who foretell the future by means of a number of willow wands. A large bundle of these wands is brought and laid on the ground. The soothsayer unties the bundle, and places each wand by itself, at the same time uttering his prophecy: then, while he is still speaking, he gathers the rods together again, and makes them up once more into a bundle. This mode of divination is of home growth in Scythia. The Enarees, or womanlike men, have another method, which they say Aphrodite taught them. It is done with the inner bark of the linden-tree. They take a piece of this bark, and, splitting it into three strips, keep twining the strips about their fingers, and untwining them, while they prophesy.

68. Whenever the Scythian king falls sick, he sends for the three soothsayers of most renown at the time, who come and make trial of their art in the mode above described. Generally they say that the king is ill, because such or such a person, mentioning his name, has sworn falsely by the royal hearth. This is the usual oath among the Scythians, when they wish to swear with very great solemnity. Then the man accused of having forsworn himself is arrested and brought before the king. The soothsayers tell him that by their art it is clear he has sworn a false oath by the royal hearth, and so caused the illness of the

king—he denies the charge, protests that he has sworn no false oath, and loudly complains of the wrong done to him. Upon this the king sends for six new soothsayers, who try the matter by soothsaying. If they too find the man guilty of the offence, straitway he is beheaded by those who first accused him, and his goods are parted among them: if, on the contrary, they acquit him, other soothsayers, and again others, are sent for, to try the case. Should the greater number decide in favour of the man's innocence, then they who first accused him forfeit their lives.

69. The mode of their execution is the following: a waggon is loaded with brushwood, and oxen are harnessed to it; the soothsayers, with their feet tied together, their hands bound behind their backs, and their mouths gagged, are thrust into the midst of the brushwood; finally the wood is set alight, and the oxen, being startled, are made to rush off with the waggon. It often happens that the oxen and the soothsayers are both consumed together, but sometimes the pole of the waggon is burnt through, and the oxen escape with a scorching. Diviners—lying diviners, they call them—are burnt in the way described, for other causes besides the one here spoken of. When the king puts one of them to death, he takes care not to let any of his sons survive: all the male offspring are slain with the father, only the females being allowed to live.

70. Oaths among the Scyths are accompanied with the following ceremonies: a large earthen bowl is filled with wine, and the parties to the oath, wounding themselves slightly with a knife or an awl, drop some of their blood into the wine; then they plunge into the mixture a scimitar, some arrows, a battle-axe, and a javelin, all the while repeating prayers; lastly the two contracting parties drink each a draught from the bowl, as do also the chief men among their followers.

71. The tombs of their kings are in the land of the Gerrhi, who dwell at the point where the Borysthenes is first navigable. Here, when the king dies, they dig a grave, which is square in shape, and of great size. When it is ready, they take the king's corpse, and, having opened the belly, and cleaned out the inside, fill the cavity with a preparation of chopped cypress, frankin-

cense, parsley-seed, and anise-seed, after which they sew up the opening, enclose the body in wax, and, placing it on a waggon, carry it about through all the different tribes. On this procession each tribe, when it receives the corpse, imitates the example which is first set by the Royal Scythians; every man chops off a piece of his ear, crops his hair close, makes a cut all round his arm, lacerates his forehead and his nose, and thrusts an arrow through his left hand. Then they who have the care of the corpse carry it with them to another of the tribes which are under the Scythian rule, followed by those whom they first visited. On completing the circuit of all the tribes under their sway, they find themselves in the country of the Gerrhi, who are the most remote of all, and so they come to the tombs of the kings. There the body of the dead king is laid in the grave prepared for it, stretched upon a mattress; spears are fixed in the ground on either side of the corpse, and beams stretched across above it to form a roof, which is covered with a thatching of twigs. In the open space around the body of the king they bury one of his concubines, first killing her by strangling, and also his cup-bearer, his cook, his groom, his lackey, his messenger, some of his horses, firstlings of all his other possessions, and some golden cups; for they use neither silver nor brass. After this they set to work, and raise a vast mound above the grave, all of them vying with each other and seeking to make it as tall as possible.

72. When a year is gone by, further ceremonies take place. Fifty of the best of the late king's attendants are taken, all native Scythians—for, as bought slaves are unknown in the country, the Scythian kings choose any of their subjects that they like, to wait on them—fifty of these are taken and strangled, with fifty of the most beautiful horses. When they are dead, their bowels are taken out, and the cavity cleaned, filled full of chaff, and straightway sewn up again. This done, a number of posts are driven into the ground, in sets of two pairs each, and on every pair half the felly of a wheel is placed archwise; then strong stakes are run lengthways through the bodies of the horses from tail to neck, and they are mounted upon the fellies, so that the felly in front supports the shoulders of the horse,

while that behind sustains the belly and quarters, the legs dangling in midair; each horse is furnished with a bit and bridle, which latter is stretched out in front of the horse, and fastened to a peg. The fifty strangled youths are then mounted severally on the fifty horses. To effect this, a second stake is passed through their bodies along the course of the spine to the neck; the lower end of which projects from the body, and is fixed into a socket, made in the stake that runs lengthwise down the horse. The fifty riders are thus ranged in a circle round the tomb, and so left.

73. Such, then, is the mode in which the kings are buried: as for the people, when any one dies, his nearest of kin lay him upon a waggon and take him round to all his friends in succession: each receives them in turn and entertains them with a banquet, whereat the dead man is served with a portion of all that is set before the others; this is done for forty days, at the end of which time the burial takes place. After the burial, those engaged in it have to purify themselves, which they do in the following way. First they well soap and wash their heads; then, in order to cleanse their bodies, they act as follows: they make a booth by fixing in the ground three sticks inclined towards one another, and stretching around them woollen felts, which they arrange so as to fit as close as possible: inside the booth a dish is placed upon the ground, into which they put a number of red-hot stones, and then add some hemp-seed.

74. Hemp grows in Scythia: it is very like flax; only that it is a much coarser and taller plant: some grows wild about the country, some is produced by cultivation: the Thracians make garments of it which closely resemble linen; so much so, indeed, that if a person has never seen hemp he is sure to think they are linen, and if he has, unless he is very experienced in such matters, he will not know of which material they are.

75. The Scythians, as I said, take some of this hemp-seed, and, creeping under the felt coverings, throw it upon the red-hot stones; immediately it smokes, and gives out such a vapour as no Grecian vapour-bath can exceed; the Scyths, delighted, shout for joy, and this vapour serves them instead of a water-

bath;[23] for they never by any chance wash their bodies with water. Their women make a mixture of cypress, cedar, and frankincense wood, which they pound into a paste upon a rough piece of stone, adding a little water to it. With this substance, which is of a thick consistency, they plaster their faces all over, and indeed their whole bodies. A sweet odour is thereby imparted to them, and when they take off the plaster on the day following, their skin is clean and glossy.

76. The Scythians have an extreme hatred of all foreign customs, particularly of those in use among the Greeks, as the instances of Anacharsis, and, more lately, of Scylas, have fully shown. The former, after he had travelled over a great portion of the world, and displayed wherever he went many proofs of wisdom, as he sailed through the Hellespont on his return to Scythia, touched at Cyzicus. There he found the inhabitants celebrating with much pomp and magnificence a festival to the Mother of the gods,[24] and was himself induced to make a vow to the goddess, whereby he engaged, if he got back safe and sound to his home, that he would give her a festival and a night-procession in all respects like those which he had seen in Cyzicus. When, therefore, he arrived in Scythia, he betook himself to the district called the Woodland, which lies opposite the Race-course of Achilles, and is covered with trees of all manner of different kinds, and there went through all the sacred rites with the tambourine in his hand, and the images tied to him. While thus employed, he was noticed by one of the Scythians, who went and told king Saulius what he had seen. Then king Saulius came in person, and when he perceived what Anacharsis was about, he shot at him with an arrow and killed him. To this day, if you ask the Scyths about Anacharsis, they pretend ignorance of him, because of his Grecian travels and adoption of the customs of foreigners. I learnt, however, from Tymnes, the

---

[23] Herodotus appears in this instance to have confounded together two things in reality quite distinct, intoxication from the fumes of hemp-seed or hashish, and indulgence in the vapour-bath.

[24] Cybele or Rhea, whose worship passed from the Phrygians to the Ionian Greeks.

steward of Ariapeithes, that Anacharsis was paternal uncle to
the Scythian king Idanthyrsus, being the son of Gnurus, who
was the son of Lycus and the grandson of Spargapeithes. If
Anacharsis were really of this house, it must have been by his
own brother that he was slain, for Idanthyrsus was a son of the
Saulius who put Anacharsis to death.

77. I have heard, however, another tale, very different from
this, which is told by the Peloponnesians: they say, that Anacharsis was sent by the king of the Scyths to make acquaintance
with Greece—that he went, and on his return home reported,
that the Greeks were all occupied in the pursuit of every kind
of knowledge, except the Lacedaemonians; who, however, alone
knew how to converse sensibly. A silly tale, this, which the
Greeks have invented for their amusement! There is no doubt
that Anacharsis suffered death in the mode already related, on
account of his attachment to foreign customs, and the intercourse which he held with the Greeks.

78. Scylas, likewise, the son of Ariapeithes, many years later,
met with almost the very same fate. Ariapeithes, the Scythian
king, had several sons, among them this Scylas, who was the
child, not of a native Scyth, but of a woman of Istria. Bred up
by her, Scylas gained an acquaintance with the Greek language
and letters. Some time afterwards, Ariapeithes was treacherously slain by Spargapeithes, king of the Agathyrsi; whereupon
Scylas succeeded to the throne, and married one of his father's
wives, a woman named Opoea. This Opoea was a Scythian by
birth, and had brought Ariapeithes a son called Oricus. Now
when Scylas found himself king of Scythia, as he disliked the
Scythic mode of life, and was attached, by his bringing up, to
the manners of the Greeks, he made it his usual practice, whenever he came with his army to the town of the Borysthenites,
who, according to their own account, are colonists of the Milesians,—he made it his practice, I say, to leave the army before
the city, and, having entered within the walls by himself, and
carefully closed the gates, to exchange his Scythian dress for
Grecian garments, and in this attire to walk about the market-
place, without guards or retinue. The Borysthenites kept watch

at the gates, that no Scythian might see the king thus apparelled. Scylas, meanwhile, lived exactly as the Greeks, and even offered sacrifices to the gods according to the Grecian rites. In this way he would pass a month, or more, with the Borysthenites, after which he would clothe himself again in his Scythian dress, and so take his departure. This he did repeatedly, and even built himself a house in Borysthenes, and married a wife there who was a native of the place.

79. But when the time came that was ordained to bring him woe, the occasion of his ruin was the following. He wanted to be initiated in the rites of the Bacchic Dionysus, and was on the point of obtaining admission to the rites, when a most strange prodigy occurred to him. The house which he possessed, as I mentioned a short time back, in the city of the Borysthenites, a building of great extent and erected at a vast cost, round which there stood a number of sphinxes and griffins carved in white marble, was struck by lightning from on high, and burnt to the ground. Scylas, nevertheless, went on, and received the initiation. Now the Scythians are wont to reproach the Greeks with their Bacchanal rage, and to say that it is not reasonable to imagine there is a god who impels men to madness. No sooner, therefore, was Scylas initiated in the Bacchic mysteries than one of the Borysthenites went and carried the news to the Scythians. "You Scyths laugh at us," he said, "because we rave when the god seizes us. But now our god has seized upon your king, who raves like us, and is maddened by the influence. If you think I do not tell you true, come with me, and I will show him to you." The chiefs of the Scythians went with the man accordingly, and the Borysthenite, conducting them into the city, placed them secretly on one of the towers. Presently Scylas passed by with the band of revellers, raving like the rest, and was seen by the watchers. Regarding the matter as a very great misfortune, they instantly departed, and came and told the army what they had witnessed.

80. When, therefore, Scylas, after leaving Borysthenes, was about returning home, the Scythians broke out into revolt. They put at their head Octamasadas, grandson (on the mother's side)

of Teres. Then Scylas, when he learned the danger with which
he was threatened, and the reason of the disturbance, made his
escape to Thrace. Octamasadas, discovering whither he had fled,
marched after him, and had reached the Ister, when he was met
by the forces of the Thracians. The two armies were about to
engage, but before they joined battle, Sitalces[25] sent a message
to Octamasadas to this effect, "Why should there be trial of
arms between us? You are my own sister's son, and you have in
your keeping my brother. Surrender him into my hands, and I
will give Scylas back to you. So neither you nor I will risk our
armies." Sitalces sent this message to Octamasadas by a herald,
and Octamasadas, with whom a brother of Sitalces had formerly
taken refuge, accepted the terms. He surrendered his own uncle
to Sitalces, and obtained in exchange his brother Scylas. Sitalces
took his brother with him and withdrew; but Octamasadas beheaded Scylas upon the spot. Thus rigidly do the Scythians
maintain their own customs, and thus severely do they punish
such as adopt foreign usages.

81. What the population of Scythia is, I was not able to
learn with certainty; the accounts which I received varied from
one another. I heard from some that they were very numerous
indeed; others made their numbers but scanty for such a nation
as the Scyths. Thus much, however, I witnessed with my own
eyes. There is a tract called Exampaeus between the Borysthenes and the Hypanis. I made some mention of it in a former
place, where I spoke of the bitter stream which rising there
flows into the Hypanis, and renders the water of that river un-
drinkable. Here then stands a brazen bowl, six times as big as
that at the entrance of the Euxine, which Pausanias, the son of
Cleombrotus, set up.[26] Such as have never seen that vessel may
understand me better if I say that the Scythian bowl holds with
ease six hundred amphorae,[27] and is of the thickness of six
fingers' breadth. The natives gave me the following account of

---

[25] Sitalces was contemporary with Herodotus. He died 424 B.C.
[26] Pausanias set up this bowl at the time that he was besieging Byzantium, 477 B.C.
[27] About 5,400 gallons.

the manner in which it was made. One of their kings, by name Ariantas, wishing to know the number of his subjects, ordered them all to bring him, on pain of death, the point off one of their arrows. They obeyed, and he collected thereby a vast heap of arrow-heads, which he resolved to form into a memorial that might go down to posterity. Accordingly he made of them this bowl, and dedicated it at Exampaeus. This was all that I could learn concerning the number of the Scythians.

82. The country has no marvels except its rivers, which are larger and more numerous than those of any other land. These, and the vastness of the great plain, are worthy of note, and one thing besides, which I am about to mention. They show a foot-mark of Heracles, impressed on a rock, in shape like the print of a man's foot, but three feet in length. It is in the neighbourhood of the Tyras. Having described this, I return to the subject on which I originally proposed to discourse.

83. The preparations of Darius against the Scythians had be-gun, messengers had been despatched on all sides with the king's commands, some being required to furnish troops, others to supply ships, others again to bridge the Thracian Bosporus, when Artabanus, son of Hystaspes and brother of Darius, en-treated the king to desist from his expedition, urging on him the great difficulty of attacking Scythia. Good, however, as the ad-vice of Artabanus was, it failed to persuade Darius. He there-fore ceased his reasonings, and Darius, when his preparations were complete, led his army forth from Susa.

84. It was then that a certain Persian, by name Oeobazus, the father of three sons, all of whom were to accompany the army, came and prayed the king that he would allow one of his sons to remain with him. Darius made answer, as if he regarded him in the light of a friend who had urged a moderate request, that he would allow them all to remain. Oeobazus was over-joyed, expecting that all his children would be excused from serving; the king however bade his attendants take the three sons of Oeobazus and forthwith put them to death. Thus they were all left behind, but not till they had been deprived of life.

85. When Darius, on his march from Susa, reached the terri-

tory of Calchedon on the shores of the Bosporus, where the bridge had been made, he took ship and sailed thence to the Cyanean islands, which, according to the Greeks, once floated. He took his seat also in the temple and surveyed the Pontus, which is indeed well worthy of consideration. There is not in the world any other sea so wonderful: it extends in length 1,280 miles, and its breadth, at the widest part, is 380 miles.[28] The mouth is but one-half mile wide, and this strait, called the Bosporus, and across which the bridge of Darius had been thrown, is fourteen miles in length,[29] reaching from the Euxine to the Propontis. The Propontis is sixty miles across, and 160 miles long.[30] Its waters flow into the Hellespont, the length of which is fifty miles, and the width no more than 1,400 yards.[31] The Hellespont opens into the wide sea called the Aegean.

86. The mode in which these distances have been measured is the following. In a long day a vessel generally accomplishes about 70,000 fathoms, in the night 60,000. Now from the mouth of the Pontus to the river Phasis, which is the extreme length of this sea, is a voyage of nine days and eight nights, which makes the distance 1,110,000 fathoms, or 11,100 furlongs.[32] Again, from Sindica to Themiscyra on the river Thermodon, where the Pontus is wider than at any other place, is a sail of three days and two nights; which makes 330,000 fathoms, or 3,300 furlongs. Such is the plan on which I have measured the Pontus, the Bosporus, and the Hellespont, and such is the account which I have to give of them. The Pontus has also a lake belonging to it, not very much inferior to itself in size.[33] The waters of this

[28] These measurements are extremely incorrect. The distance from the mouth of the Bosporus to the Phasis is little more than 630 miles. Again, the distance across from the Thermodon to the Sindic peninsula is about 270 miles.

[29] This is under the true length, which is about sixteen miles.

[30] The Propontis is nearer forty-three miles across and 110 miles long.

[31] The length is about forty miles; Herodotus' width is correct.

[32] These figures are given in miles in the preceding chapter. It will be noted that Herodotus regularly overestimates ships' speeds.

[33] It is commonly supposed that Herodotus fell here into a very gross mistake, since the Sea of Azov is not now much more than one-twelfth

lake run into the Pontus; it is called the Maeotis, and also the mother of the Pontus.

87. Darius, after he had finished his survey, sailed back to the bridge, which had been constructed for him by Mandrocles a Samian. He likewise surveyed the Bosporus, and erected upon its shores two pillars of white marble, whereupon he inscribed the names of all the nations which formed his army—on the one pillar in Greek, on the other in Assyrian characters. Now his army was drawn from all the nations under his sway, and the whole amount, without reckoning the naval forces, was 700,000 men, including cavalry. The fleet consisted of 600 ships. Some time afterwards the Byzantines removed these pillars to their own city, and used them for an altar which they erected to Orthosian Artemis. One block remained behind: it lay near the temple of Dionysus at Byzantium, and was covered with Assyrian writing. The spot where Darius bridged the Bosporus was, I think but I speak only from conjecture, half-way between the city of Byzantium and the temple at the mouth of the strait.

88. Darius was so pleased with the bridge thrown across the strait by the Samian Mandrocles, that he not only bestowed upon him all the customary presents, but gave him ten of every kind. Mandrocles, by way of offering firstfruits from these presents, caused a picture to be painted which showed the whole of the bridge, with King Darius sitting in a seat of honour, and his army engaged in the passage. This painting he dedicated in the temple of Hera at Samos, attaching to it the inscription following:

> The fish-fraught Bosporus bridged, to Hera's fane
> Did Mandrocles this proud memorial bring;
> When for himself a crown he'd skill to gain,
> For Samos praise, contenting the Great King.

Such was the memorial of his work which was left by the architect of the bridge.

of the size of the Euxine; but it is possible that Lake Maeotis may have been very greatly larger in the time of Herodotus than it is at present.

89. Darius, after rewarding Mandrocles, passed into Europe, while he ordered the Ionians to enter the Pontus, and sail to the mouth of the Ister. There he bade them throw a bridge across the stream and await his coming. The Ionians, Aeolians, and Hellespontians were the nations which furnished the chief strength of his navy. So the fleet, threading the Cyanean Isles, proceeded straight to the Ister, and, mounting the river to the point where its channels separate, a distance of two days' voyage from the sea, yoked the neck of the stream. Meantime Darius, who had crossed the Bosporus by the bridge over it, marched through Thrace; and happening upon the sources of the Tearus, pitched his camp and made a stay of three days.

90. Now the Tearus is said by those who dwell near it, to be the most healthful of all streams, and to cure, among other diseases, the scab either in man or beast. Its sources, which are thirty-eight in number, all flowing from the same rock, are in part cold, in part hot. They lie at an equal distance from the town of Heraeum near Perinthus, and Apollonia on the Euxine, a two days' journey from each. This river, the Tearus, is a tributary of the Contadesdus, which runs into the Agrianes, and that into the Hebrus. The Hebrus empties itself into the sea near the city of Aenus.

91. Here then, on the banks of the Tearus, Darius stopped and pitched his camp. The river charmed him so, that he caused a pillar to be erected in this place also, with an inscription to the following effect, "The fountains of the Tearus afford the best and most beautiful water of all rivers: they were visited, on his march into Scythia, by the best and most beautiful of men, Darius, son of Hystaspes, king of the Persians, and of the whole continent." Such was the inscription which he set up at this place.

92. Marching thence, he came to a second river, called the Artiscus, which flows through the country of the Odrysians. Here he fixed upon a certain spot, where every one of his soldiers should throw a stone as he passed by. When his orders were obeyed, Darius continued his march, leaving behind him great hills formed of the stones cast by his troops.

93. Before arriving at the Ister, the first people whom he subdued were the Getae, who believe in their immortality. The
Thracians of Salmydessus, and those who dwelt above the cities
of Apollonia and Mesembria—the Scyrmiadae and Nipsaeans,
as they are called—gave themselves up to Darius without a
struggle; but the Getae obstinately defending themselves, were
forthwith enslaved, notwithstanding that they are the noblest
as well as the most just of all the Thracian tribes.

94. The belief of the Getae in respect of immortality is the
following. They think that they do not really die, but that when
they depart this life they go to Zalmoxis, who is called also
Gebeleizis by some among them. To this god every five years
they send a messenger, who is chosen by lot out of the whole
nation, and charged to bear him their several requests. Their
mode of sending him is this. A number of them stand in order,
each holding in his hand three darts; others take the man who
is to be sent to Zalmoxis, and swinging him by his hands and
feet, toss him into the air so that he falls upon the points of the
weapons. If he is pierced and dies, they think that the god is
propitious to them; but if not, they lay the fault on the messenger, who (they say) is a wicked man: and so they choose
another to send away. The messages are given while the man is
still alive. This same people, when it lightens and thunders, aim
their arrows at the sky, uttering threats against the god; and
they do not believe that there is any god but their own.

95. I am told by the Greeks who dwell on the shores of the
Hellespont and the Pontus, that this Zalmoxis was in reality a
man, that he lived at Samos, and while there was the slave of
Pythagoras son of Mnesarchus. After obtaining his freedom he
grew rich, and leaving Samos, returned to his own country. The
Thracians at that time lived in a wretched way, and were a poor
ignorant race; Zalmoxis, therefore, who by his commerce with
the Greeks, and especially with one who was by no means their
most contemptible philosopher, Pythagoras, was acquainted
with the Ionic mode of life and with manners more refined than
those current among his countrymen, had a chamber built, in
which from time to time he received and feasted all the prin-

cipal Thracians, using the occasion to teach them that neither he, nor they, his boon companions, nor any of their posterity would ever perish, but that they would all go to a place where they would live forever in the enjoyment of every conceivable good. While he was acting in this way, and holding this kind of discourse, he was constructing an apartment underground, into which, when it was completed, he withdrew, vanishing suddenly from the eyes of the Thracians, who greatly regretted his loss, and mourned over him as one dead. He meanwhile abode in his secret chamber three full years, after which he came forth from his concealment, and showed himself once more to his country-men, who were thus brought to believe in the truth of what he had taught them. Such is the account of the Greeks.

96. I for my part neither put entire faith in this story of Zalmoxis and his underground chamber, nor do I altogether discredit it: but I believe Zalmoxis to have lived long before the time of Pythagoras. Whether there was ever really a man of the name, or whether Zalmoxis is nothing but a native god of the Getae, I now bid him farewell. As for the Getae themselves, the people who observe the practices described above, they were now reduced by the Persians, and accompanied the army of Darius.

97. When Darius, with his land forces, reached the Ister, he made his troops cross the stream, and after all were gone over gave orders to the Ionians to break the bridge, and follow him with the whole naval force in his land march. They were about to obey his command, when the general of the Mytilenaeans, Coes son of Erxander, having first asked whether it was agree-able to the king to listen to one who wished to speak his mind, addressed him in the words following, "You are about, Sire, to attack a country no part of which is cultivated, and wherein there is not a single inhabited city. Keep this bridge, then, as it is, and leave those who built it, to watch over it. So if we come up with the Scythians and succeed against them as we could wish, we may return by this route; or if we fail of finding them, our retreat will still be secure. For I have no fear lest the Scyth-ians defeat us in battle, but my dread is lest we be unable to

discover them, and suffer loss while we wander about their territory. And now, mayhap, it will be said I advise you thus in the hope of being myself allowed to remain behind; but in truth I have no other design than to recommend the course which seems to me the best; nor will I consent to be among those left behind, but my resolve is, in any case, to follow you." The advice of Coes pleased Darius highly, who thus replied to him "Dear Lesbian, when I am safe home again in my palace, be sure to come to me, and with good deeds will I recompense your good words of today."

98. Having so said, the king took a leathern thong, and tying sixty knots in it, called together the Ionian tyrants, and spoke thus to them, "Men of Ionia, my former commands to you concerning the bridge are now withdrawn. See, here is a thong; take it, and observe my bidding with respect to it. From the time that I leave you to march forward into Scythia, untie every day one of the knots. If I do not return before the last day to which the knots will hold out, then leave your station, and sail to your several homes. Meanwhile, understand that my resolve is changed, and that you are to guard the bridge with all care, and watch over its safety and preservation. By so doing you will oblige me greatly." When Darius had thus spoken, he set out on his march with all speed.

99. Before you come to Scythia, on the sea coast, lies Thrace. The land here makes a sweep, and then Scythia begins, the Ister falling into the sea at this point with its mouth facing the east. Starting from the Ister I shall now describe the measurements of the sea-shore of Scythia. Immediately that the Ister is crossed, Old Scythia begins, and continues as far as the city called Carcinitis, fronting towards the south wind and the midday. Here upon the same sea, there lies a mountainous tract [34] projecting into the Pontus, which is inhabited by the Tauri, as far as what is called the Rugged Chersonese, which runs out into the sea upon the east. For the boundaries of Scythia extend on two sides to two different seas, one upon the south, and the other

[34] The mountains lie only along the southern coast of the Crimea. All the rest of the peninsula belongs to the steppes.

towards the east, as is also the case with Attica. And the Tauri
occupy a position in Scythia like that which a people would hold
in Attica, who, being foreigners and not Athenians, should inhabit the highland of Sunium, from Thoricus to the township
of Anaphlystus, if this tract projected into the sea somewhat
further than it does. Such, to compare great things with small, is
the Tauric territory. For the sake of those who may not have
made the voyage round these parts of Attica, I will illustrate in
another way. It is as if in Iapygia a line were drawn from Port
Brundusium to Tarentum, and a people different from the
Iapygians inhabited the promontory.[35] These two instances may
suggest a number of others, where the shape of the land closely
resembles that of Taurica.

100. Beyond this tract, we find the Scythians again in possession of the country above the Tauri and the parts bordering
on the eastern sea, as also of the whole district lying west of the
Cimmerian Bosporus and Lake Maeotis, as far as the river
Tanais, which empties itself into that lake at its upper end. As
for the inland boundaries of Scythia, if we start from the Ister,
we find it enclosed by the following tribes, first the Agathyrsi,
next the Neuri, then the Man-eaters, and last of all, the Black-
cloaks.

101. Scythia then, which is square in shape, and has two of
its sides reaching down to the sea, extends inland to the same
distance that it stretches along the coast, and is equal every
way. For it is a ten days' journey from the Ister to the Borysthenes, and ten more from the Borysthenes to Lake Maeotis,
while the distance from the coast inland to the country of the
Black-cloaks, who dwell above Scythia, is a journey of twenty
days. I reckon the day's journey at twenty-five miles. Thus the
two sides which run straight inland are 500 miles each, and the
transverse sides at right angles to these are also of the same
length, which gives the full size of Scythia.

[35] This passage was evidently written for the benefit of readers in
Magna Graecia. Herodotus at Thurii would have Iapygia before his eyes,
as it were. Writing from Ionia, or even from Greece Proper, he would
never have thought of such an illustration.

102. The Scythians, reflecting on their situation, perceived that they were not strong enough by themselves to contend with the army of Darius in open fight. They, therefore, sent envoys to the neighbouring nations, whose kings had already met, and were in consultation upon the advance of so vast a host. Now they who had come together were the kings of the Tauri, the Agathyrsi, the Neuri, the Man-eaters, the Black-cloaks, the Geloni, the Budini, and the Sauromatae.

103. The Tauri have the following customs. They offer in sacrifice to the virgin goddess all shipwrecked persons, and all Greeks compelled to put into their ports by stress of weather. The mode of sacrifice is this. After the preparatory ceremonies, they strike the victim on the head with a club. Then, according to some accounts, they hurl the trunk from the precipice whereon the temple stands, and nail the head to a cross. Others grant that the head is treated in this way, but deny that the body is thrown down the cliff—on the contrary, they say, it is buried. The goddess to whom these sacrifices are offered the Tauri themselves declare to be Iphigenia[36] the daughter of Aga-memnon. When they take prisoners in war they treat them in the following way. The man who has taken a captive cuts off his head, and carrying it to his home, fixes it upon a tall pole, which he elevates above his house, most commonly over the chimney. The reason that the heads are set up so high, is (it is said) in order that the whole house may be under their protection. These people live entirely by war and plundering.

104. The Agathyrsi are a race of men very luxurious, and very fond of wearing gold on their persons. They have inter-course promiscuously, that so they may be all brothers,[37] and, as members of one family, may neither envy nor hate one an-other. In other respects their customs approach nearly to those of the Thracians.

105. The Neurian customs are like the Scythian. One gen-eration before the attack of Darius they were driven from their

---

[36] The virgin goddess of the Tauri was more generally identified by the Greeks with their own Artemis.

[37] This anticipation of the theory of Plato (*Rep.* v.) is curious.

land by a huge multitude of serpents which invaded them. Of these some were produced in their own country, while others, and those by far the greater number, came in from the deserts on the north. Suffering grievously beneath this scourge, they quitted their homes, and took refuge with the Budini. It seems that these people are conjurers: for both the Scythians and the Greeks who dwell in Scythia say, that every Neurian once a year becomes a wolf[38] for a few days, at the end of which time he is restored to his proper shape.[39] Not that I believe this, but they constantly affirm it to be true, and are even ready to back their assertion with an oath.

106. The manners of the Man-eaters are more savage than those of any other race. They neither observe justice, nor are governed by any laws. They are nomads, and their dress is Scythian; but the language which they speak is peculiar to themselves. Unlike any other nation in these parts, they are cannibals.

107. The Black-cloaks wear, all of them, black cloaks, and from this derive the name which they bear. Their customs are Scythic.

108. The Budini are a large and powerful nation: they have all deep blue eyes, and bright red hair. There is a city in their territory, called Gelonus, which is surrounded with a lofty wall, four miles each way, built entirely of wood. All the houses in the place and all the temples are of the same material. Here are temples built in honour of the Grecian gods, and adorned after the Greek fashion with images, altars, and shrines, all in wood. There is even a festival, held every third year, in honour of Dionysus, at which the natives fall into the Bacchic fury. For the fact is that the Geloni were anciently Greeks, who, being driven out of the trading-ports along the coast, fled to the Budini and took up their abode with them. They still speak a language half Greek, half Scythian.

[38] This is the earliest reference to the widespread superstition as to werewolves.

[39] As Herodotus recedes from the sea his accounts become more mythic and less trustworthy.

109. The Budini, however, do not speak the same language as the Geloni, nor is their mode of life the same. They are the aboriginal people of the country, and are nomads; unlike any of the neighbouring races, they eat lice.[40] The Geloni, on the contrary, are tillers of the soil, eat bread, have gardens, and both in shape and complexion are quite different from the Budini. The Greeks notwithstanding call these latter Geloni, but it is a mistake to give them the name. Their country is thickly planted with trees of all manner of kinds. In the very woodiest part is a broad deep lake, surrounded by marshy ground with reeds growing on it. Here otters are caught, and beavers, with another sort of animal which has a square face. With the skins of this last the natives border their leather cloaks: and their testicles provide a remedy, for diseases of the womb.

110. It is reported of the Sauromatae, that when the Greeks fought with the Amazons, whom the Scythians call Oiorpata or man-slayers, as it may be rendered, *Oior* being Scythic for man, and *pata* for to slay—it is reported, I say, that the Greeks after gaining the battle of the Thermodon, put to sea, taking with them on board three of their vessels all the Amazons whom they had made prisoners; and that these women upon the voyage rose up against the crews, and massacred them to a man. As however they were quite strange to ships, and did not know how to use either rudder, sails, or oars, they were carried, after the death of the men, where the winds and the waves listed. At last they reached the shores of Lake Maeotis and came to a place called Cremni or the Cliffs, which is in the country of the free Scythians. Here they went ashore, and proceeded by land towards the inhabited regions; the first herd of horses which they fell in with they seized, and mounting upon their backs, fell to plundering the Scythian territory.

111. The Scyths could not tell what to make of the attack upon them—the dress, the language, the nation itself, were alike unknown—whence the enemy had come even, was a marvel. Imagining, however, that they were all men of about the same age, they went out against them, and fought a battle. Some

[40] Photius defines the same word as fir-cone.

of the bodies of the slain fell into their hands, whereby they discovered the truth. Hereupon they deliberated, and made a resolve to kill no more of them, but to send against them a detachment of their youngest men, as near as they could guess equal to the women in number, with orders to encamp in their neighbourhood, and do as they saw them do—when the Amazons advanced against them, they were to retire, and avoid a fight—when they halted, the young men were to approach and pitch their camp near the camp of the enemy. All this they did on account of their strong desire to obtain children from so notable a race.

112. So the youth departed, and obeyed the orders which they had been given. The Amazons soon found out that they had not come to do them any harm, and so they on their part ceased to offer the Scythians any molestation. And now day after day the camps approached nearer to one another; both parties led the same life, neither having anything but their arms and horses, so that they were forced to support themselves by hunting and pillage.

113. The Amazons scattered by ones and twos at noon, wandering off to relieve themselves. The Scythians noticed this and did likewise; one of them attacked an Amazon who was alone; she did not resist but let him have his way. Then she bade him by signs (for they did not understand each other's language) to bring a friend the next day to the spot where they had met—promising on her part to bring with her another woman. He did so, and the woman kept her word. When the rest of the youths heard what had taken place, they had intercourse with the other Amazons.

114. The two camps were then joined in one, each Scythian having the Amazon with whom he first had intercourse as his wife. The men were unable to learn the tongue of the women, but the women soon caught up the tongue of the men. When they could thus understand one another, the Scyths addressed the Amazons in these words, "We have parents, and properties, let us therefore give up this mode of life, and return to our nation, and live with them. You shall be our wives there no less

than here, and we promise you to have no others." But the Amazons said, "We could not live with your women—our customs are quite different from theirs. To draw the bow, to hurl the javelin, to bestride the horse, these are our arts—of womanly employments we know nothing. Your women, on the contrary, do none of these things; but stay at home in their waggons, engaged in womanish tasks, and never go out to hunt, or to do anything. We should never agree together. But if you truly wish to keep us as your wives, and would conduct yourselves with strict justice towards us, go you home to your parents, bid them give you your inheritance, and then come back to us, and let us and you live together by ourselves."

115. The youths approved of the advice, and followed it. They went and got the portion of goods which fell to them, returned with it, and rejoined their wives, who then addressed them in these words following, "We are ashamed, and afraid to live in the country where we now are. Not only have we stolen you from your fathers, but we have done great damage to Scythia by our ravages. As you like us for wives, grant the request we make of you. Let us leave this country together, and go and dwell beyond the Tanais." Again the youths complied.

116. Crossing the Tanais they journeyed eastward a distance of three days' march from that stream, and again northward a distance of three days' march from Lake Maeotis. Here they came to the country where they now live, and took up their abode in it. The women of the Sauromatae have continued from that day to the present, to observe their ancient customs, frequently hunting on horseback with their husbands, sometimes even unaccompanied; in war taking the field; and wearing the very same dress as the men.

117. The Sauromatae speak the language of Scythia, but have never talked it correctly, because the Amazons learned it imperfectly at the first. Their marriage-law lays it down, that no girl shall wed till she has killed a man in battle. Sometimes it happens that a woman dies unmarried at an advanced age, having never been able in her whole lifetime to fulfil the condition.

118. The envoys of the Scythians, on being introduced into

the presence of the kings of these nations, who were assembled to deliberate, made it known to them, that the Persian, after subduing the whole of the other continent, had thrown a bridge over the strait of the Bosporus, and crossed into the continent of Europe, where he had reduced the Thracians, and was now making a bridge over the Ister, his aim being to bring under his sway all Europe also. "Stand not aloof then from this contest," they went on to say, "look not on tamely while we are perishing —but make common cause with us, and together let us meet the enemy. If you refuse, we must yield to the pressure, and either quit our country, or make terms with the invaders. For what else is left for us to do, if your aid be withheld from us? The blow, be sure, will not light on you more gently upon this account. The Persian comes against you no less than against us: and will not be content, after we are conquered, to leave you in peace. We can bring strong proof of what we here advance. Had the Persian leader indeed come to avenge the wrongs which he suffered at our hands when we enslaved his people, and to war on us only, he would have been bound to march straight upon Scythia, without molesting any nation by the way. Then it would have been plain to all, that Scythia alone was aimed at. But now, what has his conduct been? From the moment of his entrance into Europe, he has subjugated without exception every nation that lay in his path. All the tribes of the Thracians have been brought under his sway, and among them even our next neighbours, the Getae."

119. The assembled princes of the nations, after hearing all that the Scythians had to say, deliberated. At the end opinion was divided—the kings of the Geloni, Budini, and Sauromatae were of accord, and pledged themselves to give assistance to the Scythians; but the Agathyrsian and Neurian princes, together with the sovereigns of the Man-eaters, the Black-cloaks, and the Tauri, replied to their request as follows, "If you had not been the first to wrong the Persians, and begin the war, we should have thought the request you make just; we should then have complied with your wishes, and joined our arms with yours. Now, however, the case stands thus—you, independently of us,

invaded the land of the Persians, and so long as God gave you the power, lorded it over them: raised up now by the same God, they are come to do to you the like. We, on our part, did no wrong to these men in the former war, and will not be the first to commit wrong now. If they invade our land, and begin aggressions upon us, we will not suffer them; but, till we see this come to pass, we will remain at home. For we believe that the Persians are not come to attack us, but to punish those who are guilty of first injuring them."

120. When this reply reached the Scythians, they resolved, as the neighbouring nations refused their alliance, that they would not openly venture on any pitched battle with the enemy, but would retire before them, driving off their herds, choking up all the wells and springs as they retreated, and leaving the whole country bare of forage. They divided themselves into three bands, one of which, namely that commanded by Scopasis, it was agreed should be joined by the Sauromatae, and if the Persians advanced in the direction of the Tanais, should retreat along the shores of Lake Maeotis and make for that river; while if the Persians retired, they should at once pursue and harass them. The two other divisions, the principal one under the command of Idanthyrsus, and the third, of which Taxacis was king, were to unite in one, and, joined by the detachments of the Geloni and Budini, were, like the others, to keep at the distance of a day's march from the Persians, falling back as they advanced, and doing the same as the others. At first, they were to take the direction of the nations which had refused to join the alliance, and were to draw the war upon them: that so, if they would not of their own free will engage in the contest, they might by these means be forced into it. Afterwards, it was agreed that they should retire into their own land, and, should it on deliberation appear to them expedient, join battle with the enemy.

121. When these measures had been determined on, the Scythians went out to meet the army of Darius, sending on in front as scouts the fleetest of their horsemen. Their waggons, wherein their women and their children lived, and all their

cattle, except such a number as was wanted for food, which they kept with them, were made to precede them in their retreat, and departed, with orders to keep marching, without change of course, to the north.

122. The scouts of the Scythians found the Persian host advanced three days' march from the Ister, and immediately took the lead of them at the distance of a day's march, encamping from time to time, and destroying all that grew on the ground. The Persians no sooner caught sight of the Scythian horse than they pursued upon their track, while the enemy retired before them. The pursuit of the Persians was directed towards the single division of the Scythian army, and thus their line of march was eastward towards the Tanais. The Scyths crossed the river, and the Persians after them, still in pursuit. In this way they passed through the country of the Sauromatae, and entered that of the Budini.

123. As long as the march of the Persian army lay through the countries of the Scythians and Sauromatae, there was nothing which they could damage, the land being waste and barren; but on entering the territories of the Budini, they came upon the wooden fortress above mentioned, which was deserted by its inhabitants and left quite empty of everything. This place they burnt to the ground; and having so done, again pressed forward on the track of the retreating Scythians, till, having passed through the entire country of the Budini, they reached the desert, which has no inhabitants, and extends a distance of seven days' journey above the Budinian territory. Beyond this desert dwell the Thyssagetae, out of whose land four great streams flow. These rivers all traverse the country of the Maeotians, and fall into Lake Maeotis. Their names are the Lycus, the Oarus, the Tanais, and the Syrgis.

124. When Darius reached the desert, he paused from his pursuit, and halted his army upon the Oarus. Here he built eight large forts, at an equal distance from one another, eight miles apart or thereabouts, the ruins of which were still remaining in my day.[41] During the time that he was so occupied, the

[41] The conjecture is probable that these supposed "forts" were ruined

Scythians whom he had been following, made a circuit by the higher regions, and re-entered Scythia. On their complete disappearance, Darius, seeing nothing more of them, left his forts half finished, and returned towards the west. He imagined that the Scythians whom he had seen were the entire nation, and that they had fled in that direction.

125. He now quickened his march, and entering Scythia, fell in with the two combined divisions of the Scythian army, and instantly gave them chase. They kept to their plan of retreating before him at the distance of a day's march; and, he still following them hotly, they led him, as had been previously settled, into the territories of the nations that had refused to become their allies, and first of all into the country of the Black-cloaks. Great disturbance was caused among this people by the invasion of the Scyths first, and then of the Persians. So, having harassed them after this sort, the Scythians led the way into the land of the Man-eaters, with the same result as before; and thence passed onwards into Neuris, where their coming likewise spread dismay among the inhabitants. Still retreating they approached the Agathyrsi; but this people, which had witnessed the flight and terror of their neighbours, did not wait for the Scyths to invade them, but sent a herald to forbid them to cross their borders, and to forewarn them, that, if they made the attempt, it would be resisted by force of arms. The Agathyrsi then proceeded to the frontier, to defend their country against the invaders. As for the other nations, the Black-cloaks, the Man-eaters, and the Neuri, instead of defending themselves, when the Scyths and Persians overran their lands, they forgot their threats, and fled away in confusion to the deserts lying towards the north. The Scythians, when the Agathyrsi forbade them to enter their country, refrained; and led the Persians back from the Neurian district into their own land.

126. This had gone on so long, and seemed so interminable, that Darius at last sent a horseman to Idanthyrsus, the Scythian king, with the following message, "Strange man, why do you

barrows. Herodotus would hear of them from the Greek traders. His words do not necessarily imply that he had himself seen them.

keep on flying before me, when there are two things you might
do so easily? If you deem yourself able to resist my arms, cease
your wanderings and come, let us engage in battle. Or if you are
conscious that my strength is greater than yours—even so you
should cease to run away—you have but to bring your lord
earth and water, and to come at once to a conference."

127. To this message Idanthyrsus, the Scythian king, replied,
"This is my way, Persian. I never fear men or fly from them. I
have not done so in times past, nor do I now fly from you. There
is nothing new or strange in what I do; I only follow my common mode of life in peaceful years. Now I will tell you why I
do not at once join battle with you. We Scythians have neither
towns nor cultivated lands, which might induce us, through fear
of their being taken or ravaged, to be in any hurry to fight with
you. If, however, you must needs come to blows with us speedily, look you now, there are our fathers' tombs—seek them out,
and attempt to meddle with them—then you shall see whether
or no we will fight with you. Till you do this, be sure we shall
not join battle, unless it pleases us. This is my answer to the
challenge to fight. As for lords, I acknowledge only Zeus my
ancestor, and Hestia, the Scythian queen. Earth and water, the
tribute you ask, I do not send, but you shall soon receive more
suitable gifts. Last of all, in return for calling yourself my lord,
I say to you, 'Go howl.' " (This is what men mean by the Scythian mode of speech.) So the herald departed, bearing this message to Darius.

128. When the Scythian kings heard the name of slavery
they were filled with rage, and despatched the division under
Scopasis to which the Sauromatae were joined, with orders that
they should seek a conference with the Ionians, who had been
left at the Ister to guard the bridge. Meanwhile the Scythians
who remained behind resolved no longer to lead the Persians
hither and thither about their country, but to fall upon them
whenever they should be at their meals. So they waited till such
times, and then did as they had determined. In these combats
the Scythian horse always put to flight the horse of the enemy;
these last, however, when routed, fell back upon their foot, who

never failed to afford them support; while the Scythians, on
their side, as soon as they had driven the horse in, retired again,
for fear of the foot. By night too the Scythians made many similar attacks.

129. There was one very strange thing which greatly aided
the Persians, and was of equal disservice to the Scyths, in these
assaults on the Persian camp. This was the braying of the asses
and the appearance of the mules. For, as I observed before, the
land of the Scythians produces neither ass nor mule, and contains no single specimen of either animal, by reason of the cold.
So, when the asses brayed, they frightened the Scythian cavalry; and often, in the middle of a charge, the horses, hearing
the noise made by the asses, would take fright and wheel round,
pricking up their ears, and showing astonishment. This was owing to their having never heard the noise, or seen the form, of
the animal before: and it was not without some little influence
on the progress of the war.

130. The Scythians, when they perceived signs that the Persians were becoming alarmed, took steps to induce them not to
quit Scythia, in the hope, if they stayed, of inflicting on them
the greater injury, when their supplies should altogether fail.
To effect this, they would leave some of their cattle exposed
with the herdsmen, while they themselves moved away to a distance: the Persians would make a foray, and take the beasts,
whereupon they would be highly elated.

131. This they did several times, until at last Darius was at
his wits' end; hereon the Scythian princes, understanding how
matters stood, despatched a herald to the Persian camp with
presents for the king: these were, a bird, a mouse, a frog, and
five arrows. The Persians asked the bearer to tell them what
these gifts might mean, but he made answer that he had no
orders except to deliver them, and return again with all speed. If
the Persians were wise, he added, they would find out the meaning for themselves. So when they heard this, they held a council
to consider the matter.

132. Darius gave it as his opinion, that the Scyths intended a
surrender of themselves and their country, both land and water,

into his hands. This he conceived to be the meaning of the gifts, because the mouse is an inhabitant of the earth, and eats the same food as man, while the frog passes his life in the water; the bird bears a great resemblance to the horse, and the arrows might signify the surrender of all their power. To the explanation of Darius, Gobryas, one of the seven conspirators against the Magus, opposed another which was as follows, "Unless, Persians, you can turn into birds and fly up into the sky, or become mice and burrow under the ground, or make yourselves frogs, and take refuge in the fens, you will never make escape from this land, but die pierced by our arrows." Such were the meanings which the Persians assigned to the gifts.

133. The single division of the Scyths, which in the early part of the war had been appointed to keep guard about Lake Maeotis, and had now been sent to get speech of the Ionians stationed at the Ister, addressed them, on reaching the bridge, in these words, "Men of Ionia, we bring you freedom, if you will only do as we recommend. Darius, we understand, enjoined you to keep your guard here at this bridge just sixty days; then, if he did not appear, you were to return home. Now, therefore, act so as to be free from blame, alike in his sight, and in ours. Tarry here the appointed time, and at the end go your ways." Having said this, and received a promise from the Ionians to do as they desired, the Scythians hastened back with all possible speed.

134. After the sending of the gifts to Darius, the part of the Scythian army, which had not marched to the Ister, drew out in battle array horse and foot[42] against the Persians, and seemed about to come to an engagement. But as they stood in battle array, it chanced that a hare started up between them and the Persians, and set to running; when immediately all the Scyths who saw it, rushed off in pursuit, with great confusion, and loud cries and shouts. Darius, hearing the noise, inquired the cause of it, and was told that the Scythians were all engaged in hunting a

[42] We now hear for the first time of the Scythians having infantry. It is scarcely possible that they really possessed any such force. If they had had a force of foot-soldiers, Darius might have compelled them to a general engagement.

hare. On this he turned to those with whom he was wont to converse, and said, "These men do indeed despise us utterly: and now I see that Gobryas was right about the Scythian gifts. As, therefore, his opinion is now mine likewise, it is time we form some wise plan, whereby we may secure ourselves a safe return to our homes." "Sire," Gobryas rejoined, "I was almost sure, before I came here, that this was an impracticable race—since our coming I am yet more convinced of it, especially now that I see them making game of us. My advice is, therefore, that, when night falls, we light our fires as we do at other times, and leaving behind us on some pretext that portion of our army which is weak and unequal to hardship, taking care also to leave our asses tethered, retreat from Scythia, before our foes march forward to the Ister and destroy the bridge, or the Ionians come to any resolution which may lead to our ruin."

135. So Gobryas advised; and when night came, Darius followed his counsel, and leaving his sick soldiers, and those whose loss would be of least account, with the asses also tethered about the camp, marched away. The asses were left that their noise might be heard: the men, really because they were sick and useless, but under the pretence, that he was about to fall upon the Scythians with the flower of his troops, and that they meanwhile were to guard his camp for him. Having thus declared his plans to the men whom he was deserting, and having caused the fires to be lighted, Darius set forth, and marched hastily towards the Ister. The asses, aware of the departure of the host, brayed louder than ever; and the Scythians, hearing the sound, entertained no doubt of the Persians being still in the same place.

136. When day dawned, the men who had been left behind, perceiving that they were betrayed by Darius, stretched out their hands towards the Scythians, and spoke as befitted their situation. The enemy no sooner heard, than they quickly joined all their troops in one, and both portions of the Scythian army —alike that which consisted of a single division, and that made up of two, accompanied by all their allies, the Sauromatae, the Budini, and the Geloni, set off in pursuit, and made straight for the Ister. As, however, the Persian army was chiefly foot, and

had no knowledge of the routes, which are not cut out in Scythia; while the Scyths were all horsemen and well acquainted with the shortest way; it so happened that the two armies missed one another, and the Scythians, getting far ahead of their adversaries, came first to the bridge. Finding that the Persians were not yet arrived, they addressed the Ionians, who were aboard their ships, in these words, "Men of Ionia, the number of your days is out, and you do wrong to remain. Fear doubtless has kept you here hitherto: now, however, you may safely break the bridge, and hasten back to your homes, rejoicing that you are free, and thanking for it the gods and the Scythians. Your former lord and master we undertake so to handle, that he will never again make war upon any one."

137. The Ionians now held a council. Miltiades the Athenian, who was king of the Chersonesites upon the Hellespont,[43] and their commander at the Ister, recommended the other generals to do as the Scythians wished, and restore freedom to Ionia. But Histiaeus the Milesian opposed this advice. "It is through Darius," he said, "that we enjoy our thrones in our several states. If his power be overturned, I cannot continue lord of Miletus, nor you of your cities. For there is not one of them which will not prefer democracy to kingly rule." Then the other captains, who, till Histiaeus spoke, were about to vote with Miltiades, changed their minds, and declared in favour of the last speaker.

138. The following were the voters on this occasion, all men who stood high in the esteem of the Persian king: the tyrants of the Hellespont—Daphnis of Abydos, Hippoclus of Lampsacus, Herophantus of Parium, Metrodorus of Proconnesus, Aristagoras of Cyzicus, and Ariston of Byzantium; the Ionian princes —Strattis of Chios, Aeaces of Samos, Laodamas of Phocaea, and Histiaeus of Miletus, the man who had opposed Miltiades. Only one Aeolian of note was present, to wit, Aristagoras of Cyme.[44]

---

[43] Concerning this sovereignty of Miltiades see Book vi. 34-36.

[44] One cannot but suspect that the list of Herodotus is imperfect, and that more contingents were present than he names. It may be conjectured that the list came from a Hellespontine source (from the family of Mil-

139. Having resolved to follow the advice of Histiaeus, the Greek leaders further determined to speak and act as follows. In order to appear to the Scythians to be doing something, when in fact they were doing nothing of consequence, and likewise to prevent them from forcing a passage across the Ister by the bridge, they resolved to break up the part of the bridge which abutted on Scythia, to the distance of a bowshot from the river bank; and to assure the Scythians, while the demolition was proceeding, that there was nothing which they would not do to pleasure them. Such were the additions made to the resolution of Histiaeus; and then Histiaeus himself stood forth and made answer to the Scyths in the name of all the Greeks, "Good is the advice which you have brought us, Scythians, and well have you done to come here with such speed. Your efforts have now put us into the right path, and our efforts shall not be wanting to advance your cause. Your own eyes see that we are engaged in breaking the bridge, and, believe us, we will work zealously to procure our own freedom. Meantime, while we labour here at our task, be it your business to seek them out, and, when found, for our sakes, as well as your own, to visit them with the vengeance which they so well deserve."

140. Again the Scyths put faith in the promises of the Ionian chiefs, and retraced their steps, hoping to fall in with the Persians. They missed, however, the enemy's whole line of march; their own former acts being to blame for it. Had they not ravaged all the pasturages of that region, and filled in all the wells, they would have easily found the Persians whenever they chose. But, as it turned out, the measures which seemed to them so wisely planned were exactly what caused their failure. They took a route where water was to be found and fodder could be got for their horses, and on this track sought their adversaries, expecting that they too would retreat through regions where these things were to be obtained. The Persians, however, kept

tiades, most probably) ; and thus, while the catalogue of the Hellespontine cities is tolerably complete, there being no important omission but that of Calchedon, only those Ionian and Aeolian leaders who were of particular repute obtained any mention.

strictly to the line of their former march, never for a moment
departing from it; and even so gained the bridge with difficulty.
It was night when they arrived, and their terror, when they
found the bridge broken up, was great; for they thought that
perhaps the Ionians had deserted them.

141. Now there was in the army of Darius a certain man, an
Egyptian, who had a louder voice than any other man in the
world. This person was bid by Darius to stand at the water's
edge, and call Histiaeus the Milesian. The fellow did as he was
bid; and Histiaeus, hearing him at the very first summons,
brought the fleet to assist in conveying the army across, and
once more made good the bridge.

142. By these means the Persians escaped from Scythia,
while the Scyths sought for them in vain, again missing their
track. And hence the Scythians are accustomed to say of the
Ionians, by way of reproach, that, if they be looked upon as
free-men, they are the basest and most dastardly of all mankind
—but if they be considered as under servitude, they are the
faithfulest of slaves, and the most fondly attached to their
lords.

143. Darius, having passed through Thrace, reached Sestos
in the Chersonese, whence he crossed by the help of his fleet
into Asia, leaving a Persian, named Megabazus, commander on
the European side. This was the man on whom Darius once conferred special honour by a compliment which he paid him before all the Persians. He was about to eat some pomegranates,
and had opened the first, when his brother Artabanus asked him
what he would like to have in as great plenty as the seeds of the
pomegranate. Darius answered, "Had I as many men like Megabazus as there are seeds here, it would please me better than to
be lord of Greece." Such was the compliment wherewith Darius
honoured the general to whom at this time he gave the command
of the troops left in Europe, amounting in all to some 80,000
men.

144. This same Megabazus got himself an undying remembrance among the Hellespontians, by a certain speech which he
made. It came to his knowledge, while he was staying at By-

ʀantium, that the Calchedonians made their settlement seventeen years earlier than the Byzantines. "Then," said he, "the
Calchedonians must at that time have been labouring under
blindness—otherwise, when so far more excellent a site was open
to them, they would never have chosen one so greatly inferior."
Megabazus now, having been appointed to take the command
upon the Hellespont, employed himself in the reduction of all
those states which had not of their own accord joined the Medes.

145. About this very time another great expedition was undertaken against Libya, on a pretext which I will relate when I
have premised certain particulars. The descendants of the Argonauts in the third generation, driven out of Lemnos by the
Pelasgi who carried off the Athenian women from Brauron, took
ship and went to Lacedaemon, where, seating themselves on
Mount Taygetus, they proceeded to kindle their fires. The Lacedaemonians, seeing this, sent a herald to inquire of them who
they were, and from what region they had come; whereupon
they answered that they were Minyae, sons of the heroes by
whom the ship Argo was manned; for these persons had stayed
awhile in Lemnos, and had there become their progenitors. On
hearing this account of their descent, the Lacedaemonians sent
to them a second time, and asked what was their object in coming to Lacedaemon, and there kindling their fires. They answered that driven from their own land by the Pelasgi, they had
come, as was most reasonable, to their fathers; and their wish
was to dwell with them in their country, partake their privileges,
and obtain allotments of land. It seemed good to the Lacedaemonians to receive the Minyae among them on their own terms;
to assign them lands, and enrol them in their tribes. What
chiefly moved them to this was the consideration that the sons
of Tyndarus had sailed on board the Argo. The Minyae, on their
part, forthwith married Spartan wives, and gave the wives,
whom they had married in Lemnos, to Spartan husbands.

146. However, before much time had elapsed, the Minyae began to be insolent, demanded to share the throne, and committed other impieties; whereupon the Lacedaemonians passed
on them sentence of death, and, seizing them, cast them into

prison. Now the Lacedaemonians never put criminals to death in the daytime, but always at night. When the Minyae, accordingly, were about to suffer, their wives, who were not only citizens, but daughters of the chief men among the Spartans, entreated to be allowed to enter the prison, and have some talk with their lords; and the Spartans, not expecting any fraud from such a quarter, granted their request. The women entered the prison, gave their own clothes to their husbands, and received theirs in exchange: after which the Minyae, dressed in their wives' garments, and thus passing for women, went forth. Having effected their escape in this manner, they seated themselves once more upon Taygetus.

147. It happened that at this very time Theras, son of Autesion (whose father Tisamenus was the son of Thersander, and grandson of Polynices), was about to lead out a colony from Lacedaemon. This Theras, by birth a Cadmeian, was uncle on the mother's side to the two sons of Aristodemus, Procles and Eurysthenes, and, during their infancy, administered in their right the royal power. When his nephews, however, on attaining to man's estate, took the government, Theras, who could not bear to be under the authority of others after he had wielded authority so long himself, resolved to leave Sparta, and cross the sea to join his kindred. There were in the island now called Thera, but at that time Calliste, certain descendants of Membliarus, the son of Poeciles, a Phoenician. (For Cadmus, the son of Agenor, when he was sailing in search of Europa, made a landing on this island; and, either because the country pleased him, or because he had a purpose in so doing, left there a number of Phoenicians, and with them his own kinsman Membliarus. Calliste had been inhabited by this race for eight generations of men, before the arrival of Theras from Lacedaemon.)

148. Theras now, having with him a certain number of men from each of the tribes, was setting forth on his expedition hitherward. Far from intending to drive out the former inhabitants, he regarded them as his near kin, and meant to settle among them. It happened that just at this time the Minyae, having escaped from their prison, had taken up their station

upon Mount Taygetum; and the Lacedaemonians, wishing to destroy them, were considering what was best to be done, when Theras begged their lives, undertaking to remove them from the territory. His prayer being granted, he took ship, and sailed, with three thirty-oared ships, to join the descendants of Membliarus. He was not, however, accompanied by all the Minyae, but only by some few of them. The greater number fled to the land of the Paroreats, and Caucons, whom they drove out, themselves occupying the region in six bodies, by which were afterwards built the towns of Lepreum, Macistus, Phryxae, Pyrgus, Epium, and Nudium; whereof the greater part were in my day demolished by the Eleans.

149. The island was called Thera after the name of its founder. This same Theras had a son, who refused to cross the sea with him; Theras therefore left him behind, "a sheep," as he said, "among wolves." From this speech his son came to be called Oeolycus, a name which afterwards grew to be the only one by which he was known. This Oeolycus was the father of Aegeus, from whom sprang the Aegidae, a great tribe in Sparta. The men of this tribe lost at one time all their children, whereupon they were bidden by an oracle to build a temple to the furies of Laius and Oedipus; they complied, and the mortality ceased. The same thing happened in Thera to the descendants of these men.

150. Thus far the history is delivered without variation both by the Theraeans and the Lacedaemonians; but from this point we have only the Theraean narrative. Grinus (they say), the son of Aesanius, a descendant of Theras, and king of the island of Thera, went to Delphi to offer a hecatomb on behalf of his native city. He was accompanied by a large number of the citizens, and among the rest by Battus, the son of Polymnestus, who belonged to the Minyan family of the Euphemidae. On Grinus consulting the oracle about other matters, the priestess gave him for answer that he should found a city in Libya. Grinus replied to this, "I, O lord, am too far advanced in years, and too inactive, for such a work. Bid one of these youngsters undertake it." As he spoke, he pointed towards Battus; and

thus the matter rested for that time. When the embassy returned to Thera, small account was taken of the oracle by the Theraeans, as they were quite ignorant where Libya was, and were not so venturesome as to send out a colony in the dark.

151. Seven years passed from the utterance of the oracle, and not a drop of rain fell in Thera: all the trees in the island, except one, were killed with the drought. The Theraeans upon this sent to Delphi, and were reminded reproachfully, that they had never colonised Libya. So, as there was no help for it, they sent messengers to Crete, to inquire whether any of the Cretans, or of the strangers sojourning among them, had ever travelled as far as Libya: and these messengers of theirs, in their wanderings about the island, among other places visited Itanus, where they fell in with a man, whose name was Corobius, a dealer in purple. In answer to their inquiries, he told them that contrary winds had once carried him to Libya, where he had gone ashore on a certain island which was named Platea. So they hired this man's services, and took him back with them to Thera. A few persons then sailed from Thera to reconnoitre. Guided by Corobius to the island of Platea, they left him there with provisions for a certain number of months, and returned home with all speed to give their countrymen an account of the island.

152. During their absence, which was prolonged beyond the time that had been agreed upon, Corobius' provisions failed him. He was relieved, however, after a while, by a Samian vessel,[45] under the command of a man named Colaeus, which, on its way to Egypt, was forced to put in at Platea. The crew, informed by Corobius of all the circumstances, left him sufficient food for a year. They themselves quitted the island; and, anxious to reach Egypt, made sail in that direction, but were carried out of their course by a gale of wind from the east. The storm not abating, they were driven past the Pillars of Heracles, and at last, by some special guiding providence, reached Tartessus. This trading-town was in those days a virgin port, un-

---

[45] The tale which follows is of some consequence, as showing the character of the Samians for naval enterprise. Samos and Phocaea are the only Greek states reported to have reached so far west in their voyages.

frequented by the merchants. The Samians, in consequence, made by the return-voyage a profit greater than any Greeks before their day, excepting Sostratus, son of Laodamas, an Aeginetan, with whom no one else can compare. From the tenth part of their gains, amounting to six talents, the Samians made a brazen vessel, in shape like an Argive wine-bowl, adorned with the heads of griffins standing out in high relief. This bowl, supported by three kneeling colossal figures in brass, of the height of ten feet, was placed as an offering in the temple of Hera at Samos. The aid given to Corobius was the original cause of that close friendship which afterwards united the Cyrenaeans and Theraeans with the Samians.

153. The Theraeans who had left Corobius at Platea, when they reached Thera, told their countrymen that they had colonised an island on the coast of Libya. They of Thera, upon this, resolved that men should be sent to join the colony from each of their seven districts, and that the brothers in every family should draw lots to determine who were to go. Battus was chosen to be king and leader of the colony. So these men departed for Platea on board of two fifty-oared ships.

154. Such is the account which the Theraeans give. In the sequel of the history their accounts tally with those of the people of Cyrene; but in what they relate of Battus these two nations differ most widely. The following is the Cyrenaic story. There was once a king named Etearchus, who ruled over Axus, a city in Crete, and had a daughter named Phronima. This girl's mother having died, Etearchus married a second wife; who no sooner took up her abode in his house than she proved a true step-mother to poor Phronima, always vexing her, and contriving against her every sort of mischief. At last she charged her with lewd behaviour; and he, persuaded by his wife that the charge was true, thought of a most barbarous mode of punishment. There was a certain Theraean, named Themison, a merchant, living at Axus. This man Etearchus invited to be his friend and guest, and then induced him to swear that he would do him any service he might require. No sooner had he given the promise, than the king brought Phronima, and, delivering her

into his hands, told him to carry her away and throw her into the sea. Hereupon Themison, full of indignation at the fraud whereby his oath had been procured, dissolved forthwith the friendship, and, taking the girl with him, sailed away from Crete. Having reached the open main, to acquit himself of the obligation under which he was laid by his oath to Etearchus, he fastened ropes about the damsel, and, letting her down into the sea, drew her up again, and so made sail for Thera.

155. At Thera, Polymnestus, one of the chief citizens of the place, took Phronima to be his concubine. The fruit of this union was a son, who stammered and had a lisp in his speech. According to the Cyrenaeans and Theraeans, the name given to the boy was Battus: in my opinion, however, he was called at the first something else,[46] and only got the name of Battus after his arrival in Libya, assuming it either in consequence of the words addressed to him by the Delphian oracle, or on account of the office which he held. For, in the Libyan tongue, the word Battus means a king. And this, I think, was the reason why the priestess addressed him as she did: she knew he was to be a king in Libya, and so she used the Libyan word in speaking to him. For after he had grown to man's estate, he made a journey to Delphi, to consult the oracle about his voice; when, upon his putting his question, the priestess thus replied to him:

Battus, thou camest to ask of thy voice; but Phoebus Apollo
Bids thee establish a city in Libya, abounding in fleeces;

which was as if she had said in her own tongue, "King, you came to ask of your voice." Then he replied, "Lord, I did indeed come hither to consult about my voice, but you speak to me of quite other matters, bidding me colonise Libya—an impossible thing! What power have I? what followers?" Thus he spoke, but he did not persuade the priestess to give him any other response; so, when he found that she persisted in her former answer, he left her speaking, and set out on his return to Thera.

[46] The name was Aristotle, which appears in Pindar. Battus is a title that has become a name.

156. After a while, everything began to go wrong both with Battus and with the rest of the Theraeans, whereupon these last, ignorant of the cause of their sufferings, sent to Delphi to inquire for what reason they were afflicted. The priestess in reply told them that if they and Battus would make a settlement at Cyrene in Libya, things would go better with them. Upon this the Theraeans sent out Battus with two fifty-oared ships, and with these he proceeded to Libya, but within a little time, not knowing what else to do, the men returned and arrived off Thera. The Theraeans, when they saw the vessels approaching, received them with showers of missiles, would not allow them to come near the shore, and ordered the men to sail back from whence they came. Thus compelled to return, they settled on an island near the Libyan coast, which (as I have already said) was called Platea. In size it is reported to have been about equal to the city of Cyrene, as it now stands.

157. In this place they continued two years, but at the end of that time, as their ill luck still followed them, they left the island to the care of one of their number, and went in a body to Delphi, where they made complaint at the shrine, to the effect that, notwithstanding they had colonised Libya, they prospered as poorly as before. Hereon the priestess made them the following answer:

Knowest thou better than I, fair Libya abounding in fleeces?
Better the stranger than he who has trod it? O clever Theraeans!

Battus and his friends, when they heard this, sailed back to Platea: it was plain the god would not hold them acquitted of the colony till they were absolutely in Libya. So, taking with them the man whom they had left upon the island, they made a settlement on the mainland directly opposite Platea, fixing themselves at a place called Aziris, which is closed in on both sides by the most beautiful hills, and on one side is washed by a river.

158. Here they remained six years, at the end of which time the Libyans induced them to move, promising that they would

lead them to a better situation. So the Greeks left Aziris, and were conducted by the Libyans towards the west, their journey being so arranged, by the calculations of their guides, that they passed in the night the most beautiful district of that whole country, which is the region called Irasa. The Libyans brought them to a spring, which goes by the name of Apollo's fountain, and told them, "Here, Grecians, is the proper place for you to settle; for here the sky has a hole in it."

159. During the lifetime of Battus, the founder of the colony, who reigned forty years, and during that of his son Arcesilaus, who reigned sixteen, the Cyrenaeans continued at the same level, neither more nor fewer in number than they were at the first. But in the reign of the third king, Battus, surnamed the Happy, the advice of the Pythian priestess brought Greeks from every quarter into Libya, to join the settlement. The Cyrenaeans had offered to all comers a share in their lands; and the oracle had spoken as follows:

> He that is backward to share in the pleasant Libyan acres,
> Sooner or later, I warn him, will feel regret at his folly.

Thus a great multitude were collected together to Cyrene, and the Libyans of the neighbourhood found themselves stripped of large portions of their lands. So they, and their king Adicran, being robbed and insulted by the Cyrenaeans, sent messengers to Egypt, and put themselves under the rule of Apries, the Egyptian monarch; who, upon this, levied a vast army of Egyptians, and sent them against Cyrene. The inhabitants of that place left their walls and marched out in force to the district of Irasa, where, near the spring called Theste, they engaged the Egyptian host, and defeated it. The Egyptians, who had never before made trial of the prowess of the Greeks, and so thought but meanly of them, were routed with such slaughter that but a very few of them ever got back home. For this reason, the subjects of Apries, who laid the blame of the defeat on him, revolted from his authority.

160. This Battus left a son called Arcesilaus, who, when he came to the throne, had dissensions with his brothers, which

ended in their quitting him and departing to another region of Libya, where, after consulting among themselves, they founded the city, which is still called by the name then given to it, Barca. At the same time they endeavoured to induce the Libyans to revolt from Cyrene. Not long afterwards Arcesilaus made an expedition against the Libyans who had received his brothers and been prevailed upon to revolt; and they, fearing his power, fled to their countrymen who dwelt towards the east. Arcesilaus pursued, and chased them to a place called Leucon, which is in Libya, where the Libyans resolved to risk a battle. Accordingly they engaged the Cyrenaeans, and defeated them so entirely that as many as 7,000 of their heavy-armed were slain in the fight. Arcesilaus, after this blow, fell sick, and while he was under the influence of a draught which he had taken, was strangled by Learchus, one of his brothers. This Learchus was afterwards entrapped by Eryxo, the widow of Arcesilaus, and put to death.

161. Battus, Arcesilaus' son, succeeded to the kingdom, a lame man, who limped in his walk. Their late calamities now induced the Cyrenaeans to send to Delphi and inquire of the god what form of government they had best set up to secure themselves prosperity. The priestess answered by recommending them to fetch an arbitrator from Mantinea in Arcadia. Accordingly they sent, and the Mantineans gave them a man named Demonax, a person of high repute among the citizens; who, on his arrival at Cyrene, having first made himself acquainted with all the circumstances, proceeded to enrol the people in three tribes. One he made to consist of the Theraeans and their vassals; another of the Peloponnesians and Cretans; and a third of the various islanders. Besides this, he deprived the king Battus of his former privileges, only reserving for him certain sacred lands and offices, while, with respect to the powers which had hitherto been exercised by the king, he gave them all into the hands of the people.

162. Thus matters rested during the lifetime of this Battus, but when his son Arcesilaus came to the throne, great disturbance arose about the privileges. For Arcesilaus, son of Battus

the lame and Pheretima, refused to submit to the arrangements
of Demonax the Mantinean, and claimed all the powers of his
forefathers. In the contention which followed Arcesilaus was
worsted, whereupon he fled to Samos, while his mother took
refuge at Salamis in the island of Cyprus. Salamis was at that
time ruled by Evelthon, the same who offered at Delphi the
censer which is in the treasury of the Corinthians, a work deserving of admiration. Of him Pheretima made request, that he
would give her an army, whereby she and her son might regain
Cyrene. But Evelthon, preferring to give her anything rather
than an army, made her various presents. Pheretima accepted
them all, saying, as she took them, "Good is this too, king, but
better were it to give me the army which I crave at your hands."
Finding that she repeated these words each time that he presented her with a gift, Evelthon at last sent her a golden spindle
and distaff, with the wool ready for spinning. Again she uttered
the same speech as before, whereupon Evelthon rejoined, "These
are the gifts I present to women, not armies."

163. At Samos, meanwhile, Arcesilaus was collecting troops
by the promise of granting them lands. Having in this way
drawn together a vast host, he sent to Delphi to consult the
oracle about his restoration. The answer of the priestess was
this, "Loxias grants your race to rule over Cyrene, till four
kings Battus, four Arcesilaus by name, have passed away. Beyond this term of eighteen generations of men, he warns you
not to seek to extend your reign. You, for your part, be gentle,
when you are restored. If you find the oven full of jars, bake
not the jars, but be sure to speed them on their way. If, however, you heat the oven, then avoid the island—else you will die
yourself, and with you the most beautiful bull." [47]

164. So spoke the priestess. Arcesilaus upon this returned to
Cyrene, taking with him the troops which he had raised in
Samos. There he obtained possession of the supreme power;
whereupon, forgetful of the oracle, he took proceedings against
those who had driven him into banishment. Some of them fled

[47] This oracle is given in prose, but evidently contains fragments of the
hexameters in which it was delivered.

from him, and quitted the country for good; others fell into his hands and were sent to suffer death in Cyprus. These last happening on their passage to put in through stress of weather at Cnidus, the Cnidians rescued them, and sent them off to Thera. Another body found a refuge in the great tower of Aglomachus, a private edifice, and there were destroyed by Arcesilaus, who heaped wood around the place, and burned them to death. Aware, after the deed was done, that this was what the priestess meant when she warned him, if he found the jars in the oven, not to bake them, he withdrew himself of his own accord from the city of Cyrene, believing that to be the island of the oracle, and fearing to die as had been prophesied. Being married to a relation of his own, a daughter of Alazir,[48] at that time king of the Barcaeans, he took up his abode with him. At Barca, however, certain of the citizens, together with a number of Cyrenaean exiles, recognising him as he walked in the market-place, killed him; they slew also at the same time Alazir, his father-in-law. So Arcesilaus, wittingly or unwittingly, disobeyed the oracle, and thereby fulfilled his destiny.

165. Pheretima, the mother of Arcesilaus, during the time that her son, after working his own ruin, dwelt at Barca, continued to enjoy all his privileges, at Cyrene, managing the government, and taking her seat at the council-board. No sooner, however, did she hear of the death of her son at Barca, than leaving Cyrene, she fled in haste to Egypt. Arcesilaus had claims for service done to Cambyses, son of Cyrus; since it was by him that Cyrene was put under the Persian yoke, and a rate of tribute agreed upon. Pheretima therefore went straight to Egypt, and presenting herself as a suppliant before Aryandes, entreated him to avenge her wrongs. Her son, she said, had met his death on account of his being so well affected towards the Medes.

166. Now Aryandes had been made governor of Egypt by Cambyses. He it was who in after times was punished with

[48] This name is remarkable. It is clearly not Greek, and therefore is probably African. Hence it would seem that not only was Barca originally an African town, but that while falling under Greek influence, it had still retained its native princes, who intermarried with the Battiadae.

death by Darius for seeking to rival him. Aware, by report and also by his own eyesight, that Darius wished to leave a memorial of himself, such as no king had ever left before, Aryandes resolved to follow his example, and did so, till he got his reward. Darius had refined gold to the last perfection of purity in order to have coins struck of it: Aryandes, in his Egyptian government, did the very same with silver, so that to this day there is no such pure silver anywhere as the Aryandic. Darius, when this came to his ears, brought another charge, a charge of rebellion, against Aryandes, and put him to death.

167. At the time of which we are speaking, Aryandes, moved with compassion for Pheretima, granted her all the forces which there were in Egypt, both land and sea. The command of the army he gave to Amasis, a Maraphian; while Badres, one of the tribe of the Pasargadae, was appointed to lead the fleet. Before the expedition, however, left Egypt, he sent a herald to Barca to inquire, who it was that had slain king Arcesilaus. The Barcaeans replied that they, one and all, acknowledged the deed—Arcesilaus had done them many and great injuries. After receiving this reply, Aryandes gave the troops orders to march with Pheretima. Such was the cause which served as a pretext for this expedition: its real object was, I believe, the subjugation of Libya. For Libya is inhabited by many and various races, and of these but a very few were subjects of the Persian king, while by far the larger number held Darius in no manner of respect.

168. The Libyans dwell in the order which I will now describe. Beginning on the side of Egypt, the first Libyans are the Adyrmachidae. These people have, in most points, the same customs as the Egyptians, but use the costume of the Libyans. Their women wear on each leg a ring made of brass; they let their hair grow long, and when they catch any lice on their persons, bite them and throw them away. In this they differ from all the other Libyans. They are also the only tribe with whom the custom obtains of bringing all virgins about to become brides before the king, that he may take the virginity of such as are agreeable to him. The Adyrmachidae extend from the borders of Egypt to the harbour called Port Plynus.

169. Next to the Adyrmachidae are the Gilligammae, who inhabit the country westward as far as the island of Aphrodisias. Off this tract is the island of Platea, which the Cyrenaeans colonised. Here too, upon the mainland, are Port Menelaus, and Aziris, where the Cyrenaeans once lived. The silphium[49] begins to grow in this region, extending from the island of Platea on the one side to the mouth of the Syrtis on the other. The customs of the Gilligammae are like those of the rest of their countrymen.

170. The Asbystae adjoin the Gilligammae upon the west. They inhabit the regions above Cyrene, but do not reach to the coast, which belongs to the Cyrenaeans. Four-horse chariots are in more common use among them than among any other Libyans. In most of their customs they ape the manners of the Cyrenaeans.

171. Westward of the Asbystae dwell the Auschisae, who possess the country above Barca, reaching, however, to the sea at the place called Euesperides.[50] In the middle of their territory is the little tribe of the Cabalians, which touches the coast near Tauchira, a city of the Barcaeans. Their customs are like those of the Libyans above Cyrene.

172. The Nasamonians, a numerous people, are the western neighbours of the Auschisae. In summer they leave their flocks and herds upon the sea-shore, and go up the country to a place called Augila, where they gather the dates from the palms, which in those parts grow thickly, and are of great size, all of them being of the fruit-bearing kind. They also chase the locusts, and, when caught, dry them in the sun, after which they grind them to powder, and, sprinkling this upon their milk, so drink it. Each man among them has several wives; their intercourse with women is promiscuous as among the Massagetae.

[49] This famous plant which is figured upon most of the Cyrenaean and Barcaean coins, was celebrated both as an article of food and also for its medicinal virtues. It formed an important element in the ancient commerce of Cyrene.
[50] The place received the name of Berenice under the Ptolemies and is now Bengazi.

They place a staff in front of the house and then have intercourse. At the first wedding of a Nasamonian, it is customary
for the bride to have intercourse with each of the guests in turn.
After intercourse each man gives her some gift he has brought
from home. The following are their customs in the swearing of
oaths and the practice of augury. The man, as he swears, lays
his hand upon the tomb of some one considered to have been
pre-eminently just and good, and so doing swears by his name.
For divination they betake themselves to the sepulchres of their
own ancestors, and, after praying, lie down to sleep upon their
graves; by the dreams which then come to them they guide
their conduct. When they pledge their faith to one another, each
gives the other to drink out of his hand; if there be no liquid to
be had, they take up dust from the ground, and put their
tongues to it.

173. On the country of the Nasamonians borders that of the
Psylli, who were swept away under the following circumstances.
The south-wind had blown for a long time and dried up all the
tanks in which their water was stored. Now the whole region
within the Syrtis is utterly devoid of springs. Accordingly, the
Psylli took counsel among themselves, and by common consent
made war upon the south-wind (so at least the Libyans say, I
do but repeat their words) they went forth and reached the
desert, but there the south-wind rose and buried them under
heaps of sand: whereupon, the Psylli being destroyed, their
lands passed to the Nasamonians.

174. Above the Nasamonians, towards the south, in the district where the wild beasts abound, dwell the Garamantians,
who avoid all society or intercourse with their fellow-men, have
no weapon of war, and do not know how to defend themselves.

175. These border the Nasamonians on the south: westward
along the sea-shore their neighbours are the Macae, who, by letting the locks about the crown of their head grow long, while
they clip them close everywhere else, make their hair resemble
a crest. In war these people use the skins of ostriches for shields.
The river Cinyps rises among them from the height called the
Hill of the Graces, and runs from thence through their country

to the sea. The Hill of the Graces is thickly covered with wood, and is thus very unlike the rest of Libya, which is bare. It is distant twenty-five miles from the sea.[51]

176. Adjoining the Macae are the Gindanes, whose women wear on their legs anklets of leather. Each lover that a woman has gives her one, and she who can show the most is the best esteemed, as she appears to have been loved by the greatest number of men.

177. A promontory jutting out into the sea from the country of the Gindanes is inhabited by the Lotus-eaters, who live entirely on the fruit of the lotus-tree. The lotus-fruit is about the size of the lentisk berry, and in sweetness resembles the date. The Lotus-eaters even succeed in obtaining from it a sort of wine.

178. The sea-coast beyond the Lotus-eaters is occupied by the Machlyans, who use the lotus to some extent, though not so much as the people of whom we last spoke. The Machlyans reach as far as the great river called the Triton, which empties itself into the great lake Tritonis. Here, in this lake, is an island called Phla, which it is said the Lacedaemonians were to have colonised, according to an oracle.

179. The following is the story as it is commonly told. When Jason had finished building the Argo at the foot of Mount Pelion, he took on board the usual hecatomb, and moreover a brazen tripod. Thus equipped, he set sail, intending to coast round the Peloponnese, and so to reach Delphi. The voyage was prosperous as far as Malea, but at that point a gale of wind from the north came on suddenly, and carried him out of his course to the coast of Libya; where, before he discovered the land, he got among the shallows of Lake Tritonis. As he was turning it in his mind how he should find his way out, Triton (they say) appeared to him, and offered to show him the channel, and secure him a safe retreat, if he would give him the tripod. Jason complying, was shown by Triton the passage through the shallows; after which the god took the tripod, and, carrying it to his own

---

[51] This range however is now not more than five miles distant from the shore.

temple, seated himself upon it, and, filled with prophetic fury, delivered to Jason and his companions a long prediction. "When a descendant," he said, "of one of the Argo's crew should seize and carry off the brazen tripod, then by inevitable fate would a hundred Grecian cities be built around Lake Tritonis." The Libyans of that region, when they heard the words of this prophecy, took away the tripod and hid it.

180. The next tribe beyond the Machlyans, is the tribe of the Auseans. Both these nations inhabit the borders of Lake Tritonis, being separated from one another by the river Triton. Both also wear their hair long, but the Machlyans let it grow at the back of the head, while the Auseans have it long in front. The Ausean maidens keep year by year a feast in honour of Athena, whereat their custom is to draw up in two bodies, and fight with stones and clubs. They say that these are rites which have come down to them from their fathers, and that they honour with them their native goddess, who is the same as the Athena of the Grecians. If any of the maidens die of the wounds they receive, the Auseans declare that such are false virgins. Before the fight is suffered to begin, they have another ceremony. One of the virgins, the loveliest of the number, is selected from the rest; a Corinthian helmet and a complete suit of Greek armour are publicly put upon her; and, thus adorned, she is made to mount into a chariot, and led around the whole lake in a procession. What arms they used for the adornment of their damsels before the Greeks came to live in their country, I cannot say. I imagine they dressed them in Egyptian armour, for I maintain that both the shield and the helmet came into Greece from Egypt. The Auseans declare that Athena is the daughter of Poseidon and the Tritonis—they say she quarrelled with her father, and applied to Zeus, who consented to let her be his child; and so she became his adopted daughter. These people do not marry or live in families, but copulate promiscuously like cattle. When their children are well-grown, they are brought before the assembly of the men, which is held every third month, and assigned to those whom they most resemble.

181. Such are the tribes of wandering Libyans dwelling upon

the sea-coast. Above them inland is the wild-beast tract; and beyond that, a ridge of sand, reaching from Egyptian Thebes to the Pillars of Heracles. Throughout this ridge, at the distance of about ten days' journey from one another,[52] heaps of salt in large lumps lie upon hills. At the top of every hill there gushes forth from the middle of the salt a stream of water, which is both cold and sweet. Around dwell men who are the last inhabitants of Libya on the side of the desert, living, as they do, more inland than the wild-beast district. Of these nations the first is that of the Ammonians, who dwell at a distance of ten days' journey from Thebes, and have a temple derived from that of the Theban Zeus. For at Thebes likewise, as I mentioned above, the image of Zeus has a face like that of a ram. The Ammonians have another spring besides that which rises from the salt. The water of this stream is lukewarm at early dawn; at the time when the market fills it is much cooler; by noon it has grown quite cold; at this time, therefore, they water their gardens. As the afternoon advances the coldness goes off, till, about sunset, the water is once more lukewarm; still the heat increases, and at midnight it boils furiously. After this time it again begins to cool, and grows less and less hot till morning comes. This spring is called the Fountain of the Sun.

182. Next to the Ammonians, at the distance of ten days' journey along the ridge of sand, there is a second salt-hill like the Ammonian, and a second spring. The country round is inhabited, and the place bears the name of Augila. Hither it is that the Nasamonians come to gather in the dates.

183. Ten days' journey from Augila there is again a salt-hill and a spring; palms of the fruitful kind grow here abundantly, as they do also at the other salt-hills. This region is inhabited by a nation called the Garamantians, a very powerful people, who cover the salt with mould, and then sow their crops. From thence is the shortest road to the Lotus-eaters, a journey of thirty days. In the Garamantian country are found the oxen which, as they graze, walk backwards. This they do because

---

[52] There is here too much regularity and symmetry for truth, but Herodotus' description points to the fact of a caravan route.

their horns curve outwards in front of their heads, so that it is not possible for them when grazing to move forwards, since in that case their horns would become fixed in the ground. Only herein do they differ from other oxen, and further in the thickness and hardness of their hides. The Garamantians have four-horse chariots, in which they chase the cave-dwelling Ethiopians, who of all the nations whereof any account has reached our ears are by far the swiftest of foot. The Cave-dwellers feed on serpents, lizards, and other similar reptiles. Their language is unlike that of any other people; it sounds like the screeching of bats.

184. At the distance of ten days' journey from the Garamantians there is again another salt-hill and spring of water; around which dwell a people, called the Atarantians, who alone of all known nations are destitute of names. The title of Atarantians is borne by the whole race in common, but the men have no particular names of their own. The Atarantians, when the sun rises high in the heaven, curse him, and load him with reproaches, because (they say) he burns and wastes both their country and themselves. Once more at the distance of ten days' journey there is a salt-hill, a spring, and an inhabited tract. Near the salt is a mountain called Atlas, very taper and round; so lofty, moreover, that the top (it is said) cannot be seen, the clouds never quitting it either summer or winter. The natives call this mountain the Pillar of Heaven, and they themselves take their name from it, being called Atlantes. They are reported not to eat any living thing, and never to have any dreams.

185. As far as the Atlantes the names of the nations inhabiting the sandy ridge are known to me, but beyond them my knowledge fails. The ridge itself extends as far as the Pillars of Heracles, and even farther than these; and throughout the whole distance, at the end of every ten days' journey, there is a salt-mine, with people dwelling round it, who all of them build their houses with blocks of the salt. No rain falls in these parts of Libya; if it were otherwise, the walls of these houses could not stand. The salt quarried is of two colours, white and purple.

Beyond the ridge southwards, in the direction of the interior, the country is a desert,[53] with no springs, no beasts, no rain, no wood, and altogether destitute of moisture.

186. Thus from Egypt as far as Lake Tritonis Libya is inhabited by wandering tribes, whose drink is milk and their food the flesh of animals. Cow's flesh however none of these tribes ever taste, but abstain from it for the same reason as the Egyptians, neither do they any of them breed swine. Even at Cyrene, the women think it wrong to eat the flesh of the cow, honouring in this Isis, the Egyptian goddess, whom they worship both with fasts and festivals. The Barcaean women abstain, not from cow's flesh only, but also from the flesh of swine.

187. West of Lake Tritonis the Libyans are no longer wanderers, nor do they practise the same customs as the wandering people, or treat their children in the same way. For the wandering Libyans, many of them at any rate, if not all—concerning which I cannot speak with certainty—when their children come to the age of four years, burn the veins at the top of their heads with a flock from the fleece of a sheep: others burn the veins about the temples. This they do to prevent them from being plagued in their after-lives by a flow of rheum from the head; and such they declare is the reason why they are so much more healthy than other men. Certainly the Libyans are the healthiest men that I know, but whether this is what makes them so, or not, I cannot possibly say—the healthiest certainly they are. If when the children are being burnt, convulsions come on there is a remedy of which they have made discovery. It is to sprinkle goat's urine upon the child, who thus treated, is sure to recover. In all this I only repeat what is said by the Libyans.

188. The rites which the wandering Libyans use in sacrificing are the following. They begin with the ear of the victim, which they cut off and throw over their house: this done, they kill the animal by twisting the neck. They sacrifice to the Sun and Moon, but not to any other god. This worship is common to all the Libyans. The inhabitants of the parts about Lake Tritonis worship in addition Triton, Poseidon, and Athena, the last especially.

[53] He alludes to the great Sahara.

189. The dress wherewith Athena's statues are adorned, and her Aegis, were derived by the Greeks from the women of Libya. For, except that the garments of the Libyan women are of leather, and their fringes made of leathern thongs instead of serpents, in all else the dress of both is exactly alike. The name too itself shows that the mode of dressing the Pallas-statues came from Libya. For the Libyan women wear over their dress goat-skins stripped of the hair, fringed at their edges, and coloured with vermillion; and from these goat-skins the Greeks get their word Aegis (goat-harness). I think for my part that the loud cries uttered in our sacred rites came also from thence, for the Libyan women are greatly given to such cries, and utter them very sweetly. Likewise the Greeks learned from the Libyans to yoke four horses to a chariot.

190. All the wandering tribes bury their dead according to the fashion of the Greeks, except the Nasamonians. They bury them sitting, and are right careful when the sick man is at the point of giving up the ghost, to make him sit, and not let him die lying down. The dwellings of these people are made of the stems of the asphodel, and of rushes, wattled together. They can be carried from place to place. Such are the customs of the afore-mentioned tribes.

191. Westward of the river Triton, and adjoining upon the Auseans, are other Libyans who till the ground, and live in houses: these people are named the Maxyans. They let the hair grow long on the right side of their heads, and shave it close on the left; they besmear their bodies with red paint; and they say that they are descended from the men of Troy. Their country and the remainder of Libya towards the west is far fuller of wild beasts, and of wood, than the country of the wandering people. For the eastern side of Libya, where the wanderers dwell, is low and sandy, as far as the river Triton; but westward of that the land of the husbandmen is very hilly, and abounds with forests and wild beasts. For this is the tract in which the huge serpents are found, and the lions, the elephants, the bears, the asps, and the horned asses. Here too are the dog-faced creatures, and the creatures without heads, whom the

Libyans declare to have their eyes in their breasts; and also the wild men, and the wild women, and many other far less fabulous beasts.

192. Among the wanderers are none of these, but quite other animals; as antelopes, gazelles, buffaloes, and asses, not of the horned sort, but of a kind which does not need to drink; also oryxes, whose horns are used for the curved sides of lyres, and whose size is about that of the ox; foxes, hyaenas, porcupines, wild rams, dictyes, jackals, panthers, boryes, land-crocodiles about four feet in length, very like lizards, ostriches, and little snakes, each with a single horn. All these beasts are found here, and likewise those belonging to other countries, except the stag and the wild-boar; but neither stag nor wild-boar are found in any part of Libya. There are, however, three sorts of mice in these parts; the first are called two-footed;[54] the next, zegeries, which is a Libyan word meaning hills; and the third, prickly mice. Weasels also are found in the silphium region, much like the Tartessian. So many, therefore, are the beasts belonging to the land of the wandering Libyans, in so far at least as my researches have been able to reach.

193. Next to the Maxyan Libyans are the Zavecians, whose wives drive their chariots to battle.

194. On them border the Gyzantians; in whose country a vast deal of honey is made by bees; very much more, however, by the skill of men. The people all paint themselves red, and eat monkeys, whereof there is inexhaustible store in the hills.

195. Off their coast, as the Carthaginians report, lies an island, by name Cyrauis, the length of which is twenty-five miles, its breadth not great, and soon reached from the mainland. Vines and olive-trees cover the whole of it, and there is in the island a lake, from which the young maidens of the country draw up gold-dust, by dipping into the mud birds' feathers smeared with pitch. If this be true, I know not; I but write what is said. It may be even so, however, since I myself have seen pitch drawn up out of water from a lake in Zacynthus. At

[54] The jerboa's fore-legs are very diminutive, and, like the kangaroo and the squirrel, it usually sits upright.

the place I speak of there are a number of lakes, but one is larger than the rest, being seventy feet every way, and twelve feet in depth. Here they let down a pole into the water, with a bunch of myrtle tied to one end, and when they raise it again, there is pitch sticking to the myrtle, which in smell is like to bitumen, but in all else is better than the pitch of Pieria. This they pour into a trench dug by the lake's side, and when a good deal has thus been got together, they draw it off and put it up in jars. Whatever falls into the lake passes underground, and comes up in the sea, which is no less than half a mile distant. So then what is said of the island off the Libyan coast is not without likelihood.

196. The Carthaginians also relate the following: There is a country in Libya, and a nation, beyond the Pillars of Heracles, which they are wont to visit, where they no sooner arrive but forthwith they unlade their wares, and, having disposed them after an orderly fashion along the beach, leave them, and, returning aboard their ships, raise a great smoke. The natives, when they see the smoke, come down to the shore, and, laying out to view so much gold as they think the worth of the wares, withdraw to a distance. The Carthaginians upon this come ashore and look. If they think the gold enough, they take it and go their way; but if it does not seem to them sufficient, they go aboard ship once more, and wait patiently. Then the others approach and add to their gold, till the Carthaginians are content. Neither party deals unfairly by the other: for they themselves never touch the gold till it comes up to the worth of their goods, nor do the natives carry off the goods till the gold is taken away.

197. These be the Libyan tribes whereof I am able to give the names; and most of these cared little then, and indeed care little now, for the king of the Medes. One thing more also I can add concerning this region, namely, that, so far as our knowledge reaches, four nations, and no more, inhabit it; and two of these nations are indigenous, while two are not. The two indigenous are the Libyans and Ethiopians, who dwell respectively in the north and the south of Libya. The Phoenicians and the Greeks are later settlers.

198. It seems to me that Libya is not to compare for goodness of soil with either Asia or Europe, except the Cinyps-region,
which is named after the river that waters it. This land is equal
to any country in the world for cereal crops, and is in nothing
like the rest of Libya. For the soil here is black, and springs of
water abound; so that there is nothing to fear from drought;
nor do heavy rains (and it rains in that part of Libya) do any
harm when they soak the ground. The returns of the harvest
come up to the measure which prevails in Babylonia. The soil is
likewise good in the country of the Euesperites, for there the
land brings forth in the best years a hundred-fold. But the
Cinyps-region yields three hundred-fold.

199. The country of the Cyrenaeans, which is the highest
tract within the part of Libya inhabited by the wandering tribes,
has three seasons that deserve remark. First the crops along the
sea-coast begin to ripen, and are ready for the harvest and
the vintage; after they have been gathered in, the crops of the
middle tract above the coast-region (the hill-country, as they
call it) need harvesting; while about the time when this middle
crop is housed, the fruits ripen and are fit for cutting in the
highest tract of all. So that the produce of the first tract has
been all eaten and drunk by the time that the last harvest comes
in. And the harvest time of the Cyrenaeans continues thus for
eight full months. So much concerning these matters.

200. When the Persians sent from Egypt by Aryandes to help
Pheretima, reached Barca, they laid siege to the town, calling
on those within to give up the men who had been guilty of the
murder of Arcesilaus. The townspeople, however, as they had
one and all taken part in the deed, refused to entertain the prop-
osition. So the Persians beleaguered Barca for nine months, in
the course of which they dug several mines from their own lines
to the walls, and likewise made a number of vigorous assaults.
But their mines were discovered by a man who was a worker in
brass, who went with a brazen shield all round the fortress, and
laid it on the ground inside the city. In other places the shield,
when he laid it down, was quite dumb; but where the ground
was undermined, there the brass of the shield rang. Here, there-

fore, the Barcaeans countermined, and slew the Persian diggers. Such was the way in which the mines were discovered; as for the assaults, the Barcaeans beat them back.

201. When much time had thus been consumed, and great numbers had fallen on both sides, nor had the Persians lost fewer than their adversaries, Amasis, the leader of the land-army, perceiving that, though the Barcaeans would never be conquered by force, they might be overcome by fraud, contrived as follows. One night he dug a wide trench, and laid light planks of wood across the opening, after which he brought mould and placed it upon the planks, taking care to make the place level with the surrounding ground. At dawn of day he summoned the Barcaeans to a parley: and they gladly hearkening, the terms were at length agreed upon. Oaths were interchanged upon the ground over the hidden trench, and the agreement ran thus—"So long as the ground beneath our feet stands firm, the oath shall abide unchanged; the people of Barca agree to pay a fair sum to the king, and the Persians promise to cause no further trouble to the people of Barca." After the oath, the Barcaeans, relying upon its terms, threw open all their gates, went out themselves beyond the walls, and allowed as many of the enemy as chose, to enter. Then the Persians broke down their secret bridge, and rushed at speed into the town—their reason for breaking the bridge being, that so they might observe what they had sworn; for they had promised the Barcaeans that the oath should continue so long as the ground whereon they stood was firm. When, therefore, the bridge was once broken down, the oath ceased to hold.

202. Such of the Barcaeans as were most guilty the Persians gave up to Pheretima, who nailed them to crosses all round the walls of the city. She also cut off the breasts of their wives, and fastened them likewise about the walls. The remainder of the people she gave as booty to the Persians, except only the Battiadae, and those who had taken no part in the murder, to whom she handed over the possession of the town.

203. The Persians now set out on their return home, carrying with them the rest of the Barcaeans, whom they had made their

slaves. On their way they came to Cyrene, and the Cyrenaeans, out of regard for an oracle, let them pass through the town. During the passage, Bares, the commander of the fleet, advised to seize the place; but Amasis, the leader of the land-force, would not consent; "because," he said, "they had only been charged to attack the one Greek city of Barca." [55] When, however, they had passed through the town, and were encamped upon the hill of Lycaean Zeus, it repented them that they had not seized Cyrene, and they endeavoured to enter it a second time. The Cyrenaeans, however, would not suffer this; whereupon, though no one appeared to offer them battle, yet a panic came upon the Persians, and they ran a distance of eight miles before they pitched their camp. Here as they lay, a messenger came to them from Aryandes, ordering them home. Then the Persians besought the men of Cyrene to give them provisions for the way, and, these consenting, they set off on their return to Egypt. But the Libyans now beset them, and, for the sake of their clothes and harness, slew all who dropped behind and straggled, during the whole march homeward.

204. The furthest point of Libya reached by this Persian host was the city of Euesperides. The Barcaeans carried into slavery were sent from Egypt to the King; and Darius assigned them a village in Bactria for their dwelling-place.[56] To this village they gave the name of Barca, and it was to my time an inhabited place in Bactria.

205. Nor did Pheretima herself end her days happily. For on her return to Egypt from Libya, directly after taking vengeance on the people of Barca, she was overtaken by a most horrid death. Her body swarmed with worms, which ate her flesh while she was still alive. Thus do men, by over-harsh punishments, draw down upon themselves the anger of the gods. Such then, and so fierce, was the vengeance which Pheretima, daughter of Battus, took upon the Barcaeans.

[55] This whole account of the danger and escape of Cyrene is exceedingly improbable.

[56] The transplantation of nations was largely practised by the Persians, as it had been at an earlier date by the Assyrians and Babylonians.

The Fifth Book, Entitled

TERPSICHORE

1. The Persians left behind by King Darius in Europe, who had Megabazus for their general, reduced, before any other Hellespontine state, the people of Perinthus, who had no mind to become subjects of the king. Now the Perinthians had already been roughly handled by another nation, the Paeonians. For the Paeonians from about the Strymon were once bidden by an oracle to make war upon the Perinthians, and if these latter, when the camps faced one another, challenged them by name to fight, then to venture on a battle, but if otherwise, not to make the hazard. The Paeonians followed the advice. Now the men of Perinthus drew out to meet them in the skirts of their city, and a threefold single combat was fought on challenge given. Man to man and horse to horse, and dog to dog, was the strife waged; and the Perinthians, winners of two combats out of the three, in their joy had raised the paean; when the Paeonians, struck by the thought that this was what the oracle had meant, passed the word one to another, saying, "Now surely has the oracle been fulfilled for us; now our work begins." Then the Paeonians set upon the Perinthians in the midst of their paean, and defeated them utterly, leaving but few of them alive.

2. Such was the affair of the Paeonians, which happened a long time previously. At this time the Perinthians, after a brave struggle for freedom, were overcome by numbers, and yielded to Megabazus and his Persians. After Perinthus had been brought under, Megabazus led his host through Thrace, subduing to the dominion of the king all the towns and all the nations of those

parts. For the king's command to him was, that he should conquer Thrace.

3. The Thracians are the most powerful people in the world,
except, of course, the Indians; and if they had one head, or
were agreed among themselves, it is my belief that their match
could not be found anywhere, and that they would very far surpass all other nations. But such union is impossible for them,
and there are no means of ever bringing it about. Herein therefore consists their weakness. The Thracians bear many names in
the different regions of their country, but all of them have like
usages in every respect, excepting only the Getae, the Trausi,
and those who dwell above the people of Creston.

4. Now the manners and customs of the Getae, who believe
in their immortality, I have already spoken of. The Trausi in all
else resemble the other Thracians, but have customs at births
and deaths which I will now describe. When a child is born all
its kindred sit round about it in a circle and weep for the woes
it will have to undergo now that it is come into the world, making mention of every ill that falls to the lot of human kind;
when, on the other hand, a man has died, they bury him with
laughter and rejoicings, and say that now he is free from a host
of sufferings, and enjoys the completest happiness.

5. The Thracians who live above the Crestonaeans observe
the following customs. Each man among them has several wives,
and no sooner does a man die than a sharp contest ensues among
the wives upon the question, which of them all the husband
loved most tenderly; the friends of each eagerly plead on her
behalf, and she to whom the honour is adjudged, after receiving
the praises both of men and women, is slain over the grave by
the hand of her next of kin, and then buried with her husband.
The others are sorely grieved, for nothing is considered such a
disgrace.

6. The Thracians who do not belong to these tribes have the
customs which follow. They sell their children to traders. On
their maidens they keep no watch, but allow them to have intercourse with anyone they please, while on the conduct of their
wives they keep a most strict watch. Brides are purchased of

their parents for large sums of money. Tattooing among them marks noble birth, and the want of it low birth. To be idle is accounted the most honourable thing, and to be a tiller of the ground the most dishonourable. To live by war and plunder is of all things the most glorious. These are the most remarkable of their customs.

7. The gods which they worship are but three, Ares, Dionysus, and Artemis. Their kings, however, unlike the rest of the citizens, worship Hermes more than any other god, always swearing by his name, and declaring that they are themselves sprung from him.

8. Their wealthy ones are buried in the following fashion. The body is laid out for three days, and during this time they kill victims of all kinds, and feast upon them, after first bewailing the departed. Then they either burn the body or else bury it in the ground. Lastly, they raise a mound over the grave, and hold games of all sorts, wherein the single combat is awarded the highest prize. Such is the mode of burial among the Thracians.

9. As regards the region lying north of this country no one can say with any certainty what men inhabit it. It appears that you no sooner cross the Ister than you enter on an interminable wilderness. The only people of whom I can hear as dwelling beyond the Ister are the race named Sigynnae, who wear, they say, a dress like the Medes, and have horses which are covered entirely with a coat of shaggy hair, five fingers in length. They are a small breed, flat-nosed, and not strong enough to bear men on their backs; but when yoked to chariots, they are among the swiftest known, which is the reason why the people of that country use chariots. Their borders reach down almost to the Eneti upon the Adriatic Sea, and they call themselves colonists of the Medes; but how they can be colonists of the Medes I for my part cannot imagine. Still nothing is impossible in the long lapse of ages. Sigynnae is the name which the Ligurians who dwell above Massilia[1] give to traders, while among the Cyprians the word means spears.

The modern Marseilles

10. According to the account which the Thracians give, the country beyond the Ister is possessed by bees, on account of which it is impossible to penetrate farther.[2] But in this they seem to me to say what has no likelihood; for it is certain that those creatures are very impatient of cold. I rather believe that it is on account of the cold that the regions which lie under the Bear are without inhabitants. Such then are the accounts given of this country, the sea-coast whereof Megabazus was now employed in subjecting to the Persians.

11. King Darius had no sooner crossed the Hellespont and reached Sardis, than he bethought himself of the good deed of Histiaeus the Milesian, and the good counsel of the Mytilenean Coes. He therefore sent for both of them to Sardis, and bade them each crave a boon at his hands. Now Histiaeus, as he was already king of Miletus, did not make request for any government besides, but asked Darius to give him Myrcinus of the Edonians, where he wished to build him a city. Such was the choice that Histiaeus made. Coes, on the other hand, as he was a mere burgher, and not a king, requested the sovereignty of Mytilene. Both alike obtained their requests, and straightway betook themselves to the places which they had chosen.

12. It chanced in the meantime that King Darius saw a sight which determined him to bid Megabazus remove the Paeonians from their seats in Europe and transport them to Asia. There were two Paeonians, Pigres and Mantyes, whose ambition it was to obtain the sovereignty over their countrymen. As soon therefore as ever Darius crossed into Asia, these men came to Sardis, and brought with them their sister, who was a tall and beautiful woman. Having so done, they waited till a day came when the king sat in state in the suburb of the Lydians; and then dressing their sister in the richest gear they could, sent her to draw water for them. She bore a pitcher upon her head, and with one arm led a horse, while all the way as she went she span flax. Now as she passed by where the king was, Darius took notice of her; for it was neither like the Persians nor the Lydians, nor any of the dwellers in Asia, to do as she did. Darius accordingly noted her,

[2] Mosquitoes.

and ordered some of his guard to follow her steps, and watch to
see what she would do with the horse. So the spearmen went,
and the woman, when she came to the river, first watered the
horse, and then filling the pitcher, came back the same way she
had gone, with the pitcher of water upon her head, and the horse
dragging upon her arm, while she still kept twirling the spindle.

13. King Darius was full of wonder both at what they who
had watched the woman told him, and at what he had himself
seen. So he commanded that she should be brought before him.
And the woman came, and with her appeared her brothers, who
had been watching everything a little way off. Then Darius
asked them of what nation the woman was, and the young men
replied that they were Paeonians, and she was their sister.
Darius rejoined by asking, "Who the Paeonians were, and in
what part of the world they lived? And, further, what business
had brought the young men to Sardis?" Then the brothers told
him they had come to put themselves under his power, and
Paeonia was a country upon the river Strymon, and the Strymon
was at no great distance from the Hellespont. The Paeonians,
they said, were colonists of the Teucrians from Troy. When they
had thus answered his questions, Darius asked if all the women
of their country worked so hard. Then the brothers eagerly answered yes; for this was the very object with which the whole
thing had been done.

14. So Darius wrote letters to Megabazus, the commander
whom he had left behind in Thrace, and ordered him to remove
the Paeonians from their own land, and bring them into his
presence, men, women, and children. And immediately a horseman took the message, and rode at speed to the Hellespont;
and, crossing it, gave the paper to Megabazus. Then Megabazus, as soon as he had read it, and procured guides from
Thrace, made war upon Paeonia.

15. Now when the Paeonians heard that the Persians were
marching against them, they gathered themselves together, and
marched down to the sea-coast, since they thought the Persians
would endeavour to enter their country on that side. Here then
they stood in readiness to oppose the army of Megabazus. But

the Persians, who knew that they had collected, and were gone
to keep guard at the pass near the sea, got guides, and taking
the inland route before the Paeonians were aware, poured down
upon their cities, from which the men had all marched out; and
finding them empty, easily got possession of them. Then the
men, when they heard that all their towns were taken, scattered
this way and that to their homes, and gave themselves up to the
Persians. And so these tribes of the Paeonians, to wit, the Siro-
paeonians, the Paeoplians, and all the others as far as Lake
Prasias, were torn from their seats and led away into Asia.

16. They on the other hand who dwelt about Mount Pangaeum and in the country of the Doberes, the Agrianians, and
the Odomantians, and they likewise who inhabited Lake Prasias,
were not conquered by Megabazus. He sought indeed to subdue
the dwellers upon the lake, but could not effect his purpose.
Their manner of living is the following. Platforms supported
upon tall piles stand in the middle of the lake, which are approached from the land by a single narrow bridge.[3] At the first,
the piles which bear up the platforms were fixed in their places
by the whole body of the citizens, but since that time the custom
which has prevailed about fixing them is this: they are brought
from a hill called Orbelus, and every man drives in three for
each wife that he marries. Now the men have all many wives
apiece, and this is the way in which they live. Each has his own
hut, wherein he dwells, upon one of the platforms, and each has
also a trap-door giving access to the lake beneath; and their
wont is to tie their baby children by the foot with a string, to
save them from rolling into the water. They feed their horses
and their other beasts upon fish, which abound in the lake to
such a degree, that a man has only to open his trap-door and to
let down a basket by a rope into the water, and then to wait a
very short time, when up he draws it quite full of them. The
fish are of two kinds, which they call the paprax and the tilon.

17. The Paeonians therefore—at least such of them as had

---

[3] Discoveries in the lakes of Central Europe, particularly those of Switz-
erland, have confirmed in the most remarkable way this whole description of Herodotus.

been conquered—were led away into Asia. As for Megabazus he had no sooner brought the Paeonians under, than he sent into Macedonia an embassy of Persians, choosing for the purpose the seven men of most note in all the army after himself. These persons were to go to Amyntas, and require him to give earth and water to King Darius. Now there is a very short cut from the lake Prasias across to Macedonia. Quite close to the lake is the mine which yielded afterwards a talent of silver a day to Alexander; and from this mine you have only to cross the mountain called Dysorum to find yourself in the Macedonian territory.

18. So the Persians sent upon this errand, when they reached the court, and were brought into the presence of Amyntas, required him to give earth and water to King Darius. And Amyntas not only gave them what they asked, but also invited them to come and feast with him; after which he made ready the board with great magnificence, and entertained the Persians in right friendly fashion. Now when the meal was over, and they were all set to the drinking, the Persians said, "Dear Macedonian, we Persians have a custom when we make a great feast to bring with us to the board our wives and concubines, and make them sit beside us. Now then, as you have received us so kindly, and feast us so handsomely, and give moreover earth and water to King Darius, do also after our custom in this matter."

Then Amyntas answered, "Persians, we have no such custom as this, but with us men and women are kept apart. Nevertheless, since you, who are our lords, wish it, this also shall be granted to you."

When Amyntas had thus spoken, he bade some go and fetch the women. And the women came at his call and took their seats in a row over against the Persians. Then, when the Persians saw that the women were fair and comely, they spoke again to Amyntas and said, that what had been done was not wise, for it had been better for the women not to have come at all, than to come in this way, and not sit by their sides, but remain over against them, the torment of their eyes. So Amyntas was forced to bid the women sit side by side with the Persians. The women did as he ordered, and then the Persians, who had drunk more than they ought, began to put their hands on their breasts, and one tried to kiss the woman next him.

19. King Amyntas saw, but he kept silence, although sorely grieved, for he greatly feared the power of the Persians. Alexander, however, Amyntas' son, who was likewise there and witnessed the whole, being a young man and unacquainted with suffering, could not any longer restrain himself. He therefore, full of wrath, spake thus to Amyntas, "Dear father, you are old and should spare yourself. Rise up from table and go take your rest; do not stay out the drinking. I will remain with the guests and give them all that is fitting."

Amyntas, who guessed that Alexander planned some wild deed, answered, "Dear son, your words sound to me as those of one who is on fire, and I perceive you send me away that you may do some violent deed. I beseech you make no commotion about these men, lest you bring us all to ruin, but bear to look calmly on what they do. For myself, I will withdraw as you bid me."

20. Amyntas, when he had thus besought his son, went out, and Alexander said to the Persians, "Look on these ladies as your own, dear strangers, all or any of them—only tell us your wishes. But now, as the evening wears, and I see you have all had wine enough, let them, if you please, retire, and when they have bathed they shall come back again." To this the Persians agreed, and Alexander, having got the women away, sent them off to their apartment, and made ready in their stead an equal number of beardless youths, whom he dressed in the garments of the women, and then, arming them with daggers, brought them in to the Persians, saying as he introduced them, "Dear Persians, your entertainment has fallen short in nothing. We have set before you all that we had ourselves in store, and all that we could anywhere find to give to you—and now, to crown the whole, we make over to you our sisters and our mothers, that you may perceive yourselves to be entirely honoured by us, even as you deserve to be—and also that you may take back word to the king who sent you here, that there was one man, a

Greek, the satrap of Macedonia, by whom you were both feasted
and bedded handsomely." So speaking, Alexander set by the
side of each Persian one of those whom he had called Macedonian women, but who were in truth men. And these men,
when the Persians tried to lay hands on them, despatched them
with their daggers.

21. So the ambassadors perished by this death, both they and
also their followers. For the Persians had brought a great train
with them, carriages, and attendants, and baggage of every kind
—all of which disappeared at the same time as the men themselves. Not very long afterwards the Persians made strict search
for their lost embassy; but Alexander, with much wisdom,
hushed up the business, bribing those sent on the errand, partly
with money, and partly with the gift of his own sister Gygaea,
whom he gave in marriarge to Bubares, a Persian, the chief
leader of the expedition which came in search of the lost men.
Thus the death of these Persians was hushed up, and no more
was said of it.

22. Now that the men of this family are Greeks, sprung from
Perdiccas, as they themselves affirm, is a thing which I can declare of my own knowledge, and which I will hereafter make
plainly evident. That they are so has been already adjudged by
those who manage the Pan-Hellenic contest at Olympia. For
when Alexander wished to contend in the games, and had come
to Olympia with no other view, the Greeks who were about to
run against him would have excluded him from the contest—
saying that Greeks only were allowed to contend, and not barbarians. But Alexander proved himself to be an Argive, and was
distinctly adjudged a Greek; after which he entered the lists for
the footrace, and was drawn to run in the first pair. Thus was
this matter settled.

23. Megabazus, having reached the Hellespont with the
Paeonians, crossed it, and went up to Sardis. He had become
aware while in Europe that Histiaeus the Milesian was raising
a wall at Myrcinus—the town upon the Strymon which he had
obtained from King Darius as his reward for keeping the bridge.
No sooner therefore did he reach Sardis with the Paeonians than

he said to Darius, "What mad thing is this that you have done, sire, to let a Greek, a wise man and a shrewd, get hold of a town in Thrace, a place too where there is abundance of timber fit for shipbuilding, and oars in plenty, and mines of silver, and about which are many dwellers both Greek and barbarian, ready enough to take him for their chief, and by day and night to do his bidding! Make this man cease his work, if you would not be entangled in a war with your own followers. Stop him, but with a gentle message, only bidding him to come to you. Then when you once have him in your power, be sure you take good care that he never get back to Greece again."

24. With these words Megabazus easily persuaded Darius, who thought he had shown true foresight in this matter. Darius therefore sent a messenger to Myrcinus, who said, "These be the king's words to you, Histiaeus. I have looked for a man devoted to me and my greatness, and I have found none whom I can trust like you. Your deeds, and not your words only, have proved your love for me. Now then, since I have a mighty enterprise in hand, come to me, that I may show you what I purpose."

Histiaeus, when he heard this, put faith in the words of the messenger, and as it seemed a grand thing to be the king's counsellor, he went up to Sardis. Then Darius, when he was come, said to him, "Dear Histiaeus, hear why I have sent for you. No sooner did I return from Scythia, and lose you out of my sight, than I longed, as I have never longed for anything else, to see you once more, and to speak with you. Right sure I am there is nothing in all the world so precious as a friend who is at once wise and true. You are both, as I have had good proof in what you have already done for me. Now then it is well you are here, for I have an offer to make to you. Let go Miletus and your newly founded town in Thrace, and come with me up to Susa; share all that I have; live with me, and be my counsellor."

25. When Darius had thus spoken he made Artaphernes, his brother by the father's side, governor of Sardis, and taking Histiaeus with him, went up to Susa. He left as general of all the troops upon the sea-coast Otanes, son of Sisamnes, whose father

King Cambyses slew and flayed, because that he, being of the number of the royal judges, had taken money to give an unrighteous sentence. Therefore Cambyses slew and flayed Sisamnes, and cutting his skin into strips, stretched them across the seat of the throne whereon he had sat when he heard cases. Having so done Cambyses appointed the son of Sisamnes to be judge in his father's place, and bade him never forget in what way his seat was cushioned.

26. Accordingly this Otanes, who had occupied so strange a throne, became successor of Megabazus in his command, and took first of all Byzantium and Calchedon, then Antandrus in the Troas, and next Lamponium. This done, he borrowed ships of the Lesbians, and took Lemnos and Imbros, which were still inhabited by Pelasgians.

27. Now the Lemnians stood on their defence, and fought gallantly, but they were brought low in course of time. Such as outlived the struggle were placed by the Persians under the government of Lycaretus, the brother of that Maeandrius who was tyrant of Samos. (This Lycaretus died afterwards in his government.) The cause which Otanes alleged for conquering and enslaving all these nations was, that some had refused to join the king's army against Scythia, while others had molested the host on its return. Such were the exploits which Otanes performed in his command.

28. Afterwards, but for no long time, there was a respite from suffering. Then from Naxos and Miletus troubles gathered anew about Ionia. Now Naxos at this time surpassed all the other islands in prosperity, and Miletus had reached the height of her power, and was the glory of Ionia. But previously for two generations the Milesians had suffered grievously from civil disorders, which were composed by the Parians, whom the Milesians chose before all the rest of the Greeks to rearrange their government.

29. Now the way in which the Parians healed their differences was the following. A number of the chief Parians came to Miletus, and when they saw in how ruined a condition the Milesians were, they said that they would like first to go over their

country. So they went through all Milesia, and on their way, whenever they saw in the waste and desolate country any land that was well farmed, they took down the names of the owners in their tablets; and having thus gone through the whole region, and obtained after all but few names, they called the people together on their return to Miletus, and made proclamation that they gave the government into the hands of those persons whose lands they had found well farmed; for they thought it likely (they said) that the same persons who had managed their own affairs well would likewise conduct aright the business of the state. The other Milesians who in time past had been at variance they placed under the rule of these men. Thus was the Milesian government set in order by the Parians.

30. It was, however, from the two cities above mentioned that troubles began now to gather again about Ionia; and this is the way in which they arose. Certain of the rich men had been banished from Naxos by the commonalty, and, upon their banishment, had fled to Miletus. Aristagoras, son of Molpagoras, the nephew and likewise the son-in-law of Histiaeus, son of Lysagoras, who was still kept by Darius at Susa, happened to be regent of Miletus at the time of their coming. For the kingly power belonged to Histiaeus, but he was at Susa when the Naxians came. Now these Naxians had in times past been bondfriends of Histiaeus, and so on their arrival at Miletus they addressed themselves to Aristagoras and begged him to lend them such aid as his ability allowed, in hopes thereby to recover their country. Then Aristagoras, considering with himself that if the Naxians should be restored by his help he would be lord of Naxos, put forward the friendship with Histiaeus to cloak his views, and spoke as follows, "I cannot engage to furnish you with such a power as were needful to force you, against their will, upon the Naxians who hold the city; for I know they can bring into the field 8,000 bucklers, and have also a vast number of ships of war. But I will do all that lies in my power to get you some aid, and I think I can manage it in this way. Artaphernes happens to be my friend. Now he is a son of Hystaspes, and brother to King Darius. All the sea-coast of Asia is

under him, and he has a large army and numerous ships. I think
I can prevail on him to do what we require."

When the Naxians heard this they empowered Aristagoras to
manage the matter for them as well as he could, and told him to
promise gifts and pay for the soldiers, which (they said) they
would readily furnish, since they had great hope that the Naxians, so soon as they saw them returned, would render them
obedience, and likewise the other islanders. For at that time not
one of the Cyclades was subject to King Darius.

31. So Aristagoras went to Sardis and told Artaphernes that
Naxos was an island of no great size, but a fair land and fertile,
lying near Ionia, and containing much treasure and a vast number of slaves. "Make war then upon this land," he said, "and
reinstate the exiles; for if you do this, first of all, I have very
rich gifts in store for you (besides the cost of the armament,
which it is fair that we who are the authors of the war should
pay); and, secondly, you will bring under the power of the
king not only Naxos but the other islands which depend on it,
as Paros, Andros, and all the rest of the Cyclades. And when
you have gained these, you may easily go on against Euboea,
which is a large and wealthy island not less in size than Cyprus,[4]
and very easy to bring under. One hundred ships were quite
enough to subdue the whole." The other answered, "Truly you
are the author of a plan which may profit the house of the king,
and your counsel is good in all points except the number of the
ships. Instead of 100, 200 shall be at your disposal when the
spring comes. But the king himself must first approve the undertaking."

32. When Aristagoras heard this he rejoiced, and went home
to Miletus. And Artaphernes, after he had sent a messenger to
Susa to lay the plans of Aristagoras before the king, and received his approval of the undertaking, made ready a fleet of
200 triremes and a vast army of Persians and their confederates.
The command of these he gave to a Persian named Megabates,
who belonged to the house of the Achaemenids, being nephew
both to himself and to King Darius. It was to a daughter of this

[4] Cyprus is really more than twice the size of Euboea.

man that Pausanias the Lacedaemonian, the son of Cleombrotus (if at least there be any truth in the tale), was affianced many years afterwards, when he conceived the desire of becoming tyrant of Greece. Artaphernes now, having named Megabates to the command, sent forward the armament to Aristagoras.

33. Megabates set sail, and touching at Miletus, took on board Aristagoras with the Ionian troops and the Naxians; after which he steered, as he gave out, for the Hellespont; but when he reached Chios, he brought the fleet to anchor off Caucasa, being minded to wait there for a north wind, and then sail straight to Naxos. The Naxians however were not to perish at this time, and so the following events were brought about. As Megabates went his rounds to visit the watch on board the ships, he found a Myndian vessel upon which there was none set. Full of anger at such carelessness, he bade his guards to seek out the captain, one Scylax by name, and thrusting him through one of the holes in the ship's side, to fasten him there in such a way that his head might show outside the vessel, while his body remained within. When Scylax was thus fastened, one went and informed Aristagoras that Megabates had bound his Myndian friend and was treating him shamefully. So he came and asked Megabates to let the man off: but the Persian refused him; whereupon Aristagoras went himself and set Scylax free. When Megabates heard this he was still more angry than before, and spoke hotly to Aristagoras. Then the latter said to him, "What have you to do with these matters? Were you not sent here by Artaphernes to obey me, and to sail whithersoever I ordered? Why do you meddle so?"

Thus spoke Aristagoras. The other, in high dudgeon at such language, waited till the night, and then despatched a boat to Naxos, to warn the Naxians of the coming danger.

34. Now the Naxians up to this time had not had any suspicion that the armament was directed against them: as soon, therefore, as the message reached them, they brought within their walls all that they had in the open field, and made themselves ready against a siege by provisioning their town both with food and drink. Thus was Naxos placed in a posture of defence;

and the Persians, when they crossed the sea from Chios, found the Naxians fully prepared for them. However they besieged the place for four whole months. When at length all the stores which they had brought with them were exhausted, and Aristagoras had likewise spent upon the siege no small sum from his private means, and more was still needed to insure success, the Persians gave up the attempt, and first building certain forts, wherein they left the banished Naxians, withdrew to the mainland, having utterly failed in their undertaking.

35. And now Aristagoras found himself quite unable to make good his promises to Artaphernes; he was even hard pressed to meet the claims whereto he was liable for the pay of the troops; and at the same time his fear was great, lest, owing to the failure of the expedition and his own quarrel with Megabates, he should be ousted from the government of Miletus. These manifold alarms had already caused him to contemplate raising a rebellion, when the man with the marked head came from Susa, bringing him instructions on the part of Histiaeus to revolt from the king. For Histiaeus, when he was anxious to give Aristagoras orders to revolt, could find but one safe way, as the roads were guarded, of making his wishes known; which was by taking the trustiest of his slaves, shaving all the hair from off his head, and then pricking letters upon the skin, and waiting till the hair grew again. Thus accordingly he did; and as soon as the hair was grown, he sent the man to Miletus, giving him no other message than this, "When you come to Miletus, bid Aristagoras shave your head, and look at it." Now the marks on the head, as I have already mentioned, were a command to revolt. All this Histiaeus did, because it irked him greatly to be kept at Susa, and because he had strong hopes that, if troubles broke out, he would be sent down to the coast to quell them, whereas, if Miletus made no movement. he did not see a chance of his ever again returning thither.

36. Such, then, were the views which led Histiaeus to despatch his messenger; and it so chanced that all these several motives to revolt were brought to bear upon Aristagoras at one and the same time.

Accordingly, at this conjuncture Aristagoras held a council of his trusty friends, and laid the business before them, telling them his own opinion, and what message had been sent him by Histiaeus. At this council all his friends were of the same way of thinking, and recommended revolt, except only Hecataeus the historian. He, first of all, advised them by all mean. to avoid engaging in war with the king of the Persians, whose might he set forth, and whose subject nations he enumerated. As however he could not induce them to listen to his counsel, he next advised that they should do all that lay in their power to make themselves masters of the sea. "There was one only way,' he said, "so far as he could see, of their succeeding in this. Miletus was, he knew, a weak state—but if the treasures in the temple at Branchidae, which Croesus the Lydian gave to it, were seized, he had strong hopes that the mastery of the sea might be thereby gained; at least it would give them money to begin the war, and would save the treasures from falling into the hands of the enemy." Now these treasures were of very great value, as I showed in the first part of my history. The assembly, however, rejected the counsel of Hecataeus, while, nevertheless, they resolved upon a revolt. One of their number, it was agreed, should sail to Myus, where the fleet had been lying since its return from Naxos, and endeavour to seize the captains who had gone there with the vessels.

37. Iatragoras accordingly was despatched on this errand, and he took with guile Oliatus the son of Ibanolis the Mylassian, and Histiaeus the son of Tymnes the Termerean, Coes likewise, the son of Erxander, to whom Darius gave Mytilene, and Aristagoras the son of Heraclides the Cymaean, and also many others. Thus Aristagoras revolted openly from Darius, and now he set to work to scheme against him in every possible way. First of all, in order to induce the Milesians to join heartily in the revolt, he gave out, that he laid down his own despotism over Miletus, and established equality of government: after which, throughout all Ionia he did the like; for from some of the cities he drove out their tyrants, and to others, whose good will he hoped thereby to gain, he handed theirs over, thus giving up

all the men whom he had seized at the Naxian fleet, each to the city whereto he belonged.

38. Now the Mytileneans had no sooner got Coes into their power, than they led him forth from the city and stoned him; the Cymaeans, on the other hand, allowed their tyrant to go free, as likewise did most of the others. And so this form of government ceased throughout all the cities. Aristagoras the Milesian, after he had in this way put down the tyrants, and bidden the cities choose themselves governors, sailed away himself on board a trireme to Lacedaemon; for he had great need of obtaining the aid of some powerful ally.

39. At Sparta, Anaxandridas the son of Leo was no longer king: he had died, and his son Cleomenes had mounted the throne, not however by right of merit, but of birth. Anaxandridas took to wife his own sister's daughter, and was tenderly attached to her; but no children came from the marriage. Here-- upon the Ephors called him before them, and said, "If you have no care for yourself, nevertheless we cannot allow this, nor suffer the race of Eurysthenes to die out from among us. Come then, as your present wife bears you no children, put her away, and wed another. So will you do what is well-pleasing to the Spartans." Anaxandridas however refused to do as they required, and said it was no good advice the Ephors gave, to bid him put away his wife when she had done no wrong, and take to himself another. He therefore declined to obey them.

40. Then the Ephors and Elders took counsel together, and laid this proposal before the king, "Since you are so fond, as we see you to be, of your present wife, do what we now advise, and gainsay us not, lest the Spartans make some unusual decree concerning you. We ask you not now to put away your wife to whom you are married—give her still the same love and honour as ever,—but take another wife beside, who may bear you children."

When he heard this offer, Anaxandridas gave way—and henceforth he lived with two wives in two separate houses, quite against all Spartan custom.

41. In a short time, the wife whom he had last married bore

him a son, who received the name of Cleomenes; and so the heir
to the throne was brought into the world by her. After this, the
first wife also, who previously had been barren, by some strange
chance conceived, and came to be with child. Then the friends
of the second wife, when they heard a rumour of the truth, made
a great stir, and said it was a false boast, and she meant, they
were sure, to bring forward as her own a supposititious child. So
they raised an outcry against her, and therefore, when her full
time was come, the Ephors, who were themselves incredulous,
sat round her bed, and kept a strict watch on the labour. At this
time then she bore Dorieus, and after him quickly Leonidas, and
after him, again quickly, Cleombrotus. Some even say that Leonidas and Cleombrotus were twins. On the other hand, the second wife, the mother of Cleomenes (who was a daughter of
Prinetadas, the son of Demarmenus), never gave birth to a second child.

42. Now Cleomenes, it is said, was not right in his mind; indeed he verged upon madness, while Dorieus surpassed all his
co-mates, and looked confidently to receiving the kingdom on
the score of merit. When, therefore, after the death of Anaxandridas, the Spartans kept to the law, and made Cleomenes, his
eldest son, king, Dorieus, who had imagined that he should be
chosen, and who could not bear the thought of having such a
man as Cleomenes to rule over him, asked the Spartans to give
him a body of men, and left Sparta with them in order to found
a colony. However, he neither took counsel of the oracle at Delphi as to where he should go, nor observed any of the customary
usages; but left Sparta in dudgeon, and sailed away to Libya,
under the guidance of certain men who were Theraeans. These
men brought him to Cinyps, where he colonised a spot, which
has not its equal in all Libya, on the banks of a river. From this
place he was driven in the third year by the Macians, the Libyans, and the Carthaginians.

43. Dorieus returned to the Peloponnese, whereupon Antich-
ares the Eleonian, gave him a counsel (which he got from the
oracles of Laius), "Found the city of Heraclea in Sicily; the

whole country of Eryx belonged," he said, "to the Heracleids, since Heracles himself conquered it." On receiving this advice, Dorieus went to Delphi to inquire of the oracle whether he would take the place to which he was about to go. The priestess prophesied that he would; whereupon Dorieus went back to Libya, took up the men who had sailed with him at the first, and proceeded upon his way along the shores of Italy.

44. Just at this time, the Sybarites say, they and their king Telys were about to make war upon Croton, and the Crotoniats, greatly alarmed, begged Dorieus to aid them. Dorieus was prevailed upon, took part in the war against Sybaris, and had a share in taking the town. Such is the account which the Sybarites give of what was done by Dorieus and his companions. The Crotoniats, on the other hand, maintain that no foreigner lent them aid in their war against the Sybarites, except Callias the Elean, a soothsayer of the race of the Iamidae; and he only forsook Telys the Sybaritic king, and deserted to their side, when he found on sacrificing that the victims were not favourable to an attack on Croton. Such is the account which each party gives of these matters.

45. Both parties likewise adduce testimonies to the truth of what they say. The Sybarites show a temple and sacred precinct near the dry stream of the Crathis, which they declare that Dorieus, after taking their city, dedicated to Athena Crathias. And further, they bring forward the death of Dorieus as the surest proof, since he fell, they say, because he disobeyed the oracle. For had he in nothing varied from the directions given him, but confined himself to the business on which he was sent, he would assuredly have conquered the Erycian territory, and kept possession of it, instead of perishing with all his followers. The Crotoniats, on the other hand, point to the numerous allotments within their borders which were assigned to Callias the Elean by their countrymen, and which to my day remained in the possession of his family; while Dorieus and his descendants (they remark) possess nothing. Yet if Dorieus had really helped them in the Sybaritic war, he would have received very much more

than Callias. Such are the testimonies which are adduced on
either side; it is open to every man to adopt whichever view he
deems the best.

46. Certain Spartans accompanied Dorieus on his voyage as
co-founders, to wit, Thessalus, Paraebates, Celeas, and Euryleon. These men and all the troops under their command reached
Sicily, but there they fell in a battle wherein they were defeated
by the Egesteans and Phoenicians, only one, Euryleon, surviving the disaster. He then, collecting the remnants of the beaten
army, made himself master of Minoa, the Selinusian colony;
and helped the Selinusians to throw off the yoke of their tyrant
Peithagoras. Having upset Peithagoras, he sought to become tyrant in his room, and he even reigned at Selinus for a brief space
—but after a while the Selinusians rose up in revolt against him,
and though he fled to the altar of Zeus of the Market-place,
they notwithstanding put him to death.

47. Another man who accompanied Dorieus and died with
him, was Philip the son of Butacidas, a man of Croton, who,
after he had been betrothed to a daughter of Telys the Sybarite,
was banished from Croton, whereupon his marriage came to
nought: and he in his disappointment took ship and sailed to
Cyrene. From thence he became a follower of Dorieus, furnishing to the fleet a trireme of his own, the crew of which he supported at his own charge. This Philip was an Olympian victor,
and the handsomest Greek of his day. His beauty gained him
honours at the hands of the Egestaeans which they never ac-
corded to any one else; for they raised a hero-temple over his
grave, and they still worship him with sacrifices.

48. Such then was the end of Dorieus, who if he had endured
the rule of Cleomenes, and remained in Sparta, would have been
king of Lacedaemon; since Cleomenes, after reigning no great
length of time, died without male offspring, leaving behind him
a single daughter, by name Gorgo.

49. Cleomenes, however, was still king when Aristagoras, tyrant of Miletus, reached Sparta. At their interview, Aristagoras,
according to the report of the Lacedaemonians, produced a
bronze tablet, whereupon the whole circuit of the earth was en-

graved, with all its seas and rivers.[5] Discourse began between
the two, and Aristagoras addressed the Spartan king in these
words following, "Think it not strange, King Cleomenes, that I
have been at the pains to sail hither; for the state of affairs
made it fitting. Shame and grief is it indeed to none so much as
to us, that the sons of the Ionians should have lost their freedom, and come to be the slaves of others; but yet it touches you
likewise, Spartans, beyond the rest of the Greeks, inasmuch you
are leaders of all Greece. We beseech you therefore, by the common gods of the Grecians, deliver the Ionians, who are your own
kinsmen, from slavery. Truly the task is not difficult; for the
barbarians are an unwarlike people, and you are the best and
bravest warriors in the whole world. Their mode of fighting is
the following: they use bows and arrows and a short spear; they
wear trousers in the field, and cover their heads with turbans.
So easy are they to vanquish. Know too that the dwellers in
these parts have more good things than all the rest of the world
put together—gold, and silver, and brass, and embroidered garments, beasts of burden, and slaves—all which, if you only wish
it, you may soon have for your own. The nations border on one
another, in the order which I will now explain. Next to these
Ionians" (here he pointed with his finger to the map of the
world which was engraved upon the tablet that he had brought
with him) "these Lydians dwell; their soil is fertile, and few
people are so rich in silver. Next to them," he continued, "come
these Phrygians, who have more flocks and herds than any race
that I know, and more plentiful harvests. On them border the
Cappadocians, whom we Greeks know by the name of Syrians:
they are neighbours to the Cilicians, who extend all the way to
this sea, where Cyprus (the island which you see here) lies. The
Cilicians pay the king a yearly tribute of five hundred talents.
Next to them come the Armenians, who live here—they too
have numerous flocks and herds. After them come the Matieni,
inhabiting this country; then Cissia, this province, where you
see the river Choaspes marked, and likewise the town Susa upon

[5] Maps, according to Strabo, were invented about this time by Anaxi-
mander.

Its banks, where the Great King holds his court, and where the treasuries are in which his wealth is stored. Once masters of this city, you may vie with Zeus himself for riches. In the wars which you wage with your rivals of Messenia,[6] with them of Argos likewise and of Arcadia, about paltry boundaries and strips of land not so remarkably good, you contend with those who have no gold, nor silver even, which often give men heart to fight and die. Must you wage such wars, and when you might so easily be lords of Asia, will you decide otherwise?" Thus spoke Aristagoras; and Cleomenes replied to him, "Milesian stranger, three days hence I will give you an answer."

50. So they proceeded no further at that time. When, however, the day appointed for the answer came, and the two once more met, Cleomenes asked Aristagoras how many days' journey it was from the sea of the Ionians to the king's residence. Hereupon Aristagoras, who had managed the rest so cleverly, and succeeded in deceiving the king, tripped in his speech and blundered; for instead of concealing the truth, as he ought to have done if he wanted to induce the Spartans to cross into Asia, he said plainly that it was a journey of three months. Cleomenes caught at the words, and, preventing Aristagoras from finishing what he had begun to say concerning the road, addressed him thus, "Milesian stranger, quit Sparta before sunset. This is no good proposal that you make to the Lacedaemonians, to conduct them a distance of three months' journey from the sea." When he had thus spoken, Cleomenes went to his home.

51. But Aristagoras took an olive bough in his hand, and hastened to the king's house, where he was admitted by reason of his suppliant's garb. Gorgo, the daughter of Cleomenes and his only child, a girl of about eight or nine years of age, happened to be there, standing by her father's side. Aristagoras, seeing her, requested Cleomenes to send her out of the room before he began to speak with him; but Cleomenes told him to say on, and not mind the child. So Aristagoras began with a promise of ten talents if the king would grant him his request, and when Cleom-

[6] This is the only distinct reference in Herodotus to the two early Messenian wars.

enes shook his head, continued to raise his offer till it reached
fifty talents; whereupon the child spoke. "Father," she said,
"get up and go, or the stranger will certainly corrupt you." Then
Cleomenes, pleased at the warning of his child, withdrew, and
went into another room. Aristagoras quitted Sparta for good,
not being able to discourse any more concerning the road which
led up to the king.

52. Now the true account of the road in question is the following: Royal stations[7] exist along its whole length, and excellent caravanserais; and throughout, it traverses an inhabited
tract, and is free from danger. In Lydia and Phrygia there are
twenty stations within a distance of ninety-four and one-half
parasangs. On leaving Phrygia the Halys has to be crossed, and
here are gates through which you must pass before you can traverse the stream. A strong force guards this post. When you
have made the passage, and are come into Cappadocia, twenty-
eight stations and 104 parasangs bring you to the borders of
Cilicia, where the road passes through two sets of gates, at each
of which there is a guard posted. Leaving these behind, you go
on through Cilicia, where you find three stations in a distance of
fifteen and one-half parasangs. The boundary between Cilicia
and Armenia is the river Euphrates, which it is necessary to
cross in boats. In Armenia the resting-places are fifteen in number, and the distance fifty-six and one-half parasangs. There is
one place where a guard is posted. Four large streams intersect
this district, all of which have to be crossed by means of boats.
The first of these is the Tigris; the second and the third have
both of them the same name, though they are not only different
rivers, but do not even run from the same place.[8] For the one
which I have called the first of the two has its source in Armenia, while the other flows afterwards out of the country of
the Matienians. The fourth of the streams is called the Gyndes,
and this is the river which Cyrus dispersed by digging for it

---

[7] These are the abodes of the king's couriers who conveyed despatches
from their own station to the next, and then returned.

[8] What Herodotus here states is exactly true of the two Zabs.

360 channels. Leaving Armenia and entering the Matienian country, you have four stations; these passed you find yourself in Cissia, where eleven stations and forty-two and one-half parasangs bring you to another navigable stream, the Choaspes, on the banks of which the city of Susa is built. Thus the entire number of the stations is brought to 111, and so many are in fact the resting-places that one finds between Sardis and Susa.

53. If then the royal road be measured aright, and the parasang equals, as it does, thirty furlongs,[9] the whole distance from Sardis to the palace of Memnon (as it is called), amounting to 450 parasangs, would be 1,615 miles.[10] Travelling then at the rate of eighteen miles a day, one will take exactly ninety days to perform the journey.

54. Thus when Aristagoras the Milesian told Cleomenes the Lacedaemonian that it was a three months' journey from the sea up to the king, he said no more than the truth. The exact distance (if any one desires still greater accuracy) is somewhat more; for the journey from Ephesus to Sardis must be added to the foregoing account; and this will make the whole distance between the Greek Sea and Susa (or the city of Memnon, as it is called) 1,682 miles; since Ephesus is distant from Sardis sixty-seven miles. This would add three days to the three months' journey.

55. When Aristagoras left Sparta he hastened to Athens, which had been freed of its tyrants in the way that I will now describe. After the death of Hipparchus (the son of Pisistratus, and brother of the tyrant Hippias), who, in spite of the clear warning he had received concerning his fate in a dream, was slain by Harmodius and Aristogeiton (men both of the race of the Gephyraeans), the oppression of the Athenians continued

---

[9] This was the ordinary estimate of the Greeks. The truth is, that the ancient parasang, like the modern farsakh, was originally a measure of time (an hour), not a measure of distance.

[10] As usual, there is a discrepancy in the numbers. The stations, according to the previous small sums, are eighty-one instead of 111, and the parasangs 328 instead of 450.

for the space of four years;[11] and they gained nothing, but were worse used than before.

56. Now the dream of Hipparchus was the following: The night before the Panathenaic festival, he thought he saw in his sleep a tall and beautiful man, who stood over him, and read him the following riddle:

Bear thou unbearable woes with the all-bearing heart of a lion,
Never, be sure, shall wrong-doer escape the reward of wrong-
    doing.

As soon as day dawned he sent and submitted his dream to the interpreters, after which he offered the averting sacrifices, and then went and led the procession in which he perished.

57. The family of the Gephyraeans, to which the murderers of Hipparchus belonged, according to their own account, came originally from Eretria. My inquiries, however, have made it clear to me that they are in reality Phoenicians, descendants of those who came with Cadmus into the country now called Boeotia. Here they received for their portion the district of Tanagra, in which they afterwards dwelt. On their expulsion from this country by the Boeotians (which happened some time after that of the Cadmaeans from the same parts by the Argives) they took refuge at Athens. The Athenians received them among their citizens upon set terms, whereby they were excluded from a number of privileges which are not worth mentioning.

58. Now the Phoenicians who came with Cadmus, and to whom the Gephyraei belonged, introduced into Greece upon their arrival a great variety of arts, among the rest that of writing, whereof the Greeks till then had, as I think, been ignorant. And originally they shaped their letters exactly like all the other Phoenicians, but afterwards, in course of time, they changed by degrees their language, and together with it the form likewise of

---

[11] From 514 B.C. to 510 B.C. Herodotus wishes to correct the popular Athenian view that the murder of Hipparchus ended the tyranny.

their characters. Now the Greeks who dwelt about those parts at that time were chiefly the Ionians. The Phoenician letters were accordingly adopted by them, but with some variation in the shape of a few, and so they arrived at the present use, still calling the letters Phoenician, as justice required, after the name of those who were the first to introduce them into Greece. Paper rolls also were called from of old "parchments" by the Ionians, because formerly when paper was scarce they used, instead, the skins of sheep and goats—on which material many of the barbarians are even now wont to write.

59. I myself saw Cadmaean characters[12] engraved upon some tripods in the temple of Apollo Ismenias in Boeotian Thebes, most of them shaped like the Ionian. One of the tripods has the inscription following:

Me did Amphitryon place, from the far Teleboans coming.

This would be about the age of Laius, the son of Labdacus, the son of Polydorus, the son of Cadmus.

60. Another of the tripods has this legend in the hexameter measure:

I to far-shooting Phoebus was offered by Scaeus the boxer,
When he had won at the games, a wondrous beautiful offering.

This might be Scaeus, the son of Hippocoor, and the tripod, if dedicated by him, and not by another of the same name, would belong to the time of Oedipus, the son of Laius.

61. The third tripod has also an inscription in hexameters, which runs thus:

King Laodamas gave this tripod to far-seeing Apollo,
When he was set on the throne, a wondrous beautiful offering.

It was in the reign of this Laodamas, the son of Eteocles, that

[12] The old Greek letters, like the Phoenician, were written from right to left, and were nearer in shape to those of the parent alphabet.

the Cadmaeans were driven by the Argives out of their country, and found a shelter with the Encheleans. The Gephyraeans at that time remained in the country, but afterwards they retired before the Boeotians, and took refuge at Athens, where they have a number of temples for their separate use, which the other Athenians are not allowed to enter—among the rest, one of Achaean Demeter, in whose honour they likewise celebrate special orgies.

62. Having thus related the dream which Hipparchus saw, and traced the descent of the Gephyraeans, the family whereto his murderers belonged, I must proceed with the matter whereof I was intending before to speak; to wit, the way in which the Athenians got quit of their tyrants. Upon the death of Hipparchus, Hippias, who was king, grew harsh towards the Athenians; and the Alcmaeonidae, an Athenian family which had been banished by the Pisistratidae, joined the other exiles, and endeavoured to procure their own return, and to free Athens, by force. They seized and fortified Leipsydrium above Paeonia, and tried to gain their object by arms; but great disasters befell them, and their purpose remained unaccomplished. They therefore resolved to shrink from no contrivance that might bring them success, and accordingly they contracted with the Amphictyons to build the temple which now stands at Delphi, but which in those days did not exist. Having done this, they proceeded, being men of great wealth and members of an ancient and distinguished family, to build the temple much more magnificently than the plan obliged them. Besides other improvements, instead of the coarse stone whereof by the contract the temple was to have been constructed, they made the facings of Parian marble.

63. These same men, if we may believe the Athenians, during their stay at Delphi persuaded the priestess by a bribe to tell the Spartans, whenever any of them came to consult the oracle, either on their own private affairs or on the business of the state, that they must free Athens. So the Lacedaemonians, when they found no answer ever returned to them but this, sent at last Anchimolius, the son of Aster—a man of note among their cit-

izens—at the head of an army against Athens, with orders to
drive out the Pisistratidae, albeit they were bound to them by
the closest ties of friendship. For they esteemed the things of
heaven more highly than the things of men. The troops went by
sea and were conveyed in transports. Anchimolius brought them
to an anchorage at Phalerum, and there the men disembarked.
But the Pisistratidae, who had previous knowledge of their
intentions, had sent to Thessaly, between which country and
Athens there was an alliance, with a request for aid. The Thessalians, in reply to their entreaties, sent them by a public vote
1,000 horsemen, under the command of their king, Cineas, who
was a Coniaean. When this help came, the Pisistratidae laid
their plan accordingly: they cleared the whole plain about Phalerum so as to make it fit for the movements of cavalry, and
then charged the enemy's camp with their horse, which fell with
such fury upon the Lacedaemonians as to kill numbers, among
the rest Anchimolius, the general, and to drive the remainder to
their ships. Such was the fate of the first army sent from Lacedaemon, and the tomb of Anchimolius may be seen to this day
in Attica; it is at Alopecae, near the temple of Heracles in Cyno-
sargos.

64. Afterwards, the Lacedaemonians despatched a larger
force against Athens, which they put under the command of
Cleomenes, son of Anaxandridas, one of their kings. These
troops were not sent by sea, but marched by the mainland.
When they were come into Attica, their first encounter was with
the Thessalian horse, which they shortly put to flight, killing
above forty men; the remainder made good their escape, and
fled straight to Thessaly. Cleomenes proceeded to the city, and,
with the aid of such of the Athenians as wished for freedom, besieged the tyrants. who had shut themselves up in the Pelasgic
fortress.

65. And now there had been small chance of the Pisistratidae
falling into the hands of the Spartans, who did not even design
to besiege the place, which had moreover been well provisioned
beforehand with stores both of meat and drink,—nay, it is likely
that after a few days' blockade the Lacedaemonians would have

quitted Attica altogether, and gone back to Sparta—had not an event occurred most unlucky for the besieged, and most advantageous for the besiegers. The children of the Pisistratidae were made prisoners, as they were being removed out of the country. By this calamity all their plans were deranged, and as the ransom of their children they consented to the demands of the Athenians, and agreed within five days' time to quit Attica. Accordingly they soon afterwards left the country, and withdrew to Sigeum on the Scamander, after reigning thirty-six years over the Athenians. By descent they were Pylians, of the family of the Neleids, to which Codrus and Melanthus likewise belonged, men who in former times from foreign settlers became kings of Athens. And hence it was that Hippocrates came to think of calling his son Pisistratus: he named him after the Pisistratus who was a son of Nestor. Such then was the mode in which the Athenians got rid of their tyrants. What they did and suffered worthy of note from the time when they gained their freedom until the revolt of Ionia from King Darius, and the coming of Aristagoras to Athens with a request that the Athenians would lend the Ionians aid, I shall now proceed to relate.

66. The power of Athens had been great before, but now that the tyrants were gone it became greater than ever. The chief authority was lodged with two persons, Cleisthenes, of the family of the Alcmaeonids, who is said to have been the persuader of the Pythian priestess, and Isagoras, the son of Tisander, who belonged to a noble house, but whose pedigree I am not able to trace further. Howbeit his kinsmen offer sacrifice to the Carian Zeus. These two men strove together for the mastery; and Cleisthenes, finding himself the weaker, called to his aid the common people. Hereupon, instead of the four tribes among which the Athenians had been divided hitherto, Cleisthenes made ten tribes, and parcelled out the Athenians among them. He likewise changed the names of the tribes; for whereas they had till now been called after Geleon, Aegicores, Argades, and Hoples, the four sons of Ion, Cleisthenes set these names aside, and called his tribes after certain other heroes,[13] all of whom were

[13] The names of the Attic tribes were Erechtheis, Aegeis, Pandionis,

402

Herodotus

native, except Ajax. Ajax was associated because, although a foreigner, he was a neighbour and an ally of Athens.

67. My belief is that in acting thus he did but imitate his maternal grandfather, Cleisthenes, king of Sicyon. This king, when he was at war with Argos, put an end to the contest of the rhapsodists at Sicyon, because in the Homeric poems Argos and the Argives were so constantly the theme of song. He likewise conceived the wish to drive Adrastus, the son of Talaus, out of his country, seeing that he was an Argive hero. For Adrastus had a shrine at Sicyon, which yet stands in the market-place of the town. Cleisthenes therefore went to Delphi, and asked the oracle if he might expel Adrastus. To this the priestess is reported to have answered, "Adrastus is the Sicyonians' king, but you are only a robber." So when the god would not grant his request, he went home and began to think how he might contrive to make Adrastus withdraw of his own accord. After a while he hit upon a plan which he thought would succeed. He sent envoys to Thebes in Boeotia, and informed the Thebans that he wished to bring Melanippus the son of Astacus to Sicyon. The Thebans consenting, Cleisthenes carried Melanippus back with him, assigned him a precinct within the town-hall, and built him a shrine there in the safest and strongest part. The reason for his so doing (which I must not forbear to mention) was, because Melanippus was Adrastus' great enemy, having slain both his brother Mecistes and his son-in-law Tydeus. Cleisthenes, after assigning the precinct to Melanippus, took away from Adrastus the sacrifices and festivals wherewith he had till then been honoured, and transferred them to his adversary. Hitherto the Sicyonians had paid extraordinary honours to Adrastus, because the country had belonged to Polybus, and Adrastus was Polybus' daughter's son, whence it came to pass that Polybus, dying childless, left Adrastus his kingdom. Besides other ceremonies, it had been their custom to honour Adrastus with tragic choruses, which they assigned to him rather than Dionysus, on account of his calamities. Cleisthenes now gave the choruses to

Leontis, Acamantis, Oeneis, Cecropis, Hippothoontis, Aeantis, and Antiochis.

Dionysus, transferring to Melanippus the rest of the sacred rites.

68. Such were his doings in the matter of Adrastus. With respect to the Dorian tribes, not choosing the Sicyonians to have the same tribes as the Argives, he changed all the old names for new ones; and here he took special occasion to mock the Sicyonians, for he drew his new names from the words pig, and ass, adding thereto the usual tribe endings; only in the case of his own tribe he did nothing of the sort, but gave them a name drawn from his own kingly office. For he called his own tribe the Archelai, or Rulers, while the others he named Hyatae, or Pigfolk, Oneatae, or Ass-folk, and Choereatae, or Swine-folk. The Sicyonians kept these names, not only during the reign of Cleisthenes, but even after his death, for sixty years: then, however, they took counsel together, and changed to the well-known names of Hyllaeans, Pamphylians, and Dymanatae, taking at the same time, as a fourth name, the title of Aegialeans, from Aegialeus the son of Adrastus.

69. Thus had Cleisthenes the Sicyonian done. The Athenian Cleisthenes, who was grandson by the mother's side of the other, and had been named after him, resolved, from contempt (as I believe) of the Ionians,[14] that his tribes should not be the same as theirs; and so followed the pattern set him by his namesake of Sicyon. Having brought entirely over to his own side the common people of Athens, who had before lacked rights, he gave all the tribes new names, and made the number greater than formerly; instead of the four tribal presidents he established ten; he likewise placed ten demes in each of the tribes; and he was, now that the common people took his part, very much more powerful than his adversaries.

70. Isagoras in his turn lost ground, and therefore, to counterplot his enemy, he called in Cleomenes the Lacedaemonian,

[14] There can be no doubt that Cleisthenes was actuated by a higher motive. He abolished the old tribes, not because they were Ionic, but because they were exclusive; his intention was to break down an old oligarchical distinction, and to admit the more readily to the franchise fresh classes of the free inhabitants.

who had already, at the time when he was besieging the Pisistratidae, made a contract of friendship with him. A charge is
even brought against Cleomenes, that he was a lover of Isagoras'
wife. At this time the first thing that he did, was to send a herald
and require that Cleisthenes, and a large number of Athenians
besides, whom he called the Accursed, should leave Athens. This
message he sent at the suggestion of Isagoras: for in the affair
referred to, the bloodguiltiness lay on the Alcmaeonidae and
their partisans, while he and his friends were quite clear of it.

71. The way in which the Accursed at Athens got their name,
was the following. There was a certain Athenian called Cylon, a
victor at the Olympic games, who aspired to the sovereignty;
and aided by a number of his companions, who were of the
same age with himself, made an attempt to seize the citadel.
But the attack failed, and Cylon became a suppliant at the
image. Hereupon the presidents of the naval boards, who at that
time bore rule in Athens, induced the fugitives to leave by a
promise to spare their lives. Nevertheless they were all slain,
and the blame was laid on the Alcmaeonidae. All this happened
before the time of Pisistratus.

72. When the message of Cleomenes arrived, requiring Cleisthenes and the Accursed to quit the city, Cleisthenes departed
of his own accord. Cleomenes, however, notwithstanding came
to Athens, with a small band of followers; and on his arrival
sent into banishment 700 Athenian families, which were pointed
out to him by Isagoras. Succeeding here, he next endeavoured to
dissolve the council,[15] and to put the government into the hands
of 300 of the partisans of that leader. But the council resisted,
and refused to obey his orders; whereupon Cleomenes, Isagoras,
and their followers took possession of the citadel. Here they
were attacked by the rest of the Athenians, who took the side of
the council, and were besieged for the space of two days; on the
third day they accepted terms, being allowed—at least such of
them as were Lacedaemonians—to quit the country. And so the
word which came to Cleomenes received its fulfilment. For when

---

[15] The new council of 500, fifty from each local tribe, which Cleisthenes
had recently substituted for Solon's council of 400.

he first went up into the citadel, meaning to seize it, just as he
was entering the sanctuary of the goddess, in order to question
her, the priestess arose from her throne, before he had passed
the doors, and said, "Stranger from Lacedaemon, depart hence,
and presume not to enter the holy place—it is not lawful for a
Dorian to set foot there." But he answered, "Woman, I am not
a Dorian, but an Achaean." Slighting this warning, Cleomenes
made his attempt, and so he was forced to retire, together with
his Lacedaemonians. The rest were cast into prison by the Athenians, and condemned to die, among them Timasitheus the Delphian, of whose prowess and courage I have great things which
I could tell.

73. So these men died in prison. The Athenians directly afterwards recalled Cleisthenes, and the 700 families which Cleomenes had driven out; and, further, sent envoys to Sardis, to
make an alliance with the Persians, for they knew that war
would follow with Cleomenes and the Lacedaemonians. When
the ambassadors reached Sardis and delivered their message,
Artaphernes, son of Hystaspes, who was at that time governor
of the place, inquired of them who they were, and in what part
of the world they dwelt, that they wanted to become allies of the
Persians. The messengers told him, upon which he answered
them shortly—that if the Athenians chose to give earth and water to King Darius, he would conclude an alliance with them;
but if not, they might go home again. After consulting together,
the envoys, anxious to form the alliance, accepted the terms;
but on their return to Athens, they fell into deep disgrace on account of their compliance.[16]

74. Meanwhile Cleomenes, who considered himself to have
been insulted by the Athenians both in word and deed, was
drawing a force together from all parts of the Peloponnese,
without informing any one of his object; which was to revenge
himself on the Athenians, and to establish Isagoras, who had
escaped with him from the citadel, as despot of Athens. Accordingly, with a large army, he invaded the district of Eleusis, while

---

[16] Herodotus seems to have concealed Cleisthenes' part in these negotia-
tions.

the Boeotians, who had concerted measures with him, took Oenoe and Hysiae, two country-towns upon the frontier; and at the same time the Chalcideans, on another side, plundered various places in Attica. The Athenians, notwithstanding that danger threatened them from every quarter, put off all thought of the Boeotians and Chalcideans till a future time, and marched against the Peloponnesians, who were at Eleusis.

75. As the two hosts were about to engage, first of all the Corinthians, thinking that they were perpetrating a wrong, changed their minds, and drew off from the main army. Then Demaratus, son of Ariston, who was himself king of Sparta and joint leader of the expedition, and who till now had had no sort of quarrel with Cleomenes, followed their example. On account of this rupture between the kings, a law was passed at Sparta, forbidding both monarchs to go out together with the army, as had been the custom hitherto. The law also provided, that, as one of the kings was to be left behind, one of the Tyndaridae should also remain at home; whereas hitherto both had accompanied the expeditions, as auxiliaries. So when the rest of the allies saw that the Lacedaemonian kings were not of one mind, and that the Corinthian troops had quitted their post, they likewise drew off and departed.

76. This was the fourth time that the Dorians had invaded Attica: twice they came as enemies, and twice they came to do good service to the Athenian people. Their first invasion took place at the period when they founded Megara, and is rightly placed in the reign of Codrus at Athens; the second and third occasions were when they came from Sparta to drive out the Pisistratidae; the fourth was the present attack, when Cleomenes, at the head of a Peloponnesian army, entered at Eleusis. Thus the Dorians had now four times invaded Attica.

77. So when the Spartan army had broken up from its quarters thus ingloriously, the Athenians, wishing to revenge themselves, marched first against the Chalcideans. The Boeotians, however, advancing to the aid of the latter as far as the Euripus, the Athenians thought it best to attack them first. A battle was fought accordingly, and the Athenians gained a very complete

victory, killing a vast number of the enemy, and taking 700 of them alive. After this, on the very same day, they crossed into Euboea, and engaged the Chalcideans with the like success; whereupon they left 4,000 settlers[17] upon the lands of the Hippobotae, which is the name the Chalcideans give to their rich men. All the Chalcidean prisoners whom they took were put in irons, and kept for a long time in close confinement, as likewise were the Boeotians, until the ransom asked for them was paid; and this the Athenians fixed at two minae the man. The chains wherewith they were fettered the Athenians suspended in the citadel, where they were still to be seen in my day, hanging against the wall scorched by the Median flames, opposite the cell which faces the west. The Athenians made an offering of the tenth part of the ransom-money: and expended it on the brazen chariot drawn by four steeds, which stands on the left hand immediately that one enters the gateway of the citadel. The inscription runs as follows:

> When Chalcis and Boeotia dared her might,
> Athens subdued their pride in valorous fight;
> Gave bonds for insults; and, the ransom paid,
> From the full tenths these steeds for Pallas made.

78. Thus did the Athenians increase in strength. And it is plain enough, not from this instance only, but from many everywhere, that freedom is an excellent thing; since even the Athenians, who, while they continued under the rule of tyrants, were not a whit more valiant than any of their neighbours, no sooner shook off the yoke than they became decidedly the first of all. These things show that, while undergoing oppression, they let themselves be beaten, since then they worked for a master; but

---

[17] These allotment-holders are to be carefully distinguished from the ordinary colonists, who went out to find themselves a home wherever they might be able to settle, and who retained but a very slight connexion with the mother-country. The cleruchs were a military garrison planted in a conquered territory, the best portions of which were given to them. They continued Athenian subjects, and retained their full rights as Athenian citizens.

so soon as they got their freedom, each man was eager to do the best he could for himself. So fared it now with the Athenians.

79. Meanwhile the Thebans, who longed to be revenged on the Athenians, had sent to the oracle, and been told by the Pythian priestess that of their own strength they would be unable to accomplish their wish. "They must lay the matter," she said, "before the many-voiced, and ask the aid of those nearest them." The messengers, therefore, on their return, called a meeting, and laid the answer of the oracle before the people, who no sooner heard the advice to "ask the aid of those nearest them" than they exclaimed, "What! are not they who dwell the nearest to us the men of Tanagra, of Coronaea, and Thespiae? Yet these men always fight on our side, and have aided us with a good heart all through the war. Of what use is it to ask them? But maybe this is not the true meaning of the oracle."

80. As they were thus discoursing one with another, a certain man, informed of the debate, cried out, "I think I understand what course the oracle would recommend to us. Asopus, they say, had two daughters, Thebe and Aegina. The god means that, as these two were sisters, we ought to ask the Aeginetans to lend us aid." As no one was able to hit on any better explanation, the Thebans forthwith sent messengers to Aegina, and, according to the advice of the oracle, asked their aid, as the people "nearest to them." In answer to this petition the Aeginetans said, that they would give them the Aeacidae[18] for helpers.

81. The Thebans now, relying on the assistance of the Aeacidae, ventured to renew the war; but they met with so rough a reception, that they resolved to send to the Aeginetans again, returning the Aeacidae, and beseeching them to send some men instead. The Aeginetans, who were at that time a most flourishing people, elated with their greatness, and at the same time calling to mind their ancient feud with Athens, agreed to lend the Thebans aid, and forthwith went to war with the Athenians, without even giving them notice by a herald. The attention of these latter being engaged by the struggle with the Boeotians,

---

[18] Probably the images of the sons of Aeacus.

the Aeginetans in their ships of war made descents upon Attica, plundered Phalerum, and ravaged a vast number of the townships upon the sea-board, whereby the Athenians suffered very grievous damage.

82. The ancient feud between the Aeginetans and Athenians arose out of the following circumstances. Once upon a time the land of Epidaurus would bear no crops, and the Epidaurians sent to consult the oracle of Delphi concerning their affliction. The answer bade them set up the images of Damia and Auxesia, and promised them better fortune when that should be done. "Shall the images be made of bronze or stone?" the Epidaurians asked; but the priestess replied, "Of neither: but let them be made of the garden olive." Then the Epidaurians sent to Athens and asked leave to cut olive wood in Attica, believing the Athenian olives to be the holiest; or, according to others, because there were no olives at that time anywhere else in all the world but at Athens. The Athenians answered that they would give them leave, but on condition of their bringing offerings year by year to Athena Polias and to Erechtheus. The Epidaurians agreed, and having obtained what they wanted, made the images of olive wood, and set them up in their own country. Henceforth their land bore its crops, and they duly paid the Athenians what had been agreed upon.

83. Anciently, and even down to the time when this took place, the Aeginetans were in all things subject to the Epidaurians, and had to cross over to Epidaurus for the trial of all suits in which they were engaged one with another. After this, however, the Aeginetans built themselves ships, and growing proud, revolted from the Epidaurians. Having thus come to be at enmity with them, the Aeginetans, who were masters of the sea, ravaged Epidaurus, and even carried off these very images of Damia and Auxesia, which they set up in their own country, in the interior, at a place called Oea, about three miles from their city. This done, they fixed a worship for the images, which consisted in part of sacrifices, in part of female satiric choruses; while at the same time they appointed certain men to furnish the choruses, ten for each goddess. These choruses did not abuse

men, but only the women of the country. Holy rites of a similar kind were in use also among the Epidaurians, and likewise another sort of holy rites, whereof it is not lawful to speak.

84. After the robbery of the images the Epidaurians ceased to make the stipulated payments to the Athenians, wherefore the Athenians sent to Epidaurus to remonstrate. But the Epidaurians proved to them that they were not guilty of any wrong. "While the images continued in their country," they said, "they had duly paid the offerings according to the agreement; now that the images had been taken from them, they were no longer under any obligation to pay: the Athenians should make their demand of the Aeginetans, in whose possession the figures now were." Upon this the Athenians sent to Aegina, and demanded the images back, but the Aeginetans answered that the Athenians had nothing whatever to do with them.

85. After this the Athenians relate that they sent a trireme to Aegina with certain citizens on board, and that these men, who bore commission from the state, landed in Aegina, and sought to take the images away, considering them to be their own, inasmuch as they were made of their wood. And first they endeavoured to wrench them from their pedestals, and so carry them off, but failing herein, they in the next place tied ropes to them, and set to work to try if they could haul them down. In the midst of their hauling suddenly there was a thunderclap, and with the thunderclap an earthquake; and the crew of the trireme were forthwith seized with madness, and, like enemies, began to kill one another; until at last there was but one left, who returned alone to Phalerum.

86. Such is the account given by the Athenians. The Aeginetans deny that there was only a single vessel. "Had there been only one," they say, "or no more than a few, they would easily have repulsed the attack, even if they had had no fleet at all; but the Athenians came against them with a large number of ships, wherefore they gave way, and did not hazard a battle." They do not however explain clearly whether it was from a conviction of their own inferiority at sea that they yielded, or whether it was for the purpose of doing that which in fact they

did. Their account is that the Athenians, disembarking from their ships when they found that no resistance was offered, made for the statues, and failing to wrench them from their pedestals, tied ropes to them and began to haul. Then, they say—and some people will perhaps believe them, though I for my part do not— the two statues, as they were being dragged and hauled, fell down both upon their knees, in which attitude they still remain. Such, according to them, was the conduct of the Athenians; they meanwhile, having learnt beforehand what was intended, had prevailed on the Argives to hold themselves in readiness; and the Athenians accordingly were but just landed on their coasts when the Argives came to their aid. Secretly and silently they crossed over from Epidaurus, and before the Athenians were aware, cut off their retreat to their ships, and fell upon them; and the thunder came exactly at that moment, and the earthquake with it.

87. The Argives and the Aeginetans both agree in giving this account; and the Athenians themselves acknowledge that but one of their men returned alive to Attica. According to the Argives, he escaped from the battle in which the rest of the Athenian troops were destroyed by them. According to the Athenians, it was the god who destroyed their troops; and even this one man did not escape, for he perished in the following manner. When he came back to Athens, bringing word of the calamity, the wives of those who had been sent out on the expedition took it sorely to heart, that he alone should have survived the slaughter of all the rest; they therefore crowded round the man, and struck him with the brooches by which their dresses were fastened—each, as she struck, asking him, where he had left her husband. And the man died in this way. The Athenians thought the deed of the women more horrible even than the fate of the troops; as however they did not know how else to punish them, they changed their dress and compelled them to wear the costume of the Ionians. Till this time the Athenian women had worn a Dorian dress, shaped nearly like that which prevails at Corinth. Henceforth they were made to wear the linen tunic, which does not require brooches.

88. In very truth, however, this dress is not originally Ionian, but Carian; for anciently the Greek women all wore the costume which is now called the Dorian. It is said further that the Argives and Aeginetans made it a custom, on this same account, for their women to wear brooches half as large again as formerly, and to offer brooches rather than anything else in the temple of these goddesses. They also forbade the bringing of anything Attic into the temple, were it even a jar of earthenware, and made a law that none but native drinking vessels should be used there in time to come.[19] From this early age to my own day the Argive and Aeginetan women have always continued to wear their brooches larger than formerly, through hatred of the Athenians.

89. Such then was the origin of the feud which existed between the Aeginetans and the Athenians. Hence, when the Thebans made their application for succour, the Aeginetans, calling to mind the matter of images, gladly lent their aid to the Boeotians. They ravaged all the sea-coast of Attica, and the Athenians were about to attack them in return, when they were stopped by the oracle of Delphi, which bade them wait till thirty years had passed from the time that the Aeginetans did the wrong, and in the thirty-first year, having first set apart a precinct for Aeacus, then to begin the war. "So should they succeed to their wish," the oracle said; "but if they went to war at once, though they would still conquer the island in the end, yet they must go through much suffering and much exertion before taking it." On receiving this warning the Athenians set apart a precinct for Aeacus—the same which still remains dedicated to him in their market-place—but they could not hear with any patience of waiting thirty years, after they had suffered such grievous wrong at the hands of the Aeginetans.

90. Accordingly they were making ready to take their revenge when a fresh stir on the part of the Lacedaemonians hin-

[19] This law perhaps amounted to a prohibition of the Attic pottery, and was really for the protection of native industry. though it may have been professedly a war measure, like a blockade or an embargo.

dered their projects. These last had become aware of the truth—
how that the Alcmaeonidae had practised on the Pythian priestess, and the priestess had schemed against themselves, and
against the Pisistratidae; and the discovery was a double grief
to them, for while they had driven their own sworn friends into
exile, they found that they had not gained thereby a particle of
good will from Athens. They were also moved by certain prophecies, which declared that many dire calamities should befall
them at the hands of the Athenians. Of these in times past they
had been ignorant, but now they had become acquainted with
them by means of Cleomenes, who had brought them with him
to Sparta, having found them in the Athenian citadel, where
they had been left by the Pisistratidae when they were driven
from Athens: they were in the temple, and Cleomenes having
discovered them, carried them off.

91. So when the Lacedaemonians obtained possession of
the prophecies, and saw that the Athenians were growing in
strength, and had no mind to acknowledge any subjection to
their control, it occurred to them that, if the people of Attica
were free, they would be likely to be as powerful as themselves,
but if they were oppressed by a tyranny, they would be weak
and submissive. Under this feeling they sent and recalled Hippias, the son of Pisistratus, from Sigeum upon the Hellespont,
where the Pisistratidae had taken shelter. Hippias came at their
bidding, and the Spartans on his arrival summoned deputies
from all their other allies, and thus addressed the assembly:

"Friends and brothers in arms, we are free to confess that we
did lately a thing which was not right. Misled by counterfeit
oracles, we drove from their country those who were our sworn
and true friends, and who had, moreover, engaged to keep
Athens in dependence upon us; and we delivered the government into the hands of an unthankful people—a people who no
sooner got their freedom by our means, and grew in power, than
they turned us and our king, with every token of insult, out of
their city. Since then they have gone on continually raising their
thoughts higher, as their neighbours of Boeotia and Chalcis

have already discovered to their cost, and as others too will presently discover if they shall offend them. Having thus erred, we will endeavour now, with your help, to remedy the evils we have caused, and to obtain vengeance on the Athenians. For this cause we have sent for Hippias to come here, and have summoned you likewise from your several states, that we may all now with heart and hand unite to restore him to Athens, and thereby give him back that which we took from him formerly."

92. Such was the address of the Spartans. The greater number of the allies listened without being persuaded. None however broke silence, but Sosicles the Corinthian, who exclaimed:

"Surely the heaven will soon be below, and the earth above, and men will henceforth live in the sea, and fish take their place upon the dry land, since you, Lacedaemonians, propose to put down free governments in the cities of Greece, and to set up tyrannies in their stead. There is nothing in the whole world so unjust, nothing so bloody, as a tyranny. If, however, it seems to you a desirable thing to have the cities under despotic rule, begin by putting a tyrant over yourselves, and then establish despots in the other states. While you continue yourselves, as you have always been, unacquainted with tyranny, and take such excellent care that Sparta may not suffer from it, to act as you are now doing is to treat your allies unworthily. If you knew what tyranny was as well as ourselves, you would be better advised than you now are in regard to it. The government at Corinth was once an oligarchy—a single race, called Bacchiadae, who intermarried only among themselves, held the management of affairs. Now it happened that Amphion, one of these, had a daughter, named Labda, who was lame, and whom therefore none of the Bacchiadae would consent to marry; so she was taken to wife by Aetion, son of Echecrates, a man of the township of Petra, who was, however, by descent of the race of the Lapithae, and of the house of Caeneus. Aetion, as he had no child either by this wife, or by any other, went to Delphi to consult the oracle concerning the matter. Scarcely had he entered the temple when the priestess saluted him in these words:

No one honours thee now, Aetion, worthy of honour;
Labda shall soon be a mother—her offspring a rock, that will
      one day
Fall on the kingly race, and right the city of Corinth.

By some chance this address of the oracle to Aetion came to the
ears of the Bacchiadae, who till then had been unable to perceive the meaning of another earlier prophecy which likewise
bore upon Corinth, and pointed to the same event as Aetion's
prediction. It was the following:

When mid the rocks an eagle shall bear a carnivorous lion,
Mighty and fierce, he shall loosen the limbs of many beneath
      them—
Brood ye well upon this, all ye Corinthian people,
Ye who dwell by fair Peirene, and beetling Corinth.

The Bacchiadae had possessed this oracle for some time, but
they were quite at a loss to know what it meant until they heard
the response given to Aetion; then however they at once perceived its meaning, since the two agreed so well together. Nevertheless, though the bearing of the first prophecy was now clear
to them, they remained quiet, intending to put to death the
child which Aetion was expecting. As soon, therefore, as his wᵻᵉe
was delivered, they sent ten of their number to the township
where Aetion lived, with orders to make away with the baby.
So the men came to Petra, and went into Aetion's house, and
there asked if they might see the child; and Labda, who knew
nothing of their purpose, but thought their inquiries arose from
a kindly feeling towards her husband, brought the child, and
laid him in the arms of one of them. Now they had agreed by
the way that whoever first got hold of the child should dash it
against the ground. It happened, however, by a providential
chance, that the babe, just as Labda put him into the man's arms,
smiled in his face. The man saw the smile, and was touched
with pity, so that he could not kill it; he therefore passed it on

to his next neighbour, who gave it to a third; and so it went through all the ten without any one choosing to be the murderer. The mother received her child back, and the men went out of the house, and stood near the door, and there blamed and reproached one another; chiefly however accusing the man who had first had the child in his arms, because he had not done as had been agreed upon. At last, after much time had been thus spent, they resolved to go into the house again and all take part in the murder. But it was fated that evil should come upon Corinth from the progeny of Aetion, and so it chanced that Labda, as she stood near the door, heard all that the men said to one another, and fearful of their changing their mind, and returning to destroy her baby, she carried him off and hid him in what seemed to her the most unlikely place to be suspected, a cypsel or corn-bin. She knew that if they came back to look for the child, they would search all her house; and so indeed they did, but not finding the child after looking everywhere, they thought it best to go away, and declare to those by whom they had been sent that they had done their bidding. And thus they reported on their return home. Aetion's son grew up, and, in remembrance of the danger from which he had escaped, was named Cypselus, after the corn-bin. When he reached to man's estate, he went to Delphi, and on consulting the oracle, received a response which was two-sided. It was the following:

See there comes to my dwelling a man much favour'd of fortune,
Cypselus, son of Aetion, and king of the glorious Corinth,—
He and his children too, but not his children's children.

Such was the oracle; and Cypselus put so much faith in it that he forthwith made his attempt, and thereby became master of Corinth. Having thus got the tyranny, he showed himself a harsh ruler—many of the Corinthians he drove into banishment, many he deprived of their fortunes, and a still greater number of their lives. His reign lasted thirty years, and was prosperous to its close; insomuch that he left the government to Periander, his son. This prince at the beginning of his reign

was of a milder temper than his father; but after he corre-
sponded by means of messengers with Thrasybulus, tyrant of
Miletus, he became even more sanguinary. On one occasion he
sent a herald to ask Thrasybulus what mode of government it
was safest to set up in order to rule with honour. Thrasybulus
led the messenger without the city, and took him into a field of
corn, through which he began to walk, while he asked him again
and again concerning his coming from Corinth, ever as he went
breaking off and throwing away all such ears of corn as over-
topped the rest. In this way he went through the whole field,
and destroyed all the best and richest part of the crop; then,
without a word, he sent the messenger back. On the return of
the man to Corinth, Periander was eager to know what Thrasybulus had counselled, but the messenger reported that he had
said nothing; and he wondered that Periander had sent him to
so strange a man, who seemed to have lost his senses, since he
did nothing but destroy his own property. And upon this he
told how Thrasybulus had behaved at the interview. Periander,
perceiving what the action meant, and knowing that Thrasybulus advised the destruction of all the leading citizens, treated
his subjects from this time forward with the very greatest
cruelty. Where Cypselus had spared any, and had neither put
them to death nor banished them, Periander completed what his
father had left unfinished. One day he stripped all the women
of Corinth stark naked, for the sake of his own wife Melissa.
He had sent messengers into Thesprotia to consult the oracle
of the dead upon the Acheron concerning a pledge which had
been given into his charge by a stranger, and Melissa appeared,
but refused to speak or tell where the pledge was. 'She was
chill,' she said, 'having no clothes; the garments buried with
her were of no manner of use, since they had not been burnt.
And this should be her token to Periander, that what she said
was true—the oven was cold when he baked his loaves in it.'
When this message was brought him, Periander knew the token
for he had had intercourse with the dead body of Melissa;
wherefore he straightway made proclamation, that all the wives
of the Corinthians should go forth to the temple of Hera. So

the women apparelled themselves in their bravest, and went forth, as if to a festival. Then, with the help of his guards, whom he had placed for the purpose, he stripped them one and all, making no difference between the free women and the slaves; and, taking their clothes to a pit, he called on the name of Melissa, and burnt the whole heap. This done, he sent a second time to the oracle, and Melissa's ghost told him where he would find the stranger's pledge. Such, Lacedaemonians, is tyranny, and such are the deeds which spring from it. We Corinthians marvelled greatly when we first knew of your having sent for Hippias, and now it surprises us still more to hear you speak as you do. We adjure you, by the common gods of Greece, plant not despots in her cities. If however you are determined, if you persist, against all justice, in seeking to restore Hippias, know, at least, that the Corinthians will not approve your conduct."

93. When Sosicles, the deputy from Corinth, had thus spoken, Hippias replied, and, invoking the same gods, he said, "Of a surety the Corinthians will, beyond all others, regret the Pisistratidae, when the fated days come for them to be distressed by the Athenians." Hippias spoke thus because he knew the prophecies better than any man living. But the rest of the allies, who till Sosicles spoke had remained quiet, when they heard him utter his thoughts thus boldly, all together broke silence, and declared themselves of the same mind; and withal, they conjured the Lacedaemonians not to revolutionise a Grecian city. And in this way the enterprise came to nought.

94. Hippias hereupon withdrew, and Amyntas the Macedonian offered him the city of Anthemus, while the Thessalians were willing to give him Iolcos: but he would accept neither the one nor the other, preferring to go back to Sigeum, which city Pisistratus had taken by force of arms from the Mytilenaeans. Pisistratus, when he became master of the place, established there as tyrant, his own bastard son, Hegesistratus, whose mother was an Argive woman. But this prince was not allowed to enjoy peaceably what his father had made over to him; for during very many years there had been war between the Athe-

nians of Sigeum and the Mytilenaeans of the city called Achilleum. They of Mytilene insisted on having the place restored to them: but the Athenians refused, since they argued that the Aeolians had no better claim to the Trojan territory than themselves, or than any of the other Greeks who helped Menelaus on occasion of the rape of Helen.

95. War accordingly continued, with many and various incidents, whereof the following was one. In a battle which was gained by the Athenians, the poet Alcaeus took to flight, and saved himself, but lost his arms, which fell into the hands of the conquerors. They hung them up in the temple of Athena at Sigeum, and Alcaeus made a poem describing his misadventure, to his friend Melanippus, and sent it to him at Mytilene. The Mytilenaeans and Athenians were reconciled by Periander, the son of Cypselus, who was chosen by both parties as arbiter—he decided that they should each retain that of which they were at the time possessed, and Sigeum passed in this way under the dominion of Athens.

96. On the return of Hippias to Asia from Lacedaemon, he moved heaven and earth to set Artaphernes against the Athenians, and did all that lay in his power to bring Athens into subjection to himself and Darius. So when the Athenians learnt what he was about, they sent envoys to Sardis, and exhorted the Persians not to lend an ear to the Athenian exiles. Artaphernes told them in reply that if they wished to remain safe, they must receive back Hippias. The Athenians, when this answer was reported to them, determined not to consent, and therefore made up their minds to be at open enmity with the Persians.

97. The Athenians had come to this decision, and were already in bad odour with the Persians, when Aristagoras the Milesian, dismissed from Sparta by Cleomenes the Lacedaemonian, arrived at Athens. He knew that, after Sparta, Athens was the most powerful of the Grecian states. Accordingly he appeared before the people, and, as he had done at Sparta, spoke to them of the good things which there were in Asia, and of the Persian mode of fight—how they used neither shield nor spear, and were very easy to conquer. All this he urged, and reminded

them also, that Miletus was a colony from Athens, and therefore ought to receive their succour, since they were so powerful
—and in the earnestness of his entreaties, he cared little what he
promised—till, at the last, he prevailed and won them over. It
seems indeed to be easier to deceive a multitude than one man
—for Aristagoras, though he failed to impose on Cleomenes,
the Lacedaemonian, succeeded with the Athenians, who were
30,000.[20] Won by his persuasions, they voted that twenty ships
should be sent to the aid of the Ionians, under the command of
Melanthius, one of the citizens, a man of mark in every way.
These ships were the beginning of mischief both to the Greeks
and to the barbarians.[21]

98. Aristagoras sailed away in advance, and when he reached
Miletus, devised a plan, from which no manner of advantage
could possibly accrue to the Ionians; indeed, in forming it, he
did not aim at their benefit, but his sole wish was to annoy King
Darius. He sent a messenger into Phrygia to those Paeonians
who had been led away captive by Megabazus from the river
Strymon, and who now dwelt by themselves in Phrygia, having
a tract of land and a hamlet of their own. This man, when he
reached the Paeonians, spoke thus to them, "Men of Paeonia,
Aristagoras, despot of Miletus, has sent me to you, to inform
you that you may now escape, if you choose to follow the advice
he proffers. All Ionia has revolted from the king, and the way is
open to you to return to your own land. You have only to contrive to reach the sea-coast; the rest shall be our business."

When the Paeonians heard this, they rejoiced exceedingly,
and, taking with them their wives and children, they made all
speed to the coast; a few only remaining in Phrygia through
fear. The rest, having reached the sea, crossed over to Chios,
where they had just landed, when a great troop of Persian horse
came following upon their heels, and seeking to overtake them.

[20] This was the conventional estimate of the number of citizens in Herodotus' time. The census of 317 B.C. gives 21,000 but the number was
greater in the fifth century.
[21] Herodotus treats the Ionian revolt as a scheme of desperate adven-
turers despite the evidence he presents for a Persian project of conquest.

Not succeeding, however, they sent a message across to Chios, and begged the Paeonians to come back again. These last refused, and were conveyed by the Chians from Chios to Lesbos, and by the Lesbians thence to Doriscus; from which place they made their way on foot to Paeonia.

99. The Athenians now arrived with a fleet of twenty sail, and brought also in their company five triremes of the Eretrians; which had joined the expedition, not so much out of goodwill towards Athens, as to pay a debt which they already owed to the people of Miletus. For in the old war between the Chalcideans and Eretrians,[22] the Milesians fought on the Eretrian side throughout, while the Chalcideans had the help of the Samian people. Aristagoras, on their arrival, assembled the rest of his allies, and proceeded to attack Sardis, not however leading the army in person, but appointing to the command his own brother Charopinus, and Hermophantus, one of the citizens, while he himself remained behind in Miletus.

100. The Ionians sailed with this fleet to Ephesus, and, leaving their ships at Coressus in the Ephesian territory, took guides from the city, and went up the country, with a great host. They marched along the course of the river Cayster, and, crossing over the ridge of Tmolus, came down upon Sardis and took it, no man opposing them; the whole city fell into their hands, except only the citadel, which Artaphernes defended in person, having with him no contemptible force.

101. Though, however, they took the city, they did not succeed in plundering it; for, as the houses in Sardis were most of them built of reeds, and even the few which were of brick had a reed thatching for their roof, one of them was no sooner fired by a soldier than the flames ran speedily from house to house, and spread over the whole place. As the fire raged, the Lydians, and such Persians as were in the city, inclosed on every side by the flames, which had seized all the outskirts of the town, and finding themselves unable to get out, came in crowds into the market-place, and gathered themselves upon the banks of the

[22] In the seventh century the commercial rivalry of these two cities apparently involved most of Greece in the struggle.

Pactolus. This stream, which comes down from Mount Tmolus,
and brings the Sardians a quantity of gold-dust, runs directly
through the market-place of Sardis, and joins the Hermus, before that river reaches the sea. So the Lydians and Persians,
prought together in this way in the market-place and about the
Pactolus, were forced to stand on their defence; and the Ionians,
when they saw the enemy in part resisting, in part pouring towards them in dense crowds, took fright, and drawing off to the
ridge which is called Tmolus, when night came, went back to
their ships.

102. Sardis however was burnt, and, among other buildings,
a temple of the native goddess Cybele was destroyed; which was
the reason afterwards alleged by the Persians for setting on fire
the temples of the Greeks. As soon as what had happened was
known, all the Persians who were stationed on this side the
Halys drew together, and brought help to the Lydians. Finding
however, when they arrived, that the Ionians had already withdrawn from Sardis, they set off, and, following close upon their
track, came up with them at Ephesus. The Ionians drew out
against them in battle array, and a fight ensued, wherein the
Greeks had very greatly the worse. Vast numbers were slain by
the Persians: among other men of note, they killed the captain
of the Eretrians, a certain Eualcidas, a man who had gained
crowns at the games, and received much praise from Simonides
the Cean. Such as made their escape from the battle, dispersed
among the several cities.

103. So ended this encounter. Afterwards the Athenians quite
forsook the Ionians, and, though Aristagoras besought them
much by his ambassadors, refused to give him any further help.
Still the Ionians, notwithstanding this desertion, continued unceasingly their preparations to carry on the war against the Persian king, which their late conduct towards him had rendered
unavoidable. Sailing into the Hellespont, they brought Byzantium, and all the other cities in that quarter, under their sway.
Again, quitting the Hellespont, they went to Caria, and won the
greater part of the Carians to their side; while Caunus, which

had formerly refused to join with them, after the burning of
Sardis, came over likewise.

104. All the Cyprians too, excepting those of Amathus, of
their own proper motion espoused the Ionian cause. The occasion of their revolting from the Medes was the following. There
was a certain Onesilus, younger brother of Gorgus, king of
Salamis, and son of Chersis, who was son of Siromus, and grandson of Evelthon. This man had often in former times entreated
Gorgus to rebel against the king; but, when he heard of the revolt of the Ionians, he left him no peace with his importunity.
As, however, Gorgus would not hearken to him, he watched his
occasion, and when his brother had gone outside the town, he
with his partisans closed the gates upon him. Gorgus, thus deprived of his city, fled to the Medes; and Onesilus, being now
king of Salamis, sought to bring about a revolt of the whole of
Cyprus. All were prevailed on except the Amathusians, who refused to listen to him; whereupon Onesilus sat down before
Amathus, and laid siege to it.

105. While Onesilus was engaged in the siege of Amathus,
King Darius received tidings of the taking and burning of Sardis
by the Athenians and Ionians; and at the same time he learnt
that the author of the league, the man by whom the whole matter had been planned and contrived, was Aristagoras the Milesian. It is said he no sooner understood what had happened,
than, laying aside all thought concerning the Ionians, who
would, he was sure, pay dear for their rebellion, he asked who
the Athenians were and, being informed, called for his bow, and
placing an arrow on the string, shot upward into the sky, saying, as he let fly the shaft, "Grant me, Zeus, to revenge myself
on the Athenians!" After this speech, he bade one of his servants every day, when his dinner was spread, three times repeat
these words to him, "Master, remember the Athenians."

106. Then he summoned into his presence Histiaeus of Miletus, whom he had kept at his court for so long a time; and on
his appearance addressed him thus, "I am told, Histiaeus, that
your lieutenant, to whom you gave Miletus in charge, has raised

a rebellion against me. He has brought men from the other continent to contend with me, and, prevailing on the Ionians—whose conduct I shall know how to recompense—to join with this force, he has robbed me of Sardis. Is this as it should be, do you think? Or can it have been done without your knowledge and advice? Beware lest it be found hereafter that the blame of these acts is yours."

Histiaeus answered, "What words are these, O king, to which you have uttered? I advise aught from which unpleasantness of any kind, little or great, should come to you! What could I gain by so doing? Or what is there that I lack now? Have I not all that you have, and am I not thought worthy to partake all your counsels? If my lieutenant has indeed done as you say, be sure he has done it all of his own head. For my part, I do not think it can really be that the Milesians and my lieutenant have raised a rebellion against you. But if they have indeed done so, and the tidings are true which have come to you, judge how ill-advised you were to remove me from the sea-coast. The Ionians, it seems, have waited till I was no longer in sight, and then sought to execute that which they long ago desired; whereas, if I had been there, not a single city would have stirred. Let me then hasten at my best speed to Ionia, that I may place matters there upon their former footing, and deliver up to you the deputy of Miletus, who has caused all the troubles. Having managed this business to your heart's content, I swear by all the gods of the royal house, I will not put off the clothes in which I reach Ionia, till I have made Sardinia, the biggest island in the world, your tributary."

107. Histiaeus spoke thus, wishing to deceive the king; and Darius, persuaded by his words, let him go; only bidding him be sure to do as he had promised, and afterwards come back to Susa.

108. In the mean time—while the tidings of the burning of Sardis were reaching the king, and Darius was shooting the arrow and having the conference with Histiaeus, and the latter, by permission of Darius, was hastening down to the sea—in Cyprus the following events took place. Tidings came to Onesilus, the

Salaminian, who was still besieging Amathus, that a certain
Artybius, a Persian, was looked for to arrive in Cyprus with a
great Persian armament. So Onesilus, when the news reached
him, sent off heralds to all parts of Ionia, and begged the Ionians
to give him aid. After brief deliberation, these last in full force
passed over into the island, and the Persians about the same
time crossed in their ships from Cilicia, and proceeded by land
to attack Salamis, while the Phoenicians, with the fleet, sailed
round the promontory which goes by the name of the Keys of
Cyprus.

109. In this posture of affairs the princes of Cyprus called
together the captains of the Ionians, and thus addressed them,
"Men of Ionia, we Cyprians leave it to you to choose whether
you will fight with the Persians or with the Phoenicians. If it be
your pleasure to try your strength on land against the Persians,
come on shore at once, and array yourselves for the battle; we
will then embark aboard your ships and engage the Phoenicians
by sea. If, on the other hand, you prefer to encounter the
Phoenicians, let that be your task; only be sure, whichever part
you choose, to acquit yourselves so that Ionia and Cyprus, as
far as depends on you, may preserve their freedom."

The Ionians answered, "The commonwealth of Ionia sent us
here to guard the sea, not to make over our ships to you, and
engage with the Persians on shore. We will therefore keep the
post which has been assigned to us, and seek therein to be of
some service. Do you, remembering what you suffered when you
were the slaves of the Medes, behave like brave warriors."

110. Such was the reply of the Ionians. Not long afterwards
the Persians advanced into the plain before Salamis, and the
Cyprian kings ranged their troops in order of battle against
them, placing them so that while the rest of the Cyprians were
drawn up against the auxiliaries of the enemy, the choicest
troops of the Salaminians and the Solians were set to oppose the
Persians. At the same time Onesilus, of his own accord, took
post opposite to Artybius, the Persian general.

111. Now Artybius rode a horse which had been trained to
rear up against a foot-soldier. Onesilus, informed of this, called

to him his shieldbearer, who was a Carian by nation, a man well skilled in war, and of daring courage; and thus addressed him, "I hear," he said, "that the horse which Artybius rides, rears up and attacks with his fore-legs and teeth the man against whom his rider urges him. Consider quickly therefore and tell me which you will undertake to encounter, the steed or the rider?" Then the squire answered him, "Both, my liege, or either, am I ready to undertake, and there is nothing that I will shrink from at your bidding. But I will tell you what seems to me to make most for your interest. As you are a prince and a general, I think you should engage with one who is himself both a prince and also a general. For then, if you slay your adversary, it will redound to your honour, and if he slays you, which may Heaven forefend, yet to fall by the hand of a worthy foe makes death lose half its horror. Leave his war-horse and his retinue to us. And have no fear of the horse's tricks. I promise that this is the last time he will stand up against any one."

112. Thus the Carian spoke, and shortly after, the two hosts joined battle both by sea and land. And here it chanced that by sea the Ionians, who that day fought as they have never done either before or since, defeated the Phoenicians, the Samians especially distinguishing themselves. Meanwhile the combat had begun on land, and the two armies were engaged in a sharp struggle, when thus it fell out in the matter of the generals. Artybius, astride upon his horse, charged down upon Onesilus, who, as he had agreed with his shieldbearer, aimed his blow at the rider; the horse reared and placed his forefeet upon the shield of Onesilus, when the Carian cut at him with a reaping-hook, and severed the two legs from the body. The horse fell upon the spot, and Artybius, the Persian general, with him.

113. In the thick of the fight, Stesanor, tyrant of Curium, who commanded no inconsiderable body of troops, went over with them to the enemy. On this desertion of the Curians—Argive colonists, if report says true—forthwith the war-chariots of the Salaminians followed the example set them, and went over likewise; whereupon victory declared in favour of the Persians;

and the army of the Cyprians being routed, vast numbers were
slain, and among them Onesilus, the son of Chersis, who was the
author of the revolt, and Aristocyprus, king of the Solians. This
Aristocyprus was son of Philocyprus, whom Solon the Athenian,
when he visited Cyprus, praised in his poems beyond all other
sovereigns.

114. The Amathusians, because Onesilus had laid siege to
their town, cut the head off his corpse, and took it with them to
Amathus, where it was set up over the gates. Here it hung till it
became hollow; whereupon a swarm of bees took possession of
it, and filled it with a honeycomb. On seeing this the Amathusians consulted the oracle, and were commanded to take down
the head and bury it, and thenceforth to regard Onesilus as a
hero, and offer sacrifice to him year by year; so it would go the
better with them. And to this day the Amathusians do as they
were then bidden.

115. As for the Ionians who had gained the sea-fight, when
they found that the affairs of Onesilus were utterly lost and
ruined, and that siege was laid to all the cities of Cyprus excepting Salamis, which the inhabitants had surrendered to Gorgus,
the former king—forthwith they left Cyprus, and sailed away
home. Of the cities which were besieged, Soli held out the longest: the Persians took it by undermining the wall in the fifth
month from the beginning of the siege.

116. Thus, after enjoying a year of freedom, the Cyprians
were enslaved for the second time. Meanwhile Daurises, who
was married to one of the daughters of Darius, together with
Hymeas, Otanes, and other Persian captains, who were likewise
married to daughters of the king, after pursuing the Ionians who
had fought at Sardis, defeating them, and driving them to their
ships, divided their efforts against the different cities, and proceeded in succession to take and sack them all.

117. Daurises attacked the towns upon the Hellespont, and
took in as many days the five cities of Dardanus, Abydus, Per-
cote, Lampsacus, and Paesus. From Paesus he marched against
Parium, but on his way receiving intelligence that the Carians

had made common cause with the Ionians, and thrown off the Persian yoke, he turned round, and leaving the Hellespont, marched away towards Caria.

118. The Carians by some chance got information of this movement before Daurises arrived, and drew together their strength to a place called the White Columns, which is on the river Marsyas, a stream running from the Idrian country, and emptying itself into the Maeander. Here when they were met, many plans were put forth; but the best, in my judgment, was that of Pixodarus, the son of Mausolus, a Cindyan, who was married to a daughter of Syennesis, the Cilician king. His advice was, that the Carians should cross the Maeander, and fight with the river at their back; that so, all chance of flight being cut off, they might be forced to stand their ground, and have their natural courage raised to a still higher pitch.[23] His opinion, however, did not prevail; it was thought best to make the enemy have the Maeander behind them; that so, if they were defeated in the battle and put to flight, they might have no retreat open, but be driven headlong into the river.

119. The Persians soon afterwards approached, and, crossing the Maeander, engaged the Carians upon the banks of the Marsyas; where for a long time the battle was stoutly contested, but at last the Carians were defeated, being overpowered by numbers. On the side of the Persians there fell 2,000, while the Carians had not fewer than 10,000 slain. Such as escaped from the field of battle collected together at Labranda, in the vast precinct of Zeus lord of Armies—a deity worshipped only by the Carians—and in the sacred grove of plane-trees. Here they deliberated as to the best means of saving themselves, doubting whether they would fare better if they gave themselves up to the Persians, or if they abandoned Asia for ever.

120. As they were debating these matters a body of Milesians and allies came to their assistance; whereupon the Carians, dismissing their former thoughts, prepared themselves afresh for war, and on the approach of the Persians gave them battle a

---

[23] Herodotus really thinks that an army should fight where no retreat is possible.

second time. They were defeated, however, with still greater loss than before; and while all the troops engaged suffered severely, the blow fell with most force on the Milesians.

121. The Carians, some while after, repaired their ill fortune in another action. Understanding that the Persians were about to attack their cities, they laid an ambush for them on the road which leads to Pedasus; the Persians, who were making a night-march, fell into the trap, and the whole army was destroyed, together with the generals, Daurises, Amorges, and Sisimaces: Myrsus too, the son of Gyges, was killed at the same time. The leader of the ambush was Heraclides, the son of Ibanolis a man of Mylasa. Such was the way in which these Persians perished.

122. In the meantime Hymeas, who was likewise one of those by whom the Ionians were pursued after their attack on Sardis, directing his course towards the Propontis, took Cius, a city of Mysia. Learning, however, that Daurises had left the Hellespont, and was gone into Caria, he in his turn quitted the Propontis, and marching with the army under his command to the Hellespont, reduced all the Aeolians of the Troad, and likewise conquered the Gergithae, a remnant of the ancient Teucrians. He did not, however, quit the Troad, but, after gaining these successes, was himself carried off by disease.

123. After his death, which happened as I have related, Artaphernes, the satrap of Sardis, and Otanes, the third general, were directed to undertake the conduct of the war against Ionia and the neighbouring Aeolis. By them Clazomenae in the former, and Cyme in the latter, were recovered.

124. As the cities fell one after another, Aristagoras the Milesian (who was in truth, as he now plainly showed, a man of but little courage), notwithstanding that it was he who had caused the disturbances in Ionia and made so great a commotion, began, seeing his danger, to look about for means of escape. Being convinced that it was in vain to endeavour to overcome King Darius, he called his brothers-in-arms together, and laid before them the following project: "It would be well," he said, "to have some place of refuge, in case they were driven out of Miletus. Should he go out at the head of a colony to

Sardinia, or should he sail to Myrcinus in Edonia, which Histiaeus had received as a gift from King Darius, and had begun to fortify?"

125. To this question of Aristagoras, Hecataeus, the historian, son of Hegesander, made answer, that in his judgment neither place was suitable. "Aristagoras should build a fort," he said, "in the island of Leros, and if driven from Miletus, should go there and bide his time; from Leros attacks might readily be made, and he might re-establish himself in Miletus." Such was the advice given by Hecataeus.

126. Aristagoras, however, was bent on retiring to Myrcinus. Accordingly he put the government of Miletus into the hands of one of the chief citizens, named Pythagoras, and taking with him all who liked to go, sailed to Thrace, and there made himself master of the place in question. From thence he proceeded to attack the Thracians, but here he was cut off with his whole army, while besieging a city whose defenders were anxious to accept terms of surrender.

The Sixth Book, Entitled

ERATO

1. Aristagoras, the author of the Ionian revolt, perished in the way which I have described. Meanwhile Histiaeus, tyrant of Miletus, who had been allowed by Darius to leave Susa, came down to Sardis. On his arrival, being asked by Artaphernes, the Sardian satrap, what he thought was the reason that the Ionians had rebelled, he made answer that he could not conceive, and it had astonished him greatly, pretending to be quite unconscious of the whole business. Artaphernes, however, who perceived that he was dealing dishonestly, and who had in fact full knowledge of the whole history of the outbreak, said to him, "I will tell you how the case stands, Histiaeus: this shoe is your stitching; Aristagoras only put it on."

2. Such was the remark made by Artaphernes concerning the rebellion. Histiaeus, alarmed at the knowledge which he displayed, as soon as night fell, fled away to the coast. Thus he forfeited his word to Darius; for though he had pledged himself to bring Sardinia, the biggest island in the whole world, under the Persian yoke, he in reality sought to obtain the direction of the war against the king. Crossing over to Chios, he was there laid in bonds by the inhabitants, who accused him of intending some mischief against them in the interest of Darius. However, when the whole truth was laid before them, and they found that Histiaeus was in reality a foe to the king, they forthwith set him at large again.

3. After this the Ionians inquired of him for what reason he

had so strongly urged Aristagoras to revolt from the king, thereby doing their nation so ill a service. In reply, he took good care not to disclose to them the real cause, but told them that King Darius had intended to remove the Phoenicians from their own country, and place them in Ionia, while he planted the Ionians in Phoenicia, and that it was for this reason he sent Aristagoras the order. Now it was not true that the king had entertained any such intention, but Histiaeus succeeded hereby in arousing the fears of the Ionians.

4. After this, Histiaeus, by means of a certain Hermippus, a native of Atarneus, sent letters to many of the Persians in Sardis, who had before held some discourse with him concerning a revolt. Hermippus, however, instead of conveying them to the persons to whom they were addressed, delivered them into the hands of Artaphernes, who, perceiving what was on foot, commanded Hermippus to deliver the letters according to their addresses, and then bring him back the answers which were sent to Histiaeus. The traitors being in this way discovered, Artaphernes put a number of Persians to death, and caused a commotion in Sardis.

5. As for Histiaeus, when his hopes in this matter were disappointed, he persuaded the Chians to carry him back to Miletus; but the Milesians were too well pleased at having got quit of Aristagoras to be anxious to receive another tyrant into their country; besides which, they had now tasted liberty. They therefore opposed his return; and when he endeavoured to force an entrance during the night, one of the inhabitants even wounded him in the thigh. Having been thus rejected from his country, he went back to Chios; whence, after failing in an attempt to induce the Chians to give him ships, he crossed over to Mytilene, where he succeeded in obtaining vessels from the Lesbians. They fitted out a squadron of eight triremes, and sailed with him to the Hellespont, where they took up their station, and proceeded to seize all the vessels which passed out from the Euxine, unless the crews declared themselves ready to obey his orders.

6. While Histiaeus and the Mytilenaeans were thus em-

ployed, Miletus was expecting an attack from a vast armament, which comprised both a fleet and also a land force. The Persian captains had drawn their several detachments together, and formed them into a single army; and had resolved to pass over all the other cities, which they regarded as of lesser account, and to march straight on Miletus. Of the naval states, Phoenicia showed the greatest zeal; but the fleet was composed likewise of the Cyprians (who had so lately been brought under), the Cilicians, and also the Egyptians.

7. While the Persians were thus making preparations against Miletus and Ionia, the Ionians, informed of their intent, sent their deputies to the Panionium, and held a council upon the state of their affairs. Here it was determined that no land force should be collected to oppose the Persians, but that the Milesians should be left to defend their own walls as they could;[1] at the same time they agreed that the whole naval force of the states, not excepting a single ship, should be equipped, and should muster at Lade, a small island lying off Miletus—to give battle on behalf of the place.

8. Presently the Ionians began to assemble in their ships, and with them came the Aeolians of Lesbos; and in this way they marshalled their line: The wing towards the east was formed of the Milesians themselves, who furnished eighty ships; next to them came the Prienians with twelve, and the Myusians with three ships; after the Myusians were stationed the Teians, whose ships were seventeen; then the Chians, who furnished 100. The Erythraeans and Phocaeans followed, the former with eight, the latter with three ships; beyond the Phocaeans were the Lesbians, furnishing seventy; last of all came the Samians, forming the western wing, and furnishing sixty vessels. The fleet amounted in all to 353 triremes. Such was the number on the Ionian side.

[1] There is no reason to suppose that the Ionians came to this decision from jealousy of Milesian influence. They always recognised the sea as their own proper element, and they knew, as well as the Persians, that so long as they could maintain the mastery at sea, Miletus and the other maritime towns were safe.

9. On the side of the barbarians the number of vessels was 600. These assembled off the coast of Milesia, while the land army collected upon the shore; but the leaders, learning the strength of the Ionian fleet, began to fear lest they might fail to defeat them, in which case, not having the mastery at sea, they would be unable to reduce Miletus, and might in consequence receive rough treatment at the hands of Darius. So when they thought of all these things, they resolved on the following course: Calling together the Ionian tyrants, who had fled to the Medes for refuge when Aristagoras deposed them from their governments, and who were now in camp, having joined in the expedition against Miletus, the Persians addressed them thus, "Men of Ionia, now is the fit time to show your zeal for the house of the king. Use your best efforts, every one of you, to detach your fellow-countrymen from the general body. Hold forth to them the promise that if they submit, no harm shall happen to them on account of their rebellion; their temples shall not be burnt, nor any of their private buildings; neither shall they be treated with greater harshness than before the outbreak. But if they refuse to yield, and determine to try the chance of a battle, threaten them with the fate which shall assuredly overtake them in that case. Tell them, when they are vanquished in fight, they shall be enslaved; their boys shall be made eunuchs, and their maidens transported to Bactra; while their country shall be delivered into the hands of foreigners."

10. Thus spoke the Persians. The Ionian tyrants sent accordingly by night to their respective citizens, and reported the words of the Persians; but the people were all obstinate, and refused to betray their countrymen, those of each state thinking that they alone had had overtures made to them. Now these events happened on the first appearance of the Persians before Miletus.

11. Afterwards, while the Ionian fleet was still assembled at Lade, councils were held, and speeches made by various persons —among the rest by Dionysius, the Phocaean captain, who thus expressed himself, "Our affairs hang on the razor's edge, men of Ionia, either to be free or to be slaves; and slaves, too, who

have shown themselves runaways. Now then you have to choose
whether you will endure hardships, and so for the present lead a
life of toil, but thereby gain ability to overcome your enemies
and establish your own freedom; or whether you will persist in
this slothfulness and disorder, in which case I see no hope of
your escaping the king's vengeance for your rebellion. I beseech
you, be persuaded by me, and trust yourselves to my guidance.
Then, if the gods only hold the balance fairly between us, I
undertake to say that our foes will either decline a battle, or, if
they fight, suffer complete discomfiture."

12. These words prevailed with the Ionians, and forthwith
they committed themselves to Dionysius; whereupon he proceeded every day to make the ships move in column, and the
rowers ply their oars, and exercise themselves in breaking the
line;[2] while the marines were held under arms, and the vessels
were kept, till evening fell, upon their anchors, so that the men
had nothing but toil from morning even to night. Seven days did
the Ionians continue obedient, and do whatsoever he bade
them; but on the eighth day, worn out by the hardness of the
work and the heat of the sun, and quite unaccustomed to such
fatigues, they began to confer together, and to say one to another, "What god have we offended to bring upon ourselves such
a punishment as this? Fools and distracted that we were, to put
ourselves into the hands of this Phocaean braggart, who furnishes but three ships to the fleet. He, now that he has got us,
plagues us in the most desperate fashion; many of us, in consequence, have fallen sick already—many more expect to follow.
We had better suffer anything rather than these hardships; even
the slavery with which we are threatened, however harsh, can be
no worse that our present thraldom. Come, let us refuse him
obedience." So saying, they ceased to obey his orders, and
pitched their tents, as if they had been soldiers, upon the island,
where they reposed under the shade all the day, and refused to
go aboard the ships and train themselves.

[2] This was the most important naval manoeuvre with which the Greeks
were acquainted. It consisted in breaking through and then turning rapidly to ram the enemy ship on its defenceless side or stern.

13. Now when the Samian captains perceived what was taking place, they were more inclined than before to accept the terms which Aeaces, the son of Syloson, had been authorised by the Persians to offer them, on condition of their deserting from the confederacy. For they saw that all was disorder among the Ionians, and they felt also that it was hopeless to contend with the power of the king; since if they defeated the fleet which had been sent against them, they knew that another would come five times as great. So they took advantage of the occasion which now offered; and as soon as ever they saw the Ionians refuse to work, hastened gladly to provide for the safety of their temples and their properties. This Aeaces, who made the overtures to the Samians, was the son of Syloson, and grandson of the earlier Aeaces. He had formerly been tyrant of Samos, but was ousted from his government by Aristagoras the Milesian, at the same time with the other tyrants of the Ionians.

14. The Phoenicians soon afterwards sailed to the attack, and the Ionians likewise put themselves in line, and went out to meet them. When they had now neared one another, and joined battle, which of the Ionians fought like brave men and which like cowards, I cannot declare with any certainty, for charges are brought on all sides; but the tale goes that the Samians, according to the agreement which they had made with Aeaces, hoisted sail, and quitting their post bore away for Samos, except eleven ships, whose captains gave no heed to the orders of the commanders, but remained and took part in the battle. The state of Samos, in consideration of this action, granted to these men, as an acknowledgment of their bravery, the honour of having their names, and the names of their fathers, inscribed upon a pillar, which still stands in the market-place. The Lesbians also, when they saw the Samians, who were drawn up next them, begin to fly, themselves did the like; and the example, once set, was followed by the greater number of the Ionians.

15. Of those who remained and fought, none were so rudely handled as the Chians, who displayed prodigies of valour, and disdained to play the part of cowards. They furnished to the

common fleet, as I mentioned above, 100 ships, having each of them forty armed citizens, and those picked men, on board; and when they saw the greater portion of the allies betraying the common cause, they for their part, scorning to imitate the base conduct of these traitors, although they were left almost alone and unsupported, a very few friends continuing to stand by them, notwithstanding went on with the fight, and ofttimes cut the line of the enemy, until at last, after they had taken very many of their adversaries' ships, they ended by losing more than half of their own. Hereupon, with the remainder of their vessels, the Chians fled away to their own country.

16. As for such of their ships as were damaged and disabled, these, being pursued by the enemy, made straight for Mycale, where the crews ran them ashore, and abandoning them began their march along the continent. Happening in their way upon the territory of Ephesus, they tried to cross it; but here a dire misfortune befell them. It was night, and the Ephesian women chanced to be engaged in celebrating the Thesmophoria—the previous calamity of the Chians had not been heard of—so when the Ephesians saw their country invaded by an armed band, they made no question of the new-comers being robbers who purposed to carry off their women; and accordingly they marched out against them in full force, and slew them all. Such were the misfortunes which befell them of Chios.

17. Dionysius, the Phocaean, when he perceived that all was lost, having first captured three ships from the enemy, himself took to flight. He would not, however, return to Phocaea, which he well knew must fall again, like the rest of Ionia, under the Persian yoke; but immediately, as he was, he set sail for Phoeni-cia, and there sunk a number of merchantmen, and gained a great booty; after which he directed his course to Sicily, where he established himself as a pirate, and plundered the Carthaginians and Tyrrhenians, but did no harm to the Greeks.

18. The Persians, when they had vanquished the Ionians in the sea-fight, besieged Miletus both by land and sea, driving mines under the walls, and making use of every known device,

until at length they took the whole town, six years from the time when the revolt first broke out under Aristagoras.[3] All the inhabitants of the city they reduced to slavery, and thus the event tallied with the announcement which had been made by the oracle.

19. For once upon a time, when the Argives had sent to Delphi to consult the god about the safety of their own city, a prophecy was given them, in which others besides themselves were interested; for while it bore in part upon the fortunes of Argos, it touched in a by-clause the fate of the men of Miletus. I shall set down the portion which concerned the Argives when I come to that part of my history, mentioning at present only the passage in which the absent Milesians were spoken of. This passage was as follows:

Then shalt thou, Miletus, so oft the contriver of evil,
Be to many, thyself, a feast and an excellent booty:
Then shall thy matrons wash the feet of long-haired masters;
Others shall then possess our lov'd Didymian temple.

Such a fate now befell the Milesians; for the Persians, who wore their hair long, after killing most of the men, made the women and children slaves; and the sanctuary at Didyma, the oracle no less than the temple, was plundered and burnt; of the riches whereof I have made frequent mention in other parts of my history.

20. Those of the Milesians whose lives were spared, being carried prisoners to Susa, received no ill treatment at the hands of King Darius, but were established by him in Ampe, a city on the shores of the Red sea, near the spot where the Tigris flows into it. Miletus itself, and the plain about the city, were kept by the Persians for themselves, while the hill-country was assigned to the Carians of Pedasus.

21. And now the Sybarites, who after the loss of their city occupied Laus and Scidrus, failed duly to return the former kindness of the Milesians. For these last, when Sybaris was

[3] 494 B.C.

taken by the Crotoniats, made a great mourning, all of them,
youths as well as men, shaving their heads; since Miletus and
Sybaris were, of all the cities whereof we have any knowledge,
the two most closely united to one another. The Athenians, on
the other hand, showed themselves beyond measure afflicted at
the fall of Miletus, in many ways expressing their sympathy,
and especially by their treatment of Phrynichus. For when this
poet brought out upon the stage his drama, *The Capture of
Miletus,* the whole theatre burst into tears, and the people sentenced him to pay a fine of a thousand drachmas, for recalling
to them their own misfortunes. They likewise made a law, that
no one should ever again exhibit that piece.

22. Thus was Miletus bereft of its inhabitants. In Samos, the
people of the richer sort were much displeased with the doings
of the captains, and the dealings they had had with the Medes;
they therefore held a council, very shortly after the sea-fight,
and resolved that they would not remain to become the slaves
of Aeaces and the Persians, but before the tyrant set foot in
their country, would sail away and found a colony in another
land. Now it chanced that about this time the Zanclaeans of
Sicily had sent ambassadors to the Ionians, and invited them to
the Fair Coast, where they wished an Ionian city to be founded.
This place, Fair Coast as it is called, is in the country of the
Sicilians, and is situated in the part of Sicily which looks towards Tyrrhenia. The offer thus made to all the Ionians was
embraced only by the Samians, and by such of the Milesians as
had contrived to effect their escape.

23. Hereupon this is what ensued. The Samians on their voyage reached the country of the Epizephyrian Locrians, at a time
when the Zanclaeans and their king Scythas were engaged in the
siege of a Sicilian town which they hoped to take. Anaxilaus,
tyrant of Rhegium, who was on ill terms with the Zanclaeans,
knowing how matters stood, made application to the Samians,
and persuaded them to give up the thought of Fair Coast, the
place to which they were bound, and to seize Zancle itself, which
was left without men. The Samians followed this counsel and
possessed themselves of the town, which the Zanclaeans no

sooner heard than they hurried to the rescue, calling to their aid
Hippocrates, tyrant of Gela, who was one of their allies. Hippocrates came with his army to their assistance; but on his arrival he seized Scythas, the Zanclaean king, who had just lost
his city, and sent him away in chains, together with his brother
Pythogenes, to the town of Inycus; after which he came to an
understanding with the Samians, exchanged oaths with them,
and agreed to betray the people of Zancle. The reward of his
treachery was to be one-half of the goods and chattels, including
slaves, which the town contained, and all that he could find in
the open country. Upon this Hippocrates seized and bound the
greater number of the Zanclaeans as slaves; delivering, however,
into the hands of the Samians 300 of the principal citizens, to
be slaughtered; but the Samians spared the lives of these persons.

24. Scythas, the king of the Zanclaeans, made his escape
from Inycus, and fled to Himera; whence he passed into Asia,
and went up to the court of Darius. Darius thought him the
most upright of all the Greeks to whom he afforded a refuge, for
with the king's leave he paid a visit to Sicily, and thence returned back to Persia, where he lived in great comfort, and died
by a natural death at an advanced age.

25. Thus did the Samians escape the yoke of the Medes, and
possess themselves without any trouble of Zancle,[4] a most beautiful city. At Samos itself the Phoenicians, after the fight which
had Miletus for its prize was over, re-established Aeaces, the son
of Syloson, upon his throne. This they did by the command of
the Persians, who looked upon Aeaces as one who had rendered
them a high service and therefore deserved well at their hands.
They likewise spared the Samians, on account of the desertion
of their vessels, and did not burn either their city or their temples, as they did those of the other rebels. Immediately after the
fall of Miletus the Persians recovered Caria, bringing some of
the cities over by force, while others submitted of their own
accord.

26. Meanwhile tidings of what had befallen Miletus reached

---

[4] Zancle, the modern Messina.

Histiaeus the Milesian, who was still at Byzantium, employed in intercepting the Ionian merchantmen as they issued from the Euxine. Histiaeus had no sooner heard the news than he gave the Hellespont in charge to Bisaltes, son of Apollophanes, a native of Abydos, and himself, at the head of his Lesbians, set sail for Chios. One of the Chian garrisons which opposed him he engaged at a place called The Hollows, situated in the Chian territory, and of these he slaughtered a vast number; afterwards, by the help of his Lesbians, he reduced all the rest of the Chians, who were weakened by their losses in the sea-fight, Polichne, a city of Chios, serving him as headquarters.

27. It mostly happens that there is some warning when great misfortunes are about to befall a state or nation; and so it was in this instance, for the Chians had previously had some strange tokens sent to them. A choir of 100 of their youths had been dispatched to Delphi, and of these only two had returned, the remaining ninety-eight having been carried off by a pestilence. Likewise, about the same time, and very shortly before the sea-fight, the roof of a school-house had fallen in upon a number of their boys, who were at lessons, and out of 120 children there was but one left alive. Such were the signs which God sent to warn them. It was very shortly afterwards that the sea-fight happened, which brought the city down upon its knees; and after the sea-fight came the attack of Histiaeus and his Lesbians, to whom the Chians, weakened as they were, furnished an easy conquest.

28. Histiaeus now led a numerous army, composed of Ionians and Aeolians, against Thasos,[5] and had laid siege to the place when news arrived that the Phoenicians were about to quit Miletus and attack the other cities of Ionia. On hearing this, Histiaeus raised the siege of Thasos, and hastened to Lesbos with all his forces. There his army was in great straits for want of food; whereupon Histiaeus left Lesbos and went across to the mainland, intending to cut the crops which were growing in the Atarnean territory, and likewise in the plain of the Caicus, which belonged to Mysia. Now it chanced that a certain Persian

---

[5] The gold mines of Thasos perhaps formed the chief attraction.

named Harpagus was in these regions at the head of an army of
no little strength. He, when Histiaeus landed, marched out to
meet him, and engaging with his forces, destroyed the greater
number of them, and took Histiaeus himself prisoner.

29. Histiaeus fell into the hands of the Persians in the following manner. The Greeks and Persians engaged at Malena,
in the region of Atarneus, and the battle was for a long time
stoutly contested, till at length the cavalry came up, and charging the Greeks, decided the conflict. The Greeks fled, and Histiaeus, who thought that Darius would not punish his fault with
death, showed how he loved his life by the following conduct.
Overtaken in his flight by one of the Persians, who was about
to run him through, he cried aloud in the Persian tongue that he
was Histiaeus the Milesian.

30. Now had he been taken before King Darius I verily believe that he would have received no hurt, but the king would
have freely forgiven him. Artaphernes, however, satrap of Sardis, and his captor Harpagus, on this very account, because they
were afraid that, if he escaped, he would be again received into
high favour by the king, put him to death as soon as he arrived
at Sardis. His body they impaled at that place, while they embalmed his head and sent it up to Susa to the king. Darius, when
he learnt what had taken place, found great fault with the men
engaged in this business for not bringing Histiaeus alive into his
presence, and commanded his servants to wash and dress the
head with all care, and then bury it, as the head of a man who
had been a great benefactor to himself and the Persians. Such
was the sequel of the history of Histiaeus.

31. The naval armament of the Persians wintered at Miletus,
and in the following year proceeded to attack the islands off the
coast, Chios, Lesbos, and Tenedos, which were reduced without
difficulty. Whenever they became masters of an island, the barbarians, in every single instance, netted the inhabitants. Now
the mode in which they practise this netting is the following.
Men join hands, so as to form a line across from the north coast
to the south, and then march through the island from end to end
and hunt out the inhabitants. In like manner the Persians took

also the Ionian towns upon the mainland, not however netting the inhabitants, as it was not possible.

32. And now their generals made good all the threats wherewith they had menaced the Ionians before the battle. For no sooner did they get possession of the towns than they chose out all the best favoured boys, castrated them and made them eunuchs, while the most beautiful of the girls they tore from their homes and sent as presents to the king, at the same time burning the cities themselves, with their temples. Thus were the Ionians for the third time reduced to slavery; once by the Lydians, and a second, and now a third time, by the Persians.

33. The sea force, after quitting Ionia, proceeded to the Hellespont, and took all the towns which lie on the left shore as one sails into the straits. For the cities on the right bank had already been reduced by the land force of the Persians. Now these are the places which border the Hellespont on the European side; the Chersonese, which contains a number of cities, Perinthus, the forts in Thrace, Selybria, and Byzantium. The Byzantines at this time, and their opposite neighbours, the Calchedonians, instead of awaiting the coming of the Phoenicians, quitted their country, and sailing into the Euxine, took up their abode at the city of Mesembria. The Phoenicians, after burning all the places above mentioned, proceeded to Proconnesus and Artaca, which they likewise delivered to the flames; this done, they returned to the Chersonese, being minded to reduce those cities which they had not ravaged in their former cruise. Upon Cyzicus they made no attack at all, as before their coming the inhabitants had made terms with Oebares, the son of Megabazus, and satrap of Dascyleium, and had submitted themselves to the king. In the Chersonese the Phoenicians subdued all the cities, excepting Cardia.

34. Up to this time the cities of the Chersonese had been under the government of Miltiades, the son of Cimon, and grandson of Stesagoras, to whom they had descended from Miltiades, the son of Cypselus, who obtained possession of them in the following manner. The Dolonci, a Thracian tribe, to whom the Chersonese at that time belonged, being harassed by a war in

which they were engaged with the Apsinthians, sent their princes
to Delphi to consult the oracle about the matter. The reply of
the priestess bade them take back with them as a colonist into
their country the man who should first offer them hospitality
after they quitted the temple. The Dolonci, following the sacred
road,[6] passed through the regions of Phocis and Boeotia; after
which, as still no one invited them in, they turned aside, and
travelled to Athens.

35. Now Pisistratus was at this time sole lord of Athens, but
Miltiades, the son of Cypselus, was likewise a person of much
distinction. He belonged to a family which kept four-horse chariots, and traced its descent to Aeacus and Aegina, but which,
from the time of Philaeus, the son of Ajax, who was the first
Athenian citizen of the house, had been naturalised at Athens.
It happened that as the Dolonci passed his door Miltiades
was sitting in his vestibule, which caused him to remark them,
dressed as they were in outlandish garments, and armed moreover with lances. He therefore called to them, and, on their
approach, invited them in, offering them lodging and entertainment. The strangers accepted his hospitality, and, after the
banquet was over, they laid before him in full the directions of
the oracle, and besought him on their own part to yield obedience to the god. Miltiades was persuaded as soon as he heard
their request, for the government of Pisistratus was irksome to
him, and he wanted to be beyond the tyrant's reach. He therefore went straightway to Delphi, and inquired of the oracle
whether he should do as the Dolonci desired.

36. As the priestess backed their request, Miltiades, son of
Cypselus, who had already won the four-horse chariot-race at
Olympia, left Athens, taking with him as many of the Athenians
as liked to join in the enterprise, and sailed away with the Dolonci. On his arrival at the Chersonese, he was made despot by
those who had invited him. After this his first act was to build
a wall across the neck of the Chersonese from the city of Cardia
to Pactya, to protect the country from the incursions and rav-

---

[6] By "the sacred road" is meant apparently the road which led from
Delphi eastward, in the direction of Lebadea and Orchomenus.

ages of the Apsinthians. The breadth of the isthmus at this part
is four miles, the whole length of the peninsula within the isthmus being fifty-three miles.

37. When he had finished carrying the wall across the isthmus, and had thus secured the Chersonese against the Apsinthians, Miltiades proceeded to engage in other wars, and first of
all attacked the Lampsacenians; but falling into an ambush
which they had laid he had the misfortune to be taken prisoner.
Now it happened that Miltiades stood high in the favour of
Croesus, king of Lydia. When Croesus therefore heard of his
calamity he sent and commanded the men of Lampsacus to give
Miltiades his freedom. "If they refused," he said, "he would destroy them like a fir." Then the Lampsacenians were somewhile
in doubt about this speech of Croesus, and could not tell how to
construe his threat "that he would destroy them like a fir"; but
at last one of their elders divined the true sense, and told them
that the fir is the only tree which, when cut down, makes no
fresh shoots, but forthwith dies outright. So the Lampsacenians
being greatly afraid of Croesus, released Miltiades, and let him
go free.

38. Thus did Miltiades, by the help of Croesus, escape this
danger. Some time afterwards he died childless, leaving his kingdom and his riches to Stesagoras, who was the son of Cimon, his
half-brother. Ever since his death the people of the Chersonese
have offered him the customary sacrifices of a founder; and they
have further established in his honour a gymnic contest and a
chariot-race, in neither of which is it lawful for any Lampsa-
cenian to contend. Before the war with Lampsacus was ended
Stesagoras too died childless: he was sitting in the hall of justice when he was struck upon the head with a hatchet by a man
who pretended to be a deserter, but was in actuality an enemy,
and a bitter one.

39. Thus died Stesagoras, and upon his death the Pisistratidae fitted out a trireme, and sent Miltiades, the son of Cimon,
and brother of the deceased, to the Chersonese, that he might
undertake the management of affairs in that quarter. They had
already shown him much favour at Athens, as if, indeed, they

had been no parties to the death of his father Cimon—a matter whereof I will give an account in another place. He upon his arrival remained shut up within the house, pretending to do honour to the memory of his dead brother; whereupon the chief people of the Chersonese gathered themselves together from all the cities of the land, and came in a procession to the place where Miltiades was, to condole with him upon his misfortune. Miltiades commanded them to be seized and thrown into prison; after which he made himself master of the Chersonese, maintained a body of 500 mercenaries, and married Hegesipyla, daughter of the Thracian king Olorus.

40. This Miltiades, the son of Cimon, had not been long in the country[7] when a calamity befell him yet more grievous than those in which he was now involved; for three years earlier he had had to fly before an incursion of the Scyths. These nomads, angered by the attack of Darius, collected in a body and marched as far as the Chersonese. Miltiades did not await their coming, but fled, and remained away until the Scyths retired, when the Dolonci sent and fetched him back. All this happened three years before the events which befell Miltiades at the present time.

41. He now no sooner heard that the Phoenicians were attacking Tenedos than he loaded five triremes with his goods and chattels, and set sail for Athens. Cardia was the point from which he took his departure; and as he sailed down the gulf of Melas, along the shore of the Chersonese, he came suddenly upon the whole Phoenician fleet. However he himself escaped, with four of his vessels, and got into Imbrus, one trireme only falling into the hands of his pursuers. This vessel was under the command of his eldest son Metiochus, whose mother was not the daughter of the Thracian king Olorus, but a different woman. Metiochus and his ship were taken; and when the Phoenicians found out that he was a son of Miltiades they resolved to convey him to the king, expecting thereby to rise high in the royal favour. For they remembered that it was Miltiades who coun-

[7] Herodotus seems to have confused the sequence of events in this chapter.

selled the Ionians to hearken when the Scyths prayed them to
break up the bridge and return home. Darius, however, when
the Phoenicians brought Metiochus into his presence, was so far
from doing him any hurt, that he loaded him with benefits. He
gave him a house and estate, and also a Persian wife, by whom
there were children born to him who were accounted Persians.
As for Miltiades himself, from Imbrus he made his way in safety
to Athens.

42. At this time the Persians did no more hurt to the Ionians,
but on the contrary, before the year was out, they carried into
effect the following measures, which were greatly to their advantage. Artaphernes, satrap of Sardis, summoned deputies
from all the Ionian cities, and forced them to enter into agree-
ments with one another, not to harass each other by force of
arms, but to settle their disputes by legal means. He likewise
took the measurement of their whole country in parasangs—
such is the name which the Persians give to a distance of thirty
furlongs—and settled the tributes which the several cities were
to pay, at a rate that has continued unaltered from the time
when Artaphernes fixed it down to the present day. The rate was
very nearly the same as that which had been paid before the revolt. Such were the peaceful dealings of the Persians with the
Ionians.

43. The next spring Darius superseded all the other generals,
and sent down Mardonius, the son of Gobryas, to the coast, and
with him a vast body of men, some fit for sea, others for land
service. Mardonius was a youth at this time, and had only lately
married Artazostra, the king's daughter. When Mardonius, accompanied by this numerous host, reached Cilicia, he took ship,
and proceeded along shore with his fleet, while the land army
marched under other leaders towards the Hellespont. In the
course of his voyage along the coast of Asia he came to Ionia;
and here I have a marvel to relate which will greatly surprise
those Greeks who cannot believe that Otanes advised the seven
conspirators to make Persia a commonwealth.[8] Mardonius put

[8] It would seem that the tale related by Herodotus in Book iii, had
appeared incredible to the Greeks themselves. The story does not really

down all the despots throughout Ionia, and established democracies. Having so done, he hastened to the Hellespont, and when a vast multitude of ships had been brought together, and likewise a powerful land force, he conveyed his troops across the strait by means of his vessels, and proceeded through Europe against Eretria and Athens.

44. At least these towns served as a pretext for the expedition, the real purpose of which was to subjugate as great a number as possible of the Grecian cities; and this became plain when the Thasians, who did not even lift a hand in their defence, were reduced by the sea force, while the land army added the Macedonians to the former slaves of the king. All the tribes on the hither side of Macedonia had been reduced previously. From Thasos the fleet stood across to the mainland, and sailed along shore to Acanthus, whence an attempt was made to double Mount Athos. But here a violent north wind sprang up, against which nothing could contend, and handled a large number of the ships with much rudeness, shattering them and driving them aground upon Athos. It is said the number of the ships destroyed was little short of 300, and the men who perished were more than 20,000. For the sea about Athos abounds in monsters beyond all others, and so a portion were seized and devoured by these animals, while others were dashed violently against the rocks; some, who did not know how to swim, were engulfed, and some died of the cold.

45. While thus it fared with the fleet, on land Mardonius and his army were attacked in their camp during the night by the Brygi, a tribe of Thracians, and here vast numbers of the Persians were slain, and even Mardonius himself received a wound. The Brygi, nevertheless, did not succeed in maintaining their own freedom: for Mardonius would not leave the country till he had subdued them and made them subjects of Persia. Still,

derive any support from the policy here pursued by Mardonius. The Persians had learnt that they lost more by upholding the tyrants, than they gained by the convenience of having the government of the Greek states assimilated to their own. To allow Greeks democratic institutions, was a very different thing from contemplating the adoption of such institutions among themselves.

though he brought them under the yoke, the blow which his land force had received at their hands, and the great damage done to his fleet off Athos, induced him to set out upon his retreat; and so this armament, having failed disgracefully, returned to Asia.

46. The year after these events, Darius received information from certain neighbours of the Thasians that those islanders were making preparations for revolt; he therefore sent a herald, and bade them dismantle their walls, and bring all their ships to Abdera. The Thasians, at the time when Histiaeus the Milesian made his attack upon them, had resolved that, as their income was very great, they would apply their wealth to building ships of war, and surrounding their city with another and a stronger wall. Their revenue was derived partly from their possessions upon the mainland, partly from the mines which they owned. They were masters of the gold mines at Scapte Hyle, the yearly produce of which amounted in all to eighty talents. Their mines in Thasos yielded less, but still were so far prolific that, besides being entirely free from land-tax, they had a surplus income, derived from the two sources of their territory on the main and their mines, in common years of 200, and in the best years of 300 talents.

47. I myself have seen the mines in question: by far the most curious of them are those which the Phoenicians discovered at the time when they went with Thasus and colonised the island, which afterwards took its name from him. These Phoenician workings are in Thasos itself, between Coenyra and a place called Aenyra, over against Samothrace: a huge mountain has been turned upside down in the search for ores. Such then was the source of their wealth. On this occasion no sooner did the Great King issue his commands than the Thasians dismantled their wall, and took their whole fleet to Abdera.

48. After this Darius resolved to prove the Greeks, and try the bent of their minds, whether they were inclined to resist him in arms or prepared to make their submission. He therefore sent out heralds in divers directions round about Greece, with orders to demand everywhere earth and water for the king. At the same time he sent other heralds to the various seaport towns which

paid him tribute, and required them to provide a number of
ships of war and horse-transports.

49. These towns accordingly began their preparations, and
the heralds who had been sent into Greece obtained what the
king had bid them ask from a large number of the states upon
the mainland, and likewise from all the islanders whom they
visited. Among these last were included the Aeginetans, who,
equally with the rest, consented to give earth and water to the
Persian king.

When the Athenians heard what the Aeginetans had done, believing that it was from enmity to themselves that they had
given consent, and that the Aeginetans intended to join the Persian in his attack upon Athens, they straightway took the matter in hand. In good truth they greatly rejoiced to have so fair
a pretext, and accordingly they sent frequent embassies to
Sparta,[9] and made it a charge against the Aeginetans that their
conduct in this matter proved them to be traitors to Greece.

50. Hereupon Cleomenes, the son of Anaxandridas, who was
then king of the Spartans, went in person to Aegina, intending
to seize those whose guilt was the greatest. As soon however as
he tried to arrest them, a number of the Aeginetans made resistance, a certain Crius, son of Polycritus, being the foremost
in violence. This person told him he should not carry off a single Aeginetan without it costing him dear—the Athenians had
bribed him to make this attack, for which he had no warrant
from his own government—otherwise both the kings would have
come together to make the seizure. This he said in consequence
of instructions which he had received from Demaratus. Hereupon Cleomenes, finding that he must quit Aegina, asked Crius
his name; and when Crius told him, "Get your horns tipped
with brass with all speed, Crius," [10] he said, "for you will have
to struggle with a great danger."

[9] This appeal raised Sparta to the general protectorate of Greece. Hitherto she had been a leading power, frequently called in to aid the weaker
against the stronger, but with no definite hegemony, excepting over the
states of the Peloponnese.

[10] Cleomenes puns upon the name Crius, which means ram in Greek.

51. Meanwhile Demaratus, son of Ariston, was bringing charges against Cleomenes at Sparta. He too, like Cleomenes, was king of the Spartans, but he belonged to the lower house— not indeed that his house was of any lower origin than the other, for both houses are of one blood—but the house of Eurysthenes is the more honoured of the two, inasmuch as it is the elder branch.

52. The Lacedaemonians declare, contradicting therein all the poets, that it was king Aristodemus himself, son of Aristomachus, grandson of Cleodaeus, and great-grandson of Hyllus, who conducted them to the land which they now possess, and not the sons of Aristodemus. The wife of Aristodemus, whose name (they say) was Argeia, and who was daughter of Autesion, son of Tisamenus, grandson of Thersander, and great-grandson of Polynices, within a little while after their coming into the country gave birth to twins. Aristodemus just lived to see his children, but died soon afterwards oᶠ a disease. The Lacedaemonians of that day determined, according to custom, to take for their king the elder of the two children, but they were so alike, and so exactly of one size, that they could not possibly tell which of the two to choose; so when they found themselves unable to make a choice, or even earlier, they went to the mother and asked her to tell them which was the elder, whereupon she declared that she herself did not know the children apart, although in truth she knew them very well, and only feigned ignorance in order that, if it were possible, both of them might be made kings of Sparta. The Lacedaemonians were now at a loss; so they sent to Delphi and inquired of the oracle how they should deal with the matter. The priestess answered, "Let both be taken to be kings, but let the elder have the greater honour." So the Lacedaemonians were in as great a strait as before, and could not conceive how they were to discover which was the first-born, till at length a certain Messenian, by name Panites, suggested to them to watch and see which of the two the mother washed and fed first; if they found she always gave one the preference, that fact would tell them all they wanted to know; if, on the contrary, she herself varied, and sometimes

took the one first, sometimes the other, it would be plain that she knew as little as they; in which case they must try some other plan. The Lacedaemonians did according to the advice of the Messenian, and, without letting her know why, kept a watch upon the mother; by which means they discovered that, whenever she either washed or fed her children, she always gave the same child the preference. So they took the boy whom the mother honoured the most, and regarding him as the first-born, brought him up in the palace; and the name which they gave to the elder boy was Eurysthenes, while his brother they called Procles. When the brothers grew up, there was always, so long as they lived, enmity between them; and the houses sprung from their loins have continued the feud to this day.

53. Thus much is related by the Lacedaemonians, but not by any of the other Greeks; in what follows I give the tradition of the Greeks generally. The kings of the Dorians (they say)—counting up to Perseus, son of Danae, and so omitting the god—are rightly given in the common Greek lists, and rightly considered to have been Greeks themselves, for even at this early time they ranked among that people. I say up to Perseus, and not further, because Perseus has no mortal father by whose name he is called, as Heracles has in Amphitryon; whereby it appears that I have reason on my side, and am right in saying up to Perseus. If we follow the line of Danae, daughter of Acrisius, and trace her progenitors, we shall find that the chiefs of the Dorians are really genuine Egyptians.[11] In the genealogies here given I have followed the common Greek accounts.

54. According to the Persian story, Perseus was an Assyrian who became a Greek; his ancestors, therefore, according to them, were not Greeks. They do not admit that the forefathers of Acrisius were in any way related to Perseus, but say they were Egyptians, as the Greeks likewise testify.

55. Enough however of this subject. How it came to pass that Egyptians obtained the kingdoms of the Dorians, and what they did to raise themselves to such a position, these are questions which, as they have been treated by others, I shall say nothing.

[11] Herodotus believes in the tale which brings Danaus from Egypt.

I proceed to speak of points on which no other writer has touched.

56. The prerogatives which the Spartans have allowed their kings are the following. In the first place, two priesthoods, those (namely) of Lacedaemonian and of Celestial Zeus; also the right of making war on what country soever they please, without hindrance from any of the other Spartans, under pain of outlawry; on service the privilege of marching first in the advance and last in the retreat, and of having 100 picked men for their body-guard while with the army; likewise the liberty of sacrificing as many cattle in their expeditions as it seems them good, and the right of having the skins and the chines of the slaughtered animals for their own use.

57. Such are their privileges in war; in peace their rights are as follows. When a citizen makes a public sacrifice the kings are given the first seats at the banquet; they are served before any of the other guests, and have a double portion of everything; they take the lead in the libations, and the hides of the sacrificed beasts belong to them. Every month, on the first day, and again on the seventh of the first decade, each king receives a beast without blemish at the public cost, which he offers up to Apollo; likewise a medimnus of meal, and of wine a Laconian quart. In the contests of the games they have always the seat of honour; they appoint the citizens who have to entertain foreigners;[12] they also nominate, each of them, two of the Pythians, officers whose business it is to consult the oracle at Delphi, who eat with the kings, and, like them, live at the public charge. If the kings do not come to the public supper, each of them must have two choenixes of meal and a cotyle of wine sent home to him at his house; if they come, they are given a double quantity of each, and the same when any private man invites

[12] The Proxeni, whose special duty was to receive and entertain ambassadors from foreign states. The chief states of Greece had generally a proxenus at all the more important towns, who undertook this duty. He was always a native of the place, and, except at Sparta, was nominated to his office by the state whose proxenus he was. At Sparta, in consequence of the greater jealousy of foreigners, the state insisted on itself appointing the proxeni.

them to his table. They have the custody of all the oracles which are pronounced, but the Pythians must likewise have knowledge of them. They have the whole decision of certain causes, which are these, and these only: When a maiden is left the heiress of her father's estate, and has not been betrothed by him to any one, they decide who is to marry her; in all matters concerning the public highways they judge; and if a person wants to adopt a child, he must do it before the kings. They likewise have the right of sitting in council with the twenty-eight senators; and if they are not present, then the senators nearest of kin to them have their privileges, and give two votes as the royal proxies, besides a third vote, which is their own.

58. Such are the honours which the Spartan people have allowed their kings during their lifetime; after they are dead other honours await them. Horsemen carry the news of their death through all Laconia, while in the city the women go hither and thither drumming upon a kettle. At this signal, in every house two free persons, a man and a woman, must put on mourning, or else be subject to a heavy fine. The Lacedaemonians have likewise a custom at the demise of their kings which is common to them with the barbarians of Asia—indeed with the greater number of the barbarians everywhere—that when one of their kings dies, not only the Spartans, but a certain number of the country people from every part of Laconia are forced, whether they will or no, to attend the funeral. So these persons and the Helots, and likewise the Spartans themselves,[13] flock together to the number of several thousands, men and women intermingled, and all of them smite their foreheads violently, and weep and wail without stint, saying always that their last king was the best. If a king dies in battle, then they make a statue

[13] The three classes of which the Lacedaemonian population consisted are here very clearly distinguished from one another: 1. The Perioeci, or free inhabitants of the country districts, the descendants in the main of the submitted Achaeans; 2. The Helots, or serfs who tilled the soil upon the estates of their Dorian lords, descended in part from Achaeans taken with arms in their hands, but chiefly from the conquered Messenians; and 3. The Spartans, or Dorian conquerors, who were the only citizens, and who lived most exclusively in the capital.

of him, and placing it upon a couch right bravely decked, so
carry it to the grave. After the burial, for the space of ten days
there is no assembly, nor do they elect magistrates, but continue
mourning the whole time.

59. They hold with the Persians also in another custom.
When a king dies, and another comes to the throne, the newly
made monarch forgives all the Spartans the debts which they
owe either to the king or to the public treasury. And in like manner among the Persians each king when he begins to reign re-
mits the tribute due from the provinces.

60. In one respect the Lacedaemonians resemble the Egyptians. Their heralds and flute-players, and likewise their cooks,
take their trades by succession from their fathers. A flute-player
must be the son of a flute-player, a cook of a cook, a herald of a
herald; and other people cannot take advantage of the loudness
of their voice to come into the profession and shut out the heralds' sons, but each follows his father's business.[14] Such are the
customs of the Lacedaemonians.

61. At the time of which we are speaking, while Cleomenes
in Aegina was labouring for the general good of Greece, Demaratus at Sparta continued to bring charges against him, moved
not so much by love of the Aeginetans as by jealousy and hatred
of his colleague. Cleomenes therefore was no sooner returned
from Aegina than he considered with himself how he might deprive Demaratus of his kingly office; and here the following
circumstance furnished a ground for him to proceed upon. Ariston, king of Sparta, had been married to two wives, but neither
of them had borne him any children; as however he still thought
it was possible he might have offspring, he resolved to wed a
third; and this was how the wedding was brought about. He
had a certain friend, a Spartan, with whom he was more intimate than with any other citizen. This friend was married to a
wife whose beauty far surpassed that of all the other women in
Sparta; and what was still more strange, she had once been as
ugly as she now was beautiful. For her nurse, seeing how ill-

[14] No general caste system should be inferred; this is merely the tend
ency of a society as conservative as Sparta's.

favoured she was, and how sadly her parents, who were wealthy people, took her bad looks to heart, bethought herself of a plan, which was to carry the child every day to the temple of Helen at Therapna, which stands above the Phoebeum, and there to place her before the image, and beseech the goddess to take away the child's ugliness. One day, as she left the temple, a woman appeared to her, and begged to know what it was she held in her arms. The nurse told her it was a child, on which she asked to see it, but the nurse refused; the parents, she said, had forbidden her to show the child to any one. However, the woman would not take a denial, and the nurse, seeing how highly she prized a look, at last let her see the child. Then the woman gently stroked its head, and said, "One day this child shall be the fairest dame in Sparta." And her looks began to change from that very day. When she was of marriageable age, Agetus, son of Alcides, the same whom I have mentioned above as the friend of Ariston, made her his wife.

62. Now it chanced that Ariston fell in love with this person, and his love so preyed upon his mind that at last he devised as follows. He went to his friend, who was the woman's husband, and proposed to him that they should exchange gifts, each taking that which pleased him best out of all the possessions of the other. His friend, who felt no alarm about his wife, since Ariston was also married, consented readily; and so the matter was confirmed between them by an oath. Then Ariston gave Agetus the present, whatever it was, of which he had made choice, and when it came to his turn to name the present which he was to receive in exchange, required to be allowed to carry home with him Agetus' wife. But the other demurred, and said he might have anything else except his wife; however, as he could not resist the oath which he had sworn, or the trickery which had been practised on him, at last he suffered Ariston to carry her away to his house.

63. Ariston hereupon put away his second wife and took for his third this woman, and she, in less than the due time, when she had not yet reached her full term of ten months, gave birth to a child, the Demaratus of whom we have spoken. Then one

of his servants came and told him the news, as he sat in council
with the Ephors; whereat, remembering when it was that the
woman became his wife, he counted the months upon his fingers,
and having so done, cried out with an oath, "The boy cannot be
mine." This was said in the hearing of the Ephors, but they
made no account of it at the time. The boy grew up, and Ariston
repented of what he had said, for he became altogether convinced that Demaratus was truly his son. The reason why he
named him Demaratus was the following. Some time before
these events the whole Spartan people, looking upon Ariston as
a man of mark beyond all the kings that had reigned at Sparta
before him, had offered up a prayer that he might have a son.
On this account, therefore, the name Demaratus[15] was given.

64. In course of time Ariston died, and Demaratus received
the kingdom; but it was fated, as it seems, that these words,
when bruited abroad, should strip him of his sovereignty. This
was brought about by means of Cleomenes, whom he had twice
sorely vexed, once when he led the army home from Eleusis, and
a second time when Cleomenes was gone across to Aegina
against such as had espoused the side of the Medes.

65. Cleomenes now, being resolved to have his revenge upon
Demaratus, went to Leotychides, the son of Menares, and
grandson of Agis, who was of the same family as Demaratus,
and made agreement with him to this tenor following. Cleomenes was to lend his aid to make Leotychides king in place of
Demaratus, and then Leotychides was to take part with Cleomenes against the Aeginetans. Now Leotychides hated Demaratus chiefly on account of Percalus, the daughter of Chilon, son
of Demarmenus: she had been betrothed to Leotychides; but
Demaratus laid a plot, and robbed him of his bride, forestalling
him in carrying her off, and marrying her. Such was the origin
of the enmity. At the time of which we speak, Leotychides was
prevailed upon by the earnest desire of Cleomenes to come forward against Demaratus and make oath "that Demaratus was
not rightful king of Sparta, since he was not the true son of

[15] Dem-aratus is the "People-prayed-for" king. The ten months are
lunar, reckoned inclusively.

Ariston." After he had thus sworn, Leotychides sued Demaratus, and brought up against him the phrase which Ariston had let drop when, on the coming of his servant to announce to him the birth of his son, he counted the months, and cried out with an oath that the child was not his. It was on this speech of Ariston's that Leotychides relied to prove that Demaratus was not his son, and therefore not rightful king of Sparta; and he produced as witnesses the Ephors who were sitting with Ariston at the time and heard what he said.

66. At last, as there came to be much strife concerning this matter, the Spartans made a decree that the Delphic oracle should be asked to say whether Demaratus were Ariston's son or no. Cleomenes set them upon this plan, and no sooner was the decree passed than he made a friend of Cobon, the son of Aristophantus, a man of the greatest weight among the Delphians; and this man prevailed upon Perialla, the prophetess, to give the answer which Cleomenes wished. Accordingly, when the sacred messengers came and put their question, the priestess answered that Demaratus was not Ariston's son. Some time afterwards all this became known, and Cobon was forced to fly from Delphi, while Perialla the prophetess was deprived of her office.

67. Such were the means whereby the deposition of Demaratus was brought about; but his flying from Sparta to the Medes was by reason of the following reproach. On losing his kingdom he had been made a magistrate; and in that office soon afterwards, when the feast of the Naked Youths came round, he took his station among the lookers-on; whereupon Leotychides, who was now king in his stead, sent a servant to him and asked him, by way of insult and mockery how it felt to be a magistrate after one had been a king. Demaratus, who was hurt at the question, answered, "Tell him I have tried them both, but he has not. However this speech will be the cause to Sparta of infinite blessings or else of infinite woes." Having thus spoken he wrapped his head in his robe, and leaving the theatre, went home to his own house, where he prepared an ox for sacrifice, and offered it to Zeus, after which he called for his mother.

68. When she appeared, he took of the entrails, and placing

them in her hand, besought her in these words following, "Dear
mother, I beseech you, by all the gods, and chiefly by our own
hearth-god Zeus, tell me the truth, who was really my father.
For Leotychides, in the suit which we had together, declared,
that when you became Ariston's wife you were already pregnant
by your former husband; and others repeat a yet more disgraceful tale, that our groom seduced you, and that I am his
son. I entreat you therefore by the gods to tell me the truth.
For if you went astray, you did no more than many a woman;
and the Spartans remark it as strange, if I am Ariston's son,
that he had no children by his other wives."

69. Thus spoke Demaratus, and his mother replied as follows,
"Dear son, since you beg so earnestly for the truth, it shall indeed be fully told to you. When Ariston brought me to his
house, on the third night after my coming, there appeared to
me one like to Ariston, who, after lying with me, rose, and taking
the garlands from his own brows placed them upon my head,
and so went away. Presently Ariston entered, and when he saw
the garlands which I still wore, asked me who gave them to me.
I said they were his; but this he stoutly denied, whereupon I sol-
emnly swore that it was none other, and told him he did not do
well to dissemble when he had so lately lain with me and left
the garlands with me. Then Ariston, when he heard my oath,
understood that there was something beyond nature in what had
taken place. And indeed it appeared that the garlands had come
from the hero-temple which stands by our court gates, the
temple of him they call Astrabacus, and the soothsayers, moreover, declared that the apparition was that very person. And
now, my son, I have told you all you wished to know. Either
you are the son of that hero—you may call Astrabacus sire, or
else Ariston was your father. As for that matter which they who
hate you urge the most, the words of Ariston, who, when the
messenger told him of your birth, declared before many witnesses that you were not his son, forasmuch as the ten months
were not fully out, it was a random speech, uttered from mere
ignorance. The truth is, children are born not only at ten
months, but at nine, and even at seven. You were, my son, a

seven months' child. Ariston acknowledged, no long time afterwards, that his speech sprang from thoughtlessness. Hearken
not then to other tales concerning your birth, my son; for be
assured you have the whole truth. As for grooms, pray heaven
Leotychides and all who speak as he does may suffer wrong
from them." Such was the mother's answer.

70. Demaratus, having learned all that he wished to know,
took with him provisions for the journey, and went into Elis,
pretending that he proposed to proceed to Delphi and there
consult the oracle. The Lacedaemonians, however, suspecting
that he meant to fly his country, sent men in pursuit of him; but
Demaratus hastened, and leaving Elis before they arrived, sailed
across to Zacynthus. The Lacedaemonians followed, and sought
to lay hands upon him, and to separate him from his retinue;
but the Zacynthians would not give him up to them; so he
escaping, made his way afterwards by sea to Asia, and presented
himself before King Darius, who received him generously, and
gave him both lands and cities. Such was the chance which drove
Demaratus to Asia, a man distinguished among the Lacedaemonians for many noble deeds and wise counsels, and who
alone of all the Spartan kings brought honour to his country by
winning at Olympia the prize in the four-horse chariot-race.

71. After Demaratus was deposed, Leotychides, the son of
Menares, received the kingdom. He had a son, Zeuxidamus,
called Cyniscus by many of the Spartans. This Zeuxidamus did
not reign at Sparta, but died before his father, leaving a son,
Archidamus. Leotychides, when Zeuxidamus was taken from
him, married a second wife, named Eurydame, the sister of
Menius and daughter of Diactorides. By her he had no male offspring, but only a daughter called Lampito, whom he gave in
marriage to Archidamus, Zeuxidamus' son.

72. Even Leotychides, however, did not spend his old age
in Sparta, but suffered a punishment whereby Demaratus was
fully avenged. He commanded the Lacedaemonians when they
made war against Thessaly, and might have conquered the
whole of it, but was bribed by a large sum of money. It chanced
that he was caught in the fact, being found sitting in his tent

on a gauntlet quite full of silver. Upon this he was brought to trial and banished from Sparta; his house was razed to the ground; and he himself fled to Tegea, where he ended his days. But these events took place long afterwards.

73. At the time of which we are speaking Cleomenes, having carried his proceedings in the matter of Demaratus to a prosperous issue, forthwith took Leotychides with him, and crossed over to attack the Aeginetans; for his anger was hot against them on account of the affront which they had formerly put upon him. Hereupon the Aeginetans, seeing that both the kings were come against them, thought it best to make no further resistance. So the two kings picked out from all Aegina the ten men who for wealth and birth stood the highest, among whom were Crius, son of Polycritus, and Casambus, son of Aristocrates, who wielded the chief power; and these men they carried with them to Attica, and there deposited them in the hands of the Athenians, the great enemies of the Aeginetans.

74. Afterwards, when it came to be known what evil arts had been used against Demaratus, Cleomenes was seized with fear of his own countrymen, and fled into Thessaly. From thence he passed into Arcadia, where he began to stir up troubles, and endeavoured to unite the Arcadians against Sparta. He bound them by various oaths to follow him whithersoever he should lead, and was even desirous of taking their chief leaders with him to the city of Nonacris, that he might swear them to his cause by the waters of the Styx. For the waters of Styx, as the Arcadians say, are in that city; and this is the appearance they present: you see a little water, dripping from a rock into a basin, which is fenced round by a low wall. Nonacris, where this fountain is to be seen, is a city of Arcadia near Pheneus.

75. When the Lacedaemonians heard how Cleomenes was engaged, they were afraid, and agreed with him that he should come back to Sparta and be king as before. So Cleomenes came back, but had no sooner returned than he, who had never been altogether of sound mind, was smitten with downright madness. This he showed by striking every Spartan he met upon the face with his sceptre. On his behaving thus, and showing that he was

gone quite out of his mind, his kindred imprisoned him, and even put his feet in the stocks. While so bound, finding himself left alone with a single keeper, he asked the man for a knife. The keeper at first refused, whereupon Cleomenes began to threaten him, until at last he was afraid, being only a Helot, and gave him what he required. Cleomenes had no sooner got the steel than, beginning at his legs, he horribly disfigured himself, cutting gashes in his flesh, along his legs, thighs, hips, and loins, until at last he reached his belly, which he likewise began to gash, whereupon in a little time he died. The Greeks generally think that this fate came upon him because he induced the priestess to pronounce against Demaratus; the Athenians differ from all others in saying that it was because he cut down the sacred grove of the goddesses when he made his invasion by Eleusis; while the Argives ascribed it to his having taken from their refuge and cut to pieces certain Argives who had fled from battle into a precinct sacred to Argus, where Cleomenes slew them, burning likewise at the same time, through irreverence, the grove itself.

76. For once, when Cleomenes had sent to Delphi to consult the oracle, it was prophesied to him that he should take Argos; upon which he went out at the head of the Spartans, and led them to the river Erasinus. This stream is reported to flow from the Stymphalian lake, the waters of which empty themselves into a pitch-dark chasm, and then (as they say) reappear in Argos, where the Argives call them the Erasinus. Cleomenes, having arrived up the banks of this river, proceeded to offer sacrifice to it, but, in spite of all that he could do, the victims were not favourable to his crossing. So he said that he admired the god for refusing to betray his countrymen, but still the Argives should not escape him for all that. He then withdrew his troops, and led them down to Thyrea, where he sacrificed a bull to the sea, and conveyed his men on shipboard to Nauplia in the Tirynthian territory.

77. The Argives, when they heard of this, marched down to the sea, to defend their country; and arriving in the neighbourhood of Tiryns, at the place which bears the name of Sepeia,

they pitched their camp opposite to the Lacedaemonians, leaving no great space between the hosts. And now their fear was not so much lest they should be worsted in open fight as lest some trick should be practised on them; for such was the danger which the oracle given to them in common with the Milesians seemed to intimate. The oracle ran as follows:

Time shall be when the female shall conquer the male, and shall
    chase him
Far away, gaining so great praise and honour in Argos;
Then full many an Argive woman her cheeks shall mangle;
Hence, in the times to come 'twill be said by the men who are
    unborn,
"Tamed by the spear expired the coiled terrible serpent."

At the coincidence of all these things the Argives were greatly cast down, and so they resolved that they would follow the signals of the enemy's herald. Having made this resolve, they proceeded to act as follows: whenever the herald of the Lacedaemonians gave any order to the soldiers of his own army, the Argives did the like on their side.

78. Now when Cleomenes heard that the Argives were acting thus, he commanded his troops that, so soon as the herald gave the word for the soldiers to go to dinner, they should instantly seize their arms and charge the host of the enemy. Which the Lacedaemonians did accordingly, and fell upon the Argives just as, following the signal, they had begun their repast; whereby vast numbers of the Argives were slain, while the rest, who were more than they which died in the fight, were driven to take refuge in the grove of Argus hard by, where they were surrounded, and watch kept upon them.

79. When things were at this pass Cleomenes acted as follows: Having learnt the names of the Argives who were shut up in the sacred precinct from certain deserters who had come over to him, he sent a herald to summon them one by one, on pretence of having received their ransoms. Now the ransom of prisoners among the Peloponnesians is fixed at two minae the man. So Cleomenes had these persons called forth severally, to the

number of fifty, or thereabouts, and massacred them. All this while they who remained in the enclosure knew nothing of what was happening, for the grove was so thick that the people inside were unable to see what was taking place without. But at last one of their number climbed up into a tree and spied the treachery; after which none of those who were summoned would go forth.

80. Then Cleomenes ordered all the Helots to bring brushwood, and heap it around the grove, which was done accordingly, and Cleomenes set the grove on fire. As the flames spread he asked a deserter who was the god of the grove, whereto the other answered, "Argus." So he, when he heard that, uttered a loud groan, and said, "Greatly you deceived me, Apollo, god of prophecy, in saying that I should take Argos. I fear your oracle has now got its accomplishment."

81. Cleomenes now sent home the greater part of his army, while with a thousand of his best troops he proceeded to the temple of Hera,[16] to offer sacrifice. When however he would have slain the victim on the altar himself, the priest forbade him, as it was not lawful (he said) for a foreigner to sacrifice in that temple. At this Cleomenes ordered his Helots to drag the priest from the altar and scourge him, while he performed the sacrifice himself, after which he went back to Sparta.

82. Thereupon his enemies brought him up before the Ephors, and made it a charge against him that he had allowed himself to be bribed, and on that account had not taken Argos when he might have captured it easily. To this he answered, whether truly or falsely I cannot say with certainty, but at any rate his answer to the charge was, that so soon as he discovered the sacred precinct which he had taken to belong to Argus, he directly imagined that the oracle had received its accomplishment; he therefore thought it not good to attempt the town, at the least until he had inquired by sacrifice, and ascertained if the god meant to grant him the place, or was determined to oppose

---

[16] This temple of Juno, one of the most famous in antiquity, was situated between Mycenae and Argos, at a distance of less than two miles from the former place.

his taking it. So he offered in the temple of Hera, and when the omens were propitious, immediately there flashed forth a flame of fire from the breast of the image; wherefrom he knew that he was not to take Argos. For if the flash had come from the head, he would have gained the town, citadel and all; but as it shone from the breast, he had done as much as the god intended. And his words seemed to the Spartans so true and reasonable, that he came clear off from his adversaries.

83. Argos however was left so bare of men, that the slaves managed the state, filled the offices, and administered everything until the sons of those who were slain by Cleomenes grew up. Then these latter cast out the slaves, and got the city back under their own rule; while the slaves who had been driven out, fought a battle and won Tiryns. After this for a time there was peace between the two; but a certain man, a soothsayer, named Cleander, who was by race a Phigalean from Arcadia, joined himself to the slaves, and stirred them up to make a fresh attack upon their lords. Then were they at war with one another for many years; but at length the Argives with much trouble gained the upper hand.

84. The Argives say that Cleomenes lost his senses, and died so miserably, on account of these doings. But his own countrymen declare that his madness proceeded not from any supernatural cause whatever, but only from the habit of drinking wine unmixed with water, which he learnt of the Scyths. These nomads, from the time that Darius made his inroad into their country, had always had a wish for revenge. They therefore sent ambassadors to Sparta to conclude a league, proposing to endeavour themselves to enter Media by the Phasis, while the Spartans should march inland from Ephesus, and then the two armies should join together in one. When the Scyths came to Sparta on this errand Cleomenes was with them continually; and growing somewhat too familiar, learned of them to drink his wine without water, a practice which is thought by the Spartans to have caused his madness. From this distance of time the Spartans, according to their own account, have been accustomed, when they want to drink purer wine than common, to

give the order to fill Scythian fashion. The Spartans then speak
thus concerning Cleomenes; but for my own part I think his
death was a judgment on him for wronging Demaratus.

85. No sooner did the news of Cleomenes' death reach Aegina
than straightway the Aeginetans sent ambassadors to Sparta to
complain of the conduct of Leotychides in respect of their hostages, who were still kept at Athens. So they of Lacedaemon assembled a court of justice and gave sentence upon Leotychides,
that whereas he had grossly affronted the people of Aegina, he
should be given up to the ambassadors, to be led away, in place
of the men whom the Athenians had in their keeping. Then the
ambassadors were about to lead him away; but Theasides, the
son of Leoprepes, who was a man greatly esteemed in Sparta,
interfered, and said to them, "What do you intend to do, men of
Aegina? To lead away captive the king of the Spartans, whom
his countrymen have given into your hands? Though now in
their anger they have passed this sentence, yet the time will
come when they will punish you, if you act thus, by bringing
utter destruction upon your country."

The Aeginetans, when they heard this, changed their plan,
and, instead of leading Leotychides away captive, agreed with
him that he should come with them to Athens and give them
back their men.

86. When however he reached that city, and demanded the
restoration of his pledge, the Athenians, being unwilling to
comply, proceeded to make excuses, saying that two kings had
come and left the men with them, and they did not think it right
to give them back to the one without the other. So when the
Athenians refused plainly to restore the men, Leotychides said
to them:

"Men of Athens, act which way you choose—give me up the
hostages, and be righteous, or keep them, and be the contrary.
I wish, however, to tell you what happened once in Sparta about
a pledge. The story goes among us that three generations back
there lived in Lacedaemon one Glaucus, the son of Epicydes, a
man who in every other respect was on a par with the first in the
kingdom, and whose character for justice was such as to place

him above all the other Spartans. Now to this man at the appointed season the following events happened. A certain Milesian came to Sparta and having desired to speak with him, said, 'I am of Miletus, and I have come here, Glaucus, in the hope of profiting by your honesty. For when I heard much talk in Ionia and through all the rest of Greece, and when I observed that whereas Ionia is always insecure, the Peloponnese stands firm and unshaken, and noted likewise how wealth is continually changing hands in our country, I took counsel with myself and resolved to turn one-half of my substance into money, and place it in your hands, since I am well assured that it will be safe in your keeping. Here then is the silver—take it—and take likewise these tokens, and be careful of them; remember you are to give back the money to the person who shall bring you their fellows.' Such were the words of the Milesian stranger; and Glaucus took the deposit on the terms expressed to him. Many years had gone by when the sons of the man by whom the money was left came to Sparta, and had an interview with Glaucus, whereat they produced the tokens, and asked to have the money returned to them. But Glaucus sought to refuse, and answered them, 'I have no recollection of the matter, nor can I bring to mind any of those particulars whereof you speak. When I remember, I will certainly do what is just. If I had the money, you have a right to receive it back; but if it was never given to me, I shall put the Greek law in force against you. For the present I give you no answer, but four months hence I will settle the business.' So the Milesians went away sorrowful, considering that their money was utterly lost to them. As for Glaucus, he made a journey to Delphi, and there consulted the oracle. To his question if he should swear,[17] and so make prize of the money, the priestess returned for answer these lines following:

Best for the present it were, Glaucus, to do as thou wishest,
Swearing an oath to prevail, and so to make prize of the money.

[17] The Greek law allowed an accused person, with the consent of the accuser, to clear himself of a crime imputed to him, by taking an oath that the charge was false.

Swear then—death is the lot e'en of those who never swear
    falsely.
Yet hath the Oath-God a son who is nameless, footless, and
    handless;
Mighty in strength he approaches to vengeance, and whelms in
    destruction
All who belong to the race, or the house of the man who is per-
    jured.
But oath-keeping men leave behind them a flourishing offspring.

Glaucus when he heard these words earnestly besought the god
to pardon his question; but the priestess replied that it was as
bad to have tempted the god as it would have been to have done
the deed. Glaucus, however, sent for the Milesian strangers, and
gave them back their money. And now I will tell you, Athenians,
what my purpose has been in recounting to you this history.
Glaucus at the present time has not a single descendant, nor is
there any family known as his—root and branch has he been
removed from Sparta. It is a good thing, therefore, when a
pledge has been left with one, not even in thought to doubt
about restoring it."

Thus spoke Leotychides; but, as he found that the Athenians
would not listen to him, he left them and went his way.

87. The Aeginetans had never been punished for the wrongs
which, to please the Thebans, they had committed upon Athens.
Now, however, conceiving that they were themselves wronged,
and had a fair ground of complaint against the Athenians, they
instantly prepared to revenge themselves. As it chanced that the
Athenians were holding a quadrennial festival at Sunium, the
Aeginetans contrived an ambush, and made themselves masters
of the embassy vessel, on board of which were a number of
Athenians of the highest rank, whom they took and threw into
prison.

88. At this outrage the Athenians no longer delayed, but set
to work to scheme their worst against the Aeginetans; and as
there was in Aegina at that time a man of mark, Nicodromus by
name, the son of Cnoethus, who was on ill terms with his countrymen because on a former occasion they had driven him into

banishment, they listened to overtures from this man, who had heard how determined they were to harm the Aeginetans, and agreed with him that on a certain day he should be ready to betray the island into their hands, and they would come with a body of troops to his assistance. And Nicodromus, some time after, holding to the agreement, made himself master of what is called the old town.

89. The Athenians, however, did not come to the day; for their own fleet was not of force sufficient to engage the Aeginetans, and while they were begging the Corinthians to lend them some ships, the failure of the enterprise took place. In those days the Corinthians were on the best of terms with the Athenians, and accordingly they now yielded to their request and furnished them with twenty ships; but, as their law did not allow the ships to be given for nothing, they sold them to the Athenians for five drachmas apiece. As soon then as the Athenians had obtained this aid, and, by manning also their own ships, had equipped a fleet of seventy sail, they crossed over to Aegina, but arrived a day later than the time agreed upon.

90. Meanwhile Nicodromus, when he found the Athenians did not come at the time appointed, took ship and made his escape from the island. The Aeginetans who accompanied him were settled by the Athenians at Sunium, whence they were wont to issue forth and plunder the Aeginetans of the island. But this took place at a later date.

91. When the wealthier Aeginetans had thus obtained the victory over the common people who had revolted with Nicodromus, they laid hands on a certain number of them, and led them out to death. But here they were guilty of a sacrilege, which, notwithstanding all their efforts, they were never able to atone, being driven from the island[18] before they had appeased the goddess whom they provoked. Seven hundred of the common people had fallen alive into their hands, and they were all being let out to death, when one of them escaped from his chains, and flying to the gateway of the temple of Demeter the

---

[18] Herodotus refers to the expulsion of the Aeginetans by the Athenians in the first year of the Peloponnesian war, 431 B.C.

Lawgiver, laid hold of the door-handles, and clung to them. The others sought to drag him from his refuge, but finding themselves unable to tear him away, they cut off his hands, and so took him, leaving the hands still tightly grasping the handles.

92. Such were the doings of the Aeginetans among themselves. When the Athenians arrived, they went out to meet them with seventy ships, and a battle took place, wherein the Aeginetans suffered a defeat. Hereupon they had recourse again to their old allies the Argives; but these latter refused now to lend them any aid, being angry because some Aeginetan ships, which Cleomenes had taken by force, accompanied him in his invasion of Argolis, and joined in the disembarkation. The same thing had happened at the same time with certain vessels of the Sicyonians, and the Argives had laid a fine of 1,000 talents upon the misdoers, 500 upon each; whereupon the Sicyonians acknowledged themselves guilty, and agreed with the Argives to pay them 100 talents, and so be quit of the debt; but the Aeginetans would make no acknowledgment at all, and showed themselves proud and stiff-necked. For this reason, when they now prayed the Argives for aid, the state refused to send them a single soldier. Notwithstanding, volunteers joined them from Argos to the number of 1,000, under a captain, Eurybates, a man skilled in the pentathlon.[19] Of these men the greater part never returned, but were slain by the Athenians in Aegina. Eurybates, their captain, fought a number of single combats, and after killing three men in this way, was himself slain by the fourth, who was a Decelean, named Sophanes.

93. Afterwards the Aeginetans fell upon the Athenian fleet when it was in some disorder and beat it, capturing four ships with their crews.

94. Thus did war rage between the Aeginetans and Athenians. Meantime the Persian pursued his own design, from day to day exhorted by his servant to remember the Athenians, and likewise urged continually by the Pisistratidae, who were ever accusing their countrymen. Moreover it pleased him well to

[19] This consisted of the five sports of jumping, running, throwing the discus, hurling the spear, and wrestling.

have a pretext for carrying war into Greece, that so he might reduce all those who had refused to give him earth and water. As for Mardonius, since his expedition had succeeded so ill, Darius took the command of the troops from him, and appointed other generals in his stead, who were to lead the host against Eretria and Athens; Datis, who was by descent a Mede, and Artaphernes, the son of Artaphernes, his own nephew. These men received orders to carry Athens and Eretria away captive, and to bring the prisoners into his presence.

95. So the new commanders took their departure from the court and went down to Cilicia, to the Aleian plain, having with them a numerous and well-appointed land army. Encamping here, they were joined by the sea force which had been required of the several states, and at the same time by the horse-transports which Darius had, the year before, commanded his tributaries to make ready. Aboard these the horses were embarked, and the troops were received by the ships of war; after which the whole fleet, amounting in all to 600 triremes, made sail for Ionia. Thence, instead of proceeding with a straight course along the shore to the Hellespont and to Thrace, they loosed from Samos and voyaged across the Icarian sea through the midst of the islands; mainly, as I believe, because they feared the danger of doubling Mount Athos, where the year before they had suffered so grievously on their passage; but a constraining cause also was their former failure to take Naxos.

96. When the Persians, therefore, approaching from the Icarian sea, cast anchor at Naxos, which, recollecting what there befell them formerly, they had determined to attack before any other state, the Naxians, instead of encountering them, took to flight, and hurried off to the hills. The Persians however succeeded in laying hands on some, and them they carried away captive, while at the same time they burnt all the temples together with the town. This done, they left Naxos, and sailed away to the other islands.

97. While the Persians were thus employed, the Delians likewise quitted Delos, and took refuge in Tenos. And now the expedition drew near, when Datis sailed forward in advance of the

other ships; which he commanded, instead of anchoring at Delos, to rendezvous at Rhenea, over against Delos, while he himself proceeded to discover whither the Delians had fled, after which he sent a herald to them with this message:

"Why have you fled, O holy men? Why have you judged me so harshly and so wrongfully? I have surely sense enough, even had not the king so ordered, to spare the country which gave birth to the two gods, to spare, I say, both the country and its inhabitants. Come back therefore to your dwellings, and once more inhabit your island." Such was the message which Datis sent by his herald to the Delians. He likewise placed upon the altar 300 talents' weight of frankincense, and offered it.

98. After this he sailed with his whole host against Eretria, taking with him both Ionians and Aeolians. When he was departed, Delos (as the Delians told me) was shaken by an earthquake, the first and last shock that has been felt to this day. And truly this was a prodigy whereby the god warned men of the evils that were coming upon them. For in the three following generations of Darius the son of Hystaspes, Xerxes the son of Darius, and Artaxerxes the son of Xerxes, more woes befell Greece than in the twenty generations preceding Darius;[20] woes caused in part by the Persians, but in part arising from the contentions among their own chief men respecting the supreme power. Wherefore it is not surprising that Delos, though it had never before been shaken, should at that time have felt the shock of an earthquake. And indeed there was an oracle, which said of Delos:

Delos self will I shake, which never yet has been shaken.

Of the above names Darius may be rendered Worker, Xerxes Warrior, and Artaxerxes Great Warrior. And so we might call these kings in our own language with propriety.

99. The barbarians, setting out from Delos, proceeded to

* Darius reigned 522-486 B.C., Xerxes 486-465 B.C. and Artaxerxes 465-424 B.C. Artaxerxes may have been alive still when Herodotus wrote this passage.

touch at the other islands, and took troops from each, and likewise carried off a number of the children as hostages. Going thus
from one to another, they came at last to Carystus; but here the
hostages were refused by the Carystians, who said they would
neither give any, nor consent to bear arms against the cities of
their neighbours, meaning Athens and Eretria. Hereupon the
Persians laid siege to Carystus, and wasted the country round,
until at last the inhabitants were brought over and agreed to do
what was required of them.

100. Meanwhile the Eretrians, understanding that the Persian armament was coming against them, besought the Athenians for assistance. Nor did the Athenians refuse their aid, but
assigned to them as auxiliaries the 4,000 landholders to whom
they had allotted the estates of the Chalcidean Hippobatae. At
Eretria, however, things were in no healthy state; for though
they had called in the aid of the Athenians, yet they were not
agreed among themselves how they should act; some of them
being minded to leave the city and to take refuge in the heights
of Euboea, while others, who looked to receiving a reward from
the Persians, were making ready to betray their country. So
when these things came to the ears of Aeschines, the son of
Nothon, one of the first men in Eretria, he made known the
whole state of affairs to the Athenians who were already arrived,
and urged them to return home to their own land, and not perish
with his countrymen. And the Athenians followed his advice,
and crossing over to Oropus, in this way escaped the danger.

101. The Persian fleet now drew near and anchored at Tamy-
nae, Choereae, and Aegilia, three places in the territory of
Eretria. Once masters of these posts, they proceeded forthwith
to disembark their horses, and made ready to attack the enemy.
But the Eretrians were not minded to sally forth and offer
battle; their only care, after it had been resolved not to quit the
city, was, if possible, to defend their walls. And now the fortress
was assaulted in good earnest, and for six days there fell on both
sides vast numbers, but on the seventh day Euphorbus, the son
of Alcimachus, and Philagrus, the son of Cyneas, who were both
citizens of good repute, betrayed the place to the Persians.

These were no sooner entered within the walls than they plundered and burnt all the temples that there were in the town, in revenge for the burning of their own temples at Sardis; moreover, they did according to the orders of Darius, and carried away captive all the inhabitants.

102. The Persians, having thus brought Eretria into subjection, after waiting a few days, sailed for Attica, greatly straitening the Athenians as they approached, and thinking to deal with them as they had dealt with the people of Eretria. And because there was no place in all Attica so convenient for their horse as Marathon, and it lay moreover quite close to Eretria, therefore Hippias, the son of Pisistratus, conducted them thither.

103. When intelligence of this reached the Athenians, they likewise marched their troops to Marathon, and there stood on the defensive, having at their head ten generals, of whom one was Miltiades.

Now this man's father, Cimon, the son of Stesagoras, was banished from Athens by Pisistratus, the son of Hippocrates. In his banishment it was his fortune to win the four-horse chariot-race at Olympia, whereby he gained the very same honour which had before been carried off by Miltiades, his half-brother on the mother's side. At the next Olympiad he won the prize again with the same mares, upon which he caused Pisistratus to be proclaimed the winner, having made an agreement with him that on yielding him this honour he should be allowed to come back to his country. Afterwards, still with the same mares, he won the prize a third time, whereupon he was put to death by the sons of Pisistratus, whose father was no longer living. They set men to lie in wait for him secretly, and these men slew him near the town-hall in the night-time. He was buried outside the city, beyond what is called the Valley Road, and right opposite his tomb were buried the mares which had won the three prizes. The same success had likewise been achieved once previously, to wit, by the mares of Evagoras the Lacedaemonian, but never except by them. At the time of Cimon's death, Stesagoras, the elder of his two sons, was in the Chersonese, where he lived with Miltiades his uncle; the younger, who was called Miltiades after the

founder of the Chersonesite colony, was with his father in
Athens.

104. It was this Miltiades who now commanded the Athenians, after escaping from the Chersonese, and twice nearly losing his life. First he was chased as far as Imbrus by the Phoenicians, who had a great desire to take him and carry him up to
the king; and when he had avoided this danger, and, having
reached his own country, thought himself to be altogether in
safety, he found his enemies waiting for him, and was cited by
them before a court and impeached for his tyranny in the Chersonese. But he came off victorious here likewise, and was there
upon made general of the Athenians by the free choice of the
people.

105. And first, before they left the city, the generals sent off
to Sparta a herald, one Philippides, who was by birth an Athenian, and by profession and practice a trained runner. This man,
according to the account which he gave to the Athenians on his
return, when he was near Mount Parthenium, above Tegea, fell
in with the god Pan, who called him by his name, and bade him
ask the Athenians, "Why they neglected him so entirely, when
he was kindly disposed towards them, and had often helped
them in times past, and would do so again in time to come?"
The Athenians, entirely believing in the truth of this report, as
soon as their affairs were once more in good order, set up a
temple to Pan under the Acropolis, and, in return for the message which I have recorded, established in his honour yearly
sacrifices and a torch-race.

106. On the occasion of which we speak, when Philippides
was sent by the Athenian generals, and, according to his own
account, saw Pan on his journey, he reached Sparta on the very
next day after quitting the city of Athens. Upon his arrival he
went before the rulers, and said:

"Men of Lacedaemon, the Athenians beseech you to hasten to
their aid, and not allow that state, which is the most ancient in
all Greece, to be enslaved by the barbarians. Eretria is already
carried away captive, and Greece weakened by the loss of no
mean city."

Thus did Philippides deliver the message committed to him. And the Spartans wished to help the Athenians, but were unable to give them any present aid, as they did not like to break their established law. It was the ninth day of the month, and they could not march out of Sparta on the ninth, when the moon had not reached the full. So they waited for the full of the moon.

107. The barbarians were conducted to Marathon by Hippias, the son of Pisistratus, who the night before had seen a strange vision in his sleep. He seemed to have intercourse with his mother, and conjectured the dream to mean that he would be restored to Athens, recover the power which he had lost, and afterwards live to a good old age in his native country. Such was the sense in which he interpreted the vision. He now proceeded to act as guide to the Persians, and in the first place he landed the prisoners taken from Eretria upon the island that is called Aegileia, belonging to the Styreans, after which he brought the fleet to anchor off Marathon, and marshalled the bands of the barbarians as they disembarked. As he was thus employed it chanced that he sneezed and at the same time coughed with more violence than was his wont. Now as he was a man advanced in years, and the greater number of his teeth were loose, it so happened that one of them was driven out with the force of the cough, and fell down into the sand. Hippias took all the pains he could to find it, but the tooth was nowhere to be seen; whereupon he fetched a deep sigh, and said to the bystanders, "After all the land is not ours, and we shall never be able to bring it under. All my share in it is the portion of which my tooth has possession."

So Hippias believed that this fulfilled his dream.

108. The Athenians were drawn up in order of battle in a precinct belonging to Heracles, when they were joined by the Plataeans, who came in full force to their aid. Some time before,[21] the Plataeans had put themselves under the rule of the Athenians, and these last had already undertaken many labours on their behalf. The occasion of the surrender was the following.

[21] 519 B.C. if we accept the date of Thucydides (iii. 68); but 509 B.C. is more probable.

The Plataeans suffered grievous things at the hands of the men of Thebes; so, as it chanced that Cleomenes, the son of Anaxandridas, and the Lacedaemonians were in their neighbourhood, they first of all offered to surrender themselves to them. But the Lacedaemonians refused to receive them, and said, "We dwell too far off from you, and ours would be but cold comfort. You might oftentimes be carried into slavery before one of us heard of it. We counsel you rather to give yourselves up to the Athenians, who are your next neighbours, and well able to shelter you."

This they said, not so much out of good will towards the Plataeans as because they wished to involve the Athenians in trouble by engaging them in wars with the Boeotians. The Plataeans, however, when the Lacedaemonians gave them this counsel, complied at once; and when the sacrifice to the Twelve Gods was being offered at Athens, they came and sat as suppliants about the altar, and gave themselves up to the Athenians. The Thebans no sooner learned what the Plataeans had done than instantly they marched out against them, while the Athenians sent troops to their aid. As the two armies were about to join battle, the Corinthians, who chanced to be at hand, would not allow them to engage; both sides consented to take them for arbitrators, whereupon they made up the quarrel, and fixed the boundary-line between the two states upon this condition: that if any of the Boeotians wished no longer to belong to Boeotia, the Thebans should allow them to follow their own inclinations. The Corinthians, when they had thus decreed, departed to their homes; the Athenians likewise set off on their return, but the Boeotians fell upon them during the march, and a battle was fought wherein they were worsted by the Athenians. Hereupon these last would not be bound by the line which the Corinthians had fixed, but advanced beyond those limits, and made the Asopus the boundary-line between the country of the Thebans and that of the Plataeans and Hysians. Under such circumstances did the Plataeans give themselves up to Athens; and now they were come to Marathon to aid the Athenians.

109. The Athenian generals were divided in their opinions;

and some advised not to risk a battle, because they were too few to engage such a host as that of the Medes; while others were for fighting at once, and among these last was Miltiades. He therefore, seeing that opinions were thus divided, and that the less worthy counsel appeared likely to prevail, resolved to go to the Polemarch, and have a conference with him. For the man on whom the lot fell to be polemarch,[22] at Athens was entitled to give his vote with the ten generals, since anciently the Athenians allowed him an equal right of voting with them. The Polemarch at this juncture was Callimachus of Aphidnae; to him therefore Miltiades went, and said:

"With you it rests, Callimachus, either to bring Athens to slavery, or, by securing her freedom, to leave behind to all future generations a memory beyond even Harmodius and Aristogeiton. For never since the time that the Athenians became a people were they in so great a danger as now. If they bow their necks beneath the yoke of the Medes, the woes which they will have to suffer when given into the power of Hippias are already determined on; if, on the other hand, they fight and overcome, Athens may rise to be the very first city in Greece. How it comes to pass that these things are likely to happen, and how the determining of them in some sort rests with you, I will now proceed to make clear. We generals are ten in number, and our votes are divided; half of us wish to engage, half to avoid a combat. Now, if we do not fight, I look to see a great disturbance at Athens which will shake men's resolutions, and then I fear they will submit themselves; but if we fight the battle before any unsoundness show itself among our citizens, let the gods but give us fair play, and we are well able to overcome the enemy. On you therefore we depend in this matter, which lies wholly in your own power. You have only to add your vote to my side and your country will be free, and not free only, but

[22] The Polemarch, or War-Archon, was the third archon in dignity and before the time of Cleisthenes had constitutionally the general superintendence of all military matters, having succeeded to the office of the kings as respected war. When Herodotus wrote, the polemarch had no military functions at all, but attended to the personal and family interests of the metics and foreigners.

the first state in Greece. Or, if you prefer to give your vote to
them who would decline the combat, then the reverse will follow."

110. Miltiades by these words gained Callimachus; and the
addition of the polemarch's vote caused the decision to be in
favor of fighting. Hereupon all those generals who had been desirous of hazarding a battle, when their turn came to command
the army, gave up their right to Miltiades. He however, though
he accepted their offers, nevertheless waited, and would not
fight, until his own day of command arrived in due course.[23]

111. Then at length, when his own turn was come, the Athenian battle was set in array, and this was the order of it. Callimachus the polemarch led the right wing, for it was at that
time a rule with the Athenians to give the right wing to the
polemarch. After this followed the tribes, according as they were
numbered, in an unbroken line; while last of all came the
Plataeans, forming the left wing. And ever since that day it has
been a custom with the Athenians, in the sacrifices and assemblies held each fifth year at Athens, for the Athenian herald
to implore the blessing of the gods on the Plataeans conjointly
with the Athenians. Now as they marshalled the host upon the
field of Marathon, in order that the Athenian front might be of
equal length with the Median, the ranks of the centre were
diminished, and it became the weakest part of the line, while the
wings were both made strong with a depth of many ranks.

112. So when the battle was set in array, and the victims
showed themselves favourable, instantly the Athenians, so soon
as they were let go, charged the barbarians at a run. Now the
distance between the two armies was little short of a mile. The
Persians, therefore, when they saw the Greeks coming on at
speed, made ready to receive them, although it seemed to them
that the Athenians were bereft of their senses, and bent upon
their own destruction; for they saw a mere handful of men coming on at a run without either horsemen or archers.[24] Such was

---

[23] According to Aristotle's *Constitution of Athens* Herodotus is guilty
of an anachronism in assigning chief command to the tribal generals.

[24] It was probably on account of the deficiency of the Greeks in archers

the opinion of the barbarians; but the Athenians in close array fell upon them, and fought in a manner worthy of being recorded. They were the first of the Greeks, so far as I know, who introduced the custom of charging the enemy at a run, and they were likewise the first who dared to look upon the Median garb, and to face men clad in that fashion. Until this time the very name of the Medes had been a terror to the Greeks to hear.

113. The two armies fought together on the plain of Marathon for a length of time; and in the mid battle, where the Persians themselves and the Sacae had their place, the barbarians were victorious, and broke and pursued the Greeks into the inner country; but on the two wings the Athenians and the Plataeans defeated the enemy. Having so done, they suffered the routed barbarians to fly at their ease, and joining the two wings in one, fell upon those who had broken their own centre, and fought and conquered them. These likewise fled, and now the Athenians hung upon the runaways and cut them down, chasing them all the way to the shore, on reaching which they laid hold of the ships and called aloud for fire.

114. It was in the struggle here that Callimachus the polemarch, after greatly distinguishing himself, lost his life; Stesilaus too, the son of Thrasilaus, one of the generals, was slain; and Cynaegirus, the son of Euphorion, having seized on a vessel of the enemy's by the ornament at the stern, had his hand cut off by the blow of an axe, and so perished; as likewise did many other Athenians of note and name.

115. Nevertheless the Athenians secured in this way seven of the vessels, while with the remainder the barbarians pushed off, and taking aboard their Eretrian prisoners from the island where they had left them, doubled Cape Sunium, hoping to reach Athens before the return of the Athenians. The Alcmaeonidae were accused by their countrymen of suggesting this course to them; they had, it was said, an understanding with the Persians, and made a signal to them, by raising a shield, after they were embarked in their ships.

and cavalry that the rapid charge (actually only the last quarter-mile?) was made. There is reason to believe that the Persian horse was still in Eretria.

116. The Persians accordingly sailed round Sunium. But the Athenians with all possible speed marched away to the defence of their city, and succeeded in reaching Athens before the appearance of the barbarians; and as their camp at Marathon had been pitched in a precinct of Heracles, so now they encamped in another precinct of the same god at Cynosarges. The barbarian fleet arrived, and lay to off Phalerum, which was at that time the haven of Athens; but after resting awhile upon their oars, they departed and sailed away to Asia.

117. There fell in this battle of Marathon, on the side of the barbarians, about 6,400 men;[25] on that of the Athenians, 192. Such was the number of the slain on the one side and the other. A strange prodigy likewise happened at this fight. Epizelus, the son of Cuphagoras, an Athenian, was in the thick of the fray, and behaving himself as a brave man should, when suddenly he was stricken with blindness, without blow of sword or dart, and this blindness continued thenceforth during the whole of his after life. The following is the account which he himself, as I have heard, gave of the matter: he said that a gigantic warrior, with a huge beard, which shaded all his shield, stood over against him, but the ghostly semblance passed him by, and slew the man at his side. Such, as I understand, was the tale which Epizelus told.

118. Datis meanwhile was on his way back to Asia, and had reached Myconus, when he saw in his sleep a vision. What it was is not known; but no sooner was day come than he caused strict search to be made throughout the whole fleet, and finding on board a Phoenician vessel an image of Apollo overlaid with gold, he inquired from whence it had been taken, and learning to what temple it belonged, he took it with him in his own ship to Delos, and placed it in the temple there, enjoining the Delians, who had now come back to their island, to restore the image to the Theban Delium, which lies on the coast over against Chalcis. Having left these injunctions, he sailed away; but the Delians failed to restore the statue, and it was not till twenty years

[25] This total is a moderate one; although Herodotus gives no estimate of the Persian army at Marathon, it numbered perhaps 15,000.

afterwards that the Thebans, warned by an oracle, themselves
brought it back to Delium.

119. As for the Eretrians, whom Datis and Artaphernes had
carried away captive, when the fleet reached Asia, they were
taken up to Susa. Now king Darius, before they were made his
prisoners, nourished a fierce anger against these men for having
injured him without provocation; but now that he saw them
brought into his presence, and become his subjects, he did them
no other harm, but only settled them at one of his own stations
in Cissia, a place called Ardericca, twenty-six miles distant from
Susa, and five miles from the well which yields produce of three
different kinds. For from this well they get bitumen, salt, and
oil, procuring it in the way that I will now describe: they draw
with a swipe, and instead of a bucket make use of the half of a
wine-skin; with this the man dips, and after drawing, pours the
liquid into a reservoir, wherefrom it passes into another, and
there takes three different shapes. The salt and the bitumen
forthwith collect and harden, while the oil is drawn off into
casks. It is called by the Persians rhadinace,[26] is black, and has
an unpleasant smell. Here then king Darius established the
Eretrians, and here they continued to my time, and still spoke
their old language. So thus it fared with the Eretrians.

120. After the full of the moon 2,000 Lacedaemonians came
to Athens. So eager had they been to arrive in time, that they
took but three days to reach Attica from Sparta. They came,
however, too late for the battle; yet, as they had a longing to
behold the Medes, they continued their march to Marathon and
there viewed the slain. Then, after giving the Athenians all
praise for their achievement, they departed and returned home.

121. But it fills me with wonderment, and I cannot believe
the report, that the Alcmaeonidae had an understanding with
the Persians, and held them up a shield as a signal, wishing
Athens to be brought under the yoke of the barbarians and of
Hippias—the Alcmaeonidae, who have shown themselves at
least as bitter haters of tyrants as was Callias, the son of Phae-
nippus, and father of Hipponicus. This Callias was the only per-

[26] Petroleum.

son at Athens who, when the Pisistratidae were driven out, and
their goods were exposed for sale by the vote of the people, had
the courage to make purchases, and likewise in many other ways
to display the strongest hostility.

[122. He was a man very worthy to be had in remembrance
by all, on several accounts. For not only did he thus distinguish
himself beyond others in the cause of his country's freedom; but
likewise, by the honours which he gained at the Olympic games,
where he carried off the prize in the horse-race, and was second
in the four-horse chariot-race, and by his victory at an earlier
period in the Pythian games, he showed himself in the eyes of
all the Greeks a man most unsparing in his expenditure. He was
remarkable too for his conduct in respect of his daughters, three
in number; for when they came to be of marriageable age, he
gave to each of them a most ample dowry, and placed it at their
own disposal, allowing them to choose their husbands from
among all the citizens of Athens, and giving each in marriage to
the man of her own choice.[27]]

123. Now the Alcmaeonidae fell not a whit short of this person in their hatred of tyrants, so that I am astonished at the
charge made against them, and cannot bring myself to believe
that they held up a shield; for they were men who had remained
in exile during the whole time that the tyranny lasted, and they
even contrived the trick by which the Pisistratidae were deprived of their throne. Indeed I look upon them as the persons
who in good truth gave Athens her freedom far more than Harmodius and Aristogeiton. For these last merely exasperated the
other Pisistratidae by slaying Hipparchus, and were far from
doing anything towards putting down the tyranny; whereas the
Alcmaeonidae were manifestly the actual deliverers of Athens,
if at least it be true that the priestess was prevailed upon by
them to bid the Lacedaemonians set Athens free, as I have already related.

124. But perhaps they were offended with the people of
Athens, and therefore betrayed their country. Nay, but on the
contrary there were none of the Athenians who were held in such

[27] This chapter is an interpolation.

general esteem, or who were so laden with honours.[28] So that it is not even reasonable to suppose that a shield was held up by them on this account. A shield was shown, no doubt; that cannot be gainsaid; but who it was that showed it I cannot any further determine.

125. Now the Alcmaeonidae were, even in days of yore, a family of note at Athens, but from the time of Alcmaeon, and again of Megacles, they rose to special eminence.[29] The former of these two personages, Alcmaeon, the son of Megacles, when Croesus the Lydian sent men from Sardis to consult the Delphic oracle, gave aid gladly to his messengers, and assisted them to accomplish their task. Croesus, informed of Alcmaeon's kindnesses by the Lydians who from time to time conveyed his messages to the god, sent for him to Sardis, and, when he arrived, made him a present of as much gold as he should be able to carry at one time about his person. Finding that this was the gift assigned him, Alcmaeon took his measures, and prepared himself to receive it in the following way. He clothed himself in a loose tunic, which he made to bag greatly at the waist, and placing upon his feet the widest buskins that he could anywhere find, followed his guides into the treasure-house. Here he fell to upon a heap of gold-dust, and in the first place packed as much as he could inside his buskins, between them and his legs; after which he filled the breast of his tunic quite full of gold, and then sprinkling some among his hair, and taking some likewise in his mouth, he came forth from the treasure-house, scarcely able to drag his legs along, like anything rather than a man, with his mouth crammed full, and his bulk increased every way. On seeing him, Croesus burst into a laugh, and not only let him have all that he had taken, but gave him presents besides of fully equal worth. Thus this house became one of great wealth, and Alcmaeon was able to keep horses for the chariot-race, and won the prize at Olympia.

126. Afterwards, in the generation which followed, Cleis-

---

[28] Herodotus' defense of the Alcmaeonidae is unconvincing.
[29] The following anecdotes are popular tales Herodotus collected.

thenes, king of Sicyon, raised the family to still greater eminence among the Greeks than even that to which it had attained
before. For this Cleisthenes, who was the son of Aristonymus,
the grandson of Myron, and the great-grandson of Andreas, had
a daughter, called Agarista, whom he wished to marry to the
best husband that he could find in the whole of Greece. At the
Olympic games, therefore, having gained the prize in the chariot-
race, he caused public proclamation to be made to the following
effect, "Whoever among the Greeks deems himself worthy to
become the son-in-law of Cleisthenes, let him come, sixty days
hence, or, if he will, sooner, to Sicyon; for within a year's time,
counting from the end of the sixty days, Cleisthenes will decide on the man to whom he shall contract his daughter." So all
the Greeks who were proud of their own merit or of their country flocked to Sicyon as suitors; and Cleisthenes had a foot-
course and a wrestling-ground made ready, to try their powers.

127. From Italy there came Smindyrides, the son of Hippocrates, a native of Sybaris—which city about that time was
at the very height of its prosperity. He was a man who in luxu-
riousness of living exceeded all other persons. Likewise there
came Damasus, the son of Amyris, surnamed the Wise, a native
of Siris. These two were the only suitors from Italy. From the
Ionian Gulf appeared Amphimnestus, the son of Epistrophus,
an Epidamnian; from Aetolia Males, the brother of that Titor-
mus who excelled all the Greeks in strength, and who, wishing
to avoid his fellow-men, withdrew himself into the remotest
parts of the Aetolian territory. From the Peloponnese came several—Leocedes, son of that Pheidon, king of the Argives, who
established weights and measures throughout the Peloponnese,
and was the most insolent of all the Grecians—the same who
drove out the Elean directors of the games, and himself presided
over the contests at Olympia—Leocedes, I say, appeared, this
Pheidon's son; and likewise Amiantus, son of Lycurgus, an Arcadian of the city of Trapezus; Laphanes, an Azenian of Paeus,
whose father, Euphorion, as the story goes in Arcadia, entertained the Dioscuri at his residence, and thenceforth kept open
house for all comers; and lastly, Onomastus, the son of Agaeus,

a native of Elis. These four came from the Peloponnese. From Athens there arrived Megacles, the son of that Alcmaeon who visited Croesus, and Tisander's son, Hippocleides, the wealthiest and handsomest of the Athenians. There was likewise one Euboean, Lysanias, who came from Eretria, then a flourishing city. From Thessaly came Diactorides, a Cranonian, of the race of the Scopadae; and Alcon arrived from the Molossians. This was the list of the suitors.

128. Now when they were all come, and the day appointed had arrived, Cleisthenes first of all inquired of each concerning his country and his family; after which he kept them with him a year, and made trial of their manly bearing, their temper, their accomplishments, and their disposition, sometimes drawing them apart for converse, sometimes bringing them all together. Such as were still youths he took with him from time to time to the gymnasia; but the greatest trial of all was at the banquet-table. During the whole period of their stay he lived with them as I have said, and, further, from first to last he entertained them sumptuously. Somehow or other the suitors who came from Athens pleased him the best of all; and of these Hippocleides, Tisander's son, was specially in favour, partly on account of his manly bearing, and partly also because his ancestors were of kin to the Corinthian Cypselids.

129. When at length the day arrived which had been fixed for the espousals, and Cleisthenes had to speak out and declare his choice, he first of all made a sacrifice of 100 oxen, and held a banquet whereat he entertained all the suitors, and the whole people of Sicyon. After the feast was ended, the suitors vied with each other in music and in speaking on a given subject. Presently, as the drinking advanced, Hippocleides, who quite dumbfounded the rest, called aloud to the fluteplayer, and bade him strike up a dance; which the man did, and Hippocleides danced to it. And he fancied that he was dancing excellently well; but Cleisthenes, who was observing him, began to misdoubt the whole business. Then Hippocleides, after a pause, told an attendant to bring in a table; and when it was brought he mounted upon it and danced first of all some Laconian figures.

then some Attic ones; after which he stood on his head upon the table, and began to toss his legs about. Cleisthenes, notwithstanding that he now loathed Hippocleides for a son-in-law, by reason of his dancing and his shamelessness, still, as he wished to avoid an outbreak, had restrained himself during the first and likewise during the second dance; when, however, he saw him tossing his legs in the air, he could no longer contain himself, but cried out, "Son of Tisander, you have danced your wife away!" "What does Hippocleides care?" was the other's answer. And hence the proverb arose.

130. Then Cleisthenes commanded silence, and spake thus before the assembled company:

"Suitors of my daughter, well pleased am I with you all, and right willingly, if it were possible, would I content you all, and not by making choice of one appear to put a slight upon the rest. But as it is out of my power, seeing that I have but one daughter, to grant to all their wishes, I will present to each of you whom I must needs dismiss a talent of silver, for the honour that you have done me in seeking to ally yourselves with my house, and for your long absence from your homes. But my daughter, Agarista, I betroth to Megacles, the son of Alcmaeon, to be his wife, according to the usage and wont of Athens."

Then Megacles expressed his readiness, and Cleisthenes had the marriage solemnized.

131. Thus ended the affair of the suitors, and thus the Alcmaeonidae came to be famous throughout the whole of Greece. The issue of this marriage was the Cleisthenes—so named after his grandfather the Sicyonian—who made the tribes at Athens, and set up the popular government. Megacles had likewise another son, called Hippocrates, whose children were a Megacles and an Agarista, the latter named after Agarista the daughter of Cleisthenes. She married Xanthippus, the son of Ariphron; and when she was with child by him had a dream, wherein she fancied that she was delivered of a lion; after which, within a few days, she bore Xanthippus a son, Pericles.

132. After the blow struck at Marathon, Miltiades, who was previously held in high esteem by his countrymen, increased yet

more in influence. Hence, when he told them that he wanted a fleet of seventy ships,[30] with an armed force, and money, without informing them what country he was going to attack, but only promising to enrich them, if they would accompany him, seeing that it was a right wealthy land, where they might easily get as much gold as they cared to have—when he told them this, they were quite carried away, and gave him the whole armament which he required.

133. So Miltiades, having got the armament, sailed against Paros, with the object, as he alleged, of punishing the Parians for having gone to war with Athens, inasmuch as a trireme of theirs had come with the Persian fleet to Marathon. This, however, was a mere pretence; the truth was, that Miltiades owed the Parians a grudge, because Lysagoras, the son of Tisias, who was a Parian by birth, had told tales against him to Hydarnes the Persian. Arrived before the place against which his expedition was designed, he drove the Parians within their walls, and forthwith laid siege to the city. At the same time he sent a herald to the inhabitants, and required of them 100 talents, threatening that, if they refused, he would press the siege, and never give it over till the town was taken. But the Parians, without giving his demand a thought, proceeded to use every means that they could devise for the defence of their city, and even invented new plans for the purpose, one of which was, by working at night to raise such parts of the wall as were likely to be carried by assault to double their former height.

134. Thus far all the Greeks agree in their accounts of this business; what follows is related upon the testimony of the Parians only. Miltiades had come to his wit's end, when one of the prisoners, a woman named Timo, who was by birth a Parian, and had held the office of under-priestess in the temple of the infernal goddesses, came and conferred with him. This woman, they say, introduced into the presence of Miltiades, advised him, if he set great store by the capture of the place, to do some-

---

[30] Seventy ships appear to have been the full complement of the Athenian navy until the time when the number was raised by Themistocles to 100. Miltiades therefore took the whole Athenian navy on this expedition.

thing which she could suggest to him. When therefore she had told him what it was she meant, he betook himself to the hill which lies in front of the city, and there leaped the fence enclosing the precinct of Demeter the Lawgiver, since he was not able to open the door. After leaping into the place he went straight to the sanctuary, intending to do something within it—either to remove some of the holy things which it was not lawful to stir, or to perform some act or other, I cannot say what—and had just reached the door, when suddenly a feeling of horror came upon him, and he returned back the way he had come; but in jumping down from the outer wall, he strained his thigh, or, as some say, struck the ground with his knee.

135. So Miltiades returned home sick, without bringing the Athenians any money, and without conquering Paros, having done no more than to besiege the town for twenty-six days, and ravage the remainder of the island. The Parians, however, when it came to their knowledge that Timo, the under-priestess of the goddesses, had advised Miltiades what he should do, were minded to punish her for her crime; they therefore sent messengers to Delphi, as soon as the siege was at an end, and asked the god if they should put the under-priestess to death. "She had discovered," they said, "to the enemies of her country how they might bring it into subjection, and had exhibited to Miltiades mysteries which it was not lawful for a man to know." But the priestess forbade them, and said, "Timo was not in fault; it was decreed that Miltiades should come to an unhappy end, and she was sent to lure him to his destruction." Such was the answer given to the Parians by the priestess.

136. The Athenians, upon the return of Miltiades from Paros, had much debate concerning him; and Xanthippus, the son of Ariphron, who spoke more freely aganist him than all the rest, impeached him before the people, and brought him to trial for his life, on the charge of having dealt deceitfully with the Athenians. Miltiades, though he was present in court, did not speak in his own defence, for his thigh had begun to mortify, and disabled him from pleading his cause. He was forced to lie on a couch while his defence was made by his friends, who dwelt

at most length on the fight at Marathon, while they made mention also of the capture of Lemnos, telling how Miltiades took the island, and after executing vengeance on the Pelasgians, gave up his conquest to Athens. The judgment of the people was in his favour so far as to spare his life, but for the wrong he had done them they fined him fifty talents. Soon afterwards his thigh completely gangrened and mortified; and so Miltiades died, and the fifty talents were paid by his son Cimon.

137. Now the way in which Miltiades had made himself master of Lemnos was the following. There were certain Pelasgians whom the Athenians once drove out of Attica; whether they did it justly or unjustly I cannot say, since I only know what is reported of it, which is the following: Hecataeus, the son of Hegesander, says in his history that it was unjustly. "The Athenians," according to him, "had given to the Pelasgi a tract of land at the foot of Hymettus as payment for the wall with which the Pelasgians had surrounded their citadel. This land was barren, and little worth at the time, but the Pelasgians brought it into good condition; whereupon the Athenians begrudged them the tract, and desired to recover it. And so, without any better excuse, they took arms and drove out the Pelasgians." But the Athenians maintain that they were justified in what they did. "The Pelasgians," they say, "while they lived at the foot of Hymettus, were wont to sally forth from that region and commit outrages on their children. For the Athenians used at that time to send their sons and daughters to draw water at the fountain called the Nine Springs, inasmuch as neither they nor the other Greeks had any household slaves in those days; and the maidens, whenever they came, were used rudely and insolently by the Pelasgians. Nor were they even content thus, but at the last they laid a plot, and were caught by the Athenians in the act of making an attempt upon their city. Then the Athenians proved how much better men they were than the Pelasgians; for whereas they might justly have killed them all, having caught them in the very act of rebelling, they spared their lives, and only required that they should leave the country. Hereupon the Pelasgians quitted Attica, and settled in Lemnos and other

places." Such are the accounts respectively of Hecataeus and the Athenians.

138. These same Pelasgians, after they were settled in Lemnos, conceived the wish to be revenged on the Athenians. So, as they were well acquainted with the Athenian festivals, they manned some fifty-oared ships, and having laid an ambush to catch the Athenian women as they kept the festival of Artemis at Brauron, they succeeded in carrying off a large number, whom they took to Lemnos and there kept as concubines. After a while the women bore children, whom they taught to speak the language of Attica and observe the manners of the Athenians. These boys refused to have any commerce with the sons of the Pelasgian women; and if a Pelasgian boy struck one of their number, they all made common cause, and joined in avenging their comrade; nay, the Greek boys even set up a claim to exercise lordship over the others, and succeeded in gaining the upper hand. When these things came to the ears of the Pelasgians, they took counsel together, and on considering the matter, they grew frightened, and said one to another, "If these boys even now are resolved to make common cause against the sons of our lawful wives, and seek to exercise lordship over them, what may we expect when they grow up to be men?" Then it seemed good to the Pelasgians to kill all the sons of the Attic women; which they did accordingly, and at the same time slew likewise their mothers. From this deed, and that former crime of the Lemnian women, when they slew their husbands in the days of Thoas, it has come to be usual throughout Greece to call wicked actions by the name of Lemnian deeds.

139. When the Pelasgians had thus slain their children and their women, the earth refused to bring forth its fruits for them, and their wives bore fewer children, and their flocks and herds increased more slowly than before, till at last, sore pressed by famine and bereavement, they sent men to Delphi, and begged the god to tell them how they might obtain deliverance from their sufferings. The priestess answered, "They must give the Athenians whatever satisfaction they might demand." Then the Pelasgians went to Athens and declared their wish to give the

Athenians satisfaction for the wrong which they had done to them. So the Athenians had a couch prepared in their town-hall, and adorned it with the fairest coverlets, and set by its side a table laden with all manner of good things, and then told the Pelasgians they must deliver up their country to them in a similar condition. The Pelasgians answered and said, "When a ship comes with a north wind from your country to ours in a single day, then will we give it up to you." This they said because they knew that what they required was impossible, for Attica lies a long way to the south of Lemnos.

140. No more passed at that time. But very many years afterwards, when the Hellespontian Chersonese had been brought under the power of Athens, Miltiades, the son of Cimon, sailed, during the prevalence of the Etesian winds, from Elaeus in the Chersonese to Lemnos, and called on the Pelasgians to quit their island, reminding them of the prophecy which they had supposed it impossible to fulfil. The people of Hephaestia obeyed the call; but they of Myrina, not acknowledging the Chersonese to be any part of Attica, refused; and were besieged and brought over by force. Thus was Lemnos gained by the Athenians and Miltiades

The Seventh Book, Entitled

POLYMNIA

1. Now when tidings of the battle that had been fought at Marathon reached the ears of King Darius, the son of Hystaspes, his anger against the Athenians, which had been already roused by their attack upon Sardis, waxed still fiercer, and he became more than ever eager to lead an army against Greece. Instantly he sent off messengers to make proclamation through the several states, that fresh levies were to be raised, and these at an increased rate; while ships, horses, provisions, and transports were likewise to be furnished. So the men published his commands; and now all Asia was in commotion for three years, while everywhere, as Greece was to be attacked, the best and bravest were enrolled for the service, and had to make their preparations accordingly.

After this, in the fourth year, the Egyptians whom Cambyses had enslaved revolted from the Persians; whereupon Darius was more hot for war than ever, and earnestly desired to march an army against both adversaries.

2. Now, as he was about to lead forth his levies against Egypt and Athens, a fierce contention for the sovereign power arose among his sons; since the law of the Persians was, that a king must not go out with his army, until he has appointed one to succeed him upon the throne. Darius, before he obtained the kingdom, had had three sons born to him from his former wife, who was a daughter of Gobryas; while, since he began to reign, Atossa, the daughter of Cyrus, had borne him four. Artabazanes was the eldest of the first family, and Xerxes of the second. These two, therefore, being the sons of different mothers, were

ed the crown as the eldest of
an established custom all over
the pre-eminence; while Xerxes,
t he was sprung from Atossa, the
it was Cyrus who had won the Per-

pronounced on the matter, it happened
that D   son of Ariston, who had been deprived of
his crown a   and had afterwards, of his own accord, gone
into banishmen   came up to Susa, and there heard of the quarrel of the princes. Hereupon, as report says, he went to Xerxes,
and advised him, in addition to all that he had urged before, to
plead—that at the time when he was born Darius was already
king, and bore rule over the Persians; but when Artabazanes
came into the world, he was a mere private person. It would
therefore be neither right nor seemly that the crown should go
to another in preference to himself. "For at Sparta," said Demaratus, by way of suggestion, "the law is, that if a king has
sons before he comes to the throne, and another son is born to
him afterwards, the child so born is heir to his father's kingdom." [1] Xerxes followed this counsel, and Darius, persuaded
that he had justice on his side, appointed him his successor. For
my own part I believe that, even without this, the crown would
have gone to Xerxes; for Atossa was all-powerful.

4. Darius, when he had thus appointed Xerxes his heir, was
minded to lead forth his armies; but he was prevented by death
while his preparations were still proceeding. He died in the year
following the revolt of Egypt, and the matters here related, after
having reigned in all six and thirty years, leaving the revolted
Egyptians and the Athenians alike unpunished. At his death the
kingdom passed to his son, Xerxes.

5. Now Xerxes, on first mounting the throne, was coldly disposed towards the Grecian war, and made it his business to col-

[1] The tale here introduced does not seem to have been accepted by
Herodotus; and it is indeed very doubtful whether the law of succession
at Sparta was such as is stated. It has been remarked that anecdotes in-
vesting Demaratus with a factitious importance are frequent in Herodotus

lect an army against Egypt. But Mardonius, the son of Gobryas,
who was at the court, and had more influence with him than any
of the other Persians, being his own cousin, the child of a sister
of Darius, plied him with discourses like the following:

"Master, it is not fitting that they of Athens escape scot-free,
after doing the Persians such great injury. Complete the work
which you have in hand, and then, when the pride of Egypt is
brought down, lead an army against Athens. So shall you have
good report among men, and others shall fear hereafter to attack your country."

Thus far it was of vengeance that he spoke, but sometimes he
would vary the theme, and observe by the way that Europe was
a beautiful region, rich in all kinds of cultivated trees, and the
soil excellent: no one, save the king, was worthy to own such a
land.

6. All this he said, because he longed for adventures, and
hoped to become Satrap of Greece under the king; and after a
while he had his way, and persuaded Xerxes to do according to
his desires. Other things, however, occurring about the same
time, helped his persuasions. For, in the first place, it chanced
that messengers arrived from Thessaly, sent by the Aleuadae,
Thessalian kings, to invite Xerxes into Greece, and to promise
him all the assistance which it was in their power to give. And
further, the Pisistratidae, who had come up to Susa, used the
same language as the Aleuadae, and worked upon him even
more than they, by means of Onomacritus of Athens, an oracle-
monger, and the same who set forth the prophecies of Musaeus
in their order.[2] The Pisistratidae had previously been at enmity
with this man, but made up the quarrel before they removed to
Susa. He was banished from Athens by Hipparchus, the son of
Pisistratus, because he foisted into the writings of Musaeus a
prophecy that the islands which lie off Lemnos would one day
disappear in the sea. Lasus of Hermione[3] caught him in the act

[2] Of Musaeus all perhaps that can be said with certainty is that poems
believed to be ancient were current under his name as early as 520 B.C.
These were chiefly oracles, but not entirely so.

[3] Lasus of Hermione, a lyric and dithyrambic poet, was said to have
been the instructor of Pindar.

of so doing. For this cause Hipparchus banished him, though till then they had been the closest of friends. Now, however, he went up to Susa with the sons of Pisistratus, and they talked very grandly of him to the king; while he, for his part, whenever he was in the king's company, repeated to him certain of the oracles; and while he took care to pass over all that spoke of disaster to the barbarians, brought forward the passages which promised them the greatest success. "It was fated," he told Xerxes, "that a Persian should bridge the Hellespont, and march an army from Asia into Greece." While Onomacritus thus plied Xerxes with his oracles, the Pisistratidae and Aleuadae did not cease to press on him their advice, till at last the king yielded, and agreed to lead forth an expedition.

7. First, however, in the year following the death of Darius, he marched against those who had revolted from him; and having reduced them, and laid all Egypt under a far harder yoke than ever his father had put upon it, he gave the government to Achaemenes, who was his own brother, and son to Darius. This Achaemenes was afterwards slain in his government by Tnaros, the son of Psammetichus, a Libyan.

8. After Egypt was subdued, Xerxes, being about to take in hand the expedition against Athens, called together an assembly of the noblest Persians, to learn their opinions, and to lay before them his own designs.[4] So, when the men were met, the king spoke thus to them:

"Persians, I shall not be the first to bring in among you a new custom—I shall but follow one which has come down to us from our forefathers. Never yet, as our old men assure me, has our race reposed itself, since the time when Cyrus overcame Astyages, and so we Persians wrested the sceptre from the Medes. Now in all this God guides us, and we, obeying his guidance, prosper greatly. What need have I to tell you of the deeds of Cyrus and Cambyses, and my own father Darius, how many nations they conquered, and added to our dominions? You

[4] These speeches have no historical character but they may be considered as embodying Persian as well as Greek views of the circumstances out of which the war arose, and the feelings of those who engaged in it.

know right well what great things they achieved. But for myself,
I will say, that from the day on which I mounted the throne, I
have not ceased to consider by what means I may rival those
who have preceded me in this post of honour, and increase the
power of Persia as much as any of them. And truly I have pondered upon this, until at last I have found out a way whereby
we may at once win glory, and likewise get possession of a land
which is as large and as rich as our own—nay, which is even
more varied in the fruits it bears—while at the same time we
obtain satisfaction and revenge. For this cause I have now called
you together, that I may make known to you what I design to
do. My intent is to throw a bridge over the Hellespont and
march an army through Europe against Greece, that thereby I
may obtain vengeance from the Athenians for the wrongs committed by them against the Persians and against my father.
Your own eyes saw the preparations of Darius against these
men; but death came upon him, and balked his hopes of revenge. In his behalf, therefore, and in behalf of all the Persians,
I undertake the war, and pledge myself not to rest till I have
taken and burnt Athens, which has dared, unprovoked, to injure me and my father. Long since they came to Asia with Aristagoras of Miletus, who was one of our slaves, and entering
Sardis, burnt its temples and its sacred groves; again, more
lately, when we made a landing upon their coast under Datis
and Artaphernes, how roughly they handled us you do not need
to be told. For these reasons, therefore, I am bent upon this
war; and I see likewise therewith united no few advantages.
Once let us subdue this people, and those neighbours of theirs
who hold the land of Pelops the Phrygian, and we shall extend
the Persian territory as far as God's heaven reaches. The sun
will then shine on no land beyond our borders; for I will pass
through Europe from one end to the other, and with your aid
make of all the lands which it contains one country. For thus, if
what I hear be true, affairs stand: The nations whereof I have
spoken, once swept away, there is no city, no country left in all
the world, which will venture so much as to withstand us in
arms. By this course then we shall bring all mankind under our

yoke, alike those who are guilty and those who are innocent of doing us wrong. For yourselves, if you wish to please me, do as follows: When I announce the time for the army to meet together, hasten to the muster with a good will, every one of you; and know that to the man who brings with him the most gallant array I will give the gifts which our people consider the most honourable. This then is what you have to do. But to show that I am not self-willed in this matter I lay the business before you, and give you full leave to speak your minds upon it openly."

Xerxes, having so spoken, held his peace. ·

9. Whereupon Mardonius took the word, and said:

"Of a truth, my lord, you surpass, not only all living Persians, but likewise those yet unborn. Most true and right is each word that you have now uttered; but best of all your resolve, not to let the Ionians who live in Europe—a worthless crew—mock us any more. It were indeed a monstrous thing if, after conquering and enslaving the Sacae, the Indians, the Ethiopians, the Assyrians, and many other mighty nations, not for any wrong that they had done us, but only to increase our empire, we should then allow the Greeks, who have done us such wanton injury, to escape our vengeance. What is it that we fear in them?—not surely their numbers?—not the greatness of their wealth? We know the manner of their battle—we know how weak their power is; already have we subdued their children who dwell in our country, the Ionians, Aeolians, and Dorians. I myself have had experience of these men when I marched against them by the orders of your father; and though I went as far as Macedonia, and came but a little short of reaching Athens itself, yet not a soul ventured to come out against me to battle. And yet, I am told, these very Greeks are wont to wage wars against one another in the most foolish way, through sheer perversity and doltishness. For no sooner is war proclaimed than they search out the smoothest and fairest plain that is to be found in all the land, and there they assemble and fight; whence it comes to pass that even the conquerors depart with great loss: I say nothing of the conquered, for they are destroyed altogether. Now surely, as they are all of one speech, they ought to interchange heralds and messengers, and make up their differences by any means rather than battle; or, at the worst, if they must needs fight one against another, they ought to post themselves as strongly as possible, and so try their quarrels. But, notwithstanding that they have so foolish a manner of warfare, yet these Greeks, when I led my army against them to the very borders of Macedonia, did not so much as think of offering me battle. Who then will dare, O king, to meet you in arms, when you come with all Asia's warriors at your back, and with all her ships? For my part I do not believe the Greek people will be so foolhardy. Grant, however, that I am mistaken herein, and that they are foolish enough to meet us in open fight; in that case they will learn that there are no such soldiers in the whole world as we. Nevertheless let us spare no pains; for nothing comes without trouble, but all that men acquire is got by painstaking."

When Mardonius had in this way softened the harsh speech of Xerxes, he too held his peace.

10. The other Persians were silent, for all feared to raise their voice against the plan proposed to them. But Artabanus, the son of Hystaspes, and uncle of Xerxes, trusting to his relationship, was bold to speak:

"O king, it is impossible, if no more than one opinion is uttered, to make choice of the best: a man is forced then to follow whatever advice may have been given him; but if opposite speeches are delivered, then choice can be exercised. In like manner pure gold is not recognised by itself; but when we test it along with baser ore, we perceive which is the better. I counselled your father, Darius, who was my own brother, not to attack the Scyths, a race of people who had no town in their whole land. He thought however to subdue those wandering tribes, and would not listen to me, but marched an army against them, and before he returned home lost many of his bravest warriors. You are about, O king, to attack a people far superior to the Scyths, a people distinguished above others both by land and sea. It is fit therefore that I should tell you what danger you incur hereby. You say that you will bridge the Hellespont, and lead your troops through Europe against Greece. Now suppose some disaster befall you by land or sea, or by both. It may be even so, for the men are reputed valiant. Indeed one may measure their prowess from what they have already done; for when Datis and Artaphernes led their huge army against Attica, the Athenians singly defeated them. But grant they are not successful on both elements. Still, if they man their ships, and defeating us by sea, sail to the Hellespont, and there destroy our bridge, that, sire, were a fearful hazard. And here it is not by my own mother wit alone that I conjecture what will happen, but I remember how narrowly we escaped disaster once, when your father, after throwing bridges over the Thracian Bosporus and the Ister, marched against the Scythians, and they tried every sort of prayer to induce the Ionians, who had charge of the bridge over the Ister, to break the passage. On that day, if Histiaeus, the King of Miletus, had sided with the other princes, and not set himself to oppose their views, the empire of the Persians would have come to nought. Surely a dreadful thing is this even to hear said, that the king's fortunes depended wholly on one man.

"Think then no more of incurring so great a danger when no need presses, but follow the advice I tender. Break up this meeting, and when you have well considered the matter with yourself, and settled what you will do, declare to us your resolve. I know not of aught in the world that so profits a man as taking good counsel with himself; for even if things fall out against one's hopes, still one has counselled well, though fortune has made the counsel of no effect: whereas if a man counsels ill and luck follows, he has gotten a windfall, but his counsel is none the less silly. See how god with his lightning always smites the bigger animals, and will not suffer them to wax insolent, while those of a lesser bulk chafe him not. How likewise his bolts fall ever on the highest houses and the tallest trees? So plainly does he love to bring down everything that exalts itself. Thus often a mighty host is discomfited by a few men, when god in his jealousy sends fear or storm from heaven, and they perish in a way unworthy of them. For god allows no one to have high thoughts but himself. Again, hurry always brings about disasters, from which huge sufferings are wont to arise; but in delay lie many advantages, not apparent (it may be) at first sight, but such as in course of time are seen of all. Such then is my counsel, O king.

"And you, Mardonius, son of Gobryas, forbear to speak foolishly concerning the Greeks, who are men that ought not to be lightly esteemed by us. For while you revile the Greeks, you encourage the king to lead his own troops against them; and this, as it seems to me, is what you are specially striving to accomplish. Heaven grant you succeed not in your wish! For slander is of all evils the most terrible. In it two men do wrong, and one man has wrong done to him. The slanderer does wrong, for he abuses a man behind his back; and the hearer, for he believes what he has not searched into thoroughly. The man slandered in his absence suffers wrong at the hands of both; for one brings against him a false charge, and the other thinks him an evil-doer. If, however, it must needs be that we go to war with this people, at least allow the king to abide at home in Persia. Then let us both stake our children on the issue, and you choose out your men, and taking with you whatever number of troops you like, lead forth our armies to battle. If things go well for the king, as you say they will, let me and my children be put to death; but if they fall out as I prophesy, let your children suffer, and you too, if you come back alive. But should you refuse this wager, and still resolve to march an army against Greece, sure I am that some of those whom you leave behind you here will one day receive the sad tidings, that Mardonius has brought a great disaster upon the Persian people, and lies a prey to dogs and birds somewhere in the land of the Athenians, or else in that of the Lacedaemonians; unless indeed you have perished sooner by the way, experiencing in your own person the might of those men on whom you would induce the king to make war."

11. Thus Artabanus spoke. But Xerxes, full of wrath, replied to him:

"Artabanus, you are my father's brother—that shall save you from receiving the proper reward for your silly words. One shame however I will lay upon you, coward and faint-hearted as you are—you shall not come with me to fight these Greeks, but shall tarry here with the women. Without your aid I will accomplish all of which I spoke. For let me not be thought the child of Darius, the son of Hystaspes, the son of Arsames, the son of Ariaramnes, the son of Teispes, nor of Cyrus, the son of Cambyses, the son of Teispes, the son of Achaemenes, if I take not vengeance on the Athenians. Full well I know that, were we to remain at rest, yet would not they, but would most certainly invade our country, if at least it be right to judge from what they have already done; for, remember, it was they who fired Sardis and attacked Asia. So now retreat is on both sides impossible, and the choice lies between doing and suffering injury; either our empire must pass under the dominion of the Greeks, or their land become the prey of the Persians; for there is no middle course left in this quarrel. It is right then that we, who have in times past received wrong, should now avenge it, and that I should thereby discover, what that great risk is, which I run in marching against these men—men whom Pelops the Phrygian, a vassal of my forefathers, subdued so utterly, that to this day both the land, and the people who dwell therein, alike bear the name of the conqueror."

12. Thus far did the speaking proceed. Afterwards evening fell, and Xerxes began to find the advice of Artabanus greatly disquiet him. So he thought upon it during the night, and concluded at last that it was not for his advantage to lead an army 'nto Greece. When he had thus made up his mind anew, he fell asleep. And now he saw in the night, as the Persians declare, a vision of this nature—he thought a tall and beautiful man stood over him and said, "Have you then changed your mind, Persian, and will you not lead forth your host against the Greeks, after commanding the Persians to gather together their levies? Be sure you do not well to change; nor is there a man here who will approve your conduct. The course that you determined on during the day, let that be followed." After thus speaking the man seemed to Xerxes to fly away.

13. Day dawned, and the king made no account of this dream, but called together the same Persians as before, and spoke to them as follows:

"Men of Persia, forgive me if I alter the resolve to which I came so lately. Consider that I have not yet reached the full growth of my wisdom, and that they who urge me to engage in this war leave me not to myself for a moment. When I heard the advice of Artabanus, my young blood suddenly boiled, and I spoke words against him little befitting his years; now however I confess my fault, and am resolved to follow his counsel. Understand then that I have changed my intent with respect to carrying war into Greece, and cease to trouble your selves."

When they heard these words, the Persians were full of joy, and falling down at the feet of Xerxes, made obeisance to him.

14. But when night came, again the same vision stood over Xerxes as he slept, and said, "Son of Darius, it seems you have openly before all the Persians renounced the expedition, making light of my words, as though you had not heard them spoken. Know therefore and be well assured, that unless you go forth to the war, this thing shall happen to you—as you are grown mighty and puissant in a short space, so likewise shall you within a little time be brought low indeed."

15. Then Xerxes, greatly frightened at the vision which he had seen, sprang from his couch, and sent a messenger to call Artabanus, who came at the summons, when Xerxes spoke to him in these words:

"Artabanus, at the moment I acted foolishly, when I gave you ill words in return for your good advice. However I soon repented, and was convinced that your counsel was such as I ought to follow. But I may not now act in this way, greatly as I desire to do so. For ever since I repented and changed my mind a dream has haunted me, which disapproves my intentions, and has now just gone from me with threats. Now if this dream is sent to me from god, and if it is indeed his will that our troops should march against Greece, you too will have the same dream come to you and receive the same commands as myself. And this will be most sure to happen, I think, if you put on the dress which I wear, and then, after taking your seat upon my throne, lie down to sleep on my bed."

16. Such were the words of Xerxes. Artabanus would not at

first yield to the command of the king, for he considered himself unworthy to sit upon the royal throne. At the last however
he was forced to give way, and did as Xerxes bade him; but first
he spoke thus to the king:

"To me, sire, it seems to matter little whether a man is wise
himself or willing to hearken to such as give good advice. In you
truly are found both tempers, but the counsels of evil men lead
you astray; they are like the gales of wind which vex the sea—
else the most useful thing for man in the whole world—and suffer it not to follow the bent of its own nature. For myself, it
irked me not so much to be reproached by you, as to observe,
that when two courses were placed before the Persian people,
one of a nature to increase their pride, the other to humble it,
by showing them how hurtful it is to allow one's heart always
to covet more than one at present possesses, you chose that
which was the worse both for yourself and for the Persians.
Now you say, that from the time when you approved the better
course, and gave up the thought of warring against Greece, a
dream has haunted you, sent by some god or other, which will
not suffer you to lay aside the expedition. But such things, my
son, have of a truth nothing divine in them. The dreams, that
wander to and fro among mankind, I will tell you their nature,
—I who have seen so many more years than you. Whatever a
man has been thinking of during the day, is likely to hover
round him in the visions of his dreams at night. Now we during
these many days past have had our hands full of this enterprise.
If however the matter be not as I suppose, but god has indeed
some part therein, you have in brief declared the whole that can
be said concerning it—let it appear to me as it has to you. and
lay on me the same injunctions. But it ought not to appear to
me any the more if I put on your clothes than if I wear my own,
nor if I go to sleep in your bed than if I do so in mine—supposing, I mean, that it is about to appear at all. For this thing, be
it what it may, that visits you in your sleep, surely is not so far
gone in folly as to see me, and because I am dressed in your
clothes, straightway to mistake me for you. Now however our
business is to see if it will regard me as of small account, and

not vouchsafe to appear to me, whether I wear mine own clothes or yours, while it keeps on haunting you continually. If it does so, and appears often, I should myself say that it was from god. For the rest, if your mind is fixed, and it is not possible to turn you from your design, but I must go and sleep in your bed, well and good, let it be even so; and when I have done as you wish, then let the dream appear to me. Till such time, however, I shall keep to my former opinion."

17. Thus Artabanus spoke; and, thinking to show Xerxes that his words were nought, he obeyed his orders. Having put on the garments which Xerxes was wont to wear, and, taken his seat upon the royal throne, he lay down to sleep upon the king's own bed. As he slept, there appeared to him the very same dream which had been seen by Xerxes; it came and stood over Artabanus, and said, "You are the man, then, who, as if concerned for Xerxes, seek to dissuade him from leading his armies against the Greeks! But you shall not escape, either now or in time to come, because you sought to prevent that which is fated to happen. As for Xerxes, it has been plainly told to himself what will befall him, if he refuses to perform my bidding."

18. In such words, as Artabanus thought, the vision threatened him, and then endeavoured to burn out his eyes with red-hot irons. At this he shrieked, and leaping from his couch, hurried to Xerxes, and, sitting down at his side, gave him a full account of the vision; after which he went on to speak in the following words:

"I, O King, am a man who have seen many mighty empires overthrown by weaker ones; and therefore it was that I sought to keep you from being carried away by your youth; since I knew how evil a thing it is to covet more than one possesses. I could remember the expedition of Cyrus against the Massagetae, and what was the issue of it; I could recollect the march of Cambyses against the Ethiops; I had taken part in the attack of Darius upon the Scyths; bearing therefore all these things in mind, I thought with myself that if you should remain at peace, all men would count you fortunate. But as this impulse has plainly come from above, and a heaven-sent destruction seems about to overtake the Greeks, behold, I change to another mind, and alter my thoughts upon the matter. Therefore make known to the Persians what the god has declared, and bid them follow the orders which were first given, and prepare their levies. Be careful to act so, that the bounty of the god may not be hindered by slackness on your part."

Thus these two spoke together; and Xerxes, encouraged by the vision, when day broke, laid all before the Persians, while Artabanus, who had formerly been the only person openly to oppose the expedition, now showed as openly that he favoured it.

19. After Xerxes had thus determined to go forth to the war, there appeared to him in his sleep yet a third vision. The Magi were consulted upon it, and said that its meaning reached to the whole earth, and that all mankind would become his servants. Now the vision which the king saw was this: he dreamed that he was crowned with a branch of an olive-tree, and that boughs spread out from the olive-branch and covered the whole earth; then suddenly the garland, as it lay upon his brow, vanished. So when the Magi had thus interpreted the vision, straightway all the Persians who were come together departed to their several governments, where each displayed the greatest zeal, on the faith of the king's offers. For all hoped to obtain for themselves the gifts which had been promised. And so Xerxes gathered together his host, ransacking every corner of the continent.

20. Reckoning from the recovery of Egypt, Xerxes spent four full years in collecting his host, and making ready all things that were needful for his soldiers. It was not till the close of the fifth year that he set forth on his march, accompanied by a mighty multitude. For of all the armaments whereof any mention has reached us, this was by far the greatest; insomuch that no other expedition compared to this seems of any account, neither that which Darius undertook against the Scythians, nor the expedition of the Scythians (which the attack of Darius was designed to avenge), when they, being in pursuit of the Cimmerians, fell upon the Median territory, and subdued and held for a time almost the whole of Upper Asia; nor, again, that of the Atreidae against Troy, of which we hear in story; nor that of the Mysians

and Teucrians, which was still earlier, wherein these nations crossed the Bosporus into Europe, and, after conquering all Thrace, pressed forward till they came to the Ionian sea, while southward they reached as far as the river Peneus.

21. All these expeditions, and others, if such there were, are as nothing compared with this. For was there a nation in all Asia which Xerxes did not bring with him against Greece? Or was there a river, except those of unusual size, which sufficed for his troops to drink? One nation furnished ships; another was arrayed among the foot-soldiers; a third had to supply horses; a fourth, transports for the horse and men likewise for the service; a fifth, ships of war towards the bridges; a sixth, ships and provisions.

22. And in the first place, because the former fleet had met with so great a disaster about Athos, preparations were made, for three years, in that quarter. A fleet of triremes lay at Elaeus in the Chersonese; and from this station detachments were sent by the various nations whereof the army was composed, which relieved one another at intervals, and worked at a trench beneath the lash of taskmasters; while the people dwelling about Athos bore likewise a part in the labour. Two Persians, Bubares, the son of Megabazus, and Artachaees, the son of Artaeus, superintended the undertaking.

Athos is a great and famous mountain, inhabited by men, and stretching far out into the sea. Where the mountain ends towards the mainland, it forms a peninsula; and in this place there is a neck of land about a mile and one-half across, the whole extent whereof from the sea of the Acanthians to that over against Torone, is a level plain, broken only by a few low hills. Here, upon this isthmus where Athos ends, is Sane, a Greek city. Inside of Sane, and upon Athos itself, are a number of towns, which Xerxes was now employed in disjoining from the continent: these are, Dium, Olophyxus, Acrothoum, Thyssus, and Cleonae. Among these cities Athos was divided.

23. Now the manner in which they dug was the following: a line was drawn across by the city of Sane; and along this the various nations parcelled out among themselves the work to be

done. When the trench grew deep, the workmen at the bottom continued to dig, while others handled the earth, as it was dug out, to labourers placed higher up upon ladders, and these taking it, passed it on further, till it came at last to those at the top, who carried it off and emptied it away. All the other nations, therefore, except the Phoenicians, had double labour; for the sides of the trench fell in continually, as could not but happen, since they made the width no greater at the top than it was required to be at the bottom. But the Phoenicians showed in this the skill which they exhibit in all their undertakings. For in the portion of the work which was allotted to them they began by making the trench at the top twice as wide as the prescribed measure, and then as they dug downwards approached the sides nearer and nearer together, so that when they reached the bottom their part of the work was of the same width as the rest. In a meadow near, there was a place of assembly and a market; and hither great quantities of corn, ready ground, was brought from Asia.

24. It seems to me, when I consider this work, that Xerxes, in making it, was actuated by a feeling of pride, wishing to display the extent of his power, and to leave a memorial behind him to posterity. For notwithstanding that it was open to him, with no trouble at all, to have had his ships drawn across the isthmus, yet he issued orders that a canal should be made through which the sea might flow, and that it should be of such a width as would allow of two triremes passing through it abreast with the oars in action. He likewise gave to the same persons who were set over the digging of the trench, the task of making a bridge across the river Strymon.

25. While these things were in progress, he was having cables prepared for his bridges, some of papyrus and some of white flax, a business which he entrusted to the Phoenicians and the Egyptians. He likewise laid up stores of provisions in many places, to save the army and the beasts of burden from suffering want upon their march into Greece. He inquired carefully about all the sites, and had the stores laid up in such as were most convenient, causing them to be brought across from various

parts of Asia and in various ways, some in transports and others in merchantmen. The greater portion was carried to the White Headland, upon the Thracian coast; some part, however, was conveyed to Tyrodiza, in the country of the Perinthians, some to Doriscus, some to Eion upon the Strymon, and some to Macedonia.

26. During the time that all these labours were in progress, the land army which had been collected was marching with Xerxes towards Sardis, having started from Critalla in Cappadocia. At this spot all the host which was about to accompany the king in his passage across the continent had been bidden to assemble. And here I have it not in my power to mention which of the satraps was adjudged to have brought his troops in the most gallant array, and on that account rewarded by the king according to his promise; for I do not know whether this matter ever came to a judgment. But it is certain that the host of Xerxes, after crossing the river Halys, marched through Phrygia till it reached the city of Celaenae. Here are the sources of the river Maeander, and likewise of another stream of no less size, which bears the name of the Cataract; the last-named river has its rise in the market-place of Celaenae, and empties itself into the Maeander. Here, too, in this market-place, is hung up to view the skin of the Silenus Marsyas, which Apollo, as the Phrygian story goes, stripped off and placed there.

27. Now there lived in this city a certain Pythius, the son of Atys, a Lydian. This man entertained Xerxes and his whole army in a most magnificent fashion, offering at the same time to give him a sum of money for the war. Xerxes, upon the mention of money, turned to the Persians who stood by, and asked of them, "Who is this Pythius, and what wealth has he, that he should venture on such an offer as this?" They answered him, "This is the man, O king, who gave your father Darius the golden plane-tree, and likewise the golden vine; and he is still the wealthiest man we know of in all the world, excepting you."

28. Xerxes marvelled at these last words, and now addressing Pythius with his own lips, he asked him, what the amount of his wealth really was. Pythius answered as follows:

"O King, I will not hide this matter from you, nor make pretence that I do not know how rich I am; but as I know perfectly, I will declare all fully before you. For when your journey was noised abroad, and I heard you were coming down to the Grecian coast, straightway, as I wished to give you a sum of money for the war, I made count of my stores, and found them to be 2,000 talents of silver, and of gold 4,000,000 of Daric staters, wanting 7,000. All this I willingly make over to you as a gift; and when it is gone, my slaves and my estates in land will be wealth enough for my wants."

29. This speech charmed Xerxes, and he replied, "Dear Lydian, since I left Persia there is no man but you who has either desired to entertain my army, or come forward of his own free will to offer me a sum of money for the war. You have done both the one and the other, feasting my troops magnificently, and now making offer of a right noble sum. In return, this is what I will bestow on you. You shall be my sworn friend from this day; and the 7,000 staters which are wanting to make up your 4,000,-000 I will supply, so that the full tale may be no longer lacking, and that you may owe the completion of the round sum to me. Continue to enjoy all that you have acquired hitherto, and be sure to remain ever such as you now are. If you do, you will not repent of it so long as your life endures."

30. When Xerxes had so spoken and had made his promises to Pythius good, he pressed forward upon his march; and passing Anaua, a Phrygian city, and a lake from which salt is gathered, he came to Colossae, a Phrygian city of great size, situated at a spot where the river Lycus plunges into a chasm and disappears. This river, after running underground a distance of about half a mile, re-appears once more, and empties itself, like the stream above mentioned, into the Maeander. Leaving Colossae, the army approached the borders of Phrygia where it abuts on Lydia; and here they came to a city called Cydrara, where was a pillar set up by Croesus, having an inscription on it, showing the boundaries of the two countries.

31. Where it quits Phrygia and enters Lydia the road separates; the way on the left leads into Caria, while that on the

right conducts to Sardis. If you follow this route, you must cross
the Maeander, and then pass by the city Callatebus, where the
men live who make honey out of wheat and the fruit of the
tamarisk. Xerxes, who chose this way, found here a plane-tree so
beautiful, that he presented it with golden ornaments, and put
it under the care of one of his Immortals. The day after, he
entered the Lydian capital.

32. Here his first care was to send off heralds into Greece,
to demand earth and water, and to require that preparations
should be made everywhere to feast the king. To Athens indeed
and to Sparta he sent no such demand; but these cities ex-
cepted, his messengers went everywhere. Now the reason why he
sent for earth and water to states which had already refused,
was this: he thought that although they had refused when
Darius made the demand, they would now be too frightened to
venture to refuse. So he sent his heralds, wishing to know for
certain how it would be.

33. Xerxes, after this, made preparations to advance to Abydos, where the bridge across the Hellespont from Asia to Europe
was lately finished. Midway between Sestos and Madytus in the
Hellespontine Chersonese, and right over against Abydos, there
is a rocky tongue of land which runs out for some distance into
the sea. This is the place where no long time afterwards the
Greeks under Xanthippus, the son of Ariphron, took Artayctes
the Persian, who was at that time governor of Sestos, and nailed
him living to a plank. He was the Artayctes who brought women
into the temple of Protesilaus at Elaeus, and there was guilty of
most unholy deeds.

34. Towards this tongue of land then, the men to whom the
business was assigned, carried out a double bridge from Abydos;
and while the Phoenicians constructed one line with cables of
white flax, the Egyptians in the other used ropes made of papyrus. Now it is about a mile across from Abydos to the opposite
coast. When, therefore, the channel had been bridged success-
fully, it happened that a great storm arising broke the whole
work to pieces, and destroyed all that had been done.

35. So when Xerxes heard of it, he was full of wrath, and

straightway gave orders that the Hellespont should receive 300 lashes, and that a pair of fetters should be cast into it. Nay, I have even heard it said, that he bade the branders take their irons and therewith brand the Hellespont. It is certain that he commanded those who scourged the waters to utter, as they lashed them, these barbarian and wicked words: "Thou bitter water, thy lord lays on thee this punishment because thou hast wronged him without a cause, having suffered no evil at his hands. Verily King Xerxes will cross thee, whether thou wilt or no. Well dost thou deserve that no man should honour thee with sacrifice; for thou art of a truth a treacherous and unsavoury river." While the sea was thus punished by his orders, he likewise commanded that the overseers of the work should lose their heads.

36. Then they, whose business it was, executed the unpleasing task laid upon them; and other master-builders were set over the work, who accomplished it in the way which I will now describe.

They joined together triremes and fifty-oared ships, 360 to support the bridge on the side of the Euxine Sea, and 314 to sustain the other; and these they placed at right-angles to the Sea, and in the direction of the current of the Hellespont, relieving by these means the tension of the shore cables. Having joined the vessels, they moored them with anchors of unusual size, that the vessels of the bridge towards the Euxine might resist the winds which blow from within the straits, and that those of the more western bridge facing the Aegean, might withstand the winds which set in from the south and from the south-east. A gap was left in the fifty-oared ships and triremes, to afford a passage for such light craft as chose to enter or leave the Euxine. When all this was done, they made the cables taut from the shore by the help of wooden capstans. This time, moreover, instead of using the two materials separately, they assigned to each bridge six cables, two of which were of white flax, while four were of papyrus. Both cables were of the same size and quality; but the flaxen were the heavier, weighing not less than fifty pounds per foot. When the bridge across the channel was thus complete, trunks of trees were sawn into planks, which were cut to the width of the bridge, and these were laid side by side upon the tightened cables, and then fastened on the top. This done, brushwood was brought, and arranged upon the planks, after which earth was heaped upon the brushwood, and the whole trodden down into a solid mass. Lastly a bulwark was set up on either side of this causeway, of such a height as to prevent the beasts of burden and the horses from seeing over it and taking fright at the water.

37. And now when all was prepared—the bridges, and the works at Athos, the breakwaters about the mouths of the cutting, which were made to hinder the surf from blocking up the entrances, and the cutting itself; and when the news came to Xerxes that this last was completely finished, then at length the host, having first wintered at Sardis, began its march towards Abydos, fully equipped, on the first approach of spring. At the moment of departure, the sun suddenly quitted his seat in the heavens, and disappeared, though there were no clouds in sight, but the sky was clear and serene.[5] Day was thus turned into night; whereupon Xerxes, who saw and remarked the prodigy, was seized with alarm, and sending at once for the Magians, inquired of them the meaning of the portent. They replied, "God is foreshowing to the Greeks the destruction of their cities; for the sun foretells for them and the moon for us." So Xerxes, thus instructed, proceeded on his way with great gladness of heart.

38. The army had begun its march, when Pythius the Lydian, frightened at the heavenly portent, and emboldened by his gifts, came to Xerxes and said, "Grant me, O my lord, a favour which is to you a light matter, but to me of vast account." Then Xerxes, who looked for nothing less than such a prayer as Pythius in fact preferred, engaged to grant him whatever he wished, and commanded him to tell his wish freely. So Pythius, full of boldness, went on to say, "My lord, I have five sons, and

---

[5] There was no eclipse of the sun visible in Western Asia this year, but there was one the year before, April 19th. Herodotus may perhaps have understood of the setting forth from Sardis, what was told him of the departure from Susa in the spring of the preceding year.

it chances that all are called upon to join you in this march against Greece. I beseech you, have compassion upon my years, and let one of my sons, the eldest, remain behind, to be my prop and stay, and the guardian of my wealth. Take with you the other four; and when you have done all that is in your heart, may you come back in safety."

39. But Xerxes was greatly angered, and replied to him, "Wretch dare you speak to me of your son, when I am myself on the march against Greece, with sons, and brothers, and kinsfolk, and friends? You are my bond-slave, and are in duty bound to follow me with all your household, not excepting your wife! Know that man's spirit dwells in his ears, and when it hears good things, straightway it fills all his body with delight; but no sooner does it hear the contrary than it heaves and swells with passion. As when you did good deeds and made good offers to me, you were not able to boast of having outdone the king in bountifulness, so now when you are changed and grown impudent, you shall not receive all your deserts, but less. For you and four of your five sons, the entertainment which I had of you shall gain protection; but as for him to whom you cling above the rest, the forfeit of his life shall be your punishment." Having thus spoken, forthwith he commanded those to whom such tasks were assigned, to seek out the eldest of the sons of Pythius, and having cut his body asunder, to place the two halves, one on the right, the other on the left of the great road, so that the army might march out between them.

40. Then the king's orders were obeyed; and the army marched out between the two halves of the body. First of all went the baggage-bearers, and the beasts of burden, and then a vast crowd of many nations mingled together without any intervals, amounting to more than one half of the army. After these troops an empty space was left, to separate between them and the king. In front of the king went first 1,000 horsemen, picked men of the Persian nation—then spearmen 1,000, likewise chosen troops, with their spear-heads pointing towards the ground—next ten of the sacred horses called Nisaean, all daintily caparisoned. (Now these horses are called Nisaean, because

they come from the Nisaean plain, a vast flat in Media, pro-
ducing horses of unusual size.) After the ten sacred horses came
the holy chariot of Zeus,[6] drawn by eight milk-white steeds,
with the charioteer on foot behind them holding the reins; for
no mortal is ever allowed to mount into the car. Next to this
came Xerxes himself, riding in a chariot drawn by Nisaean
horses, with his charioteer, Patiramphes, the son of Otanes, a
Persian, standing by his side.

41. Thus rode forth Xerxes from Sardis—but he was accustomed every now and then, when the fancy took him, to alight
from his chariot and travel in a litter. Immediately behind the
king there followed a body of 1,000 spearmen, the noblest and
bravest of the Persians, holding their lances in the usual manner—then came 1,000 Persian horse, picked men—then 10,000,
picked also after the rest, and serving on foot. Of these last
1,000 carried spears with golden pomegranates at their lower
end instead of spikes; and these encircled the other 9,000, who
bore on their spears pomegranates of silver. The spearmen too
who pointed their lances towards the ground, had golden pomegranates; and the 1,000 Persians who followed close after
Xerxes, had golden apples. Behind the 10,000 footmen came a
body of Persian cavalry, likewise 10,000; after which there was
again a void space for as much as 400 yards; and then the rest
of the army followed in a confused crowd.

42. The march of the army, after leaving Lydia, was directed
upon the river Caicus and the land of Mysia. Beyond the Caicus
the road, leaving Mount Cana upon the left, passed through the
Atarnean plain, to the city of Carina. Quitting this, the troops
advanced across the plain of Thebe, passing Adramyttium, and
Antandrus, the Pelasgic city; then, holding Mount Ida upon the
left hand, it entered the Trojan territory. On this march the Persians suffered some loss; for as they bivouacked during the night
at the foot of Ida, a storm of thunder and lightning burst upon
them, and killed no small number.

43. On reaching the Scamander, which was the first stream,
of all that they had crossed since they left Sardis, whose water

⁶ Ormazd.

failed them and did not suffice to satisfy the thirst of men and cattle, Xerxes ascended into the Citadel of Priam, since he had a longing to behold the place. When he had seen everything, and inquired into all particulars, he made an offering of 1,000 oxen to the Trojan Athena, while the Magians poured libations to the heroes who were slain at Troy. The night after, a panic fell upon the camp: but in the morning they set off with daylight, and skirting on the left hand the towns Rhoeteum, Ophryneum, and Dardanus (which borders on Abydos), on the right the Teucrians of Gergis, so reached Abydos.

44. Arrived here, Xerxes wished to look upon all his host; so, as there was a throne of white marble upon a hill near the city, which they of Abydos had prepared beforehand, by the king's bidding, for his especial use, Xerxes took his seat on it, and, gazing thence upon the shore below, beheld at one view all his land forces and all his ships. While thus employed, he felt a desire to behold a sailing-match among his ships, which accordingly took place, and was won by the Phoenicians of Sidon, much to the joy of Xerxes, who was delighted alike with the race and with his army.

45. And now, as he looked and saw the whole Hellespont covered with the vessels of his fleet, and all the shore and every plain about Abydos as full as could be of men, Xerxes congratulated himself on his good fortune; but after a little while, he wept.

46. Then Artabanus, the king's uncle (the same who at the first so freely spoke his mind to the king, and advised him not to lead his army against Greece), when he heard that Xerxes was in tears, went to him, and said, "How different, sire, is what you are now doing, from what you did a little while ago! Then you congratulated yourself, and now you weep."

"There came upon me," he replied, "a sudden pity, when I thought of the shortness of man's life, and considered that of all this host, so numerous as it is, not one will be alive when a hundred years are gone by."

"And yet there are sadder things in life than that," returned the other. "Short as our time is, there is no man, whether it be

here among this multitude or elsewhere, who is so happy, as not
to have felt the wish—I will not say once, but full many a time
—that he were dead rather than alive. Calamities fall upon us,
sicknesses vex and harass us, and make life, short though it be,
to appear long. So death, through the wretchedness of our life,
is a most sweet refuge to our race: and god, who gives us the
tastes that we enjoy of pleasant times, is seen, in his very gift, to
be envious."

47. "True," said Xerxes; "human life is even such as you
have painted it, O Artabanus. But for this very reason let us
turn our thoughts from it, and not dwell on what is so sad, when
pleasant things are in hand. Tell me rather, if the vision which
we saw had not appeared so plainly to you, would you have been
still of the same mind as formerly, and have continued to dissuade me from warring against Greece, or would you at this time
think differently? Come now, tell me this honestly."

"O King," replied the other, "may the dream which hath appeared to us have such issue as we both desire! For my own
part, I am still full of fear, and have scarcely power to control
myself, when I consider all our dangers, and especially when I
see that the two things which are of most consequence are alike
opposed to you."

48. "You strange man," said Xerxes in reply, "what, I pray
you, are the two things you speak of? Does my land army seem
to you too small in number, and will the Greeks, think you,
bring into the field a more numerous host? Or is it our fleet
which you consider weaker than theirs? Or are you fearful on
both accounts? If in your judgment we fall short in either respect, it were easy to bring together with all speed another
armament."

49. "O king," said Artabanus, "it is not possible that a man
of understanding should find fault with the size of your army or
the number of your ships. The more you add to these, the more
hostile will those two things, whereof I spoke, become. Those
two things are the land and the sea. In all the wide sea there is
not, I imagine, anywhere a harbour large enough to receive your
vessels in case a storm arise, and afford them a sure protection.

And yet you will want, not one such harbour only, but many in succession, along the entire coast by which you are about to make your advance. In default then of such harbours, it is well to bear in mind that chances rule men, and not men chances. Such is the first of the two dangers, and now I will speak to you of the second. The land will also be your enemy; for if no one resists your advance, as you proceed further and further, insensibly allured onwards (for who is ever sated with success?), you will find it more and more hostile. I mean this, that, should nothing else withstand you, yet the mere distance, becoming greater as time goes on, will at last produce a famine. I think it is best for men, when they take counsel, to be timorous, and imagine all possible calamities, but when the time for action comes, then to deal boldly."

50. Whereto Xerxes answered, "There is reason, O Artabanus, in everything which you have said; but I pray you, fear not all things alike, nor count up every risk. For if in each matter that comes before us you look to all possible chances, never you will achieve anything. Far better is it to have a stout heart always, and suffer one's share of evils, than to be ever fearing what may happen, and never incur a mischance. Moreover, if you oppose whatever is said by others, without yourself showing us the sure course which we ought to take, you are as likely to lead us into failure as they who advise differently; for you are but on a par with them. And as for that sure course, how can you show it us when you are but a man? I do not believe you can. Success for the most part attends those who act boldly, not those who weigh everything, and are slack to venture. You see to how great a height the power of Persia has now reached—never would it have grown to this point if they who sat upon the throne before me had been like-minded with you, or even, though not like-minded, had listened to counsellors of such a spirit. It was by brave ventures that they extended their sway; for great empires can only be conquered by great risks. We follow then the example of our fathers in making this march, and we set forward at the best season of the year; and when we have brought Europe under us, we shall return, without suffer-

ing from want or experiencing any other calamity. For while on the one hand we carry vast stores of provisions with us, on the other we shall have the grain of all the countries and nations that we attack; since our march is not directed against a pastoral people, but against men who are tillers of the ground."

51. Then said Artabanus, "If, sire, you are determined that we shall not fear anything, at least hearken to a counsel which I wish to offer; for when the matters in hand are so many, one cannot but have much to say. You know that Cyrus the son of Cambyses reduced and made tributary to the Persians all the race of the Ionians, except only those of Attica. Now my advice is, that you on no account lead forth these men against their fathers; since we are well able to overcome them without such aid. Their choice, if we take them with us to the war, lies between showing themselves the most wicked of men by helping to enslave their fatherland, or the most righteous by joining in the struggle to keep it free. If then they choose the side of injustice, they will do us but scant good; while if they determine to act justly, they may greatly injure our host. Lay to heart the old proverb, which says truly, 'The beginning and end of a matter are not always seen at once.' "

52. "Artabanus," answered Xerxes, "there is nothing in all that you have said wherein you are so wholly wrong as in this, that you suspect the faith of the Ionians. Have they not given us the surest proof of their attachment, a proof which you witnessed, and likewise all those who fought with Darius against the Scythians? When it lay wholly with them to save or to destroy the entire Persian army, they dealt by us honourably and with good faith, and did us no hurt at all. Besides, they will leave behind them in our country their wives, their children, and their properties—can it then be conceived that they will attempt rebellion? Have no fear, therefore, on this score; but keep a brave heart and uphold my house and empire. To you, and you only, do I entrust my sovereignty."

53. After Xerxes had thus spoken, and had sent Artabanus away to return to Susa, he summoned before him all the Persians of most repute, and when they appeared, addressed them

in these words, "Persians, I have brought you together because
I wished to exhort you to behave bravely, and not to sully with
disgrace the former achievements of the Persian people, which
are very great and famous. Rather let us, one and all, singly
and jointly, exert ourselves to the uttermost; for the matter
wherein we are engaged concerns the common weal. Strain every
nerve, then, I beseech you, in this war. Brave warriors are the
men we march against, if report says true; and such that, if we
conquer them, there is not a people in all the world which will
venture thereafter to withstand our arms. And now let us offer
prayers to the gods who watch over the welfare of Persia, and
then cross the channel."

54. All that day the preparations for the passage continued;
and on the morrow they burned all kinds of spices upon the
bridges, and strewed the way with myrtle-boughs, while they
waited anxiously for the sun, which they hoped to see as he rose.
And now the sun appeared; and Xerxes took a golden goblet
and poured from it a libation into the sea, praying with his face
turned to the sun that no misfortune might befall him such as to
hinder his conquest of Europe, until he had penetrated to its
uttermost boundaries. After he had prayed, he cast the golden
cup into the Hellespont, and with it a golden bowl, and a Persian sword of the kind which they call acinaces. I cannot say for
certain whether it was as an offering to the sun-god that he
threw these things into the deep, or whether he repented of
having scourged the Hellespont, and thought by his gifts to
make amends to the sea for what he had done.

55. When, however, his offerings were made, the army began
to cross; and the foot-soldiers, with the horsemen, passed over
by one of the bridges—that (namely) which lay towards the
Euxine—while the beasts of burden and the camp-followers
passed by the other, which looked on the Aegean. Foremost
went the Ten Thousand Persians, all wearing garlands upon
their heads; and after them a mixed multitude of many nations.
These crossed upon the first day.

On the next day the horsemen began the passage; and with

them went the soldiers who carried their spears with the point downwards, garlanded like the Ten Thousand; then came the sacred horses and the sacred chariot; next Xerxes with his lancers and the thousand horse; then the rest of the army. At the same time the ships sailed over to the opposite shore. According, however, to another account which I have heard, the king crossed the last.

56. As soon as Xerxes had reached the European side, he stood to contemplate his army as they crossed under the lash. And the crossing continued during seven days and seven nights, without rest or pause. It is said that here, after Xerxes had made the passage, a Hellespontian exclaimed, "Why, O Zeus, do you, in the likeness of a Persian man, and with the name of Xerxes instead of your own, lead the whole race of mankind to the destruction of Greece? It would have been as easy for you to destroy it without their aid!"

57. When the whole army had crossed, and the troops were now upon their march, a strange prodigy appeared to them, whereof the king made no account, though its meaning was not difficult to conjecture. Now the prodigy was this: a mare gave birth to a hare. Hereby it was shown plainly enough, that Xerxes would lead forth his host against Greece with mighty pomp and splendour, but in order to reach again the spot from which he set out, would have to run for his life. There had also been another portent, while Xerxes was still at Sardis—a mule dropped a foal with double sexual organs, the male above the female; but this likewise was disregarded.

58. So Xerxes, despising the omens, marched forwards; and his land army accompanied him. But the fleet held an opposite course, and, sailing to the mouth of the Hellespont, made its way along the shore. Thus the fleet proceeded westward, making for Cape Sarpedon, where the orders were that it should await the coming up of the troops; but the land army marched eastward along the Chersonese, leaving on the right the tomb of Helle, the daughter of Athamas, and on the left the city of Cardia. Having passed through the town which is called Agora, they

skirted the shores of the Black Gulf, and thence crossed the Black River, whence the gulf takes its name, the waters of which they found too scanty to supply the host. From this point their march was to the west; and after passing Aenos, an Aeolian settlement, and likewise lake Stentoris, they came to Doriscus.

59. The name Doriscus is given to a beach and a vast plain upon the coast of Thrace, through the middle of which flows the strong stream of the Hebrus. Here is the royal fort which is likewise called Doriscus, where Darius had maintained a Persian garrison ever since the time when he attacked the Scythians. This place seemed to Xerxes a convenient spot for reviewing and numbering his soldiers; which things accordingly he proceeded to do. The sea-captains, who had brought the fleet to Doriscus, were ordered to take the vessels to the beach adjoining, where Sale stands, a city of the Samothracians, and Zone, another city. The beach extends to Serrheum, the well-known promontory; the whole district in former times was inhabited by the Ciconians. Here then the captains were to bring their ships, and to haul them ashore for refitting, while Xerxes at Doriscus was employed in numbering the soldiers.

60. What the exact number of the troops of each nation was I cannot say with certainty—for it is not mentioned by any one —but the whole land army together was found to amount to 1,700,000 men.[7] The manner in which the numbering took place was the following. A body of 10,000 men was brought to a certain place, and the men were made to stand as close together as possible; after which a circle was drawn around them, and the men were let go: then where the circle had been, a fence was built about the height of a man's middle; and the enclosure was filled continually with fresh troops, till the whole army had in

[7] J. A. R. Munro (*Cambridge Ancient History*, IV, 271-273) has offered an interpretation of the excessive size of the Persian army. He supposes that Herodotus has listed all the military forces of the Persian empire although only three of the six army corps actually participated in the expedition. Further Herodotus apparently assigned 60,000 men, an army corps, to the divisional commanders who actually had 10,000 in their divisions. The result of these corrections would leave an army of 180,000 combatants.

this way been numbered. When the numbering was over, the troops were drawn up according to their several nations.

61. Now these were the nations that took part in this expedition. The Persians, who wore on their heads the soft hat called the tiara, and about their bodies, tunics with sleeves, of divers colours, having iron scales upon them like the scales of a fish. Their legs were protected by trousers; and they bore wicker shields for bucklers; their quivers hanging at their backs, and their arms being a short spear, a bow of uncommon size, and arrows of reed. They had likewise daggers suspended from their girdles along their right thighs. Otanes, the father of Xerxes' wife, Amestris, was their leader. This people was known to the Greeks in ancient times by the name of Cephenians; but they called themselves, and were called by their neighbours, Artaeans. It was not till Perseus, the son of Zeus and Danae, visited Cepheus the son of Belus, and, marrying his daughter Andromeda, had by her a son called Perses (whom he left behind him in the country because Cepheus had no male offspring), that the nation took from this Perses the name of Persians.

62. The Medes had exactly the same equipment as the Persians; and indeed the dress common to both is not so much Persian as Median. They had for commander Tigranes, of the race of the Achaemenids. These Medes were called anciently by all the people Arians; but when Medea, the Cochian, came to them from Athens, they changed their name. Such is the account which they themselves give.

The Cissians were equipped in the Persian fashion, except in one respect: they wore on their heads, instead of hats, fillets. Anaphes, the son of Otanes, commanded them.

The Hyrcanians were likewise armed in the same way as the Persians. Their leader was Megapanus, the same who was afterwards satrap of Babylon.

63. The Assyrians went to war with helmets upon their heads made of brass, and plaited in a strange fashion which is not easy to describe. They carried shields, lances, and daggers very like the Egyptian; but in addition they had wooden clubs knotted with iron, and linen corselets. This people, whom the Greeks

call Syrians, are called Assyrians by the barbarians. The Chaldeans served in their ranks, and they had for commander Otaspes, the son of Artachaeus.

64. The Bactrians went to the war wearing a head-dress very like the Median, but armed with bows of cane, after the custom of their country, and with short spears.

The Sacae, or Scyths, were clad in trousers, and had on their heads tall stiff caps rising to a point. They bore the bow of their country and the dagger: besides which they carried the battle-axe, or sagaris. They were in truth Amyrgian Scythians, but the Persians called them Sacae, since that is the name they give to all Scythians. The Bactrians and the Sacae had for leader Hystaspes, the son of Darius and of Atossa, the daughter of Cyrus.

65. The Indians wore cotton dresses, and carried bows of cane, and arrows also of cane, with iron at the point. Such was the equipment of the Indians, and they marched under the command of Pharnazathres the son of Artabates.

66. The Arians carried Median bows, but in other respects were equipped like the Bactrians. Their commander was Sisamnes the son of Hydarnes.

The Parthians and Chorasmians, with the Sogdians, the Gandarians, and the Dadicae, had the Bactrian equipment in all respects. The Parthians and Chorasmians were commanded by Artabazus the son of Pharnaces, the Sogdians by Azanes the son of Artaeus, and the Gandarians and Dadicae by Artyphius the son of Artabanus.

67. The Caspians were clad in cloaks of skin, and carried the cane bow of their country, and the scimitar. So equipped they went to the war, and they had for commander Ariomardus the brother of Artyphius.

The Sarangians had dyed garments which showed brightly, and buskins which reached to the knee: they bore Median bows, and lances. Their leader was Pherendates, the son of Megabazus.

The Pactyans wore cloaks of skin, and carried the bow of their country and the dagger. Their commander was Artyntes, the son of Ithamatres.

68. The Utians, the Mycians, and the Paricanians were all

equipped like the Pactyans. They had for leaders, Arsamenes the son of Darius, who commanded the Utians and Mycians; and Siromitres, the son of Oeobazus, who commanded the Paricanians.

69. The Arabians wore the zeira, or long cloak, fastened about them with a girdle; and carried at their right side long bows, which when unstrung bent backwards.

The Ethiopians were clothed in the skins of leopards and lions, and had long bows made of the stem of the palm-leaf, not less than six feet in length. On these they laid short arrows made of reed, and armed at the tip, not with iron, but with a piece of stone, sharpened to a point, of the kind used in engraving seals. They carried likewise spears, the head of which was the sharpened horn of an antelope, and in addition they had knotted clubs. When they went into battle they painted their bodies, half with chalk, and half with vermilion. The Arabians, and the Ethiopians who came from the region above Egypt, were commanded by Arsames, the son of Darius and of Artystone daughter of Cyrus. This Artystone was the best-beloved of all the wives of Darius, and it was she whose statue he caused to be made of gold wrought with the hammer. Her son Arsames commanded these two nations.

70. The eastern Ethiopians—for two nations of this name served in the army—were marshalled with the Indians. They differed in nothing from the other Ethiopians, save in their language, and the character of their hair. For the eastern Ethiopians have straight hair, while they of Libya are more woolly-haired than any other people in the world. Their equipment was in most points like that of the Indians, but they wore upon their heads the scalps of horses, with the ears and mane attached; the ears were made to stand upright, and the mane served as a crest. For shields this people made use of the skins of cranes.

71. The Libyans wore a dress of leather, and carried javelins made hard in the fire. They had for commander Massages, the son of Oarizus.

72. The Paphlagonians went to the war with plaited helmets upon their heads, and carrying small shields and spears of no

great size. They had also javelins and daggers, and wore on their feet the buskin of their country, which reached half way up the shank. In the same fashion were equipped the Ligyans, the Matienians, the Mariandynians, and the Syrians (or Cappadocians, as they are called by the Persians). The Paphlagonians and Matienians were under the command of Dotus the son of Megasidrus; while the Mariandynians, the Ligyans, and the Syrians had for leader Gobryas, the son of Darius and Artystone.

73. The dress of the Phrygians closely resembled the Paphlagonian, only in a very few points differing from it. According to the Macedonian account, the Phrygians, during the time that they had their abode in Europe and dwelt with them in Macedonia, bore the name of Brigians; but on their removal to Asia they changed their designation at the same time with their dwelling-place.

The Armenians, who are Phrygian colonists, were armed in the Phrygian fashion. Both nations were under the command of Artochmes, who was married to one of the daughters of Darius.

74. The Lydians were armed very nearly in the Grecian manner. These Lydians in ancient times were called Maeonians, but changed their name, and took their present title from Lydus the son of Atys.

The Mysians wore upon their heads a helmet made after the fashion of their country, and carried a small buckler; they used as javelins staves with one end hardened in the fire. The Mysians are Lydian colonists, and from the mountain-chain of Olympus, are called Olympieni. Both the Lydians and the Mysians were under the command of Artaphernes, the son of that Artaphernes who, with Datis, made the landing at Marathon.

75. The Thracians went to the war wearing the skins of foxes upon their heads, and about their bodies tunics, over which was thrown a long cloak of many colours. Their legs and feet were clad in buskins made from the skins of fawns; and they had for arms javelins, with light targes, and short dirks. This people, after crossing into Asia, took the name of Bithynians; before they had been called Strymonians, while they dwelt upon the

Strymon; whence, according to their own account, they had been driven out by the Mysians and Teucrians. The commander of these Asiatic Thracians was Bassaces the son of Artabanus.

76. The . . .[8] had small shields made of the hide of the ox, and carried each of them two spears such as are used in wolf-hunting. Brazen helmets protected their heads, and above these they wore the ears and horns of an ox fashioned in brass. They had also crests on their helms; and their legs were bound round with purple bands. There is an oracle of Ares in the country of this people.

77. The Cabalians, who are Maeonians, but are called Lasonians, had the same equipment as the Cilicians—an equipment which I shall describe when I come in due course to the Cilician contingent.

The Milyans bore short spears, and had their garments fastened with buckles. Some of their number carried Lycian bows. They wore about their heads skull-caps made of leather. Badres the son of Hystanes led both nations to battle.

78. The Moschians wore helmets made of wood, and carried shields and spears of a small size: their spearheads, however, were long. The Moschian equipment was that likewise of the Tibarenians, the Macronians, and the Mosynoecians. The leaders of these nations were the following: the Moschians and Tibarenians were under the command of Ariomardus, who was the son of Darius and of Parmys, daughter of Smerdis son of Cyrus; while the Macronians and Mosynoecians had for leader Artayctes, the son of Cherasmis, the governor of Sestos upon the Hellespont.

79. The Mares wore on their heads the plaited helmet peculiar to their country, and used small leathern bucklers, and javelins.

The Colchians wore wooden helmets, and carried small shields of raw hide, and short spears; besides which they had swords. Both Mares and Colchians were under the command of Pharandates, the son of Teaspes.

[8] There is a defect here in the text of Herodotus; the name of the nation has been lost.

The Alarodians and Saspirians were armed like the Colchians; their leader was Masistes, the son of Siromitras.

80. The Islanders who came from the Red Sea, where they inhabited the islands to which the king sends those whom he banishes, wore a dress and arms almost exactly like the Median. Their leader was Mardontes the son of Bagaeus, who the year after perished in the battle of Mycale, where he was one of the captains.

81. Such were the nations who fought upon the dry land, and made up the infantry of the Persians. And they were commanded by the captains whose names have been above recorded. The marshalling and numbering of the troops had been committed to them, and by them were appointed the captains over 1,000, and the captains over 10,000; but the leaders of ten men, or 100, were named by the captains over 10,000. There were other officers also, who gave the orders to the various ranks and nations; but those whom I have mentioned above were the commanders.

82. Over these commanders themselves, and over the whole of the infantry, there were set six generals, namely, Mardonius, son of Gobryas; Tritantaechmes, son of the Artabanus who gave his advice against the war with Greece; Smerdomenes son of Otanes—these two were the sons of Darius' brothers, and thus were cousins of Xerxes—Masistes, son of Darius and Atossa; Gergis son of Arizus; and Megabyzus son of Zopyrus.

83. The whole of the infantry was under the command of these generals, excepting the Ten Thousand. The Ten Thousand, who were all Persians and all picked men, were led by Hydarnes, the son of Hydarnes. They were called the Immortals, for the following reason. If one of their body failed either by the stroke of death or of disease, forthwith his place was filled up by another man, so that their number was at no time either greater or less than 10,000.

Of all the troops the Persians were adorned with the greatest magnificence, and they were likewise the most valiant. Besides their arms, which have been already described, they glittered all over with gold, vast quantities of which they wore about their

persons. They were followed by litters, wherein rode their concubines, and by a numerous train of attendants handsomely
dressed. Camels and sumpter-beasts carried their provision,
apart from that of the other soldiers.

84. All these various nations fight on horseback; they did
not, however, at this time all furnish horsemen, but only the
following:

The Persians, who were armed in the same way as their own
footmen, excepting that some of them wore upon their heads devices fashioned with the hammer in brass or steel.

85. The wandering tribe known by the name of Sagartians—
a people Persian in language, and in dress half Persian, half
Pactyan, who furnished to the army as many as 8,000 horse. It
is not the wont of this people to carry arms, either of bronze or
steel, except only a dirk; but they use lassoes made of thongs
plaited together, and trust to these whenever they go to the
wars. Now the manner in which they fight is the following:
when they meet their enemy, straightway they discharge their
lassoes, which end in a noose; then, whatever the noose en-
circles, be it man or be it horse, they drag towards them, and the
foe, entangled in the toils, is forthwith slain. Such is the manner in which this people fight, and now their horsemen were
drawn up with the Persians.

86. The Medes, and Cissians, who had the same equipment
as their foot-soldiers. The Indians, equipped as their footmen,
but some on horseback and some in chariots, the chariots drawn
either by horses, or by wild asses. The Bactrians and Caspians,
arrayed as their foot-soldiers. The Libyans, equipped as their
foot-soldiers, like the rest; but all riding in chariots. The Cas-
peirians and Paricanians, equipped as their foot-soldiers. The
Arabians, in the same array as their footmen, but all riding on
camels, not inferior in fleetness to horses.

87. These nations and these only furnished horse to the
army: and the number of the horse was 80,000, without counting camels or chariots. All were marshalled in squadrons, excepting the Arabians; who were placed last, to avoid frightening
the horses, which cannot endure the sight of the camel.

88. The horse was commanded by Armamithras and Tithaeus, sons of Datis. The other commander, Pharnuches, who was to have been their colleague, had been left sick at Sardis; since at the moment that he was leaving the city, a sad mischance befell him: a dog ran under the feet of the horse upon which he was mounted, and the horse, not seeing it coming, was startled, and, rearing bolt upright, threw his rider. After this fall Pharnuches spat blood, and fell into a consumption. As for the horse, he was treated at once as Pharnuches ordered: the attendants took him to the spot where he had thrown his master, and there cut off his four legs at the hock. Thus Pharnuches lost his command.

89. The triremes amounted in all to 1,207;[9] and were furnished by the following nations:

The Phoenicians, with the Syrians of Palestine, furnished 300 vessels, the crews of which were thus accoutred: upon their heads they wore helmets made nearly in the Grecian manner; about their bodies they had breastplates of linen; they carried shields without rims; and were armed with javelins. This nation, according to their own account, dwelt anciently upon the Red Sea, but crossing thence, they fixed themselves on the sea-coast of Syria, where they still inhabit. This part of Syria, and all the region extending from hence to Egypt, is known by the name of Palestine.

The Egyptians furnished 200 ships. Their crews had plaited helmets upon their heads, and bore concave shields with rims of unusual size. They were armed with spears suited for a sea-fight, and with huge poleaxes. The greater part of them wore breastplates, and all had long cutlasses.

90. The Cyprians furnished 150 ships, and were equipped in the following fashion. Their kings had turbans bound about

---

[9] This figure agrees with that of Aeschylus (*Persians*, 341–343) for the battle of Salamis if the 207 swift ships mentioned separately by Aeschylus are to be added to his round number of 1,000. However, Munro (*Cambridge Ancient History*, IV, 273–276) has shown that it is probable that the Greeks overestimated the size of the Persian navy, which usually consisted of five fleets containing 120 ships. The Phoenician fleet was superior both in quality and numbers, and probably consisted of the 207 ships singled out by Aeschylus.

their heads, while the people wore tunics; in other respects they
were clad like the Greeks. They are of various races; some are
sprung from Athens and Salamis, some from Arcadia, some from
Cythnus, some from Phoenicia, and a portion, according to
their own account, from Ethiopia.

91. The Cilicians furnished 100 ships. The crews wore upon
their heads the helmet of their country, and carried instead of
shields light targes made of raw hide; they were clad in woollen
tunics, and were each armed with two javelins, and a sword
closely resembling the cutlass of the Egyptians. This people bore
anciently the name of Hypachaeans, but took their present title
from Cilix, the son of Agenor, a Phoenician.

The Pamphylians furnished thirty ships, the crews of which
were armed exactly as the Greeks. This nation is descended from
those who on the return from Troy were dispersed with Amphi-
lochus and Calchas.

92. The Lycians furnished fifty ships. Their crews wore
greaves and breastplates, while for arms they had bows of cornel
wood, reed arrows without feathers, and javelins. Their outer
garment was the skin of a goat, which hung from their shoulders; their head-dress a hat encircled with plumes; and besides
their other weapons they carried daggers and falchions. This
people came from Crete, and were once called Termilae; they
got the name which they now bear from Lycus, the son of Pandion, an Athenian.

93. The Dorians of Asia furnished thirty ships. They were
armed in the Grecian fashion, inasmuch as their forefathers
came from the Peloponnese.

The Carians furnished seventy ships, and were equipped like
the Greeks, but carried, in addition, falchions and daggers.
What name the Carians bore anciently was declared in the first
part of this history.

94. The Ionians furnished 100 ships, and were armed like the
Greeks. Now these Ionians, during the time that they dwelt in
the Peloponnese and inhabited the land now called Achaea
(which was before the arrival of Danaus and Xuthus in the
Peloponnese), were called, according to the Greek account,

Aegialean Pelasgi, or Pelasgi of the Sea-shore, but afterwards, from Ion the son of Xuthus, they were called Ionians.

95. The Islanders furnished seventeen ships, and wore arms like the Greeks. They too were a Pelasgian race, who in later times took the name of Ionians for the same reason as those who inhabited the twelve cities founded from Athens.

The Aeolians furnished sixty ships, and were equipped in the Grecian fashion. They too were anciently called Pelasgians, as the Greeks declare.

The Hellespontians from the Pontus, who are colonists of the Ionians and Dorians, furnished 100 ships, the crews of which wore the Grecian armour. This did not include the Abydenians, who stayed in their own country, because the king had assigned them the special duty of guarding the bridges.

96. On board of every ship was a bànd of soldiers, Persians, Medes, or Sacans. The Phoenician ships were the best sailers in the fleet, and the Sidonian the best among the Phoenicians. The contingent of each nation, whether to the fleet or to the land army, had at its head a native leader; but the names of these leaders I shall not mention, as it is not necessary for the course of my history. For the leaders of some nations were not worthy to have their names recorded; and besides, there were in each nation as many leaders as there were cities. And it was not really as commanders that they accompanied the army, but as mere slaves, like the rest of the host. For I have already mentioned the Persian generals who had the actual command, and were at the head of several nations which composed the army.

97. The fleet was commanded by the following—Ariabignes, the son of Darius, Prexaspes, the son of Aspathines, Megabazus the son of Megabates, and Achaemenes the son of Darius. Ariabignes, who was the child of Darius by a daughter of Gobryas, was leader of the Ionian and Carian ships, Achaemenes, who was own brother to Xerxes, of the Egyptian; the rest of the fleet was commanded by the other two. Besides the triremes, there was an assemblage of thirty-oared and fifty-oared galleys, of light galleys, and transports for conveying horses, amounting in all to 3,000.

98. Next to the commanders, the following were the most re-nowned of those who sailed aboard the fleet: Tetramnestus, the son of Anysus, the Sidonian; Mapen, the son of Sirom, the Tyrian; Merbal, the son of Agbal, the Aradian; Syennesis, the son of Oromedon, the Cilician; Cyberniscus, the son of Sicas, the Lycian; Gorgus, the son of Chersis, and Timonax, the son of Timagoras, the Cyprians; and Histiaeus, the son of Timnes, Pigres, the son of Seldomus, and Damasithymus, the son of Candaules, the Carians.

99. Of the other lower officers I shall make no mention, since no necessity is laid on me; but I must speak of a certain leader named Artemisia,[10] whose participation in the attack upon Greece, notwithstanding that she was a woman, moves my special wonder. She had obtained the sovereign power after the death of her husband, and though she had now a son grown up, yet her brave spirit and manly daring sent her forth to the war, when no need required her to adventure. Her name, as I said, was Artemisia, and she was the daughter of Lygdamis; by race she was on his side a Halicarnassian, though by her mother a Cretan. She ruled over the Halicarnassians, the men of Cos, of Nisyrus, and of Calydna; and the five triremes which she furnished to the Persians were, next to the Sidonian, the most famous ships in the fleet. She likewise gave to Xerxes sounder counsel than any of his other allies. Now the cities over which I have mentioned that she bore sway, were one and all Dorian; for the Halicarnassians were colonists from Troezen, while the remainder were from Epidaurus. Thus much concerning the sea-force.

100. Now when the numbering and marshalling of the host was ended, Xerxes conceived a wish to go himself throughout the forces, and with his own eyes behold everything. Accordingly he traversed the ranks seated in his chariot, and going from nation to nation, made manifold inquiries, while his scribes wrote down the answers; till at last he had passed from end to end of the whole land army, both the horsemen and likewise the foot.

---

[10] The special notice taken of Artemisia is undoubtedly due in part to her having been queen of Halicarnassus, the native place of the historian.

This done, he exchanged his chariot for a Sidonian galley, and, seated beneath a golden awning, sailed along the prows of all his vessels (the vessels having now been hauled down and launched into the sea), while he made inquiries again, as he had done when he reviewed the land-forces, and caused the answers to be recorded by his scribes. The captains took their ships to the distance of about 400 feet from the shore, and there lay to, with their vessels in a single row, the prows facing the land, and with the fighting-men upon the decks accoutred as if for war, while the king sailed along in the open space between the ships and the shore, and so reviewed the fleet.

101. Now after Xerxes had sailed down the whole line and was gone ashore, he sent for Demaratus the son of Ariston, who had accompanied him in his march upon Greece, and addressed him thus:

"Demaratus, it is my pleasure at this time to ask you certain things which I wish to know. You are a Greek, and, as I hear from the other Greeks with whom I converse, no less than from your own lips, you are a native of a city which is not the meanest or the weakest in their land. Tell me, therefore, what do you think? Will the Greeks lift a hand against us? My own judgment is, that even if all the Greeks and all the barbarians of the west were gathered together in one place, they would not be able to abide my onset, not being really of one mind. But I would like to know what you think."

Thus Xerxes questioned; and the other replied in his turn, "O King, do you wish me to give you a true answer, or do you wish for a pleasant one?"

Then the King bade him speak the plain truth, and promised that he would not on that account hold him in less favour than heretofore.

102. So Demaratus, when he heard the promise, spoke as follows, "O King, since you bid me at all risks speak the truth, and not say what will one day prove me to have lied to you, thus I answer. Want has at all times been a fellow-dweller with us in our land, while Valour is an ally whom we have gained by dint of wisdom and strict laws. Her aid enables us to drive out want

and escape tyranny. Brave are all the Greeks who dwell in any Dorian land, but what I am about to say does not concern all, but only the Lacedaemonians. First then, come what may, they will never accept your terms, which would reduce Greece to slavery; and further, they are sure to join battle with you, though all the rest of the Greeks should submit to your will. As for their numbers, do not ask how many they are, that their resistance should be a possible thing; for if 1,000 of them should take the field, they will meet you in battle, and so will any number, be it less than this, or be it more."

103. When Xerxes heard this answer of Demaratus, he laughed and answered, "What wild words, Demaratus! 1,000 men join battle with such an army as this! Come then, will you —who were once, as you say, their king—engage to fight this very day with ten men? I think not. And yet, if all your fellow citizens be indeed such as you say they are, you ought, as their king, by your own country's usages, to be ready to fight with twice the number. If then each one of them be a match for ten of my soldiers, I may well call upon you to be a match for twenty. So would you assure the truth of what you have now said. If, however, you Greeks, who vaunt yourselves so much, are of a truth men like those whom I have seen about my court, as you, Demaratus, and the others with whom I converse, if, I say, you are really men of this sort and size, how is the speech that you have uttered more than a mere empty boast? For, to go to the very verge of likelihood,—how could 1,000 men, or 10,000, or even 50,000, particularly if they were all alike free, and not under one lord, how could such a force, I say, stand against an army like mine? Let them be 5,000, and we shall have more than 1,000 men to each one of theirs. If, indeed, like our troops, they had a single master, their fear of him might make them courageous beyond their natural bent, or they might be urged by lashes against an enemy which far outnumbered them. But left to their own free choice, assuredly they will act differently. For my own part, I believe, that if the Greeks had to contend with the Persians only, and the numbers were equal on both sides, the Greeks would find it hard to stand their ground.

We too have among us such men as those of whom you spoke—not many indeed, but still we possess a few. For instance, some of my body-guard would be willing to engage singly with three Greeks. But this you did not know, and therefore it was you talked so foolishly."

104. Demaratus answered him, "I knew, O King, at the outset, that if I told you the truth, my speech would displease your ears. But as you required me to answer you with all possible truthfulness, I informed you what the Spartans will do. And in this I speak not from any love that I bear them—for you know what my love towards them is likely to be at the present time, when they have robbed me of my rank and my ancestral honours, and made me a homeless exile, whom your father received, bestowing on me both shelter and sustenance. What likelihood is there that a man of understanding should be unthankful for kindness shown him, and not cherish it in his heart? For myself, I pretend not to cope with ten men, or with two, nay, had I the choice, I would rather not fight even with one. But, if need appeared, or if there were any great cause urging me on, I would contend with right good-will against one of those persons who boast themselves a match for any three Greeks. So likewise the Lacedaemonians, when they fight singly, are as good men as any in the world, and when they fight in a body, are the bravest of all. For though they be free men, they are not in all respects free; Law is the master whom they own, and this master they fear more than your subjects fear you. Whatever it commands they do; and its commandment is always the same: it forbids them to flee in battle, whatever the number of their foes, and requires them to stand firm, and either to conquer or die. If in these words, O King, I seem to you to speak foolishly, I am content from this time forward evermore to hold my peace. I had not now spoken unless compelled by you. But I pray that all may turn out according to your wishes."

105. Such was the answer of Demaratus, and Xerxes was not angry with him at all, but only laughed, and sent him away with words of kindness. After this interview and after he had made Mascames the son of Megadostes governor of Doriscus, setting

aside the governor appointed by Darius, Xerxes started with his army, and marched upon Greece through Thrace.

106. This man, Mascames, whom he left behind him, was a person of such merit that gifts were sent him yearly by the king as a special favour, because he excelled all the other governors that had been appointed either by Xerxes or by Darius. In like manner, Artaxerxes, son of Xerxes, sent gifts yearly to the descendants of Mascames. Persian governors had been established in Thrace and about the Hellespont before the march of Xerxes began; but these persons, after the expedition was over, were all driven from their towns by the Greeks, except the governor of Doriscus: no one succeeded in driving out Mascames, though many made the attempt. For this reason the gifts are sent him every year by the king who reigns over the Persians.

107. Of the other governors whom the Greeks drove out, there was not one who, in the judgment of Xerxes, showed himself a brave man, excepting Boges, the governor of Eion. Him Xerxes never could praise enough, and such of his sons as were left in Persia, and survived their father, he very specially honoured. And of a truth this Boges was worthy of great commendation; for when he was besieged by the Athenians under Cimon, the son of Miltiades, and it was open to him to retire from the city upon terms, and return to Asia, he refused, because he feared the king might think he had played the coward to save his own life, wherefore, instead of surrendering, he held out to the last extremity. When all the food in the fortress was gone, he raised a vast funeral pile, slew his children, his wife, his concubines, and his household slaves, and cast them all into the flames. Then collecting whatever gold and silver there was in the place, he flung it from the walls into the Strymon, and when that was done, to crown all, he himself leaped into the fire. For this action Boges is with reason praised by the Persians even at the present day.

108. Xerxes, as I have said, pursued his march from Doriscus against Greece, and on his way he forced all the nations through which he passed to take part in the expedition. For the whole country as far as the frontiers of Thessaly had been (as I have

already shown) enslaved and made tributary to the king by the conquests of Megabazus, and, more lately, of Mardonius. And first, after leaving Doriscus, Xerxes passed the Samothracian fortresses, whereof Mesembria is the furthermost as one goes towards the west. The next city is Stryme, which belongs to Thasos. Midway between it and Mesembria flows the river Lissus, which did not suffice to furnish water for the army, but was drunk up and failed. This region was formerly called Gallaica; now it bears the name of Briantica; but in strict truth it likewise is really Ciconian.

109. After crossing the dry channel of the Lissus, Xerxes passed the Grecian cities of Maroneia, Dicaea, and Abdera, and likewise the famous lakes which are in their neighbourhood, Lake Ismaris between Maroneia and Stryme, and Lake Bistonis near Dicaea, which receives the waters of two rivers, the Travus and the Compsatus. Near Abdera there was no famous lake for him to pass, but he crossed the river Nestus, which there reaches the sea. Proceeding further upon his way, he passed by several continental cities, one of them possessing a lake nearly four miles in circuit, full of fish, and very salt, of which the beasts of burden only drank, and which they drained dry. The name of this city was Pistyrus. All these towns, which were Grecian, and lay upon the coast, Xerxes kept upon his left hand as he passed along.

110. The following are the Thracian tribes through whose country he marched: the Paeti, the Ciconians, the Bistonians, the Sapaeans, the Dersaeans, the Edonians, and the Satrae. Some of these dwelt by the sea, and furnished ships to the king's fleet; while others lived in the more inland parts, and of these all the tribes which I have mentioned, except the Satrae, were forced to serve on foot.

111. The Satrae, so far as our knowledge goes, have never yet been brought under by any one, but continue to this day a free and unconquered people, unlike the other Thracians. They dwell amid lofty mountains clothed with forests of different trees and capped with snow, and are very valiant in fight. They are the Thracians who have an oracle of Dionysus in their country.

which is situated upon their highest mountain-range. The Bessi, a Satrian race, deliver the oracles; but the prophet, as at Delphi, is a woman, and her answers are not harder to read.

112. When Xerxes had passed through the region mentioned above, he came next to the Pierian fortresses, one of which is called Phagres, and another Pergamus. Here his line of march lay close by the walls, with the long high range of Pangaeum upon his right, a tract in which there are mines both of gold and silver, some worked by the Pierians and Odomantians, but the greater part by the Satrae.

113. Xerxes then marched through the country of the Paeonian tribes—the Doberians and the Paeoplae—which lay to the north of Pangaeum, and, advancing westward, reached the river Strymon and the city Eion, whereof Boges, of whom I spoke a short time ago, and who was still alive, was governor. The tract of land lying about Mount Pangaeum is called Phyllis; on the west it reaches to the river Angites, which flows into the Strymon, and on the south to the Strymon itself, where at this time the Magi were sacrificing white horses to make the stream favourable.

114. After propitiating the stream by these and many other magical ceremonies, the Persians crossed the Strymon by bridges made before their arrival, at a place called the Nine Ways, which was in the territory of the Edonians. And when they learned that the name of the place was the Nine Ways, they took nine of the youths of the land and as many of their maidens, and buried them alive on the spot. Burying alive is a Persian custom. I have heard that Amestris, the wife of Xerxes, in her old age buried alive seven pairs of Persian youths, sons of illustrious men, as a thank-offering to the god who is supposed to dwell underneath the earth.

115. From the Strymon the army, proceeding westward, came to a strip of shore, on which there stands the Grecian town of Argilus. This shore, and the whole tract above it, is called Bisaltia. Passing this, and keeping on the left hand the Gulf of Posideium, Xerxes crossed the Sylean plain, as it is called, and passing by Stagirus, a Greek city, came to Acanthus. The in

habitants of these parts, as well as those who dwelt about Mount Pangaeum, were forced to join the armament, like those others of whom I spoke before; the dwellers along the coast being made to serve in the fleet, while those who lived more inland had to follow with the land forces. The road which the army of Xerxes took remains to this day untouched: the Thracians neither plough nor sow it, but hold it in great honour.

116. On reaching Acanthus, the Persian king, seeing the great zeal of the Acanthians for his service, and hearing what had been done about the cutting, took them into the number of his sworn friends, sent them as a present a Median dress, and besides commended them highly.

117. It was while he remained here that Artachaees, who presided over the canal, a man in high repute with Xerxes, and by birth an Achaemenid, who was moreover the tallest of all the Persians, being eight feet high, and who had a stronger voice than any other man in the world, fell sick and died. Xerxes therefore, who was greatly afflicted at the mischance, carried him to the tomb and buried him with all magnificence; while the whole army helped to raise a mound over his grave. The Acanthians, in obedience to an oracle, offer sacrifice to this Artachaees as a hero, invoking him in their prayers by name. But King Xerxes sorrowed greatly over his death.

118. Now the Greeks who had to feed the army, and to entertain Xerxes, were brought thereby to the very extremity of distress, insomuch that some of them were forced even to forsake house and home. When the Thasians received and feasted the host, on account of their possessions upon the mainland, Antipater, the son of Orges, one of the citizens of best repute, and the man to whom the business was assigned, proved that the cost of the meal was 400 talents of silver.

119. And estimates almost to the same amount were made by the superintendents in other cities. For the entertainment, which had been ordered long beforehand, and was reckoned to be of much consequence, was, in the manner of it, such as I will now describe. No sooner did the heralds who brought the orders give their message, than in every city the inhabitants made a division

of their stores of corn, and proceeded to grind flour of wheat and of barley for many months together. Besides this, they purchased the best cattle that they could find, and fattened them; and fed poultry and water-fowl in ponds and buildings, to be in readiness for the army; while they likewise prepared gold and silver vases and drinking-cups, and whatsoever else is needed for the service of the table. These last preparations were made for the king only, and those who sat at meat with him; for the rest of the army nothing was made ready beyond the food for which orders had been given. On the arrival of the Persians, a tent ready pitched for the purpose received Xerxes, who took his rest therein, while the soldiers remained under the open heaven. When the dinner hour came, great was the toil of those who entertained the army; while the guests ate their fill, and then, after passing the night at the place, tore down the royal tent next morning, and seizing its contents, carried them all off, leaving nothing behind.

120. On one of these occasions Megacreon of Abdera wittily recommended his countrymen to go to the temples in a body, men and women alike, and there take their station as suppliants, and beseech the gods that they would in future always spare them one-half of the woes which might threaten their peace— thanking them at the same time very warmly for their past good- ness in that they had caused Xerxes to be content with one meal in the day. For had the order been to provide breakfast for the king as well as dinner, the Abderites must either have fled before Xerxes came, or else have awaited his coming, and been brought to absolute ruin. As it was, the nations, though suffering heavy pressure, complied nevertheless with the directions that had been given.

121. At Acanthus Xerxes separated from his fleet, bidding the captains sail on ahead and await his coming at Therma, on the Thermaic Gulf, the place from which the bay takes its name. Through this town lay, he understood, his shortest road. Pre- viously, his order of march had been the following: from Doris- cus to Acanthus his land force had proceeded in three bodies, one of which took the way along the sea-shore in company with

the fleet, and was commanded by Mardonius and Masistes, while another pursued an inland track under Tritantaechmes and Gergis; the third, with whom was Xerxes himself, marching midway between the other two, and having for its leaders Smerdomenes and Megabyzus.

122. The fleet, therefore, after leaving the king, sailed through the channel which had been cut for it by Mount Athos, and came into the bay whereon lie the cities of Assa, Pilorus, Singus, and Sarta; from all which it received contingents. Thence it stood on for the Thermaic Gulf, and rounding Cape Ampelus, the promontory of the Toronaeans, passed the Grecian cities Torone, Galepsus, Sermyla, Mecyberna, and Olynthus, receiving from each a number of ships and men. This region is called Sithonia.

123. From Cape Ampelus the fleet stretched across by a short course to Cape Canastraeum, which is the point of the peninsula of Pallene that runs out furthest into the sea, and gathered fresh supplies of ships and men from Potidaea, Aphytis, Neapolis, Aega, Therambus, Scione, Mende, and Sane. These are the cities of the tract called anciently Phlegra, but now Pallene. Hence they again followed the coast, still advancing towards the place appointed by the king, and had accessions from all the cities that lie near Pallene and border on the Thermaic Gulf, whereof the names are Lipaxus, Combreia, Lisae, Gigonus, Campsa, Smila, and Aenea. The tract where these towns lie still retains its old name of Crossaea. After passing Aenea, the city which I last named, the fleet found itself arrived in the Thermaic Gulf, off the land of Mygdonia. And so at length they reached Therma, the appointed place, and came likewise to Sindus and Chalestra upon the river Axius, which separates Bottiaea from Mygdonia. Bottiaea has a scanty seaboard, which is occupied by the two cities, Ichnae and Pella.

124. So the fleet anchored off the Axius, and off Therma, and the towns that lay between, waiting the king's coming. Xerxes meanwhile with his land force left Acanthus, and started for Therma, taking his way across the land. This road led him

through Paeonia and Crestonia to the river Echidorus, which, rising in the country of the Crestonians, flows through Mygdonia, and reaches the sea near the marsh upon the Axius.

125. Upon this march the camels that carried the provisions of the army were set upon by lions, which left their lairs and came down by night, but spared the men and the beasts of burden, while they made the camels their prey. I marvel what may have been the cause which compelled the lions to leave the other animals untouched and attack the camels, when they had never seen that beast before, or had any experience of it.

126. That whole region is full of lions, and wild bulls, with gigantic horns which are brought into Greece. The lions are confined within the tract lying between the river Nestus (which flows through Abdera) on the one side, and the Achelous (which waters Acarnania) on the other. No one ever sees a lion in the fore part of Europe east of the Nestus, or through the entire continent westward of the Achelous; but in the space between these bounds lions are found.

127. On reaching Therma Xerxes halted his army, which encamped along the coast, beginning at the city of Therma in Mygdonia, and stretching out as far as the rivers Lydias and Haliacmon, two streams which, mingling their waters in one, form the boundary between Bottiaea and Macedonia. Such was the extent of country through which the barbarians encamped. The rivers here mentioned were all of them sufficient to supply the troops, except the Echidorus, which was drunk dry.

128. From Therma Xerxes beheld the Thessalian mountains, Olympus and Ossa, which are of a wonderful height. Here, learning that there lay between these mountains a narrow gorge through which the river Peneus ran, and where there was a road that gave an entrance into Thessaly, he formed the wish to go by sea himself, and examine the mouth of the river. His design was to lead his army by the upper road through the country of the inland Macedonians, and so to enter Perrhaebia, and come down by the city of Gonnus; for he was told that that way was the most secure. No sooner therefore had he formed this wish

than he acted accordingly. Embarking, as was his wont on all such occasions, aboard a Sidonian vessel, he gave the signal to the rest of the fleet to get under way, and quitting his land army, set sail and proceeded to the Peneus. Here the view of the mouth caused him to wonder greatly, and sending for his guides, he asked them whether it were possible to turn the course of the stream, and make it reach the sea at any other point.

129. Now there is a tradition that Thessaly was in ancient times a lake, shut in on every side by huge hills. Ossa and Pelion —ranges which join at the foot—do in fact inclose it upon the east, while Olympus forms a barrier upon the north, Pindus upon the west, and Othrys towards the south. The tract contained within these mountains, which is a deep basin, is called Thessaly. Many rivers pour their waters into it, but five of them are of more note than the rest, namely, the Peneus, the Apidanus, the Onochonus, the Enipeus, and the Pamisus. These streams flow down from the mountains which surround Thessaly, and meeting in the plain, mingle their waters together, and discharge themselves into the sea by a single outlet, which is a gorge of extreme narrowness. After the junction all the other names disappear, and the river is known as the Peneus. It is said that of old the gorge which allows the waters an outlet did not exist; accordingly the rivers, which were then, as well as the Lake Boebeis, without names, but flowed with as much water as at present, made Thessaly a sea. The Thessalians tell us that the gorge through which the water escapes was caused by Poseidon, and this is likely enough; at least any man who believes that Poseidon causes earthquakes, and that chasms so produced are his handiwork, would say, upon seeing this rent, that Poseidon did it. For it plainly appeared to me that the hills had been torn asunder by an earthquake.[11]

130. When Xerxes therefore asked the guides if there were any other outlet by which the waters could reach the sea, they,

[11] Modern science will scarcely quarrel with this description of Thessaly, which shows Herodotus to have had the eye of a physical geographer, and the imagination of a geologist.

being men well acquainted with the nature of their country, answered, "O King, there is no other passage by which this stream can empty itself into the sea save that which you see. For Thessaly is girt about with a circlet of hills."

Xerxes is said to have observed upon this, "Wise men truly are they of Thessaly, and good reason had they to change their minds in time and consult for their own safety. For, to pass by other matters, they must have felt that they lived in a country which may easily be brought under and subdued. Nothing more is needed than to turn the river upon their lands by an embankment which should fill up the gorge and force the stream from its present channel, and all Thessaly, except the mountains, would at once be laid under water."

The king aimed in this speech at the sons of Aleuas, who were Thessalians, and had been the first of all the Greeks to make submission to him. He thought that they had made their friendly offers in the name of the whole people.[12] So Xerxes, when he had viewed the place, and made the above speech, went back to Therma.

131. The stay of Xerxes in Pieria lasted for several days, during which a third part of his army was employed in cutting down the woods on the Macedonian mountain-range to give his forces free passage into Perrhaebia. At this time the heralds who had been sent into Greece to require earth for the king returned to the camp, some of them empty-handed, others with earth and water.

132. Among the number of those from whom earth and water were brought, were the Thessalians, Dolopians, Enianians, Perrhaebians, Locrians, Magnetians, Malians, Achaeans of Phthiotis, Thebans, and Boeotians generally, except those of Plataea and Thespiae. These are the nations against whom the Greeks that had taken up arms to resist the barbarians swore the oath, which ran thus, "From all those of Greek blood who delivered themselves up to the Persians without necessity, when their af-

---

[12] This was not the case. It appears in the subsequent narrative, that the Thessalian people was very desirous of resisting the invasion of Xerxes

fairs were in good condition, we will take a tithe of their goods, and give it to the god at Delphi." So ran the words of the Greek oath.[13]

133. King Xerxes had sent no heralds either to Athens or Sparta to ask earth and water, for a reason which I will now relate. When Darius some time before sent messengers for the same purpose, they were thrown, at Athens, into the pit of punishment, at Sparta into a well, and bidden to take therefrom earth and water for themselves, and carry it to their king. On this account Xerxes did not send to ask them. What calamity came upon the Athenians to punish them for their treatment of the heralds I cannot say, unless it were the laying waste of their city and territory; but that I believe was not on account of this crime.

134. On the Lacedaemonians, however, the wrath of Talthybius, Agamemnon's herald, fell with violence. Talthybius has a temple at Sparta, and his descendants, who are called Talthybiadae, still live there, and have the privilege of being the only persons who discharge the office of herald. When therefore the Spartans had done the deed of which we speak, the victims at their sacrifices failed to give good tokens; and this failure lasted for a very long time. Then the Spartans were troubled, and regarding what had befallen them as a grievous calamity, they held frequent assemblies of the people, and made proclamation through the town, "Was any Lacedaemonian willing to give his life for Sparta?" Upon this two Spartans, Sperthias, the son of Aneristus, and Bulis, the son of Nicolaus, both men of noble birth, and among the wealthiest in the place, came forward and freely offered themselves as an atonement to Xerxes for the heralds of Darius slain at Sparta. So the Spartans sent them away to the Medes to undergo death.

135. Nor is the courage which these men hereby displayed alone worthy of wonder, but so likewise are the following speeches which were made by them. On their road to Susa they presented themselves before Hydarnes. This Hydarnes was a

[20] A good deal of doubt hangs about this oath. Both the time and the terms of it are differently reported.

Persian by birth, and had the command of all the nations that
dwelt along the sea-coast of Asia. He accordingly showed them
hospitality, and invited them to a banquet, where, as they
feasted, he said to them, "Men of Lacedaemon, why will you
not consent to be friends with the king? You have but to look
at me and my fortune to see that the king knows well how to
honour merit. In like manner you yourselves, were you to make
your submission to him, would receive at his hands, seeing that
he deems you men of merit, some government in Greece."

"Hydarnes," they answered, "you are a one-sided counsellor.
You have experience of half the matter, but the other half is
beyond your knowledge. A slave's life you understand, but never
having tasted liberty, you can not tell whether it be sweet or no.
Had you known what freedom is, you would have bidden us
fight for it, not with the spear only, but with the battle-axe."
So they answered Hydarnes.

136. And afterwards, when they came to Susa into the king's
presence, and the guards ordered them to fall down and do
obeisance, and went so far as to use force to compel them, they
refused, and said they would never do any such thing, even were
their heads thrust down to the ground, for it was not their custom to worship men, and they had not come to Persia for that
purpose. So they fought off the ceremony; and having done so,
addressed the king in words much like the following, "O King of
the Medes, the Lacedaemonians have sent us hither, in the place
of those heralds of yours who were slain in Sparta, to make
atonement to you on their account."

Then Xerxes answered with true greatness of soul that he
would not act like the Lacedaemonians, who, by killing the heralds, had broken the laws which all men hold in common. As he
had blamed such conduct in them, he would never be guilty of it
himself. And besides, he did not wish, by putting the two men
to death, to free the Lacedaemonians from the stain of their former outrage.

137. This conduct on the part of the Spartans caused the
anger of Talthybius to cease for a while, notwithstanding that
Sperthias and Bulis returned home alive. But many years after-

wards it awoke once more, as the Lacedaemonians themselves declare, during the war between the Peloponnesians and the Athenians. In my judgment this was a case wherein the hand of heaven was most plainly manifest. That the wrath of Talthybius should have fallen upon ambassadors, and not slacked till it had full vent, so much justice required; but that it should have come upon the sons of the very men who were sent up to the Persian king on its account—upon Nicolaus, the son of Bulis, and Aner-istus, the son of Sperthias (the same who carried off fishermen from Tiryns, when cruising in a well-manned merchant-ship), this does seem to me to be plainly a supernatural circumstance. Yet certain it is that these two men, having been sent to Asia as ambassadors by the Lacedaemonians, were betrayed by Sitalces, the son of Tereus, king of Thrace, and Nymphodorus, the son of Pythes, a native of Abdera, and being made prisoners at Bi-santhe, upon the Hellespont, were conveyed to Attica, and there put to death by the Athenians, at the same time as Aristeas, the son of Adeimantus, the Corinthian. All this happened, however, very many years after the expedition of Xerxes.[14]

138. To return, however, to my main subject, the expedition of the Persian king, though it was in name directed against Athens, threatened really the whole of Greece. And of this the Greeks were aware some time before, but they did not all view the matter in the same light. Some of them had given the Persian earth and water, and were bold on this account, deeming themselves thereby secured against suffering hurt from the bar-barian army; while others, who had refused compliance, were thrown into extreme alarm. For whereas they considered all the ships in Greece too few to engage the enemy, it was plain that the greater number of states would take no part in the war, but warmly favoured the Medes.

139. And here I feel constrained to deliver an opinion, which most men, I know, will dislike, but which, as it seems to me to be true, I am determined not to withhold. Had the Athenians,

[14] The event took place in the year 430 B.C., nearly sixty years after the murder of the Persian envoys.

from fear of the approaching danger, quitted their country, or
had they without quitting it submitted to the power of Xerxes,
there would certainly have been no attempt to resist the Persians by sea; in which case, the course of events by land would
have been the following. Though the Peloponnesians might have
carried ever so many breastworks across the Isthmus, yet their
allies would have fallen off from the Lacedaemonians, not by
voluntary desertion, but because town after town must have
been taken by the fleet of the barbarians; and so the Lacedaemonians would at last have stood alone, and, standing alone,
would have displayed prodigies of valour, and died nobly. Either
they would have done thus, or else, before it came to that extremity, seeing one Greek state after another embrace the cause
of the Medes, they would have come to terms with King Xerxes;
and thus, either way Greece would have been brought under
Persia. For I cannot understand of what possible use the
walls across the Isthmus could have been, if the King had had
the mastery of the sea.[15] If then a man should now say that the
Athenians were the saviours of Greece, he would not exceed the
truth. For they truly held the scales, and whichever side they
espoused must have carried the day. They too it was who, when
they had determined to maintain the freedom of Greece, roused
up that portion of the Greek nation which had not gone over to
the Medes, and so, next to the gods, they repulsed the invader.
Even the terrible oracles which reached them from Delphi, and
struck fear into their hearts, failed to persuade them to fly from
Greece. They had the courage to remain faithful to their land,
and await the coming of the foe.

140. When the Athenians, anxious to consult the oracle, sent
their messengers to Delphi, hardly had the envoys completed the
customary rites about the sacred precinct, and taken their seats
inside the sanctuary of the god, when the priestess, Aristonice
by name, thus prophesied:

[15] These arguments are quite unanswerable, and seem to moderns almost
too plain to be enunciated, but their force was not felt at the time.

Wretches, why sit ye here? Fly, fly to the ends of creation,
Quitting your homes, and the crags which your city crowns with
  her circlet.
Neither the head, nor the body is firm in its place, nor at bottom
Firm the feet, nor the hands, nor resteth the middle uninjur'd.
All—all ruined and lost. Since fire, and impetuous Ares,
Speeding along in a Syrian chariot, hastes to destroy her.
Not alone shalt thou suffer; full many the towers he will level,
Many the shrines of the gods he will give to a fiery destruction.
Even now they stand with dark sweat horribly dripping,
Trembling and quaking for fear, and lo! from the high roofs
  trickleth
Black blood, sign prophetic of hard distresses impending.
Get ye away from the temple. and brood on the ills that await
  ye!

141. When the Athenian messengers heard this reply, they
were filled with the deepest affliction: whereupon Timon, the
son of Androbulus, one of the men of most mark among the Delphians, seeing how utterly cast down they were at the gloomy
prophecy, advised them to take an olive-branch, and entering the sanctuary again, consult the oracle as suppliants. The
Athenians followed this advice, and going in once more, said,
"O King, we pray thee reverence these boughs of supplication
which we bear in our hands, and deliver to us something more
comforting concerning our country. Else we will not leave thy
sanctuary, but will stay here till we die." Upon this the priestess
gave them a second answer, which was the following:

Pallas has not been able to soften the lord of Olympus,
Though she has often prayed him, and urged him with excellent
  counsel.
Yet once more I address thee in words than adamant firmer.
When the foe shall have taken whatever the limit of Cecrops
Holds within it, and all which divine Cithaeron shelters,
Then far-seeing Zeus grants this to the prayers of Athena;
Safe shall the wooden wall continue for thee and thy children.
Wait not the tramp of the horse, nor the footmen mightily mov-
  ing

Over the land, but turn your back to the foe, and retire ye.
Yet shall a day arrive when ye shall meet him in battle.
Holy Salamis, thou shalt destroy the offspring of women,
When men scatter the seed, or when they gather the harvest.

142. This answer seemed, as indeed it was, gentler than the former one; so the envoys wrote it down, and went back with it to Athens. When, however, upon their arrival, they produced it before the people, and inquiry began to be made into its true meaning, many and various were the interpretations which men put on it; two, more especially, seemed to be directly opposed to one another. Certain of the old men were of opinion that the god meant to tell them the citadel would escape; for this was anciently defended by a palisade; and they supposed that barrier to be the wooden wall of the oracle. Others maintained that the fleet was what the god pointed at; and their advice was that nothing should be thought of except the ships, which had best be at once got ready. Still such as said the wooden wall meant the fleet, were perplexed by the last two lines of the oracle:

Holy Salamis, thou shalt destroy the offspring of women,
When men scatter the seed, or when they gather the harvest

These words caused great disturbance among those who took the wooden wall to be the ships; since the interpreters understood them to mean, that, if they made preparations for a sea-fight, they would suffer a defeat off Salamis.

143. Now there was at Athens a man who had lately made his way into the first rank of citizens; his true name was Themistocles, but he was known more generally as the son of Neocles. This man came forward and said, that the interpreters had not explained the oracle altogether aright, "For if," he argued, "the clause in question had really respected the Athenians, it would not have been expressed so mildly; the phrase used would have been Luckless Salamis, rather than Holy Salamis, had those to whom the island belonged been about to perish in its neighbourhood. Rightly taken, the response of the god threatened the enemy, much more than the Athenians." He therefore counselled

his countrymen to make ready to fight on board their ships, since they were the wooden wall in which the god told them to trust. When Themistocles had thus cleared the matter, the Athenians embraced his view, preferring it to that of the interpreters. The advice of these last had been against engaging in a sea-fight. "All the Athenians could do," they said, "was, without lifting a hand in their defence, to quit Attica, and make a settlement in some other country."

144. Themistocles had before this given a counsel which prevailed very seasonably. The Athenians, having a large sum of money in their treasury, the produce of the mines at Laureium, were about to share it among the full-grown citizens, who would have received ten drachmas apiece, when Themistocles persuaded them to forbear the distribution, and build with the money 200 ships,[16] to help them in their war against the Aeginetans. It was the breaking out of the Aeginetan war which was at this time the saving of Greece, for hereby were the Athenians forced to become a maritime power. The new ships were not used for the purpose for which they had been built, but became a help to Greece in her hour of need. And the Athenians had not only these vessels ready before the war, but they likewise set to work to build more; while they determined, in a council which was held after the debate upon the oracle, that, according to the advice of the god, they would embark their whole force aboard their ships, and with such Greeks as chose to join them, give battle to the barbarian invader. Such, then, were the oracles which had been received by the Athenians.

145. The Greeks who were well affected to the Grecian cause, having assembled in one place, and there consulted together, and interchanged pledges with each other, agreed that, before any other step was taken, the feuds and enmities which existed between the different nations should first of all be appeased. Many such there were; but one was of more importance than the rest.

---

[16] This is what Herodotus says, but perhaps not what he meant to say. It seems certain that the real determination was to raise their navy to the number of 200 vessels. This was the number actually employed both at Artemisium and at Salamis.

namely, the war which was still going on between the Athenians and the Aeginetans. When this business was concluded, understanding that Xerxes had reached Sardis with his army, they resolved to despatch spies into Asia to take note of the king's affairs. At the same time they determined to send ambassadors to the Argives, and conclude a league with them against the Persians; while they likewise despatched messengers to Gelo, the son of Deinomenes, in Sicily, to the people of Corcyra, and to those of Crete, exhorting them to send help to Greece. Their wish was to unite, if possible, the entire Greek name in one, and so to bring all to join in the same plan of defence, inasmuch as the approaching dangers threatened all alike. Now the power of Gelo was said to be very great, far greater than that of any single Grecian people.

146. So when these resolutions had been agreed upon, and the quarrels between the states made up, first of all they sent into Asia three men as spies. These men reached Sardis, and took note of the king's forces, but, being discovered, were examined by order of the generals who commanded the land army, and, having been condemned to suffer death, were led out to execution. Xerxes, however, when the news reached him, disapproving the sentence of the generals, sent some of his body-guard with instructions, if they found the spies still alive, to bring them into his presence. The messengers found the spies alive, and brought them before the king, who, when he heard the purpose for which they had come, gave orders to his guards to take them round the camp, and show them all the footmen and all the horse, letting them gaze at everything to their heart's content; then, when they were satisfied, to send them away unharmed to whatever country they desired.

147. For these orders Xerxes gave afterwards the following reasons. "Had the spies been put to death," he said, "the Greeks would have continued ignorant of the vastness of his army, which surpassed the common report of it; while he would have done them a very small injury by killing three of their men. On the other hand, by the return of the spies to Greece, his power would become known; and the Greeks," he expected, "would

make surrender of their freedom before he began his march, by which means his troops would be saved all the trouble of an expedition." This reasoning was like to that which he used upon another occasion. While he was staying at Abydos, he saw some corn-ships, which were passing through the Hellespont from the Euxine,[17] on their way to Aegina and the Peloponnese. His attendants, hearing that they were the enemy's, were ready to capture them, and looked to see when Xerxes would give the signal. He, however, merely asked, "Whither the ships were bound?" and when they answered, "For your foes, master, with corn on board," "We too are bound thither," he rejoined, "laden, among other things, with corn. What harm is it, if they carry our provisions for us?"

So the spies, when they had seen everything, were dismissed, and came back to Europe.

148. The Greeks who had banded themselves together against the Persian king, after despatching the spies into Asia, sent next ambassadors to Argos. The account which the Argives give of their own proceedings is the following. They say that they had information from the very first of the preparations which the barbarians were making against Greece. So, as they expected that the Greeks would come upon them for aid against the assailant, they sent envoys to Delphi to inquire of the god, what it would be best for them to do in the matter. They had lost, not long before, 6,000 citizens, who had been slain by the Lacedaemonians under Cleomenes the son of Anaxandridas; which was the reason why they now sent to Delphi. When the priestess heard their question, she replied:

Hated of all thy neighbours, beloved of the blessed Immortals,
Sit thou still, with thy lance drawn inward, patiently watching;
Warily guard thine head, and the head will take care of the
  body.

[17] The corn-growing countries upon the Black Sea, in ancient as in modern times, supplied the commercial nations with their chief article of food.

This prophecy had been given them some time before the envoys came; but still, when they afterwards arrived, it was permitted them to enter the council-house, and there deliver their message. And this answer was returned to their demands, "Argos is ready to do as you require, if the Lacedaemonians will first make a truce for thirty years, and will further divide with Argos the leadership of the allied army. Although in strict right the whole command should be hers, she will be content to have the leadership divided equally."

149. Such, they say, was the reply made by the council, in spite of the oracle which forbade them to enter into a league with the Greeks. For, while not without fear of disobeying the oracle, they were greatly desirous of obtaining a thirty years' truce, to give time for their sons to grow to man's estate. They reflected, that if no such truce were concluded, and it should be their lot to suffer a second calamity at the hands of the Persians, it was likely they would fall hopelessly under the power of Sparta. But to the demands of the Argive council the Lacedaemonian envoys answered, "They would bring before the people the question of concluding a truce. With regard to the leadership, they had received orders what to say, and the reply was, that Sparta had two kings, Argos but one—it was not possible that either of the two Spartans should be stripped of his dignity —but they did not oppose the Argive king having one vote like each of them." The Argives say, that they could not brook this arrogance on the part of Sparta, and rather than yield one jot to it, they preferred to be under the rule of the barbarians. So they told the envoys to begone, before sunset, from their territory, or they should be treated as enemies.

150. Such is the account which is given of these matters by the Argives themselves. There is another story, which is told generally through Greece, of a different tenor. Xerxes, it is said, before he set forth on his expedition against Greece, sent a herald to Argos, who on his arrival spoke as follows:

"Men of Argos, King Xerxes speaks thus to you. We Persians deem that the Perses from whom we descend was the child of

Perseus the son of Danae, and of Andromeda the daughter of Cepheus. Hereby it would seem that we come of your stock and lineage. So then it neither befits us to make war upon those from whom we spring; nor can it be right for you to fight, on behalf of others, against us. Your place is to keep quiet and hold yourselves aloof. Only let matters proceed as I wish, and there is no people whom I shall have in higher esteem than you."

This address, says the story, was highly valued by the Argives, who therefore at the first neither gave a promise to the Greeks nor yet put forward a demand. Afterwards, however, when the Greeks called upon them to give their aid, they made the claim which has been mentioned, because they knew well that the Lacedaemonians would never yield it, and so they would have a pretext for taking no part in the war.

151. Some of the Greeks say that this account agrees remarkably with what happened many years afterwards. Callias, the son of Hipponicus, and certain others with him, had gone up to Susa, the city of Memnon, as ambassadors of the Athenians, upon a business quite distinct from this. While they were there, it happened that the Argives likewise sent ambassadors to Susa, to ask Artaxerxes, the son of Xerxes, "If the friendship which they had formed with his father still continued, or if he looked upon them as his enemies?" To which King Artaxerxes replied, "Most certainly it continues; and there is no city which I reckon more my friend than Argos."

152. For my own part I cannot positively say whether Xerxes did send the herald to Argos or not; nor whether Argive ambassadors at Susa did really put this question to Artaxerxes about the friendship between them and him; neither do I deliver any opinion hereupon other than that of the Argives themselves. This, however, I know—that if every nation were to bring all its evil deeds to a given place, in order to make an exchange with some other nation, when they had all looked carefully at their neighbours' faults, they would be truly glad to carry their own back again. So, after all, the conduct of the Argives was not perhaps more disgraceful than that of others. For myself, my duty is to report all that is said, but I am not obliged to believe it all

alike—a remark which may be understood to apply to my whole History. Some even go so far as to say, that the Argives first invited the Persians to invade Greece, because of their ill success in the war with Lacedaemon, since they preferred anything to the smart of their actual sufferings. Thus much concerning the Argives.

153. Other ambassadors, among whom was Syagrus from Lacedaemon, were sent by the allies into Sicily, with instructions to confer with Gelo.

The ancestor of this Gelo, who first settled at Gela, was a native of the isle of Telos, which lies off Triopium. When Gela was colonised by Antiphemus and the Lindians of Rhodes, he likewise took part in the expedition. In course of time his descendants became the high-priests of the gods who dwell below—an office which they held continually, from the time that Telines, one of Gelo's ancestors, obtained it in the way which I will now mention. Certain citizens of Gela, worsted in a sedition, had found a refuge at Mactorium, a town situated on the heights above Gela. Telines reinstated these men, without any human help, solely by means of the sacred rites of these deities. From whom he received them, or how he himself acquired them, I cannot say; but certain it is, that relying on their power he brought the exiles back. For this his reward was to be, the office of high-priest of those gods for himself and his seed for ever. It surprises me especially that such a feat should have been performed by Telines; for I have always looked upon acts of this nature as beyond the abilities of common men, and only to be achieved by such as are of a bold and manly spirit; whereas Telines is said by those who dwell about Sicily to have been a soft-hearted and womanish person. He however obtained this office in the manner above described.

154. Afterwards, on the death of Cleander the son of Pantares, who was slain by Sabyllus, a citizen of Gela, after he had held the tyranny for seven years, Hippocrates, Cleander's brother, mounted the throne. During his reign, Gelo, a descendant of the high-priest Telines, served with many others—of whom Aenesidemus, son of Pataicus, was one—in the king's

body-guard. Within a little time his merit caused him to be raised to the command of all the horse. For when Hippocrates laid siege to Callipolis, and afterwards to Naxos, to Zancle, to Leontini, and moreover to Syracuse, and many cities of the barbarians, Gelo in every war distinguished himself above all the combatants. Of the various cities above named, there was none but Syracuse which was not reduced to slavery. The Syracusans were saved from this fate, after they had suffered defeat on the river Elorus, by the Corinthians and Corcyraeans, who made peace between them and Hippocrates, on condition of their ceding Camarina to him; for that city anciently belonged to Syracuse.

155. When, however, Hippocrates, after a reign of the same length as that of Cleander his brother, perished near the city Hybla, as he was warring with the native Sicilians, then Gelo, pretending to espouse the cause of the two sons of Hippocrates, Eucleides and Cleander, defeated the citizens who were seeking to recover their freedom, and having so done, set aside the children, and himself took the kingly power. After this piece of good fortune, Gelo likewise became master of Syracuse, in the following manner. The Syracusan landholders, as they were called, had been driven from their city by the common people assisted by their own slaves, the Cyllyrians, and had fled to Casmenae. Gelo brought them back to Syracuse, and so got possession of the town; for the people surrendered themselves, and gave up their city on his approach.

156. Being now master of Syracuse, Gelo cared less to govern Gela, which he therefore entrusted to his brother Hiero, while he strengthened the defences of his new city, which indeed was now all in all to him. And Syracuse sprang up rapidly to power and became a flourishing place. For Gelo razed Camarina to the ground, and brought all the inhabitants to Syracuse, and made them citizens; he also brought thither more than half the citizens of Gela, and gave them the same rights as the Camarinaeans. So likewise with the Megareans of Sicily—after besieging their town and forcing them to surrender, he took the rich men, who having made the war, looked now for nothing less than

death at his hands, and carrying them to Syracuse, established
them there as citizens; while the common people, who, as they
had not taken any share in the struggle, felt secure that no harm
would be done to them, he carried likewise to Syracuse, where
he sold them all as slaves to be conveyed abroad. He did the
like also by the Euboeans of Sicily, making the same difference.
His conduct towards both nations arose from his belief, that a
"people" was a most unpleasant companion. In this way Gelo
became a powerful despot.

157. When the Greek envoys reached Syracuse, and were admitted to an audience, they spoke as follows, "We have been
sent hither by the Lacedaemonians and Athenians, with their
respective allies, to ask you to join us against the barbarian.
Doubtless you have heard of his invasion, and are aware that a
Persian is about to throw a bridge over the Hellespont, and
bringing with him out of Asia all the forces of the East, to carry
war into Greece,—professing indeed that he only seeks to attack Athens, but really bent on bringing all the Greeks into subjection. Do you therefore, we beseech you, aid those who would
maintain the freedom of Greece, and yourself assist to free her;
since the power which you wield is great, and your portion in
Greece, as lord of Sicily, is no small one. For if all Greece join
together in one, there will be a mighty host collected, and we
shall be a match for our assailants; but if some turn traitors,
and others refuse their aid, and only a small part of the whole
body remains sound, then there is reason to fear that all Greece
may perish. For do not cherish a hope that the Persian, when he
has conquered our country, will be content and not advance
against you. Rather take your measure beforehand; and consider that you defend yourself when you give aid to us. Wise
counsels, be sure, for the most part have prosperous issues."

158. Thus the envoys spoke; and Gelo replied with vehe-
mence, "Greeks, you have had the face to come here with selfish
words, and exhort me to join in league with you against the barbarian. Yet when I asked you to join with me in fighting barbarians, when the quarrel broke out between me and Carthage;
and when I earnestly besought you to revenge on the men of

Egesta their murder of Dorieus, the son of Anaxandridas, promising to assist you in setting free the trading-places from which you receive great profits and advantages, you neither came hither to give me succour, nor yet to revenge Dorieus; but, for any efforts on your part to hinder it, these countries might at this time have been entirely under the barbarians. Now, however, that matters have prospered and gone well with me, while the danger has shifted its ground and at present threatens yourselves, you call Gelo to mind. But though you slighted me then, I will not imitate you now: I am ready to give you aid, and to furnish as my contribution 200 triremes, 20,000 men-at-arms, 2,000 cavalry, and an equal number of archers, slingers, and light horsemen, together with corn for the whole Grecian army so long as the war shall last. These services, however, I promise on one condition—that you appoint me chief captain and commander of the Grecian forces during the war with the barbarian. Unless you agree to this, I will neither send aid, nor come myself."

159. Syagrus, when he heard these words, was unable to contain himself, and exclaimed, "Surely a groan would burst from Pelops' son, Agamemnon, did he hear that her leadership was snatched from Sparta by Gelo and the men of Syracuse. Speak then no more of any such condition, as that we should yield you the chief command; but if you are willing to come to the aid of Greece, prepare to serve under Lacedaemonian generals. Will you not serve under a leader? Then, send no aid."

160. Hereupon Gelo, seeing the indignation which showed itself in the words of Syagrus, delivered to the envoys his final offer, "Spartan stranger," he said, "reproaches cast forth against a man are wont to provoke him to anger: but the insults you uttered in your speech shall not persuade me to outstep good breeding in my answer. Surely if you maintain so stoutly your right to the command, it is reasonable that I should be still more stiff in maintaining mine, since I am at the head of a far larger fleet and army. Since, however, the claim which I have put forward is so displeasing to you, I will yield, and be content with less. Take, if it please you. the command of the land-force, and

I will be admiral of the fleet; or assume, if you prefer it, the command by sea, and I will be leader upon the land. Unless you are satisfied with these terms, you must return home by yourselves, and lose this great alliance." Such was the offer which Gelo made.

161. The Athenian envoy broke in, before the Spartan could answer, and thus addressed Gelo, "King of the Syracusans, Greece sent us here to you to ask for an army, and not to ask for a general. You, however, do not promise to send us any army at all, if you are not made leader of the Greeks; and this command is what alone you desire. Now when your request was to have the whole command, we were content to keep silence, for well we know that we might trust the Spartan envoy to make answer for us both. But since, after failing in your claim to lead the whole armament, you now put forward a request to have the command of the fleet, know that, even should the Spartan envoy consent to this, we will not consent. The command by sea, if the Lacedaemonians do not wish for it, belongs to us. While they like to keep this command, we shall raise no dispute; but we will not yield our right to it in favour of any one else. Where would be the advantage of our having raised up a naval force greater than that of any other Greek people, if nevertheless we should suffer Syracusans to take the command away from us? From us, I say, who are Athenians, the most ancient nation in Greece, the only Greeks who have never changed their abode— the people who are said by the poet Homer to have sent to Troy the man best able of all the Greeks to array and marshal an army—so that we cannot be reproached for what we say."

162. Gelo replied, "Athenian stranger, you have, it seems, no lack of commanders; but you are likely to lack men to receive their orders. As you are resolved to yield nothing and claim everything, you had best make haste back to Greece, and say, that the spring of her year is lost to her." [18] The meaning of this expression was the following: as the spring is manifestly the

---

[18] A similar expression is said by Aristotle to have been introduced into a funeral oration of Pericles; but it does not occur in the report left by Thucydides. The explanation of the image is probably an interpolation.

finest season of the year, so (he meant to say) were his troops
the finest of the Greek army—Greece, therefore, deprived of his
alliance, would be like a year with the spring taken from it.

163. Then the Greek envoys, without having any further
dealings with Gelo, sailed away home. And Gelo, who feared
that the Greeks would be too weak to withstand the barbarians,
and yet could not any how bring himself to go to the Peloponnese, and there, though despot of Sicily, serve under the Lacedaemonians, left off altogether to contemplate that course of action, and betook himself to quite a different plan. As soon as
ever tidings reached him of the passage of the Hellespont by the
Persians, he sent off three fifty-oared galleys, under the command of Cadmus, the son of Scythas, a native of Cos; who was
to go to Delphi, taking with him a large sum of money and a
stock of friendly words: there he was to watch the war, and see
what turn it would take: if the barbarians prevailed, he was to
give Xerxes the treasure, and with it earth and water for the
lands which Gelo ruled—if the Greeks won the day, he was to
convey the treasure back.

164. This Cadmus had at an earlier time received from his
father the kingly power at Cos in a right good condition, and
had of his own free will and without the approach of any danger,
from pure love of justice, given up his power into the hands of
the people at large, and departed to Sicily; where he assisted in
the Samian seizure and settlement of Zancle, or Messana, as it
was afterwards called. Upon this occasion Gelo chose him to
send into Greece, because he was acquainted with the proofs of
honesty which he had given. And now he added to his former
honourable deeds an action which is not the least of his merits.
With a vast sum entrusted to him and completely in his power,
so that he might have kept it for his own use if he had liked, he
did not touch it; but when the Greeks gained the sea-fight and
Xerxes fled away with his army, he brought the whole treasure
back with him to Sicily.

165. They, however, who dwell in Sicily say, that Gelo,
though he knew that he must serve under the Lacedaemonians,
would nevertheless have come to the aid of the Greeks, had not

it been for Terillus, the son of Crinippus, king of Himera; who, driven from his city by Thero, the son of Aenesidemus, king of Agrigentum, brought into Sicily at this very time an army of 300,000 men, Phoenicians, Libyans, Iberians, Ligurians, Helisycians, Sardinians, and Corsicans, under the command of Hamilcar the son of Hanno, king of the Carthaginians. Terillus prevailed upon Hamilcar, partly as his sworn friend, but more through the zealous aid of Anaxilaus the son of Cretines, king of Rhegium; who, by giving his own sons to Hamilcar as hostages, induced him to make the expedition. Anaxilaus herein served his father-in-law, for he was married to a daughter of Terillus, by name Cydippe. So as Gelo could not give the Greeks any aid, he sent (they say) the sum of money to Delphi.

166. They say too, that the victory of Gelo and Thero in Sicily over Hamilcar the Carthaginian, fell out upon the very day that the Greeks defeated the Persians at Salamis. Hamilcar, who was a Carthaginian on his father's side only, but on his mother's a Syracusan, and who had been raised by his merit to the throne of Carthage, after the battle and the defeat, as I am informed, disappeared from sight: Gelo made the strictest search for him, but he could not be found anywhere, either dead or alive.

167. The Carthaginians, who take probability for their guide, give the following account of this matter: Hamilcar, they say, during all the time that the battle raged between the Greeks and the barbarians, which was from early dawn till evening, remained in the camp, sacrificing and seeking favourable omens, while he burned on a huge pyre the entire bodies of the victims which he offered. Here, as he poured libations upon the sacrifices, he saw the rout of his army; whereupon he cast himself headlong into the flames, and so was consumed and disappeared. But whether Hamilcar's disappearance was, as the Phoenicians tell us, in this way, or, as the Syracusans maintain, in some other, certain it is that the Carthaginians offer him sacrifice, and in all their colonies have monuments erected in his honour, as well as one, which is the grandest of all, at Carthage. Thus much concerning the affairs of Sicily.

168. As for the Corcyraeans, whom the envoys that visited Sicily took in their way, and to whom they delivered the same message as to Gelo, their answers and actions were the following. With great readiness they promised to come and give their help to the Greeks; declaring that the ruin of Greece was a thing which they could not tamely stand by and see; for should she fall, they must the very next day submit to slavery; so that they were bound to assist her to the very utmost of their power. But notwithstanding that they answered so smoothly, yet when the time came for aid to be sent, they were of quite a different mind; and though they manned sixty ships, it was long before they put to sea with them; and when they had so done, they went no further than the Peloponnese, where they lay to with their fleet, off the Lacedaemonian coast, about Pylos, and Taenarum, like Gelo, watching to see what turn the war would take. For they despaired altogether of the Greeks gaining the day, and expected that the Persians would win a great battle, and then be masters of the whole of Greece. They therefore acted as I have said, in order that they might be able to address Xerxes in words like these, "O King, though the Greeks sought to obtain our aid in their war with you, and though we had a force of no small size, and could have furnished a greater number of ships than any Greek state except Athens, yet we refused, since we would not fight against you, or do aught to cause you annoyance." The Corcyraeans hoped that a speech like this would gain them better treatment from the Persians than the rest of the Greeks; and it would have done so, in my judgment. At the same time, they had an excuse ready to give their countrymen, which they used when the time came. Reproached by them for sending no assistance, they replied that they had fitted out a fleet of sixty triremes, but that the Etesian winds did not allow them to double Cape Malea, and this hindered them from reaching Salamis—it was not from any bad motive that they had missed the sea-fight. In this way the Corcyraeans eluded the reproaches of the Greeks.

169. The Cretans, when the envoys sent to ask aid from them

came and made their request, acted as follows. They despatched messengers in the name of their state to Delphi, and asked the god, whether it would make for their welfare if they should lend succour to Greece. "Fools!" replied the priestess, "do you not still complain of the woes which the assisting of Menelaus cost you at the hands of angry Minos? How wroth was he, when, in spite of their having lent you no aid towards avenging his death at Camicus, you helped them to avenge the carrying off by a barbarian of a woman from Sparta!" When this answer was brought from Delphi to the Cretans, they thought no more of assisting the Greeks.

170. Minos, according to tradition, went to Sicania, or Sicily, as it is now called, in search of Daedalus, and there perished by a violent death. After a while the Cretans, warned by some god or other, made a great expedition into Sicania, all except the Polichnites and the Praesians, and besieged Camicus (which in my time belonged to Agrigentum) for five years. At last, however, failing in their efforts to take the place, and unable to carry on the siege any longer from the pressure of hunger, they departed and went their way. Voyaging homewards they had reached Iapygia, when a furious storm arose and threw them upon the coast. All their vessels were broken in pieces; and so, as they saw no means of returning to Crete, they founded the town of Hyria, where they took up their abode, changing their name from Cretans to Messapian Iapygians, and at the same time becoming inhabitants of the mainland instead of islanders. From Hyria they afterwards founded those other towns which the Tarentines at a much later period endeavoured to take, but could not, being defeated signally. Indeed so dreadful a slaughter of the Greeks never happened at any other time, so far as my knowledge extends: nor was it only the Tarentines who suffered; but the men of Rhegium too, who had been forced to go to the aid of the Tarentines by Micythus the son of Choerus, lost here 3,000 of their citizens; while the number of the Tarentines who fell was beyond all count. This Micythus had been a household slave of Anaxilaus, and was by him left in charge of Rhegium:

he is the same man who was afterwards forced to leave Rhegium, when he settled at Tegea in Arcadia, from which place he made his many offerings of statues to the shrine at Olympia.

171. This account of the Rhegians and the Tarentines is a digression from the story which I was relating. To return—the Praesians say that men of various nations now flocked to Crete, which was stripped of its inhabitants; but none came in such numbers as the Grecians. Three generations after the death of Minos the Trojan war took place; and the Cretans were not the least distinguished among the helpers of Menelaus. But on this account, when they came back from Troy, famine and pestilence fell upon them, and destroyed both the men and the cattle. Crete was a second time stripped of its inhabitants, a remnant only being left; who form, together with fresh settlers, the third Cretan people by whom the island has been inhabited. These were the events of which the priestess now reminded the men of Crete, and thereby she prevented them from giving the Greeks aid, though they wished to have gone to their assistance.

172. The Thessalians did not embrace the cause of the Medes until they were forced to do so; for they gave plain proof that the intrigues of the Aleuadae were not at all to their liking. No sooner did they hear that the Persian was about to cross over into Europe than they despatched envoys to the Greeks who were met to consult together at the Isthmus, whither all the states which were well inclined to the Grecian cause had sent their delegates. These envoys on their arrival thus addressed their countrymen, "Men of Greece, you should guard the pass of Olympus; for thus will Thessaly be placed in safety, as well as the rest of Greece. We for our parts are quite ready to take our share in this work, but you must likewise send us a strong force; otherwise we give you fair warning that we shall make terms with the Persians. For we ought not to be left, exposed as we are in front of all the rest of Greece, to die in your defence alone and unassisted. If however you do not choose to send us aid, you cannot force us to resist the enemy; for there is no force so strong as inability. We shall therefore do our best to secure our own safety." Such was the declaration of the Thessalians.

173. Hereupon the Greeks determined to send a body of foot to Thessaly by sea, which should defend the pass of Olympus. Accordingly a force was collected, which passed up the Euripus, and disembarking at Alus, on the coast of Achaea, left the ships there, and marched by land into Thessaly. Here they occupied the defile of Tempe; which leads from Lower Macedonia into Thessaly along the course of the Peneus, having the range of Olympus on the one hand and Ossa upon the other. In this place the Greek force that had been collected, amounting to about 10,000 heavy-armed men, pitched their camp; and here they were joined by the Thessalian cavalry. The commanders were, on the part of the Lacedaemonians, Evaenetus, the son of Carenus, who had been chosen out of the polemarchs, but did not belong to the blood royal; and on the part of the Athenians, Themistocles, the son of Neocles. They did not however maintain their station for more than a few days; since envoys came from Alexander, the son of Amyntas, the Macedonian, and counselled them to decamp from Tempe, telling them that if they remained in the pass they would be trodden under foot by the invading army, whose numbers they recounted, and likewise the multitude of their ships. So when the envoys thus counselled them, and the counsel seemed to be good, and the Macedonian who sent it friendly, they did even as he advised. In my opinion what chiefly wrought on them was the fear that the Persians might enter by another pass, whereof they now heard, which led from Upper Macedonia into Thessaly through the territory of the Perrhaebi, and by the town of Gonnus, the pass by which soon after the army of Xerxes actually made its entrance. The Greeks therefore went back to their ships and sailed away to the Isthmus.

174. Such were the circumstances of the expedition into Thessaly; which took place when the king was at Abydos, preparing to pass from Asia into Europe. The Thessalians, when their allies forsook them, no longer wavered, but warmly espoused the side of the Medes; and afterwards, in the course of the war, they were of the very greatest service to Xerxes.

175. The Greeks, on their return to the Isthmus, took coun-

sel together concerning the words of Alexander, and considered where they should fix the war, and what places they should occupy. The opinion which prevailed was, that they should guard the pass of Thermopylae; since it was narrower than the Thessalian defile, and at the same time nearer to them. Of the pathway, by which the Greeks who fell at Thermopylae were intercepted, they had no knowledge, until, on their arrival at Thermopylae, it was discovered to them by the Trachinians. This pass then it was determined that they should guard, in order to prevent the barbarians from penetrating into Greece through it; and at the same time it was resolved that the fleet should proceed to Artemisium, in the region of Histiaeotis; for as those places are near to one another, it would be easy for the fleet and army to hold communication. The two places may be thus described.

176. Artemisium is where the sea of Thrace contracts into a narrow channel, running between the isle of Sciathus and the mainland of Magnesia. When this narrow strait is passed you come to the line of coast called Artemisium; which is a portion of Euboea, and contains a temple of Artemis. As for the entrance into Greece by Trachis, it is, at its narrowest point, about fifty feet wide. This however is not the place where the passage is most contracted; for it is still narrower a little above and a little below Thermopylae. At Alpeni, which is lower down than that place, it is only wide enough for a single carriage; and up above, at the river Phoenix, near the town called Anthela, it is the same. West of Thermopylae rises a lofty and precipitous hill, impossible to climb, which runs up into the chain of Oeta; while to the east the road is shut in by the sea and by marshes. In this place are the warm springs, which the natives call The Cauldrons; and above them stands an altar sacred to Heracles. A wall had once been carried across the opening; and in this there had of old times been a gateway. These works were made by the Phocians, through fear of the Thessalians, at the time when the latter came from Thesprotia to establish themselves in the land of Aeolis, which they still occupy. As the Thessalians strove to

reduce Phocis, the Phocians raised the wall to protect themselves, and likewise turned the hot springs upon the pass, that so the ground might be broken up by watercourses, using thus all possible means to hinder the Thessalians from invading their country. The old wall had been built in very remote times; and the greater part of it had gone to decay through age. Now however the Greeks resolved to repair its breaches, and here make their stand against the barbarian. At this point there is a village very nigh the road, Alpeni by name, from which the Greeks reckoned on getting corn for their troops.

177. These places, therefore, seemed to the Greeks fit for their purpose. Weighing well all that was likely to happen, and considering that in this region the barbarians could make no use of their vast numbers, nor of their cavalry, they resolved to await here the invader of Greece. And when news reached them of the Persians being in Pieria, straightway they broke up from the Isthmus, and proceeded, some on foot to Thermopylae, others by sea to Artemisium.

178. The Greeks now made all speed to reach the two stations; and about the same time the Delphians, alarmed both for themselves and for their country, consulted the god, and received for answer a command to pray to the winds; for the winds would do Greece good service. So when this answer was given them, forthwith the Delphians sent word of the prophecy to the Greeks who were zealous for freedom, and cheering them thereby amid the fears which they entertained with respect to the barbarian, earned their everlasting gratitude. This done, they raised an altar to the winds at Thyia (where Thyia, the daughter of Cephissus, from whom the region takes its name, has a precinct), and worshipped them with sacrifices. And even to the present day the Delphians sacrifice to the winds, because of this oracle.

179. The fleet of Xerxes now departed from Therma; and ten of the swiftest sailing ships ventured to stretch across direct for Sciathus, at which place there were upon the look-out three vessels belonging to the Greeks, one a ship of Troezen, another

of Aegina, and the third from Athens. These vessels no sooner saw from a distance the barbarians approaching than they all hurriedly took to flight.

180. The barbarians at once pursued, and the Troezenian ship, which was commanded by Prexinus, fell into their hands. Hereupon the Persians took the handsomest of the men-at-arms, and drew him to the prow of the vessel, where they sacrificed him; for they thought the man a good omen to their cause, seeing that he was at once so beautiful, and likewise the first captive they had made. The man who was slain in this way was called Leo; and it may be that the name he bore helped him to his fate in some measure.

181. The Aeginetan trireme, under its captain, Asonides, gave the Persians no little trouble, one of the men-at-arms, Pythes, the son of Ischenous, distinguishing himself beyond all the others who fought on that day. After the ship was taken this man continued to resist, and did not cease fighting till he fell quite covered with wounds. The Persians who served as men-at-arms in the squadron, finding that he was not dead, but still breathed, and being very anxious to save his life, since he had behaved so valiantly, dressed his wounds with myrrh, and bound them up with bandages of cotton. Then, when they were returned to their own station, they displayed their prisoner admiringly to the whole host, and behaved towards him with much kindness; but all the rest of the ship's crew were treated merely as slaves.

182. Thus did the Persians succeed in taking two of the vessels. The third, a trireme commanded by Phormus of Athens, took to flight and ran aground at the mouth of the river Peneus. The barbarians got possession of the bark, but not of the men. For the Athenians had no sooner run their vessel aground than they leaped out, and made their way through Thessaly back to Athens.

When the Greeks stationed at Artemisium learned what had happened by fire-signals[19] from Sciathus, so terrified were they,

[19] The employment of fire-signals among the Greeks was very common.

that, quitting their anchorage-ground at Artemisium, and leaving scouts to watch the foe on the high lands of Euboea, they removed to Chalcis, intending to guard the Euripus.

183. Meantime three of the ten vessels sent forward by the barbarians advanced as far as the sunken rock between Sciathus and Magnesia, which is called the Ant, and there set up a stone pillar which they had brought with them for that purpose. After this, their course being now clear, the barbarians set sail with all their ships from Therma, eleven days from the time that the king quitted the town. The rock, which lay directly in their course, had been made known to them by Pammon of Scyros. A day's voyage without a stop brought them to Sepias in Magnesia, and to the strip of coast which lies between the town of Casthanaea and the promontory of Sepias.

184. As far as this point then, and on land, as far as Thermopylae, the armament of Xerxes had been free from mischance; and the numbers were still, according to my reckoning, of the following amount. First there was the ancient complement of the 1,207 vessels which came with the king from Asia—the contingents of the nations severally—amounting, if we allow to each ship a crew of 200 men,[20] to 241,400. Each of these vessels had on board, besides native soldiers, thirty fighting men, who were either Persians, Medes, or Sacans; which gives an addition of 36,210. To these two members I shall further add the crews of the fifty-oared galleys; which may be reckoned, one with another, at fourscore men each. Of such vessels there were (as I said before) 3,000; and the men on board them accordingly would be 240,000. This was the sea force brought by the king from Asia; and it amounted in all to 517,610 men. The number of the foot soldiers was 1,700,000; that of the horsemen 80,000; to which must be added the Arabs who rode on camels, and the Libyans who fought in chariots, whom I reckon at 20,000. The whole number, therefore, of the land and sea forces added together amounts to 2,317,610 men. Such was the force brought

[20] The crew of a Greek trireme seems to have been 200; 170 rowers and thirty fighters.

from Asia, without including the camp followers, or taking any
account of the provision-ships and the men whom they had on
board.

185. To the amount thus reached we have still to add the
forces gathered in Europe, concerning which I can only speak
from conjecture. The Greeks dwelling in Thrace, and in the
islands off the coast of Thrace, furnished to the fleet 120 ships;
the crews of which would amount to 24,000 men. Besides these,
footmen were furnished by the Thracians, the Paeonians, the
Eordians, the Bottiaeans, by the Chalcidean tribes, by the
Brygians, the Pierians, the Macedonians, the Perrhaebians, the
Enianians, the Dolopians, the Magnesians, the Achaeans, and
by all the dwellers upon the Thracian sea-board; and the forces
of these nations amounted, I believe, to 300,000 men. These
numbers, added to those of the force which came out of Asia,
make the sum of the fighting men 2,641,610.

186. Such then being the number of the fighting men, it is
my belief that the attendants who followed the camp, together
with the crews of the corn-barks, and of the other craft accompanying the army, made up an amount rather above than below
that of the fighting men. However I will not reckon them as
either fewer or more, but take them at an equal number. We
have therefore to add to the sum already reached an exactly
equal amount. This will give 5,283,220 as the whole number of
men brought by Xerxes, the son of Darius, as far as Sepias and
Thermopylae.[21]

187. Such then was the amount of the entire host of Xerxes.
As for the number of the women who ground the corn, of the
concubines, and the eunuchs, no one can give any sure account
of it; nor can the baggage-horses and other pack-animals, nor
the Indian hounds which followed the army, be calculated, by
reason of their multitude. Hence I am not at all surprised that
the water of the rivers was found too scant for the army in some
instances; rather it is a marvel to me how the provisions did not
fail, when the numbers were so great. For I find on calculation
that if each man consumed no more than a choenix of corn a

---

[21] See notes 7 and 9 in this book.

day, there must have been used daily by the army 110,340 medimni, and this without counting what was eaten by the women, the eunuchs, the pack-animals, and the hounds. Among all this multitude of men there was not one who, for beauty and stature, deserved more than Xerxes himself to wield so vast a power.

188. The fleet then, as I said, on leaving Therma, sailed to the Magnesian territory, and there occupied the strip of coast between the city of Casthanaea and Cape Sepias. The ships of the first row were moored to the land, while the remainder swung at anchor further off. The beach extended but a very little way, so that they had to anchor off the shore, row upon row, eight deep. In this manner they passed the night. But at dawn of day calm and stillness gave place to a raging sea, and a violent storm, which fell upon them with a strong gale from the east—a wind which the people in those parts call Hellespontias. Such of them as percieved the wind rising, and were so moored as to allow of it, forestalled the tempest by dragging their ships up on the beach, and in this way saved both themselves and their vessels. But the ships which the storm caught out at sea were driven ashore, some of them near the place called the Ovens, at the foot of Pelion; others on the strand itself; others again about Cape Sepias; while a portion were dashed to pieces near the cities of Meliboea and Casthanaea. There was no resisting the tempest.

189. It is said that the Athenians had called upon Boreas to aid the Greeks, on account of a fresh oracle which had reached them, commanding them to seek help from their son-in-law. For Boreas, according to the tradition of the Greeks, took to wife a woman of Attica, Orithyia, the daughter of Erechtheus. So the Athenians, as the tale goes, considering that this marriage made Boreas their son-in-law, and perceiving, while they lay with their ships at Chalcis of Euboea, that the wind was rising, or, it may be, even before it freshened, offered sacrifice both to Boreas and likewise to Orithyia, entreating them to come to their aid and to destroy the ships of the barbarians, as they did once before off Mount Athos. Whether it was owing to this that Boreas fell with violence on the barbarians at their anchorage I cannot

say; but the Athenians declare that they had received aid from Boreas before, and that it was he who now caused all these disasters. They therefore, on their return home, built a temple to this god on the banks of the Ilissus.

190. Such as put the loss of the Persian fleet in this storm at the lowest say that 400 of their ships were destroyed, that a countless multitude of men were slain, and a vast treasure engulfed. Ameinocles, the son of Cretines, a Magnesian, who farmed land near Cape Sepias, found the wreck of these vessels a source of great gain to him; many were the gold and silver drinking-cups, cast up long afterwards by the surf, which he gathered; while treasure-boxes too which had belonged to the Persians, and golden articles of all kinds and beyond count, came into his possession. Ameinocles grew to be a man of great wealth in this way, but in other respects things did not go over well with him; he too, like other men, had his own grief—the calamity of slaying his son.

191. As for the number of the provision craft and other merchant ships which perished, it was beyond count. Indeed, such was the loss, that the commanders of the sea force, fearing lest in their shattered condition the Thessalians should venture on an attack, raised a lofty barricade around their station out of the wreck of the vessels cast ashore. The storm lasted three days. At length the Magians, by offering victims to the Winds, and charming them with the help of conjurers, while at the same time they sacrificed to Thetis and the Nereids, succeeded in laying the storm four days after it first began; or perhaps it ceased of itself. The reason of their offering sacrifice to Thetis was this: they were told by the Ionians that here was the place whence Peleus carried her off, and that the whole promontory was sacred to her and to her sister Nereids. So the storm lulled upon the fourth day.

192. The scouts left by the Greeks about the highlands of Euboea hastened down from their stations on the day following that whereon the storm began, and acquainted their countrymen with all that had befallen the Persian fleet. These no sooner heard what had happened than straightway they returned

thanks to Poseidon the Saviour, and poured libations in his
honour; after which they hastened back with all speed to Artemisium, expecting to find a very few ships left to oppose them,
and arriving there for the second time, took up their station on
that strip of coast: nor from that day to the present have they
ceased to address Poseidon by the name then given him, of
Saviour.

193. The barbarians, when the wind lulled and the sea grew
smooth, drew their ships down to the water, and proceeded to
coast along the mainland. Having then rounded the extreme
point of Magnesia, they sailed straight into the bay that runs up
to Pagasae. There is a place in this bay, belonging to Magnesia,
where Heracles is said to have been put ashore to fetch water by
Jason and his companions; who then deserted him and went on
their way to Aea in Colchis, on board the ship Argo, in quest of
the golden fleece. From the circumstance that they intended,
after watering their vessel at this place, to quit the shore and
launch forth into the deep, it received the name of Aphetae.
Here then it was that the fleet of Xerxes came to an anchor.

194. Fifteen ships, which had lagged greatly behind the rest,
happening to catch sight of the Greek fleet at Artemisium, mistook it for their own, and sailing down into the midst of it, fell
into the hands of the enemy. The commander of this squadron
was Sandoces, the son of Thamasius, governor of Cyme, in
Aeolis. He was of the number of the royal judges, and had been
crucified by Darius some time before, on the charge of taking a
bribe to determine a cause wrongly; but while he yet hung on
the cross, Darius bethought him that the good deeds of Sandoces
towards the king's house were more numerous than his evil
deeds; and so confessing that he had acted with more haste than
wisdom, he ordered him to be taken down and set at large. Thus
Sandoces escaped destruction at the hands of Darius, and was
alive at this time; but he was not fated to come off so cheaply
from his second peril; for as soon as the Greeks saw the ships
making towards them, they guessed their mistake, and putting
to sea, took them without difficulty.

195. Aridolis, tyrant of Alabanda in Caria, was on board one

of the ships, and was made prisoner; as also was the Paphian general, Penthylus, the son of Demonous, who was on board another. This person had brought with him twelve ships from Paphos, and after losing eleven in the storm off Sepias, was taken in the remaining one as he sailed towards Artemisium. The Greeks, after questioning their prisoners as much as they wished concerning the forces of Xerxes, sent them away in chains to the Isthmus of Corinth.

196. The sea force of the barbarians, with the exception of the fifteen ships commanded (as I said) by Sandoces, came safe to Aphete. Xerxes meanwhile, with the land army, had proceeded through Thessaly and Achaea, and three days earlier, had entered the territory of the Malians. In Thessaly he matched his own horses against the Thessalian, which he heard were the best in Greece; but the Greek coursers were left far behind in the race. All the rivers in this region had water enough to supply his army, except only the Onochonus; but in Achaea, the largest of the streams, the Apidanus, barely held out.

197. On his arrival at Alus in Achaea, his guides, wishing to inform him of everything, told him the tale known to the dwellers in those parts concerning the temple of the Laphystian Zeus —how that Athamas the son of Aeolus took counsel with Ino and plotted the death of Phrixus; and how that afterwards the Achaeans, warned by an oracle, laid a forfeit upon his posterity, forbidding the eldest of the race ever to enter into the court-house (which they call the people's house), and keeping watch themselves to see the law obeyed. If one comes within the doors, he can never go out again except to be sacrificed. Further, they told him, how that many persons, when on the point of being slain, are seized with such fear that they flee away and take refuge in some other country; and that these, if they come back long afterwards, and are found to be the persons who entered the court-house, are led forth covered with chaplets, and in a grand procession, and are sacrificed. This forfeit is paid by the descendants of Cytissorus the son of Phrixus, because, when the Achaeans, in obedience to an oracle, made Athamas the son of Aeolus their sin-offering and were about to slay him, Cytissorus

came from Aea in Colchis and rescued Athamas; by which deed
he brought the anger of the god upon his own posterity. Xerxes,
therefore, having heard this story, when he reached the grove of
the god, avoided it, and commanded his army to do the like. He
also paid the same respect to the house and precinct of the descendants of Athamas.

198. Such were the doings of Xerxes in Thessaly and in
Achaea. From hence he passed on into Malis, along the shores
of a bay, in which there is an ebb and flow of the tide daily. By
the side of this bay lies a piece of flat land, in one part broad,
but in another very narrow indeed, around which runs a range
of lofty hills, impossible to climb, enclosing all Malis within
them, and called the Trachinian Cliffs. The first city upon the
bay, as you come from Achaea, is Anticyra, near which the river
Spercheius, flowing down from the country of the Enianians,
empties itself into the sea. About two miles from this stream
there is a second river, called the Dyras, which is said to have
appeared first to help Heracles when he was burning. Again, at
the distance of about two miles, there is a stream called the
Melas, near which, within half a mile, stands the city of Trachis.

199. At the point where this city is built, the plain between
the hills and the sea is broader than at any other, for it there
measures 420 miles.[22] South of Trachis there is a cleft in the
mountain-range which shuts in the territory of Trachinia, and
the river Asopus issuing from this cleft flows for a while along
the foot of the hills.

200. Further to the south, another river, called the Phoenix,
which has no great body of water, flows from the same hills, and
falls into the Asopus. Here is the narrowest place of all, for in
this part there is only a causeway wide enough for a single
carriage. From the river Phoenix to Thermopylae is a distance
of two miles; and in this space is situated the village called
Anthela, which the river Asopus passes before it reaches the sea.
The space about Anthela is of some width, and contains a temple

[22] This is certainly an incorrect reading. The plain is even now, at the
utmost, seven miles across. It is possible to understand the passage as the
whole of the plain area.

of Amphictyonian Demeter, as well as the seats of the Am-
phictyonic deputies, and a temple of Amphictyon himself.

201. King Xerxes pitched his camp in the region of Malis
called Trachinia, while on their side the Greeks occupied the
straits. These straits the Greeks in general call Thermopylae
(the Hot Gates); but the natives and those who dwell in the
neighbourhood, call them Pylae (the Gates). Here then the two
armies took their stand; the one master of all the region lying
north of Trachis, the other of the country extending southward
of that place to the verge of the continent.

202. The Greeks who at this spot awaited the coming of
Xerxes were the following: From Sparta, 300 men-at-arms:
from Arcadia, 1,000 Tegeans and Mantineans, 500 of each
people; 120 Orchomenians, from the Arcadian Orchomenus;
and 1,000 from other cities: from Corinth, 400 men: from
Phlius, 200: and from Mycenae eighty. Such was the number
from the Peloponnese. There were also present, from Boeotia,
700 Thespians and 400 Thebans.

203. Besides these troops, the Locrians of Opus and the
Phocians had obeyed the call of their countrymen, and sent, the
former all the force they had, the latter 1,000 men. For envoys
had gone from the Greeks at Thermopylae among the Locrians
and Phocians, to call on them for assistance, and to say, "They
were themselves but the vanguard of the host, sent to precede
the main body, which might every day be expected to follow
them. The sea was in good keeping, watched by the Athenians,
the Aeginetans, and the rest of the fleet. There was no cause why
they should fear; for after all the invader was not a god but a
man; and there never had been, and never would be, a man who
was not liable to misfortunes from the very day of his birth, and
those greater in proportion to his own greatness. The assailant
therefore, being only a mortal, must needs fall from his glory."
Thus urged, the Locrians and the Phocians had come with their
troops to Trachis.

204. The various nations had each captains of their own under whom they served; but the one to whom all especially looked
up, and who had the command of the entire force, was the Lace-

daemonian, Leonidas. Now Leonidas was the son of Anaxandridas, who was the son of Leo, who was the son of Eurycratidas, who was the son of Anaxander, who was the son of Eurycrates, who was the son of Polydorus, who was the son of Alcamenes, who was the son of Telecles, who was the son of Archelaus, who was the son of Agesilaus, who was the son of Doryssus, who was the son of Labotas, who was the son of Echestratus, who was the son of Agis, who was the son of Eurysthenes, who was the son of Aristodemus, who was the son of Aristomachus, who was the son of Cleodaeus, who was the son of Hyllus, who was the son of Heracles.

Leonidas had come to be king of Sparta quite unexpectedly.

205. Having two elder brothers, Cleomenes and Dorieus, he had no thought of ever mounting the throne. However when Cleomenes died without male offspring, as Dorieus was likewise deceased, having perished in Sicily, the crown fell to Leonidas, who was older than Cleombrotus, the youngest of the sons of Anaxandridas, and, moreover, was married to the daughter of Cleomenes. He had now come to Thermopylae, accompanied by the 300 men which the law assigned him, whom he had himself chosen from among the citizens, and who were all of them fathers with sons living. On his way he had taken the troops from Thebes, whose number I have already mentioned, and who were under the command of Leontiades the son of Eurymachus. The reason why he made a point of taking troops from Thebes and Thebes only was, that the Thebans were strongly suspected of being well inclined to the Medes. Leonidas therefore called on them to come with him to the war, wishing to see whether they would comply with his demand, or openly refuse, and disclaim the Greek alliance. They, however, though their wishes leant the other way, nevertheless sent the men.

206. The force with Leonidas was sent forward by the Spartans in advance of their main body, that the sight of them might encourage the allies to fight, and hinder them from going over to the Medes, as it was likely they might have done had they seen Sparta backward. They intended presently, when they had celebrated the Carneian festival, which was what now kept

them at home, to leave a garrison in Sparta, and hasten in full force to join the army. The rest of the allies also intended to act similarly; for it happened that the Olympic festival fell exactly at this same period. None of them looked to see the contest at Thermopylae decided so speedily; wherefore they were content to send forward a mere advanced guard. Such accordingly were the intentions of the allies.

207. The Greek forces at Thermopylae, when the Persian army drew near to the entrance of the pass, were seized with fear, and a council was held to consider about a retreat. It was the wish of the Peloponnesians generally that the army should fall back upon the Peloponnese, and there guard the Isthmus. But Leonidas, who saw with what indignation the Phocians and Locrians heard of this plan, gave his voice for remaining where they were, while they sent envoys to the several cities to ask for help, since they were too few to make a stand against an army like that of the Medes.

208. While this debate was going on, Xerxes sent a mounted spy to observe the Greeks, and note how many they were, and what they were doing. He had heard, before he came out of Thessaly, that a few men were assembled at this place, and that at their head were certain Lacedaemonians, under Leonidas, a descendant of Heracles. The horseman rode up to the camp, and looked about him, but did not see the whole army; for such as were on the further side of the wall (which had been rebuilt and was now carefully guarded) it was not possible for him to behold; but he observed those on the outside, who were encamped in front of the rampart. It chanced that at this time the Lacedaemonians held the outer guard, and were seen by the spy, some of them engaged in gymnastic exercises, others combing their long hair. At this the spy greatly marvelled, but he counted their number, and when he had taken accurate note of everything, he rode back quietly; for no one pursued after him, or paid any heed to his visit. So he returned, and told Xerxes all that he had seen.

209. Upon this, Xerxes, who had no means of surmising the truth—namely, that the Spartans were preparing to do or die

manfully—but thought it laughable that they should be engaged in such employments, sent and called to his presence Demaratus the son of Ariston, who still remained with the army. When he appeared, Xerxes told him all that he had heard, and questioned him concerning the news, since he was anxious to understand the meaning of such behaviour on the part of the Spartans. Then Demaratus said, "I spoke to you, O King, concerning these men long since, when we had but just begun our march upon Greece; you, however, only laughed at my words, when I told you of all this, which I saw would come to pass. Earnestly do I struggle at all times to speak truth to you, sire; and now listen to it once more. These men have come to dispute the pass with us, and it is for this that they are now making ready. It is their custom, when they are about to hazard their lives, to adorn their heads with care. Be assured, however, that if you can subdue the men who are here and the Lacedaemonians who remain in Sparta, there is no other nation in all the world which will venture to lift a hand in their defence. You have now to deal with the first kingdom and town in Greece, and with the bravest men."

Then Xerxes, to whom what Demaratus said seemed altogether to surpass belief, asked further, "How it was possible for so small an army to contend with his?"

"O King," Demaratus answered, "let me be treated as a liar, if matters fall not out as I say."

210. But Xerxes was not persuaded any the more. Four whole days he suffered to go by,[23] expecting that the Greeks would run away. When, however, he found on the fifth that they were not gone, thinking that their firm stand was mere impudence and recklessness, he grew wroth, and sent against them the Medes and Cissians, with orders to take them alive and bring them into his presence. Then the Medes rushed forward and charged the Greeks, but fell in vast numbers: others however took the places of the slain, and would not be beaten off, though they suffered terrible losses. In this way it became clear to all, and especially

[23] We may suppose that the Persian king looked at first to obtaining the co-operation of his fleet, and only began the attack when that hope failed him.

to the king, that though he had plenty of combatants, he had but very few warriors. The struggle, however, continued during the whole day.

211. Then the Medes, having met so rough a reception, withdrew from the fight; and their place was taken by the band of Persians under Hydarnes, whom the king called his Immortals: they, it was thought, would soon finish the business. But when they joined battle with the Greeks, it was with no better success than the Median detachment—things went much as before—the two armies fighting in a narrow space, and the barbarians using shorter spears than the Greeks, and having no advantage from their numbers. The Lacedaemonians fought in a way worthy of note, and showed themselves far more skilful in fight than their adversaries, often turning their backs, and making as though they were all flying away, on which the barbarians would rush after them with much noise and shouting, when the Spartans at their approach would wheel round and face their pursuers, in this way destroying vast numbers of the enemy. Some Spartans likewise fell in these encounters, but only a very few. At last the Persians, finding that all their efforts to gain the pass availed nothing, and that whether they attacked by divisions or in any other way, it was to no purpose, withdrew to their own quarters.

212. During these assaults, it is said that Xerxes, who was watching the battle, thrice leaped from the throne on which he sat, in terror for his army.

Next day the combat was renewed, but with no better success on the part of the barbarians. The Greeks were so few that the barbarians hoped to find them disabled, by reason of their wounds, from offering any further resistance; and so they once more attacked them. But the Greeks were drawn up in detachments according to their cities, and bore the brunt of the battle in turns, all except the Phocians, who had been stationed on the mountain to guard the pathway. So when the Persians found no difference between that day and the preceding, they again retired to their quarters.

213. Now, as the king was at a loss, and knew not how he

should deal with the emergency, Ephialtes, the son of Euryde-
mus, a man of Malis, came to him and was admitted to a conference. Stirred by the hope of receiving a rich reward at the
king's hands, he had come to tell him of the pathway which led
across the mountain to Thermopylae; by which disclosure he
brought destruction on the band of Greeks who had there withstood the barbarians. This Ephialtes afterwards, from fear of the
Lacedaemonians, fled into Thessaly; and during his exile, in an
assembly of the Amphictyons held at Pylae, a price was set upon
his head by the Pylagorae. When some time had gone by, he
returned from exile, and went to Anticyra, where he was slain by
Athenades, a native of Trachis. Athenades did not slay him for
his treachery, but for another reason, which I shall mention in a
later part of my history:[24] yet still the Lacedaemonians honoured him none the less. Thus then did Ephialtes perish a long
time afterwards.

214. Besides this there is another story told, which I do not at
all believe, that Onetas the son of Phanagoras, a native of
Carystus, and Corydallus, a man of Anticyra, were the persons
who spoke on this matter to the king, and took the Persians
across the mountain. One may guess which story is true, from
the fact that the deputies of the Greeks, the Pylagorae, who
must have had the best means of ascertaining the truth, did not
offer the reward for the heads of Onetas and Corydallus, but for
that of Ephialtes of Trachis; and again from the flight of
Ephialtes, which we know to have been on this account. Onetas,
I allow, although he was not a Malian, might have been acquainted with the path, if he had lived much in that part of the
country; but as Ephialtes was the person who actually led the
Persians round the mountain by the pathway, I leave his name
on record as that of the man who did the deed.

215. Great was the joy of Xerxes on this occasion; and as he
approved highly of the enterprise which Ephialtes undertook to
accomplish, he forthwith sent upon the errand Hydarnes, and
the Persians under him. The troops left the camp about the time
of the lighting of the lamps. The pathway along which they

---

[24] This promise is not fulfilled in the work as it now exists.

went was first discovered by the Malians of these parts, who soon afterwards led the Thessalians by it to attack the Phocians, at the time when the Phocians fortified the pass with a wall, and so put themselves under covert from danger. And ever since, the path has always been put to an ill use by the Malians.

216. The course which it takes is the following: Beginning at the Asopus, where that stream flows through the cleft in the hills, it runs along the ridge of the mountain (which is called, like the pathway over it, Anopaea), and ends at the city of Alpenus—the first Locrian town as you come from Malis—by the stone called Black-buttock and the seats of the Cercopians. Here it is as narrow as at any other point.

217. The Persians took this path, and crossing the Asopus, continued their march through the whole of the night, having the mountains of Oeta on their right hand, and on their left those of Trachis. At dawn of day they found themselves close to the summit. Now the hill was guarded, as I have already said, by 1,000 Phocian men-at-arms, who were placed there to defend the pathway, and at the same time to secure their own country. They had been given the guard of the mountain path, while the other Greeks defended the pass below, because they had volunteered for the service, and had pledged themselves to Leonidas to maintain the post.

218. The ascent of the Persians became known to the Phocians in the following manner: During all the time that they were making their way up, the Greeks remained unconscious of it, inasmuch as the whole mountain was covered with groves of oak; but it happened that the air was very still, and the leaves which the Persians stirred with their feet made, as it was likely they would, a loud rustling, whereupon the Phocians jumped up and flew to seize their arms. In a moment the barbarians came in sight, and perceiving men arming themselves, were greatly amazed; for they had fallen in with an enemy when they expected no opposition. Hydarnes, alarmed at the sight, and fearing lest the Phocians might be Lacedaemonians, inquired of Ephialtes to what nation these troops belonged. Ephialtes told him the exact truth, whereupon he arrayed his Persians for

battle. The Phocians, galled by the showers of arrows to which they were exposed, and imagining themselves the special object of the Persian attack, fled hastily to the crest of the mountain, and there made ready to meet death; but while their mistake continued, the Persians, with Ephialtes and Hydarnes, not thinking it worth their while to delay on account of Phocians, passed on and descended the mountain with all possible speed.

219. The Greeks at Thermopylae received the first warning of the destruction which the dawn would bring on them from the seer Megistias, who read their fate in the victims as he was sacrificing. After this deserters came in, and brought the news that the Persians were marching round by the hills: it was still night when these men arrived. Last of all, the scouts came running down from the heights, and brought in the same accounts, when the day was just beginning to break. Then the Greeks held a council to consider what they should do, and here opinions were divided: some were strong against quitting their post, while others contended to the contrary. So when the council had broken up, part of the troops departed and went their ways homeward to their several states; part however resolved to remain, and to stand by Leonidas to the last.

220. It is said that Leonidas himself sent away the troops who departed, because he tendered their safety, but thought it unseemly that either he or his Spartans should quit the post which they had been especially sent to guard. For my own part, I incline to think that Leonidas gave the order, because he perceived the allies to be out of heart and unwilling to encounter the danger to which his own mind was made up.[25] He therefore commanded them to retreat, but said that he himself could not draw back with honour; knowing that, if he stayed, glory

[25] Herodotus, by accident or design, has practically ignored the Greek plan of campaign in the relation between operations on land and sea. Leonidas was perhaps surprised that the Persians came around by the short route of the Anopaea but his main task, so far as he knew, was to hold the land route until the Greek fleet could force a decisive action. This could be done if the allies met the Persians near Mount Callidromus, the longer route to the rear of Thermopylae. Leonidas believed that he could hold the pass with his remaining force.

awaited him, and that Sparta in that case would not lose her prosperity. For when the Spartans, at the very beginning of the war, sent to consult the oracle concerning it, the answer which they received from the priestess was that either Sparta must be overthrown by the barbarians, or one of her kings must perish. The prophecy was delivered in hexameter verse, and ran thus:

Oh! ye men who dwell in the streets of broad Lacedaemon,
Either your glorious town shall be sacked by the children of
    Perseus,
Or, in exchange, must all through the whole Laconian country
Mourn for the loss of a king, descendant of great Heracles.
HE cannot be withstood by the courage of bulls or of lions,
Strive as they may; he is mighty as Zeus; there is nought that
    shall stay him,
Till he have got for his prey your king, or your glorious city.

The remembrance of this answer, I think, and the wish to secure the whole glory for the Spartans, caused Leonidas to send the allies away. This is more likely than that they quarrelled with him, and took their departure in such unruly fashion.

221. To me it seems no small argument in favour of this view, that the seer also who accompanied the army, Megistias, the Acarnanian, said to have been of the blood of Melampus, and the same who was led by the appearance of the victims to warn the Greeks of the danger which threatened them, received orders to retire (as it is certain he did) from Leonidas, that he might escape the coming destruction. Megistias, however, though bidden to depart, refused, and stayed with the army; but he had an only son present with the expedition, whom he now sent away.

222. So the allies, when Leonidas ordered them to retire, obeyed him and forthwith departed. Only the Thespians and the Thebans remained with the Spartans; and of these the Thebans were kept back by Leonidas as hostages, very much against their will. The Thespians, on the contrary, stayed entirely of their own accord, refusing to retreat, and declaring that they would not forsake Leonidas and his followers. So they abode with the

Spartans, and died with them. Their leader was Demophilus, the
son of Diadromes.

223. At sunrise Xerxes made libations, after which he waited
until the time when the market-place is wont to fill, and then began his advance. Ephialtes had instructed him thus, as the
descent of the mountain is much quicker, and the distance much
shorter, than the way round the hills, and the ascent. So the
barbarians under Xerxes began to draw nigh; and the Greeks
under Leonidas, as they now went forth determined to die, advanced much further than on previous days, until they reached
the more open portion of the pass. Hitherto they had held their
station within the wall, and from this had gone forth to fight at
the point where the pass was the narrowest. Now they joined
battle beyond the defile, and carried slaughter among the barbarians, who fell in heaps. Behind them the captains of the
squadrons, armed with whips, urged their men forward with
continual blows. Many were thrust into the sea, and there
perished; a still greater number were trampled to death by their
own soldiers; no one heeded the dying. For the Greeks, reckless
of their own safety and desperate, since they knew that, as the
mountain had been crossed, their destruction was nigh at hand,
exerted themselves with the most furious valour against the
barbarians.

224. By this time the spears of the greater number were all
shivered, and with their swords they hewed down the ranks of
the Persians; and here, as they strove, Leonidas fell fighting
bravely, together with many other famous Spartans, whose
names I have taken care to learn on account of their great
worthiness, as indeed I have those of all the 300.[26] There fell too
at the same time very many famous Persians: among them, two
sons of Darius, Abrocomes and Hyperanthes, his children by
Phratagune, the daughter of Artanes. Artanes was brother of
King Darius, being a son of Hystaspes, the son of Arsames; and
when he gave his daughter to the king, he made him heir likewise of all his substance; for she was his only child.

[26] These names were all inscribed on a pillar at Sparta, which remained
standing in the time of Pausanias.

225. Thus two brothers of Xerxes here fought and fell. And now there arose a fierce struggle between the Persians and the Lacedaemonians over the body of Leonidas, in which the Greeks four times drove back the enemy, and at last by their great bravery succeeded in bearing off the body. This combat was scarcely ended when the Persians with Ephialtes approached; and the Greeks, informed that they drew nigh, made a change in the manner of their fighting. Drawing back into the narrowest part of the pass, and retreating even behind the cross wall, they posted themselves upon a hillock, where they stood all drawn up together in one close body, except only the Thebans. The hillock whereof I speak is at the entrance of the straits, where the stone lion stands which was set up in honour of Leonidas. Here they defended themselves to the last, such as still had swords using them, and the others resisting with their hands and teeth; till the barbarians, who in part had pulled down the wall and attacked them in front, in part had gone round and now encircled them upon every side, overwhelmed and buried the remnant left beneath showers of missile weapons.

226. Thus nobly did the whole body of Lacedaemonians and Thespians behave, but nevertheless one man is said to have distinguished himself above all the rest, to wit, Dieneces the Spartan. A speech which he made before the Greeks engaged the Medes, remains on record. One of the Trachinians told him, "Such was the number of the barbarians, that when they shot forth their arrows the sun would be darkened by their multitude." Dieneces, not at all frightened at these words, but making light of the Median numbers, answered, "Our Trachinian friend brings us excellent tidings. If the Medes darken the sun, we shall have our fight in the shade." Other sayings too of a like nature are said to have been left on record by this same person.

227. Next to him two brothers, Lacedaemonians, are reputed to have made themselves conspicuous: they were named Alpheus and Maro, and were the sons of Orsiphantus. There was also a Thespian who gained greater glory than any of his countrymen: he was a man called Dithyrambus, the son of Harmatidas.

228. The slain were buried where they fell; and in their hon-

our, nor less in honour of those who died before Leonidas sent
the allies away, an inscription was set up, which said:

> Here did four thousand men from Pelops' land
> Against three hundred myriads bravely stand.

This was in honour of all. Another was for the Spartans alone:

> Go, stranger, and to Lacedaemon tell
> That here, obeying her behests, we fell.

This was for the Lacedaemonians. The seer had the following:

> The great Megistias' tomb you here may view,
>   Whom slew the Medes, fresh from Spercheius' fords.
> Well the wise seer the coming death foreknew,
>   Yet scorned he to forsake his Spartan lords.

These inscriptions, and the pillars likewise, were all set up by
the Amphictyons, except that in honour of Megistias, which was
inscribed to him (on account of their sworn friendship) by
Simonides, the son of Leoprepes.[27]

229. Two of the 300, it is said, Aristodemus and Eurytus,
having been attacked by a disease of the eyes, had received
orders from Leonidas to quit the camp, and both lay at Alpeni
in the worst stage of the malady. These two men might, had they
been so minded, have agreed together to return alive to Sparta;
or if they did not like to return, they might have gone both to
the field and fallen with their countrymen. But at this time,
when either way was open to them, unhappily they could not
agree, but took contrary courses. Eurytus no sooner heard that
the Persians had come round the mountain than straightway he
called for his armour, and having buckled it on, bade his Helot[28]

---

[27] All three inscriptions are assigned to Simonides by other writers.

[28] By the expression his Helot, we are to understand the special servant
whose business it was to attend constantly upon the Spartan warrior.

lead him to the place where his friends were fighting The Helot did so, and then turned and fled; but Eurytus plunged into the thick of the battle, and so perished. Aristodemus, on the other hand, was faint of heart, and remained at Alpeni. It is my belief that if Aristodemus only had been sick and returned, or if both had come back together, the Spartans would have been content and felt no anger; but when there were two men with the very same excuse, and one of them was chary of his life, while the other freely gave it, they could not but be very wroth with the former.

230. This is the account which some give of the escape of Aristodemus. Others say, that he, with another, had been sent on a message from the army, and, having it in his power to return in time for the battle, purposely loitered on the road, and so survived his comrades; while his fellow-messenger came back in time, and fell in the battle.

231. When Aristodemus returned to Lacedaemon, reproach and disgrace awaited him; disgrace, inasmuch as no Spartan would give him a light to kindle his fire, or so much as address a word to him; and reproach, since all spoke of him as the craven. However he wiped away all his shame afterwards at the battle of Plataea.

232. Another of the 300 is likewise said to have survived the battle, a man named Pantites, whom Leonidas had sent on an embassy into Thessaly. He, they say, on his return to Sparta, found himself in such disgrace that he hanged himself.

233. The Thebans under the command of Leontiades remained with the Greeks, and fought against the barbarians, only so long as necessity compelled them. No sooner did they see victory inclining to the Persians, and the Greeks under Leonidas hurrying with all speed towards the hillock, than they moved away from their companions, and with hands upraised advanced towards the barbarians, exclaiming, as was indeed most true, "They for their part wished well to the Medes, and had been among the first to give earth and water to the king; force alone had brought them to Thermopylae, and so they must not be blamed for the slaughter which had befallen the king's army."

These words, the truth of which was attested by the Thessalians, sufficed to obtain the Thebans the grant of their lives. However, their good fortune was not without some drawback; for several of them were slain by the barbarians on their first approach; and the rest, who were the greater number, had the royal mark branded upon their bodies by the command of Xerxes, Leontiades, their captain, being the first to suffer. (This man's son, Eurymachus, was afterwards slain by the Plataeans, when he came with a band of 400 Thebans, and seized their city.)

234. Thus fought the Greeks at Thermopylae. And Xerxes, after the fight was over, called for Demaratus to question him; and began as follows, "Demaratus, you are a worthy man; your true-speaking proves it. All has happened as you forewarned me. Now, then, tell me, how many Lacedaemonians are there left, and of those left how many are such brave warriors as these? Or are they all alike?"

"O King," replied the other, "the whole number of the Lacedaemonians is very great, and many are the cities which they inhabit. But I will tell you what you really wish to learn. There is a town of Lacedaemon called Sparta, which contains within it about 8,000 full-grown men. They are, one and all, equal to those who have fought here. The other Lacedaemonians are brave men, but not such warriors as these."

"Tell me now, Demaratus," rejoined Xerxes, "how we may with least trouble subdue these men. You must know all the paths of their counsels, as you were once their king."

235. Then Demaratus answered, "O king, since you ask my advice so earnestly, it is fitting that I should inform you what I consider to be the best course. Detach 300 vessels from the body of your fleet, and send them to attack the shores of Laconia. There is an island called Cythera in those parts, not far from the coast, concerning which Chilon, one of our wisest men, made the remark, that Sparta would gain if it were sunk to the bottom of the sea—so constantly did he expect that it would give occasion to some project like that which I now recommend to you. I mean not to say that he had a foreknowledge of your attack upon Greece; but in truth he feared all armaments. Send your

ships then to this island, and thence frighten the Spartans. If once they have a war of their own close to their doors, fear not their giving any help to the rest of the Greeks while your land-force is engaged in conquering them. In this way may all Greece be subdued; and then Sparta, left to herself, will be powerless. But if you will not take this advice, I will tell you what you may expect. When you come to the Peloponnese, you will find a narrow neck of land, where all the Peloponnesians who are leagued against you will be gathered together; and there you will have to fight bloodier battles than any which you have yet witnessed. If, however, you follow my plan, the isthmus and the cities of Peloponnese will yield to you without a battle."

236. Achaemenes, who was present at their conversation, now spoke—he was brother to Xerxes, and having the command of the fleet, feared lest Xerxes might be prevailed upon to do as Demaratus advised. "I perceive, O king," he said, "that you are listening to the words of a man who is envious of your good-fortune, and seeks to betray your cause. This is indeed the common temper of the Grecian people—they envy good-fortune, and hate power greater than their own. If in this state of our affairs, after we have lost 400 vessels by shipwreck, 300 more be sent away to make a voyage round the Peloponnese, our enemies will become a match for us. But let us keep our whole fleet in one body, and it will be dangerous for them to venture on an attack, as they will certainly be no match for us then. Besides, while our sea and land forces advance together, the fleet and army can each help the other; but if they be parted, no aid will come either from you to the fleet, or from the fleet to you. Only order your own matters well, and trouble not to inquire concerning the enemy, where they will fight, or what they will do, or how many they are. Surely they can manage their own concerns without us, as we can ours without them. If the Lacedaemonians come out against the Persians to battle, they will scarce repair the disaster which has befallen them now."

237. Xerxes replied, "Achaemenes, your counsel pleases me well, and I will do as you say. But Demaratus advised what he thought best—only his judgment was not so good as yours.

Never will I believe that he does not wish well to my cause; for that is disproved both by his former counsels, and also by the circumstances of the case. A citizen does indeed envy any fellow-citizen who is more lucky than himself, and often hates him secretly; if such a man be called on for counsel, he will not give his best thoughts, unless indeed he be a man of very exalted virtue; and such are but rarely found. But a friend of another country delights in the good fortune of his foreign bond-friend, and will give him, when asked, the best advice in his power. Therefore I warn all men to abstain henceforth from speaking ill of Demaratus, who is my bond-friend."

238. When Xerxes had thus spoken, he proceeded to pass through the slain; and finding the body of Leonidas, whom he knew to have been the Lacedaemonian king and captain, he ordered that the head should be struck off, and the trunk fastened to a cross. This proves to me most clearly, what is plain also in many other ways,—namely, that King Xerxes was more angry with Leonidas, while he was still in life, than with any other mortal. Otherwise he would not have used his body so shamefully. For the Persians usually honour those who show themselves valiant in fight more highly than any nation that I know. They, however, to whom the orders were given, obeyed the commands of the king.

239. I return now to a point in my history, which at the time I left incomplete. The Lacedaemonians were the first of the Greeks to hear of the king's design against their country; and it was at this time that they sent to consult the Delphic oracle, and received the answer of which I spoke a while ago. The discovery was made to them in a very strange way. Demaratus, the son of Ariston, after he took refuge with the Medes, was not, in my judgment, which is supported by probability, a well-wisher to the Lacedaemonians. It may be questioned, therefore, whether he did what I am about to mention from good-will or from insolent triumph. It happened that he was at Susa at the time when Xerxes determined to lead his army into Greece; and in this way becoming acquainted with his design, he resolved to send tidings of it to Sparta. So as there was no other way of

effecting his purpose, since the danger of being discovered was great, Demaratus framed the following contrivance. He took a pair of tablets, and clearing the wax away from them, wrote what the king was purposing to do upon the wood whereof the tablets were made; having done this, he spread the wax once more over the writing, and so sent it. By these means, the guards placed to watch the roads, observing nothing but a blank tablet, were sure to give no trouble to the bearer. When the tablet reached Lacedaemon, there was no one, I understand, who could find out the secret, till Gorgo, the daughter of Cleomenes and wife of Leonidas, discovered it, and told the others. "If they would scrape the wax off the tablet," she said, "they would be sure to find the writing upon the wood." The Lacedaemonians took her advice, found the writing, and read it; after which they sent it round to the other Greeks. Such then is the account which is given of this matter.

The Eighth Book, Entitled

URANIA

1. The Greeks engaged in the sea-service were the following. The Athenians furnished 127 vessels to the fleet, which were manned in part by the Plataeans, who, though unskilled in such matters, were led by their active and daring spirit to undertake this duty; the Corinthians furnished a contingent of forty vessels; the Megarians sent twenty; the Chalcideans also manned twenty, which had been furnished to them by the Athenians; the Aeginetans came with eighteen; the Sicyonians with twelve; the Lacedaemonians with ten; the Epidaurians with eight; the Eretrians with seven; the Troezenians with five; the Styreans with two; and the Ceans with two triremes and two fifty-oared galleys. Last of all, the Locrians of Opus came in aid with a squadron of seven fifty-oared galleys.

2. Such were the nations which furnished vessels to the fleet now at Artemisium; and in mentioning them I have given the number of ships furnished by each. The total number of the ships thus brought together, without counting the fifty-oared galleys, was 271; and the captain, who had the chief command over the whole fleet, was Eurybiades the son of Eurycleides. He was furnished by Sparta, since the allies had said, "If a Lacedaemonian did not take the command, they would break up the fleet, for never would they serve under the Athenians."

3. From the first, even earlier than the time when the embassy went to Sicily to solicit alliance, there had been a talk of intrusting the Athenians with the command at sea; but the allies were averse to the plan. wherefore the Athenians did not press

it; for there was nothing they had so much at heart as the salvation of Greece, and they knew that, if they quarrelled among themselves about the command, Greece would be brought to ruin. Herein they judged rightly; for internal strife is a thing as much worse than war carried on by a united people, as war itself is worse than peace. The Athenians, therefore, being so persuaded, did not push their claims, but waived them, so long as they were in such great need of aid from the other Greeks. And they afterwards showed their motive; for at the time when the Persians had been driven from Greece, and were now threatened by the Greeks in their own country, they took occasion of the insolence of Pausanias to deprive the Lacedaemonians of their leadership. This, however, happened afterwards.[1]

4. At the present time the Greeks, on their arrival at Artemisium, when they saw the number of the ships which lay at anchor near Aphetae, and the abundance of troops everywhere, feeling disappointed that matters had gone with the barbarians so far otherwise than they had expected, and full of alarm at what they saw, began to speak of drawing back from Artemisium towards the inner parts of their country. So when the Euboeans heard what was in debate, they went to Eurybiades, and besought him to wait a few days, while they removed their children and their slaves to a place of safety. But as they found that they prevailed nothing, they left him and went to Themistocles, the Athenian commander, to whom they gave a bribe of thirty talents, on his promise that the fleet should remain and risk a battle in defence of Euboea.

5. And Themistocles succeeded in detaining the fleet in the way which I will now relate. He made over to Eurybiades five talents out of the thirty paid him, which he gave as if they came from himself; and having in this way gained over the admiral, he addressed himself to Adeimantus, the son of Ocytus, the Corinthian leader, who was the only remonstrant now, and who still threatened to sail away from Artemisium and not wait for the other captains. Addressing himself to this man, Themistocles said with an oath, "You forsake us? By no means! I will pay

[1] Probably in 477 B.C.

you better for remaining than the Mede would for leaving your friends"—and straightway he sent on board the ship of Adeimantus a present of three talents of silver. So these two captains were won by gifts, and came over to the views of Themistocles, who was thereby enabled to gratify the wishes of the Euboeans. He likewise made his own gain on the occasion; for he kept the rest of the money, and no one knew of it. The commanders who took the gifts thought that the sums were furnished by Athens, and had been sent to be used in this way.

6. Thus it came to pass that the Greeks stayed at Euboea and there gave battle to the enemy. Now the battle was on this wise. The barbarians reached Aphetae early in the afternoon, and then saw (as they had previously heard reported) that a fleet of Greek ships, weak in number, lay at Artemisium. At once they were eager to engage, fearing that the Greeks would fly, and hoping to capture them before they should get away. They did not however think it wise to make straight for the Greek station, lest the enemy should see them as they bore down, and betake themselves to flight immediately; in which case night might close in before they came up with the fugitives, and so they might get clean off and make their escape from them; whereas the Persians were minded not to let even a torch-bearer slip through their hands.

7. They therefore contrived a plan, which was the following: They detached 200 of their ships from the rest, and—to prevent the enemy from seeing them start—sent them round outside the island of Sciathos, to make the circuit of Euboea by Caphareus and Geraestus, and so to reach the Euripus. By this plan they thought to enclose the Greeks on every side; for the ships detached would block up the only way by which they could retreat, while the others would press upon them in front. With these designs therefore they dispatched the two hundred ships, while they themselves waited, since they did not mean to attack the Greeks upon that day, or until they knew, by signal, of the arrival of the detachment which had been ordered to sail round Euboea. Meanwhile they made a muster of the other ships at Aphetae.

8. Now the Persians had with them a man named Scyllias, a native of Scione, who was the most expert diver of his day. At the time of the shipwreck off Mount Pelion he had recovered for the Persians a great part of what they lost, and at the same time he had taken care to obtain for himself a good share of the treasure. He had for some time been wishing to go over to the Greeks; but no good opportunity had offered till now, when the Persians were making the muster of their ships. In what way he contrived to reach the Greeks I am not able to say for certain: I marvel much if the tale that is commonly told be true. It is said he dived into the sea at Aphetae, and did not once come to the surface till he reached Artemisium, a distance of nearly ten miles. Now many things are related of this man which are plainly false, but some of the stories seem to be true. My own opinion is that on this occasion he made the passage to Artemisium in a boat.

However this might be, Scyllias no sooner reached Artemisium than he gave the Greek captains a full account of the damage done by the storm, and likewise told them of the ships sent to make the circuit of Euboea.

9. So the Greeks on receiving these tidings held a council, whereat, after much debate, it was resolved that they should stay quiet for the present where they were, and remain at their moorings, but that after midnight they should put out to sea, and encounter the ships which were on their way round the island. Later in the day, when they found that no one meddled with them, they formed a new plan, which was to wait till near evening, and then sail out against the main body of the barbarians, for the purpose of trying their mode of fighting and skill in manoeuvring.

10. When the Persian commanders and crews saw the Greeks thus boldly sailing towards them with their few ships, they thought them possessed with madness, and went out to meet them, expecting (as indeed seemed likely enough) that they would take all their vessels with the greatest ease. The Greek ships were so few, and their own so far outnumbered them, and sailed so much better, that they resolved, seeing their advantage,

to encompass their foe on every side. And now such of the Ionians as wished well to the Grecian cause and served in the Persian fleet unwillingly, seeing their countrymen surrounded, were sorely distressed; for they felt sure that not one of them would ever make his escape, so poor an opinion had they of the strength of the Greeks. On the other hand, such as saw with pleasure the attack on Greece, now vied eagerly with each other which should be the first to make prize of an Athenian ship, and thereby to secure himself a rich reward from the king. For through both the hosts none were so much talked of as the Athenians.

11. The Greeks, at a signal, brought the sterns of their ships together into a small compass, and turned their prows on every side towards the barbarians; after which, at a second signal, although inclosed within a narrow space, and closely pressed upon by the foe, yet they fell bravely to work, and captured thirty ships of the barbarians, at the same time taking prisoner Philaon, the son of Chersis, and brother of Gorgus, king of Salamis, a man of much repute in the fleet. The first who made prize of a ship of the enemy was Lycomedes the son of Aeschreas, an Athenian, who afterwards received the prize for valour. Victory however was still doubtful when night came on, and put a stop to the combat. The Greeks sailed back to Artemisium and the barbarians to Aphetae, much surprised at the result, which was far other than they had looked for. In this battle only one of the Greeks who fought on the side of the king deserted and joined his countrymen. This was Antidorus of Lemnos, whom the Athenians rewarded for his desertion by the present of a piece of land in Salamis.

12. Evening had barely closed in when a heavy rain, it was about midsummer, began to fall, which continued the whole night, with terrible thunderings and lightnings from Mount Pelion: the bodies of the slain and the broken pieces of the damaged ships were drifted in the direction of Aphetae, and floated about the prows of the vessels there, disturbing the action of the oars. The barbarians, hearing the storm, were greatly dismayed, expecting certainly to perish, as they had fallen into such a mul-

titude of misfortunes. For before they were well recovered from the tempest and the wreck of their vessels off Mount Pelion, they had been surprised by a sea-fight which had taxed all their strength, and now the sea-fight was scarcely over when they were exposed to floods of rain, and the rush of swollen streams into the sea, and violent thunderings.

13. If, however, they who lay at Aphetae passed a comfortless night, far worse were the sufferings of those who had been sent to make the circuit of Euboea; in as much as the storm fell on them out at sea, whereby the issue was indeed calamitous. They were sailing along near the Hollows of Euboea, when the wind began to rise and the rain to pour: overpowered by the force of the gale, and driven they knew not whither, at the last they fell upon rocks, Heaven so contriving, in order that the Persian fleet might not greatly exceed the Greek, but be brought nearly to its level. This squadron, therefore, was entirely lost about the Hollows of Euboea.

14. The barbarians at Aphetae were glad when day dawned, and remained in quiet at their station, content if they might enjoy a little peace after so many sufferings. Meanwhile there came to the aid of the Greeks a reinforcement of fifty-three ships from Attica.[2] Their arrival, and the news which reached Artemisium about the same time of the complete destruction by the storm of the ships sent to sail round Euboea, greatly cheered the spirits of the Greek sailors. So they waited again till the same hour as the day before, and, once more putting out to sea, attacked the enemy. This time they fell in with some Cilician vessels, which they sank; when night came on, and they withdrew to Artemisium.

15. The third day was now come, and the captains of the barbarians, ashamed that so small a number of ships should harass their fleet, and afraid of the anger of Xerxes, instead of waiting for the others to begin the battle, weighed anchor themselves, and advanced against the Greeks about the hour of noon, with

[2] It is more probable that they had been guarding the southern end of the straits of Euboea, and that they brought the news of the storm's destruction of the Persians.

shouts encouraging one another. Now it happened that these sea-fights took place on the very same days with the combats at Thermopylae;[3] and as the aim of the struggle was in the one case to maintain the pass, so in the other it was to defend the Euripus. While the Greeks, therefore, exhorted one another not to let the barbarians burst in upon Greece, these latter shouted to their fellows to destroy the Grecian fleet, and get possession of the channel.

16. And now the fleet of Xerxes advanced in good order to the attack, while the Greeks on their side remained quite motionless at Artemisium. The Persians therefore spread themselves, and came forward in a half moon, seeking to encircle the Greeks on all sides, and thereby prevent them from escaping. When they saw this, the Greeks sailed out to meet their assailants; and the battle forthwith began. In this engagement the two fleets contended with no clear advantage to either, for the armament of Xerxes injured itself by its own greatness, the vessels falling into disorder, and often running foul of one another; yet still they did not give way, but made a stout fight, since the crews felt it would indeed be a disgrace to turn and fly from a fleet so inferior in number. The Greeks therefore suffered much, both in ships and men; but the barbarians experienced a far larger loss of each. So the fleets separated after such a combat as I have described.

17. On the side of Xerxes the Egyptians distinguished themselves above all the combatants; for besides performing many other noble deeds, they took five vessels from the Greeks with their crews on board. On the side of the Greeks the Athenians bore off the meed of valour; and among them the most distinguished was Clinias, the son of Alcibiades, who served at his own

---

[3] The relation of the battle of Thermopylae to Artemisium depends on this statement. If it is true, Leonidas was still trying to block the Persians at the pass on the final day at Thermopylae; if Athenian sources concealed from Herodotus the fact that the Greek fleet withdrew one day earlier, Leonidas was simply fighting a rear-guard action to enable the allies to escape, since the Persian fleet could easily land troops behind him.

charge with 200 men, on board a vessel which he had himself furnished.

18. The two fleets, on separating, hastened very gladly to their anchorage-grounds. The Greeks, indeed, when the battle was over, became masters of the bodies of the slain and the wrecks of the vessels; but they had been so roughly handled, especially the Athenians, one-half of whose vessels had suffered damage, that they determined to break up from their station, and withdraw to the inner parts of their country.

19. Then Themistocles, who thought that if the Ionian and Carian ships could be detached from the barbarian fleet, the Greeks might be well able to defeat the rest, called the captains together. They met upon the sea-shore, where the Euboeans were now assembling their flocks and herds; and here Themistocles told them he thought that he knew of a plan whereby he could detach from the king those who were of most worth among his allies. This was all that he disclosed to them of his plan at that time. Meanwhile, looking to the circumstances in which they were, he advised them to slaughter as many of the Euboean cattle as they liked—for it was better (he said) that their own troops should enjoy them than the enemy—and to give orders to their men to kindle the fires as usual. With regard to the retreat, he said that he would take upon himself to watch the proper moment, and would manage matters so that they should return to Greece without loss. These words pleased the captains; so they had the fires lighted, and began the slaughter of the cattle.

20. The Euboeans, until now, had made light of the oracle of Bacis, as though it had been void of all significancy, and had neither removed their goods from the island, nor yet taken them into their strong places; as they would most certainly have done if they had believed that war was approaching. By this neglect they had brought their affairs into the very greatest danger. Now the oracle of which I speak ran as follows:

When o'er the main shall be thrown a byblus yoke by a stranger,
Be thou ware, and drive from Euboea the goats' loud-bleating.

So, as the Euboeans had paid no regard to this oracle when the
evils approached and impended, now that they had arrived, the
worst was likely to befall them.

21. While the Greeks were employed in the way described
above, the scout who had been on the watch at Trachis arrived
at Artemisium. For the Greeks had employed two watchers:
Polyas, a native of Anticyra, had been stationed off Artemisium,
with a row-boat at his command ready to sail at any moment,
his orders being that, if an engagement took place by sea, he
should convey the news at once to the Greeks at Thermopylae;
and in like manner Abronychus, the son of Lysicles, an Athenian, had been stationed with a thirty-oared ship near Leonidas,
to be ready, in case of disaster befalling the land force, to carry
tidings of it to Artemisium. It was this Abronychus who now arrived with news of what had befallen Leonidas and those who
were with him. When the Greeks heard the tidings they no
longer delayed to retreat, but withdrew in the order wherein
they had been stationed, the Corinthians leading, and the Athenians sailing last of all.

22. And now Themistocles chose out the swiftest sailers from
among the Athenian vessels, and, proceeding to the various
watering-places along the coast, cut inscriptions on the rocks,
which were read by the Ionians the day following, on their arrival at Artemisium. The inscriptions ran thus, "Men of Ionia,
you do wrong to fight against your own fathers, and to give your
help to enslave Greece. We beseech you therefore to come over,
if possible, to our side: if you cannot do this, then, we pray you,
stand aloof from the contest yourselves, and persuade the Carians to do the like. If neither of these things be possible, and
you are hindered, by a force too strong to resist, from venturing
upon desertion, at least when we come to blows fight backwardly, remembering that you are sprung from us, and that it
was through you we first provoked the hatred of the barbarian."
Themistocles, in putting up these inscriptions, looked, I believe,
to two chances—either Xerxes would not discover them, in
which case they might bring over the Ionians to the side of the
Greeks; or they would be reported to him and made a ground

of accusation against the Ionians, who would thereupon be distrusted, and would not be allowed to take part in the sea-fights.

23. Shortly after the cutting of the inscriptions, a man of Histiaea went in a merchant-ship to Aphetae, and told the Persians that the Greeks had fled from Artemisium. Disbelieving his report, the Persians kept the man a prisoner, while they sent some of their fastest vessels to see what had happened. These brought back word how matters stood; whereupon at sunrise the whole fleet advanced together in a body, and sailed to Artemisium, where they remained till midday; after which they went on to Histiaea. The city fell into their hands immediately; and they shortly overran the various villages upon the coast in the district of Hellopia, which was part of the Histiaean territory.

24. It was while they were at this station that a herald reached them from Xerxes, whom he had sent after making the following dispositions with respect to the bodies of those who fell at Thermopylae. Of the 20,000 who had been slain on the Persian side, he left 1,000 upon the field while he buried the rest in trenches; and these he carefully filled up with earth, and hid with foliage, that the sailors might not see any signs of them. The herald, on reaching Histiaea, caused the whole force to be collected together, and spoke thus to them, "Comrades, King Xerxes gives permission to all who please, to quit their posts, and see how he fights with the senseless men who think to overthrow his armies."

25. No sooner had these words been uttered, than it became difficult to get a boat, so great was the number of those who desired to see the sight. Such as went crossed the strait, and passing among the heaps of dead, in this way viewed the spectacle. Many Helots were included in the slain, but every one imagined that the bodies were all either Lacedaemonians or Thespians. However no one was deceived by what Xerxes had done with his own dead. It was indeed most truly a laughable device—on the one side 1,000 men were seen lying about the field, on the other 4,000 crowded together in one spot. This day then was given up to sight-seeing; on the next the seamen embarked on board their

ships and sailed back to Histiaea, while Xerxes and his army proceeded upon their march.

26. There came now a few deserters from Arcadia to join the Persians—poor men who had nothing to live on, and were in want of employment. The Persians brought them into the king's presence, and there inquired of them, by a man who acted as their spokesman what the Greeks were doing. The Arcadians answered, "They are holding the Olympic games, seeing the athletic sports and the chariot races." "And what," said the man, "is the prize for which they contend?" "An olive-wreath," returned the others, "which is given to the man who wins." On hearing this, Tritantaechmes, the son of Artabanus, uttered a speech which was in truth most noble, but which caused him to be taxed with cowardice by King Xerxes. Hearing the men say that the prize was not money but a wreath of olive, he could not forbear from exclaiming before them all, "Good heavens, Mardonius, what manner of men are these against whom you have brought us to fight—men who contend with one another, not for money, but for honour!"

27. A little before this, and just after the blow had been struck at Thermopylae, a herald was sent into Phocis by the Thessalians, who had always been on bad terms with the Phocians, and especially since their last overthrow. For it was not many years previous to this invasion of Greece by the king, that the Thessalians, with their allies, entered Phocis in full force, but were defeated by the Phocians in an engagement wherein they were very roughly handled. The Phocians, who had with them as soothsayer Tellias of Elis, were blocked up in the mountain of Parnassus, when the following stratagem was contrived for them by their Elean ally. He took 600 of their bravest men, and whitened their bodies and their arms with chalk; then instructing them to slay every one whom they should meet that was not whitened like themselves, he made a night attack upon the Thessalians. No sooner did the Thessalian sentries, who were the first to see them, behold this strange sight, than imagining it to be a prodigy, they were all filled with terror. From the sentries

the alarm spread to the army, which was seized with such a panic that the Phocians killed 4,000 of them, and became masters of their dead bodies and shields. Of the shields one-half were sent as an offering to the temple at Abae, the other half were deposited at Delphi; while from the tenth part of the booty gained in the battle, were made the gigantic figures which stand round the tripod in front of the Delphic shrine, and likewise the figures of the same size and character at Abae.

28. Besides this slaughter of the Thessalian foot, when it was blockading them, the Phocians had dealt a blow to their horse, upon its invading their territory, from which they had never recovered. There is a pass near the city of Hyampolis, where the Phocians, having dug a broad trench, filled up the void with empty wine-jars, after which they covered the place with mould, so that the ground all looked alike, and then awaited the coming of the Thessalians. These, thinking to destroy the Phocians at one sweep, rushed rapidly forward, and became entangled in the wine-jars, which broke the legs of their horses.

29. The Thessalians had therefore a double cause of quarrel with the Phocians, when they dispatched the herald above mentioned, who thus delivered his message, "At length acknowledge, men of Phocis, that you may not think to match with us. In times past, when it pleased us to hold with the Greeks, we had always the advantage over you; and now our influence is such with the Barbarian, that, if we choose it, you will lose your country, and (what is even worse) you will be sold as slaves. However, though we can now do with you exactly as we like, we are willing to forget our wrongs. Quit them with a payment of fifty talents of silver, and we undertake to ward off the evils which threaten your country."

30. Such was the message which the Thessalians sent. The Phocians were the only people in these parts who had not espoused the cause of the Medes; and it is my deliberate opinion that the motive which swayed them was none other—neither more nor less—than their hatred of the Thessalians; for had the Thessalians declared in favour of the Greeks, I believe that the men of Phocis would have joined the Median side. As it was,

when the message arrived, the Phocians made answer, "They
would not pay anything—it was open to them equally with the
Thessalians, to make common cause with the Medes, if they only
chose so to do—but they would never of their own free will become traitors to Greece."

31. On the return of this answer, the Thessalians, full of
wrath against the Phocians, offered themselves as guides to the
barbarian army, and led them forth from Trachinia into Doris.
In this place there is a narrow tongue of Dorian territory, about
four miles across, interposed between Malis and Phocis; it is the
tract in ancient times called Dryopis; and the land, of which it
is a part, is the mother-country of the Dorians in the Peloponnese. This territory the barbarians did not plunder, for the inhabitants had espoused their side; and besides, the Thessalians
wished that they should be spared.

32. From Doris they marched forward into Phocis, but here
the inhabitants did not fall into their power; for some of them
had taken refuge in the high grounds of Parnassus—one summit of which, called Tithorea, standing quite by itself, not far
from the city of Neon, is well fitted to give shelter to a large
body of men, and had now received a number of the Phocians
with their movables; while the greater portion had fled to the
country of the Ozolian Locrians, and placed their goods in the
city called Amphissa, which lies above the Crisaean plain.
The land of Phocis, however, was entirely overrun, for the
Thessalians led the Persian army through the whole of it; and
wherever they went, the country was wasted with fire and sword,
the cities and even the temples being wilfully set alight by the
troops.

33. The march of the army lay along the valley of the Cephissus; and here they ravaged far and wide, burning the towns of
Drymus, Charadra, Erochus, Tethronium, Amphicaea, Neon,
Pedieis, Triteis, Elateia, Hyampolis, Parapotamii, and Abae. At
the last-named place there was a temple of Apollo, very rich, and
adorned with a vast number of treasures and offerings. There
was likewise an oracle there in those days, as indeed there is at
present. This temple the Persians plundered and burnt; and

here they captured a number of the Phocians before they could reach the hills, and caused the death of some of their women by mass-rape.

34. After passing Parapotamii, the barbarians marched to Panopeis; and now the army separated into two bodies, whereof one, which was the more numerous and the stronger of the two, marched, under Xerxes himself, towards Athens, entering Boeotia by the country of the Orchomenians. The Boeotians had one and all embraced the cause of the Medes; and their towns were in the possession of Macedonian garrisons, whom Alexander had sent there, to make it manifest to Xerxes that the Boeotians were on the Median side. Such then was the road followed by one division of the barbarians.

35. The other division took guides, and proceeded towards the temple of Delphi, keeping Mount Parnassus on their right hand. They too laid waste such parts of Phocis as they passed through, burning the city of the Panopeans, together with those of the Daulians and of the Aeolidae. This body had been detached from the rest of the army and made to march in this direction, for the purpose of plundering the Delphian temple and conveying to King Xerxes the riches which were there laid up. For Xerxes, as I am informed, was better acquainted with what there was worthy of note at Delphi, than even with what he had left in his own house; so many of those about him were continually describing the treasures—more especially the offerings made by Croesus the son of Alyattes.

36. Now when the Delphians heard what danger they were in, great fear fell on them. In their terror they consulted the oracle concerning the holy treasures, and inquired if they should bury them in the ground, or carry them away to some other country. The god, in reply, bade them leave the treasures untouched. "He was able," he said, "without help to protect his own." So the Delphians, when they received this answer, began to think about saving themselves. And first of all they sent their women and children across the gulf into Achaea; after which the greater number of them climbed up into the tops of Parnassus, and placed their goods for safety in the Corycian cave; while

some effected their escape to Amphissa in Locris. In this way all the Delphians quitted the city, except sixty men, and the prophet.

37. When the barbarian assailants drew near and were in sight of the place, the prophet, who was named Aceratus, beheld, in front of the temple, a portion of the sacred armour, which it was not lawful for any mortal hand to touch, lying upon the ground, removed from the inner shrine where it was wont to hang. Then went he and told the prodigy to the Delphians who had remained behind. Meanwhile the enemy pressed forward briskly, and had reached the shrine of Athena Pronaia, when they were overtaken by other prodigies still more wonderful than the first. Truly it was marvel enough, when warlike harness was seen lying outside the temple, removed there by no power but its own; what followed, however, exceeded in strangeness all prodigies that had ever been seen before. The barbarians had just reached in their advance the temple of Athena Pronaia, when a storm of thunder burst suddenly over their heads—at the same time two crags split off from Mount Parnassus, and rolled down upon them with a loud noise, crushing vast numbers beneath their weight—while from the temple of Athena there went up the war-cry and the shout of victory.

38. All these things together struck terror into the barbarians, who forthwith turned and fled. The Delphians, seeing this, came down from their hiding-places, and smote them with a great slaughter, from which such as escaped fled straight into Boeotia. These men, on their return, declared (as I am told) that besides the marvels mentioned above, they witnessed also other supernatural sights. Two armed warriors, they said, of a stature more than human, pursued after their flying ranks, pressing them close and slaying them.

39. These men, the Delphians[4] maintain, were two Heroes belonging to the place—by name Phylacus and Autonous—each of whom has a sacred precinct near the temple; one, that of Phylacus, hard by the road which runs above the temple of

---

[4] The whole story is obviously a temple legend told Herodotus by the priests.

Pronaia; the other, that of Autonous, near the Castalian spring, at the foot of the peak called Hyampeia. The blocks of stone which fell from Parnassus might still be seen in my day; they lay in the precinct of Pronaia, where they stopped, after rolling through the host of the barbarians. Thus was this body of men forced to retire from the temple.

40. Meanwhile, the Grecian fleet, which had left Artemisium, proceeded to Salamis, at the request of the Athenians, and there cast anchor. The Athenians had begged them to take up this position, in order that they might convey their women and children out of Attica, and further might deliberate upon the course which it now behoved them to follow. Disappointed in the hopes which they had previously entertained, they were about to hold a council concerning the present posture of their affairs. For they had looked to see the Peloponnesians drawn up in full force to resist the enemy in Boeotia, but found nothing of what they had expected; nay, they learnt that the Greeks of those parts, only concerning themselves about their own safety, were building a wall across the Isthmus, and intended to guard the Peloponnese, and let the rest of Greece take its chance. These tidings caused them to make the request whereof I spoke, that the combined fleet should anchor at Salamis.

41. So while the rest of the fleet lay to off this island, the Athenians cast anchor along their own coast. Immediately upon their arrival, proclamation was made, that every Athenian should save his children and household as he best could; whereupon some sent their families to Aegina, some to Salamis, but the greater number to Troezen. This removal was made with all possible haste, partly from a desire to obey the advice of the oracle, but still more for another reason. The Athenians say that they have in their acropolis a huge serpent, which lives in the temple, and is the guardian of the whole place. Nor do they only say this, but, as if the serpent really dwelt there, every month they lay out its food, which consists of a honey-cake. Up to this time the honey-cake had always been consumed; but now it remained untouched. So the priestess told the people what had happened; whereupon they left Athens the more readily, since

they believed that the goddess had already abandoned the citadel. As soon as all was removed, the Athenians sailed back to their station.

42. And now, the remainder of the Grecian sea-force, hearing that the fleet which had been at Artemisium, was come to Salamis, joined it at that island from Troezen—orders having been issued previously that the ships should muster at Pogon, the port of the Troezenians. The vessels collected were many more in number than those which had fought at Artemisium, and were furnished by more cities. The admiral was the same who had commanded before, Eurybiades, the son of Eurycleides, who was a Spartan, but not of the family of the kings: the city, however, which sent by far the greatest number of ships, and the best sailers, was Athens.

43. Now these were the nations who composed the Grecian fleet. From the Peloponnese, the following—the Lacedaemonians with sixteen ships; the Corinthians with the same number as at Artemisium; the Sicyonians with fifteen; the Epidaurians with ten; the Troezenians with five; and the Hermionians with three. These were Dorians and Macedonians all of them (except those from Hermione), and had emigrated last from Erineus, Pindus, and Dryopis. The Hermionians were Dryopes, of the race which Heracles and the Malians drove out of the land now called Doris. Such were the Peloponnesian nations.

44. From the mainland of Greece beyond the Peloponnese, came the Athenians with 180 ships, a greater number than that furnished by any other people; and these were now manned wholly by themselves; for the Plataeans did not serve on board the Athenian ships at Salamis, owing to the following reason. When the Greeks, on their withdrawal from Artemisium, arrived off Chalcis, the Plataeans disembarked upon the opposite shore of Boeotia, and set to work to remove their households, whereby it happened that they were left behind. (The Athenians, when the region which is now called Greece was held by the Pelasgi, were Pelasgians, and bore the name of Cranaans; but under their king Cecrops, they were called Cecropidae; when Erechtheus got the sovereignty, they changed their name to Athe-

nians; and when Ion, the son of Xuthus, became their general,
they were named after him Ionians.)

45. The Megarians served with the same number of ships as
at Artemisium; the Ambraciots came with seven; the Leucadians (who were Dorians from Corinth) with three.

46. Of the islanders, the Aeginetans furnished thirty ships,
they had a larger number equipped, but some were kept back to
guard their own coasts, and only thirty, which however were
their best sailers, took part in the fight at Salamis. (The Aeginetans are Dorians from Epidaurus; their island was called formerly Oenone.) The Chalcideans came next in order; they
furnished the twenty ships with which they had served at Artemisium. The Eretrians likewise furnished their seven. These
races are Ionian. Ceos gave its old number, the Ceans are Ionians from Attica. Naxos furnished four: this detachment, like
those from the other islands, had been sent by the citizens at
home to join the Medes; but they made light of the orders given
them, and joined the Greeks, at the instigation of Democritus, a
citizen of good report, who was at that time captain of a trireme.
The Naxians are Ionians, of the Athenian stock. The Styreans
served with the same ships as before; the Cythnians contributed
one, and likewise a fifty-oared ship—these two nations are Dryopians: the Seriphians, Siphnians, and Melians, also served;
they were the only islanders who had not given earth and water
to the Barbarian.

47. All these nations dwelt inside the river Acheron and the
country inhabited by the Thesprotians; for that people borders
on the Ambraciots and Leucadians, who are the most remote of
all those by whom the fleet was furnished. From the countries
beyond, there was only one people which gave help to the Greeks
in their danger. This was the people of Croton, who contributed
a single ship, under the command of Phayllus, a man who had
thrice carried off the prize at the Pythian games. The Crotoniats
are, by descent, Achaeans.

48. Most of the allies came with triremes; but the Melians,
Siphnians, and Seriphians, brought fifty oared ships. The Melians, who draw their race from Lacedaemon, furnished two; the

Siphnians and Seriphians, who are Ionians of the Athenian stock, one each. The whole number of the ships, without counting the fifty-oared ships, was 378.[5]

49. When the captains from these various nations were come together at Salamis, a council of war was summoned; and Eurybiades proposed that any one who liked to advise, should say which place seemed to him the fittest, amongst those still in the possession of the Greeks, to be the scene of a naval combat. Attica, he said, was not to be thought of now; but he desired their counsel as to the remainder. The speakers mostly advised, that the fleet should sail away to the Isthmus, and there give battle in defence of the Peloponnese; and they urged as a reason for this, that if they were worsted in a sea-fight at Salamis, they would be shut up in an island, where they could get no help; but if they were beaten near the Isthmus, they could escape to their homes.

50. As the captains from the Peloponnese were thus advising, there came an Athenian to the camp, who brought word that the barbarians had entered Attica, and were ravaging and burning everything. For the division of the army under Xerxes was just arrived at Athens from its march through Boeotia, where it had burnt Thespiae and Plataea—both which cities were forsaken by their inhabitants, who had fled to the Peloponnese—and now it was laying waste all the possessions of the Athenians. Thespiae and Plataea had been burnt by the Persians, because they knew from the Thebans that neither of those cities had espoused their side.

51. Since the passage of the Hellespont and the commencement of the march upon Greece, a space of four months had gone by; one while the army made the crossing, and delayed about the region of the Hellespont; and three while they proceeded thence to Attica, which they entered in the archonship of Calliades. They found the city forsaken; a few people only remained in the temple, either keepers of the treasures, or men of the poorer sort. These persons having fortified the acropolis with

[5] The number produced by adding the several contingents together is not 378, but 366.

planks and boards, held out against the enemy. It was in some measure their poverty which had prevented them from seeking shelter in Salamis; but there was likewise another reason which in part induced them to remain. They imagined themselves to have discovered the true meaning of the oracle uttered by the priestess, which promised "The wooden wall should never be taken." The wooden wall, they thought, did not mean the ships, but the place where they had taken refuge.

52. The Persians encamped upon the hill over against the citadel, which is called Ares' hill by the Athenians, and began the siege of the place, attacking the Greeks with arrows whereto pieces of lighted tow were attached, which they shot at the barricade. And now those who were within the citadel found themselves in a most woeful case, for their wooden rampart betrayed them; still, however, they continued to resist. It was in vain that the Pisistratidae came to them and offered terms of surrender— they stoutly refused all parley, and among their other modes of defence, rolled down huge masses of stone upon the barbarians as they were mounting up to the gates: so that Xerxes was for a long time very greatly perplexed, and could not contrive any way to take them.

53. At last, however, in the midst of these many difficulties, the barbarians made discovery of an access. For verily the oracle had spoken truth; and it was fated that the whole mainland of Attica should fall beneath the sway of the Persians. Right in front of the Acropolis, but behind the gates and the common ascent—where no watch was kept, and no one would have thought it possible that any foot of man could climb—a few soldiers mounted from the sanctuary of Aglaurus, Cecrops' daughter, notwithstanding the steepness of the precipice. As soon as the Athenians saw them upon the summit, some threw themselves headlong from the wall, and so perished; while others fled for refuge to the inner part of the temple. The Persians rushed to the gates and opened them, after which they massacred the suppliants. When all were slain, they plundered the temple, and fired every part of the Acropolis.

54. Xerxes, thus completely master of Athens, dispatched a

horseman to Susa, with a message to Artabanus, informing him of his success hitherto. The day after, he collected together all the Athenian exiles who had come into Greece in his train, and bade them go up into the citadel, and there offer sacrifice after their own fashion. I know not whether he had had a dream which bade him give this order, or whether he felt some remorse on account of having set the temple on fire. However this may have been, the exiles were not slow to obey the command given them.

55. I will now explain why I have made mention of this circumstance: there is a temple of Erechtheus, the earth-born as he is called, in this citadel, containing within it an olive-tree and a salt-water pool. The tale goes among the Athenians, that they were placed there as witnesses by Poseidon and Athena, when they had their contention about the country. Now this olive-tree had been burnt with the rest of the temple when the barbarians took the place. But when the Athenians, whom the king had commanded to offer sacrifice, went up into the temple for the purpose, they found a fresh shoot, a foot and one-half in length, thrown out from the old trunk. Such at least was the account which these persons gave.

56. Meanwhile, at Salamis, the Greeks no sooner heard what had befallen the Athenian citadel, than they fell into such alarm that some of the captains did not even wait for the council to come to a vote, but embarked hastily on board their vessels, and hoisted sail as though they would take to flight immediately. The rest, who stayed at the council board, came to a vote that the fleet should give battle at the Isthmus. Night now drew on, and the captains, dispersing from the meeting, proceeded on board their respective ships.

57. Themistocles, as he entered his own vessel, was met by Mnesiphilus, an Athenian, who asked him what the council had resolved to do. On learning that the resolve was to stand away for the Isthmus, and there give battle on behalf of the Peloponnese, Mnesiphilus exclaimed, "If these men shall sail away from Salamis, you will have no fight at all for the one fatherland; for they will all scatter themselves to their own homes; and neither

Eurybiades nor any one else will be able to hinder them, or to stop the breaking up of the armament. Thus will Greece be brought to ruin through evil counsels. But hurry now; and, if there be any possible way, seek to unsettle these resolves—perhaps you might persuade Eurybiades to change his mind, and continue here."

58. The suggestion greatly pleased Themistocles; and without answering a word, he went straight to the vessel of Eurybiades. Arrived there, he let him know that he wanted to speak with him on a matter touching the public service. So Eurybiades bade him come on board, and say whatever he wished. Then Themistocles, seating himself at his side, went over all the arguments which he had heard from Mnesiphilus, pretending as if they were his own, and added to them many new ones besides; until at last he persuaded Eurybiades, by his importunity, to quit his ship and again collect the captains to council.

59. As soon as they were come, and before Eurybiades had opened to them his purpose in assembling them together, Themistocles, as men do when they are very anxious, spoke much to them; whereupon the Corinthian captain, Adeimantus, the son of Ocytus, observed, "Themistocles, at the games they who start too soon are scourged." "True," rejoined the other in his excuse, "but they who wait too late are not crowned."

60. Thus he gave the Corinthian at this time a mild answer; and towards Eurybiades himself he did not now use any of those arguments which he had urged before, or say aught of the allies betaking themselves to flight if once they broke up from Salamis; it would have been ungraceful for him, when the confederates were present, to make accusation against any; but he had recourse to quite a new sort of reasoning, and addressed him as follows:

"With you it rests, Eurybiades, to save Greece, if you will only listen to me, and give the enemy battle here, rather than yield to the advice of those among us, who would have the fleet withdrawn to the Isthmus. Hear now, I beseech you, and judge between the two courses. At the Isthmus you will fight in an open sea, which is greatly to our disadvantage, since our ships are heavier and fewer in number than the enemy's; and further, you will in any case lose Salamis, Megara, and Aegina, even if all the rest goes well with us. The land and sea force of the Persians will advance together; and your retreat will but draw them towards the Peloponnese, and so bring all Greece into peril. If, on the other hand, you do as I advise, these are the advantages which you will secure: in the first place, as we shall fight in a narrow sea with few ships against many, if the war follows the common course, we shall gain a great victory: for to fight in a narrow space is favourable to us—in an open sea, to them. Again, Salamis will in this case be preserved, where we have placed our wives and children. Nay, that very point by which you set most store, is secured as much by this course as by the other; for whether we fight here or at the Isthmus, we shall equally give battle in defence of the Peloponnese. Assuredly you will not do wisely to draw the Persians upon that region. For if things turn out as I anticipate, and we beat them by sea, then we shall have kept your Isthmus free from the barbarians, and they will have advanced no further than Attica, but from thence have fled back in disorder; and we shall, moreover, have saved Megara, Aegina, and Salamis itself, where an oracle has said that we are to overcome our enemies. When men counsel reasonably, reasonable success ensues; but when in their counsels they reject reason, God does not choose to follow the wanderings of human fancies."

61. When Themistocles had thus spoken, Adeimantus the Corinthian again attacked him, and bade him be silent, since he was a man without a city; at the same time, he called on Eurybiades not to put the question at the instance of one who had no country, and urged that Themistocles should show of what state he was envoy, before he gave his voice with the rest. This reproach he made, because the city of Athens had been taken, and was in the hands of the barbarians. Hereupon Themistocles spake many bitter things against Adeimantus and the Corinthians generally; and for proof that he had a country, reminded the captains, that with 200 ships at his command all fully manned for battle he had both city and territory as good as

theirs; since there was no Grecian state which could resist his men if they were to make a descent.

62. After this declaration, he turned to Eurybiades, and addressing him with greater warmth and earnestness, "If you stay here," he said, "and behave like a brave man, all will be well—if not, you will bring Greece to ruin. For the whole fortune of the war depends on our ships. Be persuaded by my words. If not, we will take our families on board, and go, just as we are, to Siris in Italy, which is ours from of old, and which the prophecies declare we are to colonise some day or other. You then, when you have lost allies like us, will hereafter call to mind what I have now said."

63. At these words of Themistocles, Eurybiades changed his determination; principally, as I believe, because he feared that if he withdrew the fleet to the Isthmus, the Athenians would sail away, and knew that without the Athenians, the rest of their ships could be no match for the fleet of the enemy. He therefore decided to remain, and give battle at Salamis.

64. And now, the different chiefs, notwithstanding their skirmish of words, on learning the decision of Eurybiades, at once made ready for the fight. Morning broke, and, just as the sun rose, the shock of an earthquake was felt both on shore and at sea; whereupon the Greeks resolved to approach the gods with prayer, and likewise to send and invite the Aeacids to their aid. And this they did, with as much speed as they had resolved on it. Prayers were offered to all the gods; and Telamon and Ajax were invoked at once from Salamis, while a ship was sent to Aegina to fetch Aeacus himself, and the other Aeacids.

65. The following is a tale which was told by Dicaeus, the son of Theocydes, an Athenian, who was at this time an exile, and had gained a good report among the Medes. He declared, that after the army of Xerxes had, in the absence of the Athenians, wasted Attica, he chanced to be with Demaratus the Lacedaemonian in the Thriasian plain, and that while there he saw a cloud of dust advancing from Eleusis, such as a host of 30,000 men might raise. As he and his companion were wondering who the men, from whom the dust came, could possibly be, a sound

of voices reached his ear, and he thought that he recognised the
mystic hymn to Iacchus. Now Demaratus was unacquainted
with the rites of Eleusis, and so he inquired of Dicaeus what the
voices were saying. Dicaeus answered, "Demaratus, beyond a
doubt some mighty calamity is about to befall the king's army!
For it is manifest, inasmuch as Attica is deserted by its inhabitants, that the sound which we have heard is an unearthly one,
and is now upon its way from Eleusis to aid the Athenians and
their confederates. If it descends upon the Peloponnese, danger
will threaten the king himself and his land army—if it moves
towards the ships at Salamis, it will go hard but the king's fleet
there suffers destruction. Every year the Athenians celebrate
this feast to the Mother and the Maiden; and all who wish,
whether they be Athenians or any other Greeks, are initiated.
The sound you hear is the Iacchus-song, which is wont to be
sung at the festival." "Hush now," rejoined the other, "and tell
no man of this matter. For if your words be brought to the
king's ear, you will assuredly lose your head because of them;
neither I nor any man living can then save you. Hold your peace
therefore. The gods will see to the king's army." Thus Demaratus counselled him; and they looked and saw the dust, from
which the sound arose, become a cloud, and the cloud rise up
into the air and sail away to Salamis, making for the station of
the Grecian fleet. Then they knew that it was the fleet of Xerxes
which would suffer destruction. Such was the tale told by Dicaeus the son of Theocydes; and he appealed for its truth to
Demaratus and other eye-witnesses.

66. The men belonging to the fleet of Xerxes, after they had
seen the Spartan dead at Thermopylae, and crossed the channel
from Trachis to Histiaea, waited there for three days, and then
sailing down through the Euripus, in three more came to Phalerum. In my judgment, the Persian forces both by land and sea
when they invaded Attica, were not less numerous than they had
been on their arrival at Sepias and Thermopylae. For against the
Persian loss in the storm and at Thermopylae, and again in the
sea-fights off Artemisium, I set the various nations which had
since joined the king,—as the Malians, the Dorians, the Lo-

crians, and the Boeotians—each serving in full force in his army
except the last, who did not number in their ranks either the
Thespians or the Plataeans; and together with these, the Carystians, the Andrians, the Tenians, and the other people of the
islands, who all fought on this side except the five states already
mentioned. For as the Persians penetrated further into Greece,
they were joined continually by fresh nations.

67. Reinforced by the contingents of all these various states,
except Paros, the barbarians reached Athens. As for the Parians,
they tarried at Cythnus, waiting to see how the war would go.
The rest of the sea forces came safe to Phalerum; where they
were visited by Xerxes, who had conceived a desire to go aboard
and learn the wishes of the fleet. So he came and sat in a seat of
honour; and the sovereigns of the nations, and the captains of
the ships, were sent for to appear before him, and as they arrived took their seats according to the rank assigned them by the
king. In the first seat sat the king of Sidon; after him, the king
of Tyre; then the rest in their order. When the whole had taken
their places, one after another, and were set down in orderly
array, Xerxes, to try them, sent Mardonius and questioned each,
whether a sea-fight should be risked or no.

68. Mardonius accordingly went round the entire assemblage,
beginning with the Sidonian monarch, and asked this question;
to which all gave the same answer, advising to engage the
Greeks, except only Artemisia, who spoke as follows:

"Say to the king, Mardonius, that these are my words to him:
I was not the least brave of those who fought at Euboea, nor
were my achievements there among the meanest; it is my right,
therefore, O my lord, to tell you plainly, what I think to be
most for your advantage now. This then is my advice. Spare
your ships, and do not risk a battle; for these people are as much
superior to your people in seamanship, as men to women. What
so great need is there for you to incur hazard at sea? Are you
not master of Athens, for which you undertook the expedition?
Is not Greece subject to you? Not a soul now resists your advance. They who once resisted, were handled even as they deserved. Now learn how I expect that affairs will go with your

adversaries. If you are not over-hasty to engage with them by sea, but keep your fleet near the land, then whether you abide as you are, or march forward towards the Peloponnese, you will easily accomplish all for which you came hither. The Greeks cannot hold out against you very long; you will soon part them asunder, and scatter them to their several homes. In the island where they lie, I hear they have no food in store; nor is it likely, if your land force begins its march towards the Peloponnese, that they will remain quietly where they are—at least such as come from that region. Of a surety they will not greatly trouble themselves to give battle on behalf of the Athenians. On the other hand, if you are hasty to fight, I tremble lest the defeat of your sea force bring harm likewise to your land army. This, too, you should remember, O King; good masters are apt to have bad servants, and bad masters good ones. Now, as you are the best of men, your servants must needs be a sorry set. These Egyptians, Cyprians, Cilicians, and Pamphylians, who are counted in the number of subject-allies, of how little service are they to you!"

69. As Artemisia spoke, they who wished her well were greatly troubled concerning her words, thinking that she would suffer some hurt at the king's hands, because she exhorted him not to risk a battle; they, on the other hand, who disliked and envied her, favoured as she was by the king above all the rest of the allies, rejoiced at her declaration, expecting that her life would be the forfeit. But Xerxes, when the words of the several speakers were reported to him, was pleased beyond all others with the reply of Artemisia; and whereas, even before this, he had always esteemed her much, he now praised her more than ever. Nevertheless, he gave orders that the advice of the greater number should be followed; for he thought that at Euboea the fleet had not done its best, because he himself was not there to see—whereas this time he resolved that he would be an eye-witness of the combat.

70. Orders were now given to stand out to sea; and the ships proceeded towards Salamis, and took up the stations to which they were directed, without let or hindrance from the enemy.

The day, however, was too far spent for them to begin the battle, since night already approached: so they prepared to engage upon the morrow. The Greeks, meanwhile, were in great distress and alarm, more especially those of the Peloponnese; who were troubled that they had been kept at Salamis to fight on behalf of the Athenian territory; and feared that, if they should suffer defeat, they would be pent up and besieged in an island, while their own country was left unprotected.

71. The same night the land army of the barbarians began its march towards the Peloponnese, where, however, all that was possible had been done to prevent the enemy from forcing an entry by land. As soon as ever news reached the Peloponnese, of the death of Leonidas and his companions at Thermopylae, the inhabitants flocked together from the various cities, and encamped at the Isthmus, under the command of Cleombrotus, son of Anaxandridas, and brother of Leonidas. Here their first care was to block up the Scironian way; after which it was determined in council to build a wall across the Isthmus. As the number assembled amounted to many tens of thousands, and there was not one who did not give himself to the work, it was soon finished. Stones, bricks, timber, baskets filled full of sand, were used in the building; and not a moment was lost by those who gave their aid, for they laboured without ceasing either by night or day.

72. Now the nations who gave their aid, and who had flocked in full force to the Isthmus, were the following: the Lacedaemonians, all the tribes of the Arcadians, the Eleans, the Corinthians, the Sicyonians, the Epidaurians, the Phliasians, the Troezenians, and the Hermionians. These all gave their aid, being greatly alarmed at the danger which threatened Greece. But the other inhabitants of the Peloponnese took no part in the matter; though the Olympic and Carneian festivals were now over.

73. Seven nations inhabit the Peloponnese. Two of them are aboriginal, and still continue in the regions where they dwelt at the first, the Arcadians and the Cynurians. A third, that of the Achaeans, has never left the Peloponnese, but has been dis-

lodged from its own proper country, and inhabits a district which once belonged to others. The remaining nations, four out of the seven, are all immigrants—namely, the Dorians, the Aetolians, the Dryopians, and the Lemnians. To the Dorians belong several very famous cities; to the Aetolians one only, that is, Elis; to the Dryopians, Hermione and that Asine which lies over against Cardamyle in Laconia; to the Lemnians, all the towns of the Paroreats. The aboriginal Cynurians alone seem to be Ionians; even they, however, have, in course of time, grown to be Dorians, under the government of the Argives, whose Orneats and vassals they were. All the cities of these seven nations, except those mentioned above, stood aloof from the war; and by so doing, if I may speak freely, they in fact took part with the Medes.

74. So the Greeks at the Isthmus toiled unceasingly as though in the greatest peril; since they never imagined that any great success would be gained by the fleet. The Greeks at Salamis, on the other hand, when they heard what the rest were about, felt greatly alarmed; but their fear was not so much for themselves, as for the Peloponnese. At first they conversed together in low tones, each man with his fellow, secretly, and marvelled at the folly shown by Eurybiades; but presently the smothered feeling broke out, and another assembly was held; whereat the old subjects provoked much talk from the speakers, one side maintaining that it was best to sail to the Peloponnese and risk battle for that, instead of abiding at Salamis and fighting for a land already taken by the enemy; while the other, which consisted of the Athenians, Aeginetans, and Megarians, was urgent to remain and have the battle fought where they were.

75. Then Themistocles, when he saw that the Peloponnesians would carry the vote against him, went out secretly from the council, and instructing a certain man what he should say,[6] sent him on board a merchant ship to the fleet of the Medes. The man's name was Sicinnus; he was one of Themistocles' household slaves, and acted as tutor to his sons; in after times, when

[6] The fact of the stratagem is witnessed by Thucydides as well as Aeschylus.

the Thespians were admitting persons to citizenship, Themistocles made him a Thespian, and a rich man to boot. The ship brought Sicinnus to the Persian fleet, and there he delivered his message to the leaders in these words:

"The Athenian commander has sent me to you without the knowledge of the other Greeks. He is a well-wisher to the king's cause, and would rather success should attend on you than on his countrymen; wherefore he bids me tell you, that fear has seized the Greeks and they are meditating a hasty flight. Now then it is open to you to achieve the best feat you ever accomplished, if only you hinder their escaping. They no longer agree among themselves, so that they will not now make any resistance—indeed you may see a fight already begun between such as favour and such as oppose your cause." The messenger, when he had thus expressed himself, departed and was seen no more.

76. Then the captains, believing all that the messenger had said, proceeded to land a large body of Persian troops on the islet of Psyttaleia, which lies between Salamis and the mainland; after which, about the hour of midnight, they advanced their western wing towards Salamis, so as to inclose the Greeks. At the same time the force stationed about Ceos and Cynosura moved forward, and filled the whole strait as far as Munychia with their ships. This advance was made to prevent the Greeks from escaping by flight, and to block them up in Salamis, where it was thought that vengeance might be taken upon them for the battles fought near Artemisium. The Persian troops were landed on the islet of Psyttaleia, because, as soon as the battle began, the men and wrecks were likely to be drifted thither, as the isle lay in the very path of the coming fight, and they would thus be able to save their own men and destroy those of the enemy. All these movements were made in silence, that the Greeks might have no knowledge of them; and they occupied the whole night, so that the men had no time to get their sleep.

77. I cannot say that there is no truth in prophecies, or feel inclined to call in question those which speak with clearness, when I think of the following:

When they shall bridge with their ships to the sacred strand of
   Artemis
Girt with the golden falchion, and eke to marine Cynosura,
Mad hope swelling their hearts at the downfall of beautiful
   Athens—
Then shall godlike Right extinguish haughty Presumption,
Insult's furious offspring, who thinketh to overthrow all things.
Brass with brass shall mingle, and Ares with blood shall em-
   purple
Ocean's waves. Then—then shall the day of Grecia's freedom
Come from Victory fair, and Cronus' son all-seeing.

When I look to this, and perceive how clearly Bacis spoke, I
neither venture myself to say anything against prophecies, nor
do I approve of others impugning them.

78. Meanwhile, among the captains at Salamis, the strife of
words grew fierce. As yet they did not know that they were encompassed, but imagined that the barbarians remained in the
same places where they had seen them the day before.

79. In the midst of their contention, Aristides, the son of
Lysimachus, who had crossed from Aegina, arrived in Salamis.
He was an Athenian, and had been ostracised by the commonalty;[7] yet I believe, from what I have heard concerning his
character, that there was not in all Athens a man so worthy or
so just as he. He now came to the council, and standing outside,
called for Themistocles. Now Themistocles was not his friend,
but his most determined enemy. However, under the pressure of
the great dangers impending, Aristides forgot their feud, and
called Themistocles out of the council, since he wished to confer with him. He had heard before his arrival of the impatience
of the Peloponnesians to withdraw the fleet to the Isthmus. As
soon therefore as Themistocles came forth, Aristides addressed
him in these words, "Our rivalry at all times, and especially at

---

[7] Aristides had been ostracised through the influence of Themistocles,
three years earlier, 483 B.C. When Xerxes was in Thessaly, all exiles
whose banishment was only for a term of years, were recalled. Themistocles himself moving the decree for the purpose.

the present season, ought to be a struggle, which of us shall most advantage our country. Let me then say to you, that so far as regards the departure of the Peloponnesians from this place, much talk and little will be found precisely alike. I have seen with my own eyes that which I now report; that, however much the Corinthians or Eurybiades himself may wish it, they cannot now retreat; for we are inclosed on every side by the enemy. Go in to them, and make this known."

80. "Your advice is excellent," answered the other, "and your tidings are also good. That which I earnestly desired to happen, your eyes have beheld accomplished. Know that what the Medes have now done was at my instance; for it was necessary, as our men would not fight here at their own free will, to make them fight whether they would or no. But come now, as you have brought the good news, go in and tell it. For if I speak to them, they will think it a feigned tale, and will not believe that the barbarians have inclosed us around. Therefore you go to them, and inform them how matters stand. If they believe you, it will be for the best; but if otherwise, it will not harm. For it is impossible that they should now flee away, if we are indeed shut in on all sides, as you say."

81. Then Aristides entered the assembly, and spoke to the captains: he had come, he told them, from Aegina, and had but barely escaped the blockading vessels—the Greek fleet was entirely inclosed by the ships of Xerxes—and he advised them to get themselves in readiness to resist the foe. Having said so much, he withdrew. And now another contest arose, for the greater part of the captains would not believe the tidings.

82. But while they still doubted, a Tenian trireme, commanded by Panaetius the son of Sosimenes, deserted from the Persians and joined the Greeks, bringing full intelligence. For this reason the Tenians were inscribed upon the tripod at Delphi among those who overthrew the barbarians. With this ship, which deserted to their side at Salamis, and the Lemnian vessel which came over before at Artemisium, the Greek fleet was brought to the full number of 380 ships; otherwise it fell short by two of that amount.

83. The Greeks now, not doubting what the Tenians told them, made ready for the coming fight. At the dawn of day, all the men-at-arms were assembled together, and speeches were made to them, of which the best was that of Themistocles; who throughout contrasted what was noble with what was base, and bade them, in all that came within the range of man's nature and constitution, always to make choice of the nobler part. Having thus wound up his discourse, he told them to go at once on board their ships, which they accordingly did; and about this time the trireme, that had been sent to Aegina for the Aeacidae, returned; whereupon the Greeks put to sea with all their fleet.

84. The fleet had scarce left the land when they were attacked by the barbarians. At once most of the Greeks began to back water, and were about touching the shore, when Ameinias of Pallene, one of the Athenian captains, darted forth in front of the line, and charged a ship of the enemy. The two vessels became entangled, and could not separate, whereupon the rest of the fleet came up to help Ameinias, and engaged with the Persians. Such is the account which the Athenians give of the way in which the battle began; but the Aeginetans maintain that the vessel which had been to Aegina for the Aeacidae, was the one that brought on the fight. It is also reported, that a phantom in the form of a woman appeared to the Greeks, and, in a voice that was heard from end to end of the fleet, cheered them on to the fight; first, however, rebuking them, and saying, "Strange men, how long are you going to back water?"

85. Against the Athenians, who held the western extremity of the line towards Eleusis, were placed the Phoenicians; against the Lacedaemonians, whose station was eastward towards the Piraeus, the Ionians. Of these last a few only followed the advice of Themistocles, to fight backwardly; the greater number did far otherwise. I could mention here the names of many captains who took vessels from the Greeks, but I shall pass over all excepting Theomestor the son of Androdamus, and Phylacus the son of Histiaeus, both Samians. I show this preference to them, inasmuch as for this service Theomestor was made tyrant of Samos by the Persians, while Phylacus was enrolled among the

king's benefactors, and presented with a large estate in land. In the Persian tongue the king's benefactors are called Orosangs.

86. Far the greater number of the Persian ships engaged in this battle were disabled—either by the Athenians or by the Aeginetans. For as the Greeks fought in order and kept their line, while the barbarians were in confusion and had no plan in anything that they did, the issue of the battle could scarce be other than it was. Yet the Persians fought far more bravely here than at Euboea, and indeed surpassed themselves; each did his utmost through fear of Xerxes, for each thought that the king's eye was upon himself.

87. What part the several nations, whether Greek or barbarian, took in the combat, I am not able to say for certain; Artemisia, however, I know, distinguished herself in such a way as raised her even higher than she stood before in the esteem of the king. For after confusion had spread throughout the whole of the king's fleet, and her ship was closely pursued by an Athenian trireme, she, having no way to fly, since in front of her were a number of friendly vessels, and she was nearest of all the Persians to the enemy, resolved on a measure which in fact proved her safety. Pressed by the Athenian pursuer, she bore straight against one of the ships of her own party, a Calyndian, which had Damasithymus, the Calyndian king, himself on board. I cannot say whether she had had any quarrel with the man while the fleet was at the Hellespont, or no—neither can I decide whether she of set purpose attacked his vessel, or whether it merely chanced that the Calyndian ship came in her way—but certain it is that she bore down upon his vessel and sank it, and that thereby she had the good fortune to procure herself a double advantage. For the commander of the Athenian trireme, when he saw her bear down on one of the enemy's fleet, thought immediately that her vessel was a Greek, or else had deserted from the Persians, and was now fighting on the Greek side; he therefore gave up the chase, and turned away to attack others.

88. Thus in the first place she saved her life by the action, and was enabled to get clear off from the battle; while further, it fell out that in the very act of doing the king an injury she

raised herself to a greater height than ever in his esteem. For as Xerxes beheld the fight, he remarked (it is said) the destruction of the vessel, whereupon the bystanders observed to him, "Do you see, master, how well Artemisia fights, and how she has just sunk a ship of the enemy?" Then Xerxes asked if it were really Artemisia's doing; and they answered, "Certainly; for they knew her ensign": while all made sure that the sunken vessel belonged to the opposite side. Every thing, it is said, conspired to prosper the queen—it was especially fortunate for her, that not one of those on board the Calyndian ship survived to become her accuser. Xerxes, they say, in reply to the remarks made to him, observed, "My men have behaved like women, and my women like men!"

89. There fell in this combat Ariabignes, one of the chief commanders of the fleet, who was son of Darius and brother of Xerxes, and with him perished a vast number of men of high repute, Persians, Medes, and allies. Of the Greeks there died only a few; for as they were able to swim, all those that were not slain outright by the enemy escaped from the sinking vessels and swam across to Salamis. But on the side of the barbarians more perished by drowning than in any other way, since they did not know how to swim. The great destruction took place when the ships which had been first engaged began to fly; for they who were stationed in the rear, anxious to display their valour before the eyes of the king, made every effort to force their way to the front, and thus became entangled with such of their own vessels as were retreating.

90. In this confusion the following event occurred: certain Phoenicians belonging to the ships which had thus perished made their appearance before the king, and laid the blame of their loss on the Ionians, declaring that they were traitors, and had wilfully destroyed the vessels. But the upshot of this complaint was, that the Ionian captains escaped the death which threatened them, while their Phoenician accusers received death as their reward. For it happened that, exactly as they spoke, a Samothracian vessel bore down on an Athenian and sank it, but was attacked and crippled immediately by one of the Aeginetan

squadron. Now the Samothracians were expert with the javelin, and aimed their weapons so well, that they cleared the deck of the vessel which had disabled their own, after which they sprang on board, and took it. This saved the Ionians. Xerxes, when he saw the exploit, turned fiercely on the Phoenicians (he was ready, in his extreme vexation, to find fault with any one) and ordered their heads to be cut off, to prevent them, he said, from casting the blame of their own misconduct upon braver men. During the whole time of the battle Xerxes sat at the base of the hill called Aegaleos, over against Salamis; and whenever he saw any of his own captains perform any worthy exploit he inquired concerning him; and the man's name was taken down by his scribes, together with the names of his father and his city. Ariaramnes too, a Persian, who was a friend of the Ionians, and present at the time whereof I speak, had a share in bringing about the punishment of the Phoenicians.

91. When the rout of the barbarians began, and they sought to make their escape to Phalerum, the Aeginetans, awaiting them in the channel, performed exploits worthy to be recorded. Through the whole of the confused struggle the Athenians employed themselves in destroying such ships as either made resistance or fled to shore, while the Aeginetans dealt with those which endeavoured to escape down the straits; so that the Persian vessels were no sooner clear of the Athenians than straightway they fell into the hands of the Aeginetan squadron.

92. It chanced here that there was a meeting between the ship of Themistocles, which was hastening in pursuit of the enemy, and that of Polycritus, son of Crius the Aeginetan, which had just charged a Sidonian trireme. The Sidonian vessel was the same that captured the Aeginetan guard-ship off Sciathus, which had Pytheas, the son of Ischenous, on board—that Pytheas, I mean, who fell covered with wounds, and whom the Sidonians kept on board their ship, from admiration of his gallantry. This man afterwards returned in safety to Aegina, for when the Sidonian vessel with its Persian crew fell into the hands of the Greeks, he was still found on board. Polycritus no sooner saw the Athenian trireme, than knowing at once whose vessel it was,

as he observed that it bore the ensign of the admiral, he shouted to Themistocles jeeringly, and asked him, in a tone of reproach, if the Aeginetans did not show themselves rare friends to the Medes.[8] At the same time, while he thus reproached Themistocles, Polycritus bore straight down on the Sidonian. Such of the barbarian vessels as escaped from the battle fled to Phalerum, and there sheltered themselves under the protection of the land army.

93. The Greeks who gained the greatest glory of all in the sea-fight of Salamis were the Aeginetans, and after them the Athenians. The individuals of most distinction were Polycritus the Aeginetan, and two Athenians, Eumenes of Anagyrus, and Ameinias of Pallene; the latter of whom had pressed Artemisia so hard. And assuredly, if he had known that the vessel carried Artemisia on board, he would never have given over the chase till he had either succeeded in taking her, or else been taken himself. For the Athenian captains had received special orders touching the queen, and moreover a reward of 10,000 drachmas had been proclaimed for any one who should make her prisoner; since there was great indignation felt that a woman should appear in arms against Athens. However, as I said before, she escaped; and so did some others whose ships survived the engagement; and these were all now assembled at the port of Phalerum.

94. The Athenians say that Adeimantus, the Corinthian commander, at the moment when the two fleets joined battle, was seized with fear, and being beyond measure alarmed, spread his sails, and hasted to fly away; on which the other Corinthians, seeing their leader's ship in full flight, sailed off likewise. They had reached in their flight that part of the coast of Salamis where stands the temple of Athena Sciras, when they met a light bark, a very strange apparition: it was never discovered that any one had sent it to them, and till it appeared they were altogether ignorant how the battle was going. That there was something beyond nature in the matter they judged from this, that

---

[8] Polycritus undoubtedly spoke with special reference to the charge of Medism brought against his father (vi. 50).

when the men in the bark drew near to their ships they addressed them, saying, "Adeimantus, while you play the traitor's part, by withdrawing all these ships, and flying away from the fight, the Greeks whom you deserted are defeating their foes as completely as they ever wished in their prayers." Adeimantus, however, would not believe what the men said; whereupon they told him, "He might take them with him as hostages, and put them to death if he did not find the Greeks winning." Then Adeimantus put about, both he and those who were with him; and they rejoined the fleet when the victory was already gained. Such is the tale which the Athenians tell concerning them of Corinth; these latter however do not allow its truth.[9] On the contrary, they declare that they were among those who distinguished themselves most in the fight. And the rest of Greece bears witness in their favour.

95. In the midst of the confusion Aristides, the son of Lysimachus, the Athenian, of whom I lately spoke as a man of the greatest excellence, performed the following service. He took a number of the Athenian heavy-armed troops, who had previously been stationed along the shore of Salamis, and landing with them on the islet of Psyttaleia, slew all the Persians by whom it was occupied.

96. As soon as the sea-fight was ended,[10] the Greeks drew together to Salamis all the wrecks that were to be found in that quarter, and prepared themselves for another engagement, supposing that the king would renew the fight with the vessels which still remained to him. Many of the wrecks had been carried away by a westerly wind to the coast of Attica, where they were thrown upon the strip of shore called Colias. Thus not only were the prophecies of Bacis and Musaeus concerning this battle fulfilled completely, but likewise, by the place to

[9] There can be no doubt that the tale was altogether false, one of those calumnies which, under feelings strongly excited, men circulate against their enemies.

[10] The description of the battle of Salamis in Aeschylus (*Persians*, 359-438), as the account of an eye-witness and combatant, must always hold a primary place among the records of the time.

which the wrecks were drifted, the prediction of Lysistratus, an
Athenian soothsayer, uttered many years before these events,
and quite forgotten at the time by all the Greeks, was fully accomplished. The words were:

Then shall the sight of the oars fill Colian dames with amaze-
    ment.

Now this must have happened as soon as the king was departed.

97. Xerxes, when he saw the extent of his loss, began to be
afraid lest the Greeks might be counselled by the Ionians, or
without their advice might determine, to sail straight to the
Hellespont and break down the bridges there; in which case he
would be blocked up in Europe, and run great risk of perishing.
He therefore made up his mind to fly; but as he wished to hide
his purpose alike from the Greeks and from his own people, he
set to work to carry a mound across the channel to Salamis,[11]
and at the same time began fastening a number of Phoenician
merchant ships together, to serve at once for a bridge and a wall.
He likewise made many warlike preparations, as if he were
about to engage the Greeks once more at sea. Now, when these
things were seen, all grew fully persuaded that the king was
bent on remaining, and intended to push the war in good earnest.
Mardonius, however, was in no respect deceived; for long acquaintance enabled him to read all the king's thoughts. Meanwhile, Xerxes, though engaged in this way, sent off a messenger
to carry intelligence of his misfortune to Persia.

98. Nothing mortal travels so fast as these Persian messengers. The entire plan is a Persian invention; and this is the
method of it. Along the whole line of road there are men (they
say) stationed with horses, in number equal to the number of
days which the journey takes, allowing a man and horse to each
day; and these men will not be hindered from accomplishing at
their best speed the distance which they have to go, either by
snow, or rain, or heat, or by the darkness of night. The first
rider delivers his despatch to the second, and the second passes

[11] Other authors place this project before and not after the battle.

it to the third; and so it is borne from hand to hand along the whole line, like the light in the torch-race, which the Greeks celebrate to Hephaestus. The Persians give the riding post in this manner, the name of angareion.

99. At Susa, on the arrival of the first message, which said that Xerxes was master of Athens, such was the delight of the Persians who had remained behind, that they forthwith strewed all the streets with myrtle boughs, and burnt incense, and fell to feasting and merriment. In like manner, when the second message reached them, so sore was their dismay, that they all with one accord rent their garments, and cried aloud, and wept and wailed without stint. They laid the blame of the disaster on Mardonius; and their grief on the occasion was less on account of the damage done to their ships, than owing to the alarm which they felt about the safety of the king. Hence their trouble did not cease till Xerxes himself, by his arrival, put an end to their fears.

100. And now Mardonius, perceiving that Xerxes took the defeat of his fleet greatly to heart, and suspecting that he had made up his mind to leave Athens and fly away, began to think of the likelihood of his being visited with punishment for having persuaded the king to undertake the war. He therefore considered that it would be the best thing for him to adventure further, and either become the conqueror of Greece—which was the result he rather expected—or else die gloriously after aspiring to a noble achievement. So with these thoughts in his mind, he said one day to the king:

"Do not grieve, master, or take so greatly to heart your late loss. Our hopes hang not altogether on the fate of a few planks, but on our brave steeds and horsemen. These fellows, whom you imagine to have quite conquered us, will not venture—no, not one of them—to come ashore and contend with our land army— nor will the Greeks who are upon the mainland fight our troops; such as did so, have received their punishment. If you please, we may at once attack the Peloponnese; if you would rather wait awhile, that too is in our power. Only be not disheartened. For it is not possible that the Greeks can avoid being brought to account, alike for this and for their former injuries; nor can they any how escape being your slaves. You should therefore do as I have said. If, however, your mind is made up, and you are resolved to retreat and lead away your army, listen to the counsel which, in that case, I have to offer. Make not the Persians, O King, a laughing-stock to the Greeks. If your affairs have succeeded ill, it has not been by their fault; you cannot say that your Persians have ever shown themselves cowards. What matters it if Phoenicians and Egyptians, Cyprians and Cilicians have misbehaved? Their misconduct touches not us. Since then your Persians are without fault, be advised by me. Depart home, if you wish, and take with you the bulk of your army; but first let me choose out 300,000 troops, and let it be my task to bring Greece beneath your sway."

101. Xerxes, when he heard these words, felt a sense of joy and delight, like a man who is relieved from care. Answering Mardonius, therefore, that he would consider his counsel, and let him know which course he might prefer, Xerxes proceeded to consult with the chief men among the Persians; and because Artemisia on the former occasion had shown herself the only person who knew what was best to be done, he was pleased to summon her to advise him now. As soon as she arrived, he put forth all the rest, both councillors and body-guards, and said to her, "Mardonius wishes me to stay and attack the Peloponnese. My Persians, he says, and my other land forces, are not to blame for the disasters which have befallen our arms; and of this he declares they would very gladly give me the proof. He therefore exhorts me, either to stay and act as I have said, or to let him choose out 300,000 of my troops—wherewith he undertakes to reduce Greece beneath my sway—while I myself retire with the rest of my forces, and withdraw into my own country. You, therefore, as you counselled me so wisely to decline the sea-fight, now also advise me in this matter, and say, which course I ought to take for my own good."

102. Thus did the king ask Artemisia's counsel, and the following are the words wherewith she answered him, "It is a hard thing, O King, to give the best possible advice to one who asks

our counsel. Nevertheless, as your affairs now stand, it seems to me that you will do right to return home. As for Mardonius, if he prefers to remain, and undertakes to do as he has said, leave him behind by all means, with the troops which he desires. If his design succeeds and he subdues the Greeks, as he promises, yours is the conquest, master, for your slaves will have accomplished it. If, on the other hand, affairs run counter to his wishes, we can suffer no great loss, so long as you are safe, and your house is in no danger. The Greeks, too, while you live, and your house flourishes, must be prepared to fight full many a battle for their freedom; whereas if Mardonius fall, it matters nothing—they will have gained but a poor triumph—a victory over one of your slaves! Remember also, you go home having gained the purpose of your expedition; for you have burnt Athens!"

103. The advice of Artemisia pleased Xerxes well; for she had exactly uttered his own thoughts. I, for my part, do not believe that he would have remained, had all his counsellors, both men and women, united to urge his stay, so great was the alarm that he felt. As it was, he gave praise to Artemisia, and entrusted certain of his children to her care, ordering her to convey them to Ephesus; for he had been accompanied on the expedition by some of his bastard sons.

104. He likewise sent away at this time one of the principal of his eunuchs, a man named Hermotimus, a Pedasian, who was bidden to take charge of these sons. Now the Pedasians inhabit the region above Halicarnassus; and it is related of them, that in their country the following circumstance happens. When a mischance is about to befall any of their neighbours within a certain time, the priestess of Athena in their city grows a long beard. This has already taken place on two occasions.

105. The Hermotimus of whom I spoke above was, as I said, a Pedasian; and he, of all men whom we know, took the most cruel vengeance on the person who had done him an injury. He had been made a prisoner of war, and when his captors sold him, he was bought by a certain Panionius, a native of Chios, who made his living by a most nefarious traffic. Whenever he could

get any boys of unusual beauty, he castrated them, and carrying them to Sardis or Ephesus, sold them for large sums of money. For the barbarians value eunuchs more than others, since they regard them as more trustworthy. Many were the slaves that Panionius, who made his living by the practice, had thus treated; and among them was this Hermotimus of whom I have here made mention. However he was not without his share of good fortune; for after a while he was sent from Sardis, together with other gifts, as a present to the king. Nor was it long before he came to be esteemed by Xerxes more highly than all his eunuchs.

106. When the king was on his way to Athens with the Persian army, and abode for a time at Sardis, Hermotimus happened to make a journey upon business into Mysia; and there, in a district which is called Atarneus, but belongs to Chios, he chanced to fall in with Panionius. Recognising him at once, he entered into a long and friendly talk with him, wherein he counted up the numerous blessings he enjoyed through his means, and promised him all manner of favours in return, if he would bring his household to Sardis and live there. Panionius was overjoyed, and accepting the offer made him, came presently, and brought with him his wife and children. Then Hermotimus, when he had got Panionius and all his family into his power, addressed him in these words, "You, who make a living by viler deeds than any one else in the whole world, what wrong to you or yours had I or any of mine done, that you should have made me nothing and no longer a man? Surely you thought that the gods took no note of your crimes. But they in their justice have delivered you, the doer of unrighteousness, into my hands; and now you cannot complain of the vengeance which I am resolved to take on you."

After these reproaches, Hermotimus commanded the four sons of Panionius to be brought, and forced the father to castrate them with his own hand. Unable to resist, he did as Hermotimus required; and then his sons were made to treat him in the selfsame way. So in this way there came to Panionius requital at the hands of Hermotimus.

107. Xerxes, after charging Artemisia to convey his sons safe

to Ephesus, sent for Mardonius, and bade him choose from all his army such men as he wished, and see that he made his achievements answer to his promises. During this day he did no more; but no sooner was night come, than he issued his orders, and at once the captains of the ships left Phalerum, and bore away for the Hellespont, each making all the speed he could, and hurrying to guard the bridges against the king's return. On their way, as they sailed by Zoster, where certain narrow points of land project into the sea, they took the cliffs for vessels, and fled far away in alarm. Discovering their mistake, however, after a time, they joined company once more, and proceeded upon their voyage.

108. Next day the Greeks, seeing the land force of the bar-barians encamped in the same place, thought that their ships must still be lying at Phalerum; and expecting another attack from that quarter, made preparations to defend themselves. Soon however news came that the ships were all departed and gone away; whereupon it was instantly resolved to make sail in pursuit. They went as far as Andros; but seeing nothing of the Persian fleet, they stopped at that place, and held a council of war. At this council Themistocles advised that the Greeks should follow on through the islands, still pressing the pursuit, and making all haste to the Hellespont, there to break down the bridges. Eurybiades, however, delivered a contrary opinion. "If," he said, "the Greeks should break down the bridges, it would be the worst thing that could possibly happen for Greece. The Persian, supposing that his retreat were cut off, and he were compelled to remain in Europe, would be sure never to give them any peace. Inaction on his part would ruin all his affairs, and leave him no chance of ever getting back to Asia—nay, would even cause his army to perish by famine: whereas, if he bestirred himself, and acted vigorously, it was likely that the whole of Europe would in course of time become subject to him; since, by degrees, the various towns and tribes would either fall before his arms, or else agree to terms of submission; and in this way, his troops would find food sufficient for them, since

each year the Greek harvest would be theirs. As it was, the Persian, because he had lost the sea-fight, intended evidently to remain no longer in Europe. The Greeks ought to let him depart; and when he was gone from among them, and had returned into his own country, then would be the time for them to contend with him for the possession of that."

The other captains of the Peloponnesians declared themselves of the same mind.

109. Whereupon Themistocles, finding that the majority was against him, and that he could not persuade them to push on to the Hellespont, changed round, and addressing himself to the Athenians, who of all the allies were the most nettled at the enemy's escape, and who eagerly desired, if the other Greeks would not stir, to sail on by themselves to the Hellespont and break the bridges, spoke as follows:

"I have often myself witnessed occasions, and I have heard of many more from others, where men who had been conquered by an enemy, having been driven quite to desperation, have renewed the fight, and retrieved their former disasters. We have now had the great good luck to save both ourselves and all Greece by the repulse of this vast cloud of men; let us then be content and not press them too hard, now that they have begun to fly. Be sure we have not done this by our own might. It is the work of gods and heroes, who were jealous that one man should be king at once of Europe and of Asia—more especially a man like this, unholy and presumptuous—a man who esteems alike things sacred and things profane; who has cast down and burnt the very images of the gods themselves; who even caused the sea to be scourged with rods and commanded fetters to be thrown into it. At present all is well with us—let us then abide in Greece, and look to ourselves and to our families. The barbarian is clean gone—we have driven him off—let each now repair to his own house, and sow his land diligently. In the spring we will take ship and sail to the Hellespont and to Ionia."

All this Themistocles said in the hope of establishing a claim upon the king; for he wanted to have a safe retreat in case any mischance should befall him at Athens; which indeed came to pass afterwards.[12]

110. At present, however, he dissembled; and the Athenians were persuaded by his words. For they were ready now to do whatever he advised; since they had always esteemed him a wise man, and he had lately proved himself most truly wise and well-judging. Accordingly, they came in to his views; whereupon he lost no time in sending messengers, on board a light bark, to the king, choosing for this purpose men whom he could trust to keep his instructions secret, even although they should be put to every kind of torture. Among them was the house-slave Sicinnus, the same whom he had made use of previously. When the men reached Attica, all the others stayed with the boat; but Sicinnus went up to the king, and spake to him as follows, "I am sent to you by Themistocles, the son of Neocles, who is the leader of the Athenians, and the wisest and bravest man of all the allies, to bear you this message, 'Themistocles the Athenian, anxious to render you a service, has restrained the Greeks, who were impatient to pursue your ships, and to break up the bridges at the Hellespont. Now, therefore, return home at your leisure.' " The messengers, when they had performed their errand, sailed back to the fleet.

111. And the Greeks, having resolved that they would neither proceed further in pursuit of the barbarians, nor push forward to the Hellespont and destroy the passage, laid siege to Andros, intending to take the town by storm. For Themistocles had required the Andrians to pay down a sum of money; and they had refused, being the first of all the islanders who did so. To his declaration that the money must needs be paid, as the Athenians had brought with them two mighty gods—Persuasion and Necessity, they replied, that Athens might well be a great and glorious city, since she was blest with such excellent gods; but they were wretchedly poor, stinted for land, and cursed with

---

[12] According to Thucydides (i. 137), Themistocles did actually claim credit with the Persians for preventing the destruction of the bridge; but it is difficult to imagine him looking forward at this time to such a contingency as exile.

two unprofitable gods, who always dwelt with them, and would never quit their island, Poverty and Helplessness. These were the gods of the Andrians, and therefore they would not pay the money. For the power of Athens could not possibly be stronger than their inability. This reply, coupled with the refusal to pay the sum required, caused their city to be besieged by the Greeks.

112. Meanwhile Themistocles, who never ceased his pursuit of gain,[13] sent threatening messages to the other islanders with demands for different sums, employing the same messengers and the same words as he had used towards the Andrians. "If," he said, "they did not send him the amount required, he would bring the Greek fleet upon them, and besiege them till he took their cities." By this means he collected large sums from the Carystians and the Parians, who, when they heard that Andros was already besieged, and that Themistocles was the best es-teemed of all the captains, sent the money through fear. Whether any of the other islanders did the like, I cannot say for certain; but I think some did besides those I have mentioned. However, the Carystians, though they complied, were not spared any the more; but Themistocles was softened by the Parians' gift, and therefore they received no visit from the army. In this way it was that Themistocles, during his stay at Andros, obtained money from the islanders, unbeknown to the other captains.

113. King Xerxes and his army waited but a few days after the sea-fight, and then withdrew into Boeotia by the road which they had followed on their advance. It was the wish of Mar-donius to escort the king a part of the way; and as the time of year was no longer suitable for carrying on war, he thought it best to winter in Thessaly, and wait for the spring before he at-tempted the Peloponnese. After the army was come into Thes-saly, Mardonius made choice of the troops that were to stay with him; and, first of all, he took the whole body called the Immortals, except only their leader Hydarnes, who refused to quit the person of the king. Next, he chose the Persians who

[13] Charges of this kind against Themistocles may be partially justified but the primary purpose was to exact war indemnities to pay the crews of the fleet.

wore breastplates, and 1,000 picked horse; likewise the Medes, the Sacans, the Bactrians, and the Indians, foot and horse equally. These nations he took entire: from the rest of the allies he culled a few men, taking such as were either remarkable for their appearance, or else such as had performed, to his knowledge, some valiant deed. The Persians furnished him with the greatest number of troops, men who were adorned with chains and armlets. Next to them were the Medes, who in number equalled the Persians, but in valour fell short of them. The whole army, reckoning the horsemen with the rest, amounted to 300,000 men.

114. At the time when Mardonius was making choice of his troops, and Xerxes still continued in Thessaly, the Lacedaemonians received a message from the Delphic oracle, bidding them seek satisfaction at the hands of Xerxes for the death of Leonidas, and take whatever he chose to give them. So the Spartans sent a herald with all speed into Thessaly, who arrived while the entire Persian army was still there. This man being brought before the king, spoke as follows, "King of the Medes, the Lacedaemonians and the Heracleids of Sparta require of you the satisfaction due for bloodshed, because you slew their king, who fell fighting for Greece."

Xerxes laughed, and for a long time said not a word. At last, however, he pointed to Mardonius, who was standing by him, and said, "Mardonius here shall give them the satisfaction they deserve to get." And the herald accepted the answer, and forthwith went his way.

115. Xerxes, after this, left Mardonius in Thessaly, and marched away himself, at his best speed, toward the Hellespont. In forty-five days he reached the place of passage, where he arrived with scarce a fraction, so to speak, of his former army. All along their line of march, in every country where they chanced to be, his soldiers seized and devoured whatever corn they could find belonging to the inhabitants; while, if no corn was to be found, they gathered the grass that grew in the fields, and stripped the trees, whether cultivated or wild, alike of their bark and of their leaves, and so fed themselves. They left nothing

anywhere, so hard were they pressed by hunger. Plague too and dysentery attacked the troops while still upon their march, and greatly thinned their ranks. Many died; others fell sick and were left behind in the different cities that lay upon the route, the inhabitants being strictly charged by Xerxes to tend and feed them. Of these some remained in Thessaly, others in Macedon, others again in Siris of Paeonia. Here Xerxes, on his march into Greece, had left the sacred car and steeds of Zeus; which upon his return, he was unable to recover; for the Paeonians had disposed of them to the Thracians, and, when Xerxes demanded them back, they said, that the Thracian tribes who dwelt about the sources of the Strymon had stolen the mares as they pastured.

116. Here too a Thracian chieftain, king of the Bisaltians and of Crestonia, did a monstrous deed. He had refused to become the willing slave of Xerxes, and had fled before him into the heights of Rhodope, at the same time forbidding his sons to take part in the expedition against Greece. But they, either because they cared little for his orders, or because they wished greatly to see the war, joined the army of Xerxes. At this time they had all returned home to him—the number of the men was six—quite safe and sound. But their father took them, and punished their offence by plucking out their eyes from the sockets. Such was the treatment which these men received.

117. The Persians, having journeyed through Thrace and reached the passage, entered their ships hastily and crossed the Hellespont to Abydos. The bridges were not found stretched across the strait; since a storm had broken and dispersed them. At Abydos the troops halted, and obtaining more abundant provision than they had yet got upon their march, they fed without stint; from which cause, added to the change in their water, great numbers of those who had hitherto escaped perished. The remainder, together with Xerxes himself, came safe to Sardis.

118. There is likewise another tale told of the return of the king. It is said that when Xerxes on his way from Athens arrived at Eion upon the Strymon, he gave up travelling by land, and intrusting Hydarnes with the conduct of his forces to the

Hellespont, embarked himself on board a Phoenician ship, and so crossed into Asia. On his voyage the ship was assailed by a strong wind blowing from the mouth of the Strymon, which caused the sea to run high. As the storm increased, and the ship laboured heavily, because of the number of the Persians who had come in the king's train, and who now crowded the deck, Xerxes was seized with fear, and called out to the helmsman in a loud voice, asking him, if there were any means whereby they might escape the danger. "No means, master," the helmsman answered, "unless we could be quit of these too numerous passengers." Xerxes, they say, on hearing this, addressed the Persians as follows, "Men of Persia, now is the time for you to show what love you bear your king. My safety, as it seems, depends wholly upon you." So the king spoke; and the Persians instantly made obeisance, and then leaped over into the sea. Thus was the ship lightened, and Xerxes got safe to Asia. As soon as he had reached the shore, he sent for the helmsman, and gave him a golden crown because he had preserved the life of the king, but because he had caused the death of a number of Persians, he ordered his head to be struck from his shoulders.

119. Such is the other account which is given of the return of Xerxes; but to me it seems quite unworthy of belief, alike in other respects, and in what relates to the Persians. For had the helmsman made any such speech to Xerxes, I suppose there is not one man in 10,000 who will doubt that this is the course which the king would have followed: he would have made the men upon the ship's deck, who were not only Persians but Persians of the very highest rank, quit their place and go down below; and would have cast into the sea an equal number of the rowers, who were Phoenicians. But the truth is, that the king, as I have already said, returned into Asia by the same road as the rest of the army.

120. I will add a strong proof of this. It is certain that Xerxes on his way back from Greece passed through Abdera, where he made a contract of friendship with the inhabitants, and presented them with a golden scimitar, and a tiara broidered with gold. The Abderites declare (but I put no faith in this part of

their story) that from the time of the king's leaving Athens, he never once loosed his girdle till he came to their city, since it was not till then that he felt himself in safety. Now Abdera is nearer to the Hellespont than Eion and the Strymon, where Xerxes, according to the other tale, took ship.

121. Meanwhile the Greeks, finding that they could not capture Andros, sailed away to Carystus, and wasted the lands of the Carystians, after which they returned to Salamis. Arrived here, they proceeded, before entering on any other matter, to make choice of the first-fruits which should be set apart as offerings to the gods. These consisted of various gifts; among them were three Phoenician triremes, one of which was dedicated at the Isthmus, where it continued to my day; another at Sunium; and the third, at Salamis itself, which was devoted to Ajax. This done, they made a division of the booty, and sent away the first-fruits to Delphi. Thereof was made the statue, holding in its hand the beak of a ship, which is eighteen feet high, and which stands in the same place with the golden one of Alexander the Macedonian.

122. After the first-fruits had been sent to Delphi, the Greeks made inquiry of the god, in the name of their whole body, if he had received his full share of the spoils and was satisfied therewith. The god made answer, that all the other Greeks had paid him his full due, except only the Aeginetans; on them he had still a claim for the prize of valour which they had gained at Salamis. So the Aeginetans, when they heard this, dedicated the three golden stars which stand on the top of a bronze mast, in the corner near the bowl offered by Croesus.

123. When the spoils had been divided, the Greeks sailed to the Isthmus, where a prize of valour was to be awarded to the man who, of all the Greeks, had shown the most merit during the war. When the chiefs were all come, they met at the altar of Poseidon, and took the ballots wherewith they were to give their votes for the first and for the second in merit. Then each man gave himself the first vote, since each considered that he was himself the worthiest; but the second votes were given chiefly to Themistocles. In this way, while the others received but one

vote apiece, Themistocles had for the second prize a large majority of the suffrages.

124. Envy, however, hindered the chiefs from coming to a
decision, and they all sailed away to their homes without making
any award. Nevertheless Themistocles was regarded everywhere
as by far the wisest man of all the Greeks; and the whole country rang with his fame. As the chiefs who fought at Salamis,
notwithstanding that he was really entitled to the prize, had
withheld his honour from him, he went without delay to Lacedaemon, in the hope that he would be honoured there. And the
Lacedaemonians received him handsomely, and paid him great
respect. The prize of valour indeed, which was a crown of olive,
they gave to Eurybiades; but Themistocles was given a crown
of olive too, as the prize of wisdom and dexterity. He was likewise presented with the most beautiful chariot that could be
found in Sparta; and after receiving abundant praises, was,
upon his departure, escorted as far as the borders of Tegea, by
the 300 picked Spartans who are called the Knights. Never was
it known, either before or since, that the Spartans escorted a
man out of their city.

125. On the return of Themistocles to Athens, Timodemus of
Aphidnae, who was one of his enemies, but otherwise a man of
no repute, became so maddened with envy that he openly railed
against him, and reproaching him with his journey to Sparta,
said, "It was not his own merit that had won him honour from
the men of Lacedaemon, but the fame of Athens, his country."
Then Themistocles, seeing that Timodemus repeated this phrase
unceasingly, replied, "Thus stands the case, friend. I had never
got this honour from the Spartans, had I been a Belbinite—nor
you, had you been an Athenian!"

126. Artabazus, the son of Pharnaces, a man whom the Persians had always held in much esteem, but who, after the affair
of Plataea, rose still higher in their opinion, escorted King
Xerxes as far as the strait, with 60,000 of the chosen troops of
Mardonius. When the king was safe in Asia, Artabazus set out
upon his return; and on arriving near Pallene, and finding that
Mardonius had gone into winter quarters in Thessaly and Macedonia, and was in no hurry for him to join the camp, he thought

it his duty, as the Potidaeans had just revolted, to occupy himself in reducing them to slavery. For as soon as the king had passed beyond their territory, and the Persian fleet had made its hasty flight from Salamis, the Potidaeans revolted from the barbarians openly; as likewise did all the other inhabitants of that peninsula.

127. Artabazus, therefore, laid siege to Potidaea; and having a suspicion that the Olynthians were likely to revolt shortly, he besieged their city also. Now Olynthus was at that time held by the Bottiaeans, who had been driven from the parts about the Thermaic gulf by the Macedonians. Artabazus took the city, and having so done, led out all the inhabitants to a marsh in the neighbourhood, and there slew them. After this he delivered the place into the hands of the people called Chalcideans, having first appointed Critobulus of Torone to be governor. Such was the way in which the Chalcideans got Olynthus.

128. When this town had fallen, Artabazus pressed the siege of Potidaea all the more unremittingly; and was pushing his operations with vigour, when Timoxenus, captain of the Scionaeans, entered into a plot to betray the town to him. How the matter was managed at first, I cannot pretend to say, for no account has come down to us: but at the last this is what happened. Whenever Timoxenus wished to send a letter to Artabazus, or Artabazus to send one to Timoxenus, the letter was written on a strip of paper, and rolled round the notched end of an arrow-shaft; the feathers were then put on over the paper, and the arrow thus prepared was shot to some place agreed upon. But after a while the plot of Timoxenus to betray Potidaea was discovered in this way. Artabazus, on one occasion, shot off his arrow, intending to send it to the accustomed place, but missing his mark, hit one of the Potidaeans in the shoulder. A crowd gathered about the wounded man, as commonly happens in war; and when the arrow was pulled out, they noticed the paper, and straightway carried it to the captains, who were present from the various cities of the peninsula. The captains read the letter, and finding who the traitor was, nevertheless resolved, out of regard for the city of Scione, that as they did not wish the Scionaeans to be thenceforth branded with the name of

traitors, they would not bring against him any charge of treachery. Such accordingly was the mode in which this plot was discovered.

129. After Artabazus had continued the siege for three months, it happened that there was an unusual ebb of the tide, which lasted a long while. So when the barbarians saw that what had been sea was now no more than a swamp, they determined to push across it into Pallene. And now the troops had already made good two-fifths of their passage, and three-fifths still remained before they could reach Pallene, when the tide came in with a very high flood, higher than had ever been seen before, as the inhabitants of those parts declare, though high floods are by no means uncommon. All who were not able to swim perished immediately; the rest were slain by the Potidaeans, who bore down upon them in their sailing vessels. The Potidaeans say that what caused this swell and flood, and so brought about the disaster of the Persians which ensued therefrom, was the profanation, by the very men now destroyed in the sea, of the temple and image of Poseidon, situated in their suburb. And in this they seem to me to say well. Artabazus afterwards led away the remainder of his army, and joined Mardonius in Thessaly. Thus fared it with the Persians who escorted the king to the strait.

130. As for that part of the fleet of Xerxes which had survived the battle, when it had made good its escape from Salamis to the coast of Asia, and conveyed the king with his army across the strait from the Chersonese to Abydos, it passed the winter at Cyme. On the first approach of spring, there was an early muster of the ships at Samos, where some of them indeed had remained throughout the winter. Most of the men-at-arms who served on board were Persians, or else Medes; and the command of the fleet had been taken by Mardontes the son of Bagaeus, and Artayntes the son of Artachaeus; while there was likewise a third commander, Ithamitres the nephew of Artayntes, whom his uncle had advanced to the post. Further west than Samos, however, they did not venture to proceed; for they remembered what a defeat they had suffered, and there was no one to compel them to approach any nearer to Greece. They therefore remained at Samos, and kept watch over Ionia, to hinder it from

breaking into revolt. The whole number of their ships, including those furnished by the Ionians, was 300. It did not enter into their thoughts that the Greeks would proceed against Ionia; on the contrary, they supposed that the defence of their own country would content them, more especially as they had not pursued the Persian fleet when it fled from Salamis, but had so readily given up the chase. They despaired, however, altogether of gaining any success by sea themselves, though by land they thought that Mardonius was quite sure of victory. So they remained at Samos, and took counsel together, if by any means they might harass the enemy, at the same time that they waited eagerly to hear how matters would proceed with Mardonius.

131. The approach of spring, and the knowledge that Mardonius was in Thessaly, roused the Greeks from inaction. Their land force indeed was not yet come together; but the fleet, consisting of 110 ships, proceeded to Aegina, under the command of Leotychides. This Leotychides, who was both general and admiral, was the son of Menares, the son of Agesilaus, the son of Hippocratides, the son of Leotychides, the son of Anaxilaus, the son of Archidamus, the son of Anaxandrides, the son of Theopompus, the son of Nicander, the son of Charillus, the son of Eunomus, the son of Polydectes, the son of Prytanis, the son of Euryphon, the son of Procles, the son of Aristodemus, the son of Aristomachus, the son of Cleodaeus, the son of Hyllus, the son of Heracles. He belonged to the younger branch of the royal house. All his ancestors, except the seven next in the above list to himself, had been kings of Sparta. The Athenian vessels were commanded by Xanthippus the son of Ariphron.

132. When the whole fleet was collected together at Aegina, ambassadors from Ionia arrived at the Greek station; they had but just come from paying a visit to Sparta, where they had been entreating the Lacedaemonians to undertake the deliverance of their native land. One of these ambassadors was Herodotus, the son of Basileides. Originally they were seven in number; and the whole seven had conspired to slay Strattis the tyrant of Chios; one, however, of those engaged in the plot betrayed the enterprise; and the conspiracy being in this way discovered, Herodotus, and the remaining five, quitted Chios, and went

straight to Sparta, whence they had now proceeded to Aegina, their object being to beseech the Greeks that they would pass over to Ionia. It was not however without difficulty that they were induced to advance even so far as Delos. All beyond that seemed to the Greeks full of danger; the places were quite unknown to them, and to their fancy swarmed with Persian troops; as for Samos, it appeared to them as far off as the Pillars of Heracles. Thus it came to pass, that at the very same time the barbarians were hindered by their fears from venturing any further west than Samos, and the prayers of the Chians failed to induce the Greeks to advance any further east than Delos. Terror guarded the mid region.

133. The Greek fleet was now on its way to Delos; but Mardonius still abode in his winter-quarters in Thessaly. When he was about to leave them, he despatched a man named Mys of Europus, to go and consult the different oracles, giving him orders to put questions everywhere to all the oracles whereof he found it possible to make trial. What it was that he wanted to know, when he gave Mys these orders, I am not able to say, for no account has reached me of the matter; but for my own part, I suppose that he sent to inquire concerning the business which he had in hand, and not for any other purpose.

134. Mys, it is certain, went to Lebadeia, and by the payment of a sum of money, induced one of the inhabitants to go down to Trophonius; he likewise visited Abae of the Phocians, and there consulted the god; while at Thebes, to which place he went first of all, he not only got access to Apollo Ismenius (of whom inquiry is made by means of victims, according to the custom practised also at Olympia); but likewise prevailed on a man who was not a Theban but a foreigner, to pass the night in the temple of Amphiaraus. No Theban can lawfully consult this oracle, for the following reason: Amphiaraus by an oracle gave the Thebans their choice, to have him for their prophet or for their helper in war; he bade them elect between the two, and forego either one or the other; so they chose rather to have him for their helper. On this account it is unlawful for a Theban to sleep in his temple.

135. One thing which the Thebans declare to have happened

at this time is to me very surprising. Mys of Europus, they say, after he had gone about to all the oracles, came at last to the sacred precinct of Apollo Ptous. The place itself bears the name of Ptoum; it is in the country of the Thebans, and is situated on the mountain side overlooking Lake Copais, only a very little way from the town called Acraephia. Here Mys arrived, and entered the temple, followed by three Theban citizens—picked men whom the state had appointed to take down whatever answer the god might give. No sooner was he entered than the prophet delivered him an oracle, but in a foreign tongue; so that his Theban attendants were astonished, hearing a strange language when they expected Greek, and did not know what to do. Mys, however, the European, snatched from their hands the tablet which they had brought with them, and wrote down what the prophet uttered. The reply, he told them, was in the Carian dialect. After this, Mys departed and returned to Thessaly.

136. Mardonius, when he had read the answers given by the oracles, sent next an envoy to Athens. This was Alexander, the son of Amyntas, a Macedonian, of whom he made choice for two reasons. Alexander was connected with the Persians by family ties; for Gygaea, who was the daughter of Amyntas, and sister to Alexander himself, was married to Bubares, a Persian, and by him had a son, Amyntas of Asia; who was named after his mother's father, and enjoyed the revenues of Alabanda, a large city of Phrygia, which had been assigned him by the King. Alexander was likewise (and of this too Mardonius was well aware), both by services which he had rendered, and by formal compact of friendship, connected with Athens. Mardonius therefore thought that, by sending him, he would be most likely to gain over the Athenians to the Persian side. He had heard that they were a numerous and a warlike people, and he knew that the disasters which had befallen the Persians by sea were mainly their work; he therefore expected that, if he could form alliance with them, he would easily get the mastery of the sea (as indeed he would have done, beyond a doubt); while by land he believed that he was already greatly superior: and so he thought by this alliance to make sure of overcoming the Greeks. Perhaps too the oracles leant this way, and counselled him to make

Athens his friend: so that it may have been in obedience to them that he sent the embassy.

137. This Alexander was descended in the seventh degree from Perdiccas, who obtained the sovereignty over the Macedonians in the way which I will now relate. Three brothers, descendants of Temenus, fled from Argos to the Illyrians; their names were Gauanes, Aeropus, and Perdiccas. From Illyria they went across to Upper Macedonia, where they came to a certain town called Lebaea. There they hired themselves out to serve the king in different employs; one tended the horses; another looked after the cows; while Perdiccas, who was the youngest, took charge of the smaller cattle. In those early times poverty was not confined to the people: kings themselves were poor, and so here it was the king's wife who cooked the victuals. Now whenever she baked the bread, she always observed that the loaf of the labouring boy Perdiccas swelled to double its natural size. So the queen, finding this never to fail, spoke of it to her husband. Directly that it came to his ears, the thought struck him that it was a miracle, and boded something of no small moment. He therefore sent for the three labourers, and told them to begone out of his dominions. They said that they had a right to their wages; if he would pay them what was due, they were quite willing to go. Now it happened that the sun was shining down the chimney into the room where they were; and the king, hearing them talk of wages, lost his wits, and said, "There are the wages which you deserve; take that—I give it you," and pointed, as he spoke, to the sunshine. The two elder brothers, Gauanes and Aeropus, stood aghast at the reply, and did nothing; but the boy, who had a knife in his hand, made a mark with it round the sunshine on the floor of the room, and said, "O King, we accept your payment." Then he received the light of the sun three times into his bosom, and so went away; and his brothers went with him.

138. When they were gone, one of those who sat by told the king what the youngest of the three had done, and hinted that he must have had some meaning in accepting the wages given. Then the king, when he heard what had happened, was angry, and sent horsemen after the youths to slay them. Now there is a

river in Macedonia to which the descendants of these Argives offer sacrifice as their saviour. This stream swelled so much, as soon as the sons of Temenus were safe across, that the horsemen found it impossible to follow. So the brothers escaped into another part of Macedonia, and took up their abode near the place called the Gardens of Midas, son of Gordias. In these gardens there are roses which grow of themselves, so sweet that no others can come near them, and with blossoms that have as many as sixty petals apiece. It was here, according to the Macedonians, that Silenus was made a prisoner. Above the gardens stands a mountain called Bermius, which is so cold that none can reach the top. Here the brothers made their abode; and from this place by degrees they conquered all Macedonia.

139. From the Perdiccas, of whom we have here spoken, Alexander was descended in the following way: Alexander was the son of Amyntas, Amyntas of Alcetas; the father of Alcetas was Aeropus; of Aeropus, Philip; of Philip, Argaeus; of Argaeus, Perdiccas, the first sovereign. Such was the descent of Alexander.

140. When Alexander reached Athens as the ambassador of Mardonius, he spoke as follows:

"O men of Athens, these be the words of Mardonius. 'The king has sent a message to me, saying, "All the trespasses which the Athenians have committed against me I freely forgive. Now then, Mardonius, thus act towards them. Restore to them their territory; and let them choose for themselves whatever land they like besides, and let them dwell therein as a free people. Build up likewise all their temples which I burned, if on these terms they will consent to enter into a league with me." Such are the orders which I have received, and which I must needs obey, unless there be a hindrance on your part. And now I say to you,—why are you so mad as to levy war against the king, whom you cannot possibly overcome, or even resist for ever? You have seen the multitude and the bravery of the host of Xerxes; you know also how large a power remains with me in your land; suppose then you should get the better of us, and defeat this army—a thing whereof you will not, if you are wise, entertain the least hope—what follows even then but a contest with a still greater force? Do not, because you would fain match yourselves with the king, consent to lose your country and live in constant danger of your lives. Rather agree to make peace; which you can now do without any tarnish to your honour, since the king invites you to it. Continue free, and make an alliance with us, without fraud or deceit.'

"These are the words, O Athenians, which Mardonius has bid me speak to you. For my own part, I will say nothing of the good will I bear your nation, since you have not now for the first time to become acquainted with it. But I will add my entreaties also, and beseech you to give ear to Mardonius: for I see clearly that it is impossible for you to go on for ever contending against Xerxes. If that had appeared to me possible, I would not now have come hither the bearer of such a message. But the king's power surpasses that of man, and his arm reaches far. If then you do not hasten to conclude a peace, when such fair terms are offered you, I tremble to think of what you will have to endure—you, who of all the allies lie most directly in the path of danger, whose land will always be the chief battle-ground of the contending powers, and who will therefore constantly have to suffer alone. Hearken then, I pray you, to Mardonius. Surely it is no small matter that the Great King chooses you out from all the rest of the Greeks, to offer you forgiveness of the wrongs you have done him, and to propose himself as your friend and ally."

141. Such were the words of Alexander. Now the Lacedaemonians, when tidings reached them that Alexander had gone to Athens to bring about a league between the Athenians and the barbarians, and when at the same time they called to mind the prophecies which declared that the Dorian race should one day be driven from the Peloponnese by the Medes and the Athenians, were exceedingly afraid lest the Athenians might consent to the alliance with Persia. They therefore lost no time in sending envoys to Athens, and it so happened that these envoys were given their audience at the same time with Alexander; for the Athenians had waited and made delays, because they felt sure that the Lacedaemonians would hear that an ambassador had come to them from the Persians, and as soon as they heard it

would with all speed send an embassy. They contrived matters therefore of set purpose, so that the Lacedaemonians might hear them deliver their sentiments on the occasion.

142. As soon as Alexander had finished speaking, the ambassadors from Sparta took the word and said, "We are sent here by the Lacedaemonians to beg of you not to do a new thing in Greece, nor agree to the terms which are offered you by the barbarian. Such conduct on the part of any of the Greeks were alike unjust and dishonourable; but in you it would be worse than in others, for divers reasons. It was by you that this war was kindled at the first among us—our wishes were in no way considered; the contest began for your territory—now the fate of Greece is involved in it. Besides, it were surely an intolerable thing that the Athenians, who have always hitherto been known as a nation to which many men owed their freedom, should now become the means of bringing all other Greeks into slavery. We feel, however, for the heavy calamities which press on you—the loss of your harvest these two years, and the ruin in which your homes have lain for so long a time. We offer you, therefore, on the part of the Lacedaemonians and the allies, sustenance for your women and for the unwarlike portion of your households, so long as the war endures. Do not be seduced by Alexander the Macedonian, who softens down the rough words of Mardonius. He does as is natural for him to do—a tyrant himself, he helps forward a tyrant's cause. But you, Athenians, should do differently, at least if you be truly wise; for you should know that with barbarians there is neither faith nor truth."

143. Thus the envoys spoke. After which the Athenians returned this answer to Alexander, "We know, as well as you do, that the power of the Mede is many times greater than our own: we did not need to have that cast in our teeth. Nevertheless we cling so to freedom that we shall offer what resistance we may Seek not to persuade us into making terms with the barbarian— say what you will, you will never gain our assent. Return rather at once, and tell Mardonius that our answer to him is this, 'So long as the sun keeps his present course, we will never join alliance with Xerxes. Nay, we shall oppose him unceasingly, trusting in the aid of those gods and heroes whom he has lightly

esteemed, whose houses and whose images he has burnt with fire.' And come not again to us with words like these; nor, thinking to do us a service, persuade us to unholy actions. You are the guest and friend of our nation—we would not that you should receive hurt at our hands."

144. Such was the answer which the Athenians gave to Alexander. To the Spartan envoys they said, "It was natural no doubt that the Lacedaemonians should be afraid we might make terms with the barbarian; but nevertheless it was a base fear in men who knew so well of what temper and spirit we are. Not all the gold that the whole earth contains—not the fairest and most fertile of all lands—would bribe us to take part with the Medes and help them to enslave our countrymen. Even could we have brought ourselves to such a thing, there are many very powerful motives which would now make it impossible. The first and chief of these is the burning and destruction of our temples and the images of our gods, which forces us to make no terms with their destroyer, but rather to pursue him with our resentment to the uttermost. Again, there is our common brotherhood with the Greeks: our common language, the altars and the sacrifices of which we all partake, the common character which we bear—did the Athenians betray all these, of a truth it would not be well. Know then now, if you have not known it before, that while one Athenian remains alive, we will never join alliance with Xerxes. We thank you, however, for your forethought on our behalf, and for your wish to give our families sustenance, now that ruin has fallen on us—the kindness is complete on your part; but for ourselves, we will endure as we may, and not be burdensome to you. Such then is our resolve. Be it your care with all speed to lead out your troops; for if we surmise aright, the barbarian will not wait long before invading our territory, but will set out so soon as he learns our answer to be, that we will do none of those things which he requires of us. Now then is the time for us, before he enters Attica, to go ourselves into Boeotia, and give him battle."

When the Athenians had thus spoken, the ambassadors from Sparta departed, and returned to their own country.

The Ninth Book, Entitled

CALLIOPE

1. Mardonius, when Alexander upon his return made known to him the answer of the Athenians, forthwith broke up from Thessaly, and led his army with all speed against Athens; forcing the several nations through whose land he passed to furnish him with additional troops. The chief men of Thessaly, far from repenting of the part which they had taken in the war hitherto, urged on the Persians to the attack more earnestly than ever. Thorax of Larissa in particular, who had helped to escort Xerxes on his flight to Asia, now openly encouraged Mardonius in his march upon Greece.

2. When the army reached Boeotia, the Thebans sought to induce Mardonius to make a halt. "He would not," they told him, "find anywhere a more convenient place in which to pitch his camp, and their advice to him was, that he should go no further, but fix himself there, and thence take measures to subdue all Greece without striking a blow. If the Greeks, who had held together hitherto, still continued united among themselves, it would be difficult for the whole world to overcome them by force of arms. But if you will do as we advise," they went on to say, "you may easily obtain the direction of all their counsels. Send presents to the men of most weight in the several states, and by so doing you will sow division among them. After that, it will be a light task, with the help of such as side with you, to bring under all your adversaries."

3. Such was the advice of the Thebans: but Mardonius did not follow it. A strong desire of taking Athens a second time

possessed him, in part arising from his inborn stubbornness, in part from a wish to inform the king at Sardis, by fire-signals along the islands, that he was master of the place. However, he did not, on his arrival in Attica, find the Athenians in their country—they had again withdrawn, some to their ships, but the greater part to Salamis—and he only gained possession of a deserted town. It was ten months after the taking of the city by the king that Mardonius came against it for the second time.

4. Mardonius, being now in Athens, sent an envoy to Salamis, one Murychides, a Hellespontine Greek, to offer the Athenians once more the same terms which had been conveyed to them by Alexander. The reason for his sending a second time, though he knew beforehand their unfriendly feelings towards him, was, that he hoped, when they saw the whole land of Attica conquered and in his power, their stubbornness would begin to give way. On this account, therefore, he dispatched Murychides to Salamis.

5. Now, when Murychides came before the council, and delivered his message, one of the councillors, named Lycidas, gave it as his opinion that the best course would be, to admit the proposals brought by Murychides, and lay them before the assembly of the people. This he stated to be his opinion, perhaps because he had been bribed by Mardonius, or it may be because that course really appeared to him the most expedient. However, the Athenians, both those in the council, and those who stood without, when they heard of the advice, were full of wrath, and forthwith surrounded Lycidas, and stoned him to death. As for Murychides, the Hellespontine Greek, him they sent away unharmed. Now there was a stir in the island about Lycidas, and the Athenian women learned what had happened. Then each exhorted her fellow, and one brought another to take part in the deed; and they all flocked of their own accord to the house of Lycidas, and stoned to death his wife and his children.

6. The circumstances under which the Athenians had sought refuge in Salamis were the following. So long as any hope remained that a Peloponnesian army would come to give them aid, they remained in Attica; but when it appeared that the allies

were slack and slow to move, while the invader was reported to be pressing forward and to have already entered Boeotia, then they proceeded to remove their goods and chattels from the mainland, and themselves again crossed the strait to Salamis. At the same time they sent ambassadors to Lacedaemon, who were to reproach the Lacedaemonians for having allowed the barbarian to advance into Attica, instead of joining them and going out to meet him in Boeotia. They were likewise to remind the Lacedaemonians of the offers by which the Persian had sought to win Athens over to his side, and to warn them, that if no aid came from Sparta, the Athenians must consult for their own safety.

7. The truth was, the Lacedaemonians were keeping holiday at that time; for it was the feast of the Hyacinthia, and they thought nothing of so much moment as to perform the service of the god. They were also engaged in building their wall across the Isthmus, which was now so far advanced that the battlements had begun to be placed upon it.

When the envoys of the Athenians, accompanied by ambassadors from Megara and Plataea, reached Lacedaemon, they came before the Ephors, and spoke as follows:

"The Athenians have sent us to you to say the King of the Medes offers to give us back our country, and wishes to conclude an alliance with us on fair and equal terms, without fraud or deceit. He is willing likewise to bestow on us another country besides our own, and bids us choose any land that we like. But we, because we reverenced Hellenic Zeus, and thought it a shameful act to betray Greece, instead of consenting to these terms, refused them; notwithstanding that we have been wronged and deserted by the other Greeks, and are fully aware that it is far more for our advantage to make peace with the Persian, than to prolong the war with him. Still we shall not, of our own free will, consent to any terms of peace. Thus do we, in all our dealings with the Greeks, avoid what is base and counterfeit: while contrariwise, you, who but now were so full of fear lest we should make terms with the enemy, having learned of what temper we are, and assured yourselves that we shall not prove traitors to our country, having brought moreover your wall across the Isthmus to an advanced state, cease altogether to have any care for us. You agreed with us to go out and meet the Persian in Boeotia; but when the time came, you were false to your word, and looked on while the barbarian host advanced into Attica. At this time therefore the Athenians are angered with you; and justly, for you have not done what was right. They bid you, however, make haste to send forth your army, that we may even yet meet Mardonius in Attica. Now that Boeotia is lost to us, the best place for the fight within our country, will be the plain of Thria."

8. The Ephors, when they had heard this speech, delayed their answer till the morrow; and when the morrow came, till the day following. And thus they acted for ten days, continually putting off the ambassadors from one day to the next. Meanwhile the Peloponnesians generally were labouring with great zeal at the wall, and the work nearly approached completion. I can give no other reason for the conduct of the Lacedaemonians in showing themselves so anxious, at the time when Alexander came, that the Athenians should not join the Medes, and now being quite careless about it, except that at that former time the wall across the Isthmus was not complete, and they worked at it in great fear of the Persians, whereas now the bulwark had been raised, and so they imagined that they had no further need of the Athenians.

9. At last the ambassadors got an answer, and the troops marched forth from Sparta, under the following circumstances.[1] The last audience had been fixed for the ambassadors, when, the very day before it was to be given, a certain Tegean, named Chileus, a man who had more influence at Sparta than any other foreigner, learning from the Ephors exactly what the Athenians had said, addressed these words to them, "The case stands thus, Ephors. If the Athenians are not our friends, but league themselves with the barbarians, however strong our wall across the Isthmus may be, there will be doors enough, and wide enough

---

[1] Herodotus' account is inadequate; the key to the delay is probably the agreement of Argos with Mardonius, endangering Sparta's flank.

open too, by which the Persian may gain entrance to the Peloponnese. Grant their request then, before they make any fresh resolve, which may bring Greece to ruin."

10. Such was the counsel which Chileus gave: and the Ephors, taking the advice into consideration, determined forthwith, without speaking a word to the ambassadors from the three cities, to dispatch to the Isthmus a body of 5,000 Spartans; and accordingly they sent them forth the same night, appointing to each Spartan a retinue of seven Helots, and giving the command of the expedition to Pausanias the son of Cleombrotus. The chief power belonged of rights at this time to Pleistarchus, the son of Leonidas; but as he was still a child, Pausanias, his cousin, was regent in his room. For the father of Pausanias, Cleombrotus, the son of Anaxandridas, no longer lived; he had died a short time after bringing back from the Isthmus the troops who had been employed in building the wall. A prodigy had caused him to bring his army home; for while he was offering sacrifice to know if he should march out against the Persian, the sun was suddenly darkened in mid-sky.[2] Pausanias took with him, as joint-leader of the army, Euryanax, the son of Dorieus, a member of his own family.

11. The army accordingly had marched out from Sparta with Pausanias: while the ambassadors, when day came, appeared before the Ephors, knowing nothing of the march of the troops, and purposing themselves to leave Sparta forthwith, and return each man to his own country. They therefore addressed the Ephors in these words, "Lacedaemonians, as you do not stir from home, but keep the Hyacinthian festival, and amuse yourselves, deserting the cause of your confederates, the Athenians, whom your behaviour wrongs, and who have no other allies, will make such terms with the Persians as they shall find possible. Now when terms are once made, it is plain that, having become the King's allies, we shall march with the barbarians whithersoever they choose to lead. Then at length you will perceive what the consequences will be to yourselves." When the envoys had spoken, the Ephors declared to them with an oath, "Our troops

[2] A partial eclipse, October 2, 480 B.C.

must be at Oresteum by this time, on their march against the
strangers." (The Spartans say strangers for barbarians.) At
this the ambassadors, quite ignorant of what had happened,
questioned them concerning their meaning; and when, by much
questioning, they had discovered the truth, they were greatly
astonished, and forthwith set off, at their best speed, to overtake
the Spartan army. At the same time a body of 5,000 Lacedaemonian Perioeci, all picked men and fully armed, set forth from
Sparta, in the company of the ambassadors.

12. So these troops marched in haste towards the Isthmus.
Meanwhile the Argives, who had promised Mardonius that they
would stop the Spartans from crossing their borders, as soon as
they learned that Pausanias with his army had started from
Sparta, took the swiftest courier they could find, and sent him
off to Attica. The message which he delivered, on his arrival at
Athens, was the following, "Mardonius," he said, "the Argives
have sent me to tell you, that the Lacedaemonian youth are gone
forth from the city, and that the Argives are too weak to hinder
them. Take good heed therefore to yourself at this time." After
this, without a word more, he returned home.

13. When Mardonius learned that the Spartans were on the
march, he no longer cared to remain in Attica. Hitherto he had
kept quiet, wishing to see what the Athenians would do, and had
neither ravaged their territory, nor done it any the least harm;
for till now he had cherished the hope, that the Athenians would
come to terms with him. As however he found that his persuasions were of no avail, and as their whole policy was now clear
to him, he determined to withdraw from Attica before Pausanias with his army reached the Isthmus; first, however, he resolved to burn Athens, and to cast down and level with the
ground whatever remained standing of the walls, temples, and
other buildings. His reason for retreating was, that Attica was
not a country where horse could act with advantage; and
further, that if he suffered defeat in a battle, no way of escape
was open to him, except through defiles, where a handful of
troops might stop all his army. So he determined to withdraw

to Thebes, and give the Greeks battle in the neighbourhood of a friendly city, and on ground well suited for cavalry.

14. After he had quitted Attica and was already upon his march, news reached him that a body of 1,000 Lacedaemonians, distinct from the army of Pausanias, and sent on in advance, had arrived in the Megarid. When he heard it, wishing, if possible, to destroy this detachment first, Mardonius considered with himself how he might compass their ruin. With a sudden change of march he made for Megara, while the horse, pushing on in advance, entered and ravaged the Megarid. (Here was the furthest point in Europe towards the setting sun to which this Persian army ever penetrated.)

15. After this, Mardonius received another message, whereby he learned that the forces of the Greeks were collected together at the Isthmus; which tidings caused him to draw back, and leave Attica by the way of Deceleia. The chief magistrates of the Boeotians had sent for some of the neighbours of the Asopians; and these persons served as guides to the army, and led them first to Sphendale, and from thence to Tanagra, where Mardonius rested a night; after which, upon the morrow, he bent his course to Scolus, which brought him into the territory of the Thebans. And now, although the Thebans had espoused the cause of the Medes, yet Mardonius cut down all the trees in these parts; not however from any enmity towards the Thebans, but on account of his own urgent needs; for he wanted a rampart to protect his army from attack, and he likewise desired to have a place of refuge, whither his troops might flee, in case the battle should go contrary to his wishes. His army at this time lay on the Asopus, and stretched from Erythrae, along by Hysiae, to the territory of the Plataeans. The wall however was not made to extend so far, but formed a square of about a mile each way.

While the barbarians were employed in this work, a certain citizen of Thebes, Attaginus by name, the son of Phrynon, having made great preparations, gave a banquet, and invited Mardonius, together with fifty of the noblest Persians. Now the banquet was held at Thebes, and all the guests who were invited came to it.

16. What follows was recounted to me by Thersander, a native of Orchomenus, a man of the first rank in that city. Thersander told me, that he was himself among those invited to the feast, and that besides the Persians fifty Thebans were asked; and the two nations were not arranged separately, but a Persian and a Theban were set side by side upon each couch. After the feast was ended, and the drinking had begun, the Persian who shared Thersander's couch addressed him in the Greek tongue, and inquired of him, from what city he came. He answered, that he was of Orchomenus; whereupon the other said, "Since you have eaten with me at one table, and poured libation from one cup, I would fain leave with you a memorial of the belief I hold—the rather that you may have timely warning yourself, and so be able to provide for your own safety. Do you see these Persians here feasting, and the army which we left encamped yonder by the river-side? Yet a little while, and of all this number you will behold but a few surviving!"

As he spoke, the Persian let fall a flood of tears: whereon Thersander, who was astonished at his words, replied, "Surely you should say all this to Mardonius, and the Persians who are next him in honour." The other rejoined, "Dear friend, it is not possible for man to avert that which God has decreed shall happen. No one believes warnings, however true. Many of us Persians know our danger, but we are constrained by necessity to do as our leader bids us. Verily it is the sorest of all human ills, to abound in knowledge and yet have no power over action." All this I heard myself from Thersander the Orchomenian; who told me further, that he mentioned what had happened to other persons, before the battle was fought at Plataea.

17. When Mardonius formerly held his camp in Boeotia, all the Greeks of those parts who were friendly to the Medes sent troops to join his army, and these troops accompanied him in his attack upon Athens. The Phocians alone abstained, and took no part in the invasion; for, though they had espoused the Median cause warmly, it was very much against their will, and

only because they were compelled so to do. However, a few days after the arrival of the Persian army at Thebes, 1,000 of their heavy-armed soldiers came up, under the command of Harmocydes, one of their most distinguished citizens. No sooner had these troops reached Thebes, than some horsemen came to them from Mardonius, with orders that they should take up a position upon the plain, away from the rest of the army. The Phocians did so, and forthwith the entire Persian cavalry drew nigh to them: whereupon there went a rumour through the whole of the Greek force encamped with the Medes, that Mardonius was about to destroy the Phocians with missiles The same conviction ran through the Phocian troops themselves; and Harmocydes, their leader, addressed them thus with words of encouragement, "Phocians," said he, "it is plain that these men have resolved beforehand to take our lives, because of the accusations of the Thessalians, as I imagine. Now, then, is the time for you all to show yourselves brave men. It is better to die fighting and defending our lives, than tamely to allow them to slay us in this shameful fashion. Let them learn that they are barbarians, and that the men whose death they have plotted, are Greeks."

18. Thus Harmocydes spoke; and the Persian horse, having encircled the Phocians, charged towards them, as if about to deal out death, with bows bent, and arrows ready to be let fly; nay, here and there some did even discharge their weapons. But the Phocians stood firm, drawing together, and closing their ranks as much as possible: whereupon the horse suddenly wheeled round, and rode off. I cannot say with certainty whether they came, at the prayer of the Thessalians, to destroy the Phocians, but seeing them prepared to stand on their defence, and fearing to suffer damage at their hands, on that account beat a retreat, having orders from Mardonius so to act; or whether his sole intent was to try the temper of the Phocians and see whether they had any courage or no. However this may have been, when the horsemen retired, Mardonius sent a herald to the Phocians, saying, "Fear not, Phocians, you have shown yourselves valiant men, much unlike the report I had heard of

you. Now therefore be forward in the coming war. You will not readily outdo either the king or myself in services." Thus ended the affair of the Phocians.

19. The Lacedaemonians, when they reached the Isthmus, pitched their camp there; and the other Peloponnesians who had embraced the better side, hearing or else seeing that they were upon the march, thought it not right to remain behind when the Spartans were going forth to the war. So the Peloponnesians went out in one body from the Isthmus, the victims being favourable for setting forth; and marched as far as Eleusis, where again they offered sacrifices, and finding the omens still encouraging, advanced further. At Eleusis they were joined by the Athenians, who had come across from Salamis, and now accompanied the main army. On reaching Erythrae in Boeotia, they learnt that the barbarians were encamped upon the Asopus, wherefore they themselves, after considering how they should act, disposed their forces opposite to the enemy upon the slopes of Mount Cithaeron.

20. Mardonius, when he saw that the Greeks would not come down into the plain, sent all his cavalry, under Masistius (or Macistius, as the Greeks call him), to attack them where they were. Now Masistius was a man of much repute among the Persians, and rode a Nisaean charger, with a golden bit, and otherwise magnificently caparisoned. So the horse advanced against the Greeks, and made attacks upon them in divisions, doing them great damage at each charge, and insulting them by calling them women.

21. It chanced that the Megarians were drawn up in the position most open to attack, and where the ground offered the best approach to the cavalry. Finding themselves therefore hard pressed by the assaults upon their ranks, they sent a herald to the Greek leaders, who came and said to them, "This is the message of the Megarians: We cannot, brothers-in-arms, continue to resist the Persian horse in that post which we have occupied from the first, if we are left without assistance. Hitherto, although hard pressed, we have held out against them firmly and courageously. Now, however, if you do not send

others to take our place, we warn you that we shall quit our post." Such were the words of the herald. Pausanias, when he heard them, inquired among his troops if there were any who would volunteer to take the post and so relieve the Megarians. Of the rest none were willing to go, whereupon the Athenians offered themselves; and a body of picked men, 300 in number, commanded by Olympiodorus, the son of Lampo, undertook the service.

22. Selecting, to accompany them, the whole body of archers, these men relieved the Megarians, and occupied a post which all the other Greeks collected at Erythrae had shrunk from holding. After the struggle had continued for a while, it came to an end on this wise. As the barbarians continued charging in divisions, the horse of Masistius, which was in front of the others, received an arrow in his flank, the pain of which caused him to rear and throw his rider. Immediately the Athenians rushed upon Masistius as he lay, caught his horse, and when he himself made resistance, slew him. At first, however, they were not able to take his life; for his armour hindered them. He had on a breastplate formed of golden scales, with a scarlet tunic covering it. Thus the blows all falling upon his breastplate took no effect, till one of the soldiers, perceiving the reason, drove his weapon into his eye and so slew him. All this took place without any of the other horsemen seeing it: they had neither observed their leader fall from his horse, nor beheld him slain; for he fell as they wheeled round and prepared for another charge, so that they were quite ignorant of what had happened. When, however, they halted, and found that there was no one to marshal their line, Masistius was missed; and instantly his soldiers, understanding what must have befallen him, with loud cheers charged the enemy in one mass, hoping to recover the dead body.

23. So when the Athenians saw, that instead of coming up in squadrons, the whole mass of the horse was about to charge them at once, they called out to the other troops to make haste to their aid. While the rest of the infantry, however, was moving to their assistance, the contest waxed fierce about the dead body of Masistius. The 300, so long as they fought by themselves, had

greatly the worse of the encounter, and were forced to retire and yield up the body to the enemy; but when the other troops approached, the Persian horse could no longer hold their ground, but fled without carrying off the body, having incurred in the attempt a further loss of several of their number. They therefore retired about 400 yards, and consulted with each other what was best to be done. Being without a leader, it seemed to them the fittest course to return to Mardonius.

24. When the horse reached the camp, Mardonius and all the Persian army made great lamentation for Masistius. They shaved off all the hair from their own heads, and cut the manes from their war-horses and their pack-animals, while they vented their grief in such loud cries that all Boeotia resounded with the clamour, because they had lost the man who, next to Mardonius, was held in the greatest esteem, both by the king and by the Persians generally. So the barbarians, after their own fashion, paid honours to the dead Masistius.

25. The Greeks, on the other hand, were greatly emboldened by what had happened, seeing that they had not only stood their ground against the attacks of the horse, but had even compelled them to beat a retreat. They therefore placed the dead body of Masistius upon a cart, and paraded it along the ranks of the army. Now the body was a sight well deserving to be gazed upon, being remarkable both for stature and for beauty; and it was to stop the soldiers from leaving their ranks to look at it, that they resolved to carry it round. After this the Greeks determined to quit the high ground and go nearer Plataea, as the land there seemed far more suitable for an encampment than the country about Erythrae, particularly because it was better supplied with water. To this place therefore, and more especially to a spring-head which was called Gargaphia, they considered that it would be best for them to remove, after which they might once more encamp in their order. So they took their arms, and proceeded along the slopes of Cithaeron, past Hysiae, to the territory of the Plataeans; and here they drew themselves up, nation by nation, close by the fountain Gargaphia, and the sacred precinct of

the Hero Androcrates, partly along some hillocks of no great height, and partly upon the level of the plain.

26. Here, in the marshalling of the nations, a fierce battle of words arose between the Athenians and the Tegeans, both of whom claimed to have one of the wings assigned to them. On each side were brought forward the deeds which they had done, whether in earlier or in later times; and first the Tegeans urged their claim as follows:

"This post has always been considered our right, and not the right of any of the other allies, in all the expeditions which have been entered into conjointly by the Peloponnesians, both anciently and in later times. Ever since the Heracleidae made their attempt, after the death of Eurystheus, to return by force of arms into the Peloponnese, this custom has been observed. It was then that the right became ours, and this was the way in which we gained it: When, in company with the Achaeans and Ionians who then dwelt in the Peloponnese, we marched out to the Isthmus, and pitched our camp over against the invaders, then, the tale goes, that Hyllus made a proclamation, 'It needs not to imperil two armies in a general battle; rather let one be chosen from the Peloponnesian ranks, whomsoever they deem the bravest, and let him engage with me in single combat, on such terms as shall be agreed upon.' The saying pleased the Peloponnesians, and oaths were sworn to the effect following, 'If Hyllus conquer the Peloponnesian champion, the Heracleidae shall return to their inheritance; if, on the other hand, he be conquered, the Heracleidae shall withdraw, lead back their army, and engage for the next hundred years to make no further endeavours to force their return.' Hereupon Echemus, the son of Aeropus and grandson of Phegeus, who was our leader and king, offered himself, and was preferred before all his brothers-in-arms as champion, engaged in single combat with Hyllus, and slew him upon the spot. For this exploit we were rewarded by the Peloponnesians of that day with many goodly privileges, which we have ever since enjoyed; and, among the rest, we obtained the right of holding the leading post in one wing, whenever a joint expedition goes forth beyond our borders. With you, then, O Lacedaemonians, we do not claim to compete; choose you which wing you please; we yield and grant you the preference: but we maintain that the command of the other wing belongs of right to us, now no less than formerly. Moreover, set aside this exploit which we have related, and still our title to the chief post is better than that of the Athenians: witness the many glorious fights in which we have been engaged against yourselves, O Spartans, as well as those which we have maintained with others. We have therefore more right to this place than they; for they have performed no exploits to be compared to ours, whether we look to earlier or to later times."

27. Thus spoke the Tegeans; and the Athenians replied as follows, "We are not ignorant that our forces were gathered here, not for the purpose of speech-making, but for battle against the barbarian. Yet as the Tegeans have been pleased to bring into debate the exploits performed by our two nations, alike in earlier and in later times, we have no choice but to set before you the grounds on which we claim it as our heritage, deserved by our unchanging bravery, to be preferred above Arcadians. In the first place, then, those very Heracleidae, whose leader they boast to have slain at the Isthmus, and whom the other Greeks would not receive when they asked a refuge from the bondage wherewith they were threatened by the people of Mycenae, were given a shelter by us; and we brought down the insolence of Eurystheus, and helped to gain the victory over those who were at that time lords of the Peloponnese. Again, when the Argives led their troops with Polynices against Thebes, and were slain and refused burial, it is our boast that we went out against the Cadmeians, recovered the bodies, and buried them at Eleusis in our own territory. Another noble deed of ours was that against the Amazons, when they came from their seats upon the Thermodon, and poured their hosts into Attica; and in the Trojan war too we were not a whit behind any of the Greeks. But what boots it to speak of these ancient matters? A nation which was brave in those days might have grown cowardly since, and a nation of cowards then might now be

valiant. Enough therefore of our ancient achievements. Had we performed no other exploit than that at Marathon—though in truth we have performed exploits as many and as noble as any of the Greeks—yet had we performed no other, we should deserve this privilege, and many a one beside. There we stood alone, and singly fought with the Persians; nay, and venturing on so dangerous a cast, we overcame the enemy, and conquered on that day forty-six nations. Does not this one achievement suffice to make good our title to the post we claim? Nevertheless, Lacedaemonians, as to strive concerning place at such a time as this is not right, we are ready to do as you command, and to take our station at whatever part of the line, and face whatever nation, you think most expedient. Wheresoever you place us, it will be our endeavour to behave as brave men. Only declare your will, and we shall at once obey you."

28. Such was the reply of the Athenians; and forthwith all the Lacedaemonian troops cried out with one voice, that the Athenians were worthier to have the left wing than the Arcadians. In this way were the Tegeans overcome, and the post was assigned to the Athenians.

When this matter had been arranged, the Greek army, which was in part composed of those who came at the first, in part of such as had flocked in from day to day, drew up in the following order: 10,000 Lacedaemonian troops held the right wing, 5,000 of whom were Spartans; and these 5,000 were attended by a body of 35,000 Helots, who were only lightly armed—seven Helots to each Spartan. The place next to themselves the Spartans gave to the Tegeans, on account of their courage and of the esteem in which they held them. They were all fully armed, and numbered 1,500 men. Next in order came the Corinthians, 5,000 strong; and with them Pausanias had placed, at their request, the band of 300 which had come from Potidaea in Pallene. The Arcadians of Orchomenus, in number 600, came next; then the Sicyonians, 3,000; then the Epidaurians, 800; then the Troezenians, 1,000; then the Lepreats, 200; the Mycenaeans and Tirynthians, 400; the Phliasians, 1,000; the Hermionians, 300; the Eretrians and Styreans, 600; the Chalcideans, 400; and the Ambraciots, 500. After these came the Leucadians and Anactorians, who numbered 800; the Paleans of Cephallenia, 200; the Aeginetans, 500; the Megarians, 3,000; and the Plataeans, 600. Last of all, but first at their extremity of the line, were the Athenians, who, to the number of 8,000, occupied the left wing, under the command of Aristides, the son of Lysimachus.

29. All these, except the Helots—seven of whom, as I said, attended each Spartan—were heavy-armed troops, and they amounted to 38,700 men. This was the number of Hoplites, or heavy-armed soldiers, which was brought together against the barbarian. The light-armed troops consisted of the 35,000 ranged with the Spartans, seven in attendance upon each, who were all well equipped for war; and of 34,500 others, belonging to the Lacedaemonians and the rest of the Greeks, at the rate (nearly) of one light to one heavy-armed. Thus the entire number of the light-armed was 69,500.

30. The Greek army, therefore, which mustered at Plataea, counting light-armed as well as heavy-armed, was but 1,800 men short of 110,000; and this amount was exactly made up by the Thespians who were present in the camp; for 1,800 Thespians, being the whole number left, were likewise with the army; but these men were without arms. Such was the array of the Greek troops when they took post on the Asopus.

31. The barbarians under Mardonius, when the mourning for Masistius was at an end, and they learned that the Greeks were in the Plataean territory, moved likewise towards the river Asopus, which flows in those parts.[3] On their arrival Mardonius marshalled them against the Greeks in the following order: Against the Lacedaemonians he posted his Persians; and as the Persians were far more numerous, he drew them up with their ranks deeper than common, and also extended their front so that part faced the Tegeans; and here he took care to choose out the best troops to face the Lacedaemonians, whilst against

---

[3] Herodotus' account of the battle of Plataea is full of details but the gaps in the narrative and the impossibility of identifying some of the places make the problem of reconstruction difficult.

the Tegeans he arrayed those on whom he could not so much depend. This was done at the suggestion and by the advice of the Thebans. Next to the Persians he placed the Medes, facing the Corinthians, Potidaeans, Orchomenians, and Sicyonians; then the Bactrians, facing the Epidaurians, Troezenians, Lepreats, Tirynthians, Mycenaeans, and Phliasians; after them the Indians, facing the Hermionians, Eretrians, Styreans, and Chalcideans; then the Sacans, facing the Ambraciots, Anactorians, Leucadians, Paleans, and Aeginetans; last of all, facing the Athenians, the Plataeans, and the Megarians, he placed the troops of the Boeotians, Locrians, Malians, and Thessalians, and also the thousand Phocians. The whole nation of the Phocians had not joined the Medes: on the contrary there were some who had gathered themselves into bands about Parnassus, and made expeditions from thence, whereby they distressed Mardonius and the Greeks who sided with them, and so did good service to the Grecian cause. Besides those mentioned above, Mardonius likewise arrayed against the Athenians the Macedonians and the tribes dwelling about Thessaly.

32. I have named here the greatest of the nations which were marshalled by Mardonius on this occasion, all those of most renown and account. Mixed with these, however, were men of divers other peoples, as Phrygians, Thracians, Mysians, Paeonians, and the like; Ethiopians again, and Egyptians, both of the Hermotybian and Calasirian races, whose weapon is the sword, and who are the only fighting men in that country. These persons had formerly served on board the fleet of Xerxes, but Mardonius disembarked them before he left Phalerum; in the land force which Xerxes brought to Athens there were no Egyptians. The number of the barbarians, as I have already mentioned, was 300,000; that of the Greeks who had made alliance with Mardonius is known to none, for they were never counted: I should guess that they mustered nearly 50,000 strong. The troops thus marshalled were all foot soldiers. As for the horse, it was drawn up by itself.

33. When the marshalling of Mardonius' troops by nations and by battalions was ended, the two armies proceeded on the

next day to offer sacrifice. The Grecian sacrifice was offered by Tisamenus, the son of Antiochus, who accompanied the army as soothsayer: he was an Elean, and belonged to the Clytiad branch of the Iamidae, but had been admitted among their own citizens by the Lacedaemonians. Now his admission among them was on this wise: Tisamenus had gone to Delphi to consult the god concerning his lack of offspring, when it was declared to him by the priestess that he would win five very glorious combats. Misunderstanding the oracle, and imagining that he was to win combats in the games, Tisamenus at once applied himself to the practice of gymnastics. He trained himself for the Pentathlon, and, on contending at Olympia, came within a little of winning it; for he was successful in everything, except the wrestling-match, which was carried off by Hieronymus the Andrian. Hereon the Lacedaemonians perceived that the combats of which the oracle spoke were not combats in the games, but battles: they therefore sought to induce Tisamenus to hire out his services to them, in order that they might join him with their Heracleid kings in the conduct of their wars. He however, when he saw that they set great store by his friendship, forthwith raised his price, and told them if they would receive him among their citizens, and give him equal rights with the rest, he was willing to do as they desired, but on no other terms would they ever gain his consent. The Spartans, when they heard this, at first thought it monstrous, and ceased to implore his aid. Afterwards, however, when the fearful danger of the Persian war hung over their heads, they sent for him and agreed to his terms; but Tisamenus now, perceiving them so changed, declared he could no longer be content with what he had asked before: they must likewise make his brother Hagias a Spartan, with the same rights as himself.

34. In acting thus he did but follow the example once set by Melampus, at least if kingship may be compared with citizenship. For when the women of Argos were seized with madness, and the Argives would have hired Melampus to come from Pylos and heal them of their disease, he demanded as his reward one-half of the kingdom; but as the Argives disdained to stoop to

this, they left him and went their way. Afterwards, however,
when many more of their women were seized, they brought
themselves to agree to his terms; and accordingly they went
again to him, and said they were content to give what he required. Hereon Melampus, seeing them so changed, raised his
demand, and told them that unless they would give his brother
Bias one-third of the kingdom likewise, he would not do as they
wished. So, as the Argives were in a strait, they consented even
to this.

35. In like manner the Spartans, as they were in great need of
Tisamenus, yielded everything: and Tisamenus the Elean, having in this way become a Spartan citizen afterwards, in the
capacity of soothsayer, helped the Spartans to gain five very
glorious combats. He and his brother were the only men whom
the Spartans ever admitted to citizenship. The five combats were
these following: The first was the combat at Plataea; the
second, that near Tegea, against the Tegeans and the Argives;
the third, that at Dipaeeis, against all the Arcadians excepting
those of Mantinea; the fourth, that at the Isthmus, against the
Messenians; and the fifth, that at Tanagra, against the Athenians and the Argives. The battle here fought was the last of all
the five.

36. The Spartans had now brought Tisamenus with them to
the Plataean territory, where he acted as soothsayer for the
Greeks. He found the victims favourable, if the Greeks stood
on the defensive, but not if they began the battle or crossed the
river Asopus.

37. With Mardonius also, who was very eager to begin the
battle, the victims were not favourable for so doing; but he
likewise found they bode him well, if he was content to stand on
his defence. He too had made use of the Grecian rites; for
Hegesistratus, an Elean, and the most renowned of the Telliads,
was his soothsayer. This man had once been taken captive by
the Spartans, who, considering that he had done them many
grievous injuries, laid him in bonds, with the intent to put him
to death. Thereupon Hegesistratus, finding himself in so sore a
case, since not only was his life in danger, but he knew that he

would have to suffer torments of many kinds before his death,
Hegesistratus, I say, did a deed for which no words suffice. He
had been set with one foot in the stocks, which were of wood
but bound with iron bands; and in this condition received from
without an iron implement, wherewith he contrived to accomplish the most courageous deed upon record. Calculating how
much of his foot he would be able to draw through the hole, he
cut off the front portion with his own hand; and then, as he
was guarded by watchmen, forced a way through the wall of
his prison, and made his escape to Tegea, travelling during the
night, but in the daytime stealing into the woods, and staying
there. In this way, though the Lacedaemonians went out in full
force to search for him, he nevertheless escaped, and arrived the
third evening at Tegea. So the Spartans were amazed at the
man's endurance, when they saw on the ground the piece which
he had cut off his foot, and yet for all their seeking could not
find him anywhere. Hegesistratus having thus escaped the
Lacedaemonians, took refuge in Tegea; for the Tegeans at that
time were ill friends with the Lacedaemonians. When his wound
was healed, he procured himself a wooden foot, and became an
open enemy to Sparta. At the last, however, this enmity brought
him to trouble; for the Spartans took him captive as he was
exercising his office in Zacynthus, and forthwith put him to
death. But these things happened some while after the fight at
Plataea. At present he was serving Mardonius on the Asopus,
having been hired at no inconsiderable price; and here he offered
sacrifice with a right good will, in part from his hatred of the
Lacedaemonians, in part for profit.

38. So when the victims did not allow either the Persians or
their Greek allies to begin the battle—these Greeks had their
own soothsayer in the person of Hippomachus, a Leucadian—
and when soldiers continued to pour into the opposite camp and
the numbers on the Greek side to increase continually, Timagenidas, the son of Herpys, a Theban, advised Mardonius to
keep a watch on the passes of Cithaeron, telling him how supplies of men kept flocking in day after day, and assuring him
that he might cut off large numbers.

39. It was eight days after the two armies first encamped opposite to one another when this advice was given by Timagenidas. Mardonius, seeing it to be good, as soon as evening came, sent his cavalry to that pass of Mount Cithaeron, which opens out upon Plataea, a pass called by the Boeotians the Three Heads, but called the Oak-Heads by the Athenians. The horse sent on this errand did not make the movement in vain. They came upon a body of 500 pack-animals which were just entering the plain, bringing provisions to the Greek camp from the Peloponnese, with a number of men driving them. Seeing this prey in their power, the Persians set upon them and slaughtered them, sparing none, neither man nor beast; till at last, when they had had enough of slaying, they secured such as were left, and bore them off to the camp to Mardonius.

40. After this they waited again for two days more, neither army wishing to begin the fight. The barbarians indeed advanced as far as the Asopus, and endeavoured to tempt the Greeks to cross; but neither side actually passed the stream. Still the cavalry of Mardonius harassed and annoyed the Greeks incessantly; for the Thebans, who were zealous in the cause of the Medes, pressed the war forward with all eagerness, and often led the charge till the lines met, when the Medes and Persians took their place, and displayed, many of them, uncommon valour.

41. For ten days nothing was done more than this; but on the eleventh day from the time when the two hosts first took station, one over against the other, near Plataea—the number of the Greeks being now much greater than it was at the first, and Mardonius being impatient of the delay—there was a conference held between Mardonius, son of Gobryas, and Artabazus, son of Pharnaces, a man who was esteemed by Xerxes more than almost any of the Persians. At this consultation the following were the opinions delivered: Artabazus thought it would be best for them to break up from their quarters as soon as possible, and withdraw the whole army to the fortified town of Thebes, where they had abundant stores of corn for themselves, and of fodder for their beasts of burden. There, he said, they had only to sit

quiet, and the war might be brought to an end on this wise:
Coined gold was plentiful in the camp, and uncoined gold too;
they had silver moreover in great abundance, and drinking-cups.
Let them not spare to take of these, and distribute them among
the Greeks, especially among the leaders in the several cities; it
would not be long before the Greeks gave up their liberty, without risking another battle for it. Thus the opinion of Artabazus
agreed with that of the Thebans; for he too had more foresight
than some. Mardonius, on the other hand, expressed himself
with more fierceness and obstinacy, and was utterly disinclined
to yield. "Their army," he said, "was vastly superior to that of
the Greeks; and they had best engage at once, and not wait till
greater numbers were gathered against them. As for Hegesistratus and his victims, they should let them pass unheeded, not
seeking to force them to be favourable, but, according to the
old Persian custom, hastening to join battle."

42. When Mardonius had thus declared his sentiments, no
one ventured to disagree; and accordingly his opinion prevailed,
for it was to him, and not to Artabazus, that the king had given
the command of the army.

Mardonius now sent for the captains of the squadrons, and
the leaders of the Greeks in his service, and asked them if they
knew of any prophecy which said that the Persians were to be
destroyed in Greece. All were silent; some because they did not
know the prophecies, but others, who knew them full well, because they did not think it safe to speak out. So Mardonius,
when none answered, said, "Since you know of no such oracle,
or do not dare to speak of it, I, who know it well, will myself
declare it to you. There is an oracle which says that the Persians
shall come into Greece, sack the temple at Delphi, and when
they have so done, perish one and all. Now we, as we are aware
of the prediction, will neither go against the temple nor make
any attempt to sack it: we therefore shall not perish for this
trespass. Rejoice then thus far, all who are well-wishers to the
Persians, and doubt not we shall get the better of the Greeks."
When he had so spoken, he further ordered them to prepare

themselves, and to put all in readiness for a battle upon the morrow.

43. As for the oracle of which Mardonius spoke, and which he referred to the Persians, it did not, I am well assured, mean them, but the Illyrians and the Enchelean host. There are, however, some verses of Bacis which did speak of this battle:

By Thermodon's stream, and the grass-clad banks of Asopus,
See where gather the Grecians, and hark to the foreigners' war-
    shout—
There in death shall lie, ere fate or Lachesis doomed him,
Many a bow-bearing Mede, when the day of calamity cometh.

These verses, and some others like them which Musaeus wrote, referred, I well know, to the Persians. The river Thermodon flows between Tanagra and Glisas.

44. After Mardonius had put his question about the prophecies, and spoken the above words of encouragement, night drew on apace, and on both sides the watches were set. As soon then as there was silence throughout the camp, the night being now well advanced, and the men seeming to be in their deepest sleep, Alexander, the son of Amyntas, king and leader of the Macedonians, rode up on horseback to the Athenian outposts, and desired to speak with the generals. Hereupon, while the greater part continued on guard, some of the watch ran to the chiefs, and told them a horseman had come from the Median camp who would not say a word, except that he wished to speak with the generals, of whom he mentioned the names.

45. They at once, hearing this, made haste to the outpost, where they found Alexander, who addressed them as follows, "Men of Athens, that which I am about to say I trust to your honour; and I charge you to keep it secret from all excepting Pausanias, if you would not bring me to destruction. Had I not greatly at heart the common welfare of Greece, I should not have come to tell you; but I am myself a Greek by descent, and I would not willingly see Greece exchange freedom for slavery.

Know then that Mardonius and his army cannot obtain favour-able omens; had it not been for this, they would have fought with you long ago. Now, however, they have determined to let the victims pass unheeded; and, as soon as day dawns, to engage in battle. Mardonius, I imagine, is afraid that, if he delays, you will increase in number. Make ready then to receive him. Should he however still defer the combat, do you abide where you are; for his provisions will not hold out many more days. If you prosper in this war, forget not to do something for my freedom; consider the risk I have run, out of zeal for the Greek cause, to acquaint you with what Mardonius intends, and to save you from being surprised by the barbarians. I am Alexan-der of Macedon." As soon as he had said this, Alexander rode back to the camp, and returned to the station assigned him.

46. Meanwhile the Athenian generals hastened to the right wing, and told Pausanias all that they had learnt from Alexan-der. Hereupon Pausanias, who no sooner heard the intention of the Persians than he was struck with fear, addressed the gen-erals, and said, "Since the battle is to come with tomorrow's dawn, it were well that you Athenians should stand opposed to the Persians, and we Spartans to the Boeotians and the other Greeks; for you know the Medes and their manner of fight, since you have already fought with them once at Marathon, but we are quite ignorant and without any experience of their war-fare. While, however, there is not a Spartan here present who has ever fought against a Mede, of the Boeotians and Thes-salians we have had experience. Take then your arms, and march over to our post upon the right, while we supply your place in the left wing."

47. Both sides agreeing hereto, at the dawn of day the Spartans and Athenians changed places. But the movement was perceived by the Boeotians, and they gave notice of it to Mar-donius; who at once, on hearing what had been done, made a change in the disposition of his own forces, and brought the Persians to face the Lacedaemonians. Then Pausanias, finding that his design was discovered, led back his Spartans to the

right wing; and Mardonius, seeing this, replaced his Persians upon the left of his army.

48. When the troops again occupied their former posts, Mardonius sent a herald to the Spartans, who spoke as follows, "Lacedaemonians, in these parts the men say that you are the bravest of mankind, and admire you because you never turn your backs in flight or quit your ranks, but always stand firm, and either die at your posts or else destroy your adversaries. But in all this which they say concerning you there is not one word of truth; for now have we seen you, before battle was joined or our two hosts had come to blows, flying and leaving your posts, wishing the Athenians to make the first trial of our arms, and taking your own station against our slaves. Surely these are not the deeds of brave men. Much do we find ourselves deceived in you; for we believed the reports of you that reached our ears, and expected that you would send a herald with a challenge to us, proposing to fight by yourselves against our division of native Persians. We for our part were ready to have agreed to this; but you have made us no such offer—nay, you seem rather to shrink from meeting us. However, as no challenge of this kind comes from you to us, we send a challenge to you. Why should not you on the part of the Greeks, as you are thought to be the bravest of all, and we on the part of the barbarians, fight a battle with equal numbers on both sides? Then, if it seems good to the others to fight likewise, let them engage afterwards, but if not, if they are content that we should fight on behalf of all, let us so do and whichever side wins the battle, let them win it for their whole army."

49. When the herald had thus spoken, he waited a while, but as no one made him any answer, he went back, and told Mardonius what had happened. Mardonius was full of joy thereat, and so puffed up by the empty victory, that he at once gave orders to his horse to charge the Greek line. Then the horsemen drew near, and with their javelins and their arrows—for though horsemen they used the bow—sorely distressed the Greek troops, which could not bring them to close combat. The foun-

tain of Gargaphia, whence the whole Greek army drew its water, they at this time choked up and spoiled. The Lacedaemonians were the only troops who had their station near this fountain; the other Greeks were more or less distant from it, according to their place in the line; they however were not far from the Asopus. Still, as the Persian horse with their missile weapons did not allow them to approach, and so they could not get their water from the river, these Greeks, no less than the Lacedaemonians, resorted at this time to the fountain.

50. When the fountain was choked, the Grecian captains, seeing that the army had no longer a watering-place, and observing moreover that the cavalry greatly harassed them, held a meeting on these and other matters at the head-quarters of Pausanias upon the right. For besides the above-named difficulties, which were great enough, other circumstances added to their distress. All the provisions that they had brought with them were gone; and the attendants who had been sent to fetch supplies from the Peloponnese, were prevented from returning to camp by the Persian horse, which had now closed the passage.

51. The captains therefore held a council, whereat it was agreed, that if the Persians did not give battle that day, the Greeks should move to the Island—a tract of ground which lies in front of Plataea, at the distance of a mile from the Asopus and fount Gargaphia, where the army was encamped at that time. This tract was a sort of island in the continent: for there is a river which, dividing near its source, runs down from Mount Cithaeron into the plain below in two streams, flowing in channels about 600 yards apart, which after a while unite and become one. The name of this river is Oeroe, and the dwellers in those parts call it, the daughter of the Asopus. This was the place to which the Greeks resolved to remove; and they chose it, first because they would there have no lack of water, and secondly, because the horse could not harass them as when it was drawn up right in their front. They thought it best to begin their march at the second watch of the night, lest the Persians should see them as they left their station, and should follow and harass them with their cavalry. It was agreed likewise, that

after they had reached the place, which the Asopus-born Oeroe
surrounds, as it flows down from Cithaeron, they should dispatch, the very same night, one-half of their army towards that
mountain-range, to relieve those whom they had sent to procure
provisions, and who were now blocked up in that region.

52. Having made these resolves, they continued during that
whole day to suffer beyond measure from the attacks of the
enemy's horse. At length when towards dusk the attacks of the
horse ceased, and night having closed in, the hour arrived at
which the army was to commence its retreat, the greater number
struck their tents and began the march towards the rear. They
were not minded, however, to make for the place agreed upon;
but in their anxiety to escape from the Persian horse, no sooner
had they begun to move than they fled straight to Plataea;
where they took post at the temple of Hera, which lies outside
the city, at the distance of about three miles from Gargaphia,
and here they pitched their camp in front of the sacred building.

53. As soon as Pausanias saw a portion of the troops in motion, he issued orders to the Lacedaemonians to strike their
tents and follow those who had been the first to depart, supposing that they were on their march to the place agreed upon. All
the captains but one were ready to obey his orders: Amompharetus, however, the son of Poliadas, who was leader of the Pitanate
cohort, refused to move, saying he for one would not fly from
the strangers, or of his own will bring disgrace upon Sparta. It
had happened that he was absent from the former conference of
the captains, and so what was now taking place astonished him.
Pausanias and Euryanax thought it a monstrous thing that
Amompharetus would not hearken to them; but considered that
it would be yet more monstrous, if, when he was so minded, they
were to leave the Pitanates to their fate; seeing that if they forsook them to keep their agreement with the other Greeks,
Amompharetus and those with him, might perish. On this account, therefore, they kept the Lacedaemonian force in its place,
and made every endeavour to persuade Amompharetus that he
was wrong to act as he was doing.

54. While the Spartans were engaged in these efforts to turn

Amompharetus, the only man unwilling to retreat either in their own army or in that of the Tegeans, the Athenians on their side did as follows. Knowing that it was the Spartan temper to say one thing and do another, they remained quiet in their station until the army began to retreat, when they dispatched a horseman to see whether the Spartans really meant to set forth, or whether after all they had no intention of moving. The horseman was also to ask Pausanias, what he wished the Athenians to do.

55. The herald on his arrival found the Lacedaemonians drawn up in their old position, and their leaders quarrelling with one another. Pausanias and Euryanax had gone on urging Amompharetus not to endanger the lives of his men by staying behind while the others drew off, but without succeeding in persuading him; until at last the dispute had waxed hot between them just at the moment when the Athenian herald arrived. At this point Amompharetus, who was still disputing, took up with both his hands a vast rock, and placed it at the feet of Pausanias, saying, "With this pebble I give my vote not to run away from the strangers." (By strangers he meant barbarians.) Pausanias, in reply, called him a fool and a madman, and turning to the Athenian herald, who had made the inquiries with which he was charged, bade him tell his countrymen how he was occupied, and ask them to approach nearer, and retreat or not according to the movements of the Spartans.

56. So the herald went back to the Athenians; and the Spartans continued to dispute till morning began to dawn upon them. Then Pausanias, who as yet had not moved, gave the signal for retreat, expecting (and rightly, as the event proved) that Amompharetus, when he saw the rest of the Lacedaemonians in motion, would be unwilling to be left behind. No sooner was the signal given, than all the army except the Pitanates began their march, and retreated along the line of the hills; the Tegeans accompanying them. The Athenians likewise set off in good order, but proceeded by a different way from the Lacedaemonians. For while the latter clung to the hilly ground and the skirts of Mount Cithaeron, on account of the fear which they

entertained of the enemy's horse, the former betook themselves to the low country and marched through the plain.

57. As for Amompharetus, at first he did not believe that Pausanias would really dare to leave him behind; he therefore remained firm in his resolve to keep his men at their post; when, however, Pausanias and his troops were now some way off, Amompharetus, thinking himself forsaken in good earnest, ordered his band to take their arms, and led them at a walk towards the main army. Now the army was waiting for them at a distance of about a mile, having halted upon the river Moloeis at a place called Argiopius, where stands a temple dedicated to Eleusinian Demeter. They had stopped here, that, in case Amompharetus and his band should refuse to quit the spot where they were drawn up, and should really not stir from it, they might have it in their power to move back and lend them assistance. Amompharetus, however, and his companions rejoined the main body; and at the same time the whole mass of the barbarian cavalry arrived and began to press hard upon them. The horsemen had followed their usual practice and ridden up to the Greek camp, when they discovered that the place, where the Greeks had been posted hitherto, was deserted. Hereupon they pushed forward without stopping, and as soon as they overtook the enemy, pressed heavily on them.

58. Mardonius, when he heard that the Greeks had retired under cover of the night, and beheld the place, where they had been stationed, empty, called to him Thorax of Larissa, and his brethren, Eurypylus and Thrasideius, and said, "O sons of Aleuas, what will you say now, when you see yonder place empty? Why, you who dwell in their neighbourhood, told me the Lacedaemonians never fled from battle, but were brave beyond all the rest of mankind. Lately, however, you yourselves beheld them change their place in the line; and here, as all may see, they have run away during the night. Verily, when their turn came to fight with those, who are of a truth the bravest warriors in all the world, they showed plainly enough, that they are men of no worth, who have distinguished themselves among

Greeks—men likewise of no worth at all. However I can readily excuse you, who, knowing nothing of the Persians, praised these men from your acquaintance with certain exploits of theirs; but I marvel all the more at Artabazus, that he should have been afraid of the Lacedaemonians, and have therefore given us so dastardly a counsel, bidding us, as he did, break up our camp, and remove to Thebes, and there allow ourselves to be besieged by the Greeks, advice whereof I shall take care to inform the king. But of this hereafter. Now we must not allow them to escape us, but must pursue after them till we overtake them; and then we must exact vengeance for all the wrongs, which have been suffered at their hands by the Persians."

59. When he had so spoken, he crossed the Asopus, and led the Persians forward at a run directly upon the track of the Greeks, whom he believed to be in actual flight. He could not see the Athenians; for as they had taken the way of the plain, they were hidden from his sight by the hills; he therefore led on his troops against the Lacedaemonians and the Tegeans only. When the commanders of the other divisions of the barbarians saw the Persians pursuing the Greeks so hastily, they all forthwith seized their standards, and hurried after at their best speed, in great disorder and disarray. On they went with loud shouts and in a wild rout, thinking to swallow up the runaways.

60. Meanwhile Pausanias had sent a horseman to the Athenians, at the time when the cavalry first fell upon him, with this message, "Men of Athens, now that the great struggle has come, which is to decide the freedom or the slavery of Greece, we two, Lacedaemonians and Athenians, are deserted by all the other allies, who have fled away from us during the past night. Nevertheless, we are resolved what to do—we must endeavour, as best we may, to defend ourselves and to aid one another. Now, had the horse fallen upon you first, we ourselves with the Tegeans (who remain faithful to the Greek cause) would have been bound to render you assistance against them. As however the entire body has advanced upon us, it is your place to come to our aid, sore pressed as we are by the enemy. Should you yourselves be so straitened that you cannot come, at least

send us your archers, and be sure you will earn our gratitude. We acknowledge that throughout this whole war there has been no zeal to be compared to yours—we therefore doubt not that you will do us this service."

61. The Athenians, as soon as they received this message, were anxious to go to the aid of the Spartans, and to help them to the uttermost of their power; but, as they were upon the march, the Greeks on the king's side, whose place in the line had been opposite theirs, fell upon them, and so harassed them by their attacks that it was not possible for them to give the succour they desired. Accordingly the Lacedaemonians, and the Tegeans—whom nothing could induce to quit their side—were left alone to resist the Persians. Including the light-armed, the number of the former was 50,000; while that of the Tegeans was 3,000. Now, therefore, as they were about to engage with Mardonius and the troops under him, they made ready to offer sacrifice. The victims, however, for some time were not favourable; and during the delay, many fell on the Spartan side, and a still greater number were wounded. For the Persians had made a rampart of their wicker shields, and shot from behind them such clouds of arrows, that the Spartans were sorely distressed. The victims continued unpropitious; till at last Pausanias raised his eyes to the Heraeum of the Plataeans, and calling the goddess to his aid, besought her not to disappoint the hopes of the Greeks.

62. As he offered his prayer, the Tegeans, advancing before the rest, rushed forward against the enemy; and the Lacedaemonians, who had obtained favourable omens the moment that Pausanias prayed, at length, after their long delay, advanced to the attack; while the Persians, on their side, left shooting, and prepared to meet them. And first the combat was at the wicker shields. Afterwards, when these were swept down, a fierce contest took place by the side of the temple of Demeter, which lasted long, and ended in a hand-to-hand struggle. The barbarians many times seized hold of the Greek spears and broke them; for in boldness and warlike spirit the Persians were not a whit inferior to the Greeks; but they were without bucklers, un-

trained, and far below the enemy in respect of skill in arms.
Sometimes singly, sometimes in bodies of ten, now fewer and
now more in number, they dashed forward upon the Spartan
ranks, and so perished.

63. The fight went most against the Greeks, where Mardonius, mounted upon a white horse, and surrounded by the
bravest of all the Persians, the 1,000 picked men, fought in person. So long as Mardonius was alive, this body resisted all attacks, and, while they defended their own lives, struck down no
small number of Spartans; but after Mardonius fell, and the
troops with him, which were the main strength of the army,
perished, the remainder yielded to the Lacedaemonians, and
took to flight. Their light clothing, and want of bucklers, were
of the greatest hurt to them: for they had to contend against
men heavily armed, while they themselves were without any
such defence.

64. Then was the warning of the oracle fulfilled, and the vengeance which was due to the Spartans for the slaughter of Leonidas was paid them by Mardonius—then too did Pausanias, the
son of Cleombrotus, and grandson of Anaxandridas (I omit to
recount his other ancestors, since they are the same with those
of Leonidas), win a victory exceeding in glory all those to which
our knowledge extends. Mardonius was slain by Aeimnestus, a
man famous in Sparta—the same who in the Messenian war,
which came after the struggle against the Medes, fought a battle
near Stenyclerus with but 300 men against the whole force of
the Messenians, and himself perished, and the 300 with him.

65. The Persians, as soon as they were put to flight by the
Lacedaemonians, ran hastily away, without preserving any order, and took refuge in their own camp, within the wooden defence which they had raised in the Theban territory. It is a
marvel to me how it came to pass, that although the battle was
fought quite close to the grove of Demeter, yet not a single Persian appears to have died on the sacred soil, or even to have set
foot upon it, while round about the precinct, in the unconse-
crated ground, great numbers perished. I imagine—if it is lawful, in matters which concern the gods, to imagine anything—

that the goddess herself kept them out, because they had burnt her dwelling at Eleusis. Such, then, was the issue of this battle.

66. Artabazus, the son of Pharnaces, who had disapproved from the first of the king's leaving Mardonius behind him, and had made great endeavours, but all in vain, to dissuade Mardonius from risking a battle, when he found that the latter was bent on acting otherwise than he wished, did as follows. He had a force under his orders which was far from inconsiderable, amounting, as it did, to nearly 40,000 men. Being well aware, therefore, how the battle was likely to go, as soon as the two armies began to fight, he led his soldiers forward in an orderly array, bidding them one and all proceed at the same pace, and follow him with such celerity as they should observe him to use. Having issued these commands, he pretended to lead them to the battle. But when, advancing before his army, he saw that the Persians were already in flight, instead of keeping the same order, he wheeled his troops suddenly round, and beat a retreat; nor did he even seek shelter within the palisade or behind the walls of Thebes, but hurried on into Phocis, wishing to make his way to the Hellespont with all possible speed. Such accordingly was the course which these Persians took.

67. As for the Greeks upon the king's side, while most of them played the coward purposely, the Boeotians, on the contrary, had a long struggle with the Athenians. Those of the Thebans who were attached to the Medes, displayed especially no little zeal; far from playing the coward, they fought with such fury that 300 of the best and bravest among them were slain by the Athenians in this passage of arms. But at last they too were routed, and fled away—not, however, in the same direction as the Persians and the crowd of allies, who, having taken no part in the battle, ran off without striking a blow—but to the city of Thebes.

68. To me it shows very clearly how completely the rest of the barbarians were dependent upon the Persian troops, that here they all fled at once, without ever coming to blows with the enemy, merely because they saw the Persians running away. And so it came to pass that the whole army took to flight, ex-

cept only the horse, both Persian and Boeotian. These did good service to the flying foot-men, by advancing close to the enemy, and separating between the Greeks and their own fugitives.

69. The victors however pressed on, pursuing and slaying the remnant of the king's army. Meantime, while the flight continued, tidings reached the Greeks who were drawn up round the Heraeum, and so were absent from the battle, that the fight was begun, and that Pausanias was gaining the victory. Hearing this, they rushed forward without any order, the Corinthians taking the upper road across the skirts of Cithaeron and the hills, which led straight to the temple of Demeter; while the Megarians and Phliasians followed the level route through the plain. These last had almost reached the enemy, when the Theban horse espied them, and observing their disarray, dispatched against them the squadron of which Asopodorus, the son of Timander, was captain. Asopodorus charged them with such effect that he left 600 of their number dead upon the plain, and, pursuing the rest, compelled them to seek shelter in Cithaeron. So these men perished without honour.

70. The Persians, and the multitude with them, who fled to the wooden fortress, were able to ascend into the towers before the Lacedaemonians came up. Thus placed, they proceeded to strengthen the defences as well as they could; and when the Lacedaemonians arrived, a sharp fight took place at the rampart. So long as the Athenians were away, the barbarians kept off their assailants, and had much the best of the combat, since the Lacedaemonians were unskilled in the attack of walled places: but on the arrival of the Athenians, a more violent assault was made, and the wall was for a long time attacked with fury. In the end the valour of the Athenians and their perseverance prevailed—they gained the top of the wall, and, breaking a breach through it, enabled the Greeks to pour in. The first to enter here were the Tegeans, and they it was who plundered the tent of Mardonius; where among other booty they found the manger from which his horses ate, all made of solid brass, and well worth looking at. This manger was given by the Tegeans to the temple of Athena Alea, while the remainder of

their booty was brought into the common stock of the Greeks. As soon as the wall was broken down, the barbarians no longer kept together in any array, nor was there one among them who thought of making further resistance—in good truth they were all half dead with fright, huddled as so many thousands were into so narrow and confined a space. With such tameness did they submit to be slaughtered by the Greeks, that of the 300,000 men who composed the army—omitting the 40,000 by whom Artabazus was accompanied in his flight—no more than 3,000 outlived the battle.[4] Of the Lacedaemonians from Sparta there perished in this combat ninety-one; of the Tegeans sixteen; of the Athenians, fifty-two.[5]

71. On the side of the barbarians, the greatest courage was manifested, among the foot-soldiers, by the Persians; among the horse, by the Sacae; while Mardonius himself, as a man, bore off the palm from the rest. Among the Greeks, the Athenians and the Tegeans fought well; but the prowess shown by the Lacedaemonians was beyond either. Of this I have but one proof to offer, since all the three nations overthrew the force opposed to them, which is, that the Lacedaemonians fought and conquered the best troops. The bravest man by far on that day was, in my judgment, Aristodemus—the same who alone escaped from the slaughter of the 300 at Thermopylae, and who on that account had endured disgrace and reproach: next to him were Posidonius, Philocyon, and Amompharetus the Spartan. The Spartans, however, who took part in the fight, when the question of who had distinguished himself most, came to be talked over among them, decided that Aristodemus, who, on account of the blame which attached to him, had manifestly courted death, and had therefore left his place in the line and behaved like a madman, had done of a truth very notable deeds; but that Posidonius, who, with no such desire to lose his life, had quitted himself no less gallantly, was by so much a braver man than he.

---

[4] It cannot be doubted that there was an enormous carnage, though this statement exceeds the truth in the number of dead as in the number of the Persian army.

[5] Plutarch states that the whole number of Greeks slain was 1,360.

Perchance, however, it was envy that made them speak after this sort. Of those whom I have named above as slain in this battle, all, save and except Aristodemus, received public honours: Aristodemus alone had no honours, because he courted death for the reason which I have mentioned.

72. These then were the most distinguished of those who fought at Plataea. As for Callicrates, the most beautiful man, not among the Spartans only, but in the whole Greek camp, he was not killed in the battle; for it was while Pausanias was still consulting the victims, that as he sat in his proper place in the line, an arrow struck him on the side. While his comrades advanced to the fight, he was borne out of the ranks, very loath to die, as he showed by the words which he addressed to Arimnestus, one of the Plataeans, "I grieve," said he, "not because I have to die for my country, but because I have not lifted my arm against the enemy, or done any deed worthy of me, much as I have desired to achieve something."

73. The Athenian who is said to have distinguished himself the most was Sophanes, the son of Eutychides, of the Decelean deme. The men of this deme, once upon a time, did a deed, which (as the Athenians themselves confess) has ever since been serviceable to them. When the Tyndaridae, in days of yore, invaded Attica with a mighty army to recover Helen, and not being able to find out whither she had been carried, desolated the demes, at this time, they say, the Deceleans (or Decelus himself, according to some), displeased at the rudeness of Theseus, and fearing that the whole territory would suffer, discovered everything to the enemy, and even showed them the way to Aphidnae; which Titacus, a native of the place, betrayed into their hands. As a reward for this action, Sparta has always, from that time to the present, allowed the Deceleans to be free from all dues, and to have seats of honour at their festivals; and hence too, in the war which took place many years after these events between the Peloponnesians and the Athenians, the Lacedaemonians, while they laid waste all the rest of Attica, spared the lands of the Deceleans.[6]

---

[6] The reference is probably to a sparing of Decelea in the first year of the war.

74. Of this canton was Sophanes, the Athenian who most distinguished himself in the battle. Two stories are told concerning
him: according to the one, he wore an iron anchor fastened to
the belt which secured his breastplate, by a brazen chain; and
this, when he came near the enemy, he threw out; to the intent
that, when they made their charge, it might be impossible for
him to be driven from his post: as soon, however, as the enemy
fled, his wont was to take up his anchor and join the pursuit.
Such, then, is one of the said stories. The other, which is con-
tradictory to the first, relates, that Sophanes, instead of having
an iron anchor fastened to his breastplate, bore the device of an
anchor upon his shield, which he never allowed to rest, but
made to run round continually.

75. Another glorious deed was likewise performed by this
same Sophanes. At the time when the Athenians were laying
siege to Aegina, he took up the challenge of Eurybates the Argive, a winner of the Pentathlon, and slew him. The fate of
Sophanes in after times was the following: he was leader of an
Athenian army in conjunction with Leagrus, the son of Glaucon,
and in a battle with the Edonians near Datum, about the gold-
mines there, he was slain, after displaying uncommon bravery.

76. As soon as the Greeks at Plataea had overthrown the barbarians, a woman came over to them from the enemy. She was
one of the concubines of Pharandates, the son of Teaspes, a Persian; and when she heard that the Persians were all slain and
that the Greeks had carried the day, forthwith she adorned herself and her maids with many golden ornaments, and with the
bravest of the apparel that she had brought with her, and,
alighting from her litter, came forward to the Lacedaemonians,
ere the work of slaughter was well over. When she saw that all
the orders were given by Pausanias, with whose name and country she was well acquainted, as she had oftentimes heard tell of
them, she knew who he must be: wherefore she embraced his
knees, and said:

"O King of Sparta, save me, a suppliant, from the slavery that
awaits the captive. Already I am indebted to you for one service
—the slaughter of these men, wretches who had no regard either
for gods or spirits. I am by birth a Coan, the daughter of Hege-

toridas, son of Antagoras. The Persian seized me by force in Cos, and kept me against my will."

"Lady," answered Pausanias, "fear nothing: as a suppliant you are safe—and still more, if you have spoken truth, and Hegetoridas of Cos is your father—for he is bound to me by closer ties of friendship than any other man in those regions."

When he had thus spoken, Pausanias placed the woman in the charge of some of the Ephors who were present, and afterwards sent her to Aegina, where she wished to go.

77. About the time of this woman's coming, the Mantineans arrived upon the field, and found that all was over, and that it was too late to take any part in the battle. Greatly distressed hereat, they declared themselves to deserve a fine, as laggards; after which, learning that a portion of the Medes had fled away under Artabazus, they were anxious to go after them as far as Thessaly. The Lacedaemonians however would not suffer the pursuit; so they returned again to their own land, and sent the leaders of their army into banishment. Soon after the Mantineans, the Eleans likewise arrived, and showed the same sorrow; after which they too returned home, and banished their leaders. But enough concerning these nations.

78. There was a man at Plataea among the troops of the Aeginetans, whose name was Lampon; he was the son of Pytheas, and a person of the first rank among his countrymen. Now this Lampon went about this same time to Pausanias, and counselled him to do a deed of exceeding wickedness. "Son of Cleombrotus," he said very earnestly, "what you have already done is passing great and glorious. By the favour of heaven you have saved Greece, and gained a renown beyond all the Greeks of whom we have any knowledge. Now then so finish your work, that your own fame may be increased thereby, and that henceforth barbarians may fear to commit outrages on the Grecians. When Leonidas was slain at Thermopylae, Xerxes and Mardonius commanded that he should be beheaded and crucified. You do the like at this time to Mardonius, and you will have glory in Sparta, and likewise through the whole of Greece. For by hanging him upon a cross, you will avenge Leonidas, who was your father's brother."

79. Thus spoke Lampon, thinking to please Pausanias; but Pausanias answered him, "My Aeginetan friend, for your foresight and your friendliness I am much beholden to you: but the counsel which you have offered is not good. First you lifted me up to the skies, by your praise of my country and my achievement; and then you cast me down to the ground, by bidding me maltreat the dead, and saying that thus I shall raise myself in men's esteem. Such doings befit barbarians rather than Greeks; and even in barbarians we detest them. On such terms then I could not wish to please the Aeginetans, or those who think as they think—enough for me to gain the approval of my own countrymen, by righteous deeds as well as by righteous words. Leonidas, whom you would have me avenge, is, I maintain, abundantly avenged already. Surely the countless lives here taken are enough to avenge not him only, but all those who fell at Thermopylae. Come not before me again with such a speech, or with such counsel; and thank my forbearance that you are not now punished." Then Lampon, having received this answer, departed, and went his way.

80. After this Pausanias caused proclamation to be made, that no one should lay hands on the booty, but that the Helots should collect it and bring it all to one place. So the Helots went and spread themselves through the camp, wherein were found many tents richly adorned with furniture of gold and silver, many couches covered with plates of the same, and many golden bowls, goblets, and other drinking-vessels. On the carriages were bags containing silver and golden kettles; and the bodies of the slain furnished bracelets and chains, and scimitars with golden ornaments—not to mention embroidered apparel, of which no one made any account. The Helots at this time stole many things of much value, which they sold in after times to the Aeginetans; however they brought in likewise no small quantity, chiefly such things as it was not possible for them to hide. And this was the beginning of the great wealth of the Aeginetans, who bought the gold of the Helots as if it had been mere brass.

81. When all the booty had been brought together, a tenth of the whole was set apart for the Delphian god; and hence was

made the golden tripod, which stands on the bronze serpent with the three heads, quite close to the altar. Portions were also set apart for the gods of Olympia, and of the Isthmus; from which were made, in the one case, a bronze Zeus fifteen feet high; and in the other, a bronze Poseidon of ten feet. After this, the rest of the spoil was divided among the soldiers, each of whom received less or more according to his deserts; and in this way was a distribution made of the Persian concubines, of the gold, the silver, the beasts of burden, and all the other valuables. What special gifts were presented to those who had most distinguished themselves in the battle, I do not find mentioned by any one; but I should suppose that they must have had some gifts beyond the others. As for Pausanias, the portion which was set apart for him consisted of ten specimens of each kind of thing—women, horses, talents, camels, or whatever else there was in the spoil.

82. It is said that the following circumstance happened like-wise at this time. Xerxes, when he fled away out of Greece, left his war-tent with Mardonius: when Pausanias, therefore, saw the tent with its adornments of gold and silver, and its hangings of divers colours, he gave commandment to the bakers and the cooks to make him ready a banquet in such fashion as was their wont for Mardonius. Then they made ready as they were bidden, and Pausanias, beholding the couches of gold and silver daintily decked out with their rich covertures, and the tables of gold and silver laid, and the feast itself prepared with all magnificence, was astonished at the good things which were set before him, and, being in a pleasant mood, gave commandment to his own followers to make ready a Spartan supper. When the suppers were both served, and it was apparent how vast a difference lay between the two, Pausanias laughed, and sent his servants to call to him the Greek generals. On their coming, he pointed to the two boards, and said, "I sent for you, O Greeks, to show you the folly of this Median captain, who, when he enjoyed such fare as this, must needs come here to rob us of our penury." Such, it is said, were the words of Pausanias to the Grecian generals.

83. During many years afterwards, the Plataeans used often to find upon the field of battle concealed treasures of gold, and silver, and other valuables. More recently they likewise made discovery of the following: the flesh having all fallen away from the bodies of the dead, and their bones having been gathered together into one place, the Plataeans found a skull without any seam, made entirely of a single bone; likewise a jaw, both the upper bone and the under, wherein all the teeth, front and back, were joined together and made of one bone; also, the skeleton of a man not less than eight feet in height.

84. The body of Mardonius disappeared the day after the battle; but who it was that stole it away I cannot say with certainty. I have heard tell of a number of persons, and those too of many different nations, who are said to have given him burial; and I know that many have received large sums on this score from Artontes the son of Mardonius: but I cannot discover with any certainty which of them it was who really took the body away and buried it. Among others, Dionysophanes, an Ephesian, is rumoured to have been the actual person.

85. The Greeks, after sharing the booty upon the field of Plataea, proceeded to bury their own dead, each nation apart from the rest. The Lacedaemonians made three graves; in one they buried their youths, among whom were Posidonius, Amompharetus, Philocyon, and Callicrates; in another, the rest of the Spartans; and in the third, the Helots. Such was their mode of burial. The Tegeans buried all their dead in a single grave; as likewise did the Athenians theirs, and the Megarians and Phliasians those who were slain by the horse. These graves, then, had bodies buried in them: as for the other tombs which are to be seen at Plataea, they were raised, as I understand, by the Greeks whose troops took no part in the battle; and who, being ashamed of themselves, erected empty barrows upon the field, to obtain credit with those who should come after them. Among others, the Aeginetans have a grave there, which goes by their name; but which, as I learn, was made ten years later by Cleades, the son of Autodicus, a Plataean, at the request of the Aeginetans, whose agent he was.

86. After the Greeks had buried their dead at Plataea, they presently held a council, whereat it was resolved to make war upon Thebes, and to require that those who had joined the Medes should be delivered into their hands. Two men, who had been the chief leaders on the occasion, were especially named, Timagenidas and Attaginus. If the Thebans should refuse to give these men up, it was determined to lay siege to their city, and never stir from before it till it should surrender. After this resolve, the army marched upon Thebes; and having demanded the men, and been refused, began the siege, laying waste the country all around, and making assaults upon the wall in divers places.

87. When twenty days were gone by, and the violence of the Greeks did not slacken, Timagenidas thus addressed his countrymen, "Men of Thebes, since the Greeks have so decreed, that they will never desist from the siege till either they take Thebes or we are delivered to them, we would not that the land of Boeotia should suffer any longer on our behalf. If it be money that they in truth desire, and their demand of us be no more than a pretext, let money from the treasury of the state be given them; for the state, and not we alone, embraced the cause of the Medes. If, however, they really want our persons, and on that account press this siege, we are ready to be delivered to them and to stand our trial."

The Thebans thought this offer very right and seasonable; wherefore they dispatched a herald without any delay to Pausanias, and told him they were willing to deliver up the men.

88. As soon as an agreement had been concluded upon these terms, Attaginus made his escape from the city; his sons, however, were surrendered in his place; but Pausanias refused to hold them guilty, since children (he said) could have had no part in such an offence. The rest of those whom the Thebans gave up had expected to obtain a trial, and in that case their trust was to escape by means of bribery; but Pausanias, afraid of this, dismissed at once the whole army of allies, and took the men with him to Corinth, where he slew them all. Such were the events which happened at Plataea and at Thebes.

89. Artabazus, the son of Pharnaces, who fled away from Plataea, was soon far sped on his journey. When he reached Thessaly, the inhabitants received him hospitably, and made inquiries of him concerning the rest of the army, since they were still altogether ignorant of what had taken place at Plataea: whereupon the Persian, knowing well that if he told them the truth, he would run great risk of perishing himself, together with his whole army—for if the facts were once blazoned abroad, all who learned them would be sure to fall upon him—the Persian, I say, considering this, as he had before kept all secret from the Phocians, so now answered the Thessalians in the following fashion, "I myself, Thessalians, am hastening, as you see, into Thrace; and I must use all possible dispatch, as I am sent with this force on special business from the main army. Mardonius and his host are close behind me, and may be looked for shortly. When he comes, receive him as you have received me, and show him every kindness. Be sure you will never hereafter regret it, if you so do."

With these words he took his departure, and marched his troops at their best speed through Thessaly and Macedon straight upon Thrace, following the inland route which was the shortest, and, in good truth, using all possible dispatch. He himself succeeded in reaching Byzantium; but a great part of his army perished upon the road—many being cut to pieces by the Thracians, and others dying from hunger and excess of toil. From Byzantium Artabazus set sail, and crossed the strait; returning into Asia in the manner which has been here described.

90. On the same day that the blow was struck at Plataea, another defeat befell the Persians at Mycale in Ionia. While the Greek fleet under Leotychides the Lacedaemonian was still lying inactive at Delos, there arrived at that place an embassy from Samos, consisting of three men, Lampon the son of Thrasycles, Athenagoras the son of Archestratidas, and Hegesistratus the son of Aristagoras. The Samians had sent them secretly, concealing their departure both from the Persians and from their own tyrant Theomestor, the son of Androdamas, whom the Persians had made ruler of Samos. When the ambassadors came be-

fore the Greek captains, Hegesistratus spoke, and urged them with many and various arguments, saying that the Ionians only needed to see them arrive in order to revolt from the Persians; and that the Persians would never abide their coming; or if they did, it would be to offer them the finest booty that they could anywhere expect to gain; while at the same time he made appeal to the gods of their common worship, and besought them to deliver from bondage a Grecian race, and withal to drive back the barbarians. "This," he said, "might very easily be done, for the Persian ships were bad sailers, and far from a match for theirs"; adding, moreover, "that if there was any suspicion lest the Samians intended to deal treacherously, they were themselves ready to become hostages, and to return on board the ships of their allies to Asia."

91. When the Samian stranger continued importunately beseeching him, Leotychides, either because he wanted an omen, or by a mere chance, as God guided him, asked the man, "Samian stranger, what is your name?" "Hegesistratus (army-leader)," answered the other, and might have said more, but Leotychides stopped him by exclaiming, "I accept, O Samian, the omen which your name affords. Only, before you go back, swear to us, you and your brother envoys, that the Samians will indeed be our warm friends and allies."

92. No sooner had he thus spoken than he proceeded to hurry forward the business. The Samians pledged their faith upon the spot, and oaths of alliance were exchanged between them and the Greeks. This done, two of the ambassadors forthwith sailed away; as for Hegesistratus, Leotychides kept him to accompany his own fleet, for he considered his name to be a good omen. The Greeks abode where they were that day, and on the morrow sacrificed, and found the victims favourable. Their soothsayer was Deiphonus, the son of Evenius, a man of Apollonia—I mean the Apollonia which lies upon the Ionian Gulf.

93. A strange thing happened to this man's father, Evenius. The Apolloniats have a flock of sheep sacred to the sun. During the daytime these sheep graze along the banks of the river, which flows from Mount Lacmon through their territory, and

empties itself into the sea by the port of Oricus; while at night they are guarded by the richest and noblest of the citizens, who are chosen to serve the office, and who keep the watch each for one year. Now the Apolloniats set great store by these sheep, on account of an oracle which they received concerning them. The place where they are folded at night is a cavern, a long way from the town. Here it happened that Evenius, when he was chosen to keep the watch, by some accident fell asleep upon his guard; and while he slept, the cave was entered by wolves, which destroyed some sixty of the flock under his care. Evenius, when he woke and found what had occurred, kept silence about it and told no one; for he thought to buy other sheep and put them in the place of the slain. But the matter came to the ears of the Apolloniats, who forthwith brought Evenius to trial, and condemned him to lose his eyes, because he had gone to sleep upon his post. Now when Evenius was blinded, straightway the sheep had no young, and the land ceased to bear its wonted harvests. Then the Apolloniats sent to Dodona, and to Delphi, and asked the prophets, what had caused the woes which so afflicted them. The answer which they received was this, "The woes were come for Evenius, the guardian of the sacred sheep, whom the Apolloniats had wrongfully deprived of sight. They (the gods) had themselves sent the wolves; nor would they ever cease to exact vengeance for Evenius, till the Apolloniats made him whatever atonement he liked to ask. When this was paid, they would like-wise give him a gift, which would make many men call him blessed."

94. Such was the tenor of the prophecies. The Apolloniats kept them close, but charged some of their citizens to go and make terms with Evenius; and these men managed the business for them in the way which I will now describe. They found Evenius sitting upon a bench, and, approaching him, they sat down by his side, and began to talk: at first they spoke of quite other matters, but in the end they mentioned his misfortune, and offered him their condolence. Having thus beguiled him, at last they put the question, "What atonement would he desire, if the Apolloniats were willing to make him satisfaction for the

wrongs which they had done to him?" Hereupon Evenius, who had not heard of the oracle, answered, "If I were given the lands of this man and that—" (here he named the two men whom he knew to have the finest farms in Apollonia), "and likewise the house of this other—" (and here he mentioned the house which he knew to be the handsomest in the town), "I would, when master of these, be quite content, and my wrath would cease altogether." As soon as Evenius had thus spoken, the men who sat by him rejoined, "Evenius, the Apolloniats give you the atonement which you desire, according to the bidding of the oracles." Then Evenius understood the whole matter, and was enraged that they had deceived him so; but the Apolloniats bought the farms from their owners, and gave Evenius what he had chosen. After this was done, straightway Evenius had the gift of prophecy, insomuch that he became a famous man in Greece.

95. Deiphonus, the son of this Evenius, had accompanied the Corinthians, and was soothsayer, as I said before, to the Greek armament. One account, however, which I have heard, declares, that he was not really the son of this man, but only took the name, and then went about Greece and let out his services for hire.

96. The Greeks, as soon as the victims were favourable, put to sea, and sailed across from Delos to Samos. Arriving off Calami, a place upon the Samian coast, they brought the fleet to an anchor near the temple of Hera which stands there, and prepared to engage the Persians by sea. These latter, however, no sooner heard of the approach of the Greeks, than, dismissing the Phoenician ships, they sailed away with the remainder to the main land. For it had been resolved in council not to risk a battle, since the Persian fleet was thought to be no match for that of the enemy. They fled, therefore, to the main, to be under the protection of their land army, which now lay at Mycale, and consisted of the troops left behind by Xerxes to keep guard over Ionia. This was an army of 60,000 men, under the command of Tigranes, a Persian of more than common beauty and stature. The captains resolved therefore to betake themselves to these

troops for defence, to drag their ships ashore, and to build a rampart around them, which might at once protect the fleet, and serve likewise as a place of refuge for themselves.

97. Having so resolved, the commanders put out to sea; and passing the temple of the August Goddesses, arrived at Gaesor and Scolopoeis, which are in the territory of Mycale. Here is a temple of Eleusinian Demeter, built by Philistus the son of Pasicles, who came to Asia with Nileus the son of Codrus, when he founded Miletus. At this place they drew the ships up on the beach, and surrounded them with a rampart made of stones and trunks of trees, cutting down for this purpose all the fruit-trees which grew near, and defending the barrier by means of stakes firmly planted in the ground. Here they were prepared either to win a battle or undergo a siege—their thoughts embracing both chances.

98. The Greeks, when they understood that the barbarians had fled to the main land, were sorely vexed at their escape: nor could they determine at first what they should do, whether they should return home, or proceed to the Hellespont. In the end, however, they resolved to do neither, but to sail for the continent. So they made themselves ready for a sea-fight by the preparation of boarding-bridges, and what else was necessary; provided with which they sailed to Mycale. Now when they came to the place where the camp was, they found no one ventured out to meet them, but observed the ships all dragged ashore within the barrier, and a strong land-force drawn up in battle array upon the beach; Leotychides therefore sailed along the shore in his ship, keeping as close hauled to the land as possible, and by the voice of a herald thus addressed the Ionians, "Men of Ionia, you who can hear me speak—take heed to what I say: for the Persians will not understand a word that I utter. When we join battle with them, before aught else, remember Freedom—and next, recollect our watchword, which is Hebe. If there be any who hear me not, let those who hear report my words to the others."

In all this Leotychides had the very same design which Themistocles entertained at Artemisium. Either the barbarians would not know what he had said, and the Ionians would be persuaded to revolt from them; or if his words were reported to the former, they would mistrust their Greek soldiers.

99. After Leotychides had made this address, the Greeks brought their ships to the land, and, having disembarked, arrayed themselves for the battle. When the Persians saw them marshalling their array, and thought of the advice which had been offered to the Ionians, their first act was to disarm the Samians, whom they suspected of complicity with the enemy. For it had happened lately that a number of the Athenians who lingered in Attica, having been made prisoners by the troops of Xerxes, were brought to Asia on board the barbarian fleet; and these men had been ransomed, one and all, by the Samians, who sent them back to Athens, well furnished with provisions for the way. On this account, as much as on any other, the Samians were suspected, as men who had paid the ransom of 500 of the king's enemies. After disarming them, the Persians next dispatched the Milesians to guard the paths which lead up into the heights of Mycale, because (they said) the Milesians were well acquainted with that region. Their true object, however, was to remove them to a distance from the camp. In this way the Persians sought to secure themselves against such of the Ionians as they thought likely, if occasion offered, to make rebellion. They then joined shield to shield, and so made themselves a breastwork against the enemy.

100. The Greeks now, having finished their preparations, began to move towards the barbarians; when as they advanced, a rumour flew through the host from one end to the other—that the Greeks had fought and conquered the army of Mardonius in Boeotia. At the same time a herald's wand was observed lying upon the beach. Many things prove to me that the gods take part in the affairs of man. How else, when the battles of Mycale and Plataea were about to happen on the self-same day, should such a rumour have reached the Greeks in that region, greatly cheering the whole army, and making them more eager than before to risk their lives?

101. A strange coincidence too it was, that both the battles

should have been fought near a precinct of Eleusinian Demeter. The fight at Plataea took place, as I said before, quite close to one of Demeter's temples; and now the battle at Mycale was to be fought hard by another. Rightly too did the rumour run, that the Greeks with Pausanias had gained their victory; for the fight at Plataea fell early in the day, whereas that at Mycale was towards evening. That the two battles were really fought on the same day of the same month became apparent when inquiries were made a short time afterwards. Before the rumour reached them, the Greeks were full of fear, not so much on their own account, as for their countrymen, and for Greece herself, lest she should be worsted in her struggle with Mardonius. But when the voice fell on them, their fear vanished, and they charged more vigorously and at a quicker pace. So the Greeks and the barbarians rushed with like eagerness to the fray; for the Hellespont and the islands formed the prize for which they were about to fight.

102. The Athenians, and the force drawn up with them, who formed one-half of the army, marched along the shore, where the country was low and level; but the way for the Lacedaemonians, and the troops with them, lay across hills and a torrent-course. Hence, while the Lacedaemonians were effecting their passage round, the Athenians on the other wing had already closed with the enemy. So long as the wicker bucklers of the Persians continued standing, they made a stout defence, and had not even the worst of the battle; but when the Athenians, and the allies with them, wishing to make the victory their own, and not share it with the Lacedaemonians, cheered each other on with shouts and attacked them with the utmost fierceness, then at last the face of things became changed. For, bursting through the line of shields, and rushing forwards in a body, the Greeks fell upon the Persians; who, though they bore the charge and for a long time maintained their ground, yet at length took refuge in their intrenchment. Here the Athenians themselves, together with those who followed them in the line of battle, the Corinthians, the Sicyonians, and the Troezenians, pressed so closely on the steps of their flying foes, that they entered along with them into

the fortress. And now, when even their fortress was taken, the barbarians no longer offered resistance, but fled hastily away, all save only the Persians. They still continued to fight in knots of a few men against the Greeks, who kept pouring into the in-trenchment. And here, while two of the Persian commanders fled, two fell upon the field: Artayntes and Ithamitres, who were leaders of the fleet, escaped; Mardontes, and the com-mander of the land force, Tigranes, died fighting.

103. The Persians still held out, when the Lacedaemonians, and their part of the army, reached the camp, and joined in the remainder of the battle. The number of Greeks who fell in the struggle here was not small; the Sicyonians especially lost many, and, among the rest, Perilaus their general.

The Samians, who served with the Medes, and who, although disarmed, still remained in the camp, seeing from the very be-ginning of the fight that the victory was doubtful, did all that lay in their power to render help to the Greeks. And the other Ionians likewise, beholding their example, revolted and attacked the Persians.

104. As for the Milesians, who had been ordered, for the bet-ter security of the Persians, to guard the mountain-paths, that, in case any accident befell them such as had now happened, they might not lack guides to conduct them into the high tracts of Mycale, and who had also been removed to hinder them from making an outbreak in the Persian camp; they, instead of obey-ing their orders, broke them in every respect. For they guided the flying Persians by wrong roads, which brought them into the presence of the enemy; and at last they set upon them with their own hands, and showed themselves the hottest of their adversaries. Ionia, therefore, on this day revolted a second time from the Persians.

105. In this battle the Greeks who behaved with the greatest bravery were the Athenians; and among them the palm was borne off by Hermolycus, the son of Euthynus, a man accom-plished in the pancratium.[7] This Hermolycus was afterwards

---

[7] The pancratium was a contest in which wrestling and boxing were united.

slain in the war between the Athenians and Carystians. He fell
in the fight near Cyrnus in the Carystian territory, and was
buried in the neighbourhood of Geraestus. After the Athenians,
the most distinguished on the Greek side were the Corinthians
the Troezenians, and the Sicyonians.

106. The Greeks, when they had slaughtered the greater portion of the barbarians, either in the battle or in the rout, set fire
to their ships and burnt them, together with the bulwark which
had been raised for their defence, first however removing therefrom all the booty, and carrying it down to the beach. Besides
other plunder, they found here many caskets of money. When
they had burnt the rampart and the vessels, the Greeks sailed
away to Samos, and there took counsel together concerning the
Ionians, whom they thought of removing out of Asia. Ionia they
proposed to abandon to the barbarians, and their doubt was, in
what part of their own possessions in Greece they should settle
its inhabitants. For it seemed to them a thing impossible that
they should be ever on the watch to guard and protect Ionia;
and yet otherwise there could be no hope that the Ionians would
escape the vengeance of the Persians. Hereupon the Peloponnesian leaders proposed, that the seaport-towns of such Greeks
as had sided with the Medes should be taken away from them,
and made over to the Ionians. The Athenians, on the other hand,
were very unwilling that any removal at all should take place,
and disliked the Peloponnesians holding councils concerning
their colonists. So, as they set themselves against the change, the
Peloponnesians yielded with a good will. Hereupon the Samians, Chians, Lesbians, and other islanders, who had helped the
Greeks at this time, were received into the league of the allies;
and took the oaths, binding themselves to be faithful, and not
desert the common cause. Then the Greeks sailed away to the
Hellespont, where they meant to break down the bridges, which,
they supposed to be still extended across the strait.

107. The barbarians who escaped from the battle—a scanty
remnant—took refuge in the heights of Mycale, whence they
made good their retreat to Sardis. During the march, Masistes,
the son of Darius, who had been present at the disaster, had

words with Artayntes, the general, on whom he showered many reproaches. He called him, among other things, worse than a woman, for the way in which he had exercised his command, and said there was no punishment which he did not deserve to suffer for doing the king's house such grievous hurt. Now with the Persians there is no greater insult than to call a man worse than a woman. So when Artayntes had borne the reproaches for some while, at last he fell in a rage, and drew his scimitar upon Masistes, to kill him. But a certain Halicarnassian, Xenagoras by name, the son of Praxilaus, who stood behind Artayntes at the time, seeing him in the act of rushing forward, seized him suddenly round the waist, and, lifting him from his feet, dashed him down upon the ground; which gave time for the spearmen who guarded Masistes to come to his aid. By his conduct here Xenagoras gained the favour, not of Masistes only, but likewise of Xerxes himself, whose brother he had preserved from death; and the king rewarded his action by setting him over the whole land of Cilicia. Except this, nothing happened upon the road; and the men continued their march and came all safe to Sardis. At Sardis they found the king, who had been there ever since he lost the sea-fight and fled from Athens to Asia.

108. During the time that Xerxes abode at this place, he fell in love with the wife of Masistes, who was likewise staying in the city. He therefore sent her messages, but failed to win her consent; and he could not dare to use violence, out of regard to Masistes, his brother. This the woman knew well enough, and hence it was that she had the boldness to resist him. So Xerxes, finding no other way open, devised a marriage between his own son Darius and a daughter of this woman and Masistes—thinking that he might better obtain his ends if he effected this union. Accordingly he betrothed these two persons to one another, and, after the usual ceremonies were completed, took his departure for Susa. When he was come there, and had received the woman into his palace as his son's bride, a change came over him, and, losing all love for the wife of Masistes, he conceived a passion for his son's bride, Masistes' daughter. And Artaynta—for so was she called—very soon returned his love.

109. After a while the thing was discovered in the way which I will now relate. Amestris, the wife of Xerxes, had woven with her own hands, a long robe of many colours, and very curious, which she presented to her husband as a gift. Xerxes, who was greatly pleased with it, forthwith put it on; and went in it to visit Artaynta, who happened likewise on this day to please him greatly. He therefore bade her ask him whatever boon she liked, and promised that, whatever it was, he would assuredly grant her request. Then Artaynta, who was doomed to suffer calamity together with her whole house, said to him, "Will you indeed give me whatever I like to ask?" So the king, suspecting nothing less than that her choice would fall where it did, pledged his word, and swore to her. She then, as soon as she heard his oath, asked boldly for the robe. Hereupon Xerxes tried all possible means to avoid the gift; not that he grudged to give it, but because he dreaded Amestris, who already suspected, and would now, he feared, detect his love. So he offered her cities instead, and heaps of gold, and an army which should obey no other leader. (The last of these is a thoroughly Persian gift.) But, as nothing could prevail on Artaynta to change her mind, at the last he gave her the robe. Then Artaynta very greatly rejoiced, and she often wore the garment and was proud of it. And so it came to the ears of Amestris that the robe had been given to her.

110. Now when Amestris learnt the whole matter, she felt no anger against Artaynta; but, looking upon her mother, the wife of Masistes, as the cause of all the mischief, she determined to compass her death. She waited, therefore, till her husband gave the great royal banquet, a feast which takes place once every year, in celebration of the king's birthday, tykta the feast is called in the Persian tongue, which in our language may be rendered perfect, and this is the only day in all the year on which the king soaps his head, and distributes gifts to the Persians. Amestris waited, accordingly, for this day, and then made request of Xerxes that he would please to give her, as her present, the wife of Masistes. But he refused; for it seemed to him shocking and monstrous to give into the power of another a woman, who was not only his brother's wife, but was likewise

wholly guiltless of what had happened—the more especially as he knew well enough with what intent Amestris had preferred her request.

111. At length, however, wearied by her importunity, and constrained moreover by the law of the feast, which required that no one who asked a boon that day at the king's board should be denied his request, he yielded, but with a very ill will, and gave the wife of Masistes into her power. Having so done, and told Amestris she might deal with her as she chose, the king called his brother into his presence, and said, "Masistes, you are my brother, the son of my father Darius; and, what is more, you are a good man. I pray you, live no longer with the wife whom you now have. Behold, I will give you instead my own daughter in marriage; take her to live with you. But part first with the wife you now have—I like not that you keep to her."

To this Masistes, greatly astonished, answered, "My lord and master, how strange a speech you have uttered! You bid me put away my wife, who has borne me three goodly youths, and daughters besides, whereof you have taken one and espoused her to a son of your own—you bid me put away this wife, notwithstanding that she pleases me greatly, and marry a daughter of yours! In truth, O King, that I am accounted worthy to wed your daughter, is an honour which I mightily esteem; but yet to do as you say am I in no wise willing. I pray you, use not force to compel me to yield to your prayer. Be sure your daughter will find a husband, to the full as worthy as myself. Suffer me then to live on with my own wife."

Thus did Masistes answer; and Xerxes, in wrath, replied, "I will tell you, Masistes, what you have gained by these words. I will not give you my daughter; nor shall you live any longer with your own wife. So you may learn, in time to come, to take what is offered you." Masistes, when he heard this, withdrew, only saying, "Master, you have not yet taken my life."

112. While these things were passing between Xerxes and his brother Masistes, Amestris sent for the spearmen of the royal body-guard, and caused the wife of Masistes to be mutilated in a horrible fashion. Her breasts, her nose, ears, and lips were cut

off and thrown to the dogs; her tongue was torn out by the roots, and thus disfigured she was sent back to her home.

113. Masistes, who knew nothing of what had happened, but was fearful that some calamity had befallen him, ran hastily to his house. There, finding his wife so savagely used, he forthwith took counsel with his sons, and accompanied by them and certain others also, set forth on his way to Bactria, intending to stir up revolt in that province, and hoping to do great hurt to Xerxes: all which, I believe, he would have accomplished, if he had once reached the Bactrian and Sacan people; for he was greatly beloved by them both, and was moreover satrap of Bactria. But Xerxes, hearing of his designs, sent an armed force upon his track, and slew him while he was still upon the road, with his sons and his whole army. Such is the tale of King Xerxes' love and of the death of his brother Masistes.

114. Meanwhile the Greeks, who had left Mycale, and sailed for the Hellespont, were forced by contrary winds to anchor near Lectum; from which place they afterwards sailed on to Abydos. On arriving here, they discovered that the bridges, which they had thought to find standing, and which had been the chief cause of their proceeding to the Hellespont, were already broken up and destroyed. Upon this discovery, Leotychides, and the Peloponnesians under him, were anxious to sail back to Greece; but the Athenians, with Xanthippus their captain, decided to remain, and resolved to make an attempt upon the Chersonese. So, while the Peloponnesians sailed away to their homes, the Athenians crossed over from Abydos to the Chersonese, and there laid siege to Sestos.

115. Now as Sestos was the strongest fortress in all that region, the rumour had no sooner gone forth that the Greeks were arrived at the Hellespont, than great numbers flocked thither from all the towns in the neighbourhood. Among the rest there came a certain Oeobazus, a Persian, from the city of Cardia, where he had laid up the shore-cables which had been used in the construction of the bridges. The town was guarded by its own Aeolian inhabitants, but contained also some Persians, and a great multitude of their allies.

116. The whole district was under the rule of Artayctes, one of the king's satraps; who was a Persian, but a wicked and cruel man. At the time when Xerxes was marching against Athens, he had craftily possessed himself of the treasures belonging to Protesilaus the son of Iphiclus, which were at Elaeus in the Chersonese. For at this place is the tomb of Protesilaus, surrounded by a sacred precinct; and here there was great store of wealth, vases of gold and silver, works in brass, garments, and other offerings, all which Artayctes made his prey, having got the king's consent by thus cunningly addressing him, "Master, there is in this region the house of a Greek, who, when he attacked your territory, met his due reward, and perished. Give me his house, I pray you, that hereafter men may fear to carry arms against your land."

By these words he easily persuaded Xerxes to give him the man's house; for there was no suspicion of his design in the king's mind. And he could say in a certain sense that Protesilaus had borne arms against the land of the king; because the Persians consider all Asia to belong to them, and to their king for the time being. So when Xerxes allowed his request, he brought all the treasures from Elaeus to Sestos, and made the sacred land into cornfields and pasture grounds; nay, more, whenever he paid a visit to Elaeus, he polluted the shrine itself by sexual intercourse. It was this Artayctes who was now besieged by the Athenians—and he was but ill prepared for defence; since the Greeks had fallen upon him quite unawares, nor had he in the least expected their coming.

117. When it was now late in the autumn, and the siege still continued, the Athenians began to murmur that they were kept abroad so long; and, seeing that they were not able to take the place, besought their captains to lead them back to their own country. But the captains refused to move, till either the ciy had fallen, or the Athenian people ordered them to return home. So the soldiers patiently bore up against their sufferings.

118. Meanwhile those within the walls were reduced to the last straits, and forced even to boil the very thongs of their beds for food. At last, when these too failed them, Artayctes and

Oeobazus, with the native Persians, fled away from the place by night, having let themselves down from the wall at the back of the town, where the blockading force was scantiest. As soon as day dawned, they of the Chersonese made signals to the Greeks from the walls, and let them know what had happened, at the same time throwing open the gates of their city. Hereupon, while some of the Greeks entered the town, others, and those the more numerous body, set out in pursuit of the enemy.

119. Oeobazus fled into Thrace; but there the Apsinthian Thracians seized him, and offered him, after their wonted fashion, to Pleistorus, one of the gods of their country. His companions they likewise put to death, but in a different manner. As for Artayctes and the troops with him, who had been the last to leave the town, they were overtaken by the Greeks, not far from Aegospotami, and defended themselves stoutly for a time, but were at last either killed or taken prisoners. Those whom they made prisoners the Greeks bound with chains, and brought with them to Sestos. Artayctes and his son were among the number.

120. Now the Chersonesites relate, that the following prodigy befell one of the Greeks who guarded the captives. He was broiling upon a fire some salted fish, when of a sudden they began to leap and quiver, as if they had been only just caught. Hereat, the rest of the guards hurried round to look, and were greatly amazed at the sight. Artayctes, however, beholding the prodigy, called the man to him, and said, "Fear not, Athenian stranger, because of this marvel. It has not appeared on your account, but on mine. Protesilaus of Elaeus has sent it to show me, that albeit he is dead and embalmed with salt, he has power from the gods to chastise his injurer. Now then I wish to pay my debt to him thus: For the riches which I took from his temple, I will fix my fine at 100 talents—while for myself and this boy of mine, I will give the Athenians 200 talents, on condition that they will spare our lives."

Such were the promises of Artayctes; but they failed to persuade Xanthippus. For the men of Elaeus, who wished to avenge Protesilaus, entreated that he might be put to death; and Xanthippus himself was of the same mind. So they led Artayctes to the tongue of land where the bridge of Xerxes had been fixed—or, according to others, to the knoll above the town of Madytus; and, having nailed him to a board, they left him hanging thereupon. As for the son of Artayctes, him they stoned to death before his eyes.

121. This done, they sailed back to Greece, carrying with them, besides other treasures, the shore-cables from the bridges of Xerxes, which they wished to dedicate in their temples. And this was all that took place that year.

122. It was the grandfather of this Artayctes, one Artembares by name, who suggested to the Persians a proposal, which they readily embraced, and thus urged upon Cyrus, "Since Zeus," they said, "has overthrown Astyages, and given the rule to the Persians, and to you chiefly, O Cyrus, come now, let us quit this land wherein we dwell—for it is a scant land and a rugged—and let us choose ourselves some other better country. Many such lie around us, some nearer, some further off: if we take one of these, men will admire us far more than they do now. Who that had the power would not so act? And when shall we have a fairer time than now, when we are lords of so many nations, and rule all Asia?" Then Cyrus, who did not greatly esteem the counsel, told them they might do so, if they liked—but he warned them not to expect in that case to continue rulers, but to prepare for being ruled by others—soft countries gave birth to soft men—there was no region which produced very delightful fruits, and at the same time men of a warlike spirit. So the Persians departed with altered minds, confessing that Cyrus was wiser than they; and chose rather to dwell in a churlish land, and exercise lordship, than to cultivate plains, and be the slaves of others.